Introduction to

Physiological psychology

Introduction to
Physiological psychology

Francis Leukel, Ph.D.

Professor of Psychology,
San Diego State University,
San Diego, California

with 177 illustrations

THIRD EDITION

The C. V. Mosby Company

Saint Louis 1976

THIRD EDITION

Previous editions copyrighted 1968, 1972

Printed in the United States of America

Distributed in Great Britain by Henry Kimpton, London

Library of Congress Cataloging in Publication Data

Leukel, Francis.
   Introduction to physiological psychology.

   Bibliography: p.
   Includes index.
   1. Psychology, Physiological. I. Title.
[DNLM: 1. Psychophysiology. WL102 L652i]
QP360.L48 1976   152   75-33031
ISBN 0-8016-2974-8

CB/CB/B 9 8 7 6 5 4 3 2 1

Preface

This book is a text for lower-division college students. It was written originally for a course required of psychology majors and developed from a syllabus that was used and revised each semester for five years. The course assumes that students in many upper-division psychology classes need an elementary background in physiological psychology to benefit most from their upper-division classes.

Most psychologists would agree that physiological psychology has developed rapidly in recent years and that an expanded use of physiological ideas has spread to many areas of psychology in which they were not common before. In addition to fields classically grounded in physiological ideas such as sensation, sleep, emotion, motivation, and learning, physiological discoveries have contributed to our understanding of perception, intelligence, "psychosomatic" disorders, stress, neurosis, "functional" psychoses, personality, and psychotherapy. Readers sophisticated in these fields can readily supply examples from their own experience.

It is not the purpose of this text, however, to treat these newer topics in more than a passing manner. This text attempts to prepare students to understand physiological concepts in other specialized fields that they will encounter in upper-division courses. The practical objective of this book is to provide a "tool course" for upper-division study in psychology. This course may be the only exposure to either physiology or physiological psychology that most students will have. The biology department in many small colleges lacks a physiologist just as the psychology department often has no physiological psychologist. Students may not have the opportunity to study either area without a text that provides limited useful background at a level that they and the nonspecialist instructor may find most comfortable. Such a course and text may also aid nursing students, students of speech pathology, premedical and predental students, and others whose crowded program would otherwise preclude study of the topic.

The book is organized in four parts. The two chapters of the first part, entitled The Organization of Life, introduce the field of physiological psychology and present some concepts of general physiology. The second part, entitled Integrating and Response Systems, treats elementarily the anatomy and physiology of the endocrine glands, nerves, muscles, and the nervous system. The third part, entitled The Senses, covers the topics of somesthesis, proprioception, the chemical senses, audition, and vision. The fourth part, entitled Adaptive Behavior, introduces the topics of motor organization, brain dynamics, states of consciousness, motivation, emotion, learning, and stress. The plan of the book shows a traditional orientation with more emphasis on physiology than is usual for texts in physiological psychology.

For the instructor who prefers a different orientation or topic emphasis than the one presented here, a list of inexpensive readings has been included at the end of each chapter, which are understandable to the student. An instructor who wishes to emphasize some chapters more than others can use these readings to do so. The readings include paperbound books of a supplementary nature, *Scientific American* articles that are available as reprints, and other commercially available reprint materials. An instructor could, for example, omit the chapters on the senses and use reprints to give a more extensive treatment to the other topics. There are, of course, other possibilities for changes in emphasis. An attempt has been made to build the book like an Erector Set so that the instructors can design their own course, yet students can read about any topic that interests them.

The illustrations are simple and are closely integrated with the text.

Two difficulties are foreseen for the student, and attempts have been made to remedy them. One of these problems is acquiring a new vocabulary. A glossary for words printed in bold-faced type in the text is provided at the end of the book. The other problem for the student is generalizing from the detailed ideas presented in each chapter—making sense out of each area covered. As an aid in orienting the student, each chapter begins with an "overview" of the ideas to be covered and how these ideas will be treated. To crystallize the student's knowledge, each chapter ends with a summary.

As in the previous editions I have made no reference to specific articles and dates, to avoid confusing the student with excessive detail; however, the most important authors are named as an aid to specific memory of their findings, as well as to give credit where credit is due. This also aids the advanced student and the instructor in finding the original literature in the reference section. The reference section has been expanded so as to include more of the original literature, as well as updated secondary sources, to make the book more useful and contemporary. The readings at the end of each chapter have also been expanded to include more modern work. A sincere attempt has been made to create a readable textbook at a level with a minimum loss of validity. However, omissions and distortions are unavoidable in giving lower-division students some of the major ideas in a very complex field at their own level. In this sense, I am writing to students rather than to colleagues. If the book succeeds in reaching this audience, the credit belongs to students, from whose "naïve" questions I have learned so much. With their assistance, and that of faculty colleagues, I have also been able to develop a teacher's manual and a study guide that have much local testing and revision. I hope that any benefit students receive from using these aids will repay them in part for what they have taught me.

Any misconceptions that remain are mine. As before, I have been helped by so many that I cannot name them all, despite owing them much for what I have learned.

Francis Leukel

Contents

part four
Adaptive behavior

part one

The organization of life

chapter 1

Introduction

This chapter will define the topic of physiological psychology and show how it will be treated in succeeding chapters. It is an introduction to what a physiological psychologist does. As in succeeding chapters, this one will begin with an overview—to indicate what will be discussed before going into detail—and end with a summary of what has been discussed so that the main ideas are not lost in the specific points that have been made.

OVERVIEW

Physiological psychology is psychology because it attempts to explain and predict behavior. It is physiological because it predicts behavior by using knowledge of how the organs and systems of the body work. The physiologist uses knowledge of anatomy (structural relationships of the body), physics, chemistry, and other related fields to study how the component cells, organs, and systems of the body work. The psychologist, on the other hand, is interested in any part of this knowledge that will help him understand and predict behavior. He uses many of the methods of the anatomist, biochemist, physiologist, and other specialists, as well as psychological techniques. His goal, however, is to understand behavior rather than the systems of the body as such.

In studying physiological mechanisms in behavior the physiological psychologist must use all the tools and methods that are available. Often he must experiment with animals rather than humans, since his operations involve damaging or stimulating parts of the brain. Although done in a humane fashion, such procedures cannot be used with human subjects for ethical reasons. However, an animal may be painlessly killed and studied anatomically after an experiment to locate the effects of brain damage or the site of brain stimulation. When accidents involving brain damage occur to humans, the extent of the damage is often unknown. Therefore it is difficult to know what kind of brain damage is causing the changes in their behavior. On the other hand, it is often risky to draw conclusions about humans from the effects of brain operations on animal behavior—physiological experiments must be interpreted with care. The chapter closes by noting some of the recent findings in the biological sciences and their implications for man.

PHYSIOLOGICAL APPROACH TO BEHAVIOR

All psychologists study **behavior,** but they are not the only students of people's actions. Philosophers, lawyers, and sociologists, among others, also concern themselves with behavior. All use observation as a basic technique—but what differentiates scientific from nonscientific approaches, one behavioral science from another, or physiological psychologists from other psychologists?

In the first place, scientists and nonscientists are trying to answer different questions. For example, philosophers concern themselves with questions of logic, ethics, and epistemology: Given a set of *assumptions,* what *consequences* follow—in argument or human life? Lawyers and social workers study the behavior of individuals as applied to the way society is organized and try to improve social organi-

3

zations or apply them to a *purpose*. By contrast, behavioral scientists study behavior for its own sake in an attempt to understand and predict behavior. The only assumptions they make or consequences they follow are supplied by what they observe; their intent is only to relate one behavioral event to another. Unlike nonscientific fields, behavioral sciences are usually classified by their subject matter rather than by their intent. For example, anthropologists and sociologists study cultures and groups, and individual behavior interests them only as it influences the group they are observing. Psychologists, on the other hand, are concerned with individual behavior as such, but psychologists must compare the behavior of the subjects they study with one another. Individual differences are as important as the "typical case" because individual differences define how variable the behavior has become.

Specialties in psychology form categories defined by the kind of behavior the specialist is interested in and by the methods he uses. The psychologist may study personality, abnormal behavior, child behavior, social behavior, learning, animal behavior, and so on. Some of the more complex kinds of behavior are too unpredictable or too variable—the individual differences are too great—for a knowledge of physiological psychology to be helpful. Nothing precise enough to be useful is known, for example, of the relations between the functioning of parts of the brain and leadership in social groups, or the development of anxiety as a result of rejection and the individual's glandular makeup. The understanding of many complex kinds of behavior is aided, however, by a knowledge of how the body—particularly the nervous system—works. Studies that relate nervous and glandular function to the areas of motivation, learning, and stress have added much to our understanding of behavior in these and other important areas.

Physiological psychology, then, relates the methods and findings of **physiology** to behavior. In so doing many fields are drawn upon: **anatomy, biochemistry,** and even physics and engineering. The **anatomist** is interested in how **organisms,** or living things, are structured. He is concerned with the structure of the differently specialized **cells,** of which the complex organism is composed, how they are organized into **tissues** of similar cells, and how different tissues are organized into **organs** and **systems.** The **biochemist** is concerned with the chemical reactions involved in the functioning of these cells, tissues, organs, and systems—the chemical reactions of life. The physiologist wants to know how all the systems of the body work—not just anatomically and biochemically, but physically as well. He makes use of the techniques of electronics, chemistry, and physics, in investigating how the cells, tissues, organs, and systems of the body function. He is interested in these phenomena for their own sake. The physiological psychologist, on the other hand, is concerned with those findings and methods of the anatomist, biochemist, physiologist, and others that will enable him to understand the behavior of the organism.

What are the mechanisms of inheritance whereby individual differences in many human behaviors can be understood? What characteristics of the nervous system govern learning and intelligence? What activities in the sense organs determine what we see, hear, smell, taste, and touch? What mechanisms in the brain and the glands enter into determining reactions to stress? These are only sample questions, and we are far from having complete answers to any of them. They serve to illustrate the fact, however, that the physiological psychologist is interested in physiology and the fields that contribute to it, mainly as they aid his understanding of human and animal behavior.

PHYSIOLOGICAL METHODS

Some of the scientific methods and techniques used by the physiological psychologist come from physiology, anatomy, and biochemistry. Other methods are more or less unique to psychology, such as the study of behavior. The techniques borrowed from other fields include **stimulation** of nerve tissue, electronic recording, ablation (destruction) of nervous and glandular tissue, anatomical methods, and clinical methods.

Stimulation. In learning how the brain deals with information sent to it from the sense organs through the nerves, it is often useful to bypass the sense organs and stimulate the nerves themselves or even parts of the brain. Small electrical current pulses are used, since they resemble most closely the impulses initiated by sense organs in nerves going to the brain. In this way any part of the nervous system may be stimulated at will. Sometimes this is done in an animal under anesthesia when much of the nervous system must be surgically exposed to trace where the nerve impulses go. In other experiments electrodes may be permanently implanted in parts of the nervous system. The electrodes do not disturb the animal after it recovers, and the subject may be "plugged in" to stimulate a part of the nervous system while the animal is behaving normally. In some cases small tubes are planted in the brain and chemical stimuli are used.

Electronic recording techniques. Electrodes may be implanted in the nerves or brain in either a temporary or permanent fashion to record the electrical activity of nerve impulses traveling from place to place in the nerves and brain. Excitation may be traced from one part of the nervous system to another in this manner, or the response of the brain to stimulation of the sense organs can be observed in animals either anesthetized or awake.

Ablation. Destruction of a gland or a part of the brain may be performed, followed by systematic observation of the animal's behavior after he recovers from the operation. Any deficiencies in activity, learning, or other kinds of behavior may be attributable to the missing structure. There are many chances for error in this technique because of the interactions of different structures. The errors possible in ablation procedure will be described as the occasion arises.

Anatomical methods. To confirm precisely where electrodes were placed for stimulation or recording during an experiment, or to determine what part of the brain was destroyed in ablation experiments, one must kill the animal after the experiment ends and study it anatomically. The brain may be cut into thin slices and studied with a microscope to show exactly where an electrode was placed or to find the limits of parts of the brain that were removed for an experiment.

Clinical methods. The experimental techniques described above have provided much information about the role of the sense organs, parts of the brain, the glands, and other structures that control the behavior of typical laboratory animals such as the rat, the cat, or the monkey. The behavior of man is more complex, however, and his sensory mechanisms and brain differ in many respects from other animals. Results obtained with laboratory animals can be applied only uncertainly to man. Occasional accidents occur that cause brain damage in man, and the effects of that brain damage on behavior may be studied with various types of tests. The brain may be exposed in a conscious subject, as during surgery for removal of a tumor, and then systematically stimulated. The subject can then report his sensations, and any observable responses to brain stimulation may be studied. In neither case is the exact site of the damage or stimulation known. The patient cannot be killed for study by anatomical methods. However, in brain-damage cases, the brain may be studied later, after death from natural causes. In such instances the lesions are never precisely where we would like them to be for the most profitable study, and changes occur between the time of the injury and the time of death.

PHYSIOLOGICAL PSYCHOLOGY: IMPLICATIONS FOR MAN

At some point in his study of physiological psychology, usually near the beginning, a student should and does ask: "What effect will research in this field have on my life?" and "Why should I study physiological psychology?"

These are not the kinds of questions a scientist asks in his formal role of research or teaching, or both. Whatever techniques he uses, the physiological psychologist, as a scientist, seeks to understand, predict, and control behavior by physiological means. His success in this attempt, however, has implications for man because this information can be used by society. Implications of this kind are beyond the purview of this book, but mention of them may give purpose to the study of this field by the nonspecialist.

Many have said that the past century was the century of the physicist and that we are entering the century of the biologist (broadly defined). The work of Einstein and his predecessors and successors on the nature of matter and energy has culminated in the discovery and use of nuclear fission and fusion. The implications of these discoveries range from a source of unlimited energy to the explosive extinction of man. The biological century begins with the discoveries of Watson and Crick on the physical basis of inheritance and the metabolic control of life; the work of Hess on implanting electrodes in the brain; the discovery of brain centers for "pleasure" and "anxiety" by Olds; remote-control stimulation by Delgado; the effects of environment on brain anatomy and biochemistry; the transfer of learning by biochemical means; and many other findings of crucial importance for man. The implications include the possibility of engineering our inheritance for desired characteristics, improving the rate at which we learn, increasing our intelligence, controlling the behavior of others against their "will," changing per-

sonality and temperament by physical means, curing insanity, and decreasing or increasing the aggressiveness of man, which leads to war. The biological century is only beginning, and the means to the above ends are only starting to be realized, but many believe that the curiosity of man will result in their realization if the race survives.

Like the scientist the student must begin at the beginning. Understanding current research requires an understanding of the sciences that have contributed to physiological psychology. At least a rudimentary understanding of anatomy, physiology, biochemistry, electricity, electronics, and techniques for the study of behavior is needed first. Thus this book begins with the promise that as your knowledge of physiological psychology increases, so will your understanding of these exciting ideas and their implications.

SUMMARY

A physiological psychologist is a scientist whose aim is to understand and predict behavior as it is controlled and regulated by the physiological systems of the body. Physiological psychology is the body of information that results from the experimental work of the physiological psychologist. Understanding physiological psychology requires some knowledge of how the body's physiological systems function. This study, undertaken for its own sake by the physiologist, depends partly on information and methods from the anatomist. He studies the structure of the cells, organs, and systems of the body. To talk about how a system functions requires a knowledge of its structure. The physiologist and physiological psychologist also depend on information and methods taken from biochemistry (the chemical reactions of life), physics, electronics, engineering, and many other fields.

In addition to the study of behavior, the physiological psychologist uses the more physiological techniques of nerve and brain

stimulation and recording in both anesthetized and awake animals, as well as ablation
of tissue, and anatomical and clinical methods. Because stimulation, recording, and
ablation techniques require surgery on living
organisms, experiments are largely confined
to laboratory animals such as the rat, the
cat, and the monkey. This limits conclusions
about man, since man's behavior and nervous system are more complex. In these
experiments, however, the physiological psychologist can be quite precise about placing
his electrodes for stimulation or recording.
He can be sure about the location and extent
of tissue ablated, because he can kill
the animal after the experiment and confirm his operations by anatomical study. In
cases of accidental brain damage to man
or of brain surgery, clinical studies can be
made by observing behavioral changes that
result. Nevertheless, the exact locations of
brain lesions are not planned and are seldom
confirmed later by anatomical study. As a
result, most of the data of physiological
psychology come from the study of laboratory animals.

The discoveries of the biological sciences
in general and of physiological psychology
in particular appear to have profound implications for man, including altering our
inheritance, intelligence, and personality, as
well as controlling our behavior. Although
these possibilities lie in the future, many
believe they will be realized. Comprehend-
ing the research that underlies such possibilities requires some understanding of
several sciences.

READINGS

Delgado, J. M. R.: Physical control of the mind,
New York, 1969, Harper & Row, Publishers.

Fuller, W., editor: The biological revolution:
Social good or social evil, Garden City, N.Y.,
1972, Doubleday & Co., Inc.

Glass, B.: The ethical basis of science, Science
150:1254-1261, 1965.

Goldsmith, M., and Mackay, A., editors: Science
and society, New York, 1964, Simon & Schuster,
Inc.

Gulick, A.: A biological prologue for human values, BioScience **18:**1109-1112, 1968.

Haskins, C. P.: Advances and challenges in science
in 1969, Amer. Sci. **58:**365-377, 1970.

Singh, D., and Avery, D.: Physiological techniques
in behavioral research, Monterey, Calif., 1975,
Brooks/Cole Publishing Co.

chapter 2

Internal environment

OVERVIEW

Nearly all living matter consists of protoplasm organized into the unit of life—the cell. Some of the simplest forms of life consist of only a single cell, but more complex forms of life, including man, are assemblies of specialized cells. In seeking to understand how the physiology of the organism determines behavior, one can begin by understanding how single cells are organized and how their functions, including behavior, demonstrate the characteristics and organization of life. Then varieties of cell specialization will be studied to learn how complex, many-celled organisms such as man are integrated. Integration is accomplished by specialized cells that assemble to form tissues, organs, and systems.

When cells specialize for a single function important to life, they carry on that function more efficiently. However, they lose part of their ability to carry on other functions that are necessary to sustain life. They depend on other cells that have specialized differently to fulfill other functions for them. The cells of a complex organism thus become dependent on each other, or *interdependent*. The cells "support" one another in various ways.

Specialization also reduces the ability to the cell to adapt to a changing environment. The internal environment surrounding the cells inside the body must be kept more constant than the external environment outside the body. All the processes of the body, including behavior, are modified to that end.

Life in all cells is carried on by a series of chemical reactions called metabolism. These reactions involve a class of chemical compounds called organic compounds. The reactions of metabolism either require or release energy in a balance that is maintained by automatic mechanisms in the body and by external behavior. Those chemical reactions that go on inside the cells are called cell metabolism, but the reactions that occur in the internal environment surrounding the cells are called intermediary metabolism—they are intermediary events between outside events and events in the cells.

The chemical reactions of metabolism are controlled in various ways. Enzymes are compounds that control metabolism by determining the rate at which many chemical reactions occur, both inside and outside the cells. Enzymes selectively determine which needed chemical events occur in the body and when they occur. Enzymes also determine the unique characteristics of specialized cells. In a similar way enzyme-manufacturing arrangements in the cells determine heredity—whether the offspring is to be a man or a pig, or have brown hair or blue eyes. The circulatory system has much to do with controlling intermediatry metabolism, since it is the major transportation system for energy exchanges between the cells and the outside world. Its most basic characteristics must be known before such energy exchanges can be understood. Finally, all the reactions of intermediary metabolism are directed toward maintaining a constant internal environment, an environment that must remain within narrow chemical and physical limits to support life in the specialized cells. The organization of the specialized cells into systems and the integrating effects of the endocrine glands and nervous system are critical to maintaining homeostasis. Homeostasis is a changing balance of events that protects the constancy of the internal environment. Organized reactions of the body to events in the external and internal environment range from simple reflex reactions, through inherited patterns of behavior called instincts in lower animals, to complex learned behavior in higher animals and man—all serving to maintain life by maintaining homeostasis and a constant internal environment. Ultimately, all of man's motivation and behavior is dedicated to the maintenance of homeostasis.

PROPERTIES OR FUNCTIONS OF CELLS

Living **protoplasm** is organized into cells, which show certain functions and characteristics not common to nonliving matter. The characteristics of life can be seen in their simplest form in organisms that con-

sist of a single cell. Single-celled organisms are usually found in a water environment. They are one of the least specialized forms of "animal" life. Nevertheless, various *parts* of the single cell are specialized to carry on specific functions of life. Further specialization of the parts of each cell occurs when groups of cells of differing specialization are gathered together as many-celled organisms.

The single cell (Fig. 2-1)

To oversimplify, the cell consists of a **nucleus** surrounded by liquid **cytoplasm** that contains many **inclusions.** The **cell membrane** separates the cytoplasm of a cell from the environment of the cell. Properties of each of these parts of the cell enable it to carry on the activities necessary for life.

Functions or characteristics of cells

The diverse activities carried on by the single cell, including its reaction to stimulation, demonstrate the basic characteristics

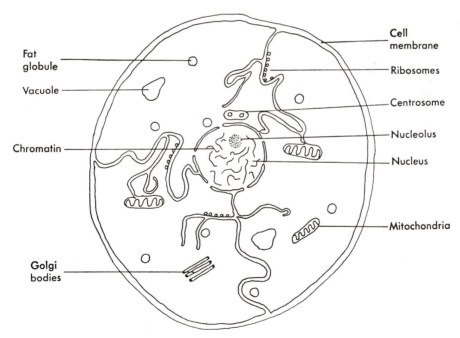

Fig. 2-1. Single cell. Semidiagrammatic sketch of a single-celled organism, showing some of its major features.

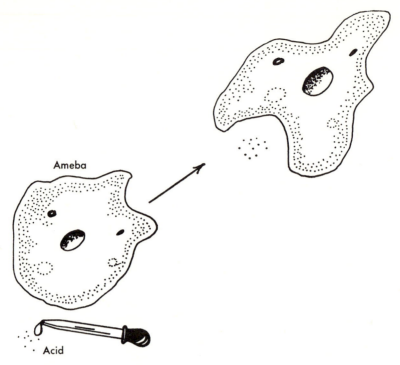

Ameba

Acid

Fig. 2-2. Reaction of a single-celled organism to an irritating stimulus.

of life. Cell activities show what part or parts of the cells are most important in carrying out each cell function.

Irritability (Fig. 2-2). When a cell such as the ameba is stimulated by a drop of acid, it reacts by changing shape to avoid the stimulus, thrusting out a **pseudopod** (false foot) and moving away. Among other things this reaction demonstrates that the cell is sensitive to the acid or is irritable to this form of **stimulus.** The cells in man that are specialized for **irritability** are found in the **sense organs.** Specialization for irritability has gone so far in man that some cells are most sensitive to **photic** stimuli (vision), **chemical** stimuli (taste, smell), **tempera-ture** (warmth, cold), or **mechanical** stimuli (touch or pressure, hearing). From the in-dependent cell to the most specialized cell, irritability persists as a property of the cell membrane. Irritability is based on a prop-erty of the cell membrane called **selective permeability.** This property enables the cell

membrane to pass some substances into the interior of the cell and to exclude oth-ers. Stimulation alters this state of affairs and results in an electrical change in the membrane (Chapter 4), which signals the effect of the stimulus on the cell.

Conduction. As Fig. 2-2 demonstrates, stimulation initiated a change in the shape of the cell; the excitation must have been conducted from one part of the cell to the other for the change to have taken place. **Conduction** is also a property of the cell membrane. It is a continuation of the elec-trical change noted previously, a change that sweeps over the entire membrane of the cell. Conduction is most highly devel-oped in the cells of man's nervous system, probably the most specialized cells of the human body. Nerve cells conduct excitation from one part of the body to another so that more widespread responses to a local stimulus may occur.

Contraction. The ability of the cell to

change shape is **contraction,** shown by the movement of the single cell away from the drop of acid. Contraction is a property of the cytoplasm of the cell and certain of its inclusions. It is most highly developed in the muscle cells of man. Threadlike inclusions running the length of each muscle cell shorten to reduce the length of muscles and move the bony levers of the body to which they are attached.

Secretion. A property of other types of cell inclusions is called **secretion.** It is carried on to provide substances necessary to the chemistry of life. They are manufactured in the cell from raw materials provided by the environment. Secretion is most highly developed by the cells that form **glands** in man. The glands secrete substances that aid in digesting food or organizing bodily changes. Glands are of two types in man: (1) **duct glands,** mostly digestive, which have tubes to carry the secretion to its site of action, and (2) **ductless glands** or **endocrine glands,** which secrete substances into the bloodstream for more widespread effects over the body. Together with the conducting cells of the nervous system, the secretions of ductless glands aid in coordinating cell activity all over the body. For example, the adrenal glands secrete a substance into the bloodstream in emergencies. This substance increases heart rate and blood pressure, and performs other functions that organize the body for physical exertion. Ductless glands are therefore both an integrating system and a response system.

Elimination. The process by which the cell rids itself of waste products is **elimination.** It is a joint property of cell inclusions that filter out the waste material and of the cell membrane, which passes it to the environment. Cells specialized in this function are found in the kidney in man, where they form urine. Although all cells rid themselves of waste products, kidney cells are specialized to clear the blood of the accumulated wastes from other cells.

Growth. **Growth** may be viewed either as an increase in the size of a single-celled organism or as an increase in the number of cells in a many-celled (multicellular) organism. When a single cell reaches a limiting size, it divides into two cells, a process called cell **mitosis,** an "unspecialized" form of cell **reproduction.** The cells in a multicellular organism likewise reproduce themselves to increase the size of each specialized part of the body during growth and to replace worn-out cells throughout life. However, reproduction of a whole new multicellular organism is a specialized function carried on by specialized cells. In either case the controlling mechanisms for reproduction are found in the cell nucleus.

Reproduction. Cell mitosis, as controlled by the nucleus, is the mechanism for cell reproduction after the single independent cell reaches a limiting size (Fig. 2-3). The cell nucleus divides along with the rest of the cell, as do specialized structures in the nucleus, the **genes.** The genes are in the DNA molecules contained in the chromosomes (colored bodies) of the cell nucleus. DNA molecules contain "patterns" for manufacturing each part of the two new cells. In man each specialized cell reproduces in a similar way, and the two new cells show the same specialized characteristics as the old cell. More complex sexual reproduction of a completely new multiple-celled organism is a more specialized function of cells in reproductive structures called the gonads. Each reproductive cell carries a "code" for the complete organism. One cell is contributed by the female and the other by the male, and they unite to form a single new cell in such a manner that each contributes some unique characteristics to the new organism. As the new cell multiplies by mitosis, the "code" in the genes of its nucleus determines whether the resulting organism will be a pig or a man, have blue or brown eyes, etc.

Metabolism. All the functions of the cell require energy. This energy is supplied by

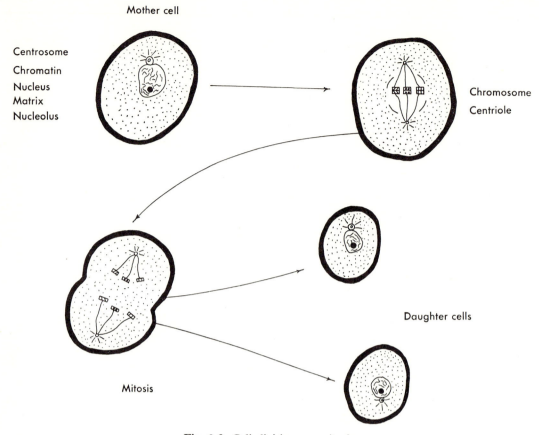

Mother cell

Centrosome
Chromatin
Nucleus
Matrix
Nucleolus

Chromosome
Centriole

Daughter cells

Mitosis

Fig. 2-3. Cell division, or mitosis.

a complex series of chemical processes called **metabolism.** Basically, metabolism involves breaking down foodstuffs (fat, proteins, and carbohydrates) into forms that the cell can utilize for energy or for part of its chemical structure. Energy for the chemical reactions of life is derived from processes such as **oxidation,** a chemical reaction similar to a fire. In this reaction oxygen combines with food to release energy and heat. The reactions of the body are like burning food, since they require the same raw materials and release similar waste products. Burning a food gives a measure of heat released, the **calorie,** and indirectly gives a measure of the energy value of that food to the body. (Those on diets know that if this energy is not utilized in exercise, the body utilizes it in building

up fat deposits!) In a complex organism such as man, food is converted into blood **glucose** (colloquially, blood sugar), which the specialized cells use as a foodstuff. To oversimplify, glucose combines with the oxygen we breathe to form carbon dioxide (released from the blood to the lungs before we exhale), heat to keep our body temperature up, waste, and water, which is eliminated by the kidney and through perspiration, and, finally, about 20% useful energy to "power" the chemical reactions of life.

VARIETIES OF CELL SPECIALIZATION
Cell colonies

Cell colonies were probably the first step toward cell specialization. Clumping together of otherwise independent cells must have had survival value among some cell species. This was a necessary first step toward cell specialization and interdependence in **multicellular organisms.**

Tissue specialization

A tissue is a group of cells that are specialized in a similar way to perform a common function. Thus all the cells of muscle tissue are specialized alike for contraction, receptor tissue for irritability, nerve tissue for conduction, glandular tissue for secretion, etc. Specialized muscle cells probably evolved first in multicellular organisms to improve mobility through efficient contracting cells. Then receptor tissue specialized to make organisms more sensitive to events in the environment. Receptor cells connected directly with muscle cells so that rapid response to such events could occur. Then nerve tissue evolved to connect receptor and **effector** (muscle and gland) cells, permitting more widespread and coordinated responses to stimuli. In man many other types of specialized tissue are found, such as bone, cartilage, connective tissue, and vascular (blood vessel) tissue.

Organ specialization

An organ is a collection of differently specialized tissues, organized for the performance of a common general function. It represents a further step in specialization and a new level of dependence of differently specialized tissues on each other. Each tissue has a different role in the overall function of the organ. For example, the stomach is a digestive organ. It is made up of connective tissue to hold it together, vascular (blood vessel) tissue to nourish it, glandular tissue to provide digestive secretions, muscle tissue to mix the food and move it into the rest of the digestive tract, etc. Other examples of organs in the body include the brain (nervous), heart (circulatory), kidney (elimination), eye (receptor), pituitary gland (endocrine), and gonads (reproductive). In each case differently specialized tissues are integrated to perform a function that a single kind of tissue would perform less efficiently.

System specialization

The highest level of integration in the body for performance of still more general functions is a system. A system consists of several organs, each of which has a limited role in the overall performance of the system. For example, the digestive system consists largely of the following organs: oral apparatus, esophagus, stomach, small and large intestines, liver, and kidneys. The general function of the system is to assimilate food, transform it into a state the body can use, store it, and eliminate that which the body cannot use. Each organ has a role in that general function; for example, the oral apparatus and esophagus specialize in ingestion, the stomach and intestines in digestion, the liver in storage, and the kidneys in elimination. The nervous system has nerves to carry excitation to and from the receptors and effectors, brain centers to make connections between incoming and outgoing excitation, and so forth. All serve the general function of carrying excitation from one part of the body to another so that response to internal and external events can occur. The circulatory system carries nourishment and removes waste, with the heart as a pumping organ, the arteries, veins, capillaries, and lymph vessels as pipelines, and so on.

EVOLUTION AND THE SPECIALIZATION OF ORGANISMS

The increased specialization and complexity of multicellular organisms resulted from **evolution** according to the principles of **random variation** and **natural selection.** The way in which these principles of inheritance are modified by the effects of the environment is the area of study called **behavior genetics.**

The characteristics of organisms are determined by genes in the reproductive cells of the sexual apparatus. Ordinarily immune to change by the environment, these genes are altered by natural and artificial radio-activity from gamma rays of the sun, atomic explosions, roentgen rays, and other "natural" causes. This alteration results in occasional organisms with novel characteristics, or **mutations.** In addition, a common physical characteristic (such as the length of a giraffe's neck) will vary randomly in the population. Both sets of events result in random variation in the physical characteristics of a species of animal.

Usually, new or extreme characteristics are unrelated to, or impair, survival in the competition between species for food supplies, space, and other necessities. Occasionally a new characteristic may aid survival—early giraffes with long necks could perhaps reach more tree leaves and therefore more food. The animal with the new characteristic may survive better and produce more offspring than his fellows. Natural selection thus prevails and the animals with the new characteristic are "selected" for survival. The new characteristic becomes more and more common among offspring as it is inherited from the larger number of surviving animals—those with the new and useful trait.

Random variation and natural selection determine the general characteristics of a species. These characteristics may set limits on the behavior of the species—birds cannot learn to read, and man cannot fly without assistance. Individual differences in behavior within a species are more subject to the interaction between inherited characteristics and environmental influences (experience). Study of this interaction lies in an area called behavior genetics. The behavior variability that results may influence random variability in a species and thus influence natural selection. To study variability in large numbers of a species involves study of a population; this field of study is called **population genetics.** Two

examples of interaction will clarify these concepts.

Genetic characteristics of the African black race are recognizably different from the genetic characteristics of some whites. One such characteristic is susceptibility to a disease called sickle cell anemia, which occurs in about 10% of the black population. Linked to this susceptibility in a complex genetic way is resistance to malaria, a characteristic of obvious survival value in Africa. The white population has evolved in areas of the world in which malaria is less common. Genetic resistance to malaria has not evolved in the white population, but neither has susceptibility to sickle cell anemia. The study of population genetics demonstrates that (1) populations adapt to their environment; (2) adaptations can be inherited, once genetically linked; and (3) adaptive characteristics sometimes exact a price in maladaptive side effects.

Mice, rats, squirrels, and other rodents exhibit hoarding behavior. In a species whose food supply is seasonal, this inherited behavior tendency has obvious survival value. It is known, however, that individual members of the population of each of these species vary in their hoarding behavior. Some of this variability depends on differences in the genes they inherit. By selective inbreeding after tests of hoarding behavior, strains of mice that differ in hoarding behavior can be developed. Statistical predictions from crossbreeding show that a third to a half of this individual difference in hoarding is under genetic control. What about the remaining difference? Can environment influence it? It has been known for a long time that depriving infant rats of food increases the amount of food they hoard as adults. Yet the extent of the same environmental influence on hoarding behavior depends on the strain and even the sex of the animal. For example, immersing mice in cold water 20 minutes before testing them increases hoarding in the males of one strain of mice but not in the males of another strain. The hoarding of females of either strain was not affected by the procedure. It is clear that inherited behavior tendencies and environmental experience interact in complex ways. It is also evident that the inherited behavior tendencies that are expressed in one environment may not be expressed in another. If the food supply of a species is abundant, hoarding behavior may be minimal. If food suddenly becomes scarce, members of the population with a greater genetic tendency to hoard may survive, whereas those with a lesser tendency to hoard may not survive. The genetic inheritance of the entire population may be changed as a result of a change in environment.

INTEGRATION OF THE COMPLEX ORGANISM: HOMEOSTASIS

As cells are organized into tissues, organs, and systems, they become more specialized and thus better able to perform certain functions. At the same time they lose part of their ability to carry on other functions necessary for life and depend on other tissues, organs, and systems to carry on these functions for them. Increased interdependence among cells results. Specialized cells are also less able to adapt to changes in their environment than are independent cells. The internal environment that surrounds the cells inside the body must be more constant than that of independent cells. An independent cell living in seawater can tolerate wider variations in salinity (saltiness), temperature, food content, and fluid pressure of the environment as compared to a specialized cell in the body. The physical and chemical conditions that surround a specialized cell in the human body must be more constant because the cell has lost its ability to cope with environmental changes. Many conditions must be kept within narrow limits inside the body to ensure the survival of its cells. The internal environment, therefore, is much more constant than is the external environment. Organization of the varied activities of the body becomes essential so that (1) the needs of functionally specialized tissues may be met by other tissues specialized in meeting such needs and (2) conditions inside the body are relatively constant in the face of varied cell activities inside the body and fluctuations in the external environment.

Integration

Activities in one part of the body are coordinated with activities in other parts of the body. A high degree of organization is necessary to permit the degree of interdependence shown by the many diverse cells, tissues, and organs. Organization is also necessary for maintenance of a constant internal environment in the face of an external environment that varies widely in temperature, food supply, and other factors. The required integration of bodily activity is carried out in three major ways: (1) the organization of tissues and organs into systems provides some coordination for a single general function such as digestion or circulation; (2) some coordination is supplied by the endocrine glands, whose secretions are carried all over the body in the bloodstream to affect widely scattered tissues in a consistent fashion; and (3) the nervous system is completely devoted to coordinating the many diverse functions of the other organs and systems of the body. Potentially, activity in nearly any part of the body can stimulate changed activity in any other part of the body because the two parts are linked by conduction through the nervous system.

When tissues and organs are organized into systems, the many steps required to carry out a complex activity take place in proper sequence. For example, in the digestive system salivary glands in the mouth begin the process of food breakdown, the stomach mixes the result and stores it, the small intestine secretes substances to complete digestion, the liver manufactures and stores blood glucose, and the kidneys and large intestine store and eliminate the waste. The circulatory system includes a pump (the heart), pipelines (arteries) to the lungs (for air), arteries running all over the body, capillaries with thin walls to release nutrition and oxygen and to recover carbon dioxide and waste in exchange with the fluid environment of the cells, and veins to return the blood to the heart.

The systems of the body are coordinated in part by the endocrine glands. Under conditions of stress, for example, the adrenal glands release a secretion into the bloodstream. This secretion increases the heart rate, breathing rate, muscle tension, and blood glucose to prepare the body for vigorous activity in the face of an emergency. The sequence of body changes in pregnancy and childbirth are controlled by other endocrine glands. The changes that occur in puberty, or sexual maturation, are also largely under the control of the endocrine system.

The nervous system, however, is the most important integrating factor in a complex organism. Every stimulus in the external environment initiates changes in the internal environment: a drop in external temperature starts a drop in internal temperature; sudden physical exertion depletes the food (glucose) and oxygen (air) content within the body. Diverse cells, tissues, organs, and systems must react all over the body to keep the internal environment relatively constant so that the specialized cells can survive. Each change in the external or internal environment, or both, makes rapid reactions all over the body necessary so that the internal environment may be held within the limits that permit life. External and internal changes are detected by sense organs reacting to conditions outside and inside the body. The nervous system conducts impulses from sense organs all over the body to effectors (muscles and glands), so that the proper tissue, organ, or system reactions will occur to maintain the constancy of the internal environment.

Every change in the external or internal environment, or both, tends to alter internal conditions from those needed by the specialized cells for adequate functioning and survival, that is, **functional integrity.** The organized reactions of the body to change maintain a *balance* among the often conflicting requirements posed by the needs of the varied cells. Such reactions are classed as homeostatic reactions, and their end result is homeostasis, a dynamic equilibrium (changing balance) that maintains conditions in the internal environment within the limits that each cell requires for functional integrity.

Homeostatic responses to environmental change involve relatively simple reflex responses, **instinctive reactions** (in lower animals), and complex **learned reactions** (in higher animals or man). For example, a drop in the external temperature sets off a variety of reflex responses: (1) the heart will beat fast to provide food and oxygen and remove wastes, sustaining a high level of metabolism throughout the body and thereby producing heat; (2) muscle cells will contract in bursts (shivering) to produce heat, and breathing will be faster to supply more oxygen; and (3) blood will be diverted from blood vessels near the surface of the body to keep it from being chilled.

Lower animals inherit complex response patterns that react to cold stresses; for example, a rat will build a nest for insulation from the cold, or a bear will reduce its body requirements and sleep (hibernation) in reaction to seasonal cold. Complex adaptive homeostatic responses of this kind are called instincts and may occur without prior learning. Man, however, acquires the complex adaptive responses called for—he *learns* to put on a coat, light a fire, and otherwise adapt to changed conditions. The maintenance of homeostasis is therefore the ultimate basis of human motivation.

The stresses imposed by a changing environment are often conflicting—to react to one stress imposes another; to adapt to one internal **need** imbalances homeostasis in another fashion. If an animal reflexly reacts to a low water supply by reducing its output of urine and perspiration, the needs of the body for removing wastes and keeping cool may be imperiled. In instances of this kind the more pressing homeostatic demands of the body are given precedence: minimum water is provided to remove waste and cool the body, since death would result from a large change in these conditions more rapidly than from thirst. Homeostasis is thus a compromise among constantly changing and often conflicting stresses imposed by the environment. Homeostatic reactions are organized responses of the organism, ranging from simple reflexes to complex learned reactions; these responses tend to keep the internal environment constant enough to maintain the functional integrity of the cells of the body.

METABOLISM OF CELLS
Cell metabolism versus intermediary metabolism

Despite their specialization, the cells of the body must obtain the food and oxygen necessary for life from their environment

inside the body (the internal environment). They must also eliminate their accumulated wastes through this environment (Fig. 2-4). The activities of the individual cell that are involved in transforming food and oxygen into cellular structure and eliminating waste from the cell are called **cell metabolism.** These activities are complex chemical reactions that go on inside the cells. The chemical reactions involve simple chemical "food" compounds—blood glucose, amino acids, fatty acids, minerals, and oxygen—that have been broken down from more complex compounds in **intermediary metabolism.** Intermediary metabolism refers to the chemical reactions that go on outside most of the cells, where the fats, proteins, and carbohydrates used by the body as food are broken down into the simple compounds specialized cells can use, and where cellular waste is transformed for removal from the bloodstream.

Chemical reaction in cells

The individual specialized cells of the body obtain predigested food material and oxygen from the internal environment of **extracellular fluid** (the fluid that surrounds all cells). These raw materials are utilized in rebuilding the structure of the cell and in supplying the chemical energy to power the reactions necessary to life, including waste elimination from the cell.

Organic compounds. The raw materials used by the cell come from a class of chemical compounds called **organic compounds.** These compounds have in common a chemical structure built of long "chains" of carbon (C) atoms. The raw materials used by the cell, the complex compounds from which they are derived in intermediary metabolism, and the structure of the cell itself are all organic compounds. In the reactions of cell metabolism, the cell uses (1) **fatty acids** derived by intermediary metabolism from **fats,** (2) **amino acids** derived from **proteins,** and (3) glucose derived from these and from **carbohydrates.** Small amounts of **minerals** (po-

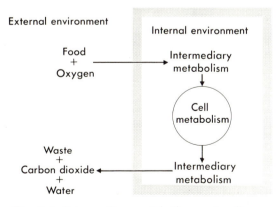

Fig. 2-4. Intermediary metabolism and cell metabolism.

tassium, calcium, and sodium) and **vitamins** are likewise needed. Fats, proteins, and minerals need no introduction. Carbohydrates are sugars and starches, and vitamins will be discussed later.

Anabolism and catabolism. The chemical reactions necessary to rebuild cellular structure and eliminate cellular waste require energy. Metabolic reactions that require energy input to proceed are collectively known as **anabolism.** The necessary energy is supplied by other chemical reactions that release energy, collectively known as **catabolism.** All organic chemical reactions either require or give off energy, that is, they are either catabolic or anabolic. Together they include all the chemical reactions of the body, which are known collectively as metabolism.

The cell as a chemical factory. Thus considered, the cell is a "chemical factory" in which the energy for each anabolic reaction is obtained from catabolic reactions. Each time a complex compound is broken down into a simpler one, energy is released and used to build complex compounds needed by the cell. The complex compounds are made from building blocks such as amino acids and fatty acids with glucose as the basic energy source. Although most of the twenty-two amino acids that the body uses are broken down from proteins in intermediary metabolism, there are ten **essential amino acids** that must be part of the diet because the body cannot manufacture them. There are likewise three **essential fatty acids** that cannot be made from fats in the diet. Small amounts of minerals—sodium, potassium, and calcium—are supplied by the diet in the form of salts. Vitamins are required to speed certain chemical reactions of life, and glucose is supplied from the carbohydrate of the diet. The cell assembles amino acids into the proteins that form the building blocks of its structure and constructs its fats from fatty acids. Glucose provides the basic energy source by catabolic reaction as it is broken down

into lactic acid, which is eliminated from the body.

INTERMEDIARY METABOLISM

The food intake of the body consists of fats, proteins, carbohydrates, essential amino and fatty acids, minerals, and vitamins. Taken in through the alimentary canal and combined with oxygen carried by the blood vessels from the lungs, these substances undergo the many chemical reactions of life referred to, collectively, as metabolism. Before the cell can utilize such raw materials, they must be broken down in a series of discrete steps into forms usable by the cells. The chemical reactions necessary to prepare raw materials for the cells are referred to as intermediary metabolism.

Oxidation

The many complex chemical reactions of intermediary and cell metabolism utilize the same raw materials and liberate the same kinds of wastes that would be involved in burning the raw material in a fire, a form of oxidation. The potential energy of a fat, protein, or carbohydrate can thus be expressed as a fraction of the energy released as heat by burning that food. The food is provided by the alimentary canal and the oxygen by the lungs. The kidneys dispose of wastes, and, together with the sweat glands and respiration, eliminate water and carbon dioxide. A simplified form of the basic equation would be as follows:

Food + Oxygen $\rightarrow$ Energy + Heat + Waste + Carbon dioxide + Water

The arrow includes hundreds of chemical reactions involved in the intermediary and cell metabolism of the body. Nevertheless, the input raw materials and output results are the same. The body is able to utilize about 20% of the potential energy of food, and the rest is given off as heat. A portion of the heat is used to keep the temperature of the body (internal environment) constant in the face of fluctuations in the (usually) colder external environment. The 20% efficiency of the body may be compared to that of a heat-operated steam engine (15%) or a gasoline motor (10%). The energy value of food can thus be measured as a fraction of the heat that would be released by burning the food. The unit involved is the calorie—the amount of heat required to raise the temperature of 1 gram of water 1 degree Celsius. The more work done by the body, the greater are the number of calories of food and volumes of oxygen required. One needs to eat more before or after exercise, as well as to breathe harder during strenuous activity to obtain more oxygen.

The basic food that is "burned" by cells is glucose, which may be formed in intermediary metabolism from either fats, proteins, or carbohydrates. Fatty acids and amino acids are needed for cellular structure, but they cannot be derived from carbohydrates. Fatty acids are derived from fats, and amino acids are from proteins. These facts have important consequences for metabolism. The Japanese had ample carbohydrates in their diet, but for many generations their growth was stunted because of dietary lack of amino acids and vitamins for cell building. The Eskimo, on the other hand, remained vigorous in the face of a hostile environment, by living on fats and proteins, from which they obtained cell-building amino and fatty acids, as well as by breaking these substances down into glucose to power the reactions of the body.

Basal metabolism

Refer again to the basic oxidation equation of metabolism given previously. It should be evident that when energy is required at a greater than normal rate by the body, more oxygen is utilized and more carbon dioxide is given off by the body. The overall rate at which metabolism is going on in the body can therefore be measured by the oxygen intake or by the carbon dioxide given off in breathing. Usually oxygen intake is measured with the subject breathing air (20% oxygen) from a measured container. When the subject exercises, he breathes harder—his metabolic rate and oxygen intake are higher because the reactions of metabolism are proceeding faster. When the subject is resting and not digesting food (a process requiring energy), an estimate of his minimum waking rate of metabolism—the **basal metabolic rate,** or BMR—is obtained. (The metabolic rate is lower during sleep.) The BMR is an important measure of the functioning of the body. It is used to test the activity of the thyroid gland (Chapter 3), whose secretions regulate the metabolic rate of the body.

Energy exchange

The digestive system must break down fat, protein, and carbohydrate into glucose to be used by the cells and must store any excess glucose in a different form to be released into the bloodstream as the cells require it. In addition, cells must store energy by "packaging" it—by building com-

$$AA \rightleftharpoons ADP \rightleftharpoons ATP \rightleftharpoons CP \text{ (energy storage—cells)}$$

$$O_2 + \text{Carbohydrate} \rightleftharpoons \text{Glucose} \rightleftharpoons \text{Glycogen (food storage—liver)}$$

$$\left.\begin{array}{l} O_2 + \text{Fat} \rightleftharpoons \text{Fatty acid} \\ O_2 + \text{Protein} \rightleftharpoons \text{Amino acid} \end{array}\right\} \rightleftharpoons \text{Pyruvic acid} \rightleftharpoons \text{Lactic acid} + CO_2 + H_2O \text{ (oxidation)}$$

Fig. 2-5. Simplified diagram of reactions involved in carbohydrate metabolism. (Double arrows refer to either chemical reactions or energy exchange.) Glucose can be manufactured from carbohydrate, fat, or protein in intermediary metabolism and stored in the liver as glycogen. When used by the cells as food, it is broken down into pyruvic acid and lactic acid before it is eliminated. These reactions release energy that the cell uses to form energy-rich phosphate bonds to store energy. *AA,* Adenylic acid (one bond); *ADP,* adenosine diphosphate (two bonds); *ATP,* adenosine triphosphate; *CP,* creatin phosphate.

Table 2-1. Summary of the vitmains: Functions, deficiency conditions, and food sources*

Vitamin	Function	Deficiency condition	Food sources
Fat soluble			
Vitamin A (retinal) and provitamin A (α,β,γ-caro-tene, crypto-xanthin)	1. Adaptation to dim light 2. Promote growth 3. Prevent keratinization of skin and eye 4. Resistance to bacterial infection	Night Xerophthalmia Hyperkeratosis Poor growth	Vitamin A Liver Egg yolk Milk, butter Provitamin A Sweet potatoes Winter squash Greens Carrots Cantaloupe
Vitamin D (calciferol)	1. Facilitate absorption of calcium and phosphorus 2. Maintenance of alkaline phosphatase for optimum calcification	Rickets Osteomalacia	Vitamin D–fortified milk Eggs Cheese, butter Fish
Vitamin E (tocopherols)	1. Antioxidant (protects vitamins A and C and unsaturated fatty acids)		Vegetable oils Greens
Vitamin K (phyllo- and farnoquinone)	1. Blood clotting (formation of pro-thrombin and proconvertin)	Hemorrhage	Greens Liver Egg yolks
Water soluble			
Thiamin	1. Coenzyme TPP (energy from carbo-hydrate and fat) 2. Formation of ribose for DNA and RNA (transketolase) 3. Conversion of tryptophan to niacin	Beriberi	Meat Whole grain and enriched cereals Milk Legumes
Riboflavin	1. FMN and FAD for releasing energy 2. Conversion of tryptophan to niacin	Ariboflavinosis	Milk Green vegetables Fish, meat, eggs
Niacin	1. NAD and NADP to release energy 2. Glycolysis 3. Fatty acid synthesis	Pellagra	Meat, poultry, fish Peanut butter Whole grain and enriched cereals Greens
Vitamin B_6 (pyridoxine)	1. Transamination and deamination of amino acid 2. Porphyrin synthesis (for hemoglobin) 3. Conversion of tryptophan to niacin 4. Energy from glycogen 5. Formation of histamine, serotonin, norepinephrine		Meats Bananas Whole grain cereals Lima beans Cabbage Potatoes Spinach
Pantothenic acid	1. CoA component (transfer 2 carbon fragments to release energy) 2. Porphyrin synthesis (hemoglobin formation) 3. Cholesterol and steroid formation		Organ meats Whole grain cereal

*Modified from Stare, F. J., and McWilliams, M.: Living nutrition, New York, 1973, John Wiley & Sons, Inc.

Table 2-1. Summary of vitamins: Functions, deficiency conditions, and food sources—cont'd

Vitamin	Function	Deficiency condition	Food sources
Water soluble—cont'd			
Biotin	1. Release energy from carbohydrate 2. Fatty acid metabolism 3. Deamination of protein		Egg yolks Milk Organ meats Cereals Legumes Nuts
Folacin (folic acid, pteroylglutamic acid)	1. Transfer of single carbon units 2. Coenzyme in synthesis of: guanine and adenine; thymine; choline; amino acids; porphyrin	Macrocytic anemia	Greens Mushrooms Liver Kidney
Vitamin B_{12} (cobalamin)	1. Maturation of red blood cells 2. Carbohydrate metabolism for energy for central nervous system 3. Formation of single carbon radicals 4. Conversion of folinic acid to folacin	Pernicious anemia	Animal foods
Ascorbic acid (vitamin C)	1. Formation of collagen 2. Utilization of calcium in bones and teeth 3. Elasticity and strength of capillaries 4. Conversion of folinic acid to folacin	Scurvy	Citrus fruits Strawberries Papayas Broccoli Cabbage Tomatoes Potatoes

plex compounds from simpler ones (anabolism). Energy is thus readily available; the complex "packages" may be broken down into simpler ones (catabolism), with the release of energy for the cells to utilize in building the proteins and fats they require.

Glucose is stored by the liver and muscles in the form of **glycogen** and released as required to keep the concentration of blood glucose for the cells within narrow limits, so that food for the cells is always available. This set of reactions occurs in intermediary metabolism. In cell metabolism the **energy-rich phosphate bond** is the chief source of energy-releasing chemical reactions that "drive" other reactions inside the cell. Such bonds hold the parts of an increasingly complex compound together (Fig. 2-5).

CONTROL OF METABOLISM
Enzymes

Every needed chemical reaction in the body must go on at a minimum rate to provide the necessary energy, structure, and food for the cell. The rate at which chemical reactions can proceed often depends on **enzymes.** Many reactions are reversible; which way the reaction goes depends on enzymes. The presence of enzymes may determine which of several alternative reactions occur. Enzymes are organic **catalysts** for the chemical reactions involved in metabolism. Catalysts are chemicals that speed up the rate at which chemical reactions go on without being used up in the reactions. Only minute amounts are needed, and since they are not consumed by the reactions they speed, catalysts can be utilized over and over again to catalyze

Table 2-2. Summary of minerals: Functions and food sources*

Mineral	Functions	Food sources
Calcium	1. Bone formation, maintenance, and growth 2. Tooth formation 3. Blood clot formation 4. Activation of pancreatic lipase 5. Absorption of vitamin B_{12} 6. Contraction of muscle	Milk, cheese, puddings, custards, chocolate beverages Fish with bones, including salmon Greens Broccoli
Chloride	1. Component of hydrochloric acid 2. Maintenance of proper osmotic pressure 3. Acid-base balance	Table salt Meats Milk Eggs
Cobalt	1. Part of vitamin B_{12} molecule	Organ meats Meats
Copper	1. Catalyst for hemoglobin formation 2. Formation of elastin (connective tissue) 3. Release of energy (in cytochrome oxidase and catalase) 4. Formation of melanin (pigment) 5. Formation of phospholipids for myelin sheath of nerves	Cereals Nuts Legumes Liver Shellfish Grapes Meats
Fluoride	1. Strengthen bones and teeth	Fluoridated water
Iodine	1. Component of thyroxine and triiodothyronine	Iodized salt Fish (salt water and anadromous)
Iron	1. Component of hemoglobin 2. Component of myoglobin 3. Component of cytochromes, cytochrome oxidase, catalase, peroxidase 4. Component of myeloperoxidase	Meats Heart, liver Clams Oysters Lima beans Spinach Dates, dried fruits Nuts Enriched and whole grain cereals
Magnesium	1. Catalyze ATP $\leftrightarrow$ ADP 2. Conduct nerve impulses 3. Retention of calcium in teeth 4. Adjust to cold environment	Milk Green vegetables Nuts Breads and cereals
Manganese	1. Bone development 2. Component of arginase 3. Promotes thiamin storage	Cereals Legumes
Molybdenum	1. Component of xanthine oxidase 2. Component of aldehyde oxidase	

Phosphorus	1. Bone formation, maintenance, and growth
	2. Tooth formation
	3. Component of DNA and RNA
	4. Component of ADP and ATP
	5. Fatty acid transport
	6. Acid-base balance
	7. Component of TPP
		Organic
		  Meats, poultry, and fish
		
		Inorganic
		  Milk, fruits and vegetables

*From Stare, F. J., and McWilliams, M.: Living nutrition, New York, 1973, John Wiley & Sons, Inc.

Table 2-2. Summary of minerals: Functions and food sources—cont'd

Mineral	Functions	Food sources
Potassium	1. Maintenance of osmotic pressure 2. Acid-base balance 3. Transmission of nerve impulses 4. Catalyst in energy metabolism 5. Formation of proteins 6. Formation of glycogen	Orange juice Dried fruits Bananas Potatoes Coffee
Selenium	1. Antioxidant	
Sodium	1. Maintenance of osmotic pressure 2. Acid-base balance 3. Relaxation of muscles 4. Absorption of glucose 5. Transmission of nerve impulses	Table salt Salted meats Milk
Sulfur	1. Component of thiamin 2. Component of some proteins (hair, nails, skin)	Meats Milk and cheese Eggs Legumes Nuts
Zinc	1. Component of carboxypeptidase 2. Component of carbonic anhydrase	Whole-grain cereals Meats Legumes

(speed up) the same reaction. The presence or absence of given catalysts, then, may decide the *direction* (anabolic or catabolic) of a reaction or which of several *alternative* reactions may occur or *selectively* speed up various metabolic reactions, according to which enzymes are present.

Vitamins

Some vitamins appear to be parts of enzymes that cannot be manufactured by the cells of the body. They must be supplied in minute amounts in the diet to form part of essential enzymes. Before the discovery of their role, deficiency symptoms from lack of vitamins were common in certain areas or diet conditions. Beriberi, with lassitude, paralysis, and convulsive reactions, was once common in the Far East because of the lack of vitamin B_1—the population ate polished rice, and vitamin B_1 was lost with the shell of the rice. Scurvy was once common in the British navy because of the lack of fresh fruit, which did not keep on ships. However, the "limeys" learned to carry lime juice to prevent scurvy. Vitamins are classified as water-soluble or fat-soluble for lack of a better basis. Table 2-1 lists the more important vitamins, together with their deficiency symptoms and mode of action. The average diet includes them all, at least in the minute amounts necessary.

Minerals

Certain minerals, in minute amounts, are also vital to normal body function and must form part of any normal diet. Table 2-2 lists these minerals, their function, and food sources. Except in a few parts of the world where the soil is deficient in one or more of the minerals listed, the average diet includes them all.

Hormones

Hormones are substances manufactured by the ductless, or endocrine, glands and secreted into the bloodstream, affecting metabolism all over the body. (The endocrine system is one of the most important integrating systems of the body and will be treated at length in Chapter 3.) The effect of hormones is selective; they act only on certain metabolic reactions in selected tissues. It appears that some hormones are enzyme inhibitors—they block certain metabolic reactions to allow competing metabolic reactions to proceed. Other hormones seem to act on the DNA or RNA molecules of cells to alter the way they govern cell function. Hormones control growth, general metabolic rate, sexual and pregnancy processes, and the metabolism of many chemicals vital to normal metabolism and behavior.

Genes, enzyme action, cell metabolism, and heredity

The nucleus of each cell in the human body contains 23 pairs of **chromosomes,** 46 in all. One of each pair of chromosomes is inherited from one parent, the other chromosome coming from the other parent. Each chromosome contains genes, complex chemicals that determine the organism's inherited characteristics. Genes also determine the particular specialization of each cell in the organism and the metabolic processes that go on within that cell. Each chromosome contains perhaps 3000 genes, and each gene is responsible for determining one or more of the characteristics of the cell. Genes are made up of a chemical called DNA (deoxyribonucleic acid), and the DNA molecule looks like a twisted ladder (Fig. 2-6), with pairs of chemical bases forming the steps of the ladder. When a cell divides to reproduce itself, the chromosomes and genes also divide, leaving two spiral "half-ladders" for each gene. Each of the two new cells thus contain 46 "half-chromosomes" containing thousands of "half-DNA" molecules. Each half-ladder of DNA forms a pattern to assemble the other half from raw materials that are readily available in the new cell. Thereby each gene reproduces itself in cell division. The specialized characteristics of the new cells are the same as those of the old cell.

The specialized features of a cell depend on the type and quantity of the proteins that are the building blocks of that cell, proteins the cell itself manufactures. The synthesis of cell proteins is controlled by the sequence of molecules in the DNA of its genes; some cells use one part of the DNA molecule to specialize as skin cells, whereas others use another part to specialize as liver cells. The DNA molecule synthesizes a **messenger RNA** (mRNA) molecule on part of its structure (Fig. 2-6). The messenger RNA moves out of the nucleus of the cell to cell inclusions in the cytoplasm called **ribosomes,** which also contain RNA. Here the messenger RNA acts as a pattern for a second kind of RNA, called **transfer RNA.** An amino acid molecule is attached to each part of the transfer RNA that is assembled on the messenger RNA. The amino acids are thereby lined up in the proper sequence to form a specific protein. The protein thus produced is an enzyme that speeds specific chemical reactions. The reactions manufacture specialized parts of the cell, making it a skin cell or a liver cell, as the case may be.

Parts of the DNA molecule also direct each metabolic reaction of the cell. Life is basically an involved set of chemical reactions directed in a little-known fashion by different segments of the DNA molecule. For example, some investigators believe that chemicals called histones cover parts of the DNA molecule whereas other nonhistone proteins uncover these locations to allow the uncovered parts to initiate chemical reactions. In trying to understand the amino acid sequence of each part of the DNA molecules that directs each chemical reaction of life, scientists face a formidable task. In attempts to "break the code" of amino acid sequences, they have turned to simpler organisms. A bacillus (germ) common to the digestive system of man and called *Escherichia coli* has been the favorite subject. A virus is a DNA molecule with a protein coat that attacks single-celled organisms like *E. coli* as readily as it infects multicellular organisms such as man. The

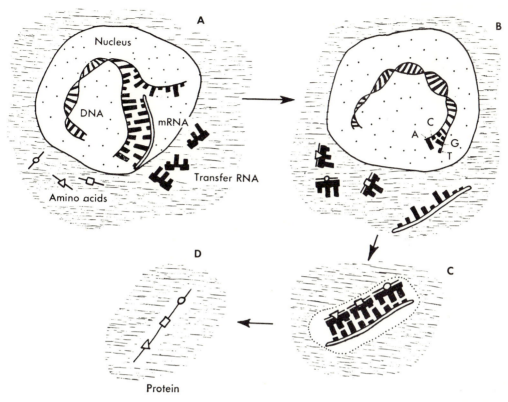

Fig. 2-6. Sequence of events in the manufacture of an enzyme by the cell. **A,** DNA molecule "divides" to form a messenger RNA (mRNA) molecule on part of its structure. The sequence of bases on the DNA molecule (*A, C, G,* and *T* labeled in **B**) determines the shape of the RNA molecule that is assembled. **B,** mRNA has left the cell nucleus. **C,** mRNA is assembling transfer RNA in a cell inclusion, called a ribosome, by serving as a template for the amino acid sequence of the transfer RNA molecule. The transfer RNA in turn is assembling three bases (represented by the *triangle, square,* and *circle*) into a protein enzyme. **D,** Enzyme has left the ribosome to catalyze a chemical reaction in another part of the cell.

virus infects by releasing its DNA into each cell, leaving its protein coat outside. Inside the cell the virus DNA uses the substance of the cell to multiply in a parasitic fashion, with each new virus DNA acquiring a protein coat. The host cell then bursts, releasing virus DNA, which infects other cells. By using components of this series of reactions, scientists have recently been able to synthesize a self-reproducing DNA molecule. This important series of experiments indicates a nearly complete understanding of the chemical mechanisms of viral DNA.

The implications of the above research are profound, for they bring us closer to an understanding of DNA mechanisms in the cells of man. After a discussion of the hereditary role of DNA, the possible applications of our new knowledge will be clearer.

Cell mechanisms in heredity

A gene is the part of a DNA molecule that determines an inherited characteristic that can be identified, such as brown hair or blue eyes. Inheritance and cell specialization depend on the DNA of genes, but genes are packaged in chromosomes, and chromosomes occur in pairs—only half of the chromosomes (23) are inherited from each parent; therefore, only half of the genes and inherited characteristics come from each parent. The chromosomes come in pairs because the half received from one parent must concern the same structures as the half the other parent contributes. If the 46 chromosomes were composed of two unpaired groups of 23 from each parent, some characteristics would be repeated and some would be missing.

Some of the cells of the body are specialized for reproduction; these cells contain the same chromosomes and genes as other cells of the body, but are isolated from them by being contained in the reproductive tissue of the male **(testes)** and female **(ovaries).** The reproductive cells of the male and female **gonads** (reproductive organs) multiply in the same fashion as other cells in the body as long as they are in an immature state; that is, each cell splits each of its 46 chromosomes and each of the DNA molecules they contain in forming two new cells by cellular mitosis, or **mitotic division** (Fig. 2-3). In the final division save one, called a *reduction division,* the chromosomes line up by pairs instead of splitting. Each cell receives only one of each pair of chromosomes, ending up with two cells of 23 chromosomes each instead of two cells of 46. Which one of each pair each new cell receives is apparently determined by chance. One of a single pair might wind up in either of the two new cells. In the male a final mitotic division produces four **sperm cells.** In the female one cell of the reduction division and one cell of the final mitotic division are discarded, so that only one **ovum** (egg cell) remains. In fertilization one of the sperm cells penetrates the ovum to contribute its 23 chromosomes to the 23 of the ovum, so that a single cell of 46 chromosomes results. It is from this cell that the mature and complex multicellular organism develops by mitotic division; half of the chromo-

somes, and therefore half of the genes of each subsequent cell, originate with the female and half with the male.

Arithmetic of heredity. The single cell that is to form the complete individual begins with 23 pairs of chromosomes and therefore 23 pairs of gene assemblies, with one member of each pair having been contributed by the mother and one by the father. Each chromosome pair contains many pairs of genes, with each gene of a pair of genes regulating the same inherited characteristics in the future offspring. To simplify, consider only one gene pair from a single pair of chromosomes that determines a given characteristic, such as eye color. Assume for the moment that the male contributed a gene for brown eyes (Br) and the female contributed a matching gene for blue eyes (bl). Further assume that the Br gene is **dominant** and the bl gene is **recessive.** This means that an individual having only Br in both members of a gene pair (BrBr) will have brown eyes, and an individual with only bl genes (blbl) will be blue-eyed, and an individual with one of each gene (Brbl) will be brown-eyed, since the brown-eyed (Br) gene is dominant over the recessive blue-eyed (bl) gene. However, the Brbl individual may contribute a bl gene to this offspring. This is true because if he carries Brbl in his genes, the reduction division will mean that half the sperm cells will carry Br and half will carry bl. Since it is a matter of chance in the reduction division which sperm or ovum gets which of the gene-chromosome groups, the odds are 50-50 that a Brbl individual will contribute a Br gene and 50-50 that he will contribute a bl gene to his offspring. To illustrate further consequences, let us consider two generations:

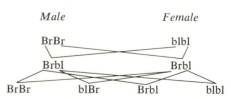

Male			*Female*
BrBr			blbl
Brbl			Brbl
BrBr	blBr	Brbl	blbl

Mating a BrBr with a blbl can only result in Brbl individuals, brown-eyed but **carriers** of the recessive gene for blue eyes. If two carriers are mated, there are four possible crosses. BrBr, blBr, Brbl, blbl. One in four (on the average) will be brown-eyed and carry only that gene, one in four will be blue-eyed and carry only that gene, and two will be brown-eyed (Br) but carriers of the recessive gene (bl) for blue eyes.

The genes of the inherited DNA molecules determine physical characteristics by the way they control the manufacture of enzymes in the cell. Enzymes that control hair and eye color are examples. In the inheritance of human characteristics some genes act as simple dominants and recessives, such as brown eye color over blue, curly hair over straight, dark hair over light. Some abnormalities may be inherited as dominants, such as short digits or hereditary cataracts, and others as recessives, such as albinism or epilepsy. In the human, however, **gene linkage, sex-linkage,** and **crossovers** complicate the picture.

Gene linkage

When the chromosomes divide by pairs, each chromosome constitutes a "package" of gene-determined characteristics. If the individual inherits chromosome A instead of B, he will receive each of the thousands of DNA genes in A. The gene for dark hair will be found in the same chromosome as the gene for brown eyes, so that both characteristics will usually be inherited, or else neither will be inherited.

Crossovers

When the chromosomes line up into pairs during reduction division, they sometimes get twisted (Fig. 2-7). When the division of genes and chromosomes occurs, its cuts across chromosome lines, and the individual may inherit some genes from chromosome A and some from B. As a result the gene for dark hair may wind up in the same chromosome as the gene for blue eyes instead of the one for brown eyes.

Sex-linked characteristics

The sex of offspring is also determined by gene pairs, with the masculine (Y) gene

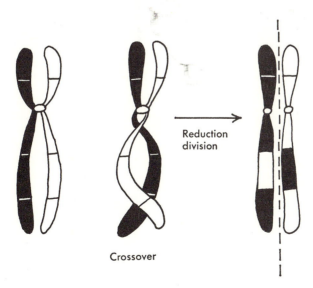

Crossover — Reduction division

Fig. 2-7. Diagram of reduction division of chromosomes showing crossover. As a result of crossover, the sperm or egg cell receives neither all the white chromosome nor all the black chromosome in the reduction division, but takes genes (DNA molecules) from each.

being dominant over the feminine gene (X). The female carries XX and the male XY. Therefore, in reduction division the female contributes only X genes, whereas the male contributes either an X or a Y, since he carries one of each:

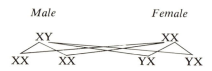

Half the offspring will be males and half females, on the average. However, other gene pairs are carried in the X chromosome and the Y chromosome besides those determining sex. These genes are called sex-linked characteristics because they are found in the same chromosomes as the genes for sex. Moreover, the Y chromosome is smaller than the X chromosome and therefore does not contain as many DNA genes. Therefore there are characteristics carried only by the larger X chromosome that are not carried by the smaller Y chromosome. Hemophilia is one of these characteristics; when the metabolism of blood is controlled by the recessive gene h, an enzyme necessary for blood clotting is missing. The dominant gene H permits normal clotting. A female never displays hemophilia if her chromosome-gene linkage is either $X_H X_h$ or $X_H X_H$, but the $X_H X_h$ female will contribute the X_h chromosome to half her offspring. The $X_h Y$ males will be hemophilic because the male has no H genes in his small Y chromosome to offset the recessive h gene, whereas the $X_H Y$ males will be normal. Therefore half of the *male* offspring $(X_h Y)$ of a hemophilic carrier female $(X_H X_h)$ will be hemophilic and half will be normal $(X_H Y)$. There is at least one famous example of this mechanism; Queen Victoria was a carrier of hemophilia, and her carrier daughters introduced the gene into the Russian and Spanish royal families. Her son, King Edward VII, was an $X_H Y$ male who did not inherit the gene

for the disease; thus it was not passed on to the English royal family.

A further genetic complexity of sexual inheritance has attracted recent attention. New techniques have enabled scientists to see certain chromosome abnormalities under the microscope. They are also able to determine which chromosomes are responsible for certain inherited characteristics. This is particularly true of the X and Y chromosomes. Studies of the population of penal institutions have turned up individual males with an extra X or Y chromosome. Their cells show an XXY or an XYY pattern, although they are biologically men, not women. They constitute less than 1% of the prison population in most studies, but the percentage found in a random sample of the law-abiding population was much lower. Subsequent studies have cast doubt on these conclusions; in any case, the percentages involved are too small to cause concern.

Other chromosome studies

Other chromosome studies have located the chromosomes responsible for certain genetic diseases, such as sickle cell anemia, which was discussed previously in this chapter. Put them together with the studies on virus DNA, which were reviewed in a preceding section, and some profound implications for the future emerge. Understanding of the genetic locus of hereditary characteristics and knowledge of DNA mechanisms may make "genetic engineering" possible. Altering the hereditary characteristics of germ tissue and artificial fertilization of the female with the altered cells could eliminate genetic disease carried by the male. One could determine the sex of offspring by sorting germ cells of both male and female, fertilizing them outside of the body, and reimplanting the germ tissue for an otherwise normal pregnancy. Sorting of germ cells could also be used to select a desirable characteristic when its chromosome locus is known.

CONTROL OF METABOLISM BY THE CIRCULATORY SYSTEM

Intermediary metabolism, which supplies the cells with food and oxygen and removes carbon dioxide and waste material, is completely dependent on the **circulatory system** as a transporting medium. The human body is 96% fluid, and the circulatory system is responsible for maintaining the chemical and physical consistency of that fluid. The fluid content of the body may be subdivided into the following: (1) the **intracellular fluid,** which is the fluid medium of the cytoplasm inside cells, a medium necessary to the chemical reactions of cell metabolism; (2) the **extracellular fluid,** outside of and surrounding the cells, which serves as a "middleman" for the physical transport of food, oxygen, waste, and carbon dioxide between the cells and the circulatory system; and (3) the blood of the circulatory system, which transports oxygen and carbon dioxide between the lungs and the extracellular fluid, transports food from the digestive system to the extracellular fluid, and transports waste from that fluid to the kidneys.

Circulatory system

The circulatory system consists of (1) the heart, which maintains the flow of blood by its pumping action; (2) the **pulmonary circulation** system of blood vessels, which carries oxygen between the heart and the lungs; and (3) the **systemic circulation** system, which carries blood from the heart to all the other tissues of the body and back again to the heart.

The pulmonary circulation is the means for loading the blood with oxygen for the tissues of the body and removing carbon dioxide from blood returned to the heart from the tissues. Inspired air contains 20% oxygen, and blood returned to the heart from the tissues is high in carbon dioxide. Blood circulated by the pulmonary circulation between heart and lungs thus loses carbon dioxide and acquires oxygen by simple diffusion of gases through the walls of the **capillaries** (thin-walled blood vessels) in the lungs. Oxygen goes into solution in the blood while carbon dioxide comes out of solution to be exhaled. Far more important, however, are chemical reactions that go on in the **red blood cells.** In the tissues they react chemically to bind carbon dioxide. After transport to the lungs the reverse chemical reaction occurs to release carbon dioxide and bind oxygen. Accompanying these reactions is a change in color, so that blood returning from the tissues (venous blood) is not as bright red as blood going to the tissues (arterial blood).

The systemic circulation moves blood between the heart and the tissues. It includes (1) the **arteries,** which carry blood from the heart to the tissues; (2) the **capillaries** in the tissues, through whose thin walls the exchange between blood and extracellular fluid occurs; (3) the **veins,** which return blood from the tissues to the heart; and (4) the **lymph vessels,** which serve as an auxiliary return system. The rhythmic contractions of the heart pump blood out through the arteries, whose muscular walls may contract or relax in reaction to vary their size and therefore the pressure of the blood within them. The pressure and rate of flow of the blood gradually diminish as the arteries branch and rebranch to finally form the thin-walled *capillaries,* through whose walls the exchange between blood and extracellular fluid occurs. Blood entering the tissue capillaries in arteries is higher in oxygen and glucose, and blood leaving the tissue capillaries in veins is high in carbon dioxide and waste. A free exchange **(diffusion)** of fluid and gases occurs between blood and extracellular fluid in the capillaries, whose thin walls retain only solid particles from the blood, such as the red cells. The red cells also react chemically to lose oxygen to the tissues and bind carbon dioxide from them. The system of diffusion is used to transport glucose from the digestive system to the blood and from the blood to the tissues, as well as to carry waste (such as lactic acid) from the cells to the blood, and from the blood to the kidneys for disposal.

Upon leaving the tissues the capillaries reform into larger veins that return the blood of the systemic circulation to the heart under low pressure. In addition, a further system of lymph vessels collects surplus extracellular fluid for return to veins near the heart. Circulation in the lymph vessels is maintained only by contraction of the muscles of the body in ordinary exercise. These contractions squeeze the thin walls of the lymph vessels passing through the muscles to move their fluid contents along.

HOMEOSTASIS AND THE
INTERNAL ENVIRONMENT
Homeostasis

Because of the extreme specialization of the cells of the body, they lose the ability to perform many functions that other (differently specialized) cells perform for them. Many conditions of the internal environment must be kept within narrow limits so that specialized cells can survive. Changes in the external environment and even internal changes caused by metabolism are reacted to by the tissues, organs, and systems of the body to keep the internal environment within narrow limits of pressure, oxygen content, acid-base balance, blood glucose level, chemical composition, and temperature. As explained before, these reactions are collectively referred to as **homeostasis.**

Blood and tissue fluid changes

Changes in blood pressure occur as a result of changes in posture and exercise, as well as from other causes. They are kept within limits by pressure receptors in the aorta (a large blood vessel) and the carotid artery. Stimulation of these receptors by an increase in blood pressure sends impulses in nerves that act to slow down the heart by way of centers in the brain. *Oxygen and carbon dioxide* content of the blood are controlled by the CO_2 level. A high level of CO_2 speeds up the heart rate (by acting on brain centers) to carry more CO_2 to the lungs for elimination. It also acts to speed up centers in the brain that control breathing. The *acidity of the blood* is also critical. Normally the blood is slightly alkaline. More CO_2 increases acidity, but the above mechanisms rid the blood of acidity. Acidity is an excess of H ions; alkalinity is an excess of OH ions. *Buffer* substances in the blood can bind either excess and deliver it to the kidneys for elimination. *Blood glucose level* is maintained between 60 and 130 mg./100 ml. of blood. Excess glucose is converted to glycogen by the liver, or it can be restored to the blood by the opposite process. The liver can also make glucose out of fat and protein. The hormone epinephrine, from the adrenal glands, stimulates glucose manufacture from glycogen, whereas insulin from the pancreas stimulates the reverse process. The endocrine glands, as well as the nervous system, organize the body's response to change. The *chemical composition* of the blood is also regulated by such mechanisms. For example, hormones of the pituitary gland regulate the potassium and calcium balance of the body fluids. The *body temperature* must be kept within narrow limits. Changes in blood temperature affect the hypothalamus (a part of the brain) so as to cause shivering (a reflex) if the body is too cold, and sweating if it is too hot. *Regulatory behavior* is a part of the homeostatic process. Changes in blood glucose may cause an animal to seek or shun food. Changes in body temperature may result in movement to sun or shade, or in nest building. Behavior is usually *aroused* by internal changes called needs; such arousal is a **drive.** For response to arousal, some lower animals have inherited patterns of behavior, called **instincts.** Man usually relies on learning to develop behavior that is appropriate to his needs and drives **(learned reactions).**

SUMMARY

All life, from single-celled organisms to man, shows the basic characteristics of irritability, conduction, contraction, secretion, elimination, growth, reproduction, and metabolism. All are necessary to behavior. Each of these characteristics depends on one or more of the specialized parts of each cell. In the course of evolution, complex, many-celled organisms have developed because they are better able to survive under the varied conditions of life. Different cells of these complex organisms have become specialized in one or more of the functions of life, depending on differently specialized cells to carry on other life functions for them. Groups of specialized cells, called tissues, are assembled into organs and systems as the many functions of the organism are integrated. Further integration is assured by the endocrine glands and nervous system.

Specialization means loss of versatility; therefore, the internal environment surrounding the cells must be held constant so that the cells can survive. The cells take food and oxygen from that environment and eliminate carbon dioxide and waste through the chemical reactions of cell metabolism. Since the cells are so specialized, other cells must provide the food and oxygen from the external environment and remove the carbon dioxide and waste in chemical reactions, called intermediary metabolism. All these reactions either store energy (anabolism) or release energy (catabolism). The source of food for the cells is glucose, and the source of energy is phosphate-bond compounds built up by anabolism from breaking down glucose (catabolism). In intermediary metabolism, glucose is provided by carbohydrates, and the amino and fatty acids the cell uses in its structure are broken down from protein and fat. Minerals and vitamins are also necessary. The whole process can be measured in terms of the oxygen consumed and carbon dioxide given off by the body in oxidation.

Metabolism includes all the chemical reactions of life. They are governed by enzymes that selectively control the speed of chemical reactions without being used up in those reactions. Enzymes control which molecules are assembled to break them down (catabolism) or build them up (anabolism). Some vitamins act as parts of enzymes.

Heredity is also determined by enzyme-manufacturing arrangements in the cell nucleus. Half the chromosomes in the nucleus of every cell are inherited from each parent. Each chromosome contains many DNA molecules that act as genes, or units of heredity. The sequence of four elements in the DNA molecule acts as a pattern to form messenger RNA molecules. Messenger RNA migrates out into the cell to assemble transfer RNA, which in turn assembles cell proteins that are enzymes. The enzymes control the nature and function of the cell.

Dominant and recessive genes may be inherited, one from each parent. If two dominant or one dominant and one recessive are inherited, the offspring will show the dominant characteristic. If one dominant gene and one recessive gene or two recessives are present, the individual may pass the recessive characteristics on to the offspring. These relationships are modified by sex-linked characteristics, gene linkage, and crossovers in the chromosomes. Population genetics and behavior genetics are areas of study concerned with more subtle interactions between heredity and environmental events.

The circulatory system is important to metabolism because it is the transportation system for interchanges between the internal and external environment. Many of the reactions of homeostasis that maintain the constancy of the internal environment are carried out by way of the circulatory system.

READINGS

Allfrey, V., and Mirsky, A.: How cells make molecules, Sci. Am. **205**:74-82, Sept. 1961. (W. H. Freeman Reprint No. 92.)

Asimov, I.: The genetic code, New York, 1962, Signet Science Library. (New American Library of World Literature, Inc., New York; also Clarkson N. Potter, Inc., N.Y.)

Asimov, I.: The human body, Boston, 1964, Houghton Mifflin Co.

Bonner, D. M., and Mills, S. E.: Heredity, Englewood Cliffs, N.J., 1964, Prentice-Hall, Inc.

Brachet, J.: The living cell, Sci. Am. **205**:50-61, Sept. 1961. (W. H. Freeman Reprint No. 90.)

Britten, R. J., and Kohne, D. E.: Repeated segments of DNA, Sci. Am. **222**:24-31, April 1970.

Carter, C. O.: Human heredity, Baltimore, 1962, Penguin Books, Inc.

Cavalli-Sforza, L.: The genetics of human populations, Sci. Am. **231**:81-89, Sept. 1974.

Changeux, J. P.: The control of biochemical reactions, Sci. Am. **212**:36-45, April 1965. (W. H. Freeman Reprint No. 1008.)

Comroe, J. H.: The lung, Sci. Am. **214**:56-68, Feb. 1966. (W. H. Freeman Reprint No. 1034.)

Crick, F. H. C.: The genetic code III, Sci. Am. **215**:55-62, Oct. 1966. (W. H. Freeman Reprint No. 1052.)

Crick, F. H. C.: Of molecules and men, Seattle, 1967, University of Washington Press.

Denenberg, V. H., and Zarrow, M. X.: Rat pax, Psychol. Today **3**:45-68, April 1970.

Fischberg, M., and Blackler, A. W.: How cells specialize, Sci. Am. **205**:124-140, Sept. 1961. (W. H. Freeman Reprint No. 94.)

Flecher, J.: The ethics of genetic control: Ending reproductive roulette, Garden City, N. Y., 1974, Doubleday Anchor Press.

Gerard, R. W.: Unresting cells, New York, 1949, Harper & Brothers.

German, J.: Studying human chromosomes today, Amer. Sci. **58**:182-201, 1970.

Goulian, M.: Synthesis of viral DNA, Sci. J. **5**:35-42, March, 1969.

Hanawalt, P. C., and Haynes, R. H.: The repair of DNA, Sci. Am. **216**:36-43, Feb. 1967. (W. H. Freeman Reprint No. 1061.)

Hurwitz, J., and Furth, J. J.: Messenger RNA, Sci. Am. **206**:41-49, Feb. 1962. (W. H. Freeman Reprint No. 119.)

Kalmas, H.: Genetics, Garden City, N. Y., 1964, Doubleday & Co., Inc.

Kornberg, A.: The synthesis of DNA, Sci. Am. **219**:64-78, Oct. 1968. (W. H. Freeman Reprint No. 1124.)

Loewenstein, W. R.: Intercellular communication, Sci. Am. **222**:79-86, May 1970.

McKusick, V. A.: The royal hemophilia, Sci. Am. **213**:88-95, Aug. 1965.

Manosevitz, M.: Hoarding—an exercise in behavior genetics, Psychol. Today **4**:55-76, Aug. 1970.

Mayerson, H. S.: The lymphatic system, Sci. Am. **208**:80-90, June 1963. (W. H. Freeman Reprint No. 158.)

Mazia, D.: How cells divide, Sci. Am. **205**:100-120, Sept. 1961. (W. H. Freeman Reprint No. 93.)

Mercer, E. H.: Cells: their structure and function, Garden City, N.Y., 1962, Doubleday & Co., Inc.

Mittwoch, U.: Sex differences in cells, Sci. Am. **209**:54-62, July 1963. (W. H. Freeman Reprint No. 161.)

Ptashne, M., and Gilbert, W.: Genetic repressors, Sci. Am. **222**:36-44, June 1970.

Ruddle, F., and Kueherlapati, R.: Hybrid cells and human genes, Sci. Am. **231**:36-44, July 1974.

Sager, R.: Genes outside the chromosomes, Sci. Am. **212**:71-79, Jan. 1965. (W. H. Freeman Reprint No. 1002.)

Schmidt-Nielson, K.: Animal physiology, Englewood Cliffs, N.J., 1960, Prentice-Hall, Inc.

Shneour, E.: The malnourished mind, Garden City, N.Y., 1974, Doubleday Anchor Press.

Siegel, P. B.: Behavior-genetics, BioScience **20**: 605-608, 1970.

Sinsheimer, R. L.: Genetic engineering: The modification of man, Impact of Science on Society **20**:279-291, 1970. Reprinted in Leukel, F., editor: Issues in physiological psychology, St. Louis, 1974, The C. V. Mosby Co.

Steen, E. B., and Montagu, A.: Anatomy and physiology, vols. 1 and 2, New York, 1959, Barnes & Noble, Inc.

Stein, G. S., Stein, J. S., and Kleinsmith, L. J.: Chromosomal proteins and gene regulation, Sci. Am. **232**:46-57, 1975.

Thurber, R. E.: Human physiology, a programmed text, New York, 1969, John Wiley & Sons, Inc.

von Koenigswald, E. H. R.: The evolution of man, Ann Arbor, 1963, University of Michigan Press.

Walker, K.: Human physiology, Baltimore, 1956, Penguin Books, Inc.

Wiggers, C. J.: The heart, Sci. Am. **196**:74-87, May 1957. (W. H. Freeman Reprint No. 62.)

Wood, J. E.: The venous system, Sci. Am. **218**: 86-96, Jan. 1968. (W. H. Freeman Reprint No. 1093.)

Yanofsky, C.: Gene structure and protein structure, Sci. Am. **216**:80-94, May 1967. (W. H. Freeman Reprint No. 1074.)

part two
Integrating and response systems

chapter 3
Endocrine glands

OVERVIEW

The cells and tissues of the body are diverse and specialized. A need for *integrating* their varied activities to maintain a *constant internal environment* has resulted. The body is integrated by (1) the organization of cells into tissues, organs, and systems, as explained in Chapter 2, (2) the integration of tissue, organ, and system activities by the nervous system, as explained in Chapter 5, and (3) the integration of these activities by the endocrine glands, whose chemical secretions may have similar effects in widely separated locations in the body.

The specialized secretions of the endocrine glands, called hormones, are carried throughout the body by the bloodstream. Some of these glands are under the control of the nervous system and are part of the organism's response to external and internal events; other glands react directly to conditions in the internal environment. In either case the endocrine glands are important to behavior.

The defining characteristics of the endocrine glands will be explained first. A few remarks on methods of investigation will follow to explain the functions of the glands and reveal the reasons for flaws in our knowledge. Then the chemical variety of the endocrine hormones can be briefly noted. The various ways in which hormones can act on their "target" cells and tissues will be explained, and the endocrine glands will then be discussed, one at a time. In each case their normal function will be explained first. The effects of undersecretion and of oversecretion of the gland

can then be appreciated. These effects show the importance of the gland to individual differences in vigor, muscle and nerve excitability, emotional balance, metabolism, growth, sexual development, and other factors important to behavior. The endocrine glands discussed will include the thyroid, parathyroids, adrenals, pancreas, pituitary, gonads, pineal gland, and thymus.

CHARACTERISTICS OF THE ENDOCRINE GLANDS
Endocrine and exocrine glands

All glands are *organs* made up of a variety of tissues that aid in *secretion* of substances needed by the body. All cells have secretory functions (Chapter 2), but glands contain cells that are specialized for secretion. Exocrine glands are duct glands, so called because they discharge their secretions into a duct, or "pipeline," that carries the secretions to their destination. The destination may be a part of the digestive tract, as in the case of the salivary glands and glands of the intestine, or it may be the surface of the body, as in the case of the sebaceous (oil-producing) and sweat glands of the skin. Only the endocrine glands are discussed in detail in this chapter. The endocrine glands, or ductless glands, have no "pipelines" for their secretions. Endocrine glands discharge their secretions directly into the blood vessels that pass through them. The endocrine gland secretions, called hormones, are carried throughout the body by the circulatory system. Depending on the nature of the hormone produced and the characteristics of the cells it encounters, an endocrine gland may affect the functioning of cells, organs, and tissues in widespread locations throughout the body. Therefore a gland is endocrine if it produces a hormone that (1) is specific to that gland, (2) is distributed by the bloodstream throughout the body, and (3) has a specific influence on some other part of the body—a **target tissue** or organ.

Hormone characteristics

Hormones are composed of a variety of compounds (for example, steroids, polypeptides, and amino acids) that have specific effects on different kinds of specialized tissue. Some hormones affect most of the cells of the body, irrespective of their specialized structure and functioning. Other hormones affect only cells that are specialized in certain ways—for example, a hormone that affects the ability of kidney tubule cells to reabsorb water from the urine. In this instance the target tissue of the hormone is found only in a single organ, the kidney. However, a given endocrine gland may produce several different hormones if it has several different kinds of secreting cells or if its cells produce more than one kind of secretion. In this case the hormones would act on a variety of target tissues, with different effects on each tissue. To fully understand the function of an endocrine gland, one would have to isolate each of its hormones and test its effects. The problem is further complicated by the fact that endocrine glands affect each other. Hormones from one endocrine gland may excite or inhibit the production of hormones by another endocrine gland—that is, *interactions* occur between endocrine glands.

Methods of investigation

Because each endocrine gland may produce several hormones and some of these hormones may affect other endocrine glands, the study of endocrine function has been a baffling and complex task. The methods that have evolved show a picture of increasingly specialized techniques. Early investigators used one of three techniques that were steps of increased knowledge about each gland: (1) removal of the gland from an animal and observation of the effects of the lack of its hormone(s) on physiology and behavior; (2) injection of a normal animal with hormones from the gland to observe the effects of an oversupply of the hormones (these hormones are obtained by "grinding up" the gland from another animal to form an extract for injection, by chemical isolation of the various hormones from the gland, or by chemically synthesizing the hormone if its structure is understood); and (3) removal of the gland and "replacement therapy," that is, injecting gland extracts, isolated hormones, or synthesized ones. Newer methods include (1) genetic studies, (2) chemical ablation, (3) chemical extraction, (4) radioactive tracers, and (5) perfusion. Genetic studies are made with strains of animals that inherit a known glandular deficiency that could not be produced by removing the gland; for example, a gland that lacks one of its hormones but not another. Chemical "ablation" may result from injecting substances known to prevent a gland from releasing a certain hormone, or use of a chemical "antihormone" that prevents a gland's hormone from affecting its target tissue. Chemical extraction involves isolating the hormone from blood or urine samples (as well as the gland itself) to study the changes in hormone output that result from experimental procedures. Radioactive tracers are made by irradiating a chemical that the gland uses to make hormones with roentgen rays. The resulting chemical is injected into the animal to be used by the gland in making its hormone. The hormone is radioactive as a result, and its distribution in target tissue can be "traced" by instruments sensitive to the radiation. Finally, the gland may be removed, and all or part of it may be perfused (circulated) with the animal's blood or a substitute solution to keep it alive for a few days outside the body (in vitro). This makes the gland tissue accessible for continuous study and stimulation as it goes about its business of making hormones. The effect of other chemicals and hormones on its function can be studied in isolation from outside influences.

The effects of the lack of only one of several hormones produced by a gland can be studied through replacement therapy. Using all the known hormones isolated from the gland, the investigator may assume that he has found them all if the animal's physiology and behavior remain normal without the gland and with replacement therapy. The errors in these methods are chiefly caused by interactions between glands. If one gland is removed and an animal develops a symptom—for example, low blood calcium and resulting irritability of the nervous system—the investigator may assume that the gland maintains the calcium level of the blood. However, the gland may produce a hormone that stimulates another gland to perform this function. Even when the hormone has been isolated or synthesized, the effect of a hormone on other glands must be understood.

Mechanisms of hormone functions

Table 3-1 lists the major endocrine glands, their hormones, the chemical nature of these hormones, the target tissue of each, their major functions, and their mode of action. There is far more detail in the table than the student needs; a knowledge of the major effects of each hormone group is sufficient. However, the details given in the table illustrate some major conclusions about the nature of hormones and their actions that *are* important. The fourteen endocrine glands listed produce at least twenty-eight different hormones, although all their effects are not fully understood. Nearly all the hormones produced have very complex molecular structures, particularly steroids or proteins and the polypeptides out of which proteins are made. The steroids are secreted by the adrenals and

gonads, and the proteins and polypeptides by the pituitary, pancreas, thyroid, and parathyroids. In recent years new methods of separating complex proteins have made it possible to isolate many protein hormones in pure form. A survey of the variety of target tissue affected by the hormones listed will show that some hormones affect only a few structures, whereas others affect most of the cells of the body. Some hormones, chiefly those of the anterior pituitary, act by stimulating or suppressing the output of other endocrine glands.

The hormones listed have a variety of effects on a variety of target tissues. Some hormones are involved in organized responses to external stimuli, such as the reaction of the adrenal medulla in sympathetic stimulation (Chapter 5). Others are concerned with the consistency of the internal environment, such as the parathyroids and calcium level or the pancreas and blood glucose level. Some endocrine glands of the latter group are stimulated directly to produce a hormone that corrects a lack of balance in internal conditions whenever the imbalance occurs; for example, the pancreas produces more insulin when the blood glucose is too high and less insulin when the blood glucose is too low. (The effect of insulin is to help cells use up blood glucose.) As would be expected from the variety of hormone effects on so many kinds of target tissue, several modes of hormone action are found, with some hormones acting in more than one of the following ways: (1) some hormones form part of *enzymes* (Chapter 2) and therefore aid in activating chemical reactions in the cells of their target tissue; for example, the thyroxin of the thyroid gland; (2) some hormones modify the membranes of the cells they encounter, adhering to the membrane to make it more or less permeable to specific substances; for example, insulin from the pancreas, which enhances the permeability of cell membranes to blood glucose; (3) some hormones act directly on structures within the cell; for

Table 3-1. Endocrine glands and their functions

Gland	Hormone(s)	Chemical nature	Target tissues
Thyroid	Thyroxin	Thyronine derivative	Probably all tissue
	Thyrocalcitonin	Polypeptide	All cells
Parathyroids	Parathormone	Protein	Gastrointestinal tract, bone, kidney
	Thyrocalcitonin-releasing factor (TCRF)		
Skin	Vitamin D		Gastrointestinal tract, kidney
Adrenal cortex	Cortisol	Steroids (enzyme)	Probably all cell membranes, liver, gonads
	Corticosterones		
	Cortisone		
	Aldosterone		
	Estrogens		
	Androgens		
Adrenal medulla	Epinephrine	Catecholamines	Heart
	Norepinephrine		Arteries
			Liver
			Anterior pituitary
Pancreas			
Alpha cells	Glucagon	Polypeptides	Liver
Beta cells	Insulin		Almost all cells
Posterior pituitary (neurohypophysis)	Vasopressin (antidiuretic hormone)	Polypeptides	Arteries
			Kidney
	Oxytocin		Uterus
			Mammary glands
Anterior pituitary (adenohypophysis)	Somatotrophic hormone (STH)	Polypeptides	Bone
	Thyrotrophic hormone (TH)	Glycoprotein	Thyroid gland
	Adrenocorticotrophic hormone (ACTH)		Adrenal cortex and fat tissues
	Follicle-stimulating hormone (FSH)	Glycoprotein	Gonads and other tissues
	Luteinizing hormone (LH)	Glycoprotein	Gonads
	Lactogenic hormone (prolactin), or	Protein	Gonads and mammary glands
	Luteotrophic hormone		
Testes	Androgens	Steroids	All tissues
	Testosterone		
	Androsterone		
Ovaries	Estrogens	Steroids	All tissues
	Estradiol		
	Estrone		
	Progesterone	Steroid	Uterus
Placenta	Anterior pituitary–like hormones (APL) or chorionic hormones	Steroids	All tissues
Pineal gland	Melatonin	Indole	Gonads
Thymus	(Not an endocrine gland—see text)		

Major function(s)	Mode of action
Raises metabolic rate, increases protein synthesis, carbohydrate synthesis, and transport	Promotes enzyme dissociation, stimulates RNA production by specific cells
Lowers blood calcium	
Raises blood calcium level, lowers phosphorus level	Stimulates calcium and decreases phosphorus absorption from the gastrointestinal tract and new bone, decreases calcium excretion, increases phosphorus secretion by kidney (by action of vitamin D)
Promotes retention of both calcium and phosphorus	
Sodium retention, potassium loss, increased carbohydrate metabolism, more glycogen produced in liver, electrolyte and estrogenic and androgenic effects	Stimulates specific RNA production
Increases heart rate	Beta receptor sites on target tissues
Vasoconstriction	Alpha receptor sites on target tissues
Release of blood glucose from liver	
Release of ACTH	
Increases production of glucose	Affects glucose transport by cell membrane by attaching to membrane, changes protein synthesis by cells through RNA mechanisms
Promotes glucose, amino acid, cation, fatty acid absorption by cells, inhibits glucogenesis by liver	
Raises blood pressure	
Stimulates water reabsorption	Attaches to cell membrane to increase permeability
Stimulates contraction of small arteries	
Stimulates milk secretion	
Stimulates growth	
Stimulates thyroxin secretion	
Stimulates steroid secretion by adrenal cortex, breaks down fat tissues	Enzyme activation
Development of ova or sperm cells	Stimulates anabolism
Stimulates estrogen and androgen output	
Corpus luteum development and milk output	
Sexual arousal; primary and secondary sex characteristics	
Sexual arousal; primary and secondary sex characteristics	Stimulates RNA production by the cell
Prepares for embryo	
Maintains pregnancy	
GTH-like effects	
Suppresses hormone output by gonads	Light to eye stimulates SNS, whose neurohumors block enzyme for hormone production

example, adrenal norepinephrine, which acts on the smooth muscle cells of the arteries; and (4) some hormones act on cells by regulating the genetic apparatus, by which they repair and reproduce themselves; for example, the androgens and estrogens of the gonads. (For a review of the operation of the genetic apparatus see Chapter 2.)

In summarizing the mode of action of hormones the following conclusions can be made: (1) steroid hormones appear to act by gene activation, (2) other hormones such as thyroxin act directly by dissociating cell enzymes to change cell reactions, (3) still other hormones such as insulin and vasopressin act on the permeability or transport features of the cell membrane, (4) additional hormones such as ACTH activate enzymes in cells to promote spe-

cific reactions, and (5) some hormones such as thyroxin have both genetic and nongenetic effects.

MAJOR ENDOCRINE GLANDS

The locations of the major endocrine glands are shown in Fig. 3-1. Some glands occur in pairs (adrenals and gonads); others form a single structure (the pineal gland). Some glands are paired parts of a single structure (adrenal cortex and medulla and anterior and posterior pituitary), or form a cluster of cells (islet cells of the pancreas). Each gland will be referred to as a single unit, whether one, a pair, or more structures are involved.

Lists of the major endocrine glands vary according to who makes the list and for what purpose. Those glands whose function is either uncertain (intermediate pituitary),

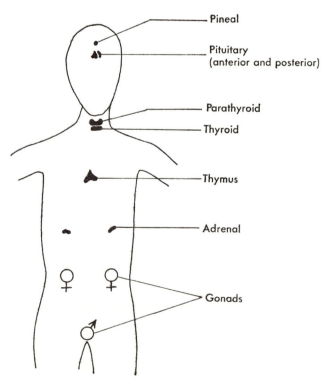

Fig. 3-1. Diagram of location of major endocrine glands in the human body.

specific to digestion (stomach gastrin and small intestine secretin), or only suspected (kidneys and blood pressure, liver and anemia) have been omitted. This leaves the following (Table 3-2 and Fig. 3-1): (1) thyroid, (2) parathyroids, (3) adrenal cortex, (4) adrenal medulla, (5) pancreas (islet alpha and beta cells), (6) posterior pituitary, (7) anterior pituitary, (8) gonads (testes, ovaries, related placenta), (9) pineal gland, and (10) thymus. The adrenal cortex, thyroid, and gonads are largely controlled by the anterior pituitary. The adrenal medulla, pancreas, posterior pituitary, and pineal gland are under nervous as well as endocrine control; thus they react to external as well as internal events. In taking up the specific function of each gland, that which is known of its normal role will be given first, followed by the effects of *hyposecretion* (undersecretion) and *hypersecretion* (oversecretion) of its hormone in cases of glandular abnormality. In each case knowledge of abnormal function helps

Table 3-2. A simplified summary of endocrine functions

Gland	*Hormone*	*Effect*
Thyroid	Thyroxin	Increases metabolism
Parathyroids	Parathormone	Increases blood calcium
		Lowers blood phosphate
	(Vitamin D)	Prevents loss of Ca and P
Adrenal cortex	Corticoids	Sodium retention
		Potassium loss
		Liver glycogen formation
		Increases carbohydrate metabolism
		Male sex hormone
Adrenal medulla	Norepinephrine	Mimics sympathetic nervous system
	Epinephrine	Raises blood pressure
		Stimulates ACTH release
Pancreas		
Alpha cells	Glucagon	Increases blood glucose level
Beta cells	Insulin	Lowers blood glucose level
Posterior pituitary	Vasopressin	Smaller arteries constrict
	Oxytocin	Kidney water reabsorption
		Uterus contracts
		Milk production increases
Anterior pituitary	STH	Stimulates growth
	TTH	Stimulates thyroid secretion
	ACTH	Stimulates adrenal cortex secretion
	Gonadotrophic	
	FSH	Develops germ cells
	LH	Stimulates sex hormones
	Lactogenic (prolactin)	Develops corpus luteum and increases milk production
Gonads	♂ Androgen	Fertility and secondary sex characteristics
	♀ Estrogen	
Pineal gland	Melatonin	Suppresses sex behavior

in understanding the role of the gland in normal control of body function and therefore behavior.

Thyroid gland

The **thyroid gland** lies on both sides of the trachea (windpipe), just below the larynx (voice box). It is a good place to begin study of the endocrine glands because its major hormone, **thyroxin,** is a relatively simple one. Thyroxin is manufactured in the gland by the combination of iodine and an amino acid (tyrosine). The hormone probably affects all the cells of the body as target tissue. Thyroxin raises the metabolic rate of all the cells of the body and therefore is necessary for a normal level of energy and activity. A minimum level of thyroxin in the blood and tissue fluid is necessary for a normal metabolic rate. Oversecretion of thyroxin raises the metabolic rate to abnormal levels. The functioning of the thyroid gland can therefore be determined by testing the metabolic rate. When the test is conducted under resting conditions, the results are called the basal metabolic rate, or BMR. As described in Chapter 2, the test measures the rate of oxygen consumption in the body caused by the metabolism of cells. (Since the hormone is made by combining an amino acid with iodine, a more direct test of protein-bound iodine content of the blood may be made.) Under normal conditions the thyroid gland may have much to do with the amount of energy and drive displayed by the individual and with how adequately he responds to stress situations that demand vigorous physical arousal. The thyroid also secretes a calcium-lowering hormone (thyrocalcitonin).

Hypothyroidism. When the thyroid does not produce enough thyroxin to maintain a normal metabolic rate, **hypothyroidism** occurs. The effects of hypothyroidism depend on whether the condition occurs during growth or after maturity. The effects are usually more severe when they occur during

childhood growth because metabolism must be higher to support growth and development than to support adult body functions; more thyroxin is therefore needed during childhood. If hypothyroidism develops at birth or during early childhood, it causes symptoms called **cretinism.** The cretin fails to develop normally either physically or mentally. He is dwarfed because of inadequate bone growth, although the connective tissue of the body is overdeveloped, resulting in a puffy face, protruding tongue, and "potbelly." He is "feebleminded" because of inadequate development of the nervous system. Cretinism can be prevented with supplementary doses of thyroxin if the hypothyroid condition is discovered in time.

Adult hypothyroidism is called **myxedema.** The name comes from the collection of body fluid in connective tissue (edema) that gives the individual a puffy, bloated appearance. Myxedema, caused by an onset of thyroid deficiency in the adult, reduces the BMR by 35% to 40%. This results in sluggishness, chills from inability to maintain body temperature, and reduced muscle tone. Motivation, vigor, and alertness diminish, and the individual sleeps much of the time. The central nervous system may deteriorate until the individual becomes an imbecile. Supplementary thyroxin can effect complete recovery.

Hyperthyroidism. Overproduction of thyroxin by the thyroid, or **hyperthyroidism,** is less common than hypothyroidism. The BMR in this condition may be 50% to 75% above normal. As a result the individual is hyperactive and "nervous." He has a huge appetite but cannot gain weight because everything he eats is consumed in maintaining a high BMR. He sleeps little, is irritable, and is unable to concentrate. Exophthalmos (bulging eyes) is a prominent symptom. Hyperthyroidism can be cured by surgically removing part of the gland. It usually leaves no permanent impairment if treated successfully.

Goiter is an enlargement of the thyroid gland that appears as a swelling in the neck region. It may, for unknown reasons, accompany hyperthyroidism, or it may result from hypothyroidism, occurring when the cells of the thyroid multiply to increase their inadequate output of thyroxin. Simple goiter used to be common and resulted from a deficiency of iodine (needed by the body to manufacture thyroxin) in the diets of goiter victims. It occurred in areas of the world where there was no iodine in the soil in which food crops were grown. Iodine is now added to most table salt (iodized salt) to prevent this condition.

Studies of abnormal thyroid conditions show, in exaggerated form, the probable importance of the thyroid to normal behavior. Individual differences in normal thyroid functioning may help account for individual differences in energy, motivation, attention, and general alertness.

Parathyroid glands

The parathyroid glands are four tiny organs shaped like slightly flattened peas and embedded in or attached to the thyroid gland. The parathyroids produce **parathormone,** a hormone essential to controlling the calcium level and calcium-to-phosphorus ratio in the blood and tissue fluid—factors required for normal nerve and muscle cell functioning and therefore normal behavior. The higher the blood calcium level, the less excitable the muscles and nervous system are; low blood calcium makes these tissues irritable and may cause convulsive seizures and muscle contractions. Parathormone acts to increase blood calcium levels, thereby decreasing nerve and muscle excitability. The parathyroids are stimulated to release this hormone by low blood calcium and suppressed by high blood calcium. This simple feedback mechanism keeps the calcium level within the narrow limits required for normal muscle and nerve excitability. Parathormone also lowers blood phosphorus levels for a proper calcium-to-phosphorus ratio.

The parathyroids require **vitamin D** to adequately regulate calcium and phosphorus levels. This vitamin stimulates the uptake of calcium from the digestive system and prevents the loss of calcium in the feces and phosphorus in the urine. Thus the vitamin and the hormone act together in maintaining calcium levels but in opposition on phosphorus levels. Vitamin D can compensate for a lack of parathormone in maintaining blood calcium, but the hormone is not effective without the vitamin. (Lack of vitamin D causes rickets in children, a bone-wasting disease caused by a loss of the calcium and phosphorus that make up bone.) Vitamin D can be considered a hormone because it is manufactured by an organ (the skin) and has an effect on other parts of the body. When the skin is exposed to sunlight, the hormone is released into the bloodstream. Because man shields his skin from the sun with clothing, a substance made by the body (a hormone) has become an essential factor (a vitamin) in the diet.

Given an adequate supply of vitamin D for retention of calcium by the body, parathormone has two mechanisms for raising the blood calcium level. One is rapid and of limited extent; the other takes more time but can cause a greater change in calcium level. Parathormone acts rapidly to increase absorption of calcium from the intestine and to prevent its loss in the urine (kidney reabsorption). The hormone acts more slowly on bone to provide a "reserve supply" of calcium. (Bone is made of calcium and phosphorus.) Parathormone breaks down bone into a form that can be taken up by the tissue fluids to supply more calcium and phosphorus. At the same time it stimulates excretion of phosphorus in the urine so that a proper calcium-phosphorus ratio is maintained; the blood calcium rises and blood phosphorus is reduced.

Hyposecretion of parathormone is rare in man (parathyroid tissue is sometimes removed in tumor operations) and is easily treated with parathormone or vitamin D. Complete removal of the parathyroids in animals has the expected effect. The nervous system and muscles become hyperexcitable because of lowered blood calcium. (Calcium is not absorbed from intestine or bone and is excreted in the urine.) Muscle twitches (clonus) result, giving way to muscle spasms (tetany), and convulsive seizures similar to epilepsy.

Hypersecretion of parathormone is equally rare in man, usually being associated with tumors that enlarge the parathyroid glands. As would be expected, an increased parathormone level in man or experimental animals raises the calcium level and lowers the phosphorus level of the blood. The calcium level may rise so high that the kidney cannot reabsorb it all, and excess calcium may be found in the urine. Calcium and phosphorus are drawn from the bones, which then become deformed. Muscle tone is reduced, the central nervous system (CNS) is less excitable, and the individual becomes dull and sluggish. Removal of part of the gland restores normality.

Note that low blood calcium with the same symptoms as hyposecretion of parathormone can result from a diet low in calcium or vitamin D, even when parathormone secretion is normal. This often happens during pregnancy and lactation (nursing) because of the need for extra calcium for milk, or for bone structure of the embryo.

Under normal conditions individual differences in parathormone and vitamin D levels in the blood could mean differences between individuals in nervous system functioning. These differences could affect all levels of behavior, from alertness and coordination to intelligence.

Adrenal cortex

The adrenal glands are named for their location atop the kidneys (renal = kidney),

but they are not directly related to the kidneys. Furthermore, the adrenals consist of two parts that bear little relation to each other. The core, or **adrenal medulla,** of each gland is derived from neural tissue and is innervated by the autonomic nervous system (Chapter 5). The covering, or **cortex,** of the gland is derived from the same type of tissue as the gonads and bears a functional relationship to them. The most important hormones produced by the **adrenal cortex** are steroids. These hormones are therefore called **corticoids.** They regulate the sodium and potassium balance of the body, govern carbohydrate metabolism, and seem to have something to do with sexual functioning. Corticoids promote sodium retention and potassium loss through the kidneys. An excess of sodium outside the cells and an excess of potassium inside the cells, where it is not available for excretion, is the basis of the excitability of the nervous system, the resting potential, and the nerve impulse (Chapter 4). Thus corticoids maintain the excitability of cells.

Corticoids also stimulate the storage of blood glucose in the liver as glycogen and increase carbohydrate metabolism to raise the basal metabolic rate. The corticoids seem to mimic the gonads in supporting vigor and secondary sex characteristics, and the adrenal cortex produces both a male sex hormone (an **androgen**) and a female sex hormone (an **estrogen**). The production of corticoids by the adrenal cortex is under the control of a stimulating hormone of the anterior pituitary gland (adrenocorticotrophic hormone, or ACTH, Table 3-2).

Hyposecretion of adrenal corticoids (Addison's disease) results in excessive elimination of sodium (Na) and chlorine (Cl) and excessive retention of potassium (K) by the kidneys. Since the excitability mechanism for all cells depends on an excess of Na outside the cell membrane and an excess of K inside (Chapter 4), the excitability of nerves and muscles is reduced. In maintaining a constant *concentration* of NaCl (salt) solution during loss of Na and Cl, the body also loses fluids. Changes in carbohydrate metabolism involve less storage of reserve blood glucose as glycogen in the liver and muscles for use when it is needed by the body. Carbohydrate utilization is also reduced, and the BMR is lowered. Lack of vigor, muscle weakness, lower body temperature, and weight loss result. Unless supplementary salt (NaCl) is available in quantities, an animal dies soon after removal of the gland. Death follows later, in any case, unless replacement therapy is given.

Hypersecretion of corticoids is rare in man. The sexual effects of the hormone are the most observable features of hypersecretion, since sexual precocity in children and masculinity in women (for example, circus bearded ladies) result. (Stimulating the adrenal cortex with pituitary ACTH has been used as a cure for rheumatism, with some unfortunate side effects!)

Normal functioning of the adrenal cortex is required for normal nerve and muscle excitability. The corticoids interact with the adrenal medulla and pituitary in the determination of resistance to environmental stress. Individual stress tolerance, sexual vigor, and nervous system efficiency are affected by the functioning of the gland.

Adrenal medulla

The "core" of the adrenal glands is closely related to the autonomic (visceral) nervous system (ANS) and is derived from the same kind of tissue (Chapter 5). The gland secretes **norepinephrine** and **epinephrine** (also called **noradrenaline** and **adrenaline**) when stimulated by sympathetic nerves of the ANS, a feature of arousal of the body in response to stress. Norepinephrine resembles the transmitter substance of sympathetic nerve endings and reinforces their effects on the viscera. This includes raising the blood pressure by constricting the arteries (vasoconstriction). Epinephrine is derived from norepinephrine and has similar effects except that it raises the

blood pressure by accelerating the heart rate rather than by vasoconstriction. There is evidence that epinephrine predominates in states of fear and norepinephrine in states of rage (Chapter 16). This could account for the "pounding heart" during fright and a "pale" appearance from vasoconstriction near the skin during anger.

Stress and alarm reactions involve both the adrenal cortex and the adrenal medulla (Fig. 3-2). Under the influence of sympathetic stimulation, epinephrine is released, with the effects noted above. Epinephrine also stimulates the anterior pituitary gland to secrete ACTH, which in turn stimulates the release of corticoids from the adrenal cortex to improve tissue excitability and increase the BMR. Norepinephrine has the same effects.

Hypersecretion of the adrenal medulla is not a known gland abnormality. It is a feature of stressful conditions, along with sympathetic arousal and the effects on the adrenal cortex previously noted.

Hyposecretion can be imitated by the removal of the gland in animals without the adrenal cortex being removed. The animal remains normal except for its inability to tolerate environmental stress. Mobilization to maintain body temperature in a cold environment, vigor, and response to arousing stimuli are reduced.

Prolonged stress causes adrenal enlargement, which probably involves both the cortex and medulla, as both are involved in the body's response to stress. The result would be an increased capacity to mobilize the resources of the body to meet future stressful conditions; this capacity would enhance chances for survival in animal or man living under primitive conditions.

Pancreas

The **pancreas** is an organ that lies in a curve of the gut between the stomach and the small intestine and has both exocrine and endocrine functions. It is a digestive gland that discharges into the small intes-

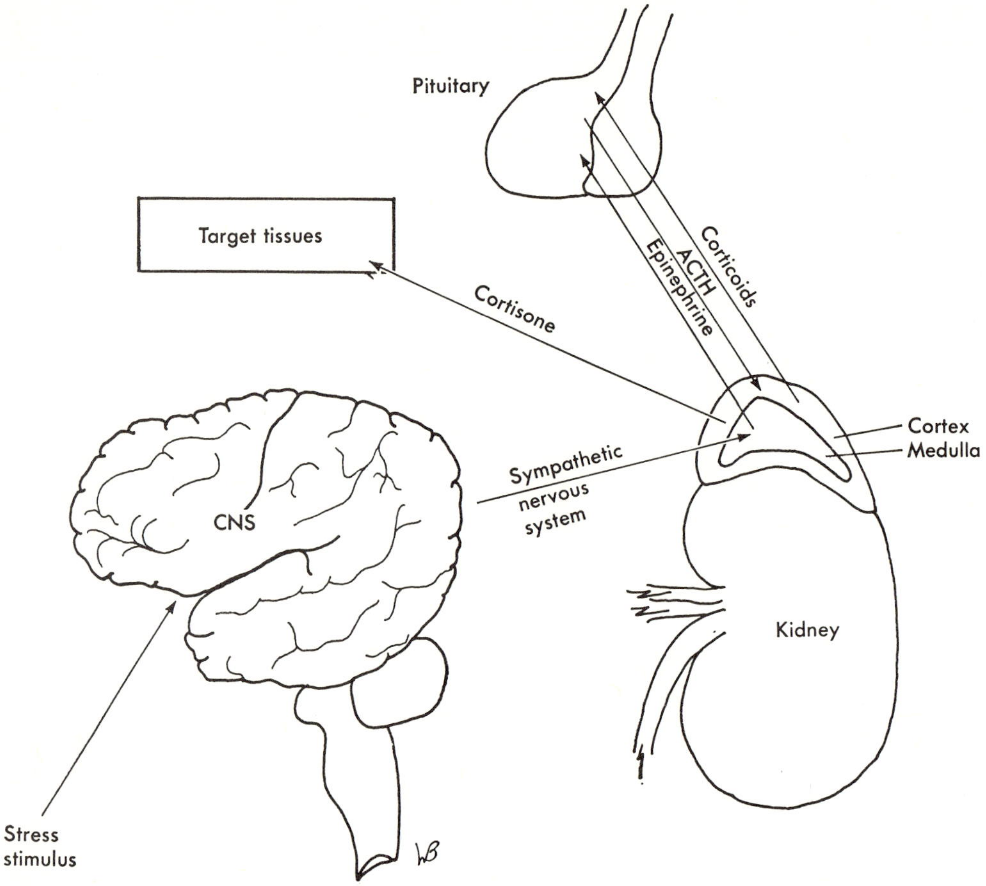

Fig. 3-2. Interaction of adrenal cortex and medulla in stress and alarm reactions. Perception of a stress stimulus results in sympathetic nervous system response, including increased epinephrine secretion by the adrenal medulla. Epinephrine stimulates ACTH output by the anterior pituitary gland. ACTH stimulates the adrenal cortex to increase corticoid output. Corticoids improve nerve tissue excitability and raise the metabolic rate, both adaptive reactions to stress.

tine, a function that is of little interest to the present topic. Embedded in the pancreas (in the islets of Langerhans) are two kinds of endocrine cells, the **alpha** and **beta cells.** The alpha cells comprise about 25% of the total endocrine cells of the pancreas and produce a hormone **(glucagon)** that opposes the action of the beta cells by stimulating the liver to produce blood glucose. Glucagon is released for a brief period by the alpha cells in response to low blood glucose, but it acts in turn, to stimulate insulin output by the beta cells.

The beta cells produce **insulin,** a hormone that inhibits the liver in either making or releasing blood glucose, and further lowers blood glucose by increasing its use by the muscles and other tissues of the body. Insulin appears to make these cells more permeable to blood glucose and is essential for blood glucose utilization. The beta cells release insulin in response to a high level of glucose in the blood; their secretion is inhibited when the blood glucose drops as a result of liver storage and muscle utilization. The gland and the effect of its secretion form a self-regulating feedback loop. Insulin is also released when the gland is stimulated by the vagus nerve (Chapter 5). The output of insulin is increased by norepinephrine and epinephrine from the adrenal medulla. Blood glucose utilization is thereby improved during stress and alarm reactions.

Hyposecretion of insulin by the beta cells of the pancreas may cause a common disorder in man called **diabetes mellitus,** although recent evidence indicates that a pituitary hormone may also cause this disorder, as will be explained later. Without sufficient insulin, blood glucose is neither used by the muscles and other tissues nor stored as glycogen by the liver. This causes an increase in the amount of glucose in the blood (blood sugar), and some of the oversupply is secreted in the urine. (Measurement of the amount of glucose in the urine is a test for diabetes.) In an attempt to rid the blood of excess glucose, the kidneys excrete more water than usual, and the individual becomes dehydrated. Poisonous waste products accumulate in the blood because the tissues cannot completely metabolize fats and proteins in place of the carbohydrate glucose (Chapter 2). A **diabetic coma** and death may ensue. Insulin replacement therapy, which can prevent these symptoms, was made possible by isolating and synthesizing the hormone. The insulin injections must be balanced against the amount and type of food intake to assure normal levels of blood glucose. (Recent research suggests that an oversupply of glucose as well as an undersupply of insulin is involved in diabetes mellitus. When the diabetic eats, the alpha cells release glucagon, which stimulates the liver to release blood glucose. The diabetic lacks the normal reaction of an extra insulin supply from beta cells to help the cells utilize the excess glucose. As a result, his blood glucose level increases even though he takes a steady supply of insulin. A substance called somastatin has been isolated from another endocrine gland—the anterior pituitary—and it prevents the release of glucagon by the alpha cells. If the diabetic takes both insulin and somastatin, his blood glucose level remains more stable than it would be if he took insulin alone.)

Hypersecretion of insulin is rare in man and is cured by removal of islet tissue. An oversupply of insulin, or an overdose of insulin in a diabetic, results in **hypoglycemia** (low blood glucose level) because all the stored blood glucose is utilized. **Insulin shock** convulsions result and cause death unless glucose is quickly administered. Induced insulin hypoglycemia and insulin shock have been used in the treatment of mental patients (Chapter 18).

It is doubtful that individual differences in insulin secretion that are within the normal range are important to behavior. The nervous system is, however, very dependent on a constant supply of blood glucose at a concentration in the body fluid that lies within the normal range. Insulin coma and insulin shock result from extremes of blood glucose concentration that affect the brain.

Posterior pituitary

The pituitary gland, or **hypophysis,** hangs from the base of the brain; it is connected to the hypothalamus by a narrow "stalk." The posterior part of the pituitary gland is called the **neurohypophysis** because it receives nerve fibers from the hypothalamus and seems to be under nervous control. Two hormones have been isolated from posterior pituitary secretions—oxytocin and vasopressin. The two hormones have the following four overlapping effects: (1) they constrict blood vessels in the smaller arteries, and therefore raise the blood pressure (a *pressor* effect); (2) they stimulate contraction of other smooth muscles besides those in the walls of arteries, particularly the uterus; (3) they stimulate ejection of milk by the mammary glands; and (4) they stimulate the kidney to reabsorb water from the urine (an antidiuretic effect). Vasopressin is more effective in causing the pressor and antidiuretic effects, whereas oxytocin has more to do with contractions of the uterus and with milk production. Oxytocin is believed to play a role in the strong uterine contractions of labor in childbirth and in subsequent readiness to nurse the young. A combination of oxytocin and vasopressin is therefore used to aid childbirth. The pressor role of these hormones in normal body functioning is little understood, but removal of the gland or injection of its hormone affects blood pressure.

The *antidiuretic* role of the **posterior pituitary** is important in controlling the water balance of the body. Vasopressin is therefore also known as **antidiuretic hormone (ADH)**. Dehydration (lack of water) in nerve cells in the hypothalamus results in stimulation of the posterior pituitary via nerves reaching it from the hypothalamus. The posterior pituitary secretes its hormones as a result. The hormones in turn stimulate the kidney to re-absorb up to a third of the water it uses to pass wastes. Hydration (the presence of water) in hypothalamic cells results. This stops the stimulation of the posterior pituitary in another interesting feedback loop. The mechanism is an important part of the thirst drive, which will be discussed in Chapter 15.

Hyposecretion of the posterior pituitary leads to **diabetes insipidus,** with the excretion of large amounts of water, together with a strong thirst and a large water intake to maintain the water balance of the body and prevent death by dehydration. The condition can be cured by the administration of posterior pituitary extract. Posterior pituitary hypersecretion is not a known disorder.

The posterior pituitary gland is also novel because its secretions are those of nerve cells **(neurohumors)** rather than gland cells. Nerve cells reaching the posterior pituitary from the hypothalamus secrete transmitter substances from their endings. (Transmitter

substances are normally chemicals that one nerve cell uses to excite another nerve cell. See Chapter 4.) The transmitter substances act as hormones do in this case, since they are distributed by the circulation to their target tissues. Posterior pituitary hormones are manufactured by the nerve cells of the hypothalamus and carried to the posterior pituitary by the long branches of these cells.

The neurohypophysis is important to the psychological areas of maternal behavior and the thirst drive. In addition, transmitter substances of the hypothalamus are released into blood vessels reaching the anterior pituitary in a **portal system** of the circulation. (A portal system carries substances in the bloodstream from one specific point to another; the substances do not reach the rest of the circulation.) The transmitter substances can excite or inhibit the secretions of the anterior pituitary. Thus the hypothalamus, which is an important center for governing motivated behavior, controls some of the secretions of both the posterior and anterior pituitary glands.

Anterior pituitary

The *anterior pituitary gland,* or **adenohypophysis,** regulates the output of three "target" endocrine glands with five "trophic" hormones through complex relationships with the nervous system and through feedback from the other endocrine glands. It controls, at least to some extent, the adrenal cortex, the thyroid, and three activities of the gonads (germ tissue growth and the production of sex and pregnancy hormones). It produces an additional hormone with widespread effects on the growth of the body. There may also be influences from the pituitary on carbohydrate metabolism and the pancreas, but they are not well enough established for discussion here. Parts of the body affected by both anterior and posterior pituitary glands are sketched in Fig. 3-3.

The **somatotrophic hormone (STH)** does not affect other glands. It acts directly to

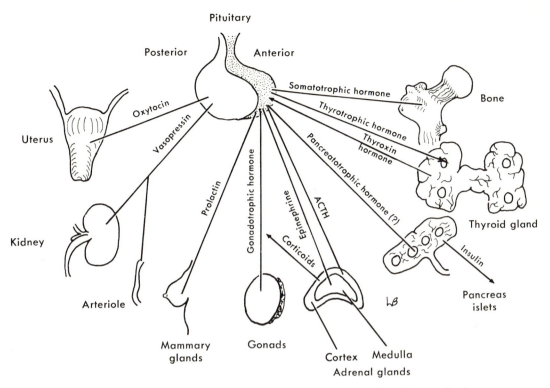

Fig. 3-3. Hormones and target tissue of anterior and posterior pituitary glands.

stimulate normal growth over the entire body in the developing organism. Growth naturally occurs by cell multiplication in all tissues, but it is most noticeable in the long bones of the body, particularly in the bones of the limbs. Growth in man seems normally to occur over two periods, the first from birth to puberty (the beginnings of adolescence) at a diminishing rate and the second a pronounced growth spurt during adolescence, the period from puberty to maturity, which is accompanied by sexual development. The timing and extent of growth is governed by STH, whereas the sexual changes are regulated by other hormones of the anterior pituitary gland.

Hyposecretion of STH inhibits growth and results in a **pituitary dwarf,** or midget. The pituitary dwarf is usually of normal intelligence and has normal body proportions; his condition should not be confused with the inherited gland abnormalities that

result in the achondroplastic dwarf, who has a normal head and body but under-developed limbs. The pituitary dwarf may or may not show retarded sexual development. He may be only 3 or 4 feet tall at maturity. Hormone therapy will prevent this condition if begun early enough.

Hypersecretion of STH varies in its effect on the body, depending on whether it begins before or after maturity. Hypersecretion during otherwise normal growth before puberty results in a **pituitary giant** of normal body proportions who may be 8 or 9 feet tall. There are no known effects on the nervous system, and the pituitary giant is usually of normal intelligence. If hypersecretion of STH begins after maturity, that is, after normal growth ends, a condition called **acromegaly** results. The cartilage at the ends of the long bones of the limbs and jaw, where growth is most noticeable, hardens into bone; normal growth in a proportionate "lengthwise" fashion is no longer possible. The bones become misshapen and thickened, especially those of the limbs, nose, and jaw. Fibrous tissue of the face and tongue is enlarged, and the abdomen protrudes. The individual has a coarse, ape-like appearance.

Recent evidence suggests that STH may have other effects beyond growth because of its interaction with the hormones of other endocrine glands. For example, (1) it aggravates diabetes, (2) it inhibits the action of insulin, and (3) it increases muscle glycogen. These effects indicate that STH antagonizes the action of the pancreatic beta cells. In addition, STH acts as a biological synergist with the trophic hormones to be discussed next; that is, it potentiates the effects of TTH, ACTH, FSH, and LH (see below). Finally, STH and thyroxin are both required for normal growth.

The **thyrotrophic hormone (TTH)** output of the anterior pituitary gland is controlled by the level of thyroxin in the blood. TTH stimulates iodine uptake and thyroxin synthesis by the thyroid gland. In an interesting feedback mechanism the increased level of blood thyroxin inhibits output of TTH by the pituitary. The blood glucose is therefore maintained at a level consistent with the needs of the body during rest or exercise.

The **adrenocorticotrophic hormone (ACTH)** stimulates and regulates the output of hormones by the adrenal cortex. As previously described, ACTH output is increased by epinephrine from the adrenal medulla under stress stimulation. Other stimuli to ACTH output are uncertain, but the hypothalamus and portal system from the posterior pituitary are probably involved. ACTH stimulates the adrenal cortex to increase corticoid output. As previously explained, the corticoids govern the sodium and potassium balance of the body for nervous system excitability, regulate carbohydrate metabolism, and support sexual vigor and the development of secondary sex characteristics.

Three **gonadotrophic hormones (GTH)** are produced by the anterior pituitary gland. Their effects on the hormone output of the gonads will be mentioned here and more thoroughly explained in the section on the gonads.

1. **Follicle-stimulating hormone (FSH)** stimulates the development of sperm cells in the testicles of the male and the development of ova, or egg cells, in the ovaries of the female. In the female, FSH also brings the follicle containing the ovum to maturity.

2. **Luteinizing hormone (LH)** stimulates the output of sex hormones by the gonads, that is, estrogens from the corpus luteum of the female ovaries and androgens from the interstitial tissue of the testes of the male. LH also causes the mature follicle of the ovary to rupture and release the ovum and then changes the follicle into the corpus luteum.

3. **Lactogenic hormone (prolactin)** brings the corpus luteum to maturity in the female and stimulates its output of progesterone. It also has a direct role in stimulating the development and milk production of the female mammary glands. Its role in the male is not clear.

The anterior pituitary gland controls the output of several other endocrine glands and is closely related to the hypothalamus, the area in the brain that governs "drives" (hunger, thirst, and so on) by way of the posterior pituitary and the portal system of blood vessels. For these two reasons the anterior pituitary probably has the most influence on behavior among the endocrine glands. By its dominance of the adrenal cortex and its feedback relationship to the adrenal medulla, it has much to do with the individual's vigor and ability to withstand stress. Its control of corticoids further governs the excitability of the nervous system, which in turn integrates behavior. Its interaction with the thyroid determines the individual's metabolic level and therefore his responsiveness to the world about him. Normal or abnormal sexual development, with its consequences for personality, depends on how the anterior pituitary governs the activity of the gonads. Physical stature depends on the growth hormone of the pituitary, and abnormalities of size have a profound influence on personality. All in all, the anterior pituitary has a pivotal role in behavior.

Gonads

The reproductive organs of the male and the female have dual roles. One function involves maturation of the reproductive organs and development of the secondary sexual characteristics (such as distribution of body fat, development of pubic, armpit, and chest hair, and deepening of the voice). The other function involves growth and development of the **germ tissue,** or **germ cells** (sperm or ova), in both sexes and an orderly sequence of reproductive events in the female.

Male reproductive system. The male reproductive system is based on paired testes contained in a sac, or **scrotum.** Their location outside the body cavity lowers the temperature to a point that permits the growth of sperm cells in the **seminiferous tubules.** The tubular tissue of the testes gives rise to the **seminal duct,** which ascends into the abdomen to unite with the duct from the other testicle and is joined here by the prostrate gland. Gland secretions and sperm form **semen,** which is collected in the **seminal vesicle.** During copulation (sexual intercourse) the vesicles and outgoing **urethra** of the **penis** contract to ejaculate the semen, which contains the sperm cells.

The male reproductive hormones are androgens, secreted by the **interstitial tissue** that surrounds the seminiferous tubules of the testes. The secretion of androgens by this tissue is stimulated by FSH from the anterior pituitary. Androgens are derived from progesterone, which is an important female sex hormone; they are also secreted in some degree by the ovaries, adrenal cortex, and female placenta.

Removal of the gonads is called castration. Lack of androgen caused by castration before puberty results in loss of vigor and failure to develop secondary sexual characteristics (that is, the person is a eunuch). Early injections of the hormones into a castrated male reverses these effects. After maturity, castration often abolishes sexual behavior in animals but merely reduces its frequency in men. (It's all in your head!) The same is true of lack of androgen production in old age.

Female reproductive system. The female reproductive system includes paired ovaries in the abdomen that contain immature **follicles,** each of' which has an ovum, or egg cell. The open ends of the **fallopian tubes** (oviducts) lie near the ovaries; when **ovulation** produces a mature ovum, a fallopian tube carries it to the **uterus.** If the ovum is fertilized by a sperm cell, it develops into an **embryo** in the wall of the uterus. At birth the **fetus** (developed embryo) is discharged through the **cervix** and **vagina.**

The female reproductive cycle is illustrated in Fig. 3-4. The cycle averages 28 days and begins at the end of menstruation with increased output of FSH by the anterior pituitary gland. The hormone causes increased growth of a follicle in the ovary. The growing follicle secretes **estrogens** which promote the growth of vascular and connective tissue in the wall of the uterus, preparing it to receive the ovum. Estrogens also stimulate LH secretion by the anterior pituitary gland.

The dual influence of pituitary LH and FSH stimulates the follicle to reach the surface of the ovary and release the ovum (ovulation) on about the fourteenth day. The ovum is carried by a fallopian tube to the uterus and buries itself in the wall of the uterus on about the seventeenth day. This interval (fourteenth to seventeenth days) is the period of greatest fertility.

Meanwhile, pituitary LH and prolactin stimulate the follicle to become an enlarged **corpus luteum** and to secrete **progesterone.** Progesterone stops the output of FSH by the pituitary to prevent further follicles

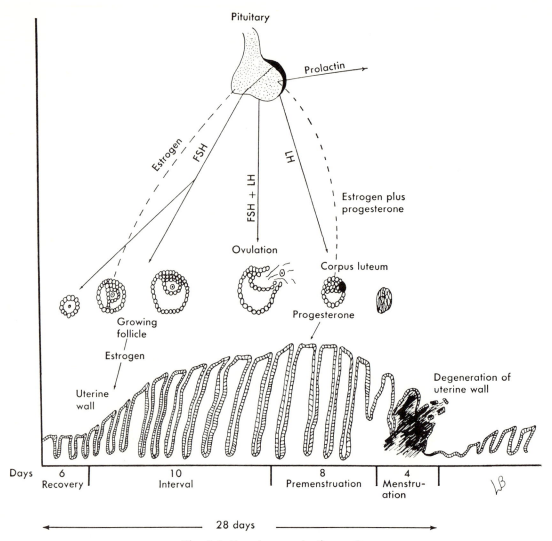

Fig. 3-4. Female reproductive cycle.

from maturing and producing eggs—the status quo is maintained. LH and prolactin also stimulate the continued output of estrogen by the corpus luteum. Estrogen acts to continue development of the wall of the uterus. Prolactin also prepares the mammary glands for milk production.

If pregnancy occurs, a **placenta** develops in the wall of the uterus to support and nourish the embryo. The placenta secretes both progesterone and **chorionic hormone.** These hormones replace progesterone from the corpus luteum, thus inhibiting FSH production and maintaining the status quo for pregnancy.

Under the influence of progesterone or chorionic hormones, or both, ovulation and further fertilizations cannot occur. The birth control pills now in wide use imitate the action of estrogen and progesterone and are taken to prevent ovulation.

If pregnancy does not occur, the corpus luteum degenerates and estrogen and progesterone production are reduced. The uterine wall sheds, causing bleeding (menstruation) from the vascular structures built up there.

Hormones of the hypothalamus

Two hormones that are released by nerve cells of the hypothalamus that affect the anterior pituitary gland have been isolated, analyzed, and synthesized. These two hormones stimulate the anterior pituitary to release TTH and LH. They are called "releasing factors" (RF) and are known as thyrotrophin releasing factor (TRF) and luteinizing hormone releasing factor (LRF). LRF stimulates the release of FSH as well as LH, but FSH may have its own releasing factor (this has not been demonstrated).

Other hypothalamic hormones are known to exist from physiological evidence, but they have not been chemically isolated as yet. These releasing factors influence anterior pituitary secretion of ACTH, prolactin, and STH. In some cases there may be two hypothalamic hormones, one stimulating the output of a specific pituitary hormone and the other inhibiting the output of that hormone. All of this was discovered because isolated lesions of specific groups of nerve cells in the hypothalamus would abolish secretion of a specific hormone by the anterior pituitary. Stimulation of the same location in the hypothalamus would increase the output of the same anterior pituitary hormone. In the *posterior* pituitary gland, nerve cells of the hypothalamus reach that structure to release hormones there (oxytocin and vasopressin), but no nerve cells reach the anterior pituitary gland from the hypothalamus. How, then, do "releasing factors" from nerve cells of the hypothalamus get to the anterior pituitary gland to stimulate the release of anterior pituitary hormones? The answer is found in some small blood vessels (capillaries) that run from the hypothalamus to the anterior pituitary gland. Neural secretions are carried by this **portal** ('pertaining to gate') **system** of blood vessels from the specific parts of the hypothalamus to specific cells of the anterior pituitary gland. There, they act as hormones (releasing factors) in stimulating the release of specific anterior pituitary hormones.

What does all of this do for man? In the first place, the releasing factor hormones are effective in quantities as small as one microgram, so it takes literally tons of brain tissue before enough can be assembled from a specific location in the hypothalamus to obtain as much as a milligram of a specific releasing factor to be analyzed. Once its molecular structure is established, however, it can be synthesized in any quantity desired. The two releasing factors produced so far are thyrotrophin releasing factor (TRF) and luteinizing hormone releasing factor (LRF). In many cases of thyroid deficiency, the thyroid gland is normal but lacks stimulation by the anterior pituitary because of a lack of TRF. TRF can be administered to cause the pituitary to stimulate the thyroid to release thyroxin instead of giving thyroxin directly—a more "natural" treatment. In the same way, many women who fail to ovulate and are therefore sterile have normal pituitary glands and ovaries. Administering LRF to stimulate the anterior pituitary release of LH results in normal ovulation by the ovaries.

Pineal gland

The **pineal gland** is a small pea-shaped structure that is found on top of the posterior part of the third ventricle of the brain (Chapter 5). In cold-blooded animals such as the lizard it is a primitive visual receptor, a "third eye." Its hormone, **melatonin,** probably acts to bleach the skin pigment cells from which the hormone takes its name. The function of the pineal gland has changed drastically in mammals through evolution, and its role in human physiology and behavior was a mystery until recently. Now it is known to govern the activity of the reproductive system in response to the light changes that accompany the light-dark cycle of each day or the changes in daylight with the seasons. The pineal gland no longer contains visual receptors in man, but it is stimulated by excitation that originates in the eye. The excitation reaches the gland by way of the sympathetic nervous system. Of the glands studied, the pineal gland is the fifth to respond to nerve stimulation (neurosecretory). The other four were the adrenal medulla, the pancreas, the posterior pituitary, and the anterior pituitary, which respond to secretions from the nerve cells of the posterior pituitary and hypothalamus.

The melatonin released by the pineal gland suppresses or inhibits the activity of the gonads and therefore affects sexual behavior. Since light suppresses the pineal gland secretion, gonadal activity is released by light. This means that sexual activity is increased by light and reduced by dark in the daily light-dark cycle. The increased sunlight of longer days during the spring triggers annual increased activity by the gonads and increased sex activity in some species of animals.

The way in which light controls gonadal activity through its effect on the pineal gland is complex. Light stimulates the retina of the eye. Excitation reaches the pineal gland by way of sympathetic nervous system fibers (from the superior cervical ganglion). These fibers release norepinephrine. Norepinephrine blocks the activity of an enzyme that is needed by the gland to make its hormone, melatonin. Melatonin production is reduced. Since melatonin normally inhibits the gonads, the gonads are released from inhibition. They secrete more sex hormones, the **estrus cycle** in the female is accelerated, germ cell production in both sexes increases, and sexual behavior is stimulated. The enzyme blocked by the sympathetic nervous system has a long and complex name (hydroxyindole-*O*-methyl transferase) that no one need learn, since it is usually known by its initials, **HIOMT.** HIOMT activity is governed directly by the light-dark cycle, which modulates rhythmic

daily activity in a control center in the hypothalamus (a "biological clock"). The pineal gland makes melatonin out of serotonin, and the serotonin supply depends on brain reactions to the light-dark cycle. Two control mechanisms are therefore possible.

Pineal gland malfunction is rare in man. It is usually caused by tumors of the gland or of adjacent tissue. If the tumor is in the gland itself, the cells multiply and secrete more melatonin; thus *hypersecretion* in children results in delayed sexual development. If the tumor is in the surrounding tissue, it interferes with the function of the gland. *Hyposecretion* of melatonin results, causing precocious puberty in children. Little is known of abnormalities of the gland in adults.

The importance of pineal function to behavior is obvious. It is an important factor governing the onset of puberty in man and may explain why sexual maturation occurs earlier in tropical regions, where there is more sunlight. It regulates the sexual behavior of some animals according to the daily light-dark cycle. It may regulate the timing of the estrus (menstrual) cycle in man as well as in animals. Finally, it governs the seasonal cycle of sexual behavior found in some animals.

Thymus gland

The **thymus gland** develops as a large "gland" of two roughly equal lobes that lie between the breastbone (sternum) and the heart. In young calves it forms a food delicacy known as sweetbread. The size of the thymus increases in step with general growth in the human until the child is 8 to 10 years old. It slowly atrophies thereafter and is not functional in the adult.

The thymus is not actually an endocrine gland, since it does not appear to produce hormones. It is included here only because it is listed with the endocrine glands in older references. Recently the thymus gland has been found to be the primary source of **lymphocytes**—white blood cells that combat disease bacteria and viruses and react to the presence of foreign proteins (infections). The lymphocytes are released into the bloodstream by the thymus and stored by the lymph glands and spleen. Production of lymphocytes by the thymus is at its peak in the last few days before birth and the first few days after birth.

Lymphocytes appear to have two functions: (1) they produce "antibodies" that neutralize disease bacteria and viruses and (2) they "recognize" and react against foreign proteins, for example, tissue transplanted from another animal or a splinter under the skin. The thymus is believed to manufacture the original lymphocytes, expose them to the body's own proteins, and destroy those that react. Then the thymus releases the rest to the spleen and lymph glands for storage and future multiplication when needed. Autoimmune diseases, in which the body reacts against its own proteins, such as leukemia and myasthenia gravis, may be caused by failure in the sorting mechanism of the thymus.

The thymus is probably of little importance to behavior except that its functioning contributes to the ability of the individual to withstand stress, particularly the stress of disease or injury.

SUMMARY

The endocrine glands are organs specialized to secrete hormones directly into the bloodstream. Hormones have a specific effect on specialized target tissue wherever they encounter it. The effect depends on both the specialized nature of the target tissue and the nature of the hormone. Hormone effects have been investigated by gland removal, by injections of natural or synthesized hormones, and by a combination of these two methods. Newer methods include genetic studies, chemical ablation, chemical extraction, radioactive tracers, and perfusion. Hormones affect their target tissues in a variety of ways, including enzyme activation or dissociation, alteration of cell membrane permeability, influence on other structures in the cell, changing of the genetic apparatus in the cell nucleus, or a combination of these effects.

Some endocrine glands are stimulated by the presence of hormones from other endocrine glands or by changes in the internal environment of the body. Other endocrine glands are under nervous as well as chemical control. The output of thyroxin from the thyroid gland is stimulated by TTH from the anterior pituitary; TTH output, in turn, is regulated by the blood thyroxin level. Thyroxin stimulates metabolism in all the cells of the body. Hypothyroidism in childhood results in cretinism, a failure to develop either physically or mentally. In the adult it causes myxedema, with subnormal vigor and alertness. Hyperthyroidism causes a high BMR, hyperactivity, nervousness, and weight loss.

The parathyroid glands produce parathormone in response to a low level of blood calcium. Parathormone, in cooperation with vitamin D, raises the blood calcium level and reduces the phosphorus level to lower nerve cell excitability. This is done by increasing calcium intake, reducing its loss, and taking reserve supplies from the bone. Hyposecretion of parathormone or lack of vitamin D causes hyperexcitability, muscle clonus, tetany, and convulsions. Hypersecretion causes sluggishness, apathy, and wasting of the bones (rickets).

The adrenal cortex secretes corticoids that regulate the sodium and potassium levels of the body, govern carbohydrate metabolism, and mimic the sex hormones. Hyposecretion of corticoids (Addison's disease) depresses the excitability of the nervous system and muscles, which is based on the sodium and potassium balance. Body fluids are lost with sodium excretion, and less blood glucose is stored. Lack of vigor, muscle weakness, low body temperature, and weight loss result. Hypersecretion causes sexual precocity in children and masculinity in women.

The adrenal medulla is stimulated by the sympathetic nervous system (SNS) to secrete norepinephrine and epinephrine (noradrenaline and adrenaline). Norepinephrine mimics SNS effects on target tissue and raises the blood pressure by vasoconstriction. Epinephrine raises blood pressure by increased heart rate and also stimulates ACTH release by the anterior pituitary. ACTH stimulates corticoid output by the adrenal cortex, which increases the BMR and improves tissue excitability. Both the adrenal cortex and medulla increase their secretions in response to stress.

The pancreas reacts to nerve excitation and to the level of blood glucose. Its major hormone is insulin, produced by the beta cells. Insulin inhibits the liver in making or releasing blood glucose and causes increased use of blood glucose by the muscles and other tissue. Hyposecretion of insulin causes diabetes mellitus, resulting in an oversupply of blood glucose (hyperglycemia), which is secreted in the urine, and an accumulation of wastes from fat and protein metabolism, which leads to diabetic coma. Hypersecretion of insulin causes hypoglycemia and insulin shock convulsions.

The posterior pituitary gland, or neurohypophysis, receives nerve fibers from the hypothalamus. Its hormones, vasopressin and oxytocin, raise the blood pressure by arterial constriction (pressor effect), cause contractions in the uterus, stimulate milk production by the mammary glands, and have an antidiuretic effect on the kidney. The main effect of hyposecretion is diabetes insipidus, with the excretion of much urine. Hypersecretion is unknown. Posterior pituitary secretions are important to the thirst drive and to maternal behavior. In addition, nerve fibers of the hypothalamus secrete neurohumors, which reach the anterior pituitary through a portal system of blood vessels and bring it under the influence of the hypothalamus, an important center for drives.

The anterior pituitary gland, or adenohypophysis, controls the activity of the thyroid gland, adrenal cortex, and gonads, in addition to secreting a somatotrophic hormone (STH) that stimulates body growth. Hyposecretion of STH in childhood results in a pituitary dwarf. Hypersecretion in childhood results in a pituitary giant, whereas adult hypersecretion causes acromegaly, with thickened bones and coarse features. The thyrotrophic hormone (TTH) output of the pituitary gland is controlled by the level of blood thyroxin and controls, in turn, the output of the thyroid gland. The adrenocorticotrophic hormone (ACTH) of the pituitary controls the adrenal output of the cortical steroids.

The gonadotrophic hormones stimulate the gonads to produce hormones and regulate sexual cycles in the female and sexual drive in the male. The follicle-stimulating hormone stimulates the development of ova by the female follicles and sperm by the male testes. Luteinizing hormone (LH) stimulates sex hormone output by both sexes and ovulation in the female. Lactogenic hormone (prolactin) aids in turning the follicle into the corpus luteum and stimulates its output of progesterone. It also stimulates female milk production. The gonads are thus under the control of the adenohypophysis. In both sexes the gonads have the two functions of producing germ tissue and sex hormones. The male testes produce androgens and sperm cells. Lack of female estrogens or male androgens in childhood results in failure to mature sexually and failure to develop a sex drive. After castration in adult animals, the sex drive often fails but is little affected in adult humans. In the female, pituitary FSH initiates the estrus cycle by stimulating the follicles of the ovaries to produce an ovum, which is carried to the uterus by a fallopian tube. The follicles secrete estrogens that stimulate growth of a placenta in the uterus and excite the pituitary to secrete LH. FSH and LH cause ovulation. Pituitary LH and prolactin change the follicle into the corpus luteum, which secretes progesterone. Progesterone stops FSH production and prevents further ovulation. LH and prolactin keep up estrogen secretion of the corpus luteum, and prolactin prepares the mammary glands for milk production. The placenta secretes chorionic hormone and progesterone to maintain the status quo if pregnancy occurs. Otherwise, the uterine wall is stripped away in menstruation.

Several transmitter substances of hypothalamic nerve cells reach the anterior hypothalamus by a portal system of capillaries. They act as hormones there, stimulating the anterior pituitary to release TTH, LH, ACTH, prolactin, and STH, depending on the hormone. They are called "releasing factors" (RF), and TRF and LRF have been isolated and used in treating hormone deficiencies.

The pineal gland produces a hormone called melatonin. SNS stimulation in response to light inhibits melatonin production by blocking its enzyme, HIOMT. Melatonin inhibits gonadal activity in the absence of light. The pineal gland helps regulate day and night cycles of sexual activity in man and other animals and regulates seasonal sexual activity in some animals.

The thymus gland is of little importance to behavior. It is not an endocrine gland, as it produces white blood cells (lymphocytes) rather than hormones. Lymphocytes are produced at birth and until 8 to 10 years of age; after this the gland atrophies. Lymphocytes react against bacteria and viruses as well as foreign proteins in the body, thereby combating infection.

READINGS

Asimov, I.: The human brain, Boston, 1964, Houghton Mifflin Co.

Burnet, M.: The thymus gland, Sci. Am. **207**:50-57, Nov. 1962.

Csapo, A.: Progesterone, Sci. Am. **198**:40-46, April 1958. (W. H. Freeman Reprint No. 138.)

Davidson, E. H.: Hormones and genes, Sci. Am. **212**:36-45, June 1965. (W. H. Freeman Reprint No. 1013.)

Edelman, G. M.: The structure and function of antibodies, Sci. Am. **223**:34-42, Aug. 1970.

Guillermin, R., and Burgus, R.: The hormones of the hypothalamus, Sci. Am. **227**:24-33, Nov. 1972.

Karmarkar, M. G., Kochupillai, N., Deo, M. G., and Ramalingaswami, V.: Adaptation of thyroid gland to iodine deficiency, Life Sci. **8**:1135-1141, 1969.

Kirshner, N., and Smith, W. J.: Metabolic requirements for secretion from the adrenal medulla, Life Sci. **8**:799-803, 1969.

Lee, J., and Knowles, F. G. W.: Animal hormones, London, 1965, Hutchinson & Co., Ltd.

Levey, R. H.: The thymus hormone, Sci. Am. **211**:66-77, July 1964. (W. H. Freeman Reprint No. 188.)

Levine, S.: Sex differences in the brain, Sci. Am. **214**:84-90, April 1966. (W. H. Freeman Reprint No. 498.)

Lewin, R.: Hormones: Chemical communication, Garden City, N.Y., 1973, Doubleday Anchor Press.

Li, C. H.: The ACTH molecule, Sci. Am. **209**:46-53, July 1963. (W. H. Freeman Reprint No. 160.)

McKusick, V. A., and Rimoin, D. L.: General Tom Thumb and other midgets, Sci. Am. **217**:103-110, July 1967.

Malvin, P. V.: Interaction between endocrine and nervous systems, BioScience **20**:595-601, 1970.

Rasmussen, H.: The parathyroid hormone, Sci. Am. **204**:56-63, April 1961. (W. H. Freeman Reprint No. 86.)

Rasmussen, H., and Pechet, M. M.: Calcitonin, Sci. Am. **223**:42-50, Oct. 1970.

Vinik, A. I., and Joubert, S. M.: Growth hormone —adrenergic relationship, Life Sci. **9**:541-546, 1970.

Wartman, S. A., Branch, B. J., George, R., and Taylor, A. N.: Evidence for a cholinergic influence in pineal hydroxyindole O-methyltransferase activity with changes in environmental lighting, Life Sci. **8**:1263-1270, 1969.

Whalen, R. E., editor: Hormones and behavior, Princeton, N.J., 1967, D. Van Nostrand Co., Inc.

Wurtman, R. J., and Axelrod, J.: The pineal gland, Sci. Am. **213**:50-60, July 1965. (W. H. Freeman Reprint No. 1015.)

chapter 4
Nerve and muscle tissue

OVERVIEW

Chapter 2 explained how cells, tissues, and organs form **systems** that integrate the diverse activities of the specialized cells. Chapter 3 demonstrated how the **hormones** of the endocrine glands organize the specialized cells and act as a response system. This chapter will explain the way in which nervous **tissue** functions and will serve as a basis for later understanding (Chapter 5) of how the nervous system integrates body function and response. At the same time this chapter briefly treats muscle tissue as it is organized for internal and external behavior.

Before the nervous system is studied as a whole (Chapter 5), the structure and functioning of its cells should be understood. The cell unit of structure and function in the nervous system is the neuron, or nerve cell. Neuron function depends on certain features of neuron structure, which will be presented first. A general idea of the methods the anatomist uses will help in the presentation, as will a section on the nature of electrical change. Then ways of measuring the electrical and chemical events that signal conduction in neurons can be explained so that the signs of neuron functioning will be meaningful. Electrical and chemical characteristics of neuron function will be outlined. A discussion of the way in which neurons pass on excitation from one cell to another at synapses concludes the section.

The nervous system controls behavior through the responses of the glands (Chapter 3) and the muscles. Muscle tissue is classified as smooth, striated, or cardiac. The differences are attributable to spe-cialization in visceral functions (smooth), movement (striated), or heart action (cardiac). A section on how the nervous system controls movement by the way it innervates (connects to) muscle concludes the chapter.

THE NEURON: ANATOMY

A simplified sketch of a "typical" **neuron** is presented in Fig. 4-1. Nerve cells in man are too small to be seen except under a microscope (see pp. 60-61) and vary widely in their characteristics, but all nerve cells feature the parts labeled in Fig. 4-1, with the exception of the neurolemma and myelin sheath. **Synapses** between two neurons are shown so that the role of certain parts of the cell may be appreciated. The nerve cell shown is a long, slender one, obviously designed to carry excitation from one part of the body to another. In life the neuron receives excitation at synapses from the **terminal arborization** of another neuron. At this point each end foot "contacts" the **dendrites** and **cell body** of the neuron, with each contact being a synapse (actually, there is a small gap between the end foot and the dendrite or cell body). The transferred excitation is focused by the **axon hillock** on the **axon** and carried down the axon to its terminal arborization at the next set of synapses. Excitation continues to be passed from cell to cell in this manner.

The axon of a neuron may or may not have a **myelin sheath,** which is a fatty covering interrupted at the **nodes of Ranvier.** Nerve cells with myelin sheaths conduct faster than nerve cells without myelin sheaths. The **neurolemma,** a covering for some neurons, is made up of a separate cell

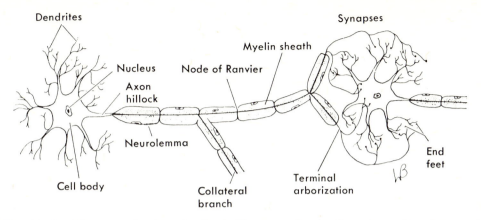

Fig. 4-1. Semidiagrammatic view of a "typical" neuron, showing its major parts and synapses with a second neuron.

(the Schwann cell). It is believed that this cell secretes the fatty myelin sheath. The main function of the neurolemma seems to be protective—it holds the long, thin axon together.

Axons and long sensory dendrites that resemble axons are often called fibers. The **nerves** of the body are bundles of fibers connecting the brain and spinal cord to the sense organs and muscles. The nerves make up the **peripheral nervous system.** Their fibers each have a neurolemma, but may or may not have a myelin sheath. The axons that lie inside the brain and spinal cord are in the **central nervous system** and have no neurolemma; they may or may not have a myelin sheath. Their myelin sheaths are believed to be secreted by glial cells, a kind of supporting cell. In any case, bundles of individually conducting fibers held together by connective tissue constitute the nerves of the peripheral nervous system. Bundles of individually conducting axons running from one part of the brain and spinal cord to another, inside the central nervous system, are called **tracts,** instead of nerves.

Types of neurons

As mentioned previously, individual nerve cells vary widely in appearance. It is useful, however, to classify them into anatomical categories that have functional significance (Fig. 4-2). Although there are many varieties of neurons, this classification types them according to the number of processes that extend directly from the cell body. The **bipolar** (two-process) **neuron,** which has a single axon and a single dendrite, is believed to be the primitive, or early, form of all nerve cells. Conduction proceeds from dendrite to cell body to axon.

Most of the nerves conducting excitation from the sense organs of the skin to the brain and spinal cord—**sensory nerves**—are made up of **unipolar neurons.** A single process connects both axon and dendrite to the cell body, and the dendrite takes on all the characteristics of an axon, including, in many cases, a myelin sheath. The direction of conduction is from dendrite to axon. (In the unipolar neuron, the axon is directly connected to the dendrite.) Since the cell body lies near the brain and spinal cord, the dendrite must be long in order to reach the skin surface and must conduct rapidly like an axon.

A **multipolar** (many-process) **neuron,** on the other hand, has several short dendrites and a single axon, and therefore many processes are connected to the cell body. Multipolar neurons are the most common, being

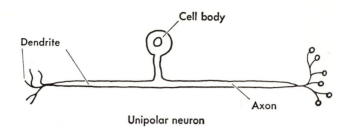

Unipolar neuron

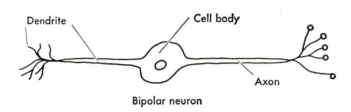

Bipolar neuron

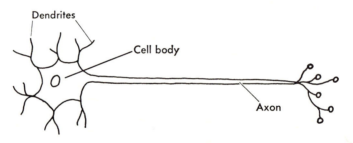

Multipolar neuron

Fig. 4-2. Types of neurons classified according to number of processes attached directly to cell body. A unipolar neuron has one, a bipolar neuron has two (one axon and one dendrite), and a multipolar neuron has several (one axon and several dendrites).

found throughout the central nervous system. Their axons make up the tracts of the brain, as well as the **motor nerves** that extend from the central nervous system to the muscles to excite muscular contraction. Multipolar neurons are classified as **Golgi type I** and **Golgi type II** according to the length and branching of their axons. If they are to carry excitation for some distance, as do tracts and motor nerves, they are Golgi type I neurons, with long axons having few branches. If their axons are short and branch repeatedly, they are Golgi type II neurons, whose function is to spread excitation to nearby neurons.

Anatomical methods for studying neurons

To appreciate what nerve cells look like and what mistakes the anatomist can make in studying their connections with one another, a simplified form of the methods used by the anatomist should be understood. It is difficult to study neurons because of their small size and still more difficult to trace their many connections with one another at synapses. To overcome these difficulties, the anatomist uses several different procedures: light microscope observations, degeneration methods, and electron microscope observations.

Light microscope observations. The largest neurons vary from 50 microns (μ) (millionths of a meter) thick at the cell body to 20 μ (about one thousandth of an inch) thick at the axon. Cells of this size can be seen only through a **microscope.** The tissue must be sliced thin enough so that light will pass through it (about 40 μ) and placed on a glass slide for observation under the microscope. Before a section of brain or spinal cord can be sliced so thin, it must be hardened with formaldehyde solution (formalin). When the animal is killed, a tube from a formalin bottle is inserted into the heart, which pumps the solution throughout the circulatory system, replacing the blood. Formalin reaches the tissue fluid through the capillary walls and hardens all the body tissues, including the nervous tissue of the brain and spinal cord. The nervous tissue is thereby hardened from the "inside out." The tissue is then removed from the animal and further hardened by freezing or embedding in paraffin, and thin cross sections are sliced from the desired portion with a **microtome,** a precision slicing instrument. The thin sections are placed in alcohol to remove water and are stained or dyed with solutions that react chemically with one part or another of the nerve cells to color them for clear observation under the microscope. For example, some stains react with the myelin sheath of axons, enabling the anatomist to trace the axons from section to section in the tracts of the brain and spinal cord. Other stains color only cells without a myelin sheath, or the cell bodies and terminal arborizations of neurons, permitting study of synapses. Many different specialized types of stains can be used. Stained sections are placed on glass slides and covered for protection. They are then ready for observation.

Degeneration methods. Even after proper staining the anatomist cannot distinguish one tract from another under the microscope because the stained axons or myelin sheaths carry no "labels" and the axons of adjoining tracts become intermingled or overlap. To overcome this difficulty the anatomist damages a tract in the living animal at a point where its location is known. After waiting for the effects of the damage to reach other levels of the brain and spinal cord, he kills the animal, makes slides, and identifies the tract at other levels by observing the effects of the original damage at these levels. For example, cutting a tract in the central nervous system will cause the axons to degenerate between the cut and their terminal arborization (wallerian degeneration). Slides of sections taken at other levels will reveal the location of the tract by the absence of its axons. The same cut will cause changes in the cell bodies of the damaged neurons (secondary, or retrograde, degeneration). When the anatomist finds a group of cell bodies (a **center,** or **nucleus**) showing the changes indicated, he knows that the axons of the tract he cut originated in that group of cell bodies. Finally, when a tract degenerates, the cell bodies of neurons on which the tract ended are deprived of synaptic connections (innervation) from the cut neurons, which sometimes causes these cells to degenerate in turn. Their axons can then be traced by their absence to the next synapses in the chain of cell connections (secondary degeneration).

Electron microscope observations. The **electron microscope** allows a magnification of ten to a hundred times that of the light microscope. Through its use in anatomy, physiology, and physiological psychology, much has been learned regarding the physical and chemical characteristics of synapses. Synapse function must be understood before one can comprehend how changes in nerve cell excitability at synapses can occur in sensitization, adaptation, and learning.

To oversimplify, the tissue is bombarded with a stream of **electrons,** or negative particles, in a vacuum. The stream of electrons can be focused by magnetic means, just as light can be focused by a lens. The resulting magnification reveals the smallest structures at the synapses. The magnified image is projected on a fluorescent screen at the end of an evacuated tube in the same manner as an image on television.

THE NEURON: FUNCTION
The nature of electrical change

Electrical currents. The flow of current through most **conductors** (such as electrical wires) is the movement of electrons, or negative particles, from a site where there are many of them to a site where there are fewer of them. A conductor is a material that allows this flow to a greater or lesser degree (an insulator is a material that prevents the flow of current). The difference in the number of electrons at two points constitutes the *voltage* (number of **volts**) difference between them. The greater the voltage difference between two points joined by a conductor, the more rapid the current flow will be, that is, the greater the *amperage* (number of **amperes**). Conversely, the greater the *resistance* (in **ohms**) to current flow offered by the conductor, the slower the current flow will be. In measuring currents in living tissue, electrical change is small so that the terms millivolt (1/1000 of a volt), microvolt (1 millionth of a volt), milliampere (1/1000 of an ampere), micro-ampere, milli- and micro-ohms are often used.

Instrumentation

The functioning of neurons in carrying nerve impulses along the length of an axon and in exciting other neurons at synapses is usually studied through the electrical activity that constitutes the nerve impulse. In the past the major obstacles to studying the electrical activity of neurons were (1) the small size of the neurons, (2) the minuteness of the electrical change (10 to 70 thousandths of a volt), and (3) recording instruments that could not follow electrical events that last only a thousandth of a second. The first problem has been solved by the development of the **microelectrode,** which is small enough to penetrate a single nerve cell, so that the difference in electrical potential between the inside and outside of the single cell can be measured. The second problem has yielded to the **vacuum-tube** or **transistor amplifier,** which can magnify voltage differences by as much as a million times. The third problem has been overcome by the **cathode-ray oscilloscope,** which measures voltage change as the movement of a stream of electrons, an event that has almost no inertia or lag.

In practice, a microelectrode is usually made by stretching a heated glass tube out until it breaks, with a hollow end as tiny as 0.5 μ thick. The tube is filled with an electrically conducting salt solution (KCl) and inserted into the tissue. When the microelectrode enters a single axon, such as a giant squid axon, a potential difference with respect to another electrode located outside the axon is registered. The difference in potential is usually about 40 millivolts (mv.) (40/1000 volt) and represents the **resting potential** of the nerve cell. The outside of the nerve cell is positively charged with respect to the inside. This **polarized condition** reverses during passage of the nerve impulse down the axon.

Recording the nerve impulse (Fig. 4-3)

The microelectrode inside the axon is negative (has surplus electrons) with respect to an electrode outside the axon. This difference in charge is magnified by the amplifier and applied to the cathode-ray oscilloscope. The cathode-ray oscilloscope amounts to a simplified version of a television set. The cathode tube itself is an elongated vacuum tube with an electron source at one end. The electron source, or cathode, discharges negative charges (electrons) at high speed, striking the face of the tube at the other end. The tube face is coated inside with a fluorescent paint so that the electrons make a bright spot on the face of the tube when they strike it. The

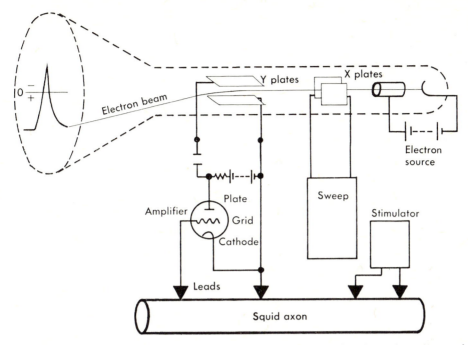

Fig. 4-3. Diagram of arrangements for recording nerve impulse. Microelectrode and operation of cathode-ray oscilloscope are described in the text. The vacuum tube controls the flow of electrons (negative charges) from a negatively charged *cathode* to a positively charged *plate* in a vacuum. Negative charges reduce the positive charge of the plate. These charges must pass through apertures in a screen *grid* to reach the plate from the cathode. The grid is connected to the microelectrode, which has a negative charge from the inside of the nerve cell. The plate is indirectly connected to the outside of the cell. The negative electrons on the grid turn back many times their number in electrons that would normally flow from cathode to plate (like charges repel each other). Thus a small charge at the grid makes a large difference in the number of electrons reaching the plate and therefore a large difference in the voltage of the plate. The voltage difference between the inside and outside of the nerve cell is therefore *amplified* many times.

spot can be made to move across the face of the tube at a known rate by charging plates positive or negative on either side of the stream of electrons to deflect the electrons back and forth (the X plates). When the amplified charge between the negative inside and positive outside of the axon is applied to plates above and below the electron stream (the Y plates), the moving spot on the face of the tube is deflected downward. If the nerve cell is stimulated, a reversal of its normal polarized condition results, and the outside of the nerve cell becomes negative with respect to the inside at that point. This change will then sweep

down the length of the axon. If the axon is stimulated at the same time that the sweep of the electron beam is started across the face of the tube, a picture of the reversal of the polarized condition of the axon as the nerve impulse passes the microelectrode will be obtained. The reversal of polarization in the axon as the electron beam passes across the face of the tube will, so to speak, "draw its own picture," with time as the horizontal axis of the graph and voltage change as the vertical axis (Figs. 4-3 and 4-8, lower diagram). Placing the microelectrode *near* the cell is enough to record nerve impulses in many experiments, as the fluid surrounding the cells is a good conductor of electrical changes.

Bioelectrical currents

Electrolytes. An **electrolyte** is a substance that breaks up into positive and negative **ions** in a water solution. Salt (NaCl) is an electrolyte; in solution it breaks up into a positively charged sodium ion (Na⁺) and a negatively charged chlorine ion (Cl⁻). The

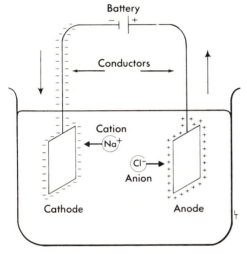

Fig. 4-4. Flow of current through a wire as electron movement, and through a salt solution (electrolyte) as ion movement.

sodium ion is positive because it lacks an electron, and the chlorine ion is negative because it has a surplus electron. Suppose that wires connected to a battery are placed in a solution of salt water. The wires serve as **electrodes** (Fig. 4-4). One wire, the **cathode,** will have more electrons than the other wire, the **anode,** Na⁺ ions will be attracted to the cathode to pick up the electron each one lacks. The Na⁺ ion is therefore a **cation.** The Cl⁻ ions will be attracted to the anode to give up the surplus electron that each one possesses. The Cl⁻ ions are therefore **anions.** A flow of current through the solution results from the movement of both positive and negative ions. Bioelectrical currents, or currents in living tissue, are the result of ion movements of this nature, rather than the movement of electrons through wires.

Resting potential. For reasons to be explained later, the fluid outside the nerve cell has more positive ions than does the fluid on the inside. The positively charged outside of the nerve cell and the negatively charged inside are separated by the **nerve** (cell) **membrane.** This state of affairs existing across the nerve membrane is termed a **polarized condition.** The difference in voltage between the positive outside and

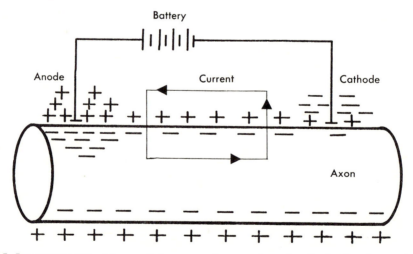

Fig. 4-5. Ion movements and current flow around an anode and cathode placed near the axon of a nerve cell.

the negative inside of the membrane of all living cells is called the **resting potential.**

Action potential. If two electrodes leading to a battery are placed near the axon of a nerve cell (in its fluid medium), the polarized condition of the nerve membrane will be changed. The polarized condition across the membrane will be increased at the anode, since any negative anions will give up their surplus electrons to the anode at this point (Fig. 4-5). The polarized condition of the membrane at the cathode will be decreased, since any positive cations will acquire electrons from the cathode. Fewer positive cations at the cathode will reduce the positive charge outside the membrane, and fewer negative anions will be attracted to this region inside the membrane (oppositely charged ions attract each other). When a critical amount of partial depolarization is reached, an explosive ion exchange occurs across the membrane. The polarized condition of the membrane will be reversed at the cathode—the membrane becomes negative on the outside and positive on the inside (Fig. 4-8). This polarization reversal will sweep along the length of the axon as the **spike potential.** Behind this moving polarization reversal, the nerve cell will recover its original polarized condition. The sequence of events is known as the **action potential** and includes other electrical changes (Fig. 4-8). Since a positive cation (Na+) initiates these events, the current flow is usually illustrated as being from positive to negative (Figs. 4-5 and 4-8). Positive and negative ions are actually moving in both directions.

All-or-none law

The nerve impulse consists of a rapid exchange of positive and negative ions across the nerve cell membrane when the degree of depolarization reaches a critical value at the cathode. That is, when the polarized condition of the nerve membrane is reduced by a certain amount, the membrane "takes over" and continues the depolarization past the neutral point, so that the outside of the nerve cell membrane becomes negative with respect to the inside. The impulse is self-propagating; that is, the energy for the polarization reversal is supplied by the nerve cell itself, and not by the

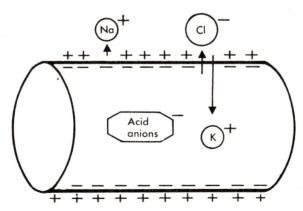

Fig. 4-6. Chemical basis of the resting potential. Negatively charged acid anions are trapped inside the cell membrane because of their size, and positive sodium cations (Na+) are actively excluded by the membrane ("sodium pump"). Concentration gradients of potassium ions (K+) and of chlorine ions (Cl-) are the result, the Cl- ions being attracted by the Na+ ions and the K+ ions being attracted by the negative acid anions. Cl- ions tend to diffuse back inside the membrane, and K+ ions diffuse back outside to some extent. As a net result the membrane is polarized, being positive on the outside with respect to the inside of the cell.

stimulus that triggers it. Once initiated, the impulse spreads along the axon by ion exchanges through the membrane down the whole length of the axon; the energy for the spread comes from the nerve cell membrane. The **all-or-none law** states that a nerve cell responds with the total voltage change that its polarized condition permits if, and only if, the stimulus intensity reaches a critical threshold value. Stronger stimuli will not result in a larger or faster nerve impulse since the nerve cell itself, and not the stimulus, provides the energy for the nerve impulse.

Chemical characteristics of resting potential and nerve impulse

Research has shown which shifts in ions, or charged chemical particles, are responsi-

ble for the resting potential and which shifts are responsible for the nerve impulse. The ionic basis of the resting potential and the ion shifts responsible for the nerve impulse have been largely worked out over the past 35 years by an ingenious set of experiments carried out on giant squid axons. These axons are unmyelinated and as large as a millimeter in diameter. As a result of their size, investigators have been able to sample and to alter the chemical and electrical characteristics of squid axons while firing them. The resulting information shows the dependence of the nervous system on the ions in its fluid environment; that is, the functioning of nerve cells and therefore sensation, imagination, thinking, and behavior all depend on that environment.

Resting potential. The polarized condi-

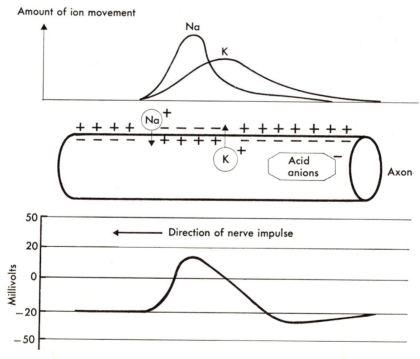

Fig. 4-7. Chemical basis of the nerve impulse. Polarization reversal is caused by an influx of sodium ions (Na+) when the membrane ceases to exclude them. Recovery of polarization occurs when potassium ions (K+) move outside the membrane to replace sodium ions. Ion movements are shown in the top graph, events in the axon are sketched in the middle, and electrical changes (millivolts of polarization) are at the bottom, with a common time axis for the three sets of events reading from left to right.

tion of the nerve cell axon is caused by certain properties of the nerve cell membrane with respect to ions—charged chemical elements and molecules. As a result of the characteristics of the nerve cell membrane, there are more positive than negative ions outside the membrane and more negative than positive ions inside the membrane. The imbalance in ions results in a positive charge outside the membrane and a negative charge inside the membrane. The ion imbalance and the consequent resting potential between the inside and outside of the cell membrane are the result of four factors (Fig. 4-6):

1. SODIUM PUMP. For reasons that are still not understood, the nerve cell membrane actively *excludes* **sodium ions (Na⁺)** from the cell. Sodium ions carry a positive charge; thus there are more positively charged sodium ions outside the membrane than inside the membrane.

2. POTASSIUM PUMP. Theorists believe that the membrane actively *includes* **potassium ions (K⁺);** That is, it takes any potassium ions encountered in the fluid environment and actively transports them into the cell. Potassium ions are positively charged, but there are not enough of them inside the cell to offset other ion differences between the inside and outside of the cell. The cell remains, on balance, more positively charged outside than inside.

3. ION SIZE. The cell contains many negatively charged acid molecules (acid anions) that are too large to pass through the pores of the cell membrane. This contributes to making the inside of the cell negative with respect to the outside.

4. PRINCIPLE OF DIFFUSION. **Chlorine ions (Cl⁻)** carry a negative charge and are free to move back and forth through the membrane. Substances tend to move from a region of high concentration to a region of low concentration, according to the principle of diffusion. To demonstrate this phenomenon, one need only place a drop of ink into a glass of water; in minutes the ink particles will diffuse throughout the water. According to the principle of diffusion, one would expect to find the same number of chlorine ions inside as there are outside the nerve cell membrane. But chlorine ions carry a negative charge and therefore are attracted by positively charged ions and repelled by negatively charged ions. As shown earlier, there are more negative acid anions inside the membrane than outside, and more positive sodium ions outside the membrane than positive ions inside the membrane. Therefore, there is an imbalance in favor of positive ions outside the membrane and negative ions inside the membrane. Negative chlorine ions are repelled by the negative ions inside the membrane and attracted by the positive ions outside the membrane; a **concentration gradient** of chlorine ions is built up, with more chlorine ions outside than inside the membrane. For reasons explained above, there is a similar concentration gradient of sodium ions (more outside) and an opposite concentration gradient of potassium ions (more inside). The measured size of these gradients of charged particles is enough to account for the size of the resting potential, which is about 40 mv. The resting potential is accounted for by the imbalance of known positive ions outside the nerve cell membrane and known negative ions inside the nerve cell membrane. These principles are not confined to nerve cells—all living cells seem to be polarized and for the same reasons. However, the specialized feature of nerve cells is their greater ability to alter their polarized condition to produce the nerve impulse.

Nerve impulse. Since a single axon rather than a bundle of axons in a nerve is being discussed, the term should be "neuron impulse." The term "nerve impulse" comes from earlier experiments in which the electrical activity of nerve trunks, rather than of a single axon, was all the experimenters could measure. To simplify, the nerve impulse in an axon occurs when its polarized condition is reduced enough to "turn off" the sodium and potassium "pumps" (Fig. 4-7). The initial result is a rapid movement of positive sodium ions (Na+) into the negatively charged interior of the axon. This event reverses the polarized condition of the membrane, so that it becomes positive inside and negative outside—the spike potential. Recovery is initiated by the movement of positive potassium ions (K+) out of the axon to replace the sodium ions. Potassium ion movement causes the recovery of the normal polarized condition of the axon, that is, the downward limb of the spike potential and parts of the negative and positive afterpotentials. The cell is depolarized by sodium ion movement and repolarized by po-

tassium ion movement through its membrane. Negative chlorine ions move first inside and then back outside the membrane in response to changes in its polarized condition. After the action potential is over, the sodium and potassium "pumps" become active again—the sodium is transferred back out of the cell and the potassium is transferred back inside the cell while the resting potential is maintained.

Electrical and excitability events

The complete sequence of electrical changes that accompany the nerve impulse is shown in Fig. 4-8. A diagram of the changes in excitability of the axon occur-

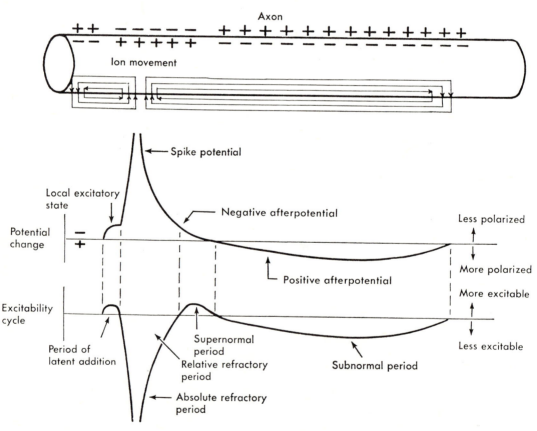

Fig. 4-8. Nerve impulse: current flow, potential changes, and excitability cycle plotted on a common time axis. (From Morgan, C. T.: Physiological psychology, ed. 3, New York, 1965, McGraw-Hill Book Co.)

ring at the same time is also shown. Finally, the current flow accompanying the various phases of the *action potential* is depicted in terms of positive-to-negative ion flow. As the current flow that causes the nerve impulse approaches the point on the axon being measured, an initial bioelectrical change in the action potential occurs; this change is called a **local excitatory state.** The membrane is partially depolarized at the point of change; that is, it is less positive outside to negative inside than normal. At the same time the excitability of the axon is increased at that point. The increase in excitability accompanying the local excitatory state is graphed as the **period of latent addition** on the excitability cycle. When the increasing excitability reaches the threshold of the nerve membrane, the membrane "takes over" and continues the electrical change. The membrane reverses potential, becoming negative on the outside and positive on the inside—an event of the action potential called the *spike potential.* During the spike potential the axon cannot be depolarized, since it has already reversed polarization—an event of the excitability cycle called the **absolute refractory period.** The axon then begins recovering its polarized condition, as indicated in the current flow diagram. This event occurs rapidly at first, and then more slowly, as shown by the action potential. The period during which the axon is recovering its normal polarized condition is the **negative afterpotential.** During the early part of the negative afterpotential, the axon has recovered enough polarization to be excitable again. However, the current flow of recovery must be reversed to excite it, so that a stronger-than-normal stimulus is required; the threshold of the axon is raised during the early part of the negative afterpotential. This part of the excitability cycle is called the **relative refractory period.** During the later part of the negative afterpotential, the current flow causing recovery slows down and is therefore easier

to reverse by a new stimulus. In addition, the axon is still partially depolarized—it has not yet recovered its fully polarized state. For these two reasons the axon is easier to stimulate (or depolarize again) than normal. The excitability cycle is therefore in a **supernormal period,** and a weaker stimulus will excite it in comparison with its resting state. Finally, the current flow involved in recovery "overshoots" the polarized condition found in the resting axon; the axon becomes more polarized than normal during the **positive afterpotential.** During the overpolarized condition of the positive afterpotential, a stronger-than-normal stimulus is required to reduce the polarized condition of the axon enough to fire it— its threshold is increased. Therefore, the **subnormal period** of the excitability cycle accompanies the positive afterpotential.

The sequence and timing of the electrical and excitatory events vary widely from one nerve cell to another. Some types of nerve cells show no positive afterpotential, or subnormal period. The duration of the phases of the action potential and excitability cycle, as well as conduction velocity, differs according to cell size and type (Table 4-1). Finally, cells in the living brain probably fire at slower rates than the excitability cycle given here would allow (the information presented has been taken from peripheral nerves). However, the principles outlined are valid and have important consequences for physiological psychology.

It is important to realize that the only information the brain receives from the outside world is coded in terms of nerve impulses. Events in the physical world stimulate the *receptors,* which in turn stimulate peripheral nerve cells whose impulses reach the brain, either directly or indirectly. Now, if the *stimulus* to the receptor is *just* strong enough to fire the sensory nerve cells —a threshold stimulus—the nerve cell will fire, and fire again only after the first part of the negative afterpotential is over and the

Table 4-1. Properties of nerve fibers*

	A	Alpha	Beta	Gamma	Delta	B	s.C†	d.r.C‡
Fiber diameter (μ)	1-22	6- 19	12-8	8-2	1-6	≤3	0.3-1.3	0.4-1.2
Conduction speed (msec.)	5-120	5-120				3-15	0.7-2.3	0.6-2.0
Spike duration (msec.)	0.4-0.5					1.2	2.0	2.0
Absolute refractory period (msec.)	0.4-1.0					1.2	2.0	2.0
Negative afterpotential amplitude, percentage of spike	3-5					None	3-5	None
Duration (msec.)	12-20						50-80	
Positive afterpotential amplitude, percentage of spike	0.2					1.5-4.0	1.5	
Duration (msec.)	40-60					100-300	300-1000	
Order of susceptibility to asphyxia	2					1	3	3
Velocity/diameter ratio	6					?	?	1.73 average

*Modified from Patton, H. D.: Special properties of nerve trunks and tracts. In Ruch, T. C., Patton, H. D., Woodbury, J. W., and Towe, A. L.: Neurophysiology, ed. 2, Philadelphia, 1965, W. B. Saunders Co.

†Unmyelinated C fibers of the sympathetic nervous system.

‡Unmyelinated sensory nerve fibers for pain.

supernormal period begins. That is, the nerve cell will have to recover full sensitivity before it can fire a second time in response to a barely sufficient, or threshold, stimulus. This means that the *frequency* of impulses will be at a *minimum*. However, the *spike size* (amount of polarization change in the nerve impulse) will be at a *maximum*. The spike will be large because the sensory nerve cell membrane will be fully repolarized, or recovered, each time it fires. Now, if the stimulus to the receptor is increased in *intensity,* how can this change be communicated to the brain? With a stimulus well above threshold, the nerve cell need not recover fully before it can be fired again—it will fire during the relative refractory period that occurs during the early part of the negative afterpotential. An increase in stimulus intensity will result in more frequent nerve impulses to the brain. Increases in intensity of stimulus can therefore be signaled to the brain by increases in the frequency of nerve impulses. Finally, receptors and sensory neurons differ in

threshold. A weak stimulus may fire only the most sensitive ones. As stimulus strength increases, more receptors and therefore more sensory neurons will be firing. Such changes must relay information to the brain as changes in the brightness of lights, loudness of sounds, intensity of pressure on the skin, etc.

Generator and graded potentials

Axons are apparently the only receptor or nervous structures that normally show spike potentials (some types of dendrites have spike potentials also). Receptors stimulate nerve cells with generator potentials, and nerve cells stimulate each other at synapses by means of graded potentials. These potentials resemble the local excitatory state previously described. They represent *partial* depolarization at the receptor or at synapses —depolarization that does not become complete. Therefore, generator and graded potentials do not follow the all-or-none law. By an increase in the *extent* and *degree* of depolarization, they signal increases in intensity of a stimulus at a receptor or increases in the number of active synapses on the cell body and dendrites of a nerve cell. The resulting ion shifts in nerve cells depolarize the axon and cause nerve impulses. Graded potentials can cause **summation** if they occur close enough together, when one partial depolarization adds to the effect of another one. In receptors, **generator potentials** usually arise only in response to the type of stimulus for which the receptor is specialized: for example, pressure on the pacinian corpuscle of the skin or light in the rods and cones of the eye. At synapses, discussed later, chemical events seem to cause **graded potentials** on the dendrites and cell bodies they contact, structures that do not normally reverse polarization in response to electrical changes. The sequence of events at the synapses would be as follows: axon spike, chemical event, graded potential, and axon spike.

THE SYNAPSE

Refer again to Fig. 4-1. Note that nerve cells contact one another when the terminal arborization of one cell "contacts" the cell body and dendrites of a second cell. Every such contact is a **synapse.** Although there are several kinds of synapses, the variety sketched here is most typical. Each branch of the terminal arborization of the first cell ends in a knoblike structure called an axon terminal, or **synaptic knob.** The synaptic knobs do not touch the surface of the dendrites or cell bodies, but come very close to them, leaving a uniform gap or about 100 angstrom units (Å, 1/10,000,000 of a millimeter). In Fig. 4-9 three types of junctions between synaptic knobs and dendrites or cell bodies are shown as they can be seen under the electron microscope. Notice the small globules that concentrate inside the synaptic knobs near the synaptic cleft, the gap between knob and cell body or dendrites. These are the **synaptic vesicles,** which are believed to contain the specific chemical substances by which one nerve cell excites another at synapses. Two of these *chemical transmitters* are known to be **norepinephrine** and **acetylcholine (ACh),** but there are others (Table 4-2). There are also neurons whose end-feet probably release inhibitory chemical transmitters, such as gamma-aminobutyric acid (GABA), that increase the polarization of dendrites and cell bodies at synapses. Increased polarization can prevent excitation at nearby synapses from excitatory neurons that end on the same cell.

Postsynaptic potentials

When an excitatory neuron releases ACh onto another neuron at its synapses, the chemical transmitter acts to partly depolarize the second cell. The resulting depolarization is called an **excitatory postsynaptic potential,** or **EPSP.** The vesicles in the synaptic knob probably release ACh molecules through the membrane of the synaptic knobs. The ACh molecules drift rapidly across the synaptic cleft to act on receptor sites in the membranes of the cell body and dendrites of the second cell. They appear to make the cell body and dendrites of the second cell more permeable to positively charged sodium and potassium ions. The result is the partial depolarization, or graded potential, described in a previous section. The cell body and dendrites do not reverse polarization immediately, as an axon does. Ions shift from the area of the axon hillock (Fig. 4-1) to replace those that move into the cell body. Depolarization of the axon hillock causes a nerve impulse in the axon. The nerve impulse sweeps down the axon to the next set of synapses. As long as a large enough negative EPSP is maintained by synapses on the dendrites and cell body, the axon will continue to fire. When fresh ACh is no longer being released at the synapses, the neuron does not continue to fire, because the remaining ACh is rapidly broken down by an enzyme, **acetylcholine esterase (AChE).**

There are types of neurons that are ex-

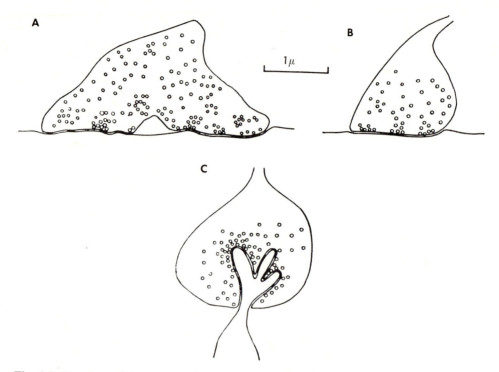

Fig. 4-9. Drawings of three types of synapses seen under the electron microscope. Presynaptic endings (synaptic knobs) are on top in each illustration, the postsynaptic endings below. **A,** Synapse on a large motoneuron cell body. **B,** Smaller interneuron synapse of the same variety. **C,** Synapse between a visual receptor cell in the retina and a nerve cell. Note synaptic vesicles of transmitter substance in each presynaptic ending. (**A** from Paley, S. L.: J. Biophys. Biochem. Cytol. **2**[supp.]:193-202, 1956; **B** from DeRobertis, E. D. P.: J. Biophys. Biochem. Cytol. **2:** 503-512, 1956; **C** from DeRobertis, E. D. P., and Franchi, C. M.: J. Biophys. Biochem. Cytol. **2:**307-317, 1956.)

Table 4-2. Known and suspected synaptic transmitters

Transmitter	Peripheral action	CNS location (order of descending concentration)
Acetylcholine	Neuromuscular junction Ganglia of sympathetic and parasympathetic nervous systems	Retina, motor cortex, caudate nucleus, occipital cortex, superior colliculus, gray matter
Norepinephrine Epinephrine Dopa catecholamines (dopamine)	Postganglionic sympathetic system Adrenal medulla	Hypothalamus, basal ganglia (dopa—caudate and lenticular gray matter)
Serotonin or 5-HT (5-hydroxytryptamine)	Adrenal medulla?	Basal ganglia, hippocampus, amygdala, caudate nucleus, putamen; highest in pineal gland and lowest in cerebral cortex; tryptophan—hypothalamus, cerebellum, pons
GABA (gamma-aminobutyric acid)	Only in CNS	Almost all gray matter

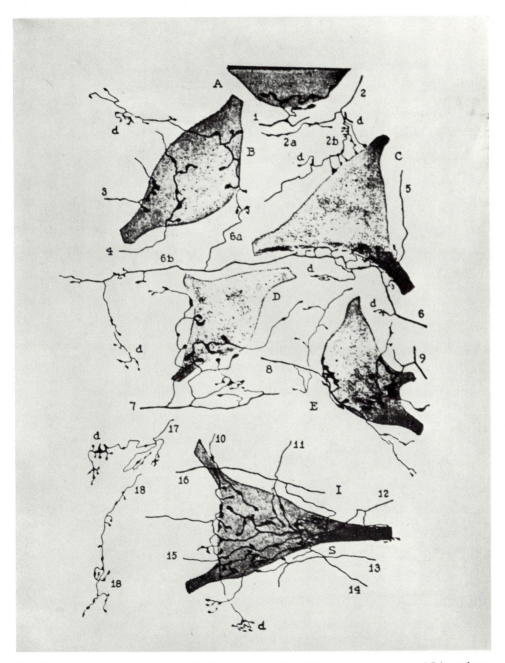

Fig. 4-10. Synapses as seen with a light microscope. **A** to **E** are motoneurons and **I** is an interneuron. Numbered fibers are presynaptic axon terminals ending in synaptic knobs on dendrites and cell bodies of **A** to **E** and **I**. (From Lorente de No, R.: J. Neurophysiol. **1:**195-206, 1938.)

cited in the normal way but act to prevent the depolarization of neurons on which they have synapses. One type of inhibitory cell known to be important in reflexes is a Golgi type II neuron called a Renshaw cell. Its synaptic knobs have vesicles that probably contain gamma-aminobutyric acid (GABA). Such transmitters *hyperpolarize,* or increase the polarized condition of, the cell body and dendrites on which they are released. The change in potential is called and **inhibitory postsynaptic potential (IPSP).** A hyperpolarized call is harder to excite with the EPSP produced at excitatory synapses. The cell body and dendrites of a cell may have both excitatory and inhibitory synapses on it; whether or not it fires depends on the algebraic sum of the EPSP and IPSP influences, which are called **facilitation** and **inhibition,** respectively.

The IPSP is believed to be caused by the effect of the inhibitory transmitter on the membrane. The transmitter probably makes the membrane permeable to potassium ions (K^+) and chlorine ions (Cl^-) encountered in the fluid environment. However, the membrane is not permeable to the slightly larger sodium ions (Na^+), which are outside the membrane. The outflow of positive potassium ions and the inflow of negative chlorine ions increase the polarized condition of the membrane, as there is no corresponding inflow of positive sodium ions. These events make the cell body and dendrites more positive outside and more negative inside. The hyperpolarized cell is more difficult to depolarize, or excite. Potassium salts have been used to hyperpolarize and therefore inhibit parts of the brain in animal learning experiments (spreading depression, Chapter 17).

The diagrams and figures used to illustrate principles of synaptic function up to this point have been oversimplified. Fig. 4-10, taken from a microscope slide, gives one some appreciation of the number and complexity of synapses on each single cell. Note also that axoaxonic synapses have been observed where the synaptic knobs

end on the terminal filaments of another fiber. Axoaxonic synapses are probably inhibitory, but until researchers agree on their mode of action, this conclusion is not certain. The importance of synaptic mechanisms to the psychologist is, however, no longer in doubt. For example, it has been shown that blocking destruction of the transmitter ACh by preventing AChE from acting not only increases the excitability of synapses but, in animals, improves the rate at which they learn (Chapter 17).

CLASSIFICATION OF MUSCLE TISSUE

Muscle tissue is made up of cells that are specialized for changing shape, which they accomplish by shortening their elongated form. When muscle cells are attached to one another and to other tissues of the body, they are organized into muscles. Muscles are made up of muscle cells (for contraction), connective tissue (to hold the cells together), vascular, or blood vessel, tissue (to nourish the other cells), etc. Muscles are therefore *organs* made up of several kinds of specialized tissue.

The way in which muscle cells and other muscle tissue have specialized hinges largely on the rate of contraction required of a given type of muscle and how dependent it is on stimulation from the nervous system. *Contraction rate* and *automaticity* (degree of independence from stimulation by the nervous system) determine the structure and function of muscle cells as organized into muscles. Three types of muscle tissue have resulted: **smooth, striated,** and **cardiac.** Smooth and cardiac (heart) muscles contract slowly and are relatively automatic, contracting without nervous stimulation. Smooth and cardiac muscle tissues are found in the *viscera* (internal organs) and therefore form **visceral muscles.** Striated muscles react rapidly and depend on the nervous system for excitation. Striated muscles move the body (Gr. *soma*) about by pulling on the bony "levers" of the skeleton and are therefore called **somatic muscles.**

Visceral muscle has often been called involuntary, since its contractions are largely automatic and one is not aware of them; the contractions involved in the beating of the heart and the digestion of food are examples. Somatic muscle has been called voluntary because one is often aware of the muscle contractions that control movements, and body movements are said to be under the control of the "will." The distinction fails in several ways. Humans and animals learn voluntary control of certain visceral smooth muscles—for example, those involved in the control of the bowel and bladder in becoming housebroken or toilet trained. Somatic (striated, or skeletal) muscles, on the other hand, often react without awareness in reflexes such as those of breathing or in more complex automatic movements such as walking.

STRUCTURE AND FUNCTION OF MUSCLES AS ORGANS
Smooth muscle

As previously explained, smooth muscle is specialized for slow, sustained, and often automatic contraction and relaxation and is the type of muscle that forms much of the viscera, or internal organs. When smooth muscle takes a tubular form, as in the arteries and intestines, the tubular structure is often made up of opposed groups of muscle fibers (Fig. 4-11). One set of fibers may be oriented in a circular fashion around the tube. Contraction of these fibers *constricts* the lumen (the "bore") of the tube to reduce the flow of blood through an artery, to reduce the flow of air through the trachea, or windpipe, or to move food along the intestine. The opposed set of fibers is oriented in a longitudinal direction. Contraction of these fibers tends to shorten the tube and, more importantly, to *increase* its lumen. Despite their automatic contractions, smooth muscles of the arteries, intestines, etc. are supplied with nerve fibers (axons) from the brain and spinal cord by the nerves of the peripheral nervous system. These motor nerves form a special subdivision of the peripheral nervous system called the **autonomic nervous system (ANS,** Chapter 5), which has two divisions, the **parasympathetic division** and the **sympathetic division.** Both divisions supply the tubular type of muscle described here, but in many cases the sympathetic

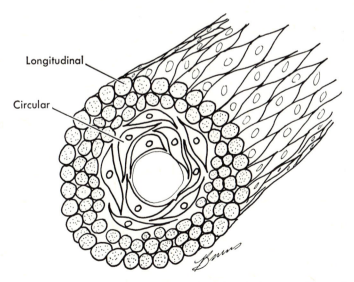

Longitudinal

Circular

Fig. 4-11. Diagram of how muscle cells are organized in tubular smooth muscle tissue, as in arteries or intestines. Contraction of circular fibers constricts the lumen of the tube, whereas contraction of longitudinal fibers has the opposite effect.

division supplies one set of fibers (for example, the circular fibers), whereas the parasympathetic division supplies the other set of fibers (for example, the longitudinal fibers). In the arteries, excitation by one division of the ANS can restrict the flow of blood to an organ by constricting the artery, whereas excitation by the other division dilates the artery to increase the flow of blood to the organ. The iris, or colored portion of the eye that surrounds the pupil, is made up of circular and radial fibers that are opposed, and the opposed fibers are supplied by the opposed divisions of the ANS. Sympathetic stimulation contracts the radial fibers, which enlarge the pupil and admit more light to the eye, whereas parasympathetic stimulation contracts the circular fibers, which constrict the pupil and admit less light to the eye.

In the case of the intestine, as previously noted, the contractions of the circular and longitudinal fibers are largely automatic, like those of the heart, although stimulated by local factors such as the presence of wastes. In this case stimulation by the parasympathetic division increases the rate of regular contractions, whereas sympathetic stimulation inhibits regular contractions.

In gross appearance, smooth muscles sometimes take a form such as that of striated muscles, with all the fibers oriented in the same direction. This is true of the piloerector muscles, which erect the body hair, and of the sphincters (all circular fibers), whose contraction closes the bowel and bladder openings. In these two cases sympathetic stimulation contracts the muscle to raise the body hair or close the sphincter opening, whereas parasympathetic stimulation inhibits contraction by these muscles. The reasons for these effects will be studied later (Chapter 5).

Cardiac muscle

Cardiac muscle is intermediate in functional characteristics between smooth and striated muscle—the heart contracts rapidly like striated muscle, but automatically like many smooth muscles. The membranes of the muscle cells are so closely interwoven that excitation spreads from cell to cell, so that the whole heart muscle contracts almost as a unit, although some parts contract before others. The heart is regularly excited by intrinsic (built-in) nerve tissue and will continue to beat if its nerve supply from the central nervous system fails. This has obvious survival value for the organism. Like smooth muscle, the heart is supplied by the ANS; sympathetic stimulation serves to increase its rate of automatic beating (pumping), whereas parasympathetic stimulation slows its rate of beat, all in response to the circulatory needs of the body.

Striated muscle

Striated, or somatic, muscle contracts most rapidly of the three types of muscle. However, it cannot maintain a strong contraction or series of contractions for as long as smooth or cardiac muscle can. Neither is it automatic in action, as is most visceral muscle; somatic muscle must receive excitation from the central nervous system, by the motor nerves of the peripheral nervous system, to contract under normal circumstances.

The way in which the cells, or fibers, are organized in striated muscle becomes important in understanding its function (Fig. 4-12). All muscle cells are oriented in the long axis of nearly all striated muscles. Connective tissue plays a major role in the structural organization of the muscle. All the cells are linked together by connective tissue, which ultimately connects to tendons on both ends of the muscle; thus shortening of the individual cells ultimately exerts a pull on the tendons and acts so as to shorten the muscle. The tendons are attached to bone at both ends, which enables one to flex or extend the arms, legs, and so forth.

Flexors and extensors. Somatic muscles occur in opposed pairs, called flexors and extensors. Flexors act to bend the digits (fingers and toes), limbs, and body; they react more rapidly than extensors. Extensors act to extend the digits, limbs, and body; they react more slowly than flexors (but can maintain contraction longer). Extensors are also called antigravity muscles, as their action in extending the limbs and body opposes the pull of gravity and maintains the upright position. An exception in man is the flexors of the arms; flexing the arm and fingers opposes the pull of gravity.

Reciprocal innervation. The muscles involved in any given body movement, whether flexors or extensors, are called the **agonist muscles** for that movement. If a flexor is the agonist muscle for a given movement (for example, bending the leg), the extensor muscle that would perform the opposite movement (straightening the leg) is the **antagonist muscle** for that movement. Since agonist and antagonist muscles occur

in opposed pairs, an antagonist muscle must relax for an agonist muscle to perform a movement. Both agonist and antagonist muscles are **innervated** (receive nerve fibers) from the central nervous system (CNS) by the motor nerves of the peripheral nervous system. The CNS is so arranged that when an agonist muscle is excited, its antagonist is inhibited. This is called **reciprocal innervation.**

INNERVATION OF STRIATED MUSCLE
Motor unit and innervation ratio

Striated muscle contraction is organized by the way it is innervated (receives nerve fibers for excitation). Each axon of the motor nerve supplying a muscle breaks up into a number of branches (Fig. 4-12). Each branch makes "contact" with a single muscle cell. If the axon of a neuron has 50 branches, that neuron contacts and excites

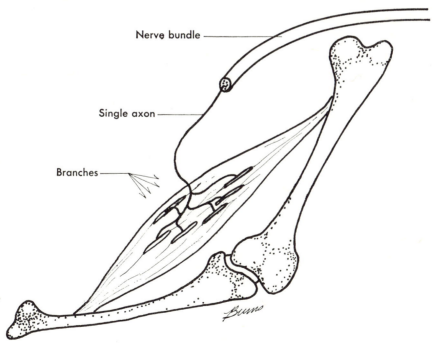

Fig. 4-12. Sketch of motor unit, consisting of single motoneuron (whose axon is shown) and individual muscle cells innervated by branches of that motoneuron.

50 muscle cells at once, whenever it fires. The single nerve cell and all the muscle cells it contacts is a **motor unit,** and this is the unit of contraction for the muscle. If on the average each axon in the motor nerve to a muscle contacts 50 muscle cells to excite them, 50 is the size of the motor unit. The minimum contraction the muscle can make would involve firing one motoneuron, which would excite 50 cells. Exciting a second neuron to increase the response would involve adding another "set" of 50 muscle cells to the muscle contraction, for a total of 100. Further increases in contraction would involve stepwise increments in motor unit involvement, 50 muscle cells at a time. This does not imply that all active motor units fire simultaneously.

The size of the motor unit in a muscle may be arrived at by the **innervation ratio,** which is the ratio between the number of nerve cell axons in a motor nerve and the number of muscle cells in the muscle it supplies. If the motor nerve to a muscle has 100 fibers (axons) and the muscle has 5000 muscle cells, the innervation ratio is 100:5000, which is expressed as 1:50. The motor unit contains 50 muscle cells supplied by each nerve cell, on the average.

The size of the innervation ratio and therefore the size of the motor unit for a given muscle depends on the kind of response that muscle will be called on to perform. Muscles involved in gross movements that require only a few gradations of contraction have large innervation ratios and large motor units. For example, in extensors such as those of the thighs and back, innervation ratios may run as high as 1:150. When only a few different strengths of contraction are needed for gross movements controlled by the muscle, the motor unit can be large. On the other hand, flexor muscles that control precise movements are called on to contract in many small gradations. The innervation ratio and motor unit must therefore be small, permitting the muscle to increase its contrac-

tion a few cells at a time. The flexors controlling the fingers may have ratios of 1:10, and the muscles controlling eye movements may have ratios running down to 1:3. Mathematically, a ratio of 1:10 is smaller than a ratio of 1:3, but size, large or small, of the innervation ratio is judged by the physiologist in terms of the size of the motor unit, the denominator of the innervation ratio.

Muscle tone and the stretch reflex

A few of the motor units of any healthy muscle are always contracting, especially in extensor muscles. This resting contraction is called **muscle tone** and gives healthy muscles their rubbery, "hard" feel to the touch. Muscle tone is increased when the muscle is stretched by body position. As an example, lay your arm on the table, relax it with the elbow bent, and feel the biceps with the other hand. Now straighten your arm out on the table, relax it again, and again feel the biceps. The stretched, or lengthened, the muscle will feel firmer to the touch—its tone has increased.

Muscle tone is the partial resting contraction of a muscle in response to a reflex called the **stretch reflex.** Receptors in the muscle respond to stretching of the muscle; sensory neurons are excited and in turn fire some of the motoneurons going to motor units in the same muscle (Chapter 8). The more the muscle is stretched, the more stretch receptors will be stimulated and the more motor units will be excited. On the other hand, if the tendon attaching a muscle is cut, the muscle will shorten by one fourth to one third of its length and will become completely "limp"—none of the stretch receptors will be firing and therefore none of the motor units of the muscle are active.

Structure and function of the myoneural junction

The **myoneural junction** is the region of contact between branches of the motor

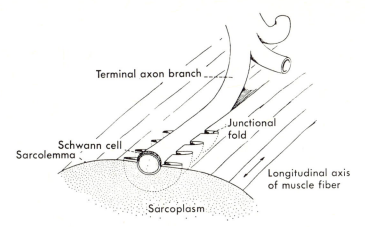

Fig. 4-13. Myoneural junction, drawn as it is seen under electron microscope. Axon branch loses its myelin sheath and runs in the longitudinal axis of the muscle fiber. Neurolemma (Schwann cell) forms a folded structure near the thickened part of the sarcolemma that forms the end plate. (After Birks, R., Huxley, H. E., and Katz, B.: J. Physiol. [London] **150**:134-144, 1960.)

nerve cell and each muscle cell in striated muscles. Recall that the axon breaks up into branches, whose number depends on the average size of the motor unit. Each branch reaches a muscle cell to establish a myoneural junction. Myoneural junctions are diagrammed in Fig. 4-13 as they are seen under the high magnification of the electron microscope. Note that the nerve branch forming the myoneural junction loses its myelin sheath covering before spreading out into a nerve ending that appears to be buried in the junctional folds of the membrane of the muscle cell at the **end plate,** or subsynaptic region. A 100 Å gap is evident between the nerve ending and the muscle end plate, and the end plate is extensively folded to increase the area exposed to the fluid of the gap. When the nerve impulse arrives and travels along the axon branch, it is unable to provide enough current to depolarize the muscle cell membrane because the membrane of the muscle cell has an area at least 1000 times larger than the nerve cell ending; therefore, a chemical event must intervene. As seen under an electron microscope, the nerve ending contains many vesicles (globules).

Chemical studies show that the vesicles probably contain acetylcholine (ACh), which acts as a chemical transmitter over the gap between nerve ending and muscle end plate. As in the case of synapses between nerve cells, arrival of the nerve impulse at the nerve ending is believed to release ACh from the vesicles into the gap between nerve ending and muscle cell end plate. Like nerve cells, the muscle cell has a polarized membrane—positive outside and negative inside—with a concentration of sodium (Na) outside the cell and potassium (K) inside the cell. The ACh *depolarizes* the end plate by making it more permeable to both of these ions; the action of ACh is the same at nerve cell synapses ("short-circuit" theory). This depolarization results in a change in potential across the end-plate region of the muscle cell membrane, called the **end-plate potential** (epp). The epp does not completely depolarize the membrane at the end plate because of the influx of ions from other regions of the membrane. Other regions, however, are depolarized enough by ion movement to initiate a **muscle action potential**—a polarization reversal that sweeps over the entire muscle cell and has the same electrical and chemical basis in excitation and recovery as described for the nerve cell. The muscle action potential activates the contraction mechanism of the cell. The sequence of events at the myoneural junction is as follows: nerve impulse → ACh transmitter release → end-plate potential → muscle action potential → muscle cell contraction. After it has acted to stimulate the end plate, ACh is destroyed by hydrolysis. The reaction is speeded by the enzyme acetylcholine esterase (AChE), which is present in the tissue fluids.

SUMMARY

This chapter has been devoted to the study of nerve and muscle tissue in order to ensure your later understanding of how the nervous system maintains homeostasis and regulates behavior.

The first section dealt with the neuron, or nerve cell, the basic unit of nervous system structure. Although neurons vary widely in appearance, they all feature a cell body, one or more dendrites, an axon, and a terminal arborization. Bundles of neuron fibers make up the nerves of the peripheral nervous system and tracts of the central nervous system. An axon may or may not have a myelin sheath, but all the axons of peripheral nerves have a neurolemma. Varied as they are, neurons can be classed as unipolar, bipolar, or multipolar, according to the number of processes attached to the cell body.

Neurons are too small to be observed except under a microscope. Even then, special hardening, staining, and slicing techniques must be used to prepare the tissue. Anatomists trace the tracts of the nervous system by observing the effect of damaging the axons of tracts at levels where their location is known—the tracts can be traced at other levels by changes in the affected cells. Extremely small parts of the neuron can be observed with the electron microscope, which is much more powerful than the light microscope.

The function of neurons is studied by observing their electrical characteristics. To understand the instruments involved, one must first understand electrical current as the flow of negative particles called electrons. Two points that differ in number of electrons differ in volts or millivolts until connected by a conductor that has some resistance (ohms) affecting the rate of current flow (amperes or milliamperes). Such observations require the use of the microelectrode, the vacuum-tube amplifier, and the cathode-ray oscilloscope. In contrast to other electrical currents, bioelectric currents in cells consists of the movement of positive and negative ions in electrolytes; positive cations are attracted to negative cathodes, negative anions to positive anodes. The neuron exhibits a resting potential, with the outside of the cell positive with respect to the inside. When stimulated, this state of affairs is reversed, and the change sweeps down the axon as the nerve impulse, or action potential. The nerve impulse obeys the all-or-none law, with the energy being supplied by bioelectrical currents of the nerve membrane.

Both the resting potential and the action potential are caused by the behavior of the nerve membrane with respect to positively and negatively charged ions, particularly the exclusion of sodium and the inclusion of potassium. The resulting differences in concentration (concentration gradient) of charged ions cause the resting potential. The action potential and nerve impulse result when the nerve membrane momentarily quits excluding sodium and including potassium—ion shifts power the nerve impulse.

The action potential shows a sequence of polarization changes, including the local excitatory state, spike potential, negative afterpotential, and positive afterpotential. The axon shows corresponding changes in excitability, including the latent addition period, absolute refractory period, relative refractory period, supernormal period, and subnormal period. These facts have important consequences because of the way the brain may detect intensity change in receptors as a function of changes in the frequency of nerve impulses. Nerve impulses are largely confined to axons. Receptors show a partial depolarization called a generator potential, and neuron cell bodies display a similar graded potential.

Nerve cells excite one another at synapses. The terminal arborization of the axon ends in synaptic knobs that contact the cell body and dendrites of second cell. These knobs contain synaptic vesicles that release either an excitatory or inhibitory transmitter when the nerve impulse reaches them. Excitatory transmitters such as ACh partly depolarize the cell body and dendrites of the second cell, causing an EPSP. The EPSP depolarizes the axon to cause a nerve impulse. Inhibitory transmitters hyperpolarize the second cell, and an IPSP results. The effect of excitatory and inhibitory synapses on the same cell is one of algebraic summation. The EPSP is caused by an increase in membrane permeability to sodium and potassium, whereas the IPSP results from an increase in permeability to potassium. The understanding of synaptic phenomena is important to the physiological psychology of sensation, perception, and learning.

Muscle cells are specialized for contraction. Muscle tissue and other types of tissue make up muscles, whose structure depends on the function they perform, primarily the *contraction rate* and the *automaticity* required for their function in the body. Visceral muscle includes smooth and cardiac muscle, which are slower in contraction and less dependent on excitation from the CNS than the somatic, or striated, muscle responsible for overt behavior. Smooth muscles often form tubes, such as arteries, with circular fibers innervated by one division of the autonomic nervous system (ANS) and with opposing longitudinal fibers innervated by the other division of the ANS. More automatic tubular muscles, such as the intestines, and other visceral muscles, such as the sphincters or piloerector fibers, may be excited by the sympathetic division of the ANS and inhibited by the parasympathetic division.

Cardiac muscle forms the blood-pumping chambers of the heart. It is intermediate in structure and function between smooth and striated muscle. It reacts fairly rapidly, as does striated muscle, but it is automatic in contraction and has intrinsic nerve tissue for timing its contractions, as does some visceral muscle.

Much of the way striated muscle functions depends on how it is innervated. Flexors and extensors perform opposite body movements and are therefore reciprocally innervated; when the agonist muscle for a movement is excited, its antagonist is inhibited. Striated muscle cells are innervated by groups, so that a motor nerve cell and the muscle cells innervated by its branches constitute the unit of contraction—the motor unit. One can compute the average number of muscle cells in the motor units of a muscle by using the ratio between the number of nerve cells going to a muscle and the number of muscle cells in the muscle; reduced to a numerator of one, this is the innervation ratio. Flexor muscles have smaller motor units and innervation ratios than do extensors because of the more precisely graded contractions they must perform.

The tone, or partial contraction of resting muscles, depends on how much the muscles are stretched, and is caused by the stretch reflex.

Each striated muscle cell is stimulated by a branch of a motor axon at the myoneural junction. A chemical event intervenes between the nerve impulse and excitation of the muscle cell membrane. The nerve ending releases acetylcholine (ACh), a transmitter that "shorts out" the end plate under the nerve ending, making it permeable to sodium and potassium and causing the end-plate potential (epp). The resulting ion shifts from all over the muscle cell membrane cause it to reverse polarization; the process is identical to that which occurs in the case of the nerve impulse. This depolarization activates the contraction mechanism of the myofibrils. The sequence of events is nerve impulse → transmitter → epp → muscle action potential → contraction.

READINGS

Axelrod, J.: Neurotransmitters, Sci. Am. **230:**59-71, June 1974.

Baker, P. F.: The nerve axon, Sci. Am. **214:**74-82, March 1966. (W. H. Freeman Reprint No. 1038.)

Eccles, J.: The synapse, Sci. Am. **212:**56-66, Jan. 1965. (W. H. Freeman Reprint No. 1001.)

Freeman, I. M.: Physics made simple, Garden City, N.Y., 1954, Doubleday & Co. Inc.

Galambos, R.: Nerves and muscles, Garden City, N.Y., 1962, Doubleday & Co. Inc.

Hayashi, T.: How cells move, Sci. Am. **205:**184-204, Sept. 1961. (W. H. Freeman Reprint No. 97.)

Hoyle, G.: How is muscle turned on and off? Sci. Am. **222:**84-93, April 1970.

Huxley, H. E.: The contraction of muscle, Sci. Am. **199:**67-82, Nov. 1958. (W. H. Freeman Reprint No. 19.)

Huxley, H. E.: The mechanism of muscular contraction, Sci. Am. **213:**18-27, Dec. 1965. (W. H. Freeman Reprint No. 1026.)

Kandel, E. R.: Nerve cells and behavior, Sci. Am. **223:**57-67, July 1970.

Katz, B.: The nerve impulse, Sci. Am. **187:**55-64, Nov. 1952. (W. H. Freeman Reprint No. 20.)

Katz, B.: Nerve, muscle, and synapse, New York, 1966, McGraw-Hill Book Co.

Keynes, R.: The nerve impulse and the squid, Sci. Am. **199:**88-90, Dec. 1958. (W. H. Freeman Reprint No. 58.)

Porter, R. E., and Franzini-Armstrong, C.: The sarcoplasmic reticulum, Sci. Am. **212:**72-80, March 1965. (W. H. Freeman Reprint No. 1007.)

Steen, E. B., and Montagu, A.: Anatomy and physiology, vol. 1, New York, 1959, Barnes & Noble, Inc.

chapter 5

Nervous system

OVERVIEW

In Chapter 4 the structure and function of the nerve cell, or neuron, was explained. Neurons, in turn, are cell units of the tissue that makes up the nervous system. The nervous system is specialized for conducting excitation from one part of the body to another so that the organism can make responses to stimuli. Such stimuli, inside or outside the body, excite receptors, or sense organs, which will be studied in Part III (Chapters 6 to 11). The organism responds by muscle contraction or gland secretion, no matter how complex the response. Muscle cells and muscle contraction were surveyed in Chapter 4. The responses of gland cells and glandular systems were explained in Chapter 3. The present chapter concentrates on the nervous system, whose structure and function enable the organism to make complex and patterned responses to a wide variety of stimuli.

The chapter begins with a simple classification of the major divisions of the nervous system—the central nervous system and the peripheral nervous system. Then the structure and function of the peripheral nervous system will be explained. Because of certain complexities of structure and function, particular attention will be given to the autonomic nervous system, which controls the smooth muscles and the glands.

The balance of the chapter will be devoted to the structure and function of the central nervous system. As a beginning model the anatomy and physiology of reflexes in the spinal cord will be outlined in simplified form. This reflex plan can be applied to the *function* of higher centers in the brain. Understanding the *structure* of the brain, however, requires a more extensive background because of the extreme complexity of the brain. The major parts of the brain are named and identified with illustrations, and the major functions of each part are briefly discussed. The cranial nerves are mentioned, and the anatomy and functions of the "highest" part of the brain, the cerebral cortex, are outlined. Some notes on the connective and circulatory tissue of the brain conclude the chapter.

CLASSIFICATION OF THE NERVOUS SYSTEM

The nervous system consists of the **brain, spinal cord,** and **nerves.** The nerves connect the brain and spinal cord to the **effectors** (muscles and glands) and **receptors (sense organs).** The brain and spinal cord constitute the **central nervous system,** studied in detail in a later section.

The nerves, made up of bundles of individually conducting parts of nerve cells, or fibers, make up the **peripheral nervous system.** The **sensory nerves** carry excitation from receptors to the central nervous system. The **motor nerves** carry excitation from the central nervous system to the glands and muscles. Sensory and motor nerves branch repeatedly as they reach receptors and effectors over the entire body, and their final branches may contain only sensory or only motor fibers and can be called sensory nerves or motor nerves, respectively. Near their origin in the brain or spinal cord, however, most nerves are *mixed* and contain both sensory and motor fibers.

PSNS AND ANS

A further distinction can be made among the independently conducting fibers of the peripheral nervous system. Those sensory fibers coming from the receptors, and those motor fibers that reach the somatic, or striated, muscles, which move the body about, form the **peripheral somatic nervous system (PSNS).** The PSNS is the part of the peripheral nervous system that is concerned with overt reactions to both internal and external stimuli. As treated here, the motor fibers to the smooth muscles and glands form the **autonomic nervous system (ANS),** a different part of the peripheral nervous system. So classified, the ANS is a *motor system only* and will be treated separately because of certain unique features of structure and function. The fibers of the PSNS and of the ANS may be mixed in nerve trunks near their origin at the brain and spinal cord. Certain features of the origin of the ANS are unique, however, as will be explained later.

Peripheral somatic nervous system. The motor nerves going to the striated muscles and the sensory nerves coming from the receptors form the PSNS. The PSNS originates in the **spinal nerves** that leave the spinal cord and the **cranial nerves** that leave the brain. Branches of the spinal and cranial nerves spread over the entire body to reach the receptors and somatic muscles. There are twelve pairs of cranial nerves (their functions will be discussed later). Both cranial and spinal nerves occur in pairs because the nervous system is **bilaterally symmetrical.** Just as you have pairs of identical arms, legs, ribs, eyes, ears, and so on, your brain and spinal cord are made up of identical halves joined at the "center." The spinal cord lies within the **vertebral column,** or backbone, of jointed **vertebrae** (Fig. 5-1). There are thirty-one pairs of spinal nerves connecting the spinal cord with receptors and effectors. The eight pairs of nerves that emerge from within the vertebral column between the neck (cervi-

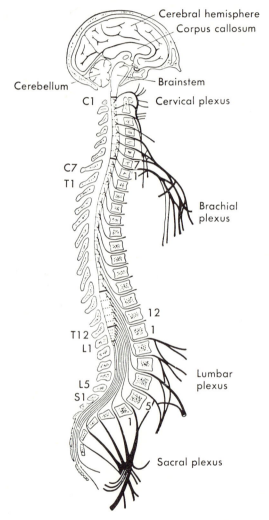

Fig. 5-1. Drawing of brain and spinal cord in situ. The brain is shown in the median plane (a midline section), the spinal cord is in external view, and the vertebrae are cut away to show the enclosed cord. Note that the cord is shorter than the vertebral column; the spinal nerves, especially those from the lower cord, must descend some distance before emerging between the vertebrae for which they are named. (From Gardner, E. O.: Fundamentals of neurology, ed. 5, Philadelphia, 1968, W. B. Saunders Co.)

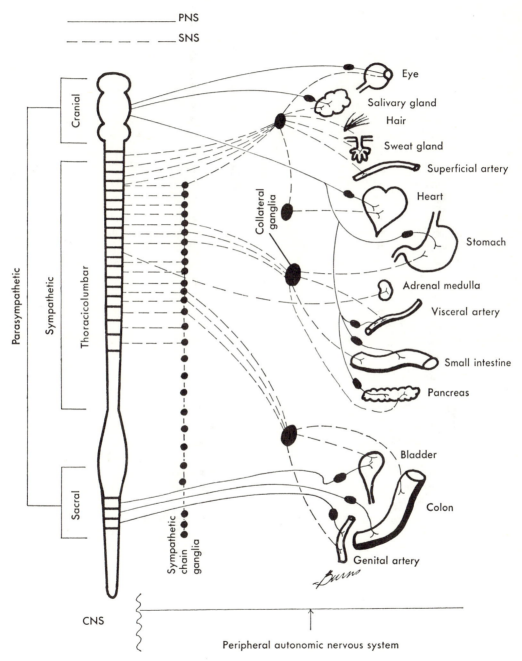

Fig. 5-2. Diagram of autonomic nervous system, showing parasympathetic (PNS) and sympathetic (SNS) divisions.

cal) vertebrae are called the **cervical** nerves (Fig. 5-1). The twelve pairs that emerge between vertebrae to which ribs are attached are called **thoracic** nerves. The five **lumbar** nerves lie between vertebrae of the lower back; the five **sacral** nerves lie between vertebrae of the hip cage, or pelvis; and a **coccygeal** pair emerges from the rudiment of a tail. The **segments** of the spinal cord to which these nerves are attached are named for the same vertebrae. The thoracic and lumbar segments of the cord contribute fibers to the autonomic nervous system (ANS), as will be explained below. The sacral segment and some of the cranial nerves also contain fibers of the ANS.

Autonomic nervous system. The ANS has been defined as a *visceral motor system,* consisting of those motor nerve fibers of the peripheral nervous system that supply the smooth muscles and glands of the viscera (Chapter 4). The ANS motor fibers differ from the motor fibers to the striated muscles in both structural and functional respects:

1. DUAL INNERVATION. There is only one system of motor fibers to the striated muscles, but each smooth muscle or gland receives two sets of fibers from the ANS (there are exceptions). One set of fibers is from the **sympathetic division** of the ANS, also called the **sympathetic nervous system (SNS).** The SNS originates in fibers leaving the spinal cord in the thoracic and lumbar regions. The other division of the ANS is the **parasympathetic division,** also called the **parasympathetic nervous system (PNS).** The PNS originates in fibers from the cranial nerves and from the sacral segment of the spinal cord. As can be seen in Fig. 5-2, each smooth muscle or gland receives both SNS and PNS fibers in a system of dual innervation.

2. PERIPHERAL ANS INHIBITION. As explained in Chapter 4, the PNS and SNS have opposite effects on the smooth muscles and glands they innervate. If the SNS excites the visceral effector or speeds up its functioning, the PNS inhibits it or slows it

down, and vice versa. For example, the SNS increases the heart rate and inhibits the digestive glands, whereas the PNS slows the heart rate and excites the digestive glands. These opposed influences act peripherally, where the nerve fibers reach the effector. By contrast, motor fibers to the striated muscles are excited or inhibited centrally, inside the brain and spinal cord. Somatic nerve fibers fire when excited and do not fire when inhibited. When they fire, a muscle contracts. Thus excitation of a somatic nerve cannot inhibit an effector.

3. TWO FIBERS IN THE ANS MOTOR PATHWAY (Fig. 5-2). Somatic motor axons have their cell bodies in the brain or spinal cord, and their fibers take an uninterrupted course through cranial and spinal nerves to the somatic muscles. In both divisions of the ANS there are two cells in the motor pathway. The **preganglionic** cells have their cell bodies in the spinal cord and brain, whereas their fibers terminate in **ganglia** (plural of ganglion), which lie outside the CNS (Fig. 5-2). Here they synapse with **postganglionic** fibers, which innervate the smooth muscles and glands. (A ganglion is a collection of nerve cell bodies lying outside the CNS). The ganglia of the sympathetic division lie along the outside of the vertebrae in an interconnected chain **(sympathetic chain ganglia)** or else among the viscera **(collateral ganglia)** in a nerve network, or **plexus.** The **parasympathetic ganglia** are found near the organs that are innervated by parasympathetic fibers.

4. AUTOMATICITY OF EFFECTORS. As noted in Chapter 4, the heart and some of the smooth muscles show automatic contractions, with their *rate* controlled by the ANS. Striated muscles do not normally contract unless they are excited by their motor nerves.

ANATOMY AND PHYSIOLOGY OF THE ANS

Details of the origin of the SNS and PNS within the brain and spinal cord will be treated in a later discussion of the reflex model of nervous system function. This section describes the anatomy and physiology of those parts of the ANS that lie outside the brain and spinal cord.

Anatomy of the sympathetic division

The cell bodies of the preganglionic fibers of the SNS lie inside the spinal cord. Their axons are myelinated and leave the spinal cord through the spinal nerves, which will be described later. The preganglionic axons synapse with unmyelinated postganglionic cells in the sympathetic ganglia. Some of these ganglia lie in an interconnected chain that lies along the length of the vertebral column and extends up into the neck and head (sympathetic chain ganglia, Fig. 5-2). Other ganglia (collateral ganglia) are found in the body cavity, as previously described. The preganglionic fibers are relatively short, reaching from the cord to nearby ganglia; the postganglionic fibers are long, reaching from ganglia to effectors. The preganglionic fibers are diffusely interconnected with many postganglionic cells, and there are more postganglionic than preganglionic fibers. This arrangement means that the SNS is anatomically connected to respond in a widespread, or diffuse, fashion—if a few of the preganglionic fibers are excited, many postganglionic fibers and effectors will respond.

Anatomy of the parasympathetic division

The PNS contains myelinated preganglionic fibers, unmyelinated postganglionic fibers, and ganglia where the two synapse, but here the resemblance to the SNS ceases. The PNS preganglionic fibers emerge from the brain in the cranial nerves and from the sacral cord in the spinal nerves. Because the PNS ganglia lie on or near the organs innervated by the PNS, the preganglionic fibers must be long, reaching from brain or cord to ganglia near the organ innervated. The postganglionic fibers are short, reaching from ganglia to nearby smooth muscles or glands. There is nearly a one-to-one relation between preganglionic and postganglionic

neurons, with no interconnection between ganglia. This means that the PNS is organized to react in a discrete fashion, and one effector can be stimulated by PNS fibers without other effectors' being stimulated.

Physiology of the ANS

The SNS and PNS differ in function by having opposed effects on the visceral organs, as previously explained—speeding or slowing the heart or digestion, causing opposed contractions in the visceral smooth muscles, and inhibiting or exciting glands. The SNS and PNS also *interact* in the complex responses involved in digestion, respiration, and other internal functions. As explained above, the SNS is organized in a diffuse manner and tends to be aroused as a whole system. The SNS sets off the widespread visceral responses characteristic of arousal and emotion—increased heart rate and rate of breathing, and widespread changes in the blood vessels to prepare for exertion. The PNS is discretely organized to influence only a few visceral structures at a time. The PNS provides for the sequence of visceral reactions involved in digestion, food metabolism, and other metabolic responses. Widespread SNS excitation does, however, stimulate more widespread PNS reactions, so that there is a continually changing balance in the influence of the two systems on the viscera.

Secretions of the ANS (Fig. 5-3)

In both the SNS and PNS there are synapses between preganglionic neurons and postganglionic neurons in peripheral ganglia. These are the only synapses between neurons that lie outside the brain and spinal cord in the peripheral nervous system. Like many synapses in the central nervous system, the preganglionic neurons stimulate the postganglionic neurons by the release of **acetylcholine (ACh)** from synaptic vesicles (Chapter 4). After exciting the postganglionic neurons, ACh is rapidly broken down under the influence of the enzyme **acetylcholine esterase (AChE),** which is

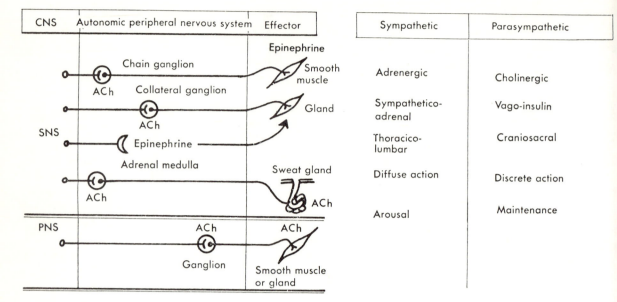

Fig. 5-3. Contrasts between sympathetic nervous system (SNS) and parasympathetic nervous system (PNS). *Left,* Aanatomical differences. *Right,* Terminology applied to each system.

always present in the tissue fluid surrounding the cells. However, at the junction between the postganglionic neurons and their effectors, the transmitter secretions of the SNS and PNS differ; thus they have opposite effects on the viscera. The PNS releases ACh to stimulate the effector. In the case of the heart the influence is inhibitory, but ACh selectively stimulates certain other smooth muscles, such as those that constrict arteries going to somatic muscle, and dilates arteries going to the digestive system. ACh also stimulates the digestive glands. Since the postganglionic fibers of the PNS excite visceral effectors by the release of acetylcholine, postganglionic PNS fibers are called **cholinergic** fibers.

By contrast the SNS acts on the effector by the release of **epinephrine** or **norepinephrine,** depending on the postganglionic neurons and the organs they innervate. Epinephrine excites the heart to increase the heart rate, excites constricting fibers in the arteries to the digestive system, and excites dilating fibers in the arteries to the

muscles to prepare the body for exertion. Norepinephrine, at other endings, inhibits the digestive glands. Since no substance such as AChE is present in the blood to speed the removal of either, *diffuse* reactions result from the spread of these transmitters to nearby effectors. Epinephrine is chemically the same as adrenaline (see below), and thus the postganglionic fibers of the SNS are often called **andrenergic** (Fig. 5-3). The only exceptions are the smooth muscles that raise the body hairs (piloerector fibers), and the sweat glands. These structures are innervated *only* by the SNS—there is no PNS innervation. The postganglionic SNS fibers release ACh to excite the piloerector fibers and sweat glands.

Glands innervated by the ANS

In addition to the digestive glands, the PNS sends fibers to the islets of Langerhans (beta cells) of the **pancreas** (Figs. 5-2 and 5-3) by way of the **vagus nerve.** The PNS stimulates the pancreas to release **insulin** into the bloodstream. Insulin is necessary for blood glucose utilization by all the cells of the body. Insulin appears to aid PNS reactions in a poorly understood fashion. Hence the PNS is sometimes called a **vago-insulin** system. The SNS, on the other hand, stimulates another gland, the **adrenal medulla,** which secretes the substances norepinephrine and epinephrine. The SNS is often called, therefore, a **sympathetico-adrenal** system. (It is interesting to note that no postganglionic fibers are involved. Since the adrenal medulla secretes epinephrine and norepinephrine, many believe it to have developed from postganglionic neurons.) The hormones secreted by the adrenal medulla circulate in the bloodstream and have widespread sympathetic effects on many visceral effectors, which, along with the diffuse anatomic arrangement of the SNS and its lack of an enzyme to destroy the hormones, increase the diffuse effects of the SNS on the viscera.

The hypothalamus

The **hypothalamus** is a part of the brain that will be discussed in more detail later. However, it is meaningful to note that the hypothalamus controls the reactions of the ANS. Most of the nerve cells involved in control of the PNS lie in the anterior and medial (central) hypothalamus; those governing the SNS are found in the posterior and lateral (to the side) hypothalamus. Both sets of centers are sensitive to the internal conditions of the brain's tissue fluid—the internal environment—and respond, for instance, to changes in blood glucose level and salinity or fluid level. The ANS is involved in maintaining homeostasis, or constant internal conditions, in the body. Changes in internal conditions set off compensating SNS or PNS reactions to restore stability, reactions governed by the hypothalamus.

FUNCTIONS OF THE ANS

To the extent that the SNS and PNS could be said to have a purpose, the function of the SNS would be to organize widespread mobilization of the resources of an animal for vigorous physical activity in an "emergency," whereas the PNS functions to conserve the resources of the animal by means of a series of discrete reflex reactions involved in digestion, food storage, and other metabolic reactions. The interactions of the SNS and PNS are involved in complex responses of motivation and emotion.

Emergency theory

The emergency theory of Cannon was proposed as an explanation for the reactions of the SNS. He stated that the SNS mobilized the resources of the animal for "fight or flight" in an emergency. Although the SNS patterns found in rage are somewhat different from those found in fear (Chapter 16), the theory predicts most SNS effects on visceral structures. The Cannon theory is therefore a useful mnemonic device for the student. Arteries contract and relax in different locations, diverting blood from the digestive system to the somatic muscles to "fuel" their exertions. Heart rate and blood pressure rise for the same reason. Breathing rate increases to provide more oxygen and the bronchial tubes to the lungs dilate. Sweating increases to cool the body, sphincters contract to "shut off" digestion, digestive contractions of stomach and intestine cease, and epinephrine and norepinephrine are released into the bloodstream by the adrenal glands to make these and other SNS reactions more widespread. To predict the SNS effect on a visceral structure, merely ask what that effect "should" be to prepare the body for exertion.

PNS effects

PNS effects can be predicted from the emergency theory; PNS effects would be the opposite of the emergency SNS effects. Thus the PNS should slow the heart rate and respiration, divert blood from the somatic muscles to the digestive system, and increase digestive functions. PNS effects can also be predicted from the reactions of the body during sleep, when automatic restorative functions such as digestion go on at an increased rate. The heart rate is slow, breathing is deep and regular, and some sweating is inhibited.

The polygraph

ANS functioning in the intact human body is most frequently measured with the **polygraph,** an instrument that measures bodily changes that result from PNS and SNS reactions and records them on moving paper tape (*poly,* 'many'; *graph,* 'writing'). Three measurements are most frequently used: (1) depth and rate of breathing **(pneumograph),** (2) heart rate and blood pressure **(sphygmomanometer),** and (3) palmar sweating (**galvanic skin response,** or **GSR**). Heart rate, blood pressure, and rate of breathing are all increased by SNS activity and decreased by PNS activity. The sweat glands are innervated only by the SNS; thus sweating of the palms provides a good measure of SNS activity undisturbed by PNS reactions. Actually, SNS reactions and PNS counterreactions and responses are going on all the time. However, a sudden increase in the SNS activity, as indicated by the polygraph, suggests arousal, mobilization of the body's resources, and perhaps an "emotional state." The indicators would be a sudden increase in the rate of breathing or else catching of the breath, an increase in heart rate and blood pressure, and the onset of palmar sweating as seen in the GSR. For this reason the polygraph is often used as a misnamed "lie detector," that is, as an instrument to detect an emotional response to a question, which would suggest that the individual is lying. Needless to say, this method of lie detection is often questionable because of individual differences in SNS reactions, the conditions under which the questioning may be done, and other factors. The use of the polygraph as a lie detector is therefore best left in the hands of experts, and the data they gather should be interpreted cautiously.

Autonomic balance

PNS functioning, typically, is a series of discrete and timed responses regulating digestion or other visceral processes that occur as a sequence of reactions. More widespread PNS reactions do occur, however, in response to diffuse SNS arousal. Diffuse SNS reactions occur in some degree to almost every stimulus. A balance between SNS and PNS arousal is therefore always present, a balance that depends on individual differences in ANS sensitivity and on the current stimulus situation. Typically there is a predominance of one system over the other (PNS or SNS dominance) in **autonomic balance ($\overline{A}$),** and **SNS reactivity** and **PNS compensation** are involved. There are individuals who show PNS dominance most of the time—they have excessive salivation, dry palms, a slow heart rate, and high intestinal motility (the stomach "growls"). Other individuals show SNS dominance most of the time—they have dry mouths, moist palms, and a fast resting heart rate. Most persons show slight dominance one way or the other and vary from day to day. Apart from autonomic balance, individuals differ in SNS reactivity—the extent to which mobilizing SNS reactions occur in response to a stimulus of a given magnitude or unexpectedness. Finally, stressful stimuli that produce extensive SNS arousal produce later PNS compensation—a reaction of the PNS. If individual PNS reactions achieve brief or lasting dominance over SNS influences, **parasympathetic overcompensation** has occurred. The PNS overcompensation may be momentary, as when a soldier relaxes his sphincters in combat and soils his trousers. It may be more lasting, as when oversecretion of digestive hydrochloric acid in the stomach produces stomach ulcers.

REFLEX PLAN OF THE CENTRAL NERVOUS SYSTEM

Despite the complexity of the responses mediated by the ANS and by the peripheral somatic nervous system, the organization of behavior must be sought in the central nervous system (CNS). The way in which neurons interconnect at synapses in the brain and spinal cord determines organized motor output in response to sensory input. Stimuli in the environment activate receptors, which leads to sensory nerve excitation and eventual motor nerve and muscle or gland response. Which stimulus leads to what response is governed by the "connections" between sensory neurons and motoneurons that are made in the CNS.

Reflex model

One of the simplest stimulus-response, or S-R, relationships that can be observed in behavior is the reflex. Even the most oversimplified diagram of reflex anatomy involves parts of both the CNS and the peripheral nervous system. A reflex mediated by the spinal cord is shown in Fig. 5-4. Five sets of component parts are involved: (1) **receptors,** (2) **sensory neurons,** (3) **association neurons,** (4) **motoneurons,** and (5) **effectors.** Stimulation of receptors leads to sensory, or **afferent,** neuron impulses,

which excite **association neurons** in the CNS. Association neurons, in turn, fire motor, or **efferent,** neurons, which excite **effectors,** which are muscles or glands. The synaptic connections between neurons are relatively fixed and invariable, so that the response to the stimulus is always the same. Examples of reflexes include jerking the hand off a painfully hot surface, blinking the eyes in response to a puff of air striking the face, and sneezing when the nasal passages are irritated. Once a given set of receptors is stimulated, the response is determined by the "fixed" synaptic connections in the pathway between stimulus and response. The reflex is then "stimulus-bound" —it is determined by the receptors stimulated. For example, stimulating pain receptors in the foot will cause an animal to reflexly withdraw his leg. Stimulating pressure receptors in the same foot will cause the animal to extend the same leg to support his weight. The pressure and pain receptors lead to different reflex pathways, so that different responses result.

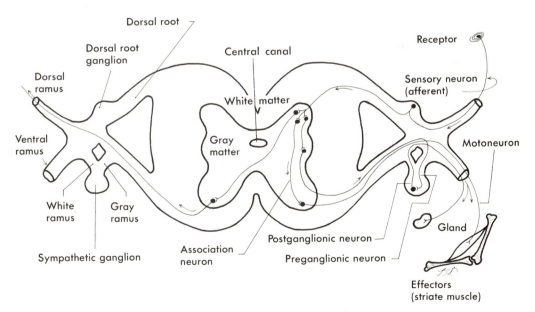

Fig. 5-4. Diagram of cross section of spinal cord, showing parts of the nervous system involved in a spinal reflex. Major parts of spinal cord and spinal nerves are labeled on the *left-hand side.* Elements involved in reflexes are labeled on the *right-hand side.*

Anatomy of the reflex

Reflexes may include pathways in the cranial nerves and synapses in the brain, or they may involve the spinal nerves and the spinal cord. **Spinal reflex** anatomy will be used as an example here because of its relative simplicity. The spinal nerves are attached to the spinal cord by two roots—the **dorsal** (toward the back) **roots** and the **ventral** (toward the front) **roots.** Now refer to Fig. 5-4, a diagram of a cross section of the spinal cord at a level that shows these features. Also shown are the **dorsal** and **ventral rami** (sing., ramus), into which the spinal nerves divide as they emerge from between the vertebrae. The cord itself is divided into the butterfly, or H-shaped, central **gray matter** and surrounding **white matter.** The white matter takes its color name from the whitish appearance of the myelin sheath coverings of its neurons. The neurons of the white matter form the **tracts** of the spinal cord, running up and down the cord to carry excitation from one level to another. The gray matter takes its color name from the grayish appearance of the unmyelinated neurons and many synaptic nerve endings found in this part of the cord. Tracts from the white matter, and sensory neurons and motoneurons from the spinal nerves, make their synaptic connections in the gray matter.

The spinal cord is connected to the receptors and effectors by way of the dorsal and ventral spinal roots and the dorsal and ventral spinal rami. The rami contain both sensory neurons and motoneurons and are merely the first of many branches of the spinal nerves that eventually reach the receptors and effectors. The dorsal roots, however, contain only incoming sensory neurons, and the ventral roots contain only outgoing motoneurons. The sensory neurons are unipolar, with one process connecting the cell body with axon and dendrite (Chapter 4). The cell bodies of the sensory neurons are found in a ganglion (a collection of cell bodies outside the CNS) on each

dorsal root, the **dorsal root ganglion.** There are thirty-one pairs of dorsal roots, ventral roots, and dorsal and ventral rami (eight cervical, twelve thoracic, five lumbar, five sacral, and one coccygeal, as previously classified).

The motoneurons to the smooth muscles and glands are also involved in reflexes. As previously explained, the motor pathway to smooth muscles and glands from the spinal cord forms the sympathetic division of the autonomic nervous system (the SNS). The SNS sends neurons, called preganglionic neurons, to the sympathetic ganglia. The preganglionic neurons have myelin sheaths and enter the sympathetic ganglia by the **white ramus** (Fig. 5-4); their myelin sheaths give the ramus its white appearance. As previously explained, the preganglionic neurons may synapse with postganglionic neurons in the sympathetic ganglia, or they may continue through the sympathetic ganglia to reach collateral ganglia in the body cavity. In either case the preganglionic neurons synapse with postganglionic neurons that have no myelin sheaths. If the synapses occur in the chain ganglia, the postganglionic neurons may rejoin the spinal nerves by way of the **gray ramus,** so-called because of the color lent to the ramus by the unmyelinated fibers. After rejoining the spinal nerves, these postganglionic fibers are distributed to smooth muscles and glands by way of the dorsal and ventral rami of the spinal nerves. If the postganglionic neurons originate in the collateral ganglia, each will reach smooth muscles and glands by way of a nerve plexus, as previously described.

Finally, the major anatomical subdivisions within the spinal cord should be described. The H-shaped gray matter includes **dorsal** and **ventral horns** (also called **dorsal** and **ventral columns**), the extensions of the gray matter on each side of the midline that reach toward the dorsal and ventral portions of the cord. The white matter is divided into three areas on either side of the cord, called funiculi (sing., funiculus). On both sides of the cord the area between the midline and the dorsal roots is called the **dorsal funiculus,** the area between the midline and the ventral roots is called the **ventral funiculus,** and the area between the dorsal and ventral roots is called the **lateral (to the side) funiculus.**

Physiology of the reflex

Refer to the right-hand side of Fig. 5-4. A **receptor** may be a separate cell or it may be a specialized ending on a nerve cell. In either case stimulation of the receptor will give rise to a **generator potential** (Chapter 4), a potential that will initiate a spike potential in the sensory, or afferent, nerve fiber. The sensory neuron may reach the spinal nerves by way of either the dorsal or the ventral ramus. In either case it will enter the cord by way of the dorsal root and synapse with association neurons in the dorsal column of the gray matter. The association neurons carry the excitation to motoneurons whose cell bodies are in the ventral horns of the gray matter. The motoneurons carry the excitation to striated muscle effectors via the ventral root and either the dorsal or the ventral rami. If a smooth muscle or gland is involved in the response, two motoneurons will carry the excitation. The preganglionic neurons will receive excitation from association neurons and transfer that excitation to postganglionic neurons through synapses located in either the sympathetic chain ganglia or collateral ganglia. The preganglionic neurons, in either case, pass out the ventral root and white ramus. Postganglionic neurons originating in the chain ganglia may rejoin the spinal nerves through the gray rami to reach effectors (smooth muscles or glands) by way of either the dorsal or ventral rami. Postganglionic neurons originating in collateral ganglia reach visceral effectors by rejoining other nerve branches in a plexus in the body cavity.

Reflex complexity

In a withdrawal reflex to pain for example, many receptors, sensory neurons, association neurons, motoneurons, and effectors are involved. Connections to the association neurons of the reflex from higher centers in the brain modify the response to conform to body position. Excitation from the sensory input to the reflex reaches higher centers to initiate further behavior. A pain, or flexion, reflex of one limb results in a **crossed-extension reflex** of the opposite limb to support the animal's weight. Association neurons reach the opposite ventral horn by way of the **gray commissure** (Fig. 5-4) to stimulate the motoneurons for extensor muscles of the opposite limb. Many other reflexes are associated with the pain reflex. Some involve the ANS, as there are changes of breathing and circulation in response to pain.

Reflex plan of higher centers

Sensory input from the receptors involved in reflexes, and from many other receptors as well, reaches higher centers in the brain by way of ascending tracts in the white matter of the spinal cord. Depending on the complexity of the brain centers involved, many thousands of association neurons may be excited. Finally, excitation will return to the spinal cord through descending tracts in the white matter. The fibers of the descending spinal cord tracts will reach the motoneurons to excite response. Considered from this oversimplified point of view, the most complex stimulus-response relations are modeled after the reflex with three major differences: (1) many more association neurons are involved at all levels of the brain and spinal cord; (2) the response is not fixed, but varies according to which association neurons intervene between stimulus and response on a given occasion; that is, the S-R pathways vary and are not fixed as in the case of a reflex; and (3) **correlation** of input and **coordination** of output are greater than in the reflex. Excitation must be focused (correlation) from many widespread receptors and tracts on a single brain **center** (collection of synapses) vital to the response. In addition, from such a single brain center, tracts lead to many motoneurons at all levels of the brain and cord. These events happen many times because many centers are involved. The widespread pattern of motoneuron excitation is such that many muscles are excited in a smooth reaction made possible by coordination of output on the motor side. The reflex model of complex S-R relationships is not adequate to describe complex behavior, but it is a useful beginning and adequate for the chapters on sensation. A more complete explanation is deferred until Chapter 13, when it is required for understanding of the last section of the text.

PARTS OF BRAIN
General plan of brain structure

The brain develops from a hollow tubular structure, as does the spinal cord. The remnants of the tubular format may be seen in the central canal of the spinal cord (Fig. 5-4). The brain is much more extensively developed than the spinal cord, however, and the hollow (tubular) parts are distorted into the **ventricles** and the **cerebral aqueduct** (Figs. 5-5 and 5-6). The parts of the brain that remain as a linear and sequential series of structures are included in the **brainstem** (like the stem of a tree). The brainstem is organized like the spinal cord only in having a central "core" of gray matter (synapses, centers, etc.) surrounded by the white matter of tracts—nerve fibers ascending and descending the brainstem to carry excitation to various levels of the brain and spinal

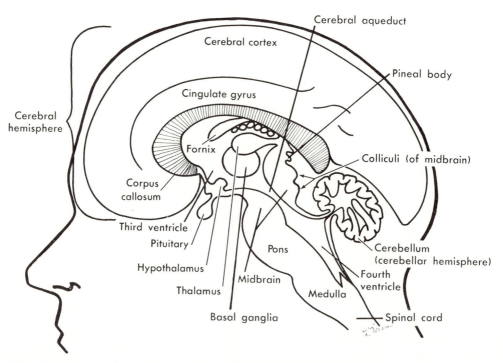

Fig. 5-5. Diagram of human brain, seen from medial plane (split down the middle). Some major features described in text are labeled in the figure.

cord. Two pairs of outgrowths from the brainstem overlie it as two **cerebral hemispheres** and two **cerebellar hemispheres.** The hemispheres are organized in an opposite fashion to the brainstem so far as gray matter and white matter are concerned. The hemispheres have surface gray matter (called **cortex**). The interior consists of the white matter of fibers reaching the surface gray matter from the brainstem that is beneath the hemispheres.

Important brain structures (see Fig. 5-5)

It is helpful to locate the major parts of the brain as "landmarks" before discussing the functions of these and related brain structures. The simplest segment of the brainstem is the **medulla,** which is continuous with the spinal cord. Next in line is the **pons.** Overlying both the medulla and pons

are the cerebellar hemispheres (see above). Between the cerebellar hemispheres above and pons and medulla below is the **fourth ventricle,** one of the "hollow" parts of the brain discussed previously. The fourth ventricle is continuous with the cerebral **aqueduct,** the hollow part of the **midbrain.** The cerebral aqueduct opens into the **third ventricle,** a tall and narrow opening, surrounded by several other brainstem structures. The floor and part of the walls of the third ventricle form the **hypothalamus.** On both sides of the ventricles lie the egg-shaped thalami (sing., **thalamus**). Lying farther to either side of the midline and embedded in the walls of the cerebral hemispheres, the **basal ganglia (corpus striatum)** are found. The **corpus callosum** is a band of white matter that interconnects corresponding parts of the surface cortex of the cerebral hemispheres. The

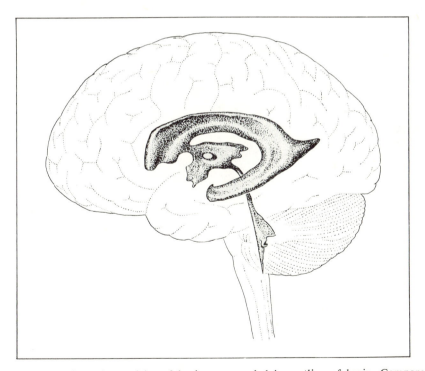

Fig. 5-6. Lateral view of ventricles of brain, surrounded by outline of brain. Compare with Fig. 5-5 to identify them. (From Vander, A. J., Sherman, J. H., and Luciano, D. S.: Human physiology: The mechanism of body function, New York, 1970, McGraw-Hill Book Co.)

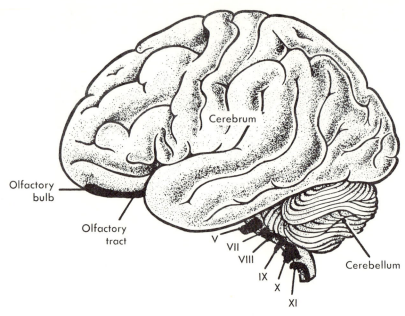

Fig. 5-7. Lateral view of brain.

cerebral hemispheres and cerebellar hemispheres have developed to such an extent that they "surround" most of the brainstem at the top and sides (Fig. 5-7). This is why Fig. 5-5 is a midline or "split-down-the-middle" view, so that the parts of the brainstem may be seen. The ventricles of the cerebral hemispheres are the **lateral ventricles.**

FUNCTIONS OF THE MAJOR PARTS OF THE BRAIN
Cerebral cortex

Fig. 5-5 should be compared with Figs. 5-6 to 5-9. The **cerebral cortex** is the highest set of integrating centers of the human brain. Through millions of synaptic connections in the gray matter of the cerebral cortex, any stimulus input can result in any response output. Excitation originating in the receptors and carried to the cerebral cortex through cranial and spinal nerves and tracts is processed by lower centers, but may eventually reach the cortex. The cerebral cortex can "connect" any part of the brain with any other part, at least indirectly.

Corpus striatum

The **corpus striatum,** located in the walls of the cerebral hemispheres, is an earlier development of a set of master correlation and coordination centers in lower animals without a cerebral cortex or without a well-developed cortex. In these animals, particularly birds, the neural connections between stimulus and response for many patterns of instinctive behavior are found in the corpus striatum (basal ganglia and tracts). In man the corpus striatum regulates the sequence and timing of movements, processes certain facial expressions in emotion, and controls "sequential acts" such as swinging the arms for balance when one walks.

Thalamus

The **thalamus** likewise serves as an integrating center. It also serves as a correlating relay center for incoming sensory input to the cerebral cortex. In addition,

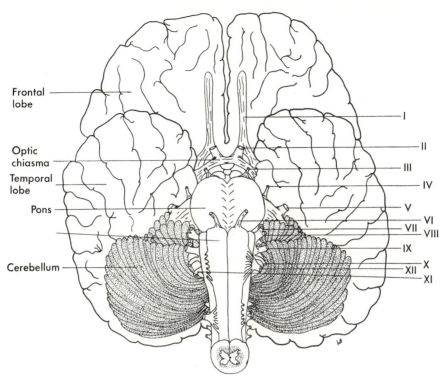

Fig. 5-8. Ventral view of human brain as seen from below, showing origins of cranial nerves and other features.

many impulses going from one area of the cerebral cortex to another travel by way of synapses in the thalamus.

Hypothalamus

The **hypothalamus** contains many centers that are sensitive to conditions in the fluid **internal environment** of the blood and **cerebrospinal fluid,** the extracellular tissue fluid of the brain and spinal cord. The neurons of these centers act as receptors and are stimulated by changes in fluid salt content and osmotic pressure, chemical composition, and other conditions. Such changes represent **need-conditions** of the tissue or disturbances in internal consistency and homeostasis (Chapter 2). The centers arouse and sustain internal and external responses until the need-condition is corrected and are therefore the basis of **drives.** The response adjustments that result may be as simple as a change in heart rate or may include complex learned behavior such as putting on a coat when one is cold.

Midbrain

The **midbrain** surrounds the cerebral aqueduct. Above the aqueduct are found the pea-shaped **colliculi** (sing., colliculus) that are visual and auditory reflex centers. The "floor" of the midbrain contains tracts of conducting fibers and a few synaptic centers.

Pons

The cerebellum is connected to the brainstem by the **pons,** a great mass of fibers that surround the brainstem and "grasp" it on the lateral and ventral aspects.

Cerebellum

The **cerebellum** regulates balance and coordination of movement. It receives input from the muscles (tension receptors) and

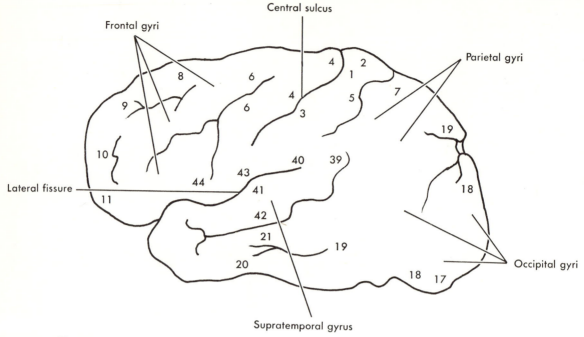

Fig. 5-9. Cerebral cortex, showing some of the major sulci and gyri and some of the principal numbered Brodmann areas.

inner ear (balance and motion receptors). Output from the cerebellum regulates muscle tone and adjustments in posture.

Medulla

The **medulla** contains many centers for the so-called "vital reflexes" of the body, which regulate, for instance, heart rate, breathing, and vomiting.

CRANIAL NERVES

Just as the spinal cord is connected to the receptors and effectors of the body by the spinal nerves, the brain is connected to the receptors and effectors of the head by the twelve **cranial nerves,** which emerge from the brainstem in pairs (Figs. 5-7 and 5-8). Unlike the spinal nerves, however, the cranial nerves do not always have separate sensory and motor roots; some pairs contain only sensory fibers, some contain only motor fibers, and some are mixed. The first two (olfactory and optic) are not a true part of the peripheral nervous system, but are extensions of the brain itself, carrying sensory pathways, or tracts. The cranial nerves are numbered in the order in which they emerge from the brainstem from anterior to posterior (Table 5-1 and Fig. 5-8). Students who wish to learn the numbers and names of the cranial nerves receive assistance from a classic bit of doggerel verse of twelve words—each word starts with the same letter as the corresponding cranial nerve from the first to the twelfth: *On old Olympus' towering top, a French-speaking German viewed some hops.*

FUNCTIONAL ANATOMY OF THE CEREBRAL CORTEX

The **cerebral cortex** undergoes greater development in man than in any lower animal. The cerebral hemispheres and covering cortex have expanded in size and area until the brainstem is almost completely covered except for the base of the

Table 5-1. Summary of the cranial nerves*

No.	Name	Origin	Primary functions
I	Olfactory	Olfactory bulb	Afferent for smell
II	Optic	Diencephalon	Afferent for vision
III	Oculomotor	Midbrain	Afferent and efferent to all eye muscles except two
IV	Trochlear	Midbrain	Afferent and efferent to one eye muscle
V	Trigeminal	Pons	Afferent from skin and mucous membranes of head and from chewing muscles Efferent to chewing muscles
VI	Abducent	Pons	Afferent and efferent to one eye muscle
VII	Facial	Medulla	Afferent from taste buds of anterior two thirds of tongue Efferent to muscles of face and salivary glands
VIII	Statoacoustic	Medulla	Afferent from the inner ear (hearing and balance)
IX	Glossopharyngeal	Medulla	Afferent from throat, rear of tongue, and taste buds of posterior one third of tongue Efferent to throat and one salivary gland
X	Vagus	Medulla	Afferent from throat, viscera, and larynx Efferent to viscera
XI	Spinal accessory	Medulla	Efferent to viscera (via vagus), throat, larynx, neck, and shoulder muscles
XII	Hypoglossal	Medulla	Afferent and efferent to tongue muscles

*Adapted from Wenger, M. A., Jones, F. N., and Jones, M. H.: Physiological psychology, New York, 1956, Holt, Rinehart & Winston, Inc.

brain. The increase in size of the cortex has resulted in a thickening that forms several *layers* of cells and synaptic connections. There is a great increase in area as well—about 2½ square feet in man. The expansion of the cortex has occurred in the face of a limited cranial capacity, the size of the bony "box" of the skull. As a result the cortex has developed folds to increase its area within the limited cranial volume, and much of the cortex is buried in the folds, or sulci (sing., **sulcus**), of the brain (Fig. 5-9). The surface areas between the sulci are called gyri (sing., **gyrus**).

Each sulcus and gyrus is named, but only the major ones are important here. The **longitudinal fissure** divides the **cerebrum** into two **cerebral hemispheres** (a fissure is a large sulcus). The **central sulcus** divides each hemisphere into an anterior one third and a posterior two thirds of cortical area. The central sulcus lies between the **precentral gyrus** (area 4 in Fig. 5-9) and the **postcentral gyrus** (areas 3, 1, and

2). The **lateral fissure** lies between area 41 and areas 44, 43, and 40.

The cortex is also divided into lobes. The **frontal lobe** is anterior to the central sulcus and includes about one third of each hemisphere. The **temporal lobe** lies below the lateral fissure—the cerebral hemispheres are shaped somewhat in the form of boxing gloves, and the temporal lobe is like the thumb of a boxing glove. The **occipital lobe** is the posterior part of the hemisphere, and the **parietal lobe** lies between the occipital lobe and the central sulcus. There is no major sulcus to mark the dividing line between occipital and parietal lobes— the parietal lobe includes area 7, and the occipital lobe, area 19.

The thickness of the cortex is caused by six well-defined cortical layers (in most areas). Functionally, the cortex is *vertically organized,* with excitation carried from cell to cell, largely in a vertical direction. Excitation reaches lower centers by way of the white matter of **projection fi-**

bers. Excitation is carried to other cortical areas by way of both lower centers and **commissural fibers** that "loop" down into the white matter and back up again. Various parts of the cortex differ in the relative thickness of the six cell layers. The **Brodmann system** of cortical areas depends on the relative thickness of the cell layers; it is a useful way to refer to a specific part of the cortex. In the Brodmann system, a cross section of the cortex was taken in the postcentral gyrus. The first arrangement of cell layers encountered was arbitrarily called area 1. With further cross sections, the first change in the relative thickness of the layers was called area 2, and so on, until the entire cortex had been classified. Sometimes these anatomical differences correspond with known functional differences in the cortex, and sometimes they do not. In any case the Brodmann system is a useful way to refer to specific parts of the cortex.

More functionally, the cortex has also been classified into sensory projection areas, motor projection areas, and association areas. **Sensory projection areas** are those parts of the cortex in which pathways from the receptors, or sense organs, terminate. Thus area 17 is the **visual projection area;** area 41, the **auditory projection area;** areas 3, 1, and 2, the **somesthetic** (skin senses) **projection area;** and so on. The **motor projection area** is the origin of fibers descending in the brainstem and spinal cord to the motor neurons of the cranial and spinal nerves that control the somatic muscles. It occupies area 4. The **association areas** are those that are not directly sensory or motor in function. Classically, they were presumed to "associate" incoming impulses to the sensory projection areas with outgoing impulses from the motor projection areas to permit responses to stimuli. Association areas are found in the cortex of all four lobes.

SUPPORTING AND NOURISHING TISSUE IN THE CNS

Nerve cell tissue is not the only tissue making up the central nervous system. Spe-

cialized tissue performs functions of food and oxygen exchange with the circulation. Other varieties of specialized tissue surround and protect the brain and spinal cord, and still other cells support and bind together the nerve cells within the CNS.

Meninges

The CNS is surrounded by three layers of connective tissue called the **meninges.** The outermost layer, the **dura mater,** is a tough fibrous covering completely enveloping the brain and spinal cord. Just inside the dura mater is a second, thinner, and more fragile layer of connective tissue, the **arachnoid layer.** The arachnoid layer contains many of the blood vessels that nourish the CNS. The **pia mater** is the layer lying next to the spinal cord and the brain, and it adheres closely to them. The space between the arachnoid layer and the pia mater is filled with **cerebrospinal fluid** (see below).

Cerebrospinal fluid (Fig. 13-11)

The brain and spinal cord are surrounded with cerebrospinal fluid, as are the ventricles and spinal canal. The fluid cushions the brain and spinal cord, keeping them away from the surrounding skull and vertebrae so as to minimize damage that could occur from blows to the head or spine. It is not known whether the cerebrospinal fluid participates in the exchange of nutrition, oxygen, and waste between the blood and the nerve cells in the same fashion as the other extracellular fluids of the CNS. However, the cerebrospinal fluid is similar to the other extracellular fluids of the nerve cells in that certain substances will not pass from the blood to either fluid. Glutamic acid and other substances that pass readily from the capillaries to extracellular fluid elsewhere in the body do not do so in the brain. Thus physiologists speak of a **blood-brain barrier,** a concept that is important in the study of the effects of various chemicals on the CNS and on behavior. If these chemicals do not pass the blood-brain barrier when they are injected into the bloodstream, they cannot affect the CNS.

Neuroglia

The various kinds of supporting cells in the CNS are collectively called **neuroglia,** or more commonly **glial cells.** Their processes weave around and between the nerve cells. The cells also attach themselves to blood vessels. Their attachment to blood vessels may indicate a role in the blood-brain barrier (see above). Substances would have to pass through the glial cells as well as the capillary walls in order to reach the CNS. Glial cells are involved in producing the myelin sheaths of axons in the tracts of the CNS. Recent work shows that some of them are mobile and can absorb damaged tissue. Glial cells may have other metabolic roles. They are clearly involved in the formation of **tumors** of the brain when they multiply in an abnormal fashion. There are ten times as many glial cells as nerve cells in the brain.

SUMMARY

The brain and spinal cord make up the central nervous system (CNS), in contrast to the peripheral nervous system, which connects the CNS to receptors and effectors. The peripheral nervous system includes the peripheral somatic nervous system (PSNS) of sensory nerves that come from the receptors and motor nerves and go to the striated, or somatic, muscles. The peripheral nervous system also includes the autonomic nervous system (ANS) of motor nerves leading to the visceral. The PSNS and ANS both originate in cranial nerves from the brain and in spinal nerves from the spinal cord; both kinds of nerves originate in pairs.

The ANS shows the unique features of (1) dual innervation of the viscera from the parasympathetic division (PNS) and from the sympathetic division (SNS), (2) peripheral inhibition, since PNS and SNS effects are opposite at the visceral effectors, (3) two fibers in the motor pathway of both

PNS and SNS via preganglionic and postganglionic neurons, and (4) automaticity of effectors, the automatic activity of which is speeded or slowed by PNS or SNS excitation.

In the SNS preganglionic fibers are short, reaching nearby sympathetic chain ganglia or collateral ganglia from the thoracic and lumbar divisions of the cord; the postganglionic fibers are long and diffusely stimulated. In the PNS the opposite condition holds, as the ganglia lie near the organs innervated. The PNS originates in cranial and sacral nerves and responds discretely. In both the PNS and SNS the preganglionic to postganglionic synapses use acetylcholine (ACh) as a transmitter, which is rapidly removed after acting because of the presence of the enzyme acetylcholine esterase (AChE). The neuroeffector junction in the PNS utilizes the same transmitter, but the postganglionic SNS fibers secrete epinephrine or norepinephrine. These secretions circulate to affect many effectors, reinforced by the presence of epinephrine and norepinephrine secreted by the adrenal medulla in response to SNS stimulation. The PNS stimulates the secretion of insulin from the pancreas by way of the vagus nerve.

The differences between SNS and PNS may be summarized by saying that the SNS is an adrenergic, sympatheticoadrenal, and thoracicolumbar system, whereas the PNS is a cholinergic, vago-insulin, and craniosacral system. Both systems are regulated by a part of the brain called the hypothalamus. The SNS acts diffusely on the viscera and stimulates relatively widespread PNS responses thereby, so that there is a constantly changing balance between the two. The SNS acts on the viscera to prepare the body for physical exertion in an "emergency," causing increased heart rate and blood pressure, rapid breathing, and increased sweating (to cool the body). Measures of these reactions on the polygraph (the so-called lie detector) have been used to indicate emotional response to questioning. The PNS has opposite effects on the viscera from those of the SNS. The PNS controls the discrete and sequential reactions of digestion and metabolism and is dominant during sleep. The PNS sometimes overreacts to SNS arousal in parasympathetic overcompensation.

The CNS determines the connections between incoming excitation from the receptors and outgoing excitation to the effectors. The CNS thus determines response to internal and external stimuli. These stimulus-response relationships are fixed in the reflex. In spinal cord reflexes, five types of elements are involved: (1) receptors, (2) sensory, or afferent, neurons, (3) association neurons, (4) motor, or efferent, neurons (motoneurons), and (5) effectors, Excitation from receptors in afferent neurons may reach the spinal nerves by either the dorsal or ventral rami, but it enters the cord by the dorsal roots. The sensory neurons excite association neurons in the dorsal columns of the gray matter. The association neurons reach motoneurons in the ventral horns of the gray matter. The axons of the motoneurons leave the cord by the ventral roots to reach somatic muscles by either the dorsal or ventral rami.

If the SNS is involved, preganglionic neurons reach sympathetic chain ganglia via the ventral roots and the white ramus. Preganglionic neurons may synapse with postganglionic fibers in the chain ganglia when the postganglionic fibers rejoin the spinal nerves via the gray ramus to reach the smooth muscles and glands. Preganglionic fibers may pass through the chain ganglia to synapse with postganglionic neurons in the collateral ganglia before excitation reaches the visceral effectors. Excitation from reflexes reaches higher centers and is returned to spinal centers via the tracts of the white matter in the dorsal, ventral, and lateral funiculi of the cord. Reflexes are fixed and determined by the receptors excited, because the "connections" between the neurons they excite are fixed. More complex and variable responses to stimuli

involving higher centers can be depicted as following the "reflex plan" if more association fibers, variability, and correlation of input and coordination of output are included.

The original hollow form of the CNS is seen in the spinal canal, ventricles, and cerebral aqueduct (Figs. 5-5 and 5-6). The linear and sequential parts of the brain form the brainstem, surmounted by the cerebral and cerebellar hemispheres. Unlike the brain and spinal cord, the hemispheres have surface gray matter and internal white matter (tracts). Important brainstem structures include the medulla, pons, fourth ventricle, cerebral aqueduct, midbrain, third ventricle, hypothalamus, basal ganglia (corpus striatum), corpus callosum, and lateral ventricles.

The cerebral cortex is the highest and most complex set of integrating centers. The corpus striatum (basal ganglia) regulate instincts in other animals and the timing and sequence of automatic movements in man. The thalamus is an integrating center; it mediates incoming sensory input to the cortex, as well as having many connections between one cortical center and another. The hypothalamus regulates the ANS and reacts to changes in the internal environment by arousing and sustaining responses that serve homeostasis, thereby serving as a center for drives. The midbrain contains tracts and visual and auditory reflex centers (the colliculi). The cerebellum regulates balance and coordination in response to input from the inner ear and muscle receptors. The medulla contains the centers mediating the vital reflexes of heart rate, breathing, and so on.

The brainstem is most directly connected to receptors and effectors by the twelve pairs of cranial nerves, which may be sensory, motor, or mixed in function. They are named as well as numbered.

The gray matter of the cerebral cortex undergoes its greatest development in man. It is folded to increase its area and thereby forms gyri, sulci, and fissures. The longitudinal fissure divides the hemispheres, the central sulcus separates the frontal lobe from the parietal lobe, and the lateral fissure lies between the frontal and parietal lobes and the temporal lobe. The occipital lobe is the posterior portion of the hemisphere. Cortical thickness is divided into six cell layers. The relative thickness of these layers is the basis for the Brodmann system of arbitrarily numbering different cortical areas. The cortex is vertically organized, with excitation reaching lower centers by way of projection fibers and reaching other cortical areas by these and commissural fibers, including the corpus callosum, which connects the two hemispheres. Areas of the cortex where sensory pathways terminate are called sensory projection areas and include those for vision (17), hearing (41), and somesthesis (3, 1, and 2). The cortical origin of motor pathways to the somatic muscles is the motor projection area (4). The remaining cortical areas of all four lobes form association areas.

The CNS is surrounded by three protective layers of connective tissue—dura mater, arachnoid, and pia mater. Cerebrospinal fluid is found between the arachnoid and pia mater and in the ventricles of the brain. Besides cushioning the brain, the cerebrospinal fluid may serve the same function of food, waste, and oxygen exchange as the other extracellular fluid of the CNS. Both fluids are not reached by some substances that readily circulate between the capillaries and other extracellular fluids of the body; physiologically there seems to be a blood-brain barrier. The various supporting cells of the CNS are referred to as neu-roglia, or glial cells. These cells may have metabolic as well as supporting roles and may be involved in the blood-brain barrier. When they proliferate abnormally, they form brain tumors.

READINGS

Asimov, I.: The human brain, Boston, 1964, Houghton Mifflin Co.

Chapman, C. B., and Mitchell, J. H.: The physiology of exercise, Sci. Am. **212**:88-96, May 1965. (W. H. Freeman Reprint No. 1011.)

Eccles, J.: The synapses, Sci. Am. **212**:56-66, Jan. 1965. (W. H. Freeman Reprint No. 1001.)

Gardner, E. D.: Fundamentals of neurology, ed. 5, Philadelphia, 1968, W. B. Saunders Co.

Gatz, A. J.: Manter's essentials of clinical neuroanatomy and neurophysiology, ed. 4, Philadelphia, 1970, F. A. Davis Co.

Gray, G. W.: The great ravelled knot, Sci. Am. **179**:27-39, Oct. 1948. (W. H. Freeman Reprint No. 13.)

Houser, R. H.: Graphic aids to neurology, ed. 2, San Diego, 1948, Scientific Illustrators.

Lewin, R.: The nervous system, Garden City, N.Y., 1972, Doubleday Anchor Press.

Matzke, H. A., and Foltz, F. M.: Synopsis of neuroanatomy, New York, 1967, Oxford University Press, Inc.

Noback, C. R., and Demarest, R. J.: The nervous system: Introduction and review, New York, 1972, McGraw-Hill Book Co.

Smith, B. M.: The polygraph, Sci. Am. **216**:25-31, Jan. 1967.

Smith, C.: The brain: Towards an understanding, New York, 1972, Capricorn books, G. P. Putnam's Sons.

Snider, R. S.: The cerebellum, Sci. Am. **199**:84-90, Aug. 1958. (W. H. Freeman Reprint No. 38.)

Sperry, R. W.: The growth of nerve circuits, Sci. Am. **201**:68-75, Nov. 1959. (W. H. Freeman Reprint No. 72.)

Wilson, J. V.: Inhibition in the central nervous system, Sci. Am. **214**:102-110, May 1966.

part three

The senses

chapter 6
Sensation and perception

OVERVIEW

This chapter introduces the third part of the text—a discussion of the senses. Subsequent chapters on the senses will cover somesthesis, proprioception, the chemical senses, audition, and vision. Before these sensory modalities are discussed, however, certain concepts that concern sensation and perception, and their measurement as well, should be mastered. These concepts are useful no matter which of the sensory modalities is discussed. The present chapter, then, covers topics that apply to all the senses.

The chapter begins by distinguishing between sensation and perception and shows how sensations can be studied through the human subject's response to perceptions as well as through animal experiments. A formal definition of a stimulus follows, together with a discussion of the implications of that definition. Then the receptor is introduced and classified in several useful ways. Attributes of the resulting sensations are noted, and the senses are classified as topographic or nontopographic. Since receptors initiate sensation in response to physical energy, the measurement of sensations, or psychophysics, is the next topic discussed. Psychophysics is the branch of science concerned with the relationship between physical energy and sensations or receptor and nervous system response. The attributes, or characteristics, that all sensations share are discussed, and their effects on nervous system activity are pointed out. Three ways of describing the relationship between stimulus intensity and sensation intensity are presented. Adapta-

tion, habituation, contrast, afterimages, compensation, and fusion are described. The chapter closes with a brief treatment of perception, with an emphasis on spatial localization.

SENSATION, PERCEPTION, AND ENERGY

To the physicist, all events in the universe make up energy of various kinds, which he classifies as light, sound, temperature, mechanical events, chemical events, and so on. A great number of these events affect man, but man can sense only a few of them. He can be sunburned by ultraviolet light he cannot see, his hearing can be damaged by air pressure changes he cannot hear as sound, or he can be poisoned by chemical substances he cannot taste. Those events that man *can* sense are those energies that affect his receptors in ways that stimulate sensory nerve cells. The nerve cells stimulate the CNS to cause sensations, which, in turn, are changed and elaborated by the CNS into perceptions.

Sensation

Receptors and sense organs stimulate the CNS when physical events affect them by stimulating their sensory nerve cells. The resulting nerve impulses provide the CNS with "information" about physical events occurring outside and inside the body. The input provides the *basis for discrimination* among stimuli in all animals and is the *basis for* conscious **sensations** that can be reported by man—the loudness of sounds, the hue of lights, and the rankness or sweetness of odors. The CNS reacts to sensory inputs in an integrated fashion. Stimuli are compared, contrasted with past stimulus events (memory), and reacted to in terms of the current internal state of the body—hunger, thirst, and so on. Responses result that reflect discrimination between stimulus events—the animal reacts to some stimuli, does not react to others, and compares present and past inputs. The responses reflect the current internal needs of the body, being appropriate to states of hunger and thirst, sexual needs, etc. *Some* of the integrative activity of the CNS that *results* from sensation seems reflected in man's reports of conscious events—comparisons, images, memories, and feelings of hunger and thirst. Such reports constitute **perception,** the conscious accompaniment of events in the CNS that *result from* sensation inputs. Our knowledge of the physiology of the sense organs and CNS tells us much about sensation, but little is known as yet about the more complex CNS events involved in perception. The distinction is a useful one, however, because the study of sensation in man almost always involves some aspect of perception.

How can the input of the sense organs be studied? There are two methods commonly used: *introspection* and *evoked potentials.* When man is the subject, the experimenter can change the stimulus and ask the subject if he is aware of the change. The experimenter varies the stimulus, and the subject attends to one attribute of his perception that depends directly on the sensation input; changes in the intensity of a sound, for example, can depend on changes in sensation input rather than on the perceptual meaning of the stimulus. The subject detects differences in his sensations by comparing perceptions. The detection of the difference in pitch between tone A and tone B, and knowing whether a light is intense enough to be perceived at all, are aspects of the subject's perception that depend directly on his sensations. (Of course we can always teach an animal subject a

response that depends on its ability to detect the difference between two stimuli and see if it responds when we change the stimulus by a certain amount.)

In animal studies, the method of evoked potentials is most commonly used. Electrodes are placed in the sense organs, sensory nerves, or brain, and the electrical response of these structures to stimulus change is recorded. This has the advantage of telling us something about what kind of "signals" the sense organ sends to the brain in response to stimulus change. It does not, of course, tell us whether the animal can detect the change, unless behavioral change also occurs.

Perception

Sensations do not impinge on a totally naïve nervous system. In lower animals patterns of reaction and therefore patterns of perception are "built into" the CNS by inheritance (instincts). In higher organisms, including man, the functioning of the CNS is frequently altered by learning. Sensations therefore interact with the memory traces of past experience to form perceptions. The perception of a stimulus and the organism's reaction to it depend on past experience with similar stimuli and on the current stimulus pattern from other sources. For example, the sound of the dinner bell to a dog or a man will vary according to past associations of the bell with eating; the perception of the sound will also depend on hunger sensations perceived at the same time. If the dog or man is hungry, the bell will sound different from the way it sounds after a full meal. Perception is the development of "meaning" that depends on past and present sensation input. As such, perception may be studied, in its own right, as the development of meaning from past stimuli. It can be more narrowly related to current stimulus input. The more narrow approach includes a study of how sensations act as cues to perception—the relation between perceived size and perceived distance of an object, for example. The chapters on the senses will include some study of perception. Only the relationships between perceptions and current sensation input will be discussed, however, because only these aspects of perception have been clearly related to physiological events.

Energy

Energy is the physical event that can initiate a sensation, and physical energy is therefore important to perception as well. The *rate* at which various forces act on the body must *change* to affect receptors most effectively. For example, man living at sea level is subject to pressure of 14.7 pounds per square inch over his entire body, but no pressure receptor response or pressure sensations result. If he puts his finger into a glass of mercury, increased pressure on the submerged part of the finger results. He senses pressure at the instant he places his finger into the mercury because of the *change* from air pressure. The sensation is brief, however. The only continuing pressure sensation comes from the "ring" about the finger where mercury meets air, that is, at the point of a *change* in the energy responsible for pressure.

Energy change is biologically very useful to the organism for survival; thus it is fortunate that our receptors are "tuned" in this fashion. A change in the stimulus events signals a *change* in the environment. Environmental change may affect survival. For example, visually detected movement is meaningful for survival to both the hungry hawk and its rabbit prey. Energy changes are much more meaningful to the organism than are sensory signals, which merely indicate that conditions are unchanged.

STIMULUS

A **stimulus** is any physical energy that excites a receptor. This statement ends, by definition, the old argument over whether a tree falling in the forest makes a noise if there is no one there to hear it. The falling tree creates an energy change that is not a stimulus because it does not excite an animal receptor. (If a "noise" is a stimulus, the tree made no noise.)

Receptors

Receptors consist of tissues or organs that are specialized to respond to a specific *form* of energy. The sensory tissue involved is not only specialized for irritability; it is specialized to be more irritable to energy change of a specific variety and range of intensity. The tissue is said to have a low **threshold** to the energy change for which it is specialized. The threshold for a receptor is the minimum energy that will stimulate that receptor. Receptors are specialized in man for five types of stimulus energy: **mechanical, thermal, chemical, acoustical,** and **photic.** Receptors specialized for mechanical stimulation include the skin receptors for pressure and pain, proprioceptive receptors in the muscles and joints that report limb position and movement, and receptors in the viscera that give sensations accompanying hunger (stomach contractions, for example). Thermal receptors in the skin report the temperature of the environment. Taste and smell are chemical receptors; that is, they respond best to substances in solution. For taste the substances are dissolved in saliva; for smell, airborne particles dissolve in the moist mucous surfaces of the nasal passages. Acoustical receptors are modified pressure receptors in the ear that respond to rapid variations in air pressure, called sound. Audition (hearing) shares with vision the function of reporting events that occur at a distance from the subject. Visual receptors are photic receptors and respond to light, a part of the spectrum of electromagnetic energy. Receptors specialize in different ways in different parts of the body, but the examples given survey most of the sensory mechanisms of the body that give rise to sensations.

Some specialized receptors in the body do not cause sensations when stimulated. These receptors stimulate reflexes and brain activity without exciting parts of the brain where activity leads to conscious awareness. (We may become aware of the responses that occur.) Some of the reflexes involved include "automatic" responses to receptors in the inner ear that help us maintain balance and coordination. Other receptors initiate reactions that regulate the consistency of the internal environment—receptors that respond to an increase in blood pressure by reflexly slowing the heart rate, for example. Still other receptors in the hypothalamus are sensitive to the internal changes that result from need states like hunger or thirst. These and other receptors may arouse the brain and change behavior without direct awareness of the internal environment—like receptors that respond to an increase in blood pressure by reflexly slowing the heart rate.

Adequate and inadequate stimuli

When a receptor is activated by the form of energy for which it is specialized, that receptor has received an **adequate stimulus.** This is true even if it is not the kind of receptor that can give rise to conscious sensations. For example, light is the adequate stimulus for the eye. When the receptor responds to a form of energy for which it is not specialized, it receives an **inadequate stimulus.** Pressure on the eyeball from a finger can cause a sensation of light, even though the eye is specialized to respond to light rather than to pressure. The eye has a low threshold to light and a high threshold to pressure, but the pressure threshold can be exceeded and thereby stimulate the retina (sensory tissue of the eye).

Law of specific nerve energies

A receptor may be a separate group of specialized cells or a specialized ending on a nerve cell, as will be explained later. Adequate stimulation of a receptor results in a **generator potential** in the specialized tissue or ending. As explained in Chapter 4, a generator potential is a change in electrical potential by the receptor. The generator potential, in turn, fires a **nerve impulse** in the sensory nerve fibers leading to the CNS. The nerve impulses result in a sensation. The form that the sensation takes—light, sound, taste, and so fourth—depends on the receptor or neuron stimulated. This statement is the **law of specific nerve energies.** The law holds because the neurons from different receptors go to different *places* in the brain. One sees light because the optic nerves lead to the visual areas of the brain, not because their nerve impulses are different from the nerve impulses reaching a different part of the brain from the ear. Electrical stimulation of the eye, the optic nerves, or the visual area of the brain causes a sensation of light. Stimulation of nerves leading to the auditory area causes a sensation of sound, even though the auditory impulses and visual impulses look the same on an oscilloscope. As Sherrington once stated, the nerve impulse is the "universal currency" of the nervous system.

CLASSIFICATION OF RECEPTORS

Sense organs and receptor tissue specialize to be irritable to a specific kind of physical energy: mechanical, thermal, chemical, acoustical, or photic. A given form of energy is the adequate stimulus for the receptor, which reacts to a limited intensity range of that form of energy. Specialization, which often involves changes in the *structure* of the receptor, adapts it to be sensitive to a given form of energy. Receptors and sense organs act as **transducers,** which are specialized to transduce, or change, the nature of physical energy. All receptors transduce some form of physical energy into nerve impulses. The physical event that is the adequate stimulus initiates processes in the receptor resulting in nerve impulses. Some receptors are more specialized in structure and function than others.

Receptors can be classified according to (1) their adequate stimulus, (2) the anatomical form that they have taken in specializing, (3) their location in the body, and (4) stimulus origin.

Classification by form

Receptors have developed as separate cells or as more or less specialized endings on neurons. Three classes are recognized (Fig. 6-1): (1) the **unspecialized nerve cell,** (2) the **specialized nerve cell,** and (3) the **specialized receptor cell.** The unspecialized endings on sensory nerves are found in great numbers just below the surface of the skin. They are also found in the viscera and muscles. This type of ending serves pain input, but similar neurons may go to areas of the brain that sense pressure and temperature as well. A number of more specialized endings on nerve cells are found beneath the surface of the skin, in the viscera, and in the joints of the skeleton. Some are known to serve pressure, and others are probably temperature receptors. The sensory cells for smell are also specialized nerve endings. Finally, some of the most specialized receptors in the body take the form of separate cells. The specialized cells respond to a specific form of energy change and excite a sensory nerve cell that they "contact." The taste receptors are a prominent example of this kind of receptor. Elaborate sense organs such as the ear and eye have specialized receptor cells along with accessory structures to assure stimulation.

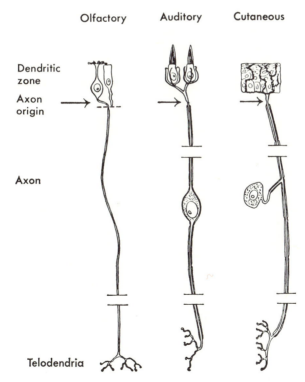

Olfactory   Auditory   Cutaneous

Dendritic zone

Axon origin

Axon

Telodendria

Fig. 6-1. Three classes of receptor structures, from left to right, are a specialized receptor structure on a neuron (a specialized nerve cell), a specialized receptor cell, and an unspecialized receptor ending on a neuron (unspecialized nerve cell). (From Bodian, D.: Science **137:**325, copyright 1962 by the American Association for the Advancement of Science.)

Classification by location

Receptors are classified as **general** if they are found throughout the body, and as **special** if they are found only in the head. The general receptors serve as a sense that is often called **somesthesis** (Gr., 'body perception'); it includes **pressure, pain, warmth, cold,** and **kinesthesis** (sense of body position and movement from the muscles and joints). Pressure, pain, warmth, and cold receptors are found just below the surface of the skin over the entire body. A less extensive distribution of poorly specialized receptors that serve these four senses are found in parts of the viscera. The special senses in the head are more highly evolved and have more complex sensory mechanisms. In the course of evolution they probably developed in the head because that end of the animal encountered the environment first as the animal moved about. (It has also been suggested that this is the reason the brain is in the head.) The special senses include **olfaction** (smell), **vision, gustation** (taste), **audition** (hearing), and **vestibular sensitivity** (head position and movement).

Classification by stimulus origin

Receptors are also classified as **exteroceptors, interoceptors,** and **proprioceptors** by the origin of their stimuli. Exteroceptors are located at or near the body surface and signal events going on in the external environment. They serve the **cutaneous general senses** of pressure, pain, warmth, and cold. The *cutaneous,* or skin, senses are the general senses located just beneath the surface of the skin; they do not include the same general senses when they are located in the viscera. The special senses of vision, audition, olfaction, and gustation are also exteroceptors when they function to detect external events. Vision and audition are served primarily by exteroceptors. Olfaction is served by an exteroceptor when the subject smells a stimulus in the external environment, and gustation is served by an exteroceptor when taste is used to explore the outside world.

Interoceptors are receptors that detect events going on inside the body. Olfaction and gustation are served by interoceptors when one smells and tastes during eating and digestion. Other interoceptors are located inside the viscera, chiefly in the walls of the digestive and urogenital tracts. They are **organic** rather than cutaneous receptors. The special senses of olfaction and gustation are therefore organic only when the stimulus comes from within the digestive tract, as in eating. The **organic general senses** of pressure, pain, warmth, and cold are included; receptors for these senses are found in the viscera.

Proprioceptors include the *general* **kinesthetic receptors** located in the muscles, tendons, and joints, as well as the *special* **vestibular receptors** found in the nonauditory inner ear. As previously explained, the kinesthetic receptors are included in the general classification because they are found throughout the body, whereas the vestibular receptors fall into the special category because they are found only in the head. Proprioceptors signal body position and movement.

ATTRIBUTES OF SENSATION

What characteristics of sensation are measurable and common to all sensory modalities? What happens in the sensory neurons, according to the law of specific nerve energies, when these attributes are varied? These are the questions attacked in this section, beginning with the four measurable attributes that all the senses have in common: (1) **quality,** (2) **intensity,** (3) **extent,** and (4) *duration.*

Sensory quality

Sensory quality is the attribute that distinguishes one sensory modality from another. It also distinguishes *qualitatively* different attributes within a sensation, such as hues for vision and tastes for gustation. For senses that have more than one quality, there are **primary qualities** and **secondary qualities.** Primary qualities are the basic differential responses of the receptor. Their combination produces all the other qualitative differences, or secondary qualities, of sensation. Whether these basic responses (sensations) depend on a single receptor or a combination of receptors, they cannot be analyzed further by the subject. To take an example from vision, the color red is primary and appears only red. The color orange is secondary, and primary yellow and primary red can be detected in orange just by looking at it.

The difference between primary and secondary qualities can be most clearly seen in further examples from various sensory modalities. Somesthesis (organic and skin sensitivity) has four primary qualities that appear to be four kinds of sensory modality: pressure, warmth, cold, and pain. Secondary somesthetic qualities such as tickle or itch are produced by combinations of these four primary qualities. The kinesthetic and vestibular senses are difficult to analyze in terms of sensory quality because they do not result in conscious sensations. Taste has four primary qualities: sweet, sour, bitter, and salt; all other tastes are combinations. Smell appears to have seven primary qualities: camphoraceous, musky, floral, pepperminty, ethereal, pungent, and putrid. Audition has but one quality—pitch—so that secondary qualities do not result. Vision has the four hue qualities of red, blue, yellow, and green; all other hues result from combinations of two or more of these qualities.

Quality indicates *what* sensory system or what *part* of a sensory system is functioning, whereas the other three attributes (intensity, extent, and duration) show only *how* it is functioning. Thus one speaks of the loudness of a pitch rather than the pitch of a loudness, or the brightness of a hue rather than the hue of a brightness. Intensity, extent, and duration modify quality, but quality does not usually modify the other three attributes in a systematic way.

Intensity

The sensed intensity of a stimulus increases with the intensity of the physical energy that is stimulating the receptor. However, the relationship is not a linear one, as will be seen in the section on psychophysics. That is, equal increases in physical energy do not lead to equal increases in sensation intensity. At low intensities a small increase in stimulus energy makes as much *difference* in the intensity sensed as a large increase in the stimulus at high intensities—a whisper can be heard in a quiet room, but one shouts to be heard over the roar of a jet engine. Furthermore, quality and intensity interact. In hearing, for example, the ear is most sensitive to tones in the middle of the musical scale of pitch (a quality), and the eye is more sensitive to some hue qualities than it is to others. Pressure, pain, warmth, and cold all vary in sensed intensity, as do taste and smell. Auditory intensity is loudness and visual intensity is brightness. The attribute of intensity, then, is important for all the senses.

Extent

Extent is the "area" of the perceptual field covered by the stimulus. This means the *size* of the area of pressure, pain, warmth, or cold on the skin, or in the viscera for somesthesis. The extent of the tongue occupied by a taste is another example. Extent has not been investigated for smell. There is, however, a dimension of auditory volume that is separated from loudness, although it interacts with both loudness and pitch. Visual extent is the proportion of the visual field occupied by a stimulus.

Duration

Duration is merely the period of time over which a sensation lasts in any of the sensory modalities.

Sensory attributes and the law of specific nerve energies

The statement has been made that all nerve impulses "look alike," whether in somesthesis, proprioception, taste, smell, audition, or vision. Sensory modalities differ according to the *place* in the brain reached by sensory neurons serving different sensory modalities—the brain has visual projection areas, auditory projection areas, etc. Stimulating the eye with light or even pressure leads to a visual sensation because the sensory nerves lead to the visual area of the brain. Differences in modality are also differences in sensory quality; thus these variations in quality may depend on the *place* in the brain reached by the fibers serving each modality. Somesthetic pressure and some proprioception reaches the somesthetic projection area; there is reason to believe that most pain and perhaps temperature excitation terminate in lower centers. Sensory modality seems to depend on the part of the brain stimulated.

Whether different qualities *within* a sense modality depend on the stimulation of different parts of their projection areas in the brain is not known. The taste receptors appear to send various *patterns* of excitation to the brain to signal salt, sweet, bitter, or sour. There seem to be seven different kinds of smell receptors for the seven olfactory qualities, but it is not known if the excitation of these receptors reaches different places in the olfactory projection areas. There appear to be three receptors serving the four primary hue qualities for vision, but the reaction of the visual projection area to these receptors is unknown. Auditory fibers excited by different pitches do reach systematically different places in the auditory area of the brain, however. There is some evidence for a "place theory" for sensory quality, but it is far from complete.

Intensity of the stimulus affects each sensory modality in the same way. As intensity is increased, more receptors and therefore more sensory neurons fire. Furthermore, each neuron fires more frequently.

Extent, logically, has a single cue—the *area,* or extent, of the receptor field stimulated, and therefore the extent, or proportion, of the projection area in the brain being excited.

Duration depends on the duration of excitation of the receptor and therefore on the duration of excitation to a projection area of the brain.

TOPOGRAPHIC AND NONTOPOGRAPHIC MODALITIES

There seem to be two basic ways in which receptors and their sensory neurons respond to a stimulus change. As a result, sensory modalities can be classified as **topographic** or **nontopographic** (Fig. 6-2). Topographic modalities are those in which single receptors and their sensory neurons respond only to a very narrow range of stimulus change. For example, a single neuron can be excited by a pressure receptor on the skin only when the stimulus is applied within 2 cm. of its location on the finger or within 5 cm. on the thorax (chest), as seen in Fig. 6-2. Different pitches of tones stimulate different input pathways, as do differently positioned vertical lines in vision. The input at the receptor, sensory pathways, and sensory projection area of the cerebral cortex is organized in an orderly spatial arrangement. A stimulus change is therefore signaled to the cortex in terms of *which* neurons are firing. Nontopographic modalities have receptors and afferent neurons that respond to a broad range of stimulus change. The individual cells are more sensitive at some points along the scale of stimulus change than at others, however. For example, the skin temperature receptor graphed in Fig. 6-2 is most sensitive to a temperature of 30° C. Temperature change is signaled to the brain by this receptor in terms of its rate of firing; the maximum rate occurs at 30° C. and diminishes at other temperatures. (This is a cold receptor; other receptors fire at higher temperatures to signal the direction of stimulus change to the brain.) Visual receptors

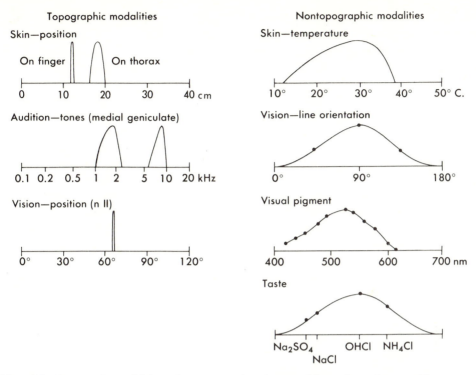

Fig. 6-2. Range of sensitivity of representative topographic and nontopographic sensory modalities. (Redrawn from Erikson, R. P.: Psychol. Rev. **75:**447-465, 1968.)

that respond to the angular position of a line, visual pigment receptors that respond to hue, and taste receptors are other examples of "broadly tuned" nontopographic receptors. In each case, there must be more than one receptor for the range of stimulus change so that the direction of stimulus change can be detected. In the case of the temperature receptor in Fig. 6-2, a decrease in the rate of firing could result from either an increase or a decrease in temperature, starting from the 30° C. maximum. In Fig. 11-9 there is an example of the three broadly tuned receptors that respond to hue. A change in hue would be signaled to the brain by the relative rate of firing of each of the three types of receptors.

It is evident that the narrowly tuned topographic input requires more receptors and sensory neurons than the broadly tuned nontopographic input, because each topographic receptor covers so little of the range of stimulus change. In either topographic or nontopographic systems, a stimulus quality change need not change the *total* frequency of neural firing, even though individual neurons may change their rate of firing. This enables the CNS to detect a change in quality (different neurons firing) that is independent of an intensity change (number of neurons firing).

Sensory inputs that involve more than one sensory quality are usually topographic in nature (color, taste, smell), but this is not universally true (skin temperature involves both warm and cold qualities, for example).

PSYCHOPHYSICS

How can the input of the sense organs to the CNS be measured? In the first place, we need to know the response characteristics of the sense organ studied. What kind of energy does it respond to—the nature of the adequate stimulus (light for the eye, sound for the ear, and so on) and what are the physical characteristics of that form of energy? Then we need to know the *sensitivity range* for intensity of the sense organ —the response limits for the brightness of lights and the loudness of sounds from the minimum sensed to the maximum experienced. Finally, we must find out what aspects of the stimulus cause differences in quality—hues for the eye and pitches for the ear. Responses to extent and duration are also measurable. The methods used are *psychophysical methods* because they compare physical change with psychological (and physiological) response.

Changes in the response of a receptor are caused by changes in the variety, intensity, extent, or duration of the physical energy stimulating that receptor. Energy changes are perceived as changes in quality, intensity, extent, or duration, respectively. By attending to the changes in perception that result from systematic changes of the stimulus, man can report the changes in sensation that accompany stimulus changes— the method of introspection. The physical energy can then be compared to the sensation reported by the subject. In the method of evoked potentials we can compare the electrical responses of sense organs or nerves with changes in the physical stimulus. In either case, the relationship between energy change and input change is seldom linear; sometimes a small stimulus change makes a difference in sensation, and sometimes it takes a large stimulus change to make a difference in sensation. The physical energy change required and the sensation or evoked potential that results must be measured separately and compared. This kind of measurement is used in the field of **psychophysics.**

Thresholds

A threshold is a limiting (minimum or maximum) energy change measured in terms of physiological recordings of receptors or nerve cells or in terms of reported sensation (in man). The questions to be asked include the following: (1) What is the minimum energy sensed **(absolute threshold)?** (2) What is the least *difference* in energy sensed **(difference threshold)?** (3) What is the maximum energy sensed, that is, when does increasing the stimulus energy not increase the sensation intensity **(terminal threshold)?** There are, then, three types of thresholds, each a measurement of physical energy as it affects sensation or receptor response. In visual intensity, for example, the absolute threshold for brightness is the dimmest light the subject can detect. The difference threshold is the smallest difference in brightness the subject can detect. The terminal threshold is the brightest light and the most intense sensation that the subject can experience; further increases in intensity do not make the light appear brighter to the subject. All three of these receptor and sensation responses have absolute and fixed values at a given moment. However, the sensitivity of the visual receptors varies from moment to moment. This will cause the absolute, difference, and terminal threshold values to vary from one measurement to the next. In addition, the subject makes *errors* in reporting his sensations, the experimenter makes errors in varying the stimulus and recording the results, and the stimulus light is not perfect. Fluctuations in receptor sensitivity and measurement error are involved. Some kind of average measurement is needed for the absolute, difference, and terminal thresholds. This means that any threshold is a derived *statistical* value rather than an absolute value for receptor sensitivity.

Absolute threshold. Frequently the absolute threshold is called "threshold," with the prefix absolute implied. The absolute threshold is most precisely defined as the minimum energy that results in a sensation (that stimulates a receptor) 50% of the time. As noted above, the 50% "average" value is used because the sensitivity of the receptor, the attention of the subject, and measurement errors fluctuate. Obviously, the more intense the energy, the greater will be the percentage of occasions that it will stimulate the subject—a more intense light will be detected more often, for example.

Difference threshold. The difference threshold is defined as the least difference between two stimuli in a given direction that can be detected 50% of the time. The same considerations requiring an average value for the absolute threshold are doubly involved for the difference threshold, since two stimuli, rather than one, are used.

Terminal threshold. At the other end of the scale from the absolute threshold is the terminal threshold. It is applied most readily to differences in the intensity and quality of stimuli. In terms of intensity it would be the stimulus whose increase in intensity leads to no increase in sensation intensity half the time. As an example from quality thresholds, when increases in the frequency of a sound pass the range where the subject can hear them 50% of the time, the terminal threshold for pitch has been reached. However, there are two difficulties with the terminal threshold: (1) as the terminal threshold for intensity is approached, pain is sensed, and damage to the receptors may result; thus for practical reasons the terminal intensity threshold is often measured in terms of the onset of pain; (2) quality and intensity interact. For example, the sensory *range* for pitch increases with increased intensity, so that both the absolute and terminal threshold values change—the subject can hear both lower and higher pitches at increased intensity.

Psychophysics and sensory attributes

Psychophysical methods can be used to determine thresholds for quality, intensity, extent, or duration in any sensory modality. Absolute, difference, and terminal thresholds can be determined for each attribute. In studying sensory quality, which stimulus value represents the absolute threshold

and which represents the terminal threshold is rather arbitrary; together they represent the *range* of qualities responded to by the receptor. In vision the hue quality is represented by a range of electromagnetic wave lengths from 400 to 750 nanometers (4000 to 7500 Å); beyond those limits the eye does not respond. Pitch, in hearing, corresponds to sound frequencies ranging from about 20 to 20,000 cycles per second (or hertz); other frequencies do not stimulate the auditory receptors, regardless of their intensity. Qualitative thresholds for somesthesis, proprioception, and the chemical senses have received little study, but measurement is at least theoretically possible.

Intensity thresholds have been studied in most sensory modalities. In vision, absolute, difference, and terminal thresholds for brightness have been established. These thresholds have also been measured for auditory loudness, intensity of each quality of taste, warmth, and pain, as well as for weight lifting (proprioception). The dimension of extent has been given the most attention in studies of visual size discrimination. Absolute thresholds of visual extent are the basis of the tests of visual *acuity* necessary in fitting eyeglasses. Difference thresholds for visual extent have been published as size judgments, but a terminal threshold merely means that the visual field is filled. The dimension of auditory extent (volume) has been scaled as it relates to pitch and loudness. Difference thresholds for extent of pressure sensations have been investigated. Absolute and difference thresholds for kinesthesis have been studied by measuring the smallest angle of arm movement detected by the subject and the smallest difference between two angles sensed.

The measurement of duration is much the same for each modality and requires little attention here. Absolute and difference thresholds are the only ones studied; logically there can be no terminal threshold for duration of a stimulus as long as the subject is awake.

Weber's law

Weber's law deals with the attribute of intensity and states that the more intense the stimulus, the greater an increase in intensity must be before the increase can be sensed. In other words, the more intense the stimulus, the greater is the difference threshold. Furthermore, the law states that this relationship is constant. If the base intensity is I, and the increase in intensity detected 50% of the time (the difference threshold) is ΔI, then $\Delta I/I = C$ when C is a constant. To use a simple example, if 1 candle must be added to 10 candles to detect an increase in the light in a room, 10 candles would have to be added to 100 candles to detect an increase. The constant in this case is $\frac{1}{10}$, or 0.1. Everyday experience attests to the general correctness of Weber's law. For example, you can whisper to a companion and be heard during a quiet solo passage at a concert, but you must shout to him to be heard above the ap-plause after the solo is over. The background noise has increased only moderately, but a greater differential increase in the intensity of your voice is needed to be heard.

Weber's law can be used to compare the sensitivity of different sensory modalities. The more sensitive the modality, the lower is its absolute threshold and the smaller is its difference threshold, ΔI. The smaller the ΔI, the smaller is the constant, C, because $\Delta I/I = C$. For example, the Weber fraction for visual brightness is about 0.016; for auditory intensity, about 0.088; for cutaneous pressure, 0.136; and for taste, 0.200.

Although Weber's law is correct in stating that the difference threshold increases with increases in base intensity, the constancy of the ratio does not hold at very low nor at very high intensities, particularly the former. In some cases the Weber fraction is largest at the low end of the intensity scale, minimum at moderate intensities, and greater than the minimum at high intensi-

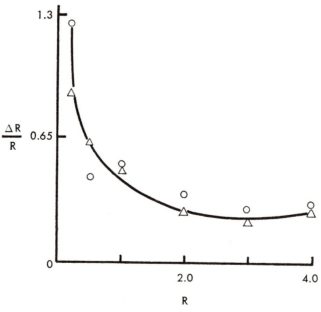

Fig. 6-3. Weber ratios for testing intensity differences in salt solutions. Expressions R and ΔR are equivalent to expressions I and ΔI in the text. (Modified from Holway, A. H., and Hurvich, L. M.: Am. J. Psychol. **49:**37-48, 1937.)

ties (Fig. 6-3). The fraction cited in comparing the sensitivity of different sensory modalities is the minimum value, where the curve dips lowest. The Weber fraction holds better for some sensory modalities than it does for others; in vision and hearing the fraction is constant over more than 99.9% of the usable range of stimulus intensities. For modalities such as taste and pressure it is quite variable.

Fechner's law

Fechner stated that the relationship between stimulus intensity and sensation intensity is a logarithmic one, when sensation intensity is scaled in differential threshold units (Fig. 6-4). He was wrong in assuming that an intensity of 20 difference threshold units is only subjectively twice 10 difference threshold units, but that is of no concern here. The most important point is that the realtionship between sensation intensity and stimulus intensity becomes nearly linear (one to one) when the stimulus values are given in log units. This is done because the increase in intensity needed to add one difference threshold unit gets larger and larger as intensity in-

creases (as Weber's law states). Furthermore, the rate of increase is logarithmic. By using a log scale for the stimulus values, the large increments at the high end of the scale are translated into smaller numbers. For example, the log of 10 is 1, the log of 100 is 2, the log of 1000 is 3, and so on. Plotted in the fashion shown in Fig. 6-4, the relationship between stimulus intensity and sensation intensity usually turns out to be a straight line. Expressed mathematically, the relationship between sensation intensity in difference threshold units *(S)*, the intensity of the stimulus *(I)*, and a constant *(K)* turns out to be $S = K \log I$, or $S = K(10^{1.2})I$, or $S = K(10^{1.3})I$ (see Fig. 6-4). Just as in Weber's law, the smaller the value of the constant, *K,* the more sensitive is the sensory modality.

General psychophysical law: Stevens' scale

Alhough Weber's law is correct enough to be useful for some senses, such as vision, it is too inaccurate for others, such as taste. Fechner's law is more generally useful because it shows that the form of the relationship between stimulus magnitude and sensation intensity is a logarithmic one. A loga-

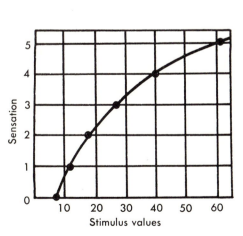

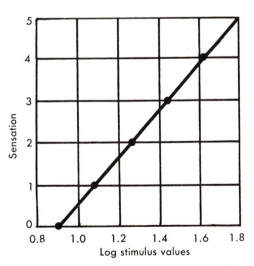

Fig. 6-4. Relationships between stimulus intensity and sensation intensity. (From Woodworth, R. S., and Schlosberg, H.: Experimental psychology, New York, 1954, Holt, Rinehart & Winston, Inc.)

rithmic function relating two measurements is one kind of *power function* because the formula that describes the function contains an *exponent*. However, using the base 10 does not provide units of intensity that are subjectively comparable for all senses. In addition, Fechner assumed that equal stimulus **ratios** led to equal sensation differences—that doubling the stimulus magnitude made the same subjective difference for a weak stimulus as a strong one. These two assumptions are corrected in Stevens' scale, where the *base* is the stimulus magnitude and the *exponent* varies with the sensitivity of the sensory modality. Thus $\psi = K\phi^n$, where ϕ (phi) is the stimulus magnitude, ψ (psi) is the sensation intensity, n varies with the sensitivity of the sensory modality, and K is a constant that depends on the size of the units used. In Stevens' formula, doubling the stimulus magnitude doubles the sensation intensity—equal stimulus ratios lead to equal sensation ratios (not equal sensation magnitudes) whether the stimulus is a strong or a weak one. However, to have a scale of measurement based on ratios is to have a scale with an absolute

zero—if 4 is to be twice 2, you must start from zero. In addition, the units must be equal. Then, having an exponent that is smaller for more sensitive sensory input, the *slope* of the straight-line relationship between stimulus magnitude and sensation intensity will be "steeper" for the less sensitive modalities (Fig. 6-5).

The state of the art of measurement in physiological psychology often confines us to "indicators" of magnitude, which have neither a true zero nor equal units. In the area of sensation, however, ratio scales are often possible for both measures of stimulus magnitude and measures of sensation intensity, or sensory nerve cell response.

SENSORY PHENOMENA

So far, sensation and perception have been treated as though constant measurements were being taken of a single quality for a single modality—for example, the response of the eye to blue light. What happens to the sensitivity of a receptor if it is stimulated at a constant rate over a period of time? What happens when one sensory quality is stimulated for a time and then

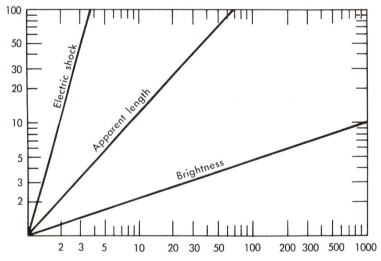

Fig. 6-5. Power functions from Stevens' scale for electric shock, apparent length, and brightness. (From Stevens, S. S.: The surprising simplicity of sensory metrics, Am. Psychol. **17:** 29-39, copyright 1962 by the American Psychological Association, Reprinted by permission.)

the stimulus for a different quality is substituted (for example, stimulating the eye with blue light for a time and then substituting yellow light)? What happens when two different qualities are presented at the same time—how does the eye respond to blue and yellow light, both presented at once? Various kinds of sensory reactions to continued stimulation and to changes in sensory quality are the subject of this section.

Adaptation

Energy of specific physical nature and amount was defined as the adequate stimulus for a given receptor—light of a specified intensity and wavelength range for the eye, air pressure changes of a specified frequency and amplitude for the ear, and so on, Increases in energy within these limits result in increases in the percieved intensity of the stimulus. In some receptors *constant* energy input over a period of time results in a *decrease* in perceived intensity. If the decrease in perceived intensity results from a decrease in receptor sensitivity, the phenomenon is called **adaptation.** For example, the smell of flowers is quite noticeable on entering a florist's shop, but it nearly disappears after remaining in the shop for 20 minutes or so. The reason is that the receptors have become insensitive to the flower odor. The extent to which receptors adapt differs from one sensory modality to another. Adaptation to a constant stimulus is nearly complete for smell under most conditions, resulting in no stimulation after a period of time. Taste adaptation is usually about half complete. Adaptation to moderate stimulus intensities is complete for temperature. Some adaptation occurs in vision and hearing. Very little adaptation occurs for pressure, pain, kinesthesis, or the vestibular senses. If the pressure receptors adapted, one would "lose touch" with his environment. If pain receptors adapted, one would become unaware of injurious stimuli. If kinesthetic receptors adapted, one would lose sensations of position and movement. If the vestibular receptors adapted, one would lose his balance. On the other hand, vision and hearing receptors must change sensitivity in order to increase their intensity range so that they can respond to intense lights and sounds without suffering damage from overstimulation; yet they must respond to faint lights and sounds when not adapted. Once smell or taste receptors have signaled the new stimuli they encounter, they can become insensitive to them without depriving the brain of useful information. Temperature receptors adapt after the body has made the adjustments to temperature change that keep the internal environment constant. If the body cannot cope with cold or warm stimuli in this manner, the receptors continue to signal this fact to the brain.

Habituation

Despite the fact that some receptors are always adapted, the brain receives more information from the remaining receptors than it can cope with at any one time. Of course, some receptors act only to set off coordinated reflexes of various kinds, and one is not aware of these imputs as such. However, the responses to them stimulate other receptors that "feed back" to contribute to the brain's information load. This load of inputs is more than the higher centers of the brain can cope with all at once. Consequently, one is not *aware* of many inputs until he turns his attention to them. This phenomenon is called **habituation.** For example, the reader is unaware of the pressure of the clothes on his back or the background noises in the room until his attention is called to them. The receptors have not adapted, because he is aware of the pressure and sound stimuli when he turns his attention to them. Habituation therefore depends on the function of higher brain centers. These centers deal with only a limited number of the inputs bombarding the brain at any given time.

Consequences of adaptation: contrast and afterimages

When a sense organ adapts to a stimulus of a given *sensory quality,* its sensitivity to other sensory qualities may be unimpaired or even enhanced. Continued stimulation of the eye with red light, for example, decreases sensitivity to red but *increases* sensitivity to green. A continuous sweet stimulus raises the taste threshold to sweet but *lowers* the threshold to sour. This phenomenon is called **contrast.** When both stimuli are present at once, **simultaneous contrast** occurs. For instance, if the subject looks at a card painted half red and half green, the red area next to the green will look redder than the remainder of the red area, and the green area next to the red will look greener than the remainder of the green. Devotees of Chinese sweet and sour spareribs are enjoying simultaneous contrast—the sweet taste is accentuated by the presence of the sour taste and vice versa.

If stimuli that mutually enhance one another are presented in succession rather than simultaneously, **successive contrast** will occur. If you look at a red card until your visual receptors have partially adapted and *then* look at a green card, the green card will look greener than it otherwise would because the eye has increased sensitivity to green. In a similar way a lemon tastes more sour after eating a candy bar.

Afterimages occur when the receptors continue to respond after the stimulus ceases acting on them. **Positive afterimages** usually result from *brief, intense* stimulation. The receptor continues to respond for a time just as it did during stimulation. For example, if you stare briefly at an unshaded light bulb and then look at a blank wall, you will continue to see the filament of the bulb for a time.

Negative afterimages result from *prolonged, moderate* stimulation of a given quality. The receptors adapt to that quality, and the threshold of another quality is lowered so that the second quality is perceived when the first is no longer sensed. When the stimulus is removed, the receptors continue to respond, not with the same quality, but with an *opposite* quality. Thus, if you stare at a green card for a minute or two and then look at a gray wall, you will perceive the image of a red card on the wall.

Compensation and fusion

If two stimuli of different quality are presented to the same receptor, either **compensation** or **fusion** may occur. Compensation occurs when the two stimuli interact to neutralize the response of the receptor. For example, the odors of balsam and beeswax are quite distinct when smelled one at a time. If both stimuli are presented at once, the subject smells nothing. Fusion occurs when the two stimuli interact so as to cause a *qualitatively* different sensation. For example, a mixture of red and yellow stimuli can result in sensation of orange.

CUES TO PERCEPTION

As previously stated, perception occurs when sensations interact together and with traces of past experiences in the central nervous system. Physiologically, little is known of how the nervous system integrates incoming sensations with the traces left by past sensations inputs. There is some knowledge of how incoming sensations interact in perception, at least so far as *cues* to the *location* of the stimulus are concerned.

Localization

How do we perceive the spatial location of stimuli? A simple example is provided by the sense of touch (pressure). When a point on the surface of the body is touched, we can locate the stimulus immediately. This can be explained by the fact that touch is a topographical sense—each point on the body that is stimulated sends nerve impulses to a corresponding point in a sensory projection area of the brain. Therefore each point touched carries its own "local sign." This is only a partial answer, however, leaving the questions of how the brain recognizes where it has been stimulated and how it deals with this information. As explained below, we have partial answers to these questions also.

To raise a more complex perceptual question, how do we localize stimuli at a distance by sight and hearing? Babies indicate by their reactions that they project visual images as distinct from themselves by 3 or 4 months of age. Perhaps this can be partially understood in terms of simpler topographic senses. If one stimulates two adjacent but separated fingertips with two vibrators, the sensation is localized by the subject in space betwen the two fingers (after some training). If one presses the tip of a screwdriver or a pencil on the table, with the other end against the palm, the sensation of pressure is felt on the palm, as its "local sign" would indicate. If one starts tapping the table with a screwdriver held in this same fashion, the sensations include movements and shock to the hand. After about 2 hours' training in this task, subjects localize the sensations at the tip of the screwdriver. Perhaps this is the way in which skilled workmen project their pressure sensations to the tips of their tools.

Lateral inhibition. The concept of **lateral inhibition** plays a role in localization because the stimulus is often more widespread that the point at which it is localized. For example, an observer walking by a row of identical loudspeakers, each producing an identical tone, perceives one loudspeaker keeping pace with him. The input from loudspeakers lateral to the one he is opposite is suppressed. A vibratory stimulus to the skin produces widespread traveling waves of skin distortion, as seen by high-spead photography. Yet the stimulus is easily localized at the point where the tim of the vibrator touches the skin. This is evidently the case because the point stimulated is surrounded by an area where skin sensations are inhibited. This inhibition requires efferent control of sensory input, a mechanism that has been clearly demonstrated for vision, hearing, and pressure sensations.

Lateral inhibition plays a role in some of the more complex phenomena of sensory contrast. One can illuminate one side of the retina (sensory tissue) of the eye with bright light, and use gradually diminishing light across the retina followed by an area of constant illumination, then diminishing light until the other side of the retina is illuminated by only a dim light. The subject sees a sudden decrease in brightness where the diminishing light becomes constant and a sudden increase in brightness where the increasing brightness becomes constant. The same intensity changes can be shown by using a gradient of amplitude of vibration applied to the skin. The contrast effect is apparently caused by inhibition of input from the area between the areas of maximum and minimum stimulation. For example, when two areas of the skin stimulated by a temperature of $39°$ C. are separated by an area stimulated by a warmer temperature of $42°$ C., heat sensations are perceived only in the $39°$ C. areas. The same demonstration is possible with taste. When two areas on the tongue are stimulated with a weak taste sensation, and a strong-tasting substance is placed between them, the strong taste is not perceived.

Localization and constancy

Differences and changes in sensory input in vision and hearing are aids to the perception of localization. In hearing, for example, the difference in the response of the two ears because of their position on either side of the head serves as a way of locating the *source* of a sound stimulus. The two eyes respond differently as a visual stimulus approaches or recedes, and each eye also makes certain adjustments that act as *cues* to the distance of an object from the viewer. In forming perceptions the brain also makes certain "inferences" about the **constancy** of stimuli. For example, a visual stimulus increases in apparent *extent* (size) as it comes closer to the subject. The subject could assume that its *apparent* size was increasing because it was actually getting bigger or because it was getting closer. The latter assumption is frequently made; objects are assumed to stay constant in size. They are also perceived as remaining constant in shape. A coin held at an angle to the eye makes an oval image on the retina —it is assumed that the oval image is caused by the position of the coin, not by a change in shape. Such assumptions are called *constancy phenomena,* and the extent to which they are the result of learned or inherited perceptual tendencies has been the subject of much research.

SUMMARY

Physical energy excites receptors when they are sensitive to the given form and intensity of energy. The resulting sensations are elaborated by the CNS into perceptions whenever several sensation inputs and CNS traces from past experience are integrated. Sensations are studied in man when a subject reports on those aspects of perception that depend on sensation. This is the method of introspection. In animal subjects, electrodes are used to detect responses of the receptors, nerves, or brain in the method of evoked potentials. The inputs from stimuli are controlled by the experimenter in both methods.

Stimuli are physical events to which receptors respond. Receptors are specialized to respond to specific forms of energy. Some specialized receptors excite those parts of the brain whose activity results in conscious sensation; some receptors cause only somatic or visceral reflexes or arouse the brain in response to needs. There are receptors specialized to respond to mechanical, thermal, chemical, acoustical, or photic energy. When a receptor is activated by the form of energy for which it is specialized, it has received an adequate stimulus; if it is excited by another form of energy, it receives an inadequate stimulus. Either stimulus causes a generator potential that fires sensory neurons.

The modality of the resulting sensation depends on what part of the brain the nerve impulses reach, according to the law of specific nerve energies. Receptors transduce physical energy into nerve impulses. Receptors may be classified by their adequate stimulus. They may be classified by form as unspecialized nerve cells, specialized nerve cells, or specialized receptor cells. They may be classified by location in the head only, or in the whole body, as special senses or general senses. The general senses are somesthesis (pressure, pain, warmth, and cold) and kinesthesis. The special senses are olfaction, vision, gustation, audition, and vestibular sensitivity. Receptors can be classified by the functional location of their stimuli as exteroceptors, interoceptors, or proprioceptors. Exteroceptors include cutaneous senses; interoceptors include organic senses. Proprioceptors respond to body position and movement.

The attributes common to all sensation are quality, intensity, extent, and duration. There are both primary and secondary qualities in sensory modalities that have more than one quality. Quality is signaled to the CNS by the arrival of nerve impulses at a given *place* in the brain when different modalities are involved, and perhaps by impulse pattern for different qualities within a modality. Intensity increases reach the CNS with the firing of more nerve cells at a faster rate. Increased extent stimulates a larger area in the brain; increased duration stimulates for a longer period of time.

Sensory modalities can be classified as topographic or nontopographic, depending on whether the receptors, sensory pathways, and cortical projection area are organized in an orderly spatial fashion. The range of stimulus change to which the receptor responds is narrow for topographic inputs and broad for nontopographic inputs. Topographic inputs require more receptors and sensory neurons to respond to the same range of stimulus change as nontopographic inputs. The total summated frequency of firing of the responding neurons need not change to signal an intensity change when the different individual neurons respond to signal a change in quality.

The study that compares changes in the physical stimulus with resulting changes in sensation is called psychophysics. Thresholds can be measured for the four attributes of sensation. The absolute threshold is the minimum level of stimulation that can be detected 50% of the time. The difference threshold is the minimum stimulus difference in a given direction that can be detected 50% of the time. The terminal threshold is the sensation intensity that cannot be exceeded 50% of the time.

Weber's law states that the relationship between the difference threshold for intensity and the stimulus level from which the increase was taken is constant for a given modality. The constant ratio is smaller the more sensitive the receptor, but the ratio increases at very high and very low intensities. Fechner's law states that the relationship between stimulus intensity and sensation intensity is a logarithmic one. The general psychophysical law gives a power function, relating stimulus magnitude and sensation intensity when ratio scales are used.

Some sensory modalities become less sensitive when they are stimulated at a constant rate for a period of time, a phenomenon called adaptation. Sensory inputs that do not adapt completely may not be attended to, a phenomenon called habituation. True adaptation to one quality in a modality may enhance sensitivity to another quality in that modality (sensory contrast). If the two stimuli are presented simultaneously, simultaneous contrast results; if they are presented successively, successive contrast results. Afterimages result when the sensation outlasts the stimulus. Positive afterimages are a continuation of the same sensation and result from brief, intense stimulation. Negative afterimages are a sensation of opposite quality from the stimulus and result from prolonged moderate stimulation. Presenting two stimuli of different qualities at once to a sense organ may cause compensation when they cancel each other out, resulting in no sensation, or

fusion when the result is a sensation having a new quality.

One way in which sensations interact to form perceptions involves the problem of localization. "Local sign" helps explain localization in topographic senses, but projection of the input in space is also involved and demonstrable. Lateral inhibition is necessary to sharpen the cues to localization. Lateral inhibition requires efferent control of sensory input, a mechanism that also explains contrast phenomena in several senses.

Sensations interact as cues when the location of the stimulus is perceived; the nature of the cues to location may be sought in some attribute of the sensation. The brain makes assumptions about the constancy of the shape, size, and so on of the stimulus (the constancy phenomena) in utilizing these cues.

READINGS

Blough, D. S.: Experiments in animal psychophysics, Sci. Am. **205:**113-122, July 1961. (W. H. Freeman Reprint No. 458.)

Boring, E. G.: The physical dimensions of consciousness, New York, 1963, Dover Publications, Inc.

Boring, E. G., Langfeld, H. S., and Weld, H. P.: Foundations of psychology, New York, 1948, John Wiley & Sons, Inc.

Case, J.: Sensory mechanisms, New York, 1966, The Macmillan Co.

Crombie, A. C.: Early concepts of the senses and the mind, Sci. Am. **210:**108-116, May 1964. (W. H. Freeman Reprint No. 184.)

Green, R. T., and Stacey, B. G.: Misapplication of the misapplied constancy hypothesis, Life Sci. **5:**1871-1880, 1966.

Held, R.: Placticity in sensory-motor systems, Sci. Am. **213:**84-94, Nov. 1965. (W. H. Freeman Reprint No. 494.)

Mueller, C. G.: Sensory psychology, Englewood Cliffs, N.J., 1965, Prentice-Hall, Inc.

Murch, G. M.: Visual and auditory perception, New York, 1973, Bobbs-Merrill Co., Inc.

Stevens, S. S.: On the psychophysical law, Psychol. Rev. **64:**153-188, 1957. (Bobbs-Merrill Reprint No. P-336.)

von Békésy, G.: Similarities of inhibition in the different sense organs, Am. Psychol. **24:**707-719, 1969.

von Buddenbrock, W.: The senses, Ann Arbor, Mich., 1958, University of Michigan Press.

chapter 7

Somesthesis

OVERVIEW

This chapter deals with the least specialized of the sensory modalities—sensations of pressure, temperature, and pain that come from the skin surface, muscles, and viscera throughout the body. Collectively these sensations are called somesthesis. The chapter begins by classifying somesthetic sensations in contrast with the proprioceptive senses of position and movement. Some of the methods used in studying somesthesis are discussed. The primary and secondary sensory qualities follow, with proofs for the primary qualities. The problems involved in specifying receptors that determine primary qualities are examined. The next section summarizes what is known of the somesthetic receptors and the sensory phenomena that result from stimulating them. Pressure, temperature, and pain inputs receive attention. The nerve pathways serving somesthesis are traced from the receptors to the brain. The chapter begins by defining somesthesis in contrast to proprioception, and it ends by contrasting the somesthetic nerve pathways to those serving proprioception. A general plan for both inputs begins the section on nerve pathways. Fiber grouping by somesthetic modality in the spinal cord is contrasted with additional fiber grouping by body location in the brain. Secondary sensory pathways are traced. A more functional classification of somesthetic and proprioceptive inputs ends the chapter.

SENSATIONS OF THE BODY

The sensations that seem to come from the body are of two general kinds: (1) those of *condition,* such as pressure, pain, or temperature sensations in some part of the body, and (2) those of *position* and *movement* of some part of the body. The sensations of *condition* are the subject of this chapter, but the sensations of position and movement will be briefly classified by way of contrast.

Somesthesis

Somesthesis (Gr., 'body perception') includes sensations of pressure, pain, and temperature and their complex combinations that come from all over the body. Somesthetic sensations are further classified according to which of the three layers of body tissue is stimulated. Sensations from the skin are called **cutaneous** somesthetic sensations, sensations from the muscles are **muscular** somesthetic sensations, and sensations from the viscera are **visceral** somesthetic sensations. In each case sensations of pressure, warmth, cold, and pain are involved.

The cutaneous sensations originate from receptors located just beneath the surface of the skin. These receptors have received the most study because they are most accessible to the investigator and because they relate to conditions at the surface of the body, where the outside world is encountered. Somesthetic receptors stimulate reflex responses from pressure receptors that affect posture; warm and cold receptors stimulate homeostatic reflexes that maintain body temperature; and pain receptors initiate protective reflexes that prevent injury. Along with other exteroceptors such as those serving vision and hearing, these receptors initiate complex adjustments to changes in the environment that are often accompanied by awareness of that environment—"touch" (pressure) sensations used in finding the way past obstacles in a dark room, temperature changes that lead one to put on or take off a coat, pain sensations that prevent one from stepping into a shower when the water is too hot, and so on.

Somesthetic sensations from the muscles also initiate reflexes. Pressure sensations in joints set off complex coordinated reflexes that make a movement depend on the initial position of a limb. Input from temperature receptors changes the blood flow to a muscle as needed. Pain reflexes in muscles can cause contractions (cramps). These simpler adjustments are usually accompanied by awareness and are followed by more complex responses to the conditions signaled by the receptors.

Visceral somesthetic sensations come from from the gut (digestive organs) and the blood vessels. Pressure sensations are often felt in digestion, and they initiate reflexes necessary for that process. Pressure receptors initiate the reflexes that empty the bladder and bowels. Temperature stimulation seems to be restricted to the mouth and esophagus, but in combination with pain, it can prevent swallowing or cause vomiting of a dangerously hot or cold substance. Visceral pain is poorly localized, but it still serves a warning function, particularly in the case of headache or stomach pain. All these sensations are interoceptive.

Somesthetic sensations—cutaneous, muscular, or visceral—can serve to arouse and sustain behavior when adverse or uncomfortable sensations are involved. This is particularly true of pain. Some somesthetic sensations can therefore act as drives since a drive is any mechanism that arouses and sustains behavior. Pressure, warmth, cold, and pain sensations are included therein. Pressure sensations from the bowel and bladder arouse and sustain behavior until evacuation reflexes are permitted to act. Our adjustments to pain and to excessive heat or cold also act as drives. Internal or external warmth, cold, or pain will sustain a high level of response activity until a comfortable temperature is found or until pain is relieved.

Proprioception

Proprioception involves sensations of *position* and *movement* rather than sensations of condition (warm, cold, pressure, or pain). Although somesthesis is a general sense involving receptors found over the entire body, proprioception involves both a general sense and special senses found only in the head.

The special senses of proprioception are the **vestibular senses.** Their receptors are found in the nonauditory labyrinth of the inner ear and will be considered in detail in Chapter 8. The vestibular senses respond to the position and movements of the head. Besides initiating reflex reactions of balance, coordination, and eye movements, they are indirectly responsible for sensations of dizziness and nausea.

The general proprioceptive sense is **kinesthesis.** Kinesthetic receptors in muscles regulate muscle tone by stimulating the **stretch reflex** (Chapters 4 and 12), which partially contracts muscles according to the degree to which they are stretched. These receptors send impulses to the **cerebellum** to regulate balance and coordination, but they do not directly result in conscious sensations. Other kinesthetic receptors in the joints, tendons, and connective tissue of muscle send impulses to the cerebral cortex and result in sensations of position and movement of the limbs. Their nervous connections will be noted later in this chapter by way of contrast with those of somesthesis. The study of muscle tonus, coordination, etc., will be deferred to Chapter 8.

METHODS OF STUDY

That which is known of somesthetic input comes from three study approaches: introspective, anatomical, and physiological.

Introspective study involves the familiar approach of stimulating a human subject under controlled conditions and asking him to report his sensations. The sensations of warmth, cold, pressure, and pain from the surface of the skin have been studied in this way. Sometimes the introspective technique has been combined with the anatomical technique, as when points on the skin sensitive to these four stimuli are mapped, after which the skin of that area is removed, stained, and sectioned for study of skin receptors under the microscope.

Anatomical study involves the tracing of tracts and centers in the brain served by sensory nerves coming from somesthetic and proprioceptive receptors. Introspective studies are subject to error because they involve only those receptor mechanisms concerned in conscious sensations and because subject reports cannot be confirmed except by other subject reports—there is no way of comparing the conscious sensations of two subjects. Anatomical studies can tell us only what receptors and tracts look like—not how they work in organizing responses. Furthermore, tracing anatomical tracts in the brain that serve sensation reveals only the most direct input pathways.

Pathways involving many synapses and diffuse inputs cannot be traced by anatomical means because they are so diffuse that they show only the many *possibilities* for input. The ones which are actually involved in receptor input can be detected only by physiological means. The favorite physiological method for this purpose is the *method of evoked potentials.* The receptors are stimulated electrically or, by use of their adequate stimuli, in an anesthetized animal. Electrodes are placed in various tracts, brain areas, and brain nuclei to detect where the input *actually* goes. New anesthetics have been developed that do not depress the excitability of the brain, yet they paralyze response on the part of the animal so that reactions of the brain to sensory input can be studied with the brain in a more or less normal condition. It is assumed that if the adequate stimuli for

pressure, temperature, and so on are used, the appropriate inputs are being stimulated. Unfortunately, the animal cannot be asked to report on what other inputs are stimulated at the same time. To that extent our data are uncertain.

The physiological methods remain, however, the ones least subject to error. The newest and most promising of these methods involves implanting electrodes in the brain of an anesthetized animal that is allowed to recover and then can be "plugged in" to record electrical activity of specific parts of the brain while the animal is responding normally to stimuli controlled by the experimenter. This is the most "true-to-life" situation; ultimately it will probably give us the most information on the way the sensory systems of the brain transact their business and control the behavior of the normal animal. Unfortunately, there is not yet as much information based on the newer methods as we would like.

SOMESTHETIC QUALITIES
Primary qualities

The primary qualities of somesthesis are pressure, cold, warmth, and pain. Introspectively, these are the irreducible qualities of somesthetic sensation, although combinations of these sensations, as well as intermittent stimulation, can produce more complex sensations. The bulk of the evidence suggests that each of the four primary qualities represents a separate sensory *modality,* that is, a pressure sense, warmth sense, cold sense, or pain sense. However, some hold that one or the other of these inputs, particularly that of pain, may represent a pattern of inputs rather than a separate modality. In any case it is evident that each of the four modalities, except pain, is served by several kinds of receptors.

Secondary qualities

Secondary qualities can result from either intermittent stimulation of one primary quality or the combination of two or more primary qualities. Examples of intermittent stimulation are the tickle sensation, which results from intermittent pressure stimulation, and the itch, which is caused by intermittent pain stimulation. A combination of primary pressure and cold sensations results in a secondary sensation of wetness from dry stimuli; weak pressure and warmth produce an oily sensation. Hardness has been produced by cold pressure with a good boundary, and softness, by an uneven warm pressure with a poor boundary. Stickiness is a variable moving pressure and clamminess can be sensed from a cold softness that is reported to be unpleasant.

Proof for four modalities of skin sensitivity

Visceral and muscle somesthesis are not ordinarily accessible to stimulation in human subjects who can report on their sensations while being stimulated. Most of the evidence was derived from experiments involving cutaneous sensitivity, and the evidence emphasizes the *punctate,* or point-to-point, distribution of spots on the skin that are most sensitive to either pressure, cold, warmth, or pain. Reliable distributions of spots that are sensitive to each primary quality have been found, despite the many kinds of receptors found in the skin.

Skin mapping. The skin on different parts of the body may be marked off in tiny (1 mm.) squares by use of a stamp pad and ink. This produces a small area marked like graph paper. Each square is then stimulated with a hair (for pressure), a warm or cold rod (for temperature), and a needle (for pain). By grading the intensity of each stimulus, absolute thresholds can be established for each square. Although nearly all spots will respond to pressure, some will have a higher threshold than others. Different spots will be *differentially sensitive* to cold, warmth, and pain as well. One spot may have a high threshold to cold and a low threshold to warmth, whereas another

may show the opposite effect. This suggests that one spot is closer to a warm receptor and the other closer to a cold receptor. Furthermore, those parts of the body that are most sensitive to cold stimulation may not be the same parts that are most sensitive to pressure or pain. For example, the face is exquisitely sensitive to cold but relatively insensitive to pain. A simple demonstration of punctate sensitivity may be made by drawing a pencil point lightly across the skin; pressure, warmth, cold, and various secondary qualities such as tickle and itch will be aroused in turn as the stimulus passes over different points of the skin. As the pencil is drawn over the fingertip, more pressure sensations will be felt; drawing it across the cheek results in more cold sensations. Again, this demonstration provides an indication of the different distribution of receptors for the four cutaneous sensations.

Spark gaps. The stimuli used so far arouse pressure sensations because they distort the skin surface. In another method of stimulation, sparks from a high-voltage source may be "jumped" to the skin in order to electrically stimulate receptors there. If the amperage (rate of current flow) is kept small, the subject does not sense a shock. Instead, from different points on the skin he will sense pressure, warmth, cold, or pain, as well as combinations of these sensations; warmth, cold, or pain can therefore be stimulated independently of pressure sensations.

Excitation and conduction time. If different kinds of receptors serve the four primary qualities, then the receptors should also differ in the rapidity with which they respond, and the sensory neurons should differ in the rapidity with which they conduct impulses to the central nervous system. Reaction time to the four kinds of stimuli should differ as a result, and this seems to be the case. Adaptation time also differs for the four stimuli, indicating receptors that adapt at different rates. Most of the nerve fibers serving pressure are large fibers of the A group (Chapter 4) that conduct rapidly, and reaction time is therefore faster in response to pressure stimuli than in response to warm, cold, or some pain stimuli. The pressure receptors adapt more rapidly than the others. Reaction time for cold is slightly faster than that for warmth—many of the fibers for both seem to be of the B group—but the cold-sensitive receptors are closer to the surface of the skin than are the warm receptors and may therefore be affected sooner by the adequate stimulus. Both adapt, but not as rapidly as pressure receptors. Cold receptors adapt more slowly than those for warmth. Pain may be served by both A and C fibers. The C fibers predominate, however, and conduction speed and reaction time for pain are usually slowest of all. Pain receptors also adapt less and more slowly than those for the other three qualities.

Different effects of cocaine and asphyxia. Cocaine affects fibers without myelin sheaths more than myelinated fibers. C fibers are anesthetized first, then B, and then A. The drug abolishes dull pain (C fibers) first, then temperature change (B fibers), then touch (pressure from A fibers), and finally sharp, or prick, pain (smaller A fibers). **Hypoxia,** or lack of oxygen, has the opposite effect. It affects myelinated fibers first. Sensations from a limb can be asphyxiated (abolished through lack of oxygen) by cutting off blood flow with a tourniquet. Hypoxia abolishes pressure (touch) first, then temperature change, and then pain. As circulation is restored, pain returns while the limb is still numb (no pressure sensations). Anyone who has had a limb "go to sleep" from poor circulation caused by an awkward position can testify that "pins and needles" (pain) sensations return before the limb senses touch.

Nerve pathways. The cutaneous somesthetic modalities are carried in different parts of the tracts of the spinal cord. The

anatomy will be considered in detail near the end of this chapter. As further proof for four modalities, however, tract location differentiates between two groups of sensory modalities. Nerve impulses resulting from pressure stimulation are carried in tracts of the dorsal and ventral funiculi of the cord; nerve impulses serving temperature and pain are carried in tracts in the lateral funiculi. Cranial nerve input for pressure goes to one nucleus, and pain and temperature go to another.

Problems of further modality specification

Despite the proofs for four somesthetic modalities, problems are involved in further specification of the receptor and neural mechanisms underlying the four primary somesthetic qualities. These problems include identifying projection areas in the brain, and receptor specificity.

Projection areas. Separate sensory projection areas in the cerebral cortex have been identified for the sensory modalities of audition and vision (Chapter 5). If pressure, warmth, cold, and pain are separate sensory modalities, their pathways should end on separate projections areas in the cerebral cortex. As far as is known, impulses for pressure arrive at areas 3, 1, and 2 on the postcentral gyrus of the cortex—the somesthetic projection area. Fibers that are carried in the dorsal columns of the spinal cord serve pressure and kinesthesis and end on different parts of the somesthetic sensory projection area. The somesthetic projection area is topographically organized, with inputs from different parts of the body surface ending on different parts of the projection area in a systematic way. Input from single fibers serving joint sensibility appears to end posterior to input serving pressure from the same body area, however. Single-fiber studies do not reveal direct pain input extending beyond the thalamus. The evidence for temperature projection is uncertain. The pain pathways have many collateral fibers to the brainstem reticular formation, which serves to arouse the cortex and other parts of the brain. Similar collateral fibers have not been found for the more discriminative pressure and kinesthetic inputs. Finally, there are indirect inputs through the thalamus for all four modalities that can arouse the secondary somesthetic sensory areas (SII and SIII).

Receptors. If pressure, cold, warmth, and pain are separate senses, then their receptors should each have specialized in different ways in order that each would be sensitive to a specific kind of physical energy. Differences in specialization would be likely to cause differences in the appearance of the various receptors. Are there four or more different kinds of sensory transducers beneath the skin that correspond to the four somesthetic modalities? Anatomical studies show that there are many different-looking receptors beneath the skin. The functions of some are understood, but the functions of others are in doubt. The most common receptor ending, an **anastomosis,** or network, of free nerve endings (Chapter 4), is the least specialized, however. It is difficult to prove four classes of specialized receptors in some areas of the body that are sensitive to the four somesthetic qualities, because *only* free nerve endings are found in these areas. For example, the pinna (external ear) is sensitive to pressure, cold, warmth, and pain; yet it contains only free nerve endings. Perhaps there are four kinds of free nerve endings that differ biochemically or in some other way that is not apparent under the microscope. Perhaps these endings differ in their "connections" to different parts of the brain and are not otherwise specialized at all. Evidence is lacking on these points. There are more specialized receptors in the more sensitive areas of the skin, and the specialized nature of some of them is understood. It may be that these specialized receptors have evolved from different kinds of free nerve endings. Others feel that some

specialized endings are merely tangled "rejects" from among free nerve endings that never reached their destination near the skin surface.

STRUCTURE OF THE SKIN

The structure of the skin must be considered to see how receptors have specialized for pressure, cold, warmth, and pain (Fig. 7-1). The skin consists of two layers, the tough outer **epidermis** and the thick fibrous inner **dermis.** Beneath these two layers is an insulating layer of **subcutaneous fat,** a layer that is thicker (and therefore softer) in women than in men. The top layer of the epidermis (corneum) is made up of dead cells because living cells cannot survive exposure to air, water, or the temperatures and pressures of the external environment. These dead cells are continually flaking off—you can see a white streak made up of these cells by raking a fingernail across your arm. The outer, dead layer of epidermis is continually replaced by living cells from the inner layer of epidermis (malpighian layer). Some of the more superficial receptors (believed to serve light pressure or touch) are found in the inner layer of epidermis, principally **free nerve endings** and **tactile disks.** Most of the cutaneous receptors are found in the dermis, whose ridged surface accounts for fingerprints and palm prints of the hand. **Meissner's corpuscles** and **basket endings** are believed to serve touch, whereas **Krause's end bulbs** may be cold receptors and **Ruffini's endings** may serve warmth. **Pacinian corpuscles** ("deep pressure" receptors) are found at the surface of the subcutaneous fat layer. The form of the receptors shown in Fig. 7-1 is an idealized one in each case; many mixed and unidentifiable forms of **encapsulated** nerve endings are found, and some areas of the body have only free nerve endings. Finally, specialized endings are constantly dying or being destroyed by direct damage or lack of an adequate local

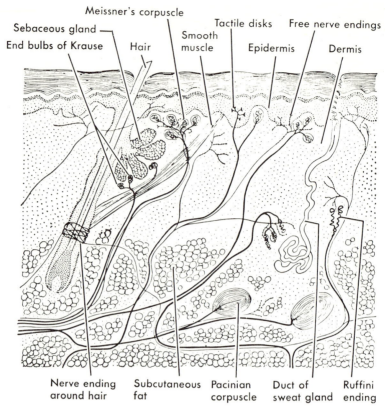

Meissner's corpuscle

Sebaceous gland

End bulbs of Krause   Hair   Smooth muscle   Tactile disks   Free nerve endings   Epidermis   Dermis

Nerve ending around hair   Subcutaneous fat   Pacinian corpuscle   Duct of sweat gland   Ruffini ending

Fig. 7-1. Composite diagram of skin and its receptors. Epidermis, dermis, and subcutaneous fat layers are shown, with receptors to be found in each layer. Not all endings shown are found in any one skin area. (From Gardner, E. O.: Fundamentals of neurology, ed. 5, Philadelphia, 1968, W. B. Saunders Co.; modified from Woolard, H. H., Weddel, G., and Harpman, J. A.: J. Anat. **74:**413-440, 1940.)

blood supply. They are replaced, however, as regenerating fibers reach peripheral tissue.

PRESSURE
Receptors

Several kinds of specialized endings appear to serve pressure sensitivity. Most of them are located near the surface of the skin, although some are located deeper beneath the skin and in the viscera, joints, and connective tissue of muscle. The adequate stimulus for each receptor seems to be a kind of mechanical deformation. Basket endings encircle the base of each body hair and are sensitive to movement of the hair, as you can discover by bending a single

hair on your arm with the point of a pencil.

Meissner's corpuscles are found in hairless regions that are particularly sensitive to touch (light pressure), such as the fingertips. This distribution suggests that they are specialized pressure-sensitive receptors. They are dermal layer receptors. Free nerve endings are found in the epidermis over the entire body. In slightly more touch-sensitive regions they become more or less specialized tactile disks. These superficially located free endings and tactile disks do not serve pain, because the superficial epidermis can be peeled off without pain sensations; their superficial location suggests that they are pressure receptors. They are found in the less pressure-sensitive areas of the skin, where more specialized-looking receptors appear to be absent.

Pacinian corpuscles are "deep pressure" receptors. They are located beneath the dermis, respond to skin deformation, and are especially sensitive to vibration. These receptors are also found in the mesenteries, sheets of transparent connective tissue from which the intestines hang beneath the stomach. Here they are sensitive to the movements of the stomach and intestines in digestion. Pacinian corpuscles are found in the walls of hollow viscera, such as the bladder and colon, and give rise to the sensations accompanying the need to urinate or defecate. They are also found near joints, where they signal position and movement of the limbs.

Most modern writers assume that there are two principal sets of cutaneous pressure receptors: (1) basket nerve ends around hair follicles and (2) Meissner's corpuscles in hairless areas. The belief is based on the distribution of pressure-sensitive "spots" on the skin, with the most sensitive spots to "windward" of the way hair leans, so that the basket ending beneath that spot is stimulated. Another reason is the greater frequency of Meissner's corpuscles in the most pressure-sensitive hairless areas. Free nerve ends in the epidermis are believed to give less discriminative pressure sensations and pacinian corpuscles can react to rapid pressure change in a brief fashion. Mechanical experiments with skin stimulation have established that the true adequate stimulus for pressure at the skin is tension or "stretch" of the skin (force per linear extent of skin contacted). A hair glued to the skin and pulled will give the same pressure sensation as pushing an equal-sized hair into the skin.

Pressure receptor as transducer

The pacinian corpuscle is the largest of the encapsulated endings and is visible to the naked eye. Its size lends it to the study of how the physical energy of pressure is transformed, or transduced, into nerve impulses, a different form of energy. The encapsulated ending looks like an onion, with a myelinated nerve fiber invading the core of the onion. Distorting the pacinian corpuscle sets up a generator potential (Chapter 4) of nonpropagated current flow in the ending, and this generator potential causes repetitive firing of the sensory neuron. The onion-shaped capsule around the nerve ending can be destroyed down to its innermost layer without impairing the generator potential. However, the capsule itself will not produce a generator potential if the neuron is destroyed. The capsule probably serves to spread pressure over a larger area of the nerve ending, which increases the size of the generator potential; several points on the nerve ending will *summate* when they are stimulated at the same time. That is, they will show increased response over pressure on a single point. The capsule may spread the stimulation in a like fashion. Greater pressure on the capsule results in a larger generator potential and a faster rate (frequency) of neuron firing to signal an increase in intensity.

Classification of pressure receptors

In animal studies, recording from single sensory nerve fibers serving the skin has revealed two types of response to pressure stimulation and therefore two kinds of receptors with different functions: (1) One type of receptor causes a rapid burst of firing in its neurons, after which the receptor adapts; sometimes a second burst of firing results when the stimulus is removed; (2) the second type of receptor reacts to stimulus onset by causing a high-frequency transient burst of firing that depends on the rate of stimulus onset; this burst of firing declines to a steady rate of discharge. Functionally, the first type of receptor acts as a movement detector. The second type reacts to both movement and the intensity of continuous skin deformity. Movement detection alerts us to pressure change on the skin, whereas a steady rate of neuron firing keeps us "in touch" with the environment.

Pressure sensitivity

The pressure sensitivity of different points on the surface of the body can be tested by using weighted rods on different contact areas. A rod (esthesiometer) is placed lightly on the skin, and weights are added until the subject reports a pressure sensation. In an older method, bristles of increasing thickness are pressed against the skin until they bend. The thinnest bristle the subject can sense under this much pressure gives a rough guide to the threshold. Some parts of the body are found to be much more sensitive than others (Table 7-1). The tongue probably has the lowest absolute threshold, and the fingertips are also sensitive. These parts have more specialized receptors than parts of the body with higher thresholds, such as the back of the forearm or the loin.

Two-point threshold. Sensitivity to pressure can also be tested by using the **two-point threshold.** This is the smallest distance between two points that can be recognized as distinct by the subject. It is therefore a difference threshold rather than an absolute threshold. However, it should in-dicate sensitivity because it is closely re-lated to pressure receptor *density* in the area tested, that is, to the number of receptors there are per square centimeter of skin surface. If two adjacent receptors are stimulated by the two points, the sensation will be that of a single point. For recognition of two distinct points, stimulated receptors must be separated by unstimulated receptors. The more pressure receptors there are in a given skin area, the closer together they will lie—and the closer together will be two points that are recognizable by the subject as separate. The results obtained by using the two-point threshold agree closely with those from absolute threshold measurements obtained in testing the relative sensitivity of various parts of the body to pressure.

Localization. The ease with which one can locate a pressure stimulus on the skin surface (localization) should also indicate receptor density. The closer together the receptors are in an area of the skin, such as the fingertip, the more nerve fibers there are to reach the central nervous system from pressure receptors in that area—and, consequently, the larger is the cortical projection area devoted to that part of the body. To simplify, the brain has more separate receptor inputs in that area and is therefore more able to locate precisely the point stimulated. Experiments on localization show that where the absolute and two-point pressure thresholds are lowest, localization is most accurate.

In contrast with the fairly accurate localization of pressure sensations on the body surface, visceral localization is very poor. Visceral sensations are felt as diffuse, partly because there are fewer pressure receptors in the viscera. On the other hand, localization of bladder pressure, for example, is quite accurate. One reason suggested for poor visceral localization is the lack of confirmation by other senses. Pressure stimuli on the skin can be confirmed by sight or touch often enough so that the subject learns

Table 7-1. Stimulus thresholds for pressure*

Body parts	Grams/mm.^{2}
Tip of tongue	2
Tip of finger	3
Back of finger	5
Front of forearm	8
Back of hand	12
Calf of leg	16
Abdomen	26
Back of forearm	33
Loin	48
Thick parts of sole	250

*From Woodworth, R. S., and Schlosberg, H.: Experimental psychology, New York, 1954, Holt, Rinehart & Winston, Inc., p. 274.

to relate small differences in skin stimulation to small differences in the point stimulated. Obviously one cannot see pressure stimulations being applied to the stomach or intestines. One can, however, sense the pressure relief in the bladder that results from urination.

Adaptation. Adaptation is partly a function of the receptor and partly a function of the stimulus. Continuous pressure stimulation of a part of the body will result in a gradual decrease in sensation, and sometimes the adaptation will be so complete that no pressure is sensed. This is true of light pressure sensations such as those commonly resulting from wearing eyeglasses or rings, the presence of which can no longer be felt after a time. It also takes a long time after a pressure stimulus is removed before the skin recovers its original shape; thus the distortion of the pressure endings continues to change after the stimulus is removed. The receptors continue to fire neurons, giving a pressure sensation that is similar to a positive aftersensation. As a result, removal of a ring or a wristwatch may leave the sensation that one is still wearing it because the skin is still distorted for a time. This may be one reason why rings and watches are so often mislaid.

TEMPERATURE

Cold and warmth appear to be separate sensory modalities, although experiments on one of these senses commonly involves the other. When cutaneous temperature sensitivity is studied, for example, local reactions in the blood vessels of the skin to a warm stimulus will change the threshold to cold, and vice versa. In response to a warm stimulus, blood vessels near the surface will dilate to cool the area; the threshold for subsequent warm stimuli will be raised and the threshold for cold stimuli lowered. In response to a cold stimulus the same vessels will constrict to preserve body heat, thereby raising the threshold to subsequent cold stimuli and lowering the threshold to

warm stimuli. The skin temperature at which neither warm nor cold sensations are experienced is called **physiological zero;** physiological zero shifts as a result of blood vessel reactions in the skin and also as a result of adaptation in the receptors themselves. The adequate stimulus for cold is a temperature at the skin surface of $35°$ to $39°$ C. or below; the adequate stimulus for warmth is a temperature of $34°$ to $35°$ C. or above. These temperatures overlap because of changes in physiological zero. The adequate stimulus temperature depends on the skin temperature itself. The sensation of *heat* is a secondary quality composed of warmth and pain stimulation; the "stinging cold" occasionally experienced in cold climates is a combination of cold and pain.

Skin mapping

Cold and warm spots on the skin can be mapped with small cold and warm stimulus points, as with the punctate stimuli used for pressure. They show a fairly reliable distribution (70% to 80%) but are not as fixed as are pressure-sensitive points. The receptors for warmth and cold are farther beneath the skin than the more superficial pressure receptors, and localization may suffer as a result. In addition, temperature changes are more diffusely spread throughout the skin than are the mechanical distortions of pressure. Table 7-2 shows that the skin is more sensitive to cold than to warmth in terms of the number of sensitive spots per square centimeter. The areas of the body most sensitive to cold, however, are usually also those most sensitive to warmth, although there are reliable exceptions to this rule. In general, the face is one of the most sensitive areas to both kinds of stimuli.

Receptor location

Cold and warm "pulses" can be applied to the outside of the prepuce (foreskin) of the penis, and their arrival at the underside of the prepuce can be measured with appropriate instruments. This procedure can be used to calculate the rate at which the change in temperature moves through the thickness of the prepuce. By timing the report of a cold or warm sensation by the subject, the depth of the cold and warm receptors can be estimated. The results suggest that the cold receptors lie about 0.1 mm. below the surface and that the warm receptors are more diffusely spread about 0.3 mm. below the surface. The experiment also shows that each type of receptor responds to the *absolute temperature* at its depth rather than to a gradient of temperature change from "outside" to "inside." The pulse may be sent through the prepuce from either the "outside" skin surface or the "inside" mucous surface without a change in threshold. The data on the depth of receptors thus obtained agree with the data from experiments with the dog and cat; in the latter experiments a cold or a warm pulse is used as a stimulus to the tongue, and the

time required for nerve impulses to begin is computed.

Receptors

There appear to be both specialized and unspecialized receptors for cold and warm stimuli. Krause's end bulbs (Fig. 7-1) are found at the proper depth (0.1 mm.) to serve as cold receptors, judging by the experiments on the prepuce that were just described. These receptors are found in mucous membrane regions and in other areas sensitive to cold, such as the face. In one experiment, tissue was removed and studied under the microscope after having been mapped and the cold spots marked. Krause's end bulbs were found nearer cold spots than spots less sensitive to cold. The experiment has been repeated on the prepuce of the penis, where the depth of the receptors has been more precisely determined. In a more daring experiment the transparent cornea of the subject's eye was stained (with methylene blue) and studied under a microscope while it was being stimulated. Only Krause's end bulbs and free nerve endings are found at the edge of the cornea. In the areas most sensitive to cold, Krause's end bulbs could be seen.

Ruffini's endings are at the proper depth (0.3 mm.) to serve as warm receptors. They are found most profusely in warmth-sensitive parts of the body. Mapping warm spots and then studying the skin under them with a microscope has been done in the same way as that described for cold. The prepuce and other warmth-sensitive parts of the skin have been studied in this manner. The results are not as clear-cut as those for cold spots. However, when Ruffini's endings are found, they usually lie near spots on the skin that are the most sensitive to warm stimuli.

If Krause's end bulbs are cold receptors and Ruffini's cylinders are warm receptors, they are not the only endings serving warm and cold. In some nonmucous areas such as the palm of the hand, there are many en-

Table 7-2. Concentrations of warm and cold spots*

Skin areas	Spots per cm.²	
	Cold	Warm
Forehead	8.0	0.6
Nose	8.0 (side)-13.0 (tip)	1.0
Upper lip	19.0	—
Chin	9.0	—
Chest	9.0	0.3
Upper arm, volar side	5.7	0.3
Upper arm, dorsal side	5.0	0.2
Bend of elbow	6.5	0.7
Forearm, volar side	6.0	0.4
Forearm, dorsal side	7.5	0.3
Back of hand	7.0	0.5
Palm	4.0	0.5
Fingers	2.0-9.0	1.6-2.0
Thigh	5.0	0.4
Lower leg	4.0-6.0	—
Sole of foot	3.0	—

*Based on data from Rein, H.: Z. Biol. **82:**513-535, 1925; and Strughold, H., and Porz, R.: Z. Biol. **91:**563-571, 1931.

capsulated endings. In these areas, however, the encapsulated endings are too varied for classification. Other areas such as the pinna (external ear) have only free nerve endings. These areas *are* sensitive to cold and warmth, but less so than areas with specialized receptors. In areas supplied only by free nerve endings, perhaps the free endings near the surface are cold receptors and those deeper beneath the skin are warm receptors. Free nerve endings may be arranged in layers: the most superficial ones for pressure, deeper ones for cold, still deeper ones serving warm, and the deepest endings serving pain. However, there are theorists who believe that the *pattern* of input from nerve endings determines all four somesthetic qualities.

Temperature phenomena

Experiments involving action potential recording from nerves serving the tongue of the cat and from nerves serving the skin have been done using cold and warm stimuli. These experiments have shown that the nerve endings serving cold and warmth respond to *absolute temperature*—the gradient of temperature change through the tissue is unimportant. In Fig. 7-2 is shown the rate of firing of a "cold neuron" and of a "warm neuron" from the cat tongue in response to rapid cooling or warming of the

tongue to the temperatures indicated. These neurons responded *only* to temperature and did not fire in response to pain or pressure stimulation.

The phenomena graphed in Fig. 7-2 can be compared with some well-known temperature phenomena. The terminal threshold for cold is usually found to be 18° C., where pain is experienced, but cold can still be sensed at that point, and Fig. 7-2 shows a cold neuron firing down to 10° C. Pain from hot stimuli is encountered at 45° to 50° C., which agrees well with the data presented. Physiological zero is around 35° C., and *both* cold and warm fibers fire at that temperature, as shown in the illustration. On the skin, warmth is sensed above 35° C., where the cold fiber does not fire; cold is sensed below 35° C., where the cold fiber is firing at a higher rate than the warm fiber.

Cold receptors can be inadequately stimulated by very warm temperatures of 43° to 51° C.; for example, when the hand is placed in hot water, a flash of cold sensation precedes the heat and pain sensations. This phenomenon is called **paradoxical cold.** Fig. 7-2 shows that the firing of the cold neuron dominates that temperature range. Producing **paradoxical warmth** with a very cold stimulus is quite difficult and the phenomenon is not reliable; it can be done on

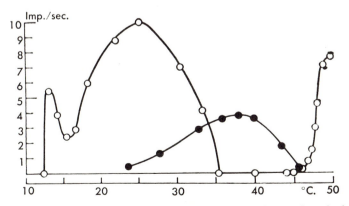

Fig. 7-2. Impulse frequency in a single cold fiber *(open circles)* and a single warm fiber *(filled circles)* as their receptors are stimulated by temperatures ranging from 10° to 50° C. (From Zotterman Y.: Annu. Rev. Physiol. **15:**357, 1953.)

some occasions, but not others. A sort of "psychological heat" can be obtained from a metal surface of 45° to 50° C. applied where there is good sensitivity to both warm and cold to arouse warm and paradoxical cold sensations at the same time. A grille of alternating warm and cold tubes will give the same sensation.

Both cold and warm aftersensations are positive and represent continued neuron firing after the stimulus has been removed.

Adaptation

All the temperature figures given for cold and warm responses are subject to change because of adaptation in the receptors and because of blood vessel constriction or dilation. As previously pointed out, continuous warm stimulation causes the warm receptors to adapt and causes the blood vessels to dilate, raising the threshold for warmth and lowering the threshold for cold. Continuous cold stimulation will cause the cold receptors to adapt and will constrict the blood vessels under the skin, thus raising the threshold for cold and lowering the threshold for warmth. These adjustments in response to temperature change can cause physiological zero to vary from 20° to 40° C. The change in physiological zero can be a general one involving the whole body, as when one adapts to a temperature change in passing from an air-conditioned room into the outdoor heat, or as when one adapts in passing from a heated house to the winter cold outdoors. On the other hand, the change in physiological zero may be restricted largely to the part of the body exposed to a temperature that necessitates adaptation. For example, the right hand can be temperature-adapted in a bowl of 40° C. water and the left hand temperature-adapted in a bowl of 20° C. water at the same time. Then if *both* hands are plunged into 30° C. water, the right hand will feel cold and the left hand will feel warm.

Muscular and visceral sensitivity

There appear to be no temperature-sensitive receptors in the muscles or their blood vessels. Visceral sensitivity seems confined to the esophagus and stomach. Hot or cold food seems to "disappear" on swallowing only to "reappear" in the stomach. The esophagus is sensitive to temperature throughout its length, but localization there is poor except at the upper and lower ends —sensations from the middle area are sensed as coming from the upper or lower part, or both.

PAIN

Pain is one of the most difficult sensory modalities to study as a sensation because the affective perceptual reactions to it are so overpowering. Pain "hurts" so much that the subject has difficulty in responding to it as a sensation. Yet pain has received much study because of the importance of the topic to the practice of medicine. Pain is useful as a diagnostic tool since it usually is set off by tissue damage. At the same time an understanding of pain is necessary to the control of pain during surgery and dental procedures. Pain, furthermore, is the most potent stimulus known to arouse and sustain behavior; it is therefore important to the study of *drives*. Pain stimuli set off somatic and visceral reflexes. The body's first "line of defense" against injury are the somatic withdrawal reflexes; the visceral, glandular, and autonomic "emergency responses" of the sympathetic nervous system form a second line of defense. The third is sensation, which leads to drives and the perception of pain. Pain will be considered first as a sensation. After the receptor, stimulus, and measurement phenomena have been studied, perceptual reactions to pain will be treated briefly as pain phenomena.

Pain as sensory modality

Pain appears to be a sensory modality, and not just a change in quality that results from overstimulation of pressure or temperature receptors. There are several lines of evidence for this point of view. Extreme pressure, warmth, or cold can produce pain, but the pain sensations will "coexist" with pressure, warmth, or cold. Furthermore, pain can be aroused by sparks "jumping" from a voltage generator to the skin without arousing sensations of pressure, cold, or warmth. Pain impulses are carried in the lateral funiculi of the spinal cord. Cutting these tracts relieves pain without disturbing touch sensations that are carried in the dorsal and ventral funiculi of the cord. As shown earlier, drugs such as cocaine affect unmyelinated pain fibers before they anesthetize the myelinated fibers carrying touch sensations; yet cutting off circulation to a limb will affect pressure sensations more than pain because this action affects myelinated fibers first.

Receptors

Some free nerve endings are known to be pain receptors. Areas of the skin having only free nerve endings are also sensitive to temperature and pressure. It is probable that the anastomoses of free nerve endings that serve pain lie deeper beneath the skin than those serving pressure. As evidence, the superficial epidermis can be peeled off without causing pain—only pressure endings seem affected. Also, a light touch to the cornea results in sensations of pressure rather than pain; the cornea contains only free nerve endings. The difference between the free endings serving pressure or temperature and those serving pain is not clear; perhaps the pain endings lie deeper beneath the skin surface than either pressure or temperature, or they differ biochemically.

There has been some debate over the possibility of two pain receptor systems. Recalling the sensations experienced the last time you "barked" a shin will reveal a "bright" first pain, followed by a "raw," burning second pain. It has been suggested that the first pain comes from lightly myelinated A-delta fibers that supply free nerve endings in the dermis near the epidermis.

These fibers conduct impulses more rapidly than do the C fibers that supply deeper free endings in the dermis. Pain stimulation without mechanical distortion of the skin in animals gives both A-delta and C action potentials in the nerve serving that area of skin, which suggests that two pain systems have been stimulated. Other investigators believe that the first pain is merely a mixture of pressure and pain sensations, the pressure being carried by A-delta and the pain by C fibers. In one experiment square-wave electrical stimuli and fine needles were used to stimulate skin pain without skin distortion (pressure), and the subjects reported only second pain. In another experiment an investigator bared a nerve in his own finger and stimulated it electrically, only to fire the lower threshold A-delta fibers. A stinging pain resulted. But when the stimulus was altered to fire C fibers as well, a severe, long-lasting, aching pain resulted. Cutting off the circulation to a limb affects myelinated fibers first and blocks "first pain," leaving only the "burning" second pain sensation. Thus the bulk of the evidence suggests two pain systems.

Pain sensitivity and localization

The distribution of pain endings and therefore the distribution of pain sensitivity varies widely from one part of the body to another. Pain sensibility is found in the hollow viscera, joints (aches), and muscles (cramping, pains), although more is known of cutaneous pain because it is the most accessible to stimulation. Cutaneous pain sensitivity varies from **analgesic** (insensitive) areas, such as Kiesow's area on the inner cheek opposite the second lower molar, to exquisitely sensitive areas, such as the "hollows" (fossae) of the body (armpit, back of knee joint, etc.). Table 7-3 gives a sample of the sensitivity of various cutaneous areas. Cutaneous pain localization is excellent; it is better than pressure localization. Muscular pain localization is accurate, as the experience of cramping pain in muscles shows.

Table 7-3. Distribution of pain sensitivity*

Skin region	Pain "points" per cm.²
Back of knee (popliteal fossa)	232
Neck region (jugular fossa)	228
Bend of elbow (cubital fossa)	224
Shoulder blade (interscapular region)	212
Volar side of forearm	203
Back of hand	188
Forehead	184
Buttocks	180
Eyelid	172
Scalp	144
Radial surface, middle finger	95
Ball of thumb	60
Sole of foot	48
Tip of nose	44

*From Strughold, H.: Z. Biol. **80:**367-380, 1924.

Visceral pain localization is poor, except for the pain receptors on the covering of bones. "Bone bruises" are quite accurately localized, for example. Visceral pain is often confused with skin or muscle pain, as will be seen later (referred pains). It is not known whether visceral pain localization is poor because of a sparse supply of pain endings in the hollow viscera, or whether pain is poorly localized because the location of the injury producing pain cannot be confirmed by the other senses. When one has a "stomachache," he cannot look to see whether the stomach or the intestine is inflamed. The location of a "bone bruise" or of pain from a cut finger can be confirmed by both touch and sight.

Adequate stimulus

The adequate stimulus for pain is unknown, despite over 40 years of diligent research. Some scientists believe that the pain endings are so unspecialized that the whole concept of an adequate stimulus for pain is meaningless. In other words, the endings respond as well to one kind of stimulus as they do to another, but their threshold is so high and they lie so deep beneath the skin that tissue damage usually occurs in the course of stimulating them. Perhaps mechanical distortion of the spray of free nerve endings is one adequate stimulus. The viscera may be cut or burned without pain to a patient undergoing surgery under local anesthesia, but stretching, twisting, and especially distention cause extreme pain from visceral pain endings. As explained below, one kind of headache is probably caused by the distention of cerebral arteries, which is the result of an increase in local blood pressure. One promising theory holds that injured tissue releases a substance called **neurokinin,** which is the adequate stimulus for pain endings. The substance is also believed to be responsible for the local vasodilation ("reddening" and swelling) that accompanies pain. Chemical analysis of the fluid of blisters, as well as other tissue fluid from injured areas, has revealed higher amounts of polypeptides of this sort than can be found in normal tissue. Pain is highly sensitive to the H^+ (hydrogen) ion of acids, but this is not the only ion stimulating pain—excess K^+ (potassium) causes exquisite pain, whereas lack of K^+ is analgesic (stops pain). This has led to the idea that the release of K^+ by injured cells causes pain, but we know that lack of K^+ affects nerve impulses of any kind (see Chapter 4).

Pain thresholds

Pain thresholds can be measured by the algesimeter, an instrument similar to the esthesiometer used for pressure thresholds. A sharp needle is substituted for a dull point. The needle can be loaded with varying weights until pain is sensed. Sensitivity measurements, as absolute thresholds for various parts of the body, agree well with the distribution of pain "points" shown in Table 7-3. The instrument of choice for measuring the effects of drugs, adaptation, etc. is the Hardy-Wolff-Gooddell apparatus. This device uses the inadequate stimulus of heat, radiated from a lamp to a black spot on the subject's forehead. The black spot absorbs all the radiant energy, and a shutter times the exposure (3 seconds). Brave subjects have established absolute and terminal (skin burn) thresholds. Difference thresholds have been established, and an equal-unit dol scale of just noticeable differences (JNDs) per unit has been established. (Dol is from Latin *dolor,* meaning 'pain.')

Adaptation. Whether pain results in adaptation depends on the stimulus and the definition one uses for adaptation. When it is defined as loss of sensitivity in the receptors and an increasing pain threshold, pain does not appear to result in adaptation, as measured by the Hardy-Wolff-Gooddell apparatus when the subject adjusts the stimulus himself to keep the pain level constant over as much as a half hour. Pain sensitivity may increase slightly under these conditions. Later experiments, using hot water as a stimulus show two kinds of pain, as far as adaptation is concerned. "Phasic" (weak) pain adapts and "static" (strong) pain that nears the intensity causing tissue damage does not adapt. Pain intensity may increase more than slightly under conditions of tissue injury. The difficulty here involves a "vicious circle" of self-stimulation that increases the pain input: pain causes reflex muscle contraction; the rigid muscle contraction reduces the blood flow to the area (ischemia), acting like a tourniquet; this causes more pain, more reflex contraction, and so on.

Habituation. Despite its insistent quality, humans can learn to ignore long-continued pain. However habituated one becomes, the pain intensity is just as great when attention is paid to it. Individuals differ widely in their ability to ignore pain. Habituation is most common under conditions of excitement and distraction—football players have been known to play almost an entire game with a broken ankle without being aware of it, only to feel intense pain when the game was over. Other motivational variables are important. For example, soldiers being evacuated from battle have been reported to deny pain from severe wounds, presumably because they were overjoyed at having escaped alive from the battlefield.

PAIN PHENOMENA
Referred pain

Referred pain occurs whenever pain sensations that originate in one part of the body are perceived as coming from another part of the body. Usually, visceral pain is referred to skin or muscle. A common example is the pain of heart disease, which is referred to the shoulder muscles (hence the name of this condition—*angina pectoris,* for pectoral muscles). In most cases the sensory neurons from the area originating the impulses and those from the area of referred pain enter the same dorsal spinal root or cranial nerve. This fact has led to speculation that a "short circuit" of the nerve impulses occurs; for example, impulses from the heart may stimulate the same area of the brain as impulses from the shoulder. Others have speculated that poor visceral localization leads the subject to locate the pain in an area more frequently stimulated and therefore more accurately localized.

Hyperalgesic pain

Hyperalgesic pain is a very painful burning sensation that surrounds an injured area. The sensation is familiar to all who have had a severe but localized wound. The threshold to pain in this area may be increased, but once stimulated, the pain sensations are persistent, strong, and unpleasant. They resemble the second pain previously described. The persistent and unpleasant quality is probably caused by the absence of competing pressure and temperature sensations from the area, because the ability of the pressure and temperature receptors to function is impaired by the injury. The deep-lying second pain endings are the only ones functioning; the superficial first pain endings near the epidermis are impaired. Competing sensations do relieve the insistent quality of pain; persons in pain clench their fists and jaw and apply pressure near the injured part to "smother" the pain input in other sensations.

Headaches

Headaches are obviously caused by stimulation of pain receptors in the head, but there are as many kinds of headaches as there are receptor locations. For example, "tension" headaches may be caused by overcontraction of muscles, particularly in the forehead. Sinus headaches may result from pressure attributable to lack of drainage of the hollows or sinuses in the bones of the head, especially the face. "Migraine" headaches are believed to be caused by dilation of blood vessels in the head that may make pain receptors in the walls of blood vessels accessible to chemicals that would otherwise not reach them—histamine, bradykinin, or neurokinin, depending on the theorist. The problem of what is the adequate stimulus for headache is as complex as the problem of the adequate stimulus for any variety of pain.

Analgesics

Analgesics are drugs that relieve pain without causing unconsciousness. Aspirin, opiates (in small doses), and various synthetic drugs are included. Experiments have shown that analgesics raise the pain threshold, as measured with the Hardy-Wolff-Gooddell apparatus.

Pain as perception

Attention is a factor that changes the response to pain in many situations. Under hypnosis pain sensations can be completely blocked—even reflex response to pain is impaired. On good subjects, hypnosis can be used rather than anesthetics for major surgery. Many reactions to pain seem to be learned ones—dogs raised in isolation show only reflex reactions to pain and do not learn to avoid painful stimuli. On a higher level, injuries that relieved soldiers of combat were perceived as less painful than similar injuries in civilian surgery. Pain thresholds, as tested on the Hardy-Wolff-Gooddell apparatus, vary considerably from day to day in normal subjects and are still more variable in psychotic persons. In one study, opiates appeared effective in 75% of the cases by relieving anxiety and producing a "bemused state" (whatever that is). In 35% of the cases a placebo (inactive drug) was successful in relieving pain reactions.

The diffuse nature of the pain pathways results in several perceptual phenomena. Cutting the pain pathways in the spinal cord (anterolateral cordotomy) relieves intractable pain; yet the pain may return, in whole or in part, after a period of years. Amputees who have lost a limb report pain referred to the absent limb—phantom limb pain—at intervals for many years. There are rare cases of congenital insensitivity to pain—people born without the ability to sense physical pain. These individuals must always be on guard to avoid seriously injuring themselves on hot or sharp objects. Some of them lack reflexes to pain. All show apparently normal nerve endings when sections of their skin are studied under a microscope. Other subjects have been found who lack only the subjective response to pain—they sense and react to pain as they do pressure or temperature, as a simple sensation. These subjects are like the isolated dogs mentioned above. They can, however, be taught to fear pain.

Pain as a sensation seems to be organized on lower levels of the brain than other somesthetic sensations; yet the perceptual reactions to it include the highest parts of the brain. Removing the cortex of one cerebral hemisphere does not interfere with the perception of pain, although it may raise the threshold. The pain pathways end on a part of the thalamus different from that of pressure pathways; pain stimulation does not result in evoked potentials of the cerebral cortex as pressure stimulation does. Pain caused by cortical stimulation or damage is rare, but pain is common when the thalamus is stimulated or damaged. Severe intractable pain may be relieved by a **prefrontal lobotomy,** a surgical procedure that severs the nerve fibers going from lower centers of the brain to the frontal lobes. The operation does not change pain thresholds, but the subject shows little subjective response to pain unless his attention is directed to it. He reports that he senses the pain but that it "doesn't bother him." When he attends to the pain sensations, his subjective response is increased, however.

THEORIES OF PAIN

Up to this point, pain has been treated as a straightforward sensory input that has powerful associated defensive reflexes and affective qualities. This seems to be the most effective point of view for explaining pain mechanisms, but the student should be aware that there are other theories.

There appear to be three major theories of pain: (1) the specificity theory, (2) the pattern theory, and (3) the gate control theory. The specificity theory is the point of view from which this chapter has been written—that pain is a sensory modality with its own receptors and brain centers like any other modality. The pattern theory holds that a nerve impulse pattern for pain is produced by intense stimulation of nonspecific receptors, as there are neither specific sensory fibers nor specific endings. The brain recognizes a high-intensity pattern of nervous input as signaling injury. One version of this approach holds that pain results from overstimulation of pressure receptors only. However, pain sensations from heat stimulation do not turn into pressure sensations as the stimulus becomes weaker. The gate control theory proposes a mutually inhibitory relationship between small-diameter and large-diameter sensory fibers. The small C fibers signal pain, and the large A fibers signal other sensory events. As shown in Fig. 7-3, both A and C fibers have branches going to the first input cells (substantia gelatinosa). A fibers excite the first input cells, which block the effect of A fibers on the dorsal horn cells by presynaptic inhibition. Thus the A fibers act to inhibit themselves by a feedback mechanism, after a brief burst of excitation to the sensory pathways. They also act to block C-fiber input by way of the first input neurons. C fibers, on the other hand, inhibit the first input neurons so that they can excite the dorsal horn cells of the sensory path-

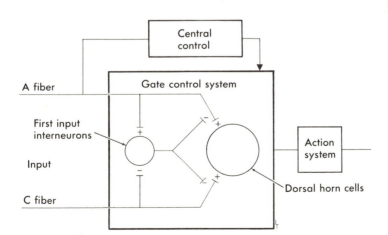

Fig. 7-3. Gate control theory of pain. "–" at a synapse means inhibition, and "+" indicates excitation. (Redrawn from Melzack, R., and Wall, P. D.: Science **150:**971-979, copyright 1965 by the American Association for the Advancement of Science.)

way. At low levels of stimulation, bursts of A-fiber input and a little C-fiber input will reach the sensory pathways. At the high levels of sensory input that accompany injury, the C fibers will fire the sensory pathways at a high rate, recognized by a central decoder mechanism as pain. Central control over this input is recognized in the scheme, as early A-fiber input can reach the brain, and the brain can respond by blocking the sensory input through a central control mechanism, preventing the frequency of input firing recognized as pain. This ingenious theory has also been used to explain the Chinese practice of acupuncture. An ancient therapy, acupuncture has been used for centuries to relieve pain, even during major surgery, by the placement of fine needles at charted locations of the skin and vibrating or twisting them. According to gate-control theory, the treatment would be more likely to stimulate large A fibers than small C fibers, thereby blocking the C fiber pain perception with additional A fiber input. Electrical stimulation that affects low-threshold A fibers but not high-threshold C fibers is a new therapy for intractable pain and is now being used with initial reports of success in controlling pain.

NERVE PATHWAYS

Further understanding of somesthetic sensibility depends on knowing the anatomy of the sensory pathways involved. As an aid to the understanding of these pathways, their common features will be presented first, together with some notes on terminology. Then three major tracts in the spinal cord that differ by modality will be described, together with three nuclei that serve the same purpose for cranial nerves. Finally, the centers that serve these pathways in the thalamus and cortex will be described. The chapter can then be concluded with a functional classification of two major sensory systems and a brief discussion of secondary sensory projection areas.

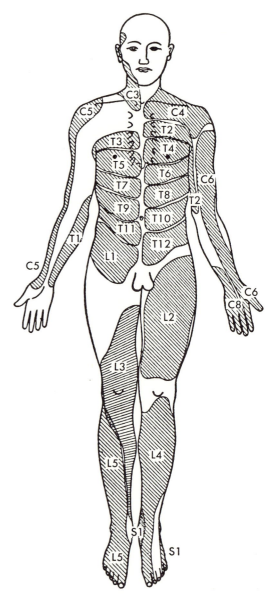

Fig. 7-4. Dermatomes of man. Successive dermatomes, labeled by spinal segment, are shown on alternate sides of the body to display the extent to which they overlap. (Based on data from Foerster, O.: Brain **56**:1-39, 1933; redrawn by Lewis, T.: Pain, New York, 1942, The Macmillan Co.)

Dermatomes

Each dorsal root in the spinal cord contains sensory neurons serving pressure, temperature, and pain receptors from the surface of the skin. The area served by a single dorsal spinal root is called a **dermatome** and is named for the spinal root. For example, L1 would be the dermatome on either side of the body, served by the first lumbar spinal root (Chapter 5). Since there are thirty-one pairs of dorsal spinal roots, there should be thirty-one pairs of dermatomes for the body and neck (except for the lack of a first cervical dorsal root). The face and most of the head are served by the fifth cranial nerve—the trigeminal nerve. Somesthetic, visceral, and muscular input is also serially arranged, according to the dorsal spinal roots and cranial nerves. The dermatomes were evolved before animals walked on four legs, as can be seen from their

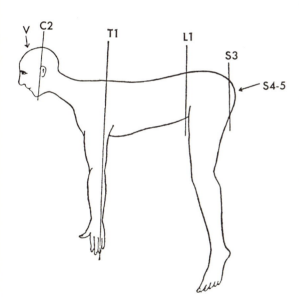

Fig. 7-5. Major dermatome boundaries in man in the quadruped (four-legged) position. **V,** Face area served by trigeminal (fifth) cranial nerve. **C2,** Anterior boundary of second cervical dermatome. **T,** Thoracic. **L,** Lumbar. **S,** Sacral. (From Monrad-Krohn, G. H.: The clinical examination of the nervous system, ed. 12, London, 1964, H. K. Lewis & Co., Ltd.)

major boundaries in man, shown in Figs. 7-4 and 7-5. Development of limbs carried the dermatome boundaries out from the body. The sizes of the dermatomes for pressure sensibility shown in Fig. 7-4 are larger than those for temperature and show more overlap; the dermatomes for pain are still smaller.

"Three-neuron" plan

Typically, a somesthetic **first-order neuron** runs from the somesthetic receptor to the spinal cord, where it enters the dorsal root, ascends, and synapses within two or three segments of the cord with **second-order neurons** in the gray matter of the dorsal horn. (Kinesthesis and some pressure inputs are exceptions; see p. 146.) The second-order neuron crosses to the opposite side of the cord, enters the white matter, and ascends to join with other neurons in the **medial lemniscus** of the brainstem. It ends on the **posteroventral nucleus** of the thalamus, synapsing with **third-order neurons.** Third-order neurons run from the thalamus to the somesthetic sensory projection area on the postcentral gyrus of the cerebral cortex (areas 3, 1, and 2—Chapter 5). In the trigeminal nerve serving the face, first-order neurons carry impulses to the sensory nuclei of the fifth nerve; second-order neurons cross the brainstem to join the medial lemniscus; and third-order neurons run from the thalamus to the cortex.

Fiber grouping

The second-order neurons, ascending the cord as tracts, are grouped by *modality*. Kinesthesis (such as joint sensibility) and fibers from specialized pressure receptors are carried in the dorsal funiculus. Fibers from less specialized (higher threshold) pressure receptors send impulses up the ventral funiculus. Pain and temperature tracts are found in the lateral funiculus. In the medial lemniscus the fibers are rearranged according to their dermatomes of

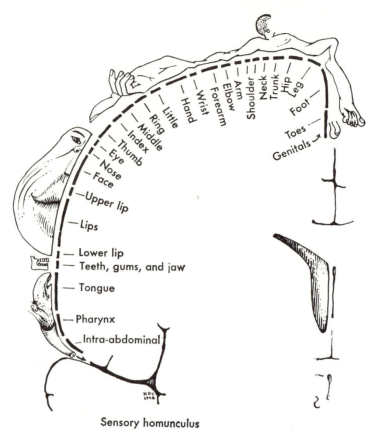

Sensory homunculus

Fig. 7-6. Sensory homunculus laid out on a cross section of one cerebral hemisphere. Length of each black line represents the proportion of sensory cortex devoted to part of body shown by labels; caricature of head and body above the lines is in about the same proportion. (From Penfield, W., and Rasmussen, T.: The cerebral cortex of man, New York, 1950, The Macmillan Co.)

origin as well, so that in the thalamus and cortex, fibers project in a **topographical organization** (Fig. 7-6). On the postcentral gyrus of the cortex the most caudal parts of the body are found at the beginning of the gyrus (in the longitudinal fissures); first the genitals and buttocks, next the feet and legs, then the body, the arms, and finally the face —compare Fig. 7-6 with Figs. 7-4 and 7-5.

Spinal tracts

Spinal tracts are typically named for their origin, their destination, and sometimes the funiculus of the cord in which they lie. Thus the lateral spinothalamic tract begins in the spinal cord, ends in the thalamus, and

lies in the lateral funiculus of the cord. We are concerned with three somesthetic tracts; two of them are named in this fashion.

Dorsal columns (Figs. 7-7 and 7-9). First-order neurons carrying kinesthetic impulses from the joints that signal limb position, from the more sensitive cutaneous pressure receptors, and from the pacinian corpuscles (deep pressure) are carried in the **dorsal columns.** These neurons enter the cord and ascend the dorsal funiculus without crossing, to end on the **gracile** and **cuneate nuclei** of the medulla. Second-order fibers from these nuclei cross and take up a ventral position in the medulla to form the **medial lemniscus.**

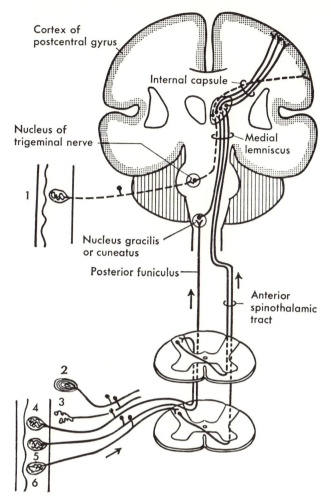

Fig. 7-7. Afferent pathways for kinesthesis and pressure sensations. Although not shown separately, the mesencephalic nucleus of trigeminal nerve is anterior part of nucleus shown, whereas main sensory nucleus is posterior part. In spinal tracts anterior is equivalent to ventral in the text, and posterior to dorsal. (From Gardner, E. O.: Fundamentals of neurology, ed. 5, Philadelphia, 1968, W. B. Saunders Co.)

Ventral spinothalamic tract (Figs. 7-7 and 7-9). First-order neurons from more crude pressure receptors synapse with second-order neurons in the dorsal gray columns of the cord. The second-order neurons cross and ascend the ventral funiculus of the cord in the **ventral spinothalamic tract,** which joins the medial lemniscus in the midbrain.

Lateral spinothalamic tract (Figs. 7-8 and 7-9). First-order neurons from pain and temperature receptors synapse with second-order fibers in the dorsal gray columns of the spinal cord. The second-order neurons cross to the opposite side of the cord and ascend the lateral funiculus as the **lateral spinothalamic tract.** Thus, in an operation to relieve intractable pain in the right leg, part of the left lateral funiculus of the cord could be cut above the level of entrance of these neurons. This would cut off pain and temperature sensation without disturbing kinesthetic and pressure path-

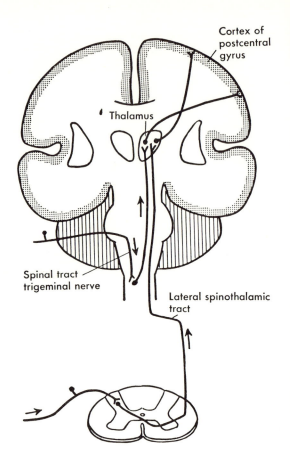

Fig. 7-8. Afferent pathways for pain and temperature. The uncrossed pathway for pain is not shown. (From Gardner, E. O.: Fundamentals of neurology, ed. 5, Philadelphia, 1968, W. B. Saunders Co.)

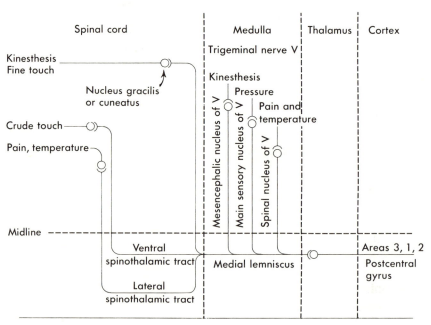

Fig. 7-9. Somesthetic and kinesthetic pathways.

ways, which are carried in the dorsal and ventral cord. The lateral and ventral spinothalamic tracts join in the medulla, and both join the medial lemniscus in the midbrain.

Cranial nerve nuclei

In the spinal cord the modalities are separated into three different spinal tracts. In the brainstem the modalities are separated into three different cranial nerve nuclei, and the separation is a little more complete. Only kinesthetic input reaches one nucleus, only pressure input the second, and only temperature and pain input the third.

Mesencephalic nucleus of fifth nerve (Figs. 7-7 and 7-9). First-order neurons of the fifth nerve from kinesthetic receptors end in the **mesencephalic** (midbrain) **nucleus of the fifth nerve.** Second-order neurons that originate here cross the brainstem to join the medial lemniscus.

Main sensory nucleus of fifth nerve. First-order neurons in the fifth nerve from pressure receptors reach the **main sensory nucleus** of that nerve. Second-order neurons originating here cross the brainstem to join the medial lemniscus.

Spinal nucleus of fifth nerve (Figs. 7-8 and 7-9). First-order neurons from pain and temperature receptors enter the brainstem and descend in the medulla as the **spinal tract of the fifth nerve.** These neurons end on the **spinal nucleus** of that nerve in the lower medulla. The second-order neurons that originate here cross to join the medial lemniscus in the midbrain.

Thalamic and cortical projection

As described in the beginning of this section, the fibers from all the somesthetic inputs are rearranged in the medial lemniscus according to origin as well as modality. The thalamic nuclei are therefore arranged topographically, and the third-order neurons and cortical projection area are also topographically ordered. There is evidence, however, that pain and tempera-

ture *sensations* are largely organized at the thalamic level, and pressure and kinesthetic sensations are organized at the cortical level.

Two sensory systems

Functionally there is evidence for two somesthetic-kinesthetic systems. The **medial lemniscal system** serves kinesthesis and more discriminative pressure sensations. Its neurons include the dorsal columns of the spinal cord and the mesencephalic and main sensory nuclei of the fifth nerve. The **spinothalamic system** serves less discriminative tactile sensations in the cord, and serves pain and temperature sensations in both the cord and brainstem. The ventral and lateral spinothalamic tracts are included in the cord, and the spinal tract and nucleus of the fifth nerve are included in the brainstem. The two systems are separate as far upward as the midbrain, where the spinothalamic tracts join the medial lemniscus.

Medial lemniscal system. The medial lemniscal system serves discriminative touch receptors and kinesthetic input for limb position. At the cortex these two inputs are in the same location for each part of the body. The two inputs may compete by mutually inhibiting one another at the cortical level. The system seems capable of the efferent control of afferent input, an important mechanism for attention that will be encountered later in other senses. Fibers run from topographically organized cortical motor projection areas down the brainstem to the mesencephalic and main sensory nuclei of the fifth nerve and to the gracile and cuneate nuclei of the spinal cord. These fibers seem able to *block* the input of parts of the system, when attention is being directed to other sensory inputs. The gracile and cuneate inhibitory synapses are of the presynaptic variety. This mechanism may sharpen topographical localization by the lateral inhibition discussed in Chapter 6. However, the most interesting feature of the medial lemniscal system is the way in which it transduces the intensity of pressure sensations. Single-fiber recording studies have established that the greater the pressure, the greater will be the generator potential in the receptor, as well as the rate of firing in sensory neurons. The relationship between intensity of pressure and rate of firing is retained in individual nerve cells of the medial lemniscal pathway, all the way to the cerebral cortex.

Spinothalamic system. The spinothalamic system seems to be the more primitive and phylogenetically older of the two. It serves less discriminative pressure, pain, and temperature sensations. The system includes impulses reaching the brain in the spinothalamic tracts and the spinal nucleus and tract of the fifth nerve. Much of the input of the system for sensation seems to be organized in the thalamus. Most of the direct pain projection probably stops at the thalamus. The destination of temperature input is not known beyond the thalamus (except for the tongue). Pressure inputs reach the cortical sensory projection area in a topographical fashion. Like the medial lemniscal system, inhibitory outputs reach the first relay nucleus of the system (the dorsal gray column nuclei of the cord). These fibers descend from the area of the motor cortex that controls the muscles of the body area from which the sensory input comes. In both medial lemniscal and spinothalamic systems, specific relay nuclei in the thalamus receive feedback fibers from the cortical areas to which they project. These projections also seem to be inhibitory in function. The spinothalamic system differs from the medial lemniscal system in one more important respect. The second-order fibers of the tracts involved give off collaterals (branches) to an important part of the brain called the **ascending reticular activating system (ARAS).** The ARAS consists of many short neurons in the core of the brainstem. They send impulses to all parts of the cortex and keep it active. Unless the ARAS is excited, either by the spinothalamic system or by descending impulses from higher brain centers, the individual goes to sleep. Widespread arousal of the brain by the spinothalamic system would be expected, as this system carries pain input that signals tissue damage and an emergency situation.

Physiological evidence. The thalamic projection of the medial lemniscal system is posterior to that of the spinothalamic system. The medial lemniscal system seems to excite neurons projecting directly to the somesthetic projection area of the cortex, whereas the spinothalamic system does not. Evoked potential studies seem to agree with these anatomical findings when the skin is stimulated in a "natural" fashion and the arrival of resulting nerve impulses at the cortical projection area is recorded. The results suggest that large-diameter fibers excite a smaller area of the cortex (receptive field) than do small-diameter sensory inputs. Evoked potentials have been recorded from joint rotation, light touch, heavy pressure, and hair movement. Thermal stimuli (except for the tongue) and pain stimuli do not result in evoked potentials from the cortex in the somesthetic projection area. The cortical "topography" (see Fig. 7-6) is orderly, but variable in size of field.

Secondary sensory projection areas

The classic somesthetic projection area on the postcentral gyrus is not the only cortical area to receive somesthetic input. The classical area is called SI. Below it is another topographically organized area called SII, which probably receives input from both the medial lemniscal and spinothalamic systems. Unlike SI, which receives input from the opposite half of the body only, SII receives input from both sides of the body. There is also a "face area," SIII, in front of the other two. It seems to receive input from SII and represents only the head regions. SII may be important to selective attention. There is some evidence that SII is active when the animal is responding to SI input. On the other hand, lesions of SII produce no observable sensory defects in monkeys or men. Lesions that destroy both SI and SII produce no worse defects than SI lesions alone. (Cortical response to pain input is found most reliably in SII. Anatomical studies suggest that these inputs are from the A-delta input of the "first pain" discussed earlier. The C-fiber input of "second pain" probably terminates in the thalamus.)

SUMMARY

Bodily sensations are classified either as somesthesis, which includes the "condition" senses of pressure, cold, warmth, and pain, or as the position and movement senses of proprioception. Somesthesis may be cutaneous, muscular, or visceral. In addition to initiating important reflexes, somesthetic inputs give rise to complex responses accompanied by awareness of the input. Since they arouse and sustain behavior, somesthetic sensations, especially pain, can act as drives. By contrast, proprioception from the special vestibular senses responding to head movement and from general kinesthetic receptors that initiate the stretch reflexes does not lead directly to awareness. However, kinesthetic (movement sense) input from receptors in the joints, tendons, and connective tissue of muscles is sensed as limb position and movement.

The methods for studying somesthetic input include introspective, anatomical, and physiological techniques. Introspective technique lacks objective confirmation, anatomical technique shows only the most obvious pathways, and physiological experiments with animals lack introspective information. Physiological methods, using implanted electrodes in the otherwise normal animal, seem to be the most promising approach.

Introspectively the primary qualities of somesthesis seem to be pressure, cold, warmth, and pain. Secondary qualities result from intermittent stimulation or combinations of primary inputs. The evidence that the primary qualities are separate modalities depends largely on experiments with cutaneous sensitivity. Experiments such as skin mapping for punctate sensitivity in different parts of the body; arousing pain, without pressure from spark-gap stimulation; determining excitation and conduction time for the four senses; recording the different effects of cocaine and asphyxia on the four senses; and locating the separate pathways of the four senses in the spinal cord all point to four modalities. Identifying specific receptors and projection areas in the brain for four separate modalities is more difficult. Projection to the postcentral gyrus of the cerebral cortex is involved, although pain probably projects directly only to lower levels. Specialized receptors have been tentatively identified in some areas, but in others free nerve endings serve all four inputs; these nerve endings may differ biochemically or in their connections to the brain.

The structure of the skin has much to do with cutaneous somesthesis. The outer layer of dead cells in the epidermis has no receptors, the inner layer of epidermis has a few free nerve ends (probably for pressure), the dermis contains most of the receptors, and subdermal cutaneous fat contains the "deep-pressure" pacinian corpuscles. Pressure receptors also include basket endings of the body hair and probably Meissner's corpuscles in hairless areas. As a sample sensory transducer, the pacinian corpuscle seems to function by spreading pressure over its included nerve ending so that the nerve ending can produce a larger generator potential to fire nerve impulses. The receptor adapts rapidly. The true adequate stimulus for pain seems to be linear stretching of the skin.

Pressure receptors can be classified as fast-adapting or slow-adapting. Pressure sensitivity can be gauged with an esthesiometer or by the two-point threshold. Either method demonstrates wide variation in pressure sensitivity over the body, from the sensitive lips and fingertips to the relatively insensitive back of the forearm or the loin. The data for localization agree with the sensitivity differences. Muscle pressure localization is good, but visceral localization is poor. Cutaneous adaptation for pressure depends on a constant degree of skin distortion; the tissue slowly recovers shape after pressure is removed, and aftersensations are therefore positive.

Although cold and warmth seem to be separate modalities, they interact because local blood vessel reactions to either stimulus changes the threshold to the other. Physiological zero is the range of skin temperature where neither cold nor warmth is sensed; it varies as a result of these vascular reactions. Cold results from temperatures below 35° to 39° C., and warmth from temperatures above 34° to 35° C., depending on physiological zero. Heat and stinging cold include pain sensations, but heat can be a combination of warm and paradoxical cold. Skin mapping shows a fairly reliable punctate distribution, with more cold spots than warm; most of the areas more sensitive to cold are also more sensitive to warmth. Timing cold and warm "pulses" traveling through the prepuce shows that cold receptors are nearer the surface than are warm receptors and that both respond to absolute temperature rather than to temperature gradients through the skin. There are both unspecialized (free nerve endings) and specialized receptors for cold and warmth. The specialized cold receptors seem to be Krause's end bulbs; the specialized warmth receptors are Ruffini's cylinder (endings). Some temperature-sensitive areas have only free nerve endings; others have encapsulated endings too varied to classify. Data on rate of firing of "cold" and "warm" neurons in the cat tongue agree with introspective findings; absolute thresholds, terminal thresholds, physiological zero, paradoxical cold and warmth, and adaptation phenomena are consistent with these data. Muscle sensitivity to temperature seems absent,

and visceral response is limited to the mouth and esophagus.

Pain is difficult to study as a sensation because of the strong reflex and affective reactions to it. Proofs for pain as a separate sensory modality include spark-gap stimulation, separate pathways in the spinal cord, and the effects of drugs and asphyxia. Some, but not all, free nerve endings are pain receptors. There appear to be two pain input systems—a rapidly conducting first-pain system of small A fibers, and a slower second-pain C-fiber system. Pain sensitivity varies from high in the fossae to analgesic areas in the cheek. Cutaneous and muscle pain localization is good, but visceral pain is poorly localized and leads to referred pain. The adequate stimulus is unknown, although there are several theories. The viscera are pain-sensitive only to distention; cerebral blood vessel distention is one cause of headache. "Weak" pain adapts but "strong" pain does not. Habituation is possible, however. Pain phenomena include referred pain, hyperalgesia, headaches, and analgesic drug effects. Perceptual studies show that many of the affective responses to pain are learned. The diffuse pathways often cause anterolateral cordotomy effects to be temporary, and phantom limb pain occurs in amputees. Congenitally insensitive persons have been found, but their cutaneous nerve endings seem normal. Most pain sensation seems subcortical. Prefrontal lobotomy reduces affective response to pain. Theories of pain include the specificity theory, the pattern theory, and the gate-control theory.

Cutaneous somesthetic nerve pathways begin with the dermatomes that are served by the dorsal spinal roots and the fifth nerve. Pressure dermatomes are the largest and overlap most, those for temperature less so, and those for pain least so. The input for the muscles and viscera is similarly organized. The input is arranged in a three-neuron plan, with synapses in the spinal cord between first- and second-order neurons, and synapses with third-order neurons in the posteroventral nucleus of the thalamus. Input is organized by modality in the spinal cord, preserving this organization while being rearranged topographically in the medial lemniscus of the brainstem below the thalamus. Accurately localized pressure and kinesthesis are carried in the first-order neurons of the dorsal columns of the spinal cord to the gracile and cuneate nuclei of the medulla; crude pressure input ascends the cord in the ventral spinothalamic tract of the ventral funiculus; temperature and pain sensations are carried in the lateral spinothalamic tract of the lateral funiculus of the cord. Two of these tracts are named for their origin, destination, and location (funiculus). The corresponding inputs for the fifth nerve are the mesencephalic (kinesthesis), main sensory (pressure), and spinal (temperature and pain) nuclei of the brainstem. The input to the brain is primarily crossed; each side of the brain serves the opposite side of the body. Functionally, two somesthetic and kinesthetic systems seem involved—the medial lemniscal system and the spinothalamic system. The former serves kinesthesis and discriminative pressure, whereas the latter serves less discriminative pressure, pain, and temperature. The medial lemniscal system seems capable of efferent inhibition of afferent input at the mesencephalic and main sensory nuclei of the fifth nerve and at the gracile and cuneate nuclei. The system translates pressure intensity as frequency of firing in a linear way, from the sensory neurons to the cortex. The spinothalamic system includes the spinal tract and nucleus of the fifth nerve. This system also inhibits input at nuclei of the dorsal columns. Evoked cortical potentials have been recorded from kinesthesis and pressure,

but not temperature and pain. The spinothalamic tracts give off many collaterals to the ascending reticular activating system (ARAS). The ARAS consists of many short neurons in the core of the brainstem that act to arouse the whole cortex to activity. When the ARAS is not aroused by the spinothalamic system or by descending impulses from higher brain centers, sleep ensues.

The primary cortical somesthetic projection area is called SI. Another topographically organized somesthetic area, SII, lies below it and receives bilateral input from the ARAS. A "face area," SIII, lies in front of the other two and is supplied by SII. SII may be important to selective attention, but cortical ablation of the area has no known sensory consequences.

READINGS

Gardner, E. D.: Fundamentals of neurology, ed. 5, Philadelphia, 1968, W. B. Saunders Co.

Livingston, W. K.: What is pain? Sci. Am. **188:** 59-66, March 1953. (W. H. Freeman Reprint No. 407.)

Loewenstein, W. R.: Biological transducers, Sci. Am. **203:**98-108, Aug. 1960. (W. H. Freeman Reprint Co. 70.)

Melzack, R.: The perception of pain, Sci. Am. **204:**41-49, Feb. 1961. (W. H. Freeman Reprint No. 457.)

Melzack, R.: How acupuncture works: A sophisticated Western theory takes the mysteries out, Psychol. Today **7:**28-38, 1973.

Melzack, R.: Phantom limbs, Psychol. Today **4:** 63-68, Oct. 1970.

Montagna, W.: The skin, Sci. Am. **212:**56-66, Feb. 1965. (W. H. Freeman Reprint No. 1003.)

Mountcastle, V. B., and Powell, T. P. S.: Neural mechanisms subserving cutaneous sensibility. In Gross, C. G., and Zeigler, H. P., editors: Readings in physiological psychology, New York, 1969, Harper & Row Publishers.

von Buddenbrock, W.: The senses, Ann Arbor, Mich., 1958, University of Michigan Press.

chapter 8

Proprioception

OVERVIEW

The two sets of receptor inputs that are sensitive to the *position* and *movement* of different parts of the body are the subjects of this chapter. Collectively, such input is known as proprioception. One set of proprioceptive receptors is found in the muscles, tendons, and joints, where they respond to muscle tension and the position and movement of the limbs. These receptors serve the sense classed as kinesthesis (Gr., 'motion perception'). The other set of receptors is in the inner ear, or vestibule. The vestibular senses respond to the position and movement of the head. Conscious sensations are not a direct result of most proprioceptive inputs. Reflex *responses to* proprioception *result* in sensory input that *is* vital to orientation. Furthermore, the reflexes set off by proprioceptors are very important to normal behavior—literally, a coordinated movement cannot be made without them.

The kinesthetic input will be considered first. Joint sensitivity results in conscious sensations of limb position because the input reaches the highest levels of the brain. The nerve pathways involved were covered in Chapter 7. The reflex input that is the basis for coordinated movement will be discussed next; this input goes primarily to the cerebellum and is not consciously sensed. The tendon jerk and stretch reflexes are used to show how posture and coordination depend on sensory input from the stretching of muscles. The sensory mechanisms in the muscle spindle and muscle tendons are examined. Mechanisms for varying the sensitivity of the muscle spindle by

contraction of its fibers are explained. Applications of the sensitivity mechanism to reciprocal innervation and to motor learning conclude the first half of the chapter.

The vestibular senses are discussed next. The semicircular canals respond to head rotation, and the sacs respond to linear (straight-line) movements of the head. The nerve pathways for reflex response to these two inputs are summarized. First, the semicircular canal receptors and their adequate stimuli are explained, and then the reflex responses to them are examined. The receptor mechanisms of the sacs and their reflex responses follow. The chapter closes with some practical applications of knowledge about the vestibular senses.

KINESTHESIS
Joint sensibility

The receptors that give conscious sensations of limb position and movement are found mainly in the joints. Some sensations of limb position and movement come from the connective tissue covering tendons and muscles and from the pull on the skin as a limb is moved or placed in an extreme position. However, if you close your eyes, rest your right arm on the table, and grasp the index finger with your left hand and flex it back and forth, the resulting sensations of movement will come primarily from the joints of the right index finger. Local anesthetics that paralyze receptors in the skin and muscles impair position sense very little, as the joint receptors are not involved. The joint receptors, as well as all the other receptors contributing to sensations of limb position and movement, appear to be pressure receptors of one kind or another. Unlike pressure receptors in other parts of the body, they adapt very little under continuous stimulation, as when the body is maintained in one position for a long time. This fact is important because constant sensory input must keep us aware of body position at all times so that movement can begin from a known posture. In the joints, most of the pressure receptors involved are pacinian corpuscles, a receptor discussed in Chapter 7. The pathway by which their excitation reaches the cerebral cortex was also discussed in Chapter 7. This pathway shares the dorsal columns of the spinal cord with pathways going to the cerebellum for reflex control of movement. The importance of the dorsal column kinesthetic pathways can be seen in victims of tabes dorsalis (destruction of the kinesthetic input by syphilis). The victim lacks knowledge of the position of his limbs because he lacks joint sensitivity; he must watch his feet in order to walk. Even then, his walk is poorly coordinated; he "throws" his legs out and his feet slap the ground at every step because kinesthetic input is not available.

The pathways from the joint receptors to the cerebral cortex are long; the input involves long conduction and synaptic delay times. Such an input can guide and direct slow and voluntary movements such as those involved in a sorting task. The input can also report on body position before, during, and after a more rapid movement. However, the pathways are too slow for rapid correction of a movement, once it is initiated. In a golfer's swing, for example, the golfer may be aware when the movement is initiated that he is going to hit the ball incorrectly, but any attempt to consciously correct his swing will only make matters worse. It appears that the movement is "programmed" by higher centers that set off a series of *reflex* reactions in lower centers. These reflex reactions automatically control a rapid sequence of movements once they are initiated. The feedback from conscious sensations in limb position and movement before, during, and after the swing may be used to correct the reflex "program" for the next try. The input cannot be used to correct the swing while it is in progress. The sensory mechanisms for reflex programs of rapid movements and for automatic postural adjustment are the topic of the remainder of the section on kinesthesis.

Tendon jerks

If the tendon of a muscle is struck with a rubber hammer or with a chopping movement of the heel of the hand, the muscle will react with a rapid and brief contraction—a **tendon jerk.** If a subject is seated with his legs dangling, striking the patellar tendon (just below the kneecap) causes a rapid contraction of the quadriceps (thigh) muscle and a kicking motion of the leg—the so-called knee jerk reflex. The quick contraction is a response to stretching of the muscle caused by hitting the tendon to which it is attached. Similar tendon jerks can be stimulated in both flexor and extensor muscles over the entire body by striking their tendons. The tendon jerk is a reflex that is stimulated by receptors in the muscles that are sensitive to the *stretch* of the muscle. Striking the tendon results in rapid stretching of the muscle to which it is attached. The same muscle responds by contracting in a reflex fashion.

The tendon jerk is, then, a reflex. Reflexes (studied in Chapter 5) are made of five elements: (1) receptors, (2) sensory neurons, (3) association neurons, (4) motoneurons, and (5) effectors. It was also pointed out that synaptic delay is responsible for most of the time required between stimulus and response. Tendon jerks require less time between stimulus and response than other reflexes because fewer synapses are involved. Measurements of the time required show that no association neurons are involved in the tendon jerk. It is a **mono-**

synaptic reflex, having only one set of synapses between the sensory neurons and motoneurons. The sensory neurons make direct functional connections with the motoneurons; thus only four reflex elements are involved.

Stretch reflex

The stretch reflex involves exactly the same elements as the tendon jerk—the same receptors, sensory neurons, motoneurons, and effectors. The **stretch reflex** is the reflex contraction of extensor muscles in response to a more gradual stretching from the pull of gravity (for example, body weight bends the knee), rather than the abnormally rapid stretching of tendon jerks. Extensor muscles are stretched when a limb is flexed by either the force of gravity or antagonist flexors. When stretched by the force of gravity as it bends a limb, the extensor muscles react by contraction and straighten the limb. Since the onset of the stretching is more gradual, stretch receptors begin to fire a few at a time as their thresholds are reached. The contraction response that straightens the limb is therefore smooth and gradual as more and more groups of muscle fibers respond. For example, as the knees bend under the weight of the body, the tendon of the quadriceps (thigh) muscle is stretched over the kneecap. The muscle reacts to stretch by contraction, which straightens the leg. With normal shifts in posture, the amount of stretching of various extensor, or antigravity, muscles changes. Their reflex contraction varies in proportion to the amount of load imposed on them, enabling the body to remain upright. If you shift your weight from your right leg to your left, the extensors of the left leg will be stretched more and will increase their contraction to compensate for the change in posture. Stretch reflexes are therefore important to normal postural adjustments.

As pointed out in Chapter 4, muscles are always stretched to some degree and are therefore always partly contracted in response, giving rise to **muscle tone,** the partial contraction of healthy muscle that varies with position (stretch). The postural changes in stretch reflex adjustment are simply increases or decreases in muscle tone. Flexor muscles are not needed for upright posture since they bend rather than extend the limbs. They have a higher response threshold to stretching than do extensor muscles, have less tone as a result, and do not show reflex contractions to gradual stretching, although they will react to the more rapid stimulus of tendon jerks. In man the flexors of the arms and hands oppose gravity rather than the extensors; for example, bending the elbow opposes gravity. The arm and hand flexors show all the characteristics of extensor muscles in the rest of the body, including postural stretch reflexes.

Muscle spindle

The receptors that excite the stretch reflex are found in structures called **muscle spindles.** Each spindle consists of a sheath of connective tissue containing two to twelve **intrafusal fibers.** The intrafusal fibers are thereby attached to connective tissue that reaches the tendons on both ends of the muscle. The stretch-sensitive intrafusal fibers are "in parallel" with the other fibers of the muscle. If the *other* muscle fibers contract, stretching of the spindle fibers is *decreased* because the spindle fibers are indirectly "attached" to both ends of the muscle, and the muscle has been shortened. As a result, stretch reflex stimulation often ceases when the muscle contracts and relieves the pull on the spindle fibers (Fig. 8-1, *A*). Since there is normally some stretch stimulation to muscles, especially the antigravity extensors, the intrafusal fiber receptors are continuously exciting a few motoneurons to contract muscle fibers even when the muscle is at rest. It is the resting level of muscle spindle firing that accounts for muscle tone.

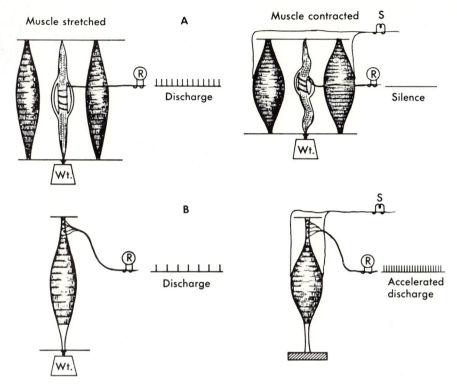

Fig. 8-1. Relationships among muscle spindle fibers, Golgi tendon organ, and muscle fibers. **A,** Muscle spindle arranged "in parallel" with muscle fibers so that muscle contraction relieves pull on muscle spindle. **B,** Golgi tendon organ arranged "in series" with muscle so that either stretch or contraction stimulates tendon organ. (From Patton, H. D.: Reflex regulation of movement and posture. In Ruch, T. C., et al.: Neurophysiology, ed. 2, Philadelphia, 1965, W. B. Saunders Co.)

As previously pointed out, tone varies with the amount of stretching imposed on the muscle.

Golgi tendon organ

The **Golgi tendon organ** is another receptor mechanism that is stimulated by stretching. This receptor is located in the tendon of the muscle, however. It is stimulated by stretching from *either* an external pull on the tendon *or* the pull that results from muscle contraction (Fig. 8-1, *B*). The intrafusal fiber, or muscle spindle, receptors are "in parallel" with the muscle; they are stimulated by stretching the muscle and they lack stimulation when the muscle contracts. The Golgi tendon organ is "in series"

with the muscle fibers and responds to pull on the tendon, whether the pull is applied by external force to the tendon or it results from contraction of the muscle itself. Stimulation of the Golgi tendon organ results in reflex *inhibition* of the fibers of the muscle. In contrast to the monosynaptic stretch reflex, the inhibitory reflex resulting from tendon stimulation includes interneurons. The sensory neurons excite Renshaw cells (Chapter 4), which inhibit the motoneurons. The pathway is therefore longer and the inhibitory response slower than stretch reflex excitation. The relative insensitivity or high threshold of the Golgi tendon organs to passive stretching led to the belief that they functioned primarily to protect the mus-

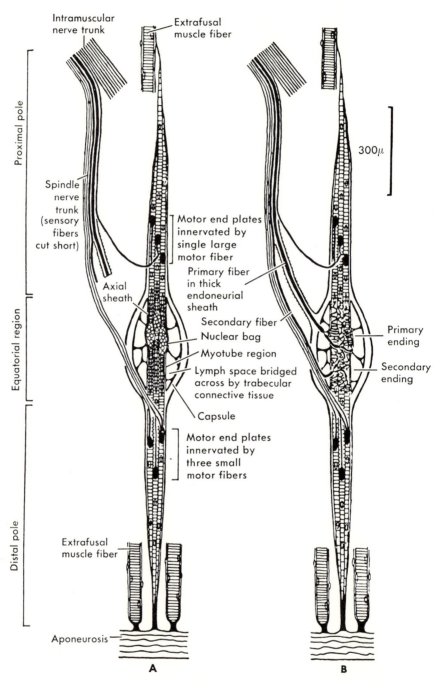

Fig. 8-2. Intrafusal fiber and its nerve supply. **A** shows only gamma efferent motor fibers to contractile ends. **B** shows also sensory supply to primary and secondary endings. (From Barker, D.: Q. J. Microsc. Sci. **89:**143-186, 1948.)

cle and tendons from damage. An extreme pull on the tendon from an imposed weight, an extreme muscle contraction, or both, would fire them in order to inhibit the muscle before the strain damaged it. Although they have a high threshold to passive stretching, the tendon organs have a low threshold to the stretching imposed by active muscle contraction. The response is a joint function of the number of muscle fibers pulling on the connective tissue where each tendon organ is found, and the strength of pull in each fiber. A single muscle fiber producing 0.1 gram of tension caused the receptor to fire its sensory neuron at 25 impulses per second in one experiment. Clearly, tendon organs are active whenever muscles contract.

Structure of the intrafusal fiber

The intrafusal fibers contain the receptors that stimulate the tendon jerk and stretch reflexes. Study of the structure of muscle spindles shows that they contain other important sensory and motor mechanisms as well. The nuclear bag type of intrafusal fiber and its nerve supply are shown in Fig. 8-2. The cell is slender, with an expanded sensory, or "equatorial," region. The striated end parts of the cell, the "polar" regions, are motor in function. The end regions resemble other muscle cells. The more central sensory area consists of a nuclear bag full of cell nuclei, surrounded by a myotube area and lymph spaces. The nuclear bag is invaded by **annulospiral,** or **primary, endings** that are responsible for the stretch reflex—they respond to the pull on the sensory region that occurs when the muscle spindle is stretched by the stretching of the whole muscle. The myotube part of the sensory region contains **secondary, or flower-spray, endings.** These endings *inhibit* the other muscle fibers in a multisynaptic reflex, just as the Golgi endings do. There is some evidence that the secondary endings are stimulated by outside pressure applied to the myotube area when the surrounding muscle cells contract. The

secondary endings seem less important than the primary endings, as some muscle spindles lack secondary endings. Finally, the striated motor ends of the intrafusal fiber can contract and are therefore invaded by the **gamma efferents,** which are small motoneurons. As will be seen later, contraction of the intrafusal fiber can stimulate the primary sensory endings of the same fiber.

Relative roles of Golgi, annulospiral, and flower-spray endings (Fig. 8-3).

There is evidence to support different roles for the three receptors in normal coordinated behavior.

1. The Golgi tendon endings register *total* tension on the tendon, although they are more sensitive to the pull caused by muscle contraction than they are to passive stretching.

2. The annulospiral endings react to the *length* of the sensory part of the muscle spindle. The extensor muscles reflexly contract in proportion to their length whenever stretching of the muscle causes the intrafusal fiber to be stretched. This action fires the monosynaptic stretch reflexes responsible for extensor tone and postural adjustments. The annulospiral endings are also excited when the intrafusal fiber contracts, as will be explained later.

3. The flower-spray endings seem to be stimulated by pressure on the fluid-filled myotube region, where these endings are found. The pressure is probably provided by the surrounding muscle fibers when they contract, shorten, and "bulge" in a contraction that shortens the muscle. It may be that their inhibition of the muscle as it shortens helps bring the movement to a smooth conclusion.

Role of the gamma efferent fibers: contraction of the intrafusal fiber

The intrafusal fiber contracts when it is excited by the motor nerves going to its polar regions—the gamma efferent fibers (Fig. 8-2, *A*). Contraction of the intrafusal

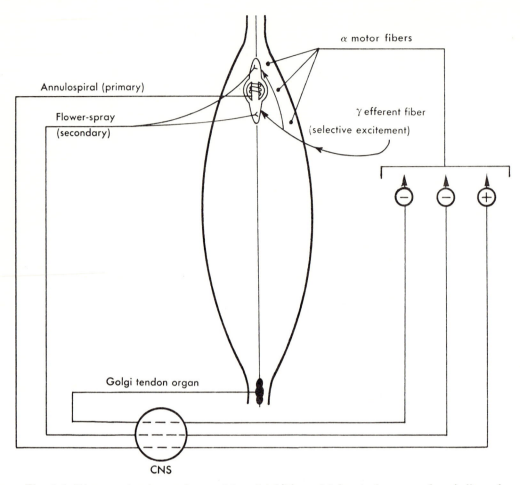

Fig. 8-3. Diagram showing excitatory (+) and inhibitory (–) inputs from muscle spindle and Golgi tendon organ as they affect alpha (α) motor fibers to muscle. Gamma (γ) efferent supply to muscle spindle is also shown.

fiber at its ends exerts a pull on the central sensory area. Stretching the intrafusal fiber also pulls on the central part of the fiber. A pull on the sensory area by either force fires the annulospiral endings, which, in turn, reflexly excites other fibers in the muscle. The stretch reflex, then, is a muscle contraction in response to the length of the sensory part of the fiber, whether the reflex is caused by stretching of the whole muscle or by contraction of the ends of the intrafusal fiber. In muscle contraction the whole muscle shortens; thus stretch to the intrafusal fiber is relieved (Fig. 8-1, *A*). If the gamma efferent fibers excite intrafusal fiber contrac-

tion while the muscle shortens, they take up the slack and maintain pull on the sensory region. The annulospiral endings remain excited and reinforce muscle contraction by their input. Contraction of the muscle spindle can therefore reinforce contraction of the muscle by shortening the intrafusal fiber as the muscle shortens, keeping tension on the annulospiral endings. Contraction of the intrafusal fibers via the gamma efferent neurons can also reinforce contraction when the muscle does not shorten. By increasing tension on the annulospiral endings, reflex muscles contraction adds to "voluntary" contraction, without change in the length of the muscle. In general, the gamma efferent mechanism acts as a "biasing" mechanism or "gain control," regulating the sensitivity of the stretch reflex; when more gamma efferents excite intrafusal fibers, more annulospiral endings are excited, and muscle contraction is greater.

Reciprocal innervation

Reciprocal innervation has been defined as the nervous mechanism that allows an antagonist muscle to relax as the agonist contracts (Chapter 4). For example, an extensor muscle must relax and not react to being stretched when the opposed flexor muscle bends a limb. If the antagonist extensors reacted with a stretch reflex when flexors contracted to bend the leg at the knee, the movement would be difficult or impossible. It is now possible to explain how reciprocal innervation occurs. When the flexor motoneurons are excited, the gamma efferents to the flexor intrafusal fibers are also excited. As previously explained, they take up the slack in the intrafusal fibers so that tension is maintained on the annulospiral endings. This input reinforces flexor contraction. The same annulospiral input from intrafusal fibers in flexor muscle spindles that excites flexor motoneurons *inhibits* the antagonist extensor motoneurons. The antagonist extensors relax to permit flexion to occur. The same reciprocal relations exist for flower-spray and Golgi tendon endings. While these inputs inhibit the motoneurons to the stimulated muscles, they excite the motoneurons of antagonists. Any flower-spray or Golgi input from a muscle that inhibits that muscle excites its antagonists; any annulospiral inputs from a muscle that excites that muscle inhibits its antagonists. As a result, when a muscle relaxes, its antagonist contracts; when a muscle contracts, its antagonist relaxes. Both may relax or contract when these mechanisms are not brought into action, of course.

Crossed extension

When one limb is flexed, the opposite limb is extended in a reflex to maintain posture and balance and to permit movements such as walking (Chapter 4). The primary, secondary, and Golgi inputs are involved in the same way as in reciprocal innervation. The pattern of reflex input from those endings that support homolateral (same side) flexion also supports contralateral (other side) extension, and vice versa.

Resting discharge

The primary and secondary endings of the intrafusal fibers are not silent when the muscle it at rest. Some stretch to the muscle always exists, and there is a **resting discharge** of input from the primary annulospiral endings to maintain muscle tone (see p. 156). The secondary endings also show a resting discharge, which reflexly inhibits some of the motoneurons of the muscle. These levels of resting discharge are modified by intermittent firing of the gamma efferents. As a result the motoneurons to a muscle are the site of a constant interplay of excitatory and inhibitory influences. Influences come from the discharge levels of the receptors in the muscle spindles of the muscle, from the discharge levels of muscle spindles in other muscles (both antagonists and agonists), from inputs to other reflexes, and from higher centers. The number of motoneurons firing at any given moment depends on the interaction of many excitatory and inhibitory influences (for examples, see Fig. 8-4).

Input to the cerebellum

The primary and secondary muscle spindle inputs and the Golgi tendon organ input set off spinal reflexes. These inputs also reach higher centers. The role of higher centers, particularly the cerebellum, is discussed in Chapter 12. Such centers are responsible for overall coordination of the body through their influence on the excitatory and inhibitory reflexes involved in

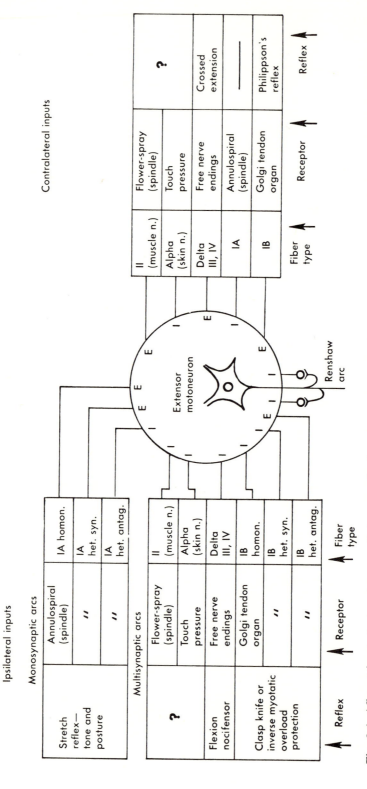

Fig. 8-4. Afferent inputs to a motoneuron that are confined to one segment of spinal cord. Influence of each input is shown as excitatory, *E*, or inhibitory, *I. Homon.*, homonomous; *het.*, heteronomous; *syn*, synergistic; *antag.*, antagonistic. (From Patton, H. D.: Reflex regulation of movement and posture. In Ruch, T. C., et al.: Neurophysiology, ed. **2**, Philadelphia, 1965, W. B. Saunders Co.)

muscle tone; the stretch reflex, and reciprocal innervation. These are the centers whose activity is "programmed" by the highest parts of the brain, as when a rapid coordinated movement such as swinging a golf club at a ball is executed. As explained at the beginning of this section, the movement is set once it is programmed and initiated by the highest parts of the brain. The movement is nevertheless dependent on the flow of input from the muscle spindles and the flow of output to the gamma efferent neurons.

Muscle spindles and motor learning

It now appears that the intrafusal fibers of the muscle spindles may be necessary for learning "voluntary" as well as reflex-controlled acts. They therefore participate in every body movement. Up to one third of all the motoneurons in the ventral roots of the spinal cord are gamma efferent motoneurons going to the muscle spindles; the rest are larger motoneurons that go to other muscle fibers. The small muscles of the digits, which require delicate control, have a greater density of spindles than the large, powerful muscles, such as those of the back. The gamma efferents regulate the sensitivity of the intrafusal fibers to stretching, and they therefore regulate most of the sensory "feedback" from movement that goes to spinal and higher reflex centers. The input from the muscle spindles seems to "decide" whether the muscle contracts in response to excitation from higher centers in so-called "voluntary" movements. If the gamma efferents contract intrafusal fibers, excitation to motoneurons of the muscle is added to their excitation by higher centers—the muscle contracts. If the intrafusal fibers do not contract and send excitation to the motoneurons, the excitation from higher centers may not be enough to cause the muscle to contract. In one experiment the role of the muscle spindles could be seen in teaching an animal to lift his leg at the sound of a tone in order to avoid a shock to his paw—a so-called **conditioned response (CR)** (Chapter 17). When the activity of the motoneurons is recorded during training, firing of gamma efferents to the muscles that lift the leg can be detected for several trials *before* the animal learns to lift his leg to avoid shock. It would therefore seem that excitation from the contraction of the muscle spindles must be added to excitation from higher centers in making the avoidance response.

VESTIBULAR SENSES
Labyrinth

The **vestibular senses** respond to head position and movement and set off many reflexes that enable us to maintain an upright posture. The receptors are located in the nonauditory part of the **labyrinth** of the inner ear, the part of the structure shown in Fig. 8-5 that is not involved in hearing. The labyrinths are located in the temporal bones, internal to the pinna, or external ear, on each side of the skull. Each labyrinth is surrounded by fluid **perilymph,** and the nonauditory parts are filled with fluid **endolymph;** thus the whole structure is cushioned by fluid. The labyrinth walls are a membranous (membrane) structure. The nonauditory part of this structure can be classified into two sets of receptor structures or both structural and functional grounds: (1) the **semicircular canals,** which respond primarily to rotation of the head, and (2) the **sacculus** and **utriculus** (collectively called **sacs**), which respond primarily to head position and linear motions of the head. The three semicircular canals have a common opening near their ampullae (sing., ampulla), the bulge on each canal at one end. There they communicate with the utriculus, which, in turn, opens into the sacculus. The ampullae, the sacculus, and the utriculus are individually served by branches of the statoacoustic, or eighth, nerve.

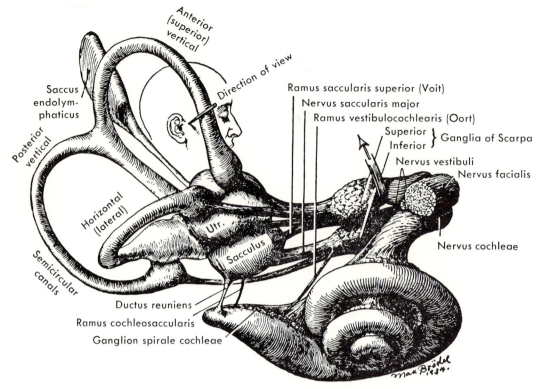

Fig. 8-5. Membranous labyrinth and its nerve supply. *Utr.,* utriculus. The saccular ramus and the saccular and vestibular nerves are parts of the vestibular nerve supply. The ampulla is the bulblike swelling on one end of each semicircular canal. Other structures are auditory in function. (Modified from Hardy, M.: Anat. Rec. **59:**404, 1934.)

Nerve pathways

Nerve fibers that respond to stimulation of the semicircular canals and sacs pass in the eighth nerve to the four **vestibular nuclei** of the medulla. Here they initiate *reflex* responses to head position and movement. The **medial longitudinal fasciculus** carries excitation from the vestibular nuclei to nuclei serving cranial nerves III, IV, and VI for reflex eye movements, and to XI for reflex head movements. The **vestibulospinal** tract carries excitation down the spinal cord to the extensor motoneurons to vary posture as a function of head position. Other pathways reach the cerebellum for more general balancing reactions. Excitation can also reach vomiting centers in the medulla (to cause motion sickness or seasickness).

Sensations

Conscious sensations do not result directly from stimulation of the nonauditory labyrinth by head position and movement. Most of the strong sensations that result from changing head position are caused by reflex *responses* to the change. For example, sensations of dizziness from spinning around and around, as children often do, come from reflex responses. The eyes move reflexly back and forth, so that the visual field seems to "swim" by. Reflex changes in extensor muscle tone cause the subject to

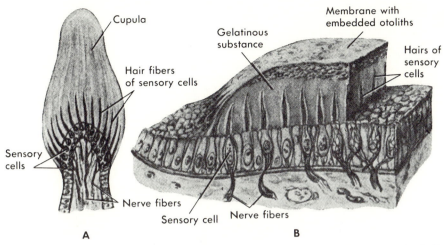

Fig. 8-6. Receptors of nonauditory labyrinth. **A,** Crista. **B,** Macula. (From Geldard, F. A.: The human senses, New York, 1953, John Wiley & Sons, Inc.)

feel that he is falling. These and other reflexes will be considered later in detail.

Semicircular canals

The semicircular canals lie in three planes of space at right angles to each other. There is a **horizontal, anterior vertical,** and **posterior vertical canal** in each labyrinth (Fig. 8-5). The horizontal canal inclines at about 30 degrees; the anterior and posterior vertical canals are at right angles to it and to each other. As a result, the anterior vertical canal on one side of the head is parallel with the posterior vertical canal on the other side of the head, and vice versa.

Ampulla. The bulblike swelling at one end of each semicircular canal where it joins the utriculus is called the **ampulla** (Fig. 8-5). Inside the ampulla is found a ridge of sensory cells, the **crista** (Fig. 8-6, *A*). These sensory cells have hair-cell endings that thrust into an overlying gelatinous (jellylike) mass called the **cupula.** Together, the cupula and crista occupy most of the internal space of the ampulla. This means that any circulation of fluid through the semicircular canals will push against

the cupula, bend the hair cells, and stimulate the fibers of the eighth nerve.

Rotational stimulation. Rotation of the head in any plane of motion will stimulate one semicircular canal more than the others because they are at right angles to one another; each canal is stimulated most by rotation parallel to it. The pattern of input from the three canals on both sides of the head can be used to detect the direction of the rotation. For example, consider stimulation of the horizontal canal by spinning around in a rotating chair. During *acceleration,* from rest to a maximum rate of spin, sudden rotation of the canal will "move the canal around its fluid" because of the inertia of the rest of the fluid (Fig. 8-7, *A*). This will cause fluid pressure against the cupula, bending the hair cells and stimulating the nerve fibers in the crista. When the rotating chair reaches a constant speed, stimulation will cease because the canal and the fluid will be rotating at the same speed and not in motion relative to each other. If the speed of rotation is too low for centrifugal force to be felt, no reflex reactions or sensations will result. When the

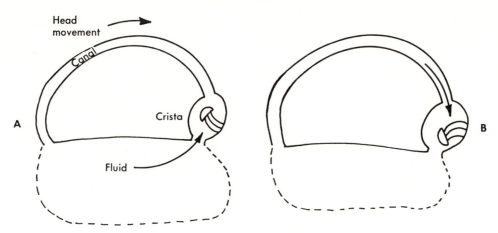

Fig. 8-7. Action of fluid motion on receptors in ampulla of semicircular canal.

rotation is suddenly *stopped* (decelerated), the horizontal semicircular canal will again be stimulated. The fluid will tend to keep moving in the direction in which the subject was rotating because of inertia of motion (Fig. 8-7, *B*). Fluid will press against the cupula from the opposite direction, as compared to acceleration. Deceleration will give the same reflexes and sensations as if the subject had *begun* rotating in the opposite direction. Excitation from the semicircular canals depends on rotational *acceleration* and *deceleration* rather than on constant motion and occurs in relatively brief periods against a resting discharge level. Nerve fibers from the crista of the ampulla show a resting discharge level of about five impulses per second, a rate that is increased by ampulla-trailing acceleration and decreased by ampulla-leading acceleration.

Rotational reflexes. Rapid rotational acceleration will cause **rotational nystagmus,** or compensating eye movement reflexes. The subject's eyes will move back and forth. If the acceleration is to the *right,* the **slow component** of the eye movement will be to the *left,* aiding him to keep a fixed visual reference point as the visual field sweeps by. The **fast component** of the back-and-forth eye movement will be to the *right,* so that he is able to pick up a new visual fixation point after his eyes have trav-

eled as far as possible to the left. Sudden stopping (deceleration) will cause **postrotational nystagmus.** The stimulus pattern would be the same if he had begun rotating in the opposite direction. Therefore, the slow component will be to the *right* and the fast component to the *left.* The student can test this assertion by spinning himself or another person, stopping suddenly, and observing the postrotational eye movements in a mirror or directly on another subject. If you test yourself, the visual field will "swim by" in the direction of the slow component of the postrotational eye movements. To avoid rotational nystagmus, dancers often turn their heads in the direction opposite to a spin; thus the semicircular canals are not stimulated, and a fixed visual reference is maintained. Head movement and visual field change are restricted to one quick motion for each revolution.

Rotation also changes extensor tone. Extensors in the limbs toward which the subject is rotating (acceleration) contract to maintain balance against the shift in weight to that side. When a person stops suddenly, it is as if he were rotating in the opposite direction. Thus, after stopping, he tends to fall in the direction in which he was spinning; if he *was* spinning to the right, his reflexes are now responding to a left-hand spin, and his left leg extends as if he had shifted his weight. He hasn't, so he staggers to the right.

Sacs

The **utriculus** communicates with the semicircular canals, and the **sacculus** communicates with the utriculus. The sacs are thus filled with the same fluid endolymph as the semicircular canals. However, their sensory structures are primarily specialized to respond to *head position* and to *linear acceleration* and *deceleration* rather than to rotary movements. The utriculus seems to be more important to behavior than the sacculus; destruction of the utriculus disturbs equilibrium and locomotion, but destruction of the sacculus does not lead to these symptoms. The input of the sacs seems more important in lower animals such as fish, amphibians, reptiles, and birds than it is to man and other mammals. Man can maintain equilibrium with vision when the sacs are destroyed, but he cannot stand erect on one foot with his eyes closed, and he loses orientation without a horizon—when swimming under water, for example.

Macula. The patch of sensory tissue on the inner surface of each of the sacs is called the **macula.** Its structure is shown in Fig. 8-6, *B.* The sensory cells extend hairlike processes into the cavity of the sac; the hairs are enveloped with a thick jellylike substance. On the free surface of the jelly rest many tiny particles of calcium carbonate (limestone "rocks"), the **otoliths.** The bases of the sensory cells are enveloped by basketlike endings of vestibular nerve fibers. These fibers are stimulated by the sensory cells when the hairlike processes are bent or pulled by movement of the "top-heavy" mass of jellylike material. Stimulation should occur whenever the hair cells are not upright or when the head is moved suddenly. The structure is like molded gelatin, with weights on top and hairs thrust into it from the bottom; movement "jiggles" the structure, and anything but an upright position displaces it to one side.

Hair cells. The hair cells are stimulated on being bent or pulled when the "top-heavy" mass of jelly that envelops them is shifted from an upright position. Motion affects the gelatinous mass in the same way that shaking or tilting a gelatin mold affects gelatin. The stimulation results from linear acceleration or deceleration of the head or from head positions that tilt the hair cells and their enveloping jelly from an upright position.

Head position. Since the postural muscles must continuously be informed of head position, the hair cells maintain a continuous or "resting" rate of neural firing, even when they are in an upright position. The **macula utriculi** in each inner ear has its hair cells upright when the head is erect. Tilting the head will result in a different direction of movement of the gelatinous mass for every different head movement. The pattern of stimulation that results depends on the fine structure of the hairs (Fig. 8-8). Each hair cell has hairs of graduated length. When head movement tilts the top-heavy gelatinous mass in the direction of the longest hair, the firing rate in nerve fibers from that receptor is *increased;* movement in the opposite fashion *decreases* the rate of firing. Since the longest cilia of hair cells in different parts of the utriculus are oriented in different directions, a different *pattern* of increases and decreases in the firing of sensory fibers will result from each different head movement. The sensory code is probably *topographic,* with a different spatial pattern of input reaching the vestibular nuclei for each position and movement of the head. The macula sacculi in each inner ear functions in the same fashion, save that its hair cells are oriented laterally (point out toward the sides) when the head is in an upright position. As previously noted, the utriculus is much more important to orientation than the sacculus.

Acceleration and deceleration. Sudden linear movement of the head stimulates the maculae, especially the macula utriculi. This

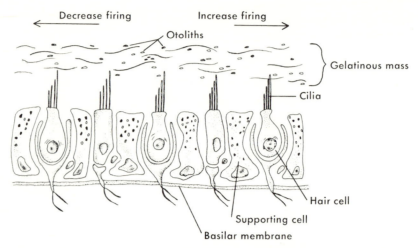

Fig. 8-8. Sketch of fine structure of macula, showing arrangement of hair cells (cilia) for each receptor. The longer hairs are responsible for sensitivity to direction of tilt. (From Flock, A., and Duvall, A. J.: The ultrastructure of the kinocilium of the sensory cells in the inner ear and lateral line organs, J. Cell Biol. **25:**1-8, 1965.)

can distort sensations of the upright position when visual cues are not a help. For example, in flying, sudden acceleration makes the pilot feel that he is climbing and sudden deceleration that he is diving, even though he is in straight and level flight.

Eye reflexes and head position. Changes in head position result in elevation of the eyes when the head is lowered, depression of the eyes when the head is raised, and rotation of the eyes when the head is tilted. All these reflexes aid the eyes in becoming oriented toward a level horizon. The eye reflexes originate in visual input as well as in the maculae. They are mediated by the medial longitudinal fasciculus pathways to the nuclei serving cranial nerves III, IV, and VI for the eye muscles. (These pathways were described earlier in the chapter.) At the same time, change from the normal erect head position stimulates the maculae to send excitation to the neck muscles in order to return the head to the erect position. Here the medial longitudinal fasciculus carries excitation to cranial nerve XI for excitation of the neck muscles.

Righting reflexes

In four-legged animals, when the neck muscles react so as to restore the upright position of the head, the neck is "twisted" if the body is not erect. This twisted position stimulates proprioceptors in the neck muscles, and the input of these proprioceptors reaches descending tracts in the spinal cord going to the motor nerve supply of the body trunk. The body muscles are then stimulated to restore the upright position of the body. The sequence involved in neck and body righting reflexes is most clearly observed by holding a cat upside down and dropping it from a position 4 or 5 feet off the floor. First the head turns toward the upright position, next the forelimbs, and then the hindlimbs. Twisting of the neck has stimulated the upper body trunk, and twisting of the upper trunk has stimulated the lower trunk, all in sequence. At the same time, extensor tone has been increased, and the animal will land with all four limbs stiffly extended to cushion the shock.

Postural reflexes. The head also "leads" (caused by visual and macular input) in regulating posture. In animals the forelimb and hindlimb extensor tone will vary with head position. If a cat lowers its head in looking under an object, forelimb extensors will relax and hindlimb extensors contract— the forepart of the body will be reflexly lowered and the hindpart elevated. If the head is raised above the normal position, preparatory to jumping up on an object, forelimb extensors will contact and hindlimb extensors relax. The forequarters will be raised and the hindquarters lowered in position for the jump. These reflexes can be demonstrated in cats with the higher parts of the brain removed as long as the connections between the sacs, medulla, and spinal cord motoneurons are intact.

Vestibular senses: practical implications

In general, the vestibular senses depend on normal conditions of gravity and acceleration to furnish accurate input for normal responses. They evolved in fish, which are thus able to orient themselves in a three-dimensional environment with little gravitational effect and little visual orientation. Evolution has adapted mammalian vestibular senses to gravity, subordinated them to accurate visual input, and developed them to respond to the amount and kind of acceleration and deceleration found in normal body movement. When their normal stimulation pattern is changed, the resulting input can cause extreme disorientation and nausea, especially when accurate visual input does not correct for their misinformation. As pointed out previously, the extreme acceleration or deceleration encountered in flying an airplane can cause a pilot in level flight to believe that he is climbing or diving if he is flying "blind," that is, without a natural visual horizon. Centrifugal forces change stimulation to the sacs in a climb, a dive, or a turn, although the semicircular canals seem little affected. A pilot who is flying upside down in a "loop" may be experiencing sufficient centrifugal force to feel that he is upright. One of the most

difficult problems in learning to fly is the necessity of disregarding vestibular input and depending strictly on vision—either a view of the horizon or, still more difficult, instrument reading when flying "blind." Research on the vestibular apparatus and the effects of weightlessness received a great deal of attention with the advent of space flight. In early experiments a weightless environment could be maintained for as long as 15 seconds by flying an aircraft with a large empty cabin in a parabolic curve—first a climb and then a dive. This method is still used in training for space flight. Orientation under conditions of weightlessness can also be taught through scuba diving; underwater the subject has the same specific gravity as the water. Neither method provides any sensations of up or down and there is no visual horizon. Space flights have resulted in initial symptoms of nausea and dizziness among some astronauts, but these seem to abate in a day or two and can be minimized by practice with the training methods described above. Given enough visual and tactual cues, space flights of over a month have produced no lasting disorders of the vestibular apparatus, although a period of some hours is required to readapt completely to normal gravity.

Finally, regular rhythmic motions that differ enough from those of walking can cause carsickness, airsickness, or seasickness, because of the nausea centers in the medulla. The primary component causing the disturbance seems to be vertical motion rather than pitch (fore and aft motion) or yaw (side-to-side motion). The frequency and amplitude of the vertical motion seem to be the important variables—frequencies near 20 per minute and amplitudes of about 7 feet being most disturbing. Drugs have proved to be of some help, and fortunately most persons adapt, as when a sailor gets his "sea legs." A combination of scopolamine and dextroamphetamine has been found recently to prevent motion sickness by action on the autonomic nervous system.

SUMMARY

Proprioception is sensory input for body position and movement. It includes kinesthesis from the general receptors in joints and muscles, and vestibular sensitivity from the nonauditory labyrinth. Kinesthesis in the limbs gives rise to conscious sensations of position and movement when receptors in the joints (mostly pacinian corpuscles) are stimulated. These receptors adapt little, so that one is always aware of limb position. Their pathways upward in the dorsal columns of the cord reach the cerebral cortex. Because many synapses are involved, cortically originated "voluntary" response to joint receptors is slow. This input can regulate slow "voluntary" reactions, but it is too slow to correct a rapid movement in progress. Rapid movements are regulated by reflexes in lower centers of the brain and spinal cord that are "programmed" by the cortex, cerebellum, and other higher centers.

Kinesthesis also includes sensory input from the muscles and tendons that does not cause conscious sensation. This input participates in the reflex "programs" mentioned above and is important to posture and coordination. One such reflex that can be shown in exaggerated form is the tendon jerk. Striking the tendon of a muscle causes a quick contraction of the muscle. This reflex is stimulated by receptors in the muscle that are sensitive to the stretching of the muscle when the tendon is struck. The reflex is rapid because it is monosynaptic.

More gradual stretching of extensor muscles elicits a more gradual extensor contraction in the stretch reflex. The stretch reflex is elicited in extensor muscles when limbs are flexed by the pull of gravity; it straightens those limbs and thus is an antigravity reflex. Shifts in posture change the pattern of stretch reflexes in extensors in normal postural adjustment. All muscles are anatomically stretched to some degree, and their stretch reflex response causes the muscle tone that varies with position (amount of stretching). Arm and hand flexors in man are antigravity muscles that react like extensors.

The receptors stimulating the stretch reflex are found in the muscle spindles. These structures each contain two to twelve intrafusal fibers. The spindle fibers are functionally attached to the ends of the muscle, and stretching of them (and therefore stretch-reflex stimulation) is relieved by muscle contraction; they are "in parallel" with the muscle. The Golgi tendon organs are found in the tendons and are "in series" with the muscle, as they react to tendon pull imposed by external force or by the muscle itself. They inhibit the muscle by a multisynaptic reflex.

The intrafusal fiber has both sensory and motor functions. In its central part, primary, or annulospiral, endings respond to pull with the stretch reflex. Secondary, or flower-spray, endings inhibit the muscle; they are probably stimulated by pressure from the contraction of surrounding muscle fibers. The striated ends of the intrafusal fiber can contract to stimulate the primary endings. They receive motor fibers, the gamma efferents. The gamma efferents can stimulate the stretch reflex. They can therefore "take up slack" on the spindle fiber as the muscle shortens in contraction to maintain stretch reflex excitation of the motoneurons. They can reinforce a static contraction by increasing stretch reflex input.

The reciprocal innervation of antagonist flexors and extensors is caused by kinesthetic input. The annulospiral input that excites a muscle inhibits its antagonist. The flower-spray and Golgi inputs that inhibit a muscle excite its antagonist. When a muscle contracts, simultaneous contraction of its gamma efferents stimulates annulospiral endings to inhibit the antagonist muscle. The same reciprocal relations hold for the crossed extension reflex. All three inputs also reach the cerebellum and other subcortical centers to regulate rapid reflex coordinations "programmed" by higher parts of the brain. Experiments seem to show that muscle spindle input is vital to learning even "voluntary" responses.

The vestibular senses are special senses located in the nonauditory part of the membranous labyrinth. The nonauditory labyrinth is surrounded by perilymph and contains endolymph. Its semicircular canals respond to head rotation, and its sacculus and utriculus to position and linear motion of the head; both are served by part of the eighth nerve that goes to the four vestibular nuclei of the medulla. The vestibular nuclei mediate reflexes rather than conscious sensations. The medial longitudinal fasciculus carries excitation to nerves III, IV, and VI for reflex eye movements, and to XI for reflex head movements. The vestibulospinal tract carries excitation to spinal extensor motoneurons for postural adjustment, and other pathways reach the cerebellum for complex coordination. The anterior vertical, posterior vertical, and horizontal semicircular canals in each temporal bone are at right angles to one another, and each canal responds most to movement in its own plane. Three-dimensional movement detection is thus provided.

The ampulla of each canal contains a crista of sensory cells, with hair endings thrust into an overlying gelatinous cupula. Fluid circulation in the semicircular canals pushes against the cupula to stimulate the hair cells. Rotary acceleration or deceleration of a canal, rather than a constant rotation, is the adequate stimulus. During rotation in a horizontal plane, the horizontal canal is stimulated. During acceleration, rotational nystagmus is produced, with the eyes showing a slow component of movement opposite to the direction of rotation and a fast component in the same direction. Deceleration reverses the direction of slow and fast components in postrotational nystagmus. Extensor tone is increased on the side toward rotation during acceleration and increased on the opposite side during deceleration.

The sacs include the sacculus and utriculus, the latter being the more important. The sensory structure in each is the macula, consisting of hair cells surrounded by a jellylike material with otoliths on its free surface. Hair cells provide continuous postural information by a resting rate of firing in their sensory fibers. Displacement of the jelly by linear acceleration and deceleration, and head positions in which the hair cells are not upright, stimulate or inhibit the hair cells for a topographically patterned input. In the utriculus the hair cells are oriented vertically, and in the sacculus they are oriented laterally, so that each head position or movement has a different pattern of stimulus input. Departures from the vertical head position cause compensating eye movements that maintain the horizon and reflex reactions of the neck muscles that return the head to the erect position. Proprioceptors in the neck muscles stimulate reflex reactions of the body muscles to restore the upright position in the righting reflexes. Forelimb and hindlimb extensors in animals adjust to head position in postural reflexes.

In general, the vestibular senses depend on normal gravity and body movements. The extreme accelerations, decelerations, and centrifugal forces that occur in flying can cause disorientation unless there are visual cues. Lack of gravitation in outer space can cause lack of orientation. Large and regular vertical movement can cause carsickness, seasickness, and airsickness through nausea reflex centers in the medulla.

READINGS

Merton, P. A.: How we control the contraction of our muscles, Sci. Am. **226**:30-37, May 1972. (W. H. Freeman Co. Reprint No. 1249.)

Mueller, C. G.: Sensory psychology, Englewood Cliffs, N.J., 1965, Prentice-Hall, Inc.

Wilson, V. J.: The labyrinth, the brain, and posture, Am. Scientist **63**:325-332, May-June 1975.

von Buddenbrock, W.: The senses, Ann Arbor, Mich., 1958, University of Michigan Press.

chapter 9

Chemical senses

OVERVIEW

The chemical senses are so named because they are normally and adequately stimulated by substances in solution. They include gustation (taste), olfaction (smell), and the common chemical sense. The common chemical sense is the simplest and will be disposed of first; it is stimulated by dissolved irritants in the eyes, nose, throat, and other mucous areas. The sensory mechanism seems identical with pain; however, the "stinging" quality of ammonia in the eyes and nose or pepper in the mouth seems different from other kinds of pain to the subject.

Gustation will be taken up next. Most of the taste receptors are confined to the tongue. Their primary qualities are sweet, salt, sour, and bitter. What is known of the adequate stimuli for these four taste qualities will be summarized. The nerve pathways for taste will be described. When receptors and nerve pathways are understood, experiments on the physiology of taste can be discussed. Phenomena of taste thresholds, adaptation, contrast, compensation, fusion, and so on conclude the section on gustation.

Olfaction is the final topic of the chapter. After some introductory remarks, the receptors and their nervous connections will be described. Some of the unique difficulties in accurately stimulating olfaction and the methods used to overcome these difficulties will precede discussion of olfactory qualities and the sensory mechanisms underlying them. Theories of olfactory sensory mechanisms will be summarized. Remarks on olfactory phenomena such as adaptation, compensation, and anosmia (smell "blindness") conclude the chapter.

COMMON CHEMICAL SENSE
Quality

The **common chemical sense** refers to the sensitivity of the mucous membranes of the body to dissolved irritants. The term is most frequently used in referring to the "stinging" quality that is aroused in the mouth by "hot" foods such as chili peppers. However, vaporizing substances such as ammonia cause stinging sensations in the eyes and nose, and these sensations are also caused by the common chemical sense. In the eyes and nose the irritants cause tears and nasal secretions, respectively, as anyone who has smelled ammonia or peeled an onion can testify. Nasal sensitivity seems the greatest (a few thousandths of 1% for some gases), eye sensitivity is intermediate, and sensations from the mouth may require a solution of 3% to 5% of some of the most irritating substances. Common chemical sensitivity is not confined to the nose, eyes, and mouth. Any mucous membrane, such as those of the anus and genitals, has common chemical sensitivity.

Common chemical sensations may be related to pain by the subject, but they seem subjectively different from pain in quality, being described as "stinging" or "burning" sensations. Common chemical sensations in the mouth may be pleasant in mild arousal —when one "tastes" peppermint or a dry martini, common chemical stimulation is the "stinging" part of the "flavor." It has been argued that the common chemical sense differs from pain because the sensory quality seems different to the subject and because drugs affect these sensations in a different way (for example, cocaine anesthetizes skin pain much more readily than the common chemical sense). The change in sensory quality can probably be explained by differences in the stimuli causing common chemical sensation from those causing skin pain; dissolved mucous irritants *should* cause a different sensation from that of skin pain stimuli, just as skin pain from a burn differs from that caused by a cut. Drugs can "deaden" skin pain more readily than they can deaden the common chemical sense. However, drugs may be less effective when the nerve endings are more directly stimulated by irritants on sensitive mucous surfaces. Finally, the anatomy of the receptors for pain and of the common chemical sense are identical, as are their pathways to the brain. It may be concluded that the common chemical sense is pain sensitivity in the mucous membranes, that is, pain stimulated by irritants dissolved in the mucus covering the mucous membranes.

Receptors

The receptors are free nerve endings distributed to the tongue, nasopharynx, orbit, and other mucous surfaces. Like other pain endings their threshold is relatively high, but the central nervous system response fatigues slowly, and the receptors adapt little under most conditions of chemical stimulation. In part, receptor adaptation is rare because the dissolved irritant is not a "constant" stimulus; the chemical changes it initiates in the tissue are a process of active change. The "bite" of a peppermint stick will not change greatly, then, no matter how long you chew on it—and your eyes will not adapt to peeling onions.

Nerve pathways

The fibers from the mouth, tongue, orbit, and nasal passages that serve pain reach the brainstem in cranial nerves V, VII, IX, and X. They are distributed with other pain fibers to the spinal tract and nucleus of the fifth nerve. The spinal nucleus relays excitation to the thalamus and, unlike other pain inputs, to the postcentral gyrus of the cerebral cortex (somesthetic projection area). As with other pain fibers, there are many collaterals to the reticular formation of the brainstem that arouse the brain to greater activity and contribute descending output to muscles. Pain input of any kind stimulates the nervous system to much activity.

GUSTATION

Taste sensitivity is caused largely by receptors on the tongue in adult man (children sometimes have taste receptors in the cheeks; these receptors later disappear). Sensitivity is also found in the palate or roof of the mouth (for sour and bitter) and the larynx. Strictly speaking, taste receptors give rise only to sensations of sweet, salt, sour, and bitter; the complex of the subtle sensations called "taste" in everyday speech includes smell, common chemical sensitivity, and somesthesis. A food is said to taste bland when "stinging" common chemical sensations are not present. Foods taste flat when one has a head cold because it is then impossible to smell food. Hold your nose and you cannot *taste* the difference between a slice of apple and a slice of raw potato—they can be distinguished only by their texture (somesthesis). Coffee tastes hot as well as bitter, and corn bread tastes "coarse" —both warmth and texture are somesthetic sensations. This shows that gourmets depend more on smell than taste. As used here, however, gustation refers only to sensations of sweet, sour, bitter, and salt.

Methods and definitions

As usual, the four primary taste qualities have been distinguished by the reports of human subjects. In the usual experiment of this kind, various solutions are applied to the tongue of the subject, and he reports on what he tastes. (The tongue is washed with water between tests to avoid interference among successive stimuli.) Agreement among subjects is the criterion for naming taste qualities, and subjects largely agree on sweet, salt, sour, and bitter, or mixtures of these, as being all they taste under such circumstances. Animal experiments often involve washing the tongue of an anesthetized animal with the same solutions while recording from the seventh or ninth cranial nerve. As will be seen later, individual receptors for each of the qualities do *not* seem indicated by the data that result from nerve cell recording. However, the *patterns* of nerve cell firing are such that the central nervous system could detect four kinds of signals corresponding to four taste qualities (three in the case of the cat, which does not respond to sweet).

Recently, an exciting method has been developed that promises subjective reports and gross neural recording at the same time. In man surgical operations on the middle ear to restore hearing, expose a branch of the sensory nerves for taste (the chorda tympani). The tongue can then be washed with various solutions, and the resulting sensory nerve impulses can be recorded at the same time. With a subject under general anesthesia, nerve firing has been recorded that resulted from a touch to the tongue, as well as from solutions of salt, sucrose and saccharine (sweet), quinine (sour), and acetic acid (bitter) applied to the tongue. The surgery can be done with the subject under local anesthesia, which offers future opportunities for the study of taste through nerve recording and the subjective report of a conscious subject at the same time.

Development

The development of taste sensitivity begins before birth, when sensory branches of nerves VII and IX invade the epithelial cells of the mucous membranes of the tongue. Under this influence (called **sensory appropriation**) the epithelial cells develop into specialized receptors. Development is complete at puberty, but the receptors begin to atrophy after about 45 years of age. These changes are related to the gonadal hormones; taste receptors atrophy after castration in animals, but they can be reestablished by injections of the missing sex hormones. Apparently taste matures at puberty and atrophies as the output of gonadal hormones falls off in middle and old age. This has important consequences for nutrition in older people, who frequently lose interest in food and do not eat enough. Recent experiments show that taste sensitivity in the aged can be restored to some degree by increasing their intake of the "trace" metals needed by the body, such as zinc and copper. This therapy does not restore atrophied taste receptors but seems to make the remaining ones more sensitive by increasing the penetration of the taste stimuli into the receptors. The discovery of sour and bitter sensitivity in the palate ("roof" of the mouth) has resulted in the redesigning of the upper plates of dentures for older people in order to admit taste stimuli to this area.

The taste receptors apparently require continuous renewal; sensory taste cells are replaced about every 7 days, on the average, like other epithelial cells. Studies that label the DNA of the taste cells with radioactive compounds confirm this finding. Furthermore the receptors may be "passed along" from one nerve fiber to another, and a single fiber may reach more than one receptor, as cells are replaced. The replacement cells become receptors under the influence of the seventh and ninth nerves and the gonadal hormones.

Receptors

The taste receptors are spindle-shaped cells, each of which has a single hair. They occur in clusters of two to twelve, surrounded by supporting cells. The whole structure is called a **taste bud** because of the resemblance to a flower bud (Fig. 9-1, *A*). The taste buds are most frequently found in the papillae of the tongue (Fig. 9-1, *B*). The papillae are structures in the tongue, made up of a "moat" surrounding an

Surface of tongue

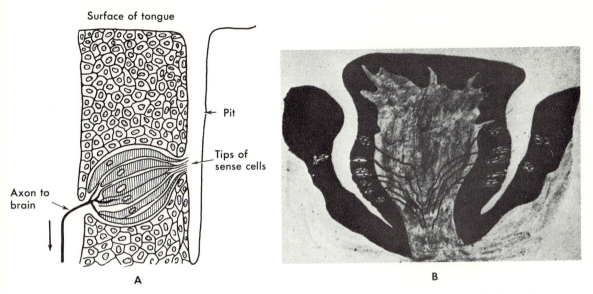

Pit

Tips of
sense cells

Axon to
brain

A

B

Fig. 9-1. Sensory structures for taste. **A,** Taste bud, with tips of sense cells extending into pit that forms the "moat" of a papilla. **B,** Circumvallate papilla seen in diagrammatic cross section, with taste buds lining the walls and their tips opening to the "moat" surrounding the papilla. (**A** from Woodworth, R. S.: Psychology, ed. 4, New York, 1940, Holt, Rinehart & Winston, Inc.; **B** from Geldard, F. A.: The human senses, New York, 1953, John Wiley & Sons, Inc.)

"island." The taste buds thrust their hairs into the moat from the sides of the island and the walls of the moat. The moat serves to contain the solution to be tasted so that it can affect the hair cells; these receptors in turn set off nerve impulses in the taste nerve fibers. There are four types of papillae on the tongue (Fig. 9-2), but those in the center of the tongue do not contain taste buds. Only the tip, sides, and back of the tongue are taste-sensitive.

Qualities. Stimulation of the tongue with various solutions identifies four primary taste qualities when smell, temperature, somesthesis, and common chemical sensitivity are ruled out. The four primary qualities are sweet, salt, sour, and bitter. The adequate stimulus for sweet is sucrose (sugar). The best salt response comes from NaCl (common table salt) solutions. Weak solutions of hydrochloric acid (HCl) provide the most adequate stimulus for sour. Bitter sensations result from stimulation with quinine solutions. In man the order of increas-

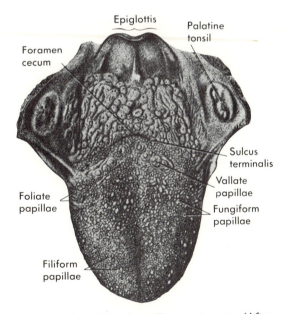

Epiglottis

Palatine
tonsil

Foramen
cecum

Sulcus
terminalis

Vallate
papillae

Foliate
papillae

Fungiform
papillae

Filiform
papillae

Fig. 9-2. Location of papillae on tongue. (After Kahn: Das Leben des Menschen, W. Keller & Co.; from Neal, H. V., and Rand, H. W.: Comparative anatomy. Copyright 1936 by McGraw-Hill Book Co., Inc. Used by permission.)

ing sensitivity to the four primary qualities is sweet, salt, sour, and bitter when the test solutions named above are used. This order of sensitivity is at body temperature—all tastes except sour change sensitivity with temperature change. (If saccharin is used to stimulate sweet, this quality has the lowest threshold except for bitter.) All the more complex tastes are compounds of these four primary qualities; an experienced taster can detect which of the four are present and which are absent in a complex taste.

Detection is aided because the tongue is not equally sensitive to the four primary qualities at the tip, sides, and back. The tongue is most sensitive to sweet at the tip, bitter at the back, and sour at the sides. Salt sensitivity is widespread, but somewhat greater at the tip. Common reactions to three of the four tastes confirm the different sensitivity of parts of the tongue. In tasting a pleasantly sweet substance, a person "purses" his lips to concentrate the solution near the tip of the tongue. In response to a very bitter substance, a person gags, which acts to remove the substance from the back of the tongue and palate. Very sour solutions cause an open-mouthed frowning expression, which removes the solution from the sides of the tongue and palate. In addition to the subjective primary nature of the four qualities and the different sensitivity of various parts of the tongue, narcotizing the tongue with cocaine gives evidence for four primary qualities. As the drug takes effect, taste sensations disappear in the following order: bitter, sweet, salt, and sour. This is not the same as their order of sensitivity—the drug is affecting the four qualities differently, and the tongue is not just losing sensitivity.

Stimuli

The nature of the adequate stimulus for two of the primary qualities is clearer than for the other two. Sour and salt are stimulated by **ions,** or electrically charged atoms or molecules, in solution. Less is known

about what affects the sweet and bitter tastes. The biggest mystery is how the receptors react to solutions to cause nerve impulses.

The sour taste is stimulated by the positively charged hydrogen ion (H^+), an ion that dissociates well from weak acids in solution. The effectiveness of the H^+ ion is modified by the **buffer** action of the saliva. Saliva contains substances that neutralize either acid H^+ ions or basic OH^- ions. The more readily an acid gives off H^+ ions in solution, the more sour it tastes. However, organic ions are more sour than inorganic ions that dissociate to give off an equal number of H^+ ions. Furthermore, not all acids are sour; for example, amino acids are sweet, and picric acid is bitter. The H^+ ion may be the most important agent in a sour stimulus, but other factors are involved.

Both the positive and negative ions of salts are important to their salty taste. (A positive ion is called a cation and a negative ion an anion—Chapter 4.) In table salt (NaCl) the cation (Na^+) seems more important than the anion (Cl^-). Other anions joined with Na^+—for example, $NaSO_4$—taste salty, and other cations joined with Cl^-, such as KCl, taste salty, although the taste varies in quality and intensity. NaCl is the most effective stimulus; the other salts taste less salty, and some have a mixed salt and bitter taste. Salts often taste bitter at threshold concentrations as well. The size of the salt molecule (its molecular weight) seems related to whether a salt will taste salty or bitter; the larger salts, such as sodium acetate, often taste bitter. As with sour, ions are the most important part of the salt stimulus, but other factors are involved.

Less is known about what makes a stimulus taste sweet. The sweetest substances are organic compounds that do not break up into ions. Most of the sugars taste sweet if the carbon chain of their molecule is not too long; sucrose is the sweetest. There are exceptions to these rules, however, Some of the inorganic lead and beryllium *salts* taste sweet, and a slight change in the molecular geometry of a sugar that does not change its carbon chain can change its sweetness. Increases in molecular size (molecular weight) can cause a compound to change from sweet to bitter. An increase in concentration of some sweet solutions can also change their taste; saccharin is the sweetest substance known when diluted, but it tastes bitter in concentrated solutions. Many bitter and sweet compounds have similar chemical and physical properties. About all that can be said is that the geometry of the molecule is the most important factor known to determine sweetness.

Of all the primary tastes the least is known about bitter. Although quinine solutions are the stimuli generally used for bitter in the laboratory, alkaloids and some complex inorganic salts are also bitter. The bitter taste does not depend on ionization, but some ionizing metals are bitter in solution. As previously noted, some salts taste bitter at threshold concentrations, some salts with large molecules taste bitter, some sugars with large molecules taste bitter, and concentrated sweet stimuli can change to bitter. Molecular size and shape are important, but that was what was said about sweet. Little is really known about either stimulus.

Nerve pathways

The nerve pathways serving taste are partly unique to taste and partly shared with somesthesis. Taste fibers from the tongue go to their own primary nucleus in the brainstem. However, the second-order fibers that arise here join second-order somesthetic fibers en route to the thalamus. The third-order fibers from the thalamus to the cortex are also anatomically mixed with somesthetic fibers. Most of the first-order taste fibers are carried in the seventh (anterior tongue) and ninth (posterior tongue) cranial nerves. Upon reaching the brainstem, they form a tract, the **tractus solitarius;** the excitation is passed on by the nu-

cleus of that tract. The second-order fibers join the medial lemniscus and end on the **arcuate** (face) **nucleus** of the thalamus, along with second-order somesthetic fibers representing the face. The third-order fibers project with somesthesis from the face on area 2 of the postcentral gyrus. They are adjacent to the part of the precentral motor area (area 4) controlling the chewing muscles. Sensory input from somesthetic sensations of the mouth, taste, and motor control of chewing are as close anatomically as they are functionally.

In agreement with the other senses, efferent pathways that control the sensory input have been found. Fibers that reach the first synapse in the pathway (nucleus of the tractus solitarius) from higher brain centers seem to be inhibitory, and fire in response to stomach distention. Perhaps this adds to adaptation effects and helps explain why food does not seem to "taste as good" near the end of a meal; it may provide part of the mechanism for controlling food intake to match the needs of the body.

Physiology of taste

The physiology of the taste receptor is largely a mystery. Substances must be in solution to stimulate the hair cells—one cannot taste a piece of stainless steel because it does not dissolve in saliva—but little else is known about how the hair cells respond. Experimenters have stimulated individual hair cells with micropipettes, and recordings have been made of the electrical responses of individual hair cells and individual afferent neurons. These experiments will be briefly described. What is confusing is that some single receptors fire neurons in response to more than one of the primary qualities. Anatomical studies using the electron microscope explain this by showing that each neuron innervates several receptor cells—the receptor cells may differ in which stimuli they respond to, but each could fire the nerve cell. Individual receptor cells of a taste bud (papilla) have been stimulated with solutions from a micro-pipette and stimulated electrically with a microelectrode. Individual receptor cells respond to a single quality only, although a single papilla may contain cells responding to different qualities. Cells responding to different qualities differ in appearance as seen through a microscope and differ in sensitivity to different electrical stimulus frequencies. What is puzzling about all this, is that a single sensory nerve fiber may be stimulated by several receptor cells, each responding to a different quality. Some more complex *pattern* of input must signal each quality. Furthermore, some receptors respond to temperature as well as to taste. Some chemical event in the receptor initiates nerve impulses in response to solutions at a specific location on the receptor cell. In the end perhaps a match can be found between the shape and charge of the molecules or ions that stimulate taste and the physical shape or charge of the receptor sites. This has been done for smell but not for taste.

Generator potential. Microelectrodes have been used to penetrate single taste receptor cells and record their generator potential in response to taste stimuli. As in other types of receptors it is the generator potential that fires the nerve impulses for taste by depolarizing the nerve cell. What is unusual about the generator potential for taste receptors is its duration—the potential requires 10 to 15 seconds to reach its maximum.

Nerve fiber recording. Single fibers from the ninth nerve of the cat respond to more than one stimulus solution washed over the tongue. Of course only the smaller fibers go to a single receptor—the larger ones go to two or more receptors. However, the only information the brain receives is nerve impulses; it cannot distinguish between two receptors served by the same fiber. The pattern of fiber response is shown in Table 9-1. Four classes of fibers were found: those responding to salt or acid (salt fiber); acid alone (acid fiber); quinine alone (quinine fiber); or acid, quinine, and water (water fiber). (Other studies show two different kinds of response to salt.) The code to the central nervous system would involve detecting salt when the salt fibers fired, sour when both salt and acid fibers fired, and bitter when the quinine fiber fired. (The cat does not sense sweet, but fibers responding to sweet have been found in the dog and rat.) Doubt has been cast on the water fiber because the saliva is a little salty, and the response of the water fiber to salt may depend on the state of adaptation of the tongue. Nerve recordings in man show no response to distilled water. It is evident in any case that the primary qualities depend on *patterns* of input rather than on single-receptor stimulation. However, there are many differences in input pattern in different species to complicate the matter. In the rat, for example, receptors have been found that are sensitive to both sweet and salt. One set of these receptors is more sensitive to

Table 9-1. Response of single fibers of taste nerves in the cat*

Stimulus	*Water fiber*	*Salt fiber*	*Acid fiber*	*Quinine fiber*		*Theoretical sensation*
H_2O (salt 0.03M)	+	0	0	0	→	Water
NaCl (0.05M)	0	+	0	0	→	Salt
HCl (pH 2.5)	+	+	+	0	→	Sour
Quinine	+	0	0	+	→	Bitter

*From Cohen, M. J., Hagiwara, S., and Zotterman, Y.: Acta Physiol. Scand. **33**:316, 1955.
Single fibers of nerve IX either do respond (+) or do not respond (0) to solutions washed over the tongue, showing *patterns* of response to primary qualities (see text).

sweet than to salt, and the other is more sensitive to salt than to sweet. The *relative* amount of input in these two sets of receptors may determine whether the rat senses salt or sweet. Further refinements of the input pattern are possible. Individual fibers in the rat differ in their response to various salts. For example, individual salt fibers differ in their response to NaCl and KCl, but give similar reactions to NH_4Cl and NaCl. Yet rats can distinguish NH_4Cl from NaCl in behavioral tests. Finally, the receptor input pattern must be quite *labile* (changeable), as tests on taste adaptation in man show quite clearly. By creating different conditions of adaptation before the test, salt (NaCl) can be made to taste salt, sweet, sour, or bitter!

Temperature response. Single afferent neurons in the cat respond to temperature as well as to taste. One investigator found that only two of twenty-eight units that he studied responded to taste alone. Some responded to taste and to cooling, others to taste, warming, and cooling, and still others to temperature changes only. Perhaps this is why taste thresholds are so intimately dependent on temperature.

Duplexity theory of taste

In agreement with the temperature response of taste cells, one investigator has devised an ingenious way of detecting which taste and temperature inputs are most closely related in sensation. He stimulated the two *sides* of the tongue with different solutions and asked the subject where the taste seemed to be located. When salt, sour, or cold stimulated one side of the tongue, and bitter, sweet, or warm stimulated the other side, the subjects localized the sensations at the sides of the tongue. The sensations seemed separate. But when salt, sour, or cold were presented in pairs, or when bitter, sweet, or warm were paired, the sensation seemed to come from the center of the tongue. These results suggest that the tongue sensations formed two groups:

(1) bitter, sweet, and warm and (2) salt, sour, and cold. The neural basis of the phenomenon is unknown, but it might be related to the receptors described in the preceding paragraph, receptors that respond to both temperature and taste.

Taste phenomena

Taste receptors are affected by temperature and prior adaptation. Temperature affects the sensitivity of the receptors and therefore their input pattern and the taste that is perceived. Furthermore, some receptors respond to both temperature and taste (see temperature response, p. 179). Adaptation to one taste can enhance or depress sensitivity to another taste, giving contrast or compensation effects. Unlike some of the other senses, the primary qualities do not fuse to give a "new" taste. There is so little fusion in taste that an experienced observer can always detect which of the four primary qualities are present and which are absent.

Taste thresholds. The threshold for taste varies according to the area of the tongue stimulated, as previously described. The tip of the tongue is most sensitive to sweet and salt, the sides to sour, and the back to bitter. For any of these areas, reliable absolute thresholds can be established for each of the four primary tastes, provided that the tongue is rinsed between stimuli to prevent adaptation effects. The temperature of the stimulus solution must also be held constant. Absolute thresholds vary with the duration of stimulation as well. Difference thresholds have also been reliably measured, and an equal-interval scale of taste units called "gusts" has been established. The absolute threshold for taste is much higher than the threshold for smell, but their difference thresholds are much the same. The Weber ratio for taste resembles smell and is not constant—it diminishes from about 1 to 0.2 for each of the four qualities. If Stevens' scaling techniques are used (see Chapter 6) linear graphs relating stimulus and sensation intensities are obtained for each of the four qualities. The slopes of the four graphs are found to differ, showing that the four qualities vary from one another in their difference threshold. The slope is smaller for bitter than for sour, smaller for sour than for salt, and smaller for salt than for sweet—the order of decreasing taste sensitivity of the four qualities (using quinine, hydrochloric acid, sodium chloride, and sugar solutions).

Temperature. Extreme hot or cold temperatures decrease sensitivity to all the primary taste qualities except sour. If sugar is added to a very cold glass of iced tea, the tea will be too sweet when it reaches room temperature—but the same is true of a very hot cup of coffee. Taste is most sensitive in a range of temperatures (17° to 42° C., or 62° to 107° F.) that is near body temperature (37° C., or 98.6° F.).

Adaptation. Taste, like most other senses, shows loss of sensitivity with continuous stimulation. Taste adaptation can be made complete for a given stimulus and area of the tongue under laboratory conditions. Adaptation is most rapid at stimulus temperatures where the receptors are most sensitive. The threshold is lower and adaptation is faster for warmer solutions (32° versus 17° C.). Thus we can be reasonably sure that it is the receptor and not the central nervous system that is adapting, because stimulus temperature affects the receptor, not the central nervous system. It has also been found, as expected, that the stronger the stimulus for any quality, the longer is the adaptation time and the longer is the period required to recover normal sensitivity. However, complete adaptation occurs only in the laboratory. A substance being tasted under normal conditions is shifted over different areas of the tongue—new receptors are continually being stimulated. Presumably, even an all-day sucker would remain somewhat sweet at the end of the day. Partial adaptation is common, however. Experts have estimated that a person is

25% to 40% adapted most of the time to the various taste qualities encountered. Of course, taste adaptation can be prevented by taste **contrast,** or mutual taste enhancement, when "opposite" qualities are involved. Adaptation results in the opposite effect— taste **compensation**—when adaptation to one taste quality raises the taste threshold to another quality. This seldom occurs except with primary tastes under laboratory conditions. Under normal conditions taste contrast is usually the rule. Adaptation to one complex of taste qualities is prevented by contrast with another complex of different taste qualities. For this reason, gourmets drink wine with food; the taste of the wine prevents adaptation to the taste of the food, and the taste of the food prevents adaptation to the taste of the wine, permitting maximum enjoyment of both. The wine is selected to match the intensity of the food stimulation so that one taste does not mask the other taste. For example, mild white wine goes with the bland taste of fish, and stronger-tasting red wine is chosen to match the more intense flavor of beefsteak. Temperature effects are also involved: the taste intensity of the white wine is reduced by chilling it, whereas red wine is served at room temperature for greater taste intensity.

Contrast. Mutual enhancement occurs when stimuli for certain of the four taste qualities are presented together **(simultaneous induction)** or successively **(successive induction).** Contrast effects of this kind depend on the intensity of the stimuli and on the specific stimulus substances used. This is evident in many food mixtures. A study done by the U.S. Army Quartermaster Corps showed that bitter (caffeine) did not affect salt or sweet but enhanced sour. Salt did not affect bitter, reduced sweet, and enhanced sour at low concentrations but reduced it at high concentrations. Sweet reduced bitter and sour, but did not affect salt. Sour enhanced bitter. These complexities depend on specific conditions however;

the evident contrast in Chinese sweet and sour spareribs disagrees with this study.

Compensation. Certain tastes raise one another's threshold, especially salt and sour, as noted above. Salted grapefruit or salted beer tastes neither as salt nor as sour as expected, for example. Compensations of this kind require stimulus intensities well above the normal threshold.

Fusion. As previously pointed out, there is little fusion in taste. In hearing, notes can blend in a chord; in vision, hues can blend to form a new color. In taste, a trained observer can usually detect which of the four primary qualities are present because they do not blend to produce novel tastes (secondary qualities).

Complex phenomena. Taste blindness **(ageusia)** for one or more of the primary tastes is unknown, although individuals differ widely in their taste thresholds. Perhaps the patterned nature of the nerve impulse "code" for the primary qualities prevents complete taste blindness when some inputs are lost.

Some data are available on the human nerve response to taste when medical patients have ear operations under local anesthetics. They are conscious and are able to report their taste sensations while the surgeon records from a branch of the seventh nerve (chorda tympani) exposed by the operation. The threshold reported by the patient for salt was accompanied by a burst of firing in the fibers of the nerve, and the reported order of sweetness of various sugars agreed with the magnitude of the response.

Another way of studying human taste (and smell) response is by injecting into a forearm vein a substance (such as neoarsphenamine) that stimulates taste and smell when it reaches the receptor area of the body (hematogenic taste and smell). (Circulation time from the forearm to the receptor area is measured in this way.) The effect is diminished (taste) or abolished (smell) in subjects with impaired or atrophied receptors.

Another curious fact worth noting and of interest to geneticists is an inherited difference in taste sensitivity to a substance called PTC (phenylthiocarbamide). People seem to fall into two groups in this respect —low-threshold "tasters" and high-threshold "nontasters." Only the "nontasters" have a correspondingly high threshold to the taste of urea. This isolated finding may yet contribute to our understanding of taste.

From a practical point of view, most tastes are bland, with preferred tastes being about halfway up the psychophysical intensity scale. This shows that their odors have more to do with their distinctiveness than with their taste.

Taste can be viewed as a factor in the control of motivated behavior rather than as a simple sensation. Since this aspect of taste involves complex brain functions in addition to the receptor input, detailed discussions will be left to Chapter 15. It is enough to note that ingestive behavior is often controlled by taste. For example, animals avoid bitter substances (which are usually nonnutritive) and accept sweet substances (which are usually nutritive). Specific hungers, or "appetites," that develop as a result of dietary deficiencies also control ingestive behavior. For example, increased avidity for salt can be produced in animals by adrenalectomy or by insulin injections, which increase the body's need for salt (Chapter 3). The result is a difference in preference behavior that does not seem to depend on any change in taste thresholds. The experimental animal selects low concentrations of salt solutions in preference to pure water more often than does the normal animal. Tests of the threshold for salt taste, using nerve cell recordings, show that the experimental animal's threshold is unchanged. The problem is one of palatability rather than taste sensitivity. Palatability changes involve higher brain centers and the whole problem of the dynamics of motivation.

OLFACTION

Smell is much more difficult to study than is taste, but it is probably a more important sense, even in man. As previously explained, odor forms a large part of the "flavor" of food, which tastes "flat" when the olfactory passages are blocked, as when one has a head cold. There would be no gourmets if it were not for smell! Smell probably accounts for as much as two fifths of the "taste" of food. This seems reasonable; smell has been estimated to be 10,000 times more sensitive than taste, as measured by stimulus concentrations, although the difference thresholds are about the same. (However, the technical difficulties of studying odor thresholds can generate threshold differences of 150 times, depending on the methods used.)

Olfaction is important in another way. It acts independently of taste, as an exteroceptor. As an exteroceptor, or distance receptor, smell joins vision, audition, and somesthesis in exploring the environment. Smell is not so important in this sense to man as it is to four-legged animals—in man the nose is not so close to the ground, from whence most odors emanate. However, human reactions to odor may be subjectively as important to man as to animals. The perfume industry spends millions of dollars on odor research, and men as well as women spend more millions on preparations that either add smell to their bodies or remove it. Man subjects the air to substances in spray cans that cover unpleasant odors or, in some cases, that make us anosmic, so that we can smell neither pleasant nor unpleasant odors. The wine industry is as interested in the smell of their product as in its taste and devotes as much energy to that end. Even used-car dealers have found that they can raise their prices and more readily sell cars when the interiors have been sprayed to give that "new-car smell."

In the face of all this activity it is only recently that two useful theories of olfaction have been possible and a list of seven primary olfactory qualities has been developed. Earlier efforts were blocked by difficulties of stimulus presentation and receptor study. The olfactory receptors are so sensitive (as little as 0.00004 mg. of mercaptan per cubic meter of air is detectable) and so inaccessible (above the nasal passages) that control of stimulus concentrations is very poor. Recording from receptors or nerve tracts is equally difficult. In animal research it is difficult surgically to "get at" the receptor or nerve tracts serving olfaction because of their location. As a result, less is known of the electrical characteristics of receptor or afferent neuron response to smell than is the case for taste.

Earlier studies of smell resorted to cataloging the thresholds of various substances in an attempt to find odor groups whose thresholds were alike. It was assumed that these groups would form the primary odor qualities. Stimulus-control difficulties impeded this approach. A theory based on examination of the physical shapes of odorous molecules has generated an acceptable list of primary qualities and some knowledge of how these molecules must affect the olfactory receptor. Other useful theories are based on temporal and spatial patterns of stimulation of the receptors. More is probably known now about receptor mechanisms in olfaction than is known about somesthesis or taste; our knowledge is more complete in the areas of vision and audition than in the area of smell, however.

Receptors

The olfactory receptors are located high in the nasal cavities (Fig. 9-3). They are specialized hairlike endings (cilia) on bipolar nerve cells (olfactory receptor, Fig. 9-4). The bipolar cells, or olfactory receptors, are surrounded by yellow-brown supporting cells, with the whole being called the **olfactory epithelium.** The olfactory epithe-

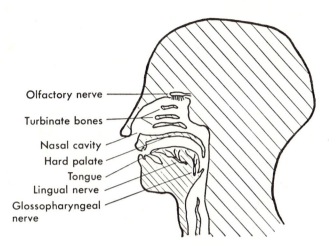

Fig. 9-3. Nasal passages. (From Pfaffman, C.: Studying the senses of taste and smell. In Andrews, R. C., editor: Methods of psychology, New York, 1948, John Wiley & Sons, Inc.)

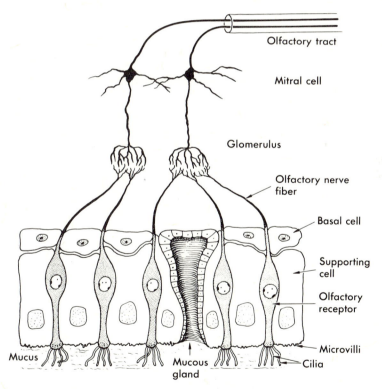

Fig. 9-4. Olfactory epithelium and neural connections to CNS. Orientation is similar to that of Fig. 9-3. (Modified by E. O. Gardner from Moulton, D. G., and Beidler, L. M.: Physiol. Rev. **47:**1-52, 1967, and from Schneider, R. A.: New Eng. J. Med. **277:**299-303, 1967. In Gardner, E. O.: Fundamentals of neurology, ed. 5, Philadelphia, 1968, W. B. Saunders Co.)

lium is located on both sides of the **nasal septum,** which completely separates two olfactory passages, one for each nostril. The two smell-sensitive areas are also called the **olfactory clefts.** Each covers about 2.5 cm.^{2} (1 inch^2) on either side of the nasal septum. The olfactory cleft is located in the "roof" of the nasal passages, high above the baffle-shaped **turbinate bones** (Fig. 9-3). Inspired air reaches this olfactory epithelium by eddy currents created by the turbinate bones, especially with vigorous sniffing. Expired air stimulates the olfactory epithelium by the rear access to the **nasopharynx** (for interoception). The olfactory epithelium is covered with mucus that bathes the odor-sensing hair endings (cilia) of the bipolar nerve cells. Presumably, odorous vapor must dissolve in mucus to reach the hairlike endings of the olfactory receptors because the hairs barely reach the surface of the mucus covering them.

Nervous system

The axonlike dendrites of smell-sensitive bipolar receptor cells pass through tiny holes in the bone that forms the roof of the nasal cavity and the floor of the braincase (Fig. 9-3). The fibers end in the **olfactory bulbs,** which are the swellings on the ends of the **olfactory tracts,** located on the base of the brain (cranial nerve I, Fig. 5-8). The short bipolar nerve cells are the true olfactory nerves that form cranial nerve I (the olfactory bulbs and tracts are part of the brain). The bipolar cells end in complex synapses in the olfactory bulbs, called **glomeruli** (Fig. 9-4). Pathways in the olfactory tracts lead from here to the **prepiriform area** of the ventral surface of the cerebral cortex. This projection area is the oldest part of the cortex, phylogenetically, since the cerebral hemispheres originated as a correlating center for smell. Olfaction also shows its antiquity in that it is the only sensory input that does not relay excitation in the thalamus or related centers. Other pathways lead from the olfactory bulb

through the olfactory tract to a "loop circuit" under the corpus callosum, involving the amygdaloid nucleus and the hypothalamus. These paths are secondary, however, and olfactory sensitivity does not depend on them. Excitation traveling back and forth in loop circuits in the olfactory bulbs may act to "amplify" the effect of receptor activity exciting the CNS.

Stimulation

Many ingenious efforts have been made to stimulate the sensitive olfactory receptors in a controlled and quantitative manner. One of the earlier devices used was an **olfactometer.** The instrument was based on a hard rubber cylinder that was impregnated with odorous material. The cylinder fitted loosely over a graduated tube, the other end of which fitted the nostril. Thrusting the tube into the cylinder exposed less of the odorous cylinder to incoming air; as the tube was withdrawn, a greater length of the cylinder was exposed to air entering the tube. In this manner absolute and difference thresholds could be obtained. A crude scale of "olfacties," or subjectively equal odor increments, was also produced. The effects of presenting the stimulus to one nostril or two, adaptation, and the presentation of different stimuli to the two nostrils were studied. Rather variable data result from the subject's uncontrolled "sniff" volume, however.

A more fruitful approach to odor investigation is the study of the interaction of odors with one another. This approach uses the **mixing olfactometer.** Air is bubbled through several odorous substances into different tubes. The tubes are led to a mixer that can select any combination of them. The result is diluted by a known flow of outside air and led to a nose cone for smelling. Proportions of odorous mixes can be rather precisely controlled in this manner.

Thresholds. The findings for absolute and difference thresholds for odor vary according to the method used; thus olfactory data are not usually very reliable. An absolute threshold as low as 0.0004 mg./M.^{3} of air has been obtained for mercaptan, one of the most odorous substances known. This is about one molecule in 50 trillion. However, a 20 cc. sniff would contain 10 trillion molecules of the substance. Calculations involving models of the nasal passages indicate that roughly 2% of inhaled molecules stimulate the receptors. Further calculations involving odor intensity and response probability suggest that only 40 cells must respond to the inhaled molecules to be detected by the subject! However, odor sensitivity does not compare with visual or auditory sensitivity for the amount of molecular energy involved in the absolute threshold, but the threshold is lower than that for taste or somesthesis. Unlike other senses with low absolute thresholds, there is a rather high difference threshold for the sense of smell. Although the absolute threshold for odor is much less than that for taste, the difference thresholds are comparable, and the Weber ratio is about the same. Determinations of $\Delta I/I$ depend on intensity. For one example, the ratio varies from about 1 at low intensities to about 0.2 at high intensities for india rubber. In free-breathing experiments, the average is about 0.2.

Sensory mechanisms

To some extent an odorous substance must be (1) volatile, (2) soluble in water, and (3) soluble in fat. A *volatile* substance evaporates molecules into the air so that they may reach the olfactory receptors. Some powerful odors such as musk are not very volatile, but since sensitivity to them is high, relatively few molecules need to reach the receptors for detection. Volatility is a necessary but not sufficient condition for odor; pure water, for example, is highly volatile, but odorless. Most of the organic compounds are both odorous and volatile, whereas most inorganic compounds are neither. *Water solubility* is also related to

odor. Presumably, odorous molecules must dissolve in the mucus covering the receptors in order to reach them, and mucus has a high water content. Exceptions can be found among the alcohols, however. *Fat solubility* may be related to odor because the cell membranes of the receptors contain fat and would be most sensitive to compounds that dissolve in cellular fat. Most fat-soluble compounds are odorous if they are also water-soluble. Yet exceptions can also be found to this rule: acetone, for example, is odorous but has low fat solubility. Fat and water solubility may, like volatility, be a necessary but not sufficient condition for odor. Very odorous compounds may require less water or fat solubility because relatively few molecules need to reach the receptors.

Recording

Recordings have been taken from the olfactory epithelium. Rabbits, fish, hedgehogs, and frogs are favorite subjects, because of the (relative) accessibility of the receptors. Records have been taken from the cat and even man (see below). Gross electrical responses of the receptor surface (the **electrooculogram,** or EOG) are somewhat unreliable, single-cell recordings are difficult because of the size of the cells (about 1 μ in diameter), and tracing evoked potentials in the sensory pathways becomes a loosing battle against background "noise." The potentials are also very sensitive to elimination by most anesthetics.

The EOG from the receptor surface is not a true generator potential for single-cell evoked potential response, but serves as a rough indicator of receptor activity. There is some evidence for a primitive spatial patterning of different odors on the receptor surface (olfactory epithelium) from degeneration studies—lesions in the olfactory bulb affect this pattern—and from single-cell evoked potentials to different odors. Although the human olfactory pathways are inaccessible in most brain surgery, one instance of recording from both bulbs comes from the Mayo Clinic. Evoked potentials were recorded from two odors (valerian and benzine) but not to breathing room air ("resting discharge," as found in the rabbit).

Theories of olfactory receptor mechanisms

There are several theories of how the olfactory receptor works, but only the most recent versions predict odors with reasonable accuracy. Some of the olfactory theories fall in two groups, one of which views the receptor mechanism as *vibrational* and the other views it as *chemical* in nature. Vibrational theories assert that the receptor acts because of the way odorous substances absorb, refract, or scatter light. For example, most odorous compounds strongly absorb infrared wavelengths, which has led to the theory that infrared ray absorption by the stimulus is the essential part of the receptor process. Most odorous substances also absorb ultraviolet light, leading to a similar theory about ultraviolet light. A third vibrational theory notes that many odorous substances reflect light of a different wavelength than they receive (the Raman effect). However, all the vibrational theories are embarrassed by several important exceptions to the rule each proposes—odorous substances that do not show appropriate vibrational characteristics. Chemical theories view the receptor event as chemical in nature. Older versions, however, were not able to classify odorous substances according to their chemical nature in any manner that did not have important exceptions. Enzyme theories came later, proposing that odorous substances interfered with or facilitated reactions in the receptor that require a catalyst. Still later work showed that no known enzyme system can account for the odors of very dilute mixtures.

One generalization of odor theory comes close, in that six of seven odorous elements can be arranged in an "electrochemical series" according to their ability to displace each other in chemically reacting to their salts in solution. There is also a theory that the stimulus "punctures" the receptor cells to cause a sodium-potassium exchange through the resulting "pores" in a millisecond or less to produce a generator potential in the same way that the nerve impulse is initiated, but this notion lacks evidence. The ideas of this and the preceding paragraph merely serve to show that there has been no lack of effort to produce a general theory of odor. Where ignorance abounds, theories do also!

The most promising efforts at theorizing are more recent. One attacks the code for smell from the point of view of the spatial and temporal (timing) characteristics of the receptor surface. The other theory rationalizes the shape and charge of the stimulating molecules. The two theories are not in conflict because they concern different aspects of the sensory code.

The first of these theories (Mozell) holds that the spatial and temporal characteristics of the receptor surface respond to different molecules in different ways, providing the brain with a "pattern" in space and time of the reaction of the surface for odor detection. This is the **gas chromatograph theory.** (Chemistry students will detect the resemblance of the pattern to a gas chromatograph.) Patterning of this sort has been recorded from branches of the olfactory nerves in the frog, and the idea is a promising one.

A later version of an old chemical theory is equally promising because it concerns the question of how the odor stimulus acts on the individual receptor cells. It is based on the *physical shape* or *electrical charge* of odorous molecules and is called the **stereochemical theory.** The theory does not specify the chemical event that is initiated in the receptor by the odorous molecule. The theory does state that the molecule must physically "fit" one or more of five *receptor sites,* or "holes," on the receptor hair endings or else be attracted by *positively* or *negatively charged* sites on the receptors. The seven sites, when individually stimulated, give rise to seven primary odor qualities. Stimulation of combinations of the primary sites gives rise to secondary, or mixed, odors. This occurs when a molecule will fit more than one site, depending on how it is oriented, or when a molecule is flexible enough to adapt itself to more than one site. More recently, the author of this theory (Amoore) has abandoned the "classical site-fitting concept" of his theory, but not the idea that the psychophysical basis for odor depends on molecular size and shape. The theory has also been modified to take into account the orientation of the molecule when it reaches the receptor surface—it might arrive "upsidedown," and probability modifications are thereby needed. Variations in stimulus volatility (vaporization) and adsorption of receptor surfaces further improve the predictive value of the theory.

Olfactory qualities: stereochemical theory. The idea that odorous substances give off molecules that must fit variously shaped "pores" in the receptors is an old one. In modern form it began with the observation that the molecules of most odorous substances had carbon chains (Chapter 2) four to eight carbons long. It was noted that a slight change in molecular geometry made a big difference in odor. The organic chemistry literature was searched for data on odors. These data are given in Table 9-2, together with familiar stimulus examples. Information was then collected on the physical shapes of molecules stimulating the seven primary odors. In five cases odors that smelled alike had molecules that were shaped alike. In the other two cases they had a similar charge. **Pungent** molecules had a deficiency of electrons and a positive charge and would be attracted to a negatively charged (excess electrons) site. **Putrid** molecules had excess electrons, were negatively charged, and presumably would be attracted to a positively charged (defi-

Table 9-2. Primary odors and familiar stimuli that resemble them*

Primary quality	Familiar stimulus
Camphoraceous	Mothballs, camphor
Musky	Angelica root oil
Floral	Roses
Minty	Peppermint candy
Ethereal	Dry-cleaning fluid
Pungent	Vinegar
Putrid	Rotten egg

*Based on data from Amoore, J. E.: Ann. New York Acad. Sci. **116**:457-476, 1964.

cient electrons) site. Models were made of the molecules stimulating primary odors, and the shape of the receptor sites that would fit such molecules was predicted and modeled (Fig. 9-5). The **ethereal** site is a narrow slot, the **camphoraceous** a hemispherical basin, the **musky** a larger elliptical flat-bottomed pan, the **floral** keyhole-shaped, and the **minty** wedge-shaped. Tests of the theory have been made in which the primary or mixed odors were predicted from the shape or charge of over 200 compounds; only one prediction seemed incorrect. When a mixing olfactometer is used to compare odors, subjects cannot tell the difference between substances whose molecules fit the same receptor site. New organic molecules have been synthesized to fit receptor site models, and the resulting odors have been correctly predicted. Complex odors have been synthesized by mixing primary odors, and the odors of the mixtures have been predicted. The theory has an impressive amount of evidence in its support. The stereochemical theory is incomplete because it does not specify the chemical event that occurs at the receptor site. However, it has produced a list of seven very promising primary olfactory qualities and has accurately described the nature of their stimuli.

Olfactory phenomena

Adaptation. In common with most other senses, olfaction adapts rather readily.

Receptor site   Odorant molecule   Site plus molecule

Ethereal

Camphor-aceous

Musky

Floral

Minty

Fig. 9-5. Models of olfactory receptor sites and of molecules that "fit" them in the stereochemical theory of odor. (From Amoore, J. E.: Ann. N. Y. Acad. Sci. **116:**457-476, 1964.)

Adaptation is complete for most single odors; the time required depends on the intensity of the odor (usually varying from 1 to 10 minutes under laboratory conditions). This fact reduces the effect of the most expensive perfume to an initial impression! On the other hand, even the odor of a fertilizer factory is unnoticeable after 20 to 30 minutes. Adaptation to single odors can be dangerous, as when miners do not detect a gradual increase in methane gas, or a leak in a household gas line allows gas to permeate the air too gradually, so that the receptors adapt before it is noticed. Absence of smell stimuli for a time results in an increased sensitivity to various odors amounting to 10% to 40%, depending on the test odor. Apparently one is partially adapted to odors most of the time, including one's own body odor, when "even our best friends won't tell us." It is difficult to predict, however, what effect adaptation to one odor will have on another odor. Adaptation to one odor may raise or lower the threshold to another odor. It may also result in a change in quality for the second odor. For example, adaptation to camphor raises the odor threshold to eau de cologne, but it does not affect the threshold for benzaldehyde. **Compensation** between odors also occurs; for example, the odors of balsam and beeswax cancel one another. Odor often changes quality with changes in stimulus intensity. Ionone, a substance used in perfume, changes its odor from cedar-wood to violets with decreasing intensity. Perhaps adaptation effects in complex odors can be rationalized in terms of the stereochemical theory, but the attempt has not yet been made.

Anosmia. Complete lack of smell sensitivity is rare, but cases are known. It seems to be an inherited defect. **Anosmia** may also result from long-standing nasal irritation or from blocking of the nasal passages, as in a head cold. The anosmic individual can still "smell" substances injected into the bloodstream, which shows that some functions of the receptors are intact. The chemical nature of the receptor process is supported by this observation and by the fact that certain odor thresholds (for example, macrocyclic lactone [Exaltolide]) vary with the estrogen level of the blood and therefore with the menstrual cycle in women. Temporary, partial, or complete anosmia can result from water in the nose, anesthesia, and other conditions. Formaldehyde in weak solution (formalin) vaporizes to cause anosmia. This, rather than adaptation, explains why the formalin you smell so strongly when you enter a biology laboratory (where it is used to preserve animals for dissection) becomes odorless so quickly. Some household deodorants use formalin together with a masking odor to "cover" the formalin smell until the receptors quit functioning. Other deodorizers, of course, use only a masking odor.

SUMMARY

The senses that are normally and adequately stimulated by substances in solution are the chemical senses. They include the common chemical sense, gustation, and olfaction. The common chemical sense is pain sensitivity to dissolved irritants in the mucous membranes. It is most frequently stimulated by spicy foods in the mouth, but irritating vapors can also stimulate the eyes, which are more sensitive, and the nasal passages, which are still more sensitive. The nerve pathways are identical with those for skin pain, but the sensory quality seems different because the usual stimulus is different from that for skin pain. Adaptation is seldom complete because chemical stimulation is a process that is seldom constant; thus the receptor has no chance to adapt.

Gustation is limited to receptors on the tongue, palate, and larynx. The sensations commonly called "taste" include common chemical sensitivity, somesthesis from the mouth, and olfaction as well. The tongue receptors give rise to primary sensations of sweet, salt, sour, and bitter, in an ascending order of sensitivity that depends on temperature, when they are stimulated by solutions of sucrose, sodium chloride, hydrochloric acid, and quinine, respectively. The taste receptors on the tongue are in papillae, which are "moatlike" and "islandlike" structures with taste buds lining their walls. The receptors developed from ordinary epithelial cells under the influence of sensory appropriation from nerves VII (anterior tongue) and IX (posterior tongue) and under the influence of the gonadal hormones. The tongue is most sensitive to salt and sweet at the tip, sour at the sides, and bitter at the back; the center is insensitive. These four primary qualities do not fuse to give novel secondary sensations.

Sour is primarily stimulated by the H^+ ion. Salt sensations are usually caused by Na^+ cations or Cl^- anions, or both. Sweet substances are organic molecules with short carbon chains, and bitter substances include quinine, alkaloids, and complex inorganic salts. Salts often taste bitter at threshold, and concentrated sweet stimuli can taste bitter. Molecular size and shape are important in sweet and bitter stimuli. The nerve pathways for taste have their own primary nucleus—the nucleus of the tractus solitarius—but the second-and third-order neurons follow the somesthetic pathways to the cortex via the thalamus. Efferent fibers respond to stomach distention by inhibiting the sensory input.

Experiments with microelectrode recording in the nerve pathway and with the stimulation of individual taste receptors by micropipettes show that gustation has unusually long generator potentials and that there are different types of taste receptors in response characteristics and anatomy. Some complex *pattern* of input signals each quality, because individual taste nerve cells respond to more than one quality. In addition, taste neurons serve two or more receptors, as shown in single-fiber experiments with cats. Other neurons respond to both temperature and taste. In man, taste stimuli applied to the sides of the tongue are separately located when salt, sour, or cold are paired or when bitter, sweet, and warm are paired; other pairings are localized in the center of the tongue.

Taste sensitivity is also dependent on stimulus temperature, with thresholds for all four qualities except sour being lowest in a range near body temperature. Within this range, difference thresholds for each quality result in Weber ratios that vary from about 1 to 0.2 as intensity is increased. The slope of Stevens' scale function differs for each of the four tastes. Taste adaptation is most rapid in the same temperature range where the receptors are most sensitive, indicating that the adaptation is caused by the receptor rather than by the central nervous system. Complete adaptation is not found outside the labatory because, under ordinary circumstances, the substance being tasted is moved about the mouth from one receptor to another.

For complex tastes, adaptation is usually prevented by mixing tastes, as in drinking wine with food. The primary qualities, however, interact to enhance or depress one another.

Human taste responses have been studied by nerve cell responses in conscious patients who have undergone brain surgery, by hematogenic taste, and by inherited sensitivity to PTC, but practically speaking, most of the preferred tastes are bland. Taste can be a controlling factor in motivated behavior. Palatability will be studied in the chapter on motivation.

Olfaction is important as an exteroceptor in exploring the environment, and important as an interoceptor because it forms part of "taste." Although olfaction as an exteroceptor is not as useful for man as for other animals, man's reactions to smell are equally important. However, research on smell has been hampered by the sensitivity of the receptor and its inaccessibility. Thus little is known of the physiology of smell. The receptors are hairlike endings on bipolar nerve cells that are bathed in mucus. They are located on both sides of the nasal septum on the roof of the nasal cavity above the turbinate bones. The two smell-sensitive areas are each called an olfactory cleft, or olfactory epithelium. Eddy currents of air created by the turbinate bones reach the receptor from the nostrils or the nasopharynx. Vaporized substances in the air stimulate the bipolar cell receptors. The axonlike dendrites of the bipolar cells reach the olfactory bulbs through holes in the bony roof of the nasal cavity and constitute cranial nerve I. Synapses, called glomeruli, transfer the excitation to second-order neurons going to the prepiriform area of the cortex. Reverberatory circuits may amplify the input.

Early attempts to stimulate the receptors in a controlled manner involved the olfactometer. Newer techniques involve the use of a mixing olfactometer. Threshold data vary widely according to the method used as well as the stimulus odor. Despite the sensitivity of the receptor, the difference thresholds are comparable to those for taste. Volatility, water solubility, and fat solubility seem necessary conditions for smell stimuli. The stimulus must reach the receptors as vapor, dissolve in watery mucus, and affect receptors whose membrane includes fat. Most organic compounds meet these conditions; most inorganic compounds do not. Recordings have been taken from the olfactory epithelium in animals (EOG) and from the nerve cells in animals and man.

Theories of how the receptor reacts have depended on vibrational, chemical, or electrochemical events, or on receptor pores. The vibrational theories have been based on infrared or ultraviolet absorption or on the Raman effect. Chemical theories have proposed that enzymes are involved. The most promising theories are the gas chromatograph and stereochemical theories. The gas chromatograph theory asserts that the sensory code has a spatiotemporal character. The stereochemical theory states that an odorous molecule must physically "fit" one of five receptor sites or be attracted to a negatively charged or a positively charged site. The seven primary odor qualities that result are ethereal, camphoraceous, musky, floral, minty, pungent, and putrid. The shapes of the receptor sites have been predicted from the shapes of the molecules. Subjects cannot tell the difference between odors whose molecules would fit the same receptor sites, and the odors of synthesized molecules have been predicted. Flexible molecules that would fit more than one site have mixed odors that are equally predict-

able. The theory is incomplete because it does not specify the chemical event that occurs at the receptor site.

In other olfactory phenomena, adaptation to single odors is complete in less than a half hour, usually in 1 to 10 minutes. An individual is usually 10% to 40% odor adapted under normal conditions. Adaptation to one odor may lower the threshold to another odor (contrast), raise the threshold to another odor (compensation), or change the quality of another odor. These effects have been unpredictable so far. Complete anosmia occurs, but this is rare. It may be inherited or caused by damage to, or blocking of, the nasal passages. Since even anosmic people can "smell" substances in the bloodstream, the receptor events are probably chemical in nature. Temporary anosmia can also be caused by vaporized formaldehyde.

READINGS

Amoore, J. E., Johnston, J. W., and Rubin, M.: The stereochemical theory of odor, Sci. Am. **210**:42-49, Feb. 1964. (W. H. Freeman Reprint No. 297.)

Haagen-Smit, A. J.: Smell and taste, Sci. Am. **186**:28-32, March 1952. (W. H. Freeman Reprint No. 404.)

Mueller, C. G.: Sensory psychology, Englewood Cliffs, N.J., 1965, Prentice-Hall, Inc.

Pfaffman, C.: The afferent code for sensory quality, Amer. Psychol. **14**:226-232, May 1959. (Bobbs-Merrill Reprint No. P-275.)

von Békésy, G.: Taste theories and the chemical stimulation of single papillae. In Gross, C. G., and Zeigler, H. P., editors: Readings in physiological psychology, New York, 1969, Harper & Row, Publishers.

von Buddenbrock, W.: The senses, Ann Arbor, 1958, University of Michigan Press.

chapter 10
Audition

OVERVIEW

The sense of hearing, called audition, is the subject of this chapter. Audition is the most complex sensory input thus far explained (vision is equally complex, if not more so). To understand audition requires some knowledge of (1) the nature of the *physical energy* that provides the sensory stimulus and (2) the anatomy of the auditory mechanism. With this background (3) the *physiology* and (4) the *psychophysics* of hearing can be understood. Finally, such topics aid study of (5) the complex phenomena of hearing. These are the topics of the chapter in their order of presentation.

The stimulus energy will be explained first in its simplest form, a sine wave of periodic changes in air pressure. The sine wave "tone" has simple characteristics of amplitude, frequency, and phase. More complex tones are also periodic waves of sound energy. Complex periodic waves are subject to a frequency analysis that reduces them to sine waves; aperiodic waves ("noise") cannot be consistently reduced to sine waves. The anatomy of the receptor mechanism that responds to sound energy is the next topic. The parts of the outer, middle, and inner ears change air pressure waves into vibrations of receptor cells in the organ of Corti. The nerve impulses that result are carried to the brain along the pathways described next. The organization of the input is further improved by output pathways from the brain back to sensory nuclei and receptors.

The physiology and psychophysics of hearing involve the study of the manner in which these sensory and nervous mecha-nisms permit the brain to analyze pitch and loudness. Pitch is analyzed by the location of stimulus effects on hair cells along the length of the organ of Corti. A different set of hair cells responds to increased vibrations of the organ of Corti in detecting loudness. Both sets of hair cells set up the "generator potential" (which can be detected as a cochlear microphonic potential), and this potential probably causes sensory nerve impulses. Disturbance of any part of the auditory mechanism can cause auditory defects. Different kinds of auditory defects result from impairment of outer, middle, or inner ear mechanisms. The psychophysics of hearing involves the following major attributes of sound: (1) quality (pitch), (2) intensity (loudness), (3) extensity (volume), (4) duration, and (5) density. Thresholds and adaptation phenomena are discussed. The chapter concludes with a discussion of the following complex auditory phenomena: (1) aural harmonics, (2) combination tones, (3) consonance and dissonance, (4) masking, (5) aftersensations, (6) speech phenomena, and (7) auditory localization.

PHYSICS OF SOUND

Any solid body will vibrate when struck, however brief its motion. The vibrations of some solid objects are regular, consistent, or periodic. This is true of a **tuning fork,** for example (Fig. 10-1). The regular movements of the tuning fork have a characteristic frequency or rate as well as a characteristic amplitude or extent. The motions of the tines of the tuning fork cause it to strike

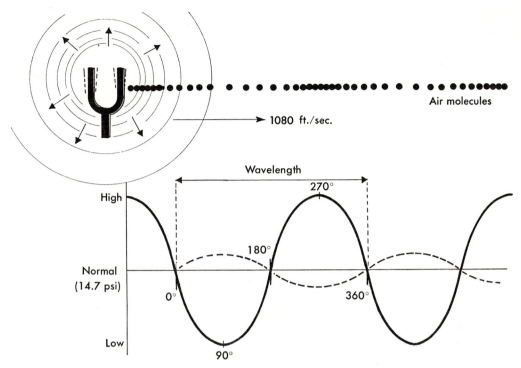

Fig. 10-1. Characteristics of sound energy. Vibrations of a tuning fork cause collisions of air molecules that radiate air pressure variations in all directions. Variations can be plotted as a simple sine wave. The sine wave has characteristics of amplitude, wavelength, frequency, and phase.

molecules of air. The air molecules collide with one another to transmit energy from molecule to molecule as the molecules vibrate back and forth. The energy radiates in all directions from the vibrating source. Since the vibrating source has a consistent frequency and amplitude of vibration, so do the air molecules. Air pressure is determined by how close together the molecules are. Since the air molecules are colliding with one another and then moving apart in a regular fashion, waves of air pressure *change* constitute sound. Pressure changes of consistent frequency and amplitude *are* the sound that radiates outward from the sound source.

Sine wave

Certain uniform bodies vibrate with a simple motion. The sound waves they produce—alternatively compressed and rarefied air molecules—have a simple pattern of air pressure change. The molecules alternately strike one another in a compressed area and are driven apart in a rarefied area. Since air pressure is merely the density of air molecules, pressure at a given point will be first above, then below, normal pressure. A graph of the pressure changes of air, with the distance from the vibrating source, gives a simple sine wave of air pressure change at any given instant (Fig. 10-1).

Amplitude. The amount of compression and rarefaction of the air molecules will depend on how hard the tuning fork is struck and therefore on how far the tines of the fork vibrate back and forth to condense and rarefy the air. **Amplitude** is the total amount of air pressure change from condensation to rarefaction (higher to lower air pressure). Changes in amplitude are detected by the ear as changes in **loudness.** (The intensity of the stimulus is proportional to the square of the amplitude of the pressure change.)

Frequency. Different tuning forks will vibrate at different rates, each having a characteristic **frequency** of vibration. Frequency, or rate of vibration, used to be stated in cycles per second, abbreviated as cps. The unit most commonly used now means the same thing. It is the **hertz,** usually abbreviated **Hz,** defined as one cycle per second. So 1 cps is 1 Hz. One Hz is one complete back-and-forth vibration of the tuning fork and results in a compression, then a rarefaction, and finally a return to normal pressure (Fig. 10-1). If the tuning fork vibrates rapidly, it has a high rate of vibration, or a high frequency; if it vibrates slowly, it has a low frequency. The **wavelength** of a sine wave of pressure change is the distance over which a single cycle of air pressure change extends at a given instant. High-frequency, or rapid, vibrations result in short wavelengths. Low-frequency vibrations have long wavelengths. (The amplitude may remain the same for high- and low-frequency vibrations.) The relationship between frequency and wavelength is usually constant because sound waves travel at a fixed rate. In air, sound travels at 1080 feet per second at sea level and 0° C. A compression and rarefaction wavelength of 1080 feet could pass a given point once each second if the sound has a frequency of 1 Hz. If the wavelength were 108 feet, the sound wave would pass a given point ten times per second, for a frequency of 10 Hz (10 Hz × 108 feet = 1080 feet per second). Frequency and wavelength can therefore be translated into one another. Frequency is usually the term used in sound. The ear detects differences in frequency as differences in **pitch.** In a denser medium than air (for example, water), sound travels at a higher rate since the molecules are closer together and need not travel so far

to strike one another. As a result, wavelengths are shorter and frequencies are higher. For example, an outboard motor has a higher-pitched sound when one listens to it with his head under water. At high altitudes in air the molecules are farther apart and must travel farther to strike one another. As a result, sound transmission is slower and apparent frequencies are lower. The rate at which sound moves in air can be appreciated by watching someone chop wood a half mile away. The sound will require more than 2 seconds to reach you after the axman swings—he may have raised the ax for a second stroke before you hear the sound of the first stroke.

Phase. A complete sound pressure wave goes from normal to compression to normal to rarefaction to normal again. The point reached by the alternating pressure wave at a given time and place can be specified in terms of 360 degrees as a complete cycle (Fig. 10-1). The beginning point could be taken as 0 degrees, with the first rarefaction peak as 90 degrees, normal as 180 degrees, compression as 270 degrees, and normal again as 360 degrees (Fig. 10-1). If one sine wave is in compression while the other is in rarefaction, the first would be at 90 degrees in the cycle and the second at 270 degrees. They would therefore be 270 minus 90 degrees, or 180 degrees, *out of phase* and exert opposite effects on air pressure at that instant.

Measurements of amplitude and loudness

Frequency is measured in hertz, and phase is measured in degrees. How, then, does one measure the amplitude of a sound wave? A complex average of the amount of pressure variation over each cycle is sometimes used by engineers, who integrate the square root of the mean square of pressure variation. This is done because a high-frequency tone has more rapid pressure variations and contains more energy than does a low-frequency tone of the same amplitude. However, most sound amplitude

Table 10-1. Sound levels of some noises found in different environments (intensities above 100 db may impair hearing)*

Overall level, db (re 0.0002 microbar)		Industrial and military	Community or outdoor	Home or indoor
130†		Armored personnel carrier (123 db)		
	Uncomfortably loud			
120		Oxygen torch (121 db) Scraper-loader (117 db) Compactor (116 db)		Rock-and-roll band (108 to 114 db)
110		Riveting machine (110 db) Textile loom (106 db)	Jet flyover, 1000 ft. (103 db)	
100	Very loud	Electric furnace area (100 db) Farm tractor (98 db) Newspaper press (97 db)	Power mower (96 db) Compressor, 20 ft. (94 db) Rock drill, 100 ft. (92 db)	Inside subway car, 35 mph (95 db) Cockpit—light aircraft (90 db)
90		Cockpit—propeller aircraft (88 db) Milling machine (85 db) Cotton spinning (83 db)	Motorcycles, 25 ft. (90 db) Propeller aircraft flyover, 1000 ft. (88 db)	Food blender (88 db) Garbage disposal (80 db) Clothes washer (78 db)
80	Moderately loud	Lathe (81 db)	Diesel truck, 40 mph, 50 ft. (84 db)	Living room music (76 db) Dishwasher (75 db)
70			Passenger car, 65 mph, 25 ft. (77 db) Near freeway, auto traffic (64 db)	TV—audio (70 db)
60			Air-conditioning unit, 20 ft. (60 db) Large transformer, 200 ft. (53 db)	Conversation (60 db)
50	Quiet		Light traffic, 100 ft. (50 db)	
40				
30	Very quiet			
20				
10	Just audible Threshold of hearing			
0	(1000 to 4000 Hz)			

*From Cohen, A., Anticaglia, J. R., and Jones, H. H.: Noise-induced hearing loss, Arch. Environ. Health **20:**614-623, 1970.

†Unless otherwise specified, listed sound levels are measured at typical operator-listener distances from source.

measurements are made to apply to human use. A physical intensity scale has therefore been developed that matches the characteristics of the human ear as closely as possible—the **decibel (db) scale.** The zero point of the scale approximates the absolute threshold of the human ear—an energy level of 0.0002 dyne/cm.^{2} for a 1000-cycle tone. (A dyne is the amount of energy required to accelerate 1 gram at 1 cm./sec.^{2}. The zero point is only 10 db above the point at which one would "hear" the random motion of molecules caused by heat!) Decibels of increase in intensity are on a scale based on the **bel** scale. The bel scale is chosen because it is a logarithmic scale in which the physical units increase in size at higher intensities (Chapter 6). The human ear requires a larger increase in sound intensity for the same loudness difference, with more intense stimuli. If zero bels is 0.0002 dyne/cm.^{2}, 1 bel is 10^1 (or 10) × 0.0002 dyne/cm.^{2} and 2 bels is 10^2 (or 100) × 0.0002 dyne/cm.^{2}, and so on. However, a smaller unit is required to match the difference threshold of the human ear; therefore the decibel, or "tenth" of a bel, is used. To be technical, the number of decibels between two sound intensities, I_1 and I_2, is 10 log I_1/I_2. The decibel intensities of certain common sounds are given in Table 10-1. In Table 10-1, the 0.0002 dyne/cm.^{2} reference is in terms of the **minimum audible field (MAF),** the pressure change in the air where the subject is located (in a theoretically echo-free open space). Sometimes sound stimuli are delivered by earphones so that the pressure delivered to the eardrum can be calibrated as the **sound pressure level (SPL),** giving lower threshold measurements.

Types of sound waves

The major characteristics of sound waves have been explained so far in terms of air pressure changes from a simple vibrating body that produces a simple **sine wave** of pressure variation with time or distance. The change is *simple* and *periodic* and re-

sults in a **simple tone** (Fig. 10-1). A complex body may vibrate with more than one frequency—and the pressure waves of sound that result may be periodic or aperiodic. If the complex vibrating body has many parts, each with its own characteristic frequency and amplitude of vibration, several sine waves of pressure variation may be produced at once (Fig. 10-2). As these sine waves come in and out of phase because of their differing frequencies of vibration, they will alternately reinforce and cancel each other, as far as air pressure changes are concerned. A complex but repeated wave pattern will result—a **complex periodic wave** that is heard as a **complex tone.**

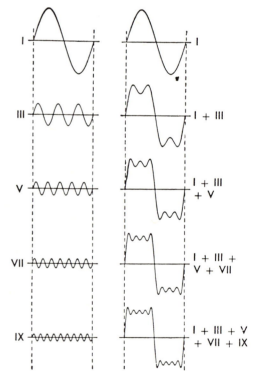

Fig. 10-2. Components of a complex sound wave. As sine waves shown on *left* are added to fundamental wave at *top,* increasingly complex periodic waves shown at *right* result. (From Newman, E. B.: Hearing. In Boring, E. G., Langfeld, H. S., and Weld, H. B., editors: Foundations of psychology, New York, 1948, John Wiley & Sons, Inc.)

However, if the component parts of the vibrating body begin and end vibrating at different times, the complex wave will not repeat itself—it will be **aperiodic.** Aperiodic complex vibrations constitute **noise,** especially when many high-frequency (high-pitched) components are in the complex. As a result, noise is harsh-sounding and variable in character.

Frequency analysis. Frequency analysis consists of analyzing a complex periodic tone to show its component sine waves of pressure change (Fig. 10-2). These sine waves have frequencies that are related to one another in a lawful way. The physical basis for the frequency analysis is best understood in terms of a simple example, such as the sound produced by plucking a violin string.

Harmonics

If a violin string is plucked, it will vibrate up and down, alternately compressing and rarefying the air molecules. The sine wave of pressure change that results will have a wavelength of twice the length of the violin string (Fig. 10-3). The length of the string can represent only the compression or the rarefaction half of the cycle of pressure change at any given moment as it vibrates back and forth. This simple vibration represents the largest movement of the string, and the resulting frequency is called the **fundamental,** or **first harmonic,** frequency. However, the string also has a smaller "double vibration"—it vibrates in halves (Fig. 10-3). The double vibration will produce a sine wave of half the wavelength and twice the frequency of the fundamental tone. The double vibration is the **first overtone,** or **second harmonic.** The string also vibrates in thirds to produce the second overtone, or third harmonic, and so on. The frequencies of these sine waves are a function of their wavelengths. If the fundamental, or first, harmonic has a frequency of n, then the first overtone, or second harmonic, has a frequency of $2n$, the second overtone, or third harmonic, has a frequency of $3n$, and so on. This relationship between the fundamental frequency and the overtone frequencies is called **Fourier's law.** (The application of Fourier's law to sound waves is

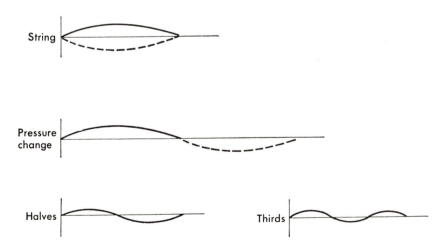

Fig. 10-3. Vibrations of violin string. String vibrates at a fundamental frequency whose corresponding wavelength is twice the string's length. Overtones occur when string also vibrates in halves, thirds, and so on.

sometimes called Ohm's acoustic law to distinguish this application from the same law applied to other periodic phenomena such as heat, where Fourier originally developed the principle.) Of course these simple sine waves combine into a complex periodic wave in the manner shown in Fig. 10-2.

Resonance

If a violin string is stretched between two points in open air, the amplitude of the fundamental frequency and the amplitude of the overtones would bear a simple relation to one another. The first overtone would be greater than the second, the second greater than the third, and so on; the complex periodic wave of pressure change would be formed accordingly. However, the string is stretched across the body of a "sound box," or resonance chamber, the violin. Each part of the violin has a frequency with which it naturally vibrates when struck. The size of the air chamber in the violin also reinforces sound waves— those whose wavelength is a multiple of the length of the sound chamber. When the parts of a violin are struck with air molecules at their natural frequency, they vibrate, or **resonate,** to amplify that frequency; thus the amplitude of certain overtone frequencies is increased. Although the fundamental frequency will be the largest component of the complex wave, various overtones will be increased in size in a pattern unique to the violin. The relative size of various overtones will be different for the same fundamental note played on a trumpet, for example. This variation in overtone pattern is recognized by the human ear as a difference in **timbre.** The violin has more parts that resonate with lower overtones; the trumpet has more parts that resonate with higher overtones. Their air chambers differ in a similar way. As a result, the overtone pattern of the violin has a louder pattern of low overtones than does the trumpet. This is why the same note played on the two instruments "sounds different" in timbre.

Beats

Two fundamental frequencies may be sounded from two sources that differ by 1 Hz in frequency. They will be in compression at the same time once each second and in rarefaction at the same time once each second. That is, one compression each second will be *in phase,* or reinforced in amplitude, as will one rarefaction each second. (At other times the two sound waves will partially cancel each other by being out of phase. You can prove this to yourself by drawing two sine waves over a distance representing 1 second—one wave of two cycles and one of three cycles.) The tone that results when two sources differ by 1 Hz will sound louder and softer once each second—one **beat** per second—because of one large pressure variation each second. If the two tones are two cycles apart, they will beat twice per second, and so on. This phenomenon is used by a piano tuner in tuning a piano string to exactly match the frequency of a tuning fork. He sounds the piano note and tuning fork together. As he tightens the string to bring its frequency up to that of the tuning fork, the difference in frequency diminishes, and the number of beats per second decrease. If he "overshoots," the number of beats per second will increase as the frequency of the piano note rises over that of the tuning fork, and the frequency difference between them increases. Beats can be heard on other occasions in everyday life; for example, the exhaust notes of two trucks traveling at nearly the same engine speed can be heard to beat.

ANATOMY OF THE AUDITORY MECHANISM

Analysis of the air pressure variations that form sound has shown the complexity of this form of stimulus. What kind of receptor apparatus can transduce differences in sound frequency, amplitude, and overtone patterns into nerve impulses in such a way that the brain can detect the corresponding differences in pitch, loudness, and timbre? As a receptor the auditory apparatus changes air pressure vibrations into vibrations of a fluid medium. The fluid vibrations in turn set off nerve impulses by acting on the hair cells of the organ of Corti, a modified "touch receptor." The timing and spatial distribution of the nerve impulses provide the brain with the cues to pitch, loudness, and timbre. Further understanding of how all this is accomplished depends on knowing the parts of the auditory apparatus and how they relate to one another.

Outer ear

The **outer ear** consists of the **pinna** (auricle), **external auditory meatus** (canal), and **tympanum,** or eardrum (Figs. 10-4 and 10-5). The pinna is what you probably refer to as your ear—the convoluted flap that extends from the side of the head. It functions to collect air vibrations and funnel them into the external auditory meatus. Man has lost most of his muscular control of the pinna (except for "wiggling" the ears

as a parlor trick), but lower animals such as dogs and donkeys move the pinna in orienting themselves toward the source of sound—they "prick up" their ears. The external auditory meatus is the canal that curves through the mastoid bone of the skull to conduct vibrations to the tympanum which seals off it's inner end. The tympanum is a membrane that vibrates in response to the pressure waves of sound. It is cone-shaped like a loudspeaker and pivots on a fold at its lower rim.

Middle ear

The **middle ear** contains the three bony **ossicles** that are vibrated mechanically by the rapid movements of the tympanum. The ossicles conduct vibrations to the fluid-filled inner ear. The **malleus,** or hammer, is connected to the eardrum. It moves the **incus** (anvil), which in turn moves the **stapes** (stirrup). The three bones are firmly connected by ligaments and vibrate almost as a unit. The stapes fits into the **oval window** of the fluid-filled inner ear and is

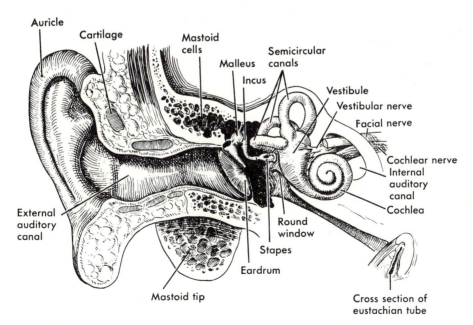

Fig. 10-4. Semidiagrammatic drawing of ear. (From Davis, H., and Silverman, S. R., editors: Hearing and deafness, New York, 1960, Holt, Rinehart & Winston, Inc.)

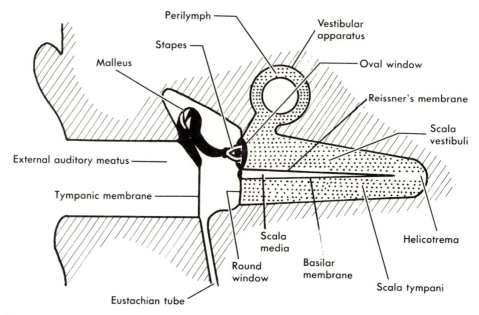

Fig. 10-5. Schematic drawing of ear. (Redrawn from von Békésy, G.: Pflueger. Arch. Ges. Physiol. **236**:58-76, 1935.)

sealed in place by a membrane. The lever system of the ossicles has little mechanical advantage, but the smaller area of the oval window and stapes, as compared to the eardrum, provides a good impedance match between air and the more resistant fluid medium of the inner ear. The small variations in air pressure, distributed over the larger eardrum, are concentrated on the smaller oval window to vibrate the fluid of the inner ear, because fluid is more resistant to movement than is air. To prevent this sensitive mechanism from being "overdriven" by loud sounds of low frequency, two muscles act to limit the motion of the ossicles. The **tensor tympani** pulls on the malleus to tighten the typanum, and the **stapedius** pulls on the stapes to limit its motion at the oval window in response to loud sounds. These muscles, especially the stapedius, contract in a reflex reaction to loud sounds at frequencies below 1000 Hz, where the amplitude of motion is greatest. The reflex may reduce sound intensity by as much as 20 db. As a chamber the middle

ear is sealed off from the outside changes in atmospheric pressure. The **eustachian tube** connects with the rear of the oral cavity (mouth) and is opened to equalized pressure with the outside air in the act of swallowing or yawning. Any pressure difference is felt in the eardrums, which explains why they seem to "pop" if you swallow or yawn after a change in altitude. Outside air pressure changes with altitude, but middle ear pressure cannot change unless the eustachian tube is opened.

Inner ear

The **inner ear** contains the **cochlea,** which is coiled (2¾ turns) like a snail shell. There are three chambers in the cochlea (Figs. 10-5 and 10-6). The **scala vestibuli** begins at the oval window and is the "upper" chamber. It communicates with the "lower" **scala tympani** at the apex of the cochlea coil via a small opening, the **helicotrema.** The membrane-covered **round window** is found at the other end of the scala tympani. Both the scala vestibuli and scala tympani are filled

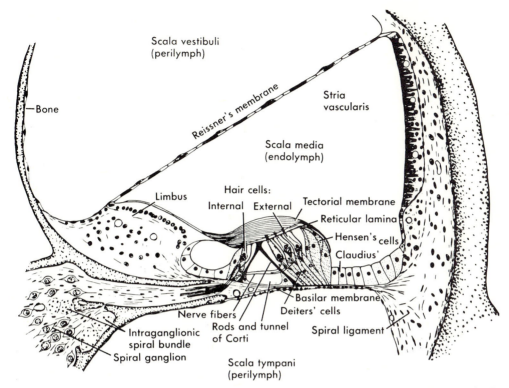

Fig. 10-6. Cross section of the cochlear duct (guinea pig). (From Davis, H. R., et al.: J. Acoust. Soc. Am. **25**:1180, 1953.)

with fluid **perilymph.** The third chamber of the cochlea is the **scala media,** or **cochlear duct.** It is filled with fluid **endolymph** and does not communicate with the other two scalae. The scala media is triangular in cross section (Fig. 10-6), with **Reissner's membrane** separating it from the scala vestibuli as a "roof." The bony **modiolus** forms part of the "floor" of the scala media, and the membranous **basilar membrane** completes the division from the scala tympani. The function of these parts of the cochlea is best appreciated in a schematic diagram such as Fig. 10-5. Air vibrations (sound) are transmitted from the eardrum to the stapes through the other ossicles. The footplate of the stapes vibrates in and out of the oval window. Pressure changes in the perilymph of the scala vestibuli result. The pressure changes are transferred to the endolymph of the scala media through the

flexible Reissner's membrane. The pressure changes in the scala media affect the scala tympani through the basilar membrane. Since fluid is incompressible, pressure changes in the scala tympani cause the membrane over the round window to bulge in and out. There is little movement of fluid through the helicotrema caused by pressure changes in the perilymph, except in response to sound of very low frequency.

Organ of Corti. The **organ of Corti** is the receptor structure that rests on the basilar membrane (Fig. 10-6). It transduces vibrations of the basilar membrane into nerve impulses when the **hair cells** are bent by the motions of the basilar membrane. The hairs of the hair cells are bent because they are thrust into an overlying **tectorial membrane.** The organ of Corti extends along the basilar membrane from its base to its apex. It is organized in a **tonotopic** fashion, with hair cells near the base of the basilar membrane (near the round and oval windows) being more affected by tones of high frequency, and hair cells near the apex (toward the helicotrema) being more affected by tones of low frequency. The reasons for this organization will be explained later. One feature of anatomy that contributes to tonotopic organization should be mentioned now, however. Although the cross section of the cochlea narrows from base to apex of its coil, the width of the modiolus narrows faster than the width of the whole cochlear duct. As a result, the basilar membrane *widens* as one traces it from the base to the apex of the cochlea. Neurons from the hair cells leave the organ of Corti all along the

basilar membrane, from base to apex. Some neurons from near the base of the basilar membrane respond more readily to high-pitched tones; some from near the apex respond more readily to low-pitched tones.

Nervous connections of the ear: the classic pathway

The nerve cells that invade the hair cells of the organ of Corti are the bipolar variety (Chapter 4). Their cell bodies are found inside the coil of the cochlea along its entire length as the **spiral ganglion** (Fig. 10-6). Their axons form the acoustic branch of the eighth, or **statoacoustic, nerve.** The first-order neurons reach the **dorsal** and **ventral cochlear nuclei** of the medulla on

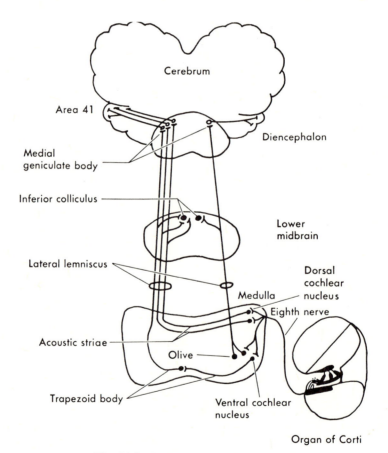

Fig. 10-7. Auditory nervous pathways.

either side of the brainstem (Fig. 10-7). Second-order neurons from the dorsal nucleus cross the floor of the fourth ventricle (a band of fibers seen as the acoustic striae). Second-order neurons from the ventral nucleus either ascend without crossing or cross (and sometimes synapse) in the trapezoid body that forms a bulge across the ventral hindbrain behind the pons. Other important connections are made to a nucleus of the medulla, called the **olive.** The ascending fibers form the **lateral lemniscus.** Synapses for reflex movements (such as turning the head in response to sound) are made in the **inferior colliculus** as well as in ascending and descending pathways going to the cranial and spinal nerves. The lateral lemniscus ends in the **medial geniculate body,** near the thalamus. From here, neurons reach the **auditory projection area** (area 41) on the temporal lobe (Chapter 5). Input from the cochlea of each ear

reaches the projection area of both hemispheres. However, the tonotopic organization of the cochlea is preserved at the cortex, with high, middle, and low tones stimulating different parts of the projection area.

Cortical areas serving audition (Fig. 10-8). Three other cortical areas that surround the classical auditory projection area respond to sound but are less precisely organized tonotopically (A II, Ep, and M I in Fig. 10-8). These areas do not receive input through the classic pathway from the medial geniculate bodies; they are probably supplied by the retricular formation—the diffuse "core" of short and many-branched fibers of the brainstem—and by nonspecific nuclei of the thalamus. These areas appear to serve higher functions associated with hearing—attention, sound recognition, and the like. They can substitute for the primary area in cats and monkeys, but not in man. Rare cases of damage to area 41 in both

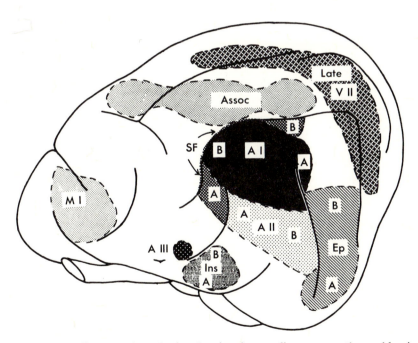

Fig. 10-8. Summary diagram of cat brain, showing four auditory areas; the cochlea is represented from apex, **A,** to base, **B,** in each area. (From Woolsey, C. N.: Organization of cortical auditory system. In Rosenblith, W. A., editor: Sensory communication, The M.I.T. Press, Cambridge, Mass. Copyright 1961 by the Massachusetts Institute of Technology.)

hemispheres in man result in nearly total deafness, as does interruption of the fibers going from the medial geniculate body to area 41. The other areas shown as responding to sound in Fig. 10-8 are not specific to audition—they are not tonotopically organized, and they respond to other sensory inputs as well as to sound.

Habituation. At successively higher levels of the auditory input system, a higher proportion of neurons responds to transient or novel sounds and a lower proportion responds to constant tones or repetitive clicks. Like other sensory systems, audition is organized to detect environmental *change;* attention to novel stimuli has obvious survival value. Monotonously repeated stimuli result in decreased auditory response at all levels. This is the phenomenon of habituation common to sensory systems.

Efferent receptor pathways. Efferent fibers reach the cochlea all along its coiled length. These fibers, the olivocochlear tract of Rasmussen, come from the olive, end in the organ of Corti, and are inhibitory in function. They probably serve to sharpen the **tonotopic organization** of the organ of Corti. In response to a high-pitched tone, for example, neurons from near the base of the cochlea fire more readily than others, but neurons along the length of the organ of Corti may also respond. Inhibition would affect the latter neurons more, and the "local sign," the location cue for pitch, would be improved. Input would be largely restricted to that coming from the base of the cochlea, a cue for high-pitched sounds.

PHYSIOLOGY OF THE COCHLEA
Tonotopic organization of the cochlea

It has already been stated that high-pitched tones stimulate the organ of Corti most near the base of the cochlea, and low-pitched tones stimulate most nearer the apex of the cochlea. There are three factors responsible for this relationship: (1) the laws of fluid motion, (2) traveling waves in the basilar membrane, and (3)

the relative width and compliance of the basilar membrane.

Fluid motion. In a fluid medium, low-frequency (long-wavelength) vibrations reach maximum amplitude farther from the source than do high-frequency vibrations. One may illustrate this by vibrating one end of a heavy water-filled balloon with a tuning fork while the forearm is resting along its length. The lower the frequency of the tuning fork, the farther away from the tuning fork will maximum vibrations be felt on the skin. In the cochlea the lower the frequency of vibration of the stapes against the oval window, the farther away from the base of the cochlea will fluid displacement of the basilar membrane be at a maximum (Fig. 10-9).

Traveling waves. The basilar membrane is under no tension and is of a limp and "leathery" consistency. However, it is stiffer near the base where the membrane is narrow than it is at the broader and more resilient apex. Because of this, the traveling waves will always move from base to apex, even if the vibrations are applied to parts of the cochlea other than their normal source at the oval window at the base of the cochlea. (This explains why bone-conducted sounds seem natural, even though the vibrations are conducted all over the cochlea. A tuning fork vibrated against the mastoid bone behind the ear does not change pitch and the bone-conducted vibrations of your own voice sound natural even though the timbre is different from listening to a recording of your voice.) Low-frequency vibrations cause maximum movement farther from the source of the vibrations (oval window); high-frequency vibrations, or fast movements, are maximum nearer the source of the movement.

Width of the basilar membrane. As previously described, the basilar membrane *widens* from base to apex of the cochlea. As a result the mass of the basilar membrane is least near the base of the cochlea and is less resistant there to rapid, high-

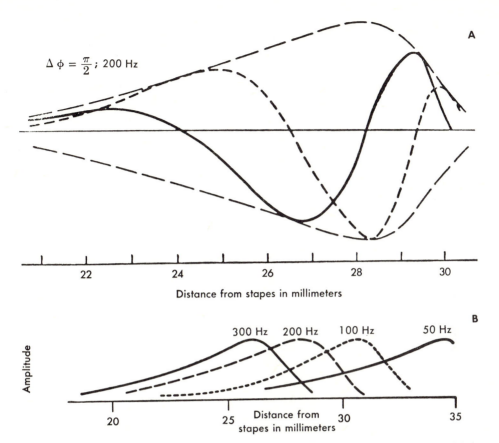

$\Delta \phi = \frac{\pi}{2}$; 200 Hz

Distance from stapes in millimeters

Amplitude

300 Hz   200 Hz   100 Hz   50 Hz

Distance from
stapes in millimeters

Fig. 10-9. A, Traveling wave on basilar membrane (really cochlear partition). *Solid line,* Pattern at one instant. *Dotted line,* Pattern a quarter-cycle later. Envelope shows maximum displacement at each point along basilar membrane at any time. **B,** Amplitude of displacement of basilar membrane (cochlear partition) for four different frequencies as a function of distance from stapes. (Modified from von Békésy, G.: J. Acoust. Soc. Am. **19:**452-460, 1947.)

frequency motion. Near the apex it is wider, has greater mass, and is therefore less resistant only to low-frequency motion. The resistance to motion of the basilar membrane changes by a factor of 100 from base to apex.

Pitch mechanisms in the organ of Corti

The location of maximum displacement of the basilar membrane is more precise for high frequencies than for low—below 50 Hz, for example, the whole basilar membrane vibrates almost as a unit. Yet pitch discrimination is excellent at low frequen-

cies. It is now believed that the efferent fibers to the organ of Corti sharpen the tonotopic input, inhibiting input from areas along the length of the organ of Corti that do not receive maximum stimulation. Single cell recordings show that the efferent fibers respond to tones of over 40 db in loudness. The fibers that fire are inhibitory fibers going to the *region* of the organ of Corti that receives maximum stimulation at a given pitch. This should assure a sharp "cut-off" of the input from sensory fibers near the place along the length of the organ of Corti where maximum stimulation occurs. Localization of the point of maximum stimulation along the organ of Corti would be thereby improved. Pitch discrimination could still, then, depend on tonotopic organization of the organ of Corti even at low frequencies.

A second factor accounts for better pitch discrimination at low frequencies than at high frequencies—the **volley theory** of pitch discrimination. It was once believed that individual nerve cells could fire at the same frequency as the sound stimulating them to carry pitch information to the brain (telephone theory). This idea came up against the absolute refractory period of nerve cells, which is at least 1 millisecond (1 msec., 1/1000 second). As a result, nerve cells could fire no more than 1000 times per second, yet we can detect frequencies of up to 20,000 Hz! At the lower frequency ranges—up to about 5000 Hz—the volley principle can explain the contradiction. A small group of nerve cells can fire in "relays" to carry the overall frequency information. By analogy, four riflemen who can each load and fire every 4 seconds can fire one round per second as a "volley." (Eight riflemen would have a two-round volley.) Frequency following of this sort has been found in groups of individual cells of the auditory nerve in the squirrel monkey for frequencies of up to 5000 Hz.

Loudness mechanisms in the organ of Corti

The detection of loudness differences depends on more hair cells firing more neurons as a result of an increase in the motion of the basilar membrane. This chain of events must occur irrespective of the location of the displacement along the basilar membrane and organ of Corti. Evoked potential measurements show that the relationship between intensity of sound stimulation and frequency of firing in individual nerve cells remains remarkably constant for the inferior colliculus, medial geniculate body, white matter of the cortex, and the cortex itself. The intensity mechanism seems to be governed by a part of the organ of Corti.

The organ of Corti includes two "rows" of hair cells (Fig. 10-6). The inner row has a single column of hair cells, and the outer row has three columns of hair cells. The outer row appears to be a loudness detection mechanism that responds to minimum intensity levels. There are two reasons for this supposition. (1) The outer row of hair cells is farthest from the "pivot points" of the basilar membrane and tectorial membrane (Fig. 10-6); as the basilar membrane and tectorial membrane "flap" up and down, they bend the hair cells in a lateral direction to fire nerve impulses. The outer-row hair cells are bent more by this motion than are the inner-row hair cells. (2) Several hair cells are innervated by each neuron going to the outer row, and an outer-row hair cell may be supplied by many nerve endings. This constitutes a *summation* mechanism; the generator potentials of several bending hair cells add their effects in order to fire a single neuron.

Differences in the innervation of the inner- and outer-row hair cells also support the idea that they function as pitch and loudness detectors, respectively. Studies with the electron microscope reveal two types of nerve cell endings that "contact" the hair cells. The small ones (type 1) are believed to be the efferent inhibitory fibers referred to in the preceding section. The larger endings (type 2) are the sensory endings. The inner-row hair cells show more large sensory endings than small inhibitory endings, in keeping with their role as detectors of the place of maximum stimulation along the basilar membrane. The outer-row hair cells show more variety in the ratio of large to small endings, corresponding to their more variable thresholds as loudness detectors.

Pitch and the hair cells

The inner row of hair cells seems designed to respond to the *place* along the length of the organ of Corti that is most displaced by sound. There are three reasons for this assumption. (1) The "traveling waves" of displacement have a maximum area of motion along the basilar membrane that depends on wavelength and therefore frequency (Fig. 10-9). (2) The inner-row hair cells seem to have a higher threshold than do the outer-row hair cells. As a result, they would respond only to the area of *maximum* displacement of the basilar membrane. As noted above, this location depends critically on pitch. (3) Each inner hair cell has 10 to 20 nerve fiber endings, and each fiber supplies 10 to 20 hair cells, providing for an overlapping "one-to-one" system. Each hair cell has a more or less "private" line in the auditory pathway to enable the brain to detect where the stimulation came from along the length of the organ of Corti. This improves discrimination by the central nervous system of which hair cells are firing neurons—and therefore where the organ of Corti was most stimulated along its length.

Action by the CNS on the tonotopic input

The accuracy of frequency discrimination is the result of the action by the CNS on a relatively crude tonotopic input. The descending pathways from higher nerve centers that were previously described seem to act on auditory input to refine its tonotopic organization. The following facts were gleaned from studies of single-fiber recordings to show the complexities involved:

1. Fibers from the basal area of the cochlea may respond to tones of any audible frequency, but apical fibers respond only to low-frequency tones. Basal fibers are most sensitive to high-frequency tones, however.

2. The range of frequencies to which a single fiber will respond broadens with increased intensity ("loudness") of the stimulus. Even at high intensity, however, these fibers show a sharp "cutoff" point as fre-

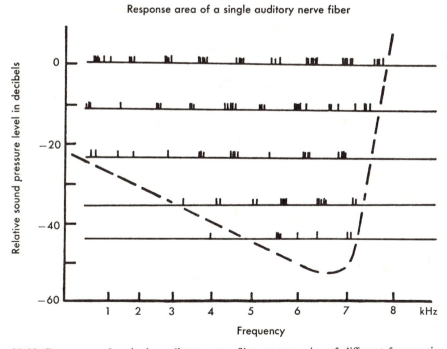

Response area of a single auditory nerve fiber

Fig. 10-10. Responses of a single auditory nerve fiber to tone pips of different frequencies and intensities. *Dotted line,* Boundary of "response area" of this fiber. (From Tasaki, I.: J. Neurophysiol. **17:**97-122, 1954.)

quency is increased, a point found just above the frequency to which they are most sensitive. (The increase in threshold at lower frequencies is more gradual—Fig. 10-10.) This cutoff is probably attributable to the tonotopically organized inhibitory efferent fibers, as previously explained.

3. How frequency-specific are individual cells? "Tuning" to a specific frequency is broader (less frequency-specific) in the cochlear nucleus than in the auditory nerve fibers. Tuning progressively narrows again up to the medial geniculate body only to become very broad at the cortex! Cells of the brainstem reticular formation that receive collaterals from the auditory pathway are not frequency-specific at all.

4. Some fibers in nerve VIII respond to all frequencies (loudness fibers from outer-row hair cells?). Some respond only to complex tones and cannot be stimulated by a sine wave "pure" tone.

5. Auditory nerve fibers show "resting" rates of firing of up to 100 per second that are not related to their frequency of firing in response to sound stimulation.

6. A frequency-specific nerve VIII fiber, firing in response to a pure tone, may be inhibited by subsequent stimulation with a higher or a lower tone.

7. A brief click stimulus produces a burst of firing in a fiber, with as little as 1 msec. between spikes; this burst of firing may outlast the stimulus by 20 to 30 msec.

8. Continued stimulation by a tone produces an irregular discharge that continues at a diminishing rate (all the impulses from a given fiber were consistent in frequency; they followed the frequency of the stimulus or a multiple of it). The diminishing response probably results from auditory adaptation to a constant stimulus.

Cochlear microphonic

The individual hair cells bend in response to sound in a manner already described. The bending of the hair cells produces a change in a current that is continually flowing through them. This *change* in current flow probably constitutes a "generator potential" that fires the sensory neurons going to the hair cells. As originally recorded from the surface of the cochlea, such electrical changes are known as the **cochlear microphonic** because they differ from nerve impulses in certain important respects: (1) they are not "all-or-none" in character (Chapter 4), but increase in size as the stimulus increases in intensity (by contrast, a nerve cell fires or does not fire with a *rate* that depends on stimulus intensity), and (2) the electrical changes faithfully reproduce the *form* as well as the frequency of the sound wave stimulus. Nerve cell firing is an electrical change that is unlike the wave form of the stimulus. The cochlear microphonic potentials act like the electrical changes produced in a microphone by sound—they can be amplified to reproduce the sound through a loudspeaker. Microelectrode recording has shown that the cochlear microphonic originates at the cuticular ("skin") surface of the hair cells. (3) The wave forms of the cochlear microphonic "follow" frequencies as high as 16,000 Hz, where nerve cell firing follows the higher frequencies only by firing in relays (volley theory). (4) Studies of strains of animals born without hair cells ("waltzing" mice) detect no cochlear microphonic, and it is abolished by certain antibiotics (such as streptomycin or neomycin) that destroy the hair cells.

Cochlear duct potential. There is a potential difference between the scala media and the other two scalae or any other indifferent point of the body fluids. The potential difference is technically known as the endolymphatic potential—a "resting" potential in which the scala media is 50 to 80 mv. positive with respect to other tissue. (The potential appears to exist because the scala media has a much higher potassium [K^+] content and only a slightly lower sodium [Na^+] content than do the other body fluids.)

Origin of nerve impulse. Absence of hair cells abolishes auditory nerve responses as well as the cochlear microphonic, so that hair cell movement in response to basilar membrane movement (the "traveling wave") seems essential to hearing. Mechanical theories propose that bending or vibration of the hair cells originates both the cochlear microphonic and nerve impulses. Chemical theories invoke a neural transmitter such as acetylcholine because of the time delays measured in neural response to sound. The most widely accepted cochlear microphonic hypothesis, states that the cochlear microphonic provides the generator potential for firing nerve impulses. In this view, bending of the hair cells changes the current flow that results from the endolymphatic or cochlear duct potential (see above). The *change* in current flow stimulates the nerve cells. Changes in the cochlear microphonic correspond well to threshold measurements for hearing. The three approaches are not mutually exclusive, and all three could be involved in the chain of events that initiates the impulse in nerve fibers.

Auditory defects

Defects in any part of the auditory mechanism, from external ear to cerebral cortex, may impair hearing, although cortical damage is often more perceptual than sensory in its effects. Sensory impairment may be too subtle to detect under ordinary circumstances. As a result, some persons are partially deaf without being aware of it. They are unable to compare their own hearing with the hearing of others, unless the defect is so striking as to make it obvious that they do not hear what others do. The nature of a sensory impairment must often be detected by **audiometry,** in which the auditory threshold is tested at selected points over a range of frequencies (Fig. 10-11). The results are plotted as an **audiogram,** which is scaled so that normal sensitivity

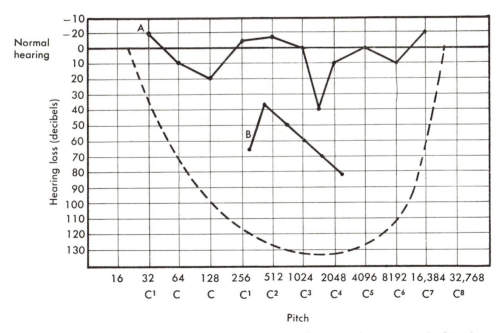

Fig. 10-11. Two fictitious but not unusual audiograms plotted on the same graph. One shows two tonal gaps, **A,** and the other is a tonal island, **B.** *Broken line,* Total loss of effective hearing.

appears as a straight line across the top of the graph.

Outer ear defects. Defects in parts of the outer ear affect all frequencies fairly evenly. The external auditory meatus may become clogged with wax, which impairs conduction of sound waves to the eardrum. The eardrum may become infected, which impairs its flexibility. Punctures of the eardrum can result in some loss of its movement in response to sound waves. Infections of the eustachian tube of the middle ear can also impair the eardrum's movement, as when an air-pressure difference builds up between the middle ear and the outer ear across the eardrum because of the infection. The infection prevents opening of the eustachian tube to equalize the pressure difference.

Middle ear defects. Apart from eustachian tube infection, defects of the middle ear result in a greater loss of sensitivity to the lower frequencies. This is because such defects affect the ossicles that transmit mechanical motion from the eardrum to the fluid of the inner ear. The *extent* of motion of the ossicles is usually greater for low frequencies than for high frequencies; impairment of the ossicles limits their motion and therefore their ability to respond to low frequencies. The ligaments holding the ossicles together may lose elasticity. More commonly, the membrane that seals the footplate of the stapes into the oval window may harden (otosclerosis), limiting the motion of the stapes. These examples of **transmission deafness** often accompany old age. In extreme cases surgery may free the junction of stapes and oval window. Another treatment consists of cutting a new window and covering it with a tiny flap of skin (fenestration). Two types of hearing aids are used to overcome these defects. One amplifies sound waves; its "loudspeaker" is placed in the external auditory meatus (air conduction). The other transmits sound vibrations to the mastoid bone behind the pinna so that vibrations reach the cochlea by bone conduction.

Inner ear defects. Inner ear defects usually arise from nerve damage or damage to the hair cells. This damage is called **nerve deafness;** it is usually localized so that it affects high frequencies more than low frequencies. Nerve deafness is the most common hearing defect of old age. When limited to specific frequencies, it is called a **tonal gap,** or a **tonal island** (Fig. 10-11). Such defects can also result from exposure to very intense sound—**exposure deafness.** The basilar membrane is overdriven by intense sound of a specific frequency range. This sound damages the hair cells in a specific region along the length of the organ of Corti, where the traveling wave of motion of the basilar membrane is at a maximum. The deafness is more or less limited to the band of frequencies produced by the exposure. High frequencies produce more damage at lower intensities because their sound waves contain more energy. Duration of exposure is also important. A "safe" level of 130 db for a 300 Hz tone (SPL) for 1½ minutes can be compared to a "safe" level of 115 db for a 3000 Hz tone of the same duration. For a 4-hour time span, 85 db at 300 Hz is comparable to 80 db at 3000 Hz. The decibel scale is exponential so that 85 db is over 1½ times 80 db. This should be taken into account in a 4-hour rock concert; rock bands have been recorded at 108 to 114 db (SPL, see Table 10-1). Safe exposure over frequencies of 100 to 10,000 Hz at this level involves durations of 15 to 30 minutes. More generalized and less frequency-specific nerve deafness also results in a symptom called *recruitment.* The threshold for hearing is raised, but when sound exceeds that threshold, it suddenly seems very loud. The experience is often reported by partially deaf people. The symptom can be explained by the summation mechanism of the outer-row hair cells. When enough undamaged hair cells are stimulated so that several fire each neuron, many neurons suddenly begin to fire—the sound therefore seem loud. The partially deaf also have difficulty distinguishing a single voice from background noise. Since they have fewer hair cells than normal, the loudness difference between the voice and the noise is harder for them to detect.

PSYCHOPHYSICS OF HEARING

Hearing demonstrates the basic attributes encountered in the other senses: (1) quality **(pitch),** (2) intensity **(loudness),** (3) extensity **(volume),** and (4) duration. A fifth psychological attribute, (5) **density,** must be added, and the attribute of volume requires some explanation. Volume is not identical with loudness, but is the perceived "size" of a tone. It qualifies as a psychological attribute because subjects can agree on comparative judgments of the sizes of tones, and an equal-interval scale can be constructed from their judgments. Apparent volume is dependent on a combination of pitch and loudness. Lower pitch and/or decreased loudness is perceived as an increase in volume. A low-pitched organ note sounds "larger" than a high-pitched flute note, but the organ note diminishes in apparent size as its intensity increases. Density is also a reliable psychological attribute that varies, in the opposite manner, with changes in pitch and loudness. Density is the apparent compactness, or hardness, of a tone—its lack of "loose," "thin," or "rare" characteristics. A high-pitched and/or intense sound appears quite dense, whereas a low-pitched and/or less loud sound is not very dense, or compact. Density qualifies as a psychological attribute for the same reason that volume does: subjects agree often enough in their judgment of tones when they compare them for density so that an equal-interval psychological scale of density can be constructed. Little need be said to define the attributes of pitch, loudness, or duration. Duration is self-explanatory. Psychologically perceived loudness varies with physical sound intensity in a manner to be described later. Psychologically perceived pitch varies with frequency in a manner that will also be described. Pitch is the *single* primary quality

of sound, whereas other senses have several primary qualities—four somesthetic qualities, several primary colors for vision, and so on. The interactions of pitch with intensity will also be discussed.

Intensity thresholds

The absolute threshold of the human ear is so low that the sound source must be calibrated at intensities well above threshold. Recent measurements on the cat eardrum with laser light interference techniques indicate threshold vibration amplitudes of the eardrum as small as 10^{-10} to 10^{-11} cm. for 1000 to 5000 Hz tones! Depending on the method used to determine threshold and the stimulus frequency, the absolute threshold may be as low as 80 db below 1 dyne/cm.^{2}. The lever system of the ossicles in the middle ear has resonant frequencies of 1200 and 800 Hz, and the external ear canal (meatus) resonates at 3000 Hz; these features largely determine the threshold curve for hearing, which is lowest in the 1000 to 5000 Hz range (Fig. 10-12). The threshold increases less rapidly for lower than for higher frequencies outside this range. The terminal threshold for loudness is much less dependent on pitch. The terminal threshold is usually set by the beginning of somesthetic sensations from the ear —the so-called threshold of feeling. The chief attribute of these sensations is pain, although tickling and itching are sensed as well. Besides being masked by somesthesis, further increments of sensed loudness require stimulus intensities that can permanently damage the organ of Corti. At low intensities the ear is most sensitive to tones in the 1000 to 5000 Hz range for the reasons given above. This means that a high- or low-pitched tone that sounds just as loud as a 1000 to 5000 Hz tone must be of greater physical intensity. High-fidelity music systems frequently have a switch on the amplifier that boosts the intensity of high and low frequencies. Its purpose is to allow music recorded at high intensity to be reproduced at low intensity without losing the

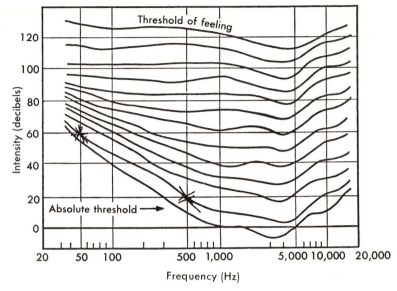

Fig. 10-12. Equal loudness contours. Lowest curve represents absolute threshold for various frequencies. Points along each of the other curves sound equally loud to the listener. (From Stevens, S. S., and Davis, H.: Hearing, New York, 1938, John Wiley & Sons, Inc.)

"natural" loudness of the high and low frequencies.

As a practical matter, differences in the loudness threshold of the two ears are common, but they are rarely large enough to cause difficulties for the subject's perception. Because of the bilateral connections of the auditory pathways from the two ears to the central nervous system, summation occurs; the two ears together have a lower threshold than one ear does, and binaural hearing is always more sensitive than monaural hearing.

Intensity discrimination

The difference threshold, or **difference limen** (DL), for intensity varies little with changes in frequency when the base intensity is below 30 db. At higher intensities the difference limen is minimal at 2500 Hz. As intensity is increased, however, the amount of further increase that one can just detect grows even faster, especially for frequencies below 2500 Hz. Weber's law of a constant $\Delta I/I$ does not hold. The best comparisons

are made by the "beat" method, with two tones of 3 Hz frequency difference being heard as "beats" three times per second when presented together at a difference in intensity level that can be detected. Using this method, $\Delta I/I$ varies from 0.2 to 7.5, depending on frequency!

Frequency thresholds and frequency discrimination

The limits—absolute and terminal thresholds—for pitch in human hearing are usually taken as 20 to 20,000 Hz. Below 20 Hz a "chugging" or a "fluttering" sound is heard. This sound acquires tonal character between 15 and 25 Hz, depending on the complexity and intensity of the tone. Above 20,000 Hz the most acute ear hears nothing, although unpleasant somesthetic "tickling" is sometimes experienced at high intensities. As noted before, little usually happens to sensitivity for lower frequencies with age, but upper-frequency limits are progressively reduced during and after middle age.

The difference threshold for pitch changes with loudness. In the first place, the difference limen for pitch increases with decreasing stimulus intensity—if you are off pitch, sing softly and others cannot tell the difference. The difference limen for pitch changes with frequency mostly between 500 and 4000 Hz, and the increase is most rapid between 2000 and 4000 Hz. This overall frequency range includes most voice fundamentals. This means that an off-pitch bass would be easier to detect than an off-pitch soprano. Finally, an odd interaction between apparent pitch and loudness occurs for pure sine wave tones, but not for complex periodic tones. With increases in intensity, pure tones higher than 2500 Hz increase in apparent pitch, whereas those below 2500 Hz decrease in pitch. No one knows the reason for this phenomenon, but it has little effect on music because musical tones are complex periodic waves; the overtones seem to keep the apparent pitch constant, whatever the loudness.

Adaptation and fatigue

The auditory threshold does increase after continuous stimulation, but the increase is very brief for sounds of moderate intensity and duration—usually less than half a second. Thus one does not notice auditory adaptation under normal circumstances. Greater intensities—a noisy office, for example—increase the threshold, so that 2 minutes or so are required for recovery in a quiet environment. Under laboratory conditions, individual subjects vary widely—some show little or no adaptation to moderate intensities—and measurement conditions make a lot of difference. Continuous stimulation for several minutes at 110 db—about all one can tolerate without ear damage—will result in impairment lasting about half an hour. The threshold for both ears is raised by stimulating one ear, which indicates that at least part of the adaptation occurs in the central nervous system because the auditory nerve pathways are shared by both ears.

COMPLEX AUDITORY PHENOMENA
Aural harmonics

In the discussion of the nature of sound, it was explained that complex structures vibrate at more than one frequency, even when the base, or fundamental frequency, is a simple sine wave. Overtones, or harmonics that determine the timbre of a sound, are thereby produced. The auditory mechanism itself is no exception to this rule, although its overtones are simple ones when the stimulus intensity is moderate. The first overtone is usually more prominent than the second, the second more prominent than the third, and so on. The more intense the auditory stimulus, the greater the amplitude and number of these **aural harmonics** and the less consistent the overtone pattern described above. Aural harmonics, because of the characteristics of the auditory mechanism, are seen in the cochlear microphonic. Even if one stimulates the ear with a pure sine-wave tone, the hair cells that probably cause the cochlear microphonic are being stimulated by a complex periodic wave. Aural harmonics are added to all sound-wave stimuli and are responsible for combination tones and other complex auditory phenomena.

Combination tones

If two pure sine-wave tones are sounded at once, the experienced observer will hear at least four. The most easily heard tone not present in the two stimulus frequencies is the **difference tone.** The frequency of the difference tone is the difference between the frequencies of the two sine-wave stimuli. The difference tone should not be confused with beats—changes in loudness in which frequency is also the difference between the stimulating frequencies. As one stimulating frequency is increased over the other, the loudness will wax and wane in beats as the two sounds come in and out of phase. As this occurs more and more often with greater separation between the frequencies, the resulting beats will be heard as a "roughness" that is quite unpleasant at high intensities. *Superimposed* on this roughness will be the difference tone. The difference tone is not caused by the beats. It is caused by the interaction of the aural harmonics of the two stimulating tones. It will be heard as a low growl when the two stimulating frequencies are about 50 Hz apart, and it will increase in frequency as the two stimulus tones differ more and more in frequency. Under these conditions it sounds somewhat like a siren.

A **summation tone** can also be heard, although it is less prominent. The summation tone is also caused by the interaction of the aural harmonics of the two stimulating frequencies. Its frequency is the *sum* of the two fundamental stimulating frequencies. If, then, the observer is stimulated with two simple sine wave tones, one of 700 Hz and one of 1000 Hz, he will hear four tones. The difference tone will be 300 Hz and the summation tone will be 1700 Hz.

Consonance and dissonance

When two tones are sounded together, the combination usually sounds either "pleasant" or "unpleasant" to most observers. The combinations that sound pleasant are **consonant frequencies**—they seem to "fuse," or blend well together. The combinations that sound "harsh" or discordant are called **dissonant frequencies.** Though musical styles change, the difference between the two frequencies (their interval) seems to be most important when consonance or dissonance is produced. The most accepted explanation states that dissonance occurs when the higher overtones of the two fundamentals are so close in frequency as to beat at a rate that gives a "rough" sound. **Consonance** occurs when the upper overtones of the two fundamentals differ enough in frequency to be distinct. Even two pure sine wave tones could be consonant or dissonant because of the interaction of the aural harmonics they produce. Con-

sonant intervals form the basis of the octave in music, and various combinations of these tones produce consonant chords.

Masking

A tone of high intensity may mask, or make inaudible, a tone of lower intensity. The low-intensity tone must be made louder in order to be heard in the presence of the high-intensity tone. The intensity required of the less intense sound in order to be heard is a measure of the **masking** effectiveness of the high-intensity tone. Masking effectiveness depends on the relative frequencies of the two tones. The effect is greatest when the two tones are close to the same frequency. However, the effect is lost when the tones are identical, and partially lost when they are close enough together to *beat* audibly. Masking effectiveness is greater in the high-frequency direction; that is, a tone will mask another tone of higher frequency more readily that it will mask a tone of lower frequency. This is because the aural harmonics (higher-frequency overtones of the auditory mechanism) from a low-frequency tone interfere with the ear's response to the higher-frequency tone. This rule will not hold when the masking tone has an overtone that is the same as the masked tone; the overtone then reinforces the masked tone instead of interfering with it.

In everyday life, masking is more frequently attributable to random frequencies, which are called noise. In masking specific pure-tone frequencies the range of frequencies in a masking noise becomes important (the critical bandwidth). Lower frequency tones are effectively masked by a smaller range of frequencies. The number of frequencies required increases for high-frequency tones that "come through" the noise more effectively.

Aftersensations

Aftersensations to "white" noise (a combination of all frequencies) are positive, but last only about 200 msec (⅕ second) at most intensities; so they are of little practical significance. The only other reliable "auditory afterimage" occurs when white noise of moderate intensity (60 db SPL) has a "gap" of a half-octave in its frequency spectrum. After about a 1-minute exposure to this stimulus ends, a pure tone is heard for 10 seconds whose sensed frequency is within the gap.

Speech

Speech is both tone and noise, that is, it has periodic vowel sounds, aperiodic sibilants (hissing sounds), and clicklike consonant sounds; the sibilants have high-frequency (noise) components. A range of 100 to 10,000 Hz contains nearly all the frequencies and overtones, but most of the sound energy output is below 1000 Hz for men or women. The sex differences include more output from 300 to 5000 Hz for men than for women and slightly more output above 5000 Hz for women. The major problem in designing communications equipment is intelligibility. Because of the great expense involved, no attempt is made to produce the whole spectrum of frequencies. Thus a range of 200 to 10,000 Hz is normally used in communications equipment.

Localization

Many complex factors may affect the localization of sound: head movements to vary the sound entering the two ears, visual cues from objects that make common sounds, such as a telephone, the complexity of the sound wave, echoes, and so on. When pure tones or "click" stimuli are used, the head is held still, and the subject is blindfolded, certain cues emerge that may be important to the initial localization of a strange sound—intensity difference and time difference. These cues are caused by the difference in sensations from the two ears when the sound source is to one side of the head or the other.

Intensity difference to the two ears occurs because the head casts a "sound shadow" if the sound comes from one side. The sound will be louder to the ear nearer the source, especially if it is a sine-wave tone above 1000 Hz. Long-wave (lower-frequency and lower-pitched) sounds "bend" around the head more readily and do not sound so different in intensity to the two ears as do higher-pitched, shorter-wave sounds.

Time difference is also important if the sound has a sharp onset, as a "click" stimulus does. The sound reaches one ear before it reaches the other. Sound travels at 1080 feet per second, but the human ears can detect a difference in sound onset of little more than half a millisecond (0.65 msec.), which is sufficient to detect which ear was stimulated first.

More complex tones, like those of music, have localization characteristics that are complicated by their overtones. Generally speaking, lower-pitched tones are less accurately localized than are high-pitched tones. This is why "stereo" (stereophonic or binaural) systems depend on overtones and higher frequencies to give the sensed difference in sound from the two loudspeaker systems.

SUMMARY

The discussion of audition included the physical energy of sound, the anatomy of the auditory mechanism, the physiology of hearing, the psychophysics of hearing, and complex auditory phenomena, in that order. Physically, sound is the alternate compression and rarefaction of air molecules caused by a vibrating body. The simplest vibrating bodies, such as a tuning fork, produce periodic variations in air pressure that can be plotted as a sine wave of pressure change over distance, depicting a simple tone. The graph (Fig. 10-1) shows simple characteristics of amplitude and wavelength. Amplitude is the amount of air pressure change, interpreted by the ear as loudness. Since sound travels at a uniform rate of 1080 feet per second, wavelength translates readily into frequency. Frequency is interpreted as pitch by the ear. Various points along the complete normal to compression to normal to rarefaction to normal sine wave can be indexed in terms of phase, the points mentioned being 0, 90, 180, 270, and 360 degrees, respectively. If one sine wave is in compression while the other is in rarefaction, they are 270 minus 90 degrees, or 180 degrees, out of phase.

The amplitude of a sound wave is measured on a log scale of pressure change constructed to match the absolute and difference thresholds of the human ear and is called the decibel scale. The zero point is an energy level of 0.0002 dyne/cm.^{2}, and there are 10 db in a bel, the exponent to the base ten multiplied by the zero point. Threshold measures are either minimum audible field or minimal audible pressure. In addition to simple periodic sine-wave tones, sound includes complex periodic tones and complex aperiodic tones. Complex periodic tones are produced by bodies such as musical instruments that vibrate with more than one frequency to produce a complex repeated wave of pressure changes made up of several sine waves. The dominant and lowest frequency is the fundamental, or first harmonic; the other frequencies are overtones, or higher harmonics, that are simple multiples of the fundamental, according to Fourier's law. The overtones are caused by the resonance of parts of the instrument and its air chambers. Differences in the relative amplitude of various overtones in different instruments are interpreted by the ear as differences in timbre. When the sine waves produced by a vibrating body are not repeated in a regular pattern, they are aperiodic and heard as noise, especially if many high-frequency components are present. Two periodic waves can come in and out of phase the same number of times per second that they differ in frequency, producing variations in loudness called beats.

The auditory mechanism transduces air pressure changes into fluid vibrations that cause the hair cells of the organ of Corti to fire nerve impulses. The outer ear funnels air pressure changes gathered by the pinna into the external auditory meatus, where they vibrate the tympanum like a drum. In the middle ear three bony ossicles, the malleus, incus, and stapes, transfer this motion to the fluid-filled inner ear; the stapes footplate is smaller than the tympanum, thus providing an impedance match between air and fluid. The motion of the ossicles resulting from loud sounds can be dampened by reflex contractions of the stapedius and tensor tympani muscles. The eustachian tube, from the middle ear to the oral cavity, equalizes middle ear pressure with the atmosphere. The coiled cochlea of the inner ear has three fluid-filled chambers. The scala vestibuli and scala tympani are filled with perilymph and communicate via the helicotrema at the cochlear apex. The scala media, or cochlear duct, is filled with endolymph. Vibrations by the stapes at the oval window cause perilymph vibrations in the scala vestibuli, and these vibrations are transmitted across Reissner's membrane to the endolymph of the scala media. The vibrations are further transmitted across the basilar membrane, which is attached to the bony shelf of the modiolus to form part of the "floor" of the scala media. The resulting pressure variations in the scala tympani cause the round-window membrane to bulge in and out.

The organ of Corti lies along the length of the basilar membrane. Its hair cells are thrust into an overlying tectorial membrane, so that as the basilar membrane moves, the hairs are bent. In response the hair cells generate firing in the nerve cells that innervate them. The hair cells are organized in a tonotopic fashion, those nearer the base of the cochlea firing more often in response to high-pitched tones and those near the apex responding to low-pitched tones. There are three reasons for this phenomenon: (1) high-frequency waves in fluid reach their maximum amplitude nearer the source than do low-frequency waves, (2) traveling waves of motion in the basilar membrane act in the same fashion, and (3) the basilar membrane widens from base to apex of the cochlea. Volley theory accounts for frequency-following by groups of nerve cells up to 5000 Hz as another pitch detector. The outer row of hair cells serves as a loudness mechanism. Several outer-row hair cells are innervated by each neuron; therefore they summate. The inner-row hair cells have high thresholds and overlapping single nerve cell innervation. Therefore they serve pitch by signaling the location of the maximum stimulus along the length of the basilar membrane. The central nervous system sharpens this tonotopic input by means of efferent pathways that inhibit input from areas not receiving maximum stimulation. Hair cells are responsible for the cochlear microphonic, which is an electrical change in the cochlea with sound, and for the firing of nerve impulses. There are mechanical, chemical, and electrical theories of impulse initiation. A potential difference between the scala media and the other scalae may provide the current flow changed by the cochlear mircrophonic, or there may be a separate generator potential.

The cell bodies of the bipolar nerve cells make up the spiral ganglion; their axons form the acoustical branch of the stato-acoustic nerve. This nerve reaches the dorsal and ventral cochlear nuclei. Fibers connecting here, both crossed and uncrossed, make up the lateral lemniscus, with synapses in its nucleus and in the olive. Collaterals reach the inferior colliculus and the path relays in the medial geniculate before reaching auditory area I in the cerebral cortex. Three areas that surround area I serve higher functions, such as sound recognition and attention.

The effect of defects in the auditory mechanism depends on where they occur. Cortical damage is more perceptual than sensory in effect. Outer ear defects such as

clogging of the meatus or eustachian tube (middle ear), or a ruptured eardrum, affect all frequencies. Ossification of middle ear bones that limits their motion or hardens the stapes to the oval window affects low frequencies most. Inner ear damage to nerves or hair cells affects high frequencies most. These symptoms may be detected by audiometry and plotted on an audiogram. Exposure damage is frequency-specific.

Psychophysically, hearing demonstrates the basic attributes of quality (pitch), intensity (loudness), extensity (volume), duration, and density. Volume increases with low pitch and less intensity; density acts in the opposite fashion. The absolute loudness threshold is a function of pitch, being lowest in the 1000 to 5000 Hz range. The terminal threshold is fixed by the onset of somesthetic sensations at 100 to 120 db, where hair cell damage can occur. Below 30 db the loudness DL varies little with pitch; at higher intensities it is minimal at 2500 Hz. The Weber ratio increases as loudness increases. The frequency limits for hearing are about 20 to 20,000 Hz. The DL for pitch improves as loudness increases and is smallest for lower frequencies below 4000 Hz. Auditory fatigue is brief for all but extreme loudness and seems to be partly a phenomenon of the central nervous system.

Complex auditory phenomena are often caused by overtones, or aural harmonics, created by the hearing mechanism itself. Difference and summation tones are caused by this mechanism. Dissonance, on the other hand, is believed to be caused by the beating of two sets of overtones, with consonance occurring when they do not beat. A lower-pitched tone can mask a higher-pitched tone more readily than the reverse; masking is less effective when overtones reinforce, or beat. Masking is most effective when the frequency difference is small. Noise masking requires a narrower bandwidth for low-pitch tones than for high-pitched tones. Speech includes both tones and noise in the range of 100 to 10,000 Hz. Sex differences are small. Aftersensations to white noise are brief and positive, but a prolonged aftersensation exists in response to a gap in the white-noise spectrum. Auditory localization is binaural and depends on (1) intensity differences and (2) time differences.

READINGS

Alpern, M., Lawrence, M., and Wolsk, D.: Sensory processes, Belmont, Calif., 1967, Brooks-Cole Publishing Co., Division of Wadsworth Publishing Co.

Beranek, L. L.: Noise, Sci. Am. **215**:66-74, Dec. 1966. (W. H. Freeman Reprint No. 306.)

Kellogg, W. N.: Porpoises and sonar, Chicago, 1961, Phoenix Books.

Mueller, C. G.: Sensory psychology, Englewood Cliffs, N.J., 1965, Prentice-Hall, Inc.

Oster, G.: Auditory beats in the brain, Sci. Am. **229**:94-102, Oct. 1973. (W. H. Freeman Reprint No. 1282.)

Rosensweig, M. R.: Auditory localization, Sci. Am. **205**:132-142, Oct. 1961. (W. H. Freeman Reprint No. 501.)

Stevens, S. S., and Newman, E. B.: The localization of actual sources of sound, Am. J. Psychol. **48**:297-306, 1936. (Bobbs-Merrill Reprint No. P-335.)

van Bergeijk, W. A., Pierce, J. R., and David, E. E.: Waves and the ear, Garden City, N.Y., 1960, Doubleday & Co., Inc.

von Békésy, G.: The ear, Sci. Am. **197**:66-78, Aug. 1957. (W. H. Freeman Reprint No. 44.)

von Békésy, G.: Similarities between hearing and skin sensations, Psychol. Rev. **66**:1-22, 1959. (Bobbs-Merrill Reprint No. P-31.)

von Buddenbrock, W.: The senses, Ann Arbor, Mich., 1958, The University of Michigan Press.

Wightman, F. L., and Green, D. M.: The perception of pitch, Am. Scientist **62**:208-215, 1974.

chapter 11

Vision

OVERVIEW

The topic of vision, like audition, can be considered from three points of view: (1) the anatomy and physiology of the eye and its nervous connections, (2) the physical energy that provides the stimulus, and (3) the psychophysics of interaction between the stimulus and the visual mechanism that provides a sensation. The anatomy and physiology of the eye will be discussed before covering the nature of light because many aspects of the stimulus energy are easier to understand after one learns how the eye reacts to stimuli and sends signals to the brain. A simplified explanation of the physical nature of light follows, including a discussion of the most common units of light measurement. Light interacts with visual anatomy as explained in the section on visual physiology, providing explanations for day and night vision, chemical reactions of the receptors, and the electrical responses of parts of the visual system that result in sensations of hue and brightness. Then visual sensations can be surveyed by using units of physical measurement and units of psychological response in visual psychophysics. Finally, various visual phenomena will be described and their basis in visual physiology given when it is known. In visual psychophysics, the way in which light reaches the eye determines the colors that are seen. Newton's laws of color and the visual dimensions of hue, brightness, and saturation explain the basis of color mixing by addition and subtraction. The visual phenomena discussed include adaptation, aftersensations, contrast, acuity, critical flicker frequency, apparent movement, cues to depth and distance, and color vision defects.

ANATOMY OF THE EYE

The eye is a sense organ and therefore an organization of different kinds of tissue; each tissue has a role to play in the eye's response to light. The tissues are organized into parts of the eye, each of which contributes to vision in unique ways. The various parts of the eye will be discussed first and the function of each part noted. Then the interaction of these parts in accommodation, convergence, and the pupillary reflexes will be described.

Extrinsic muscles of the eye

There are six muscles that originate in the bony orbit, or eye socket, and insert on the eyeball. Their function is to move the eyeball—to "point" it in various directions. The **extrinsic** eye muscles train the eye on objects in reflex and in learned responses to light, movement, and the input from other senses. The extrinsic eye muscles are named by contrast with the **intrinsic** muscles inside the eyeball that control the lens and the pupil.

Layers, or coats, of the eye

One way to understand some parts of the eye is to consider the eyeball as consisting of three layers—the sclerotic coat, the choroid coat, and the retina (Fig. 11-1). The **sclerotic coat,** or **sclera,** is the tough opaque outer fibrous tissue that forms the "white" of the eye. It serves a protective and binding function and, to some extent, prevents light from entering the eye except by way of the pupil. The sclera is continuous with the **cornea** at the front of the eye. Light first enters the interior of the eye through the transparent cornea. The cornea begins the focusing job that the **lens** completes by bringing light rays into focus on the retina.

The **choroid coat** is the middle layer of the eyeball. It contains many blood vessels that nourish the other tissues of the eye. It is pigmented, or dark-colored, on its inner surface to minimize the scattering of light by reflection inside the eyeball. The choroid coat is continuous with the **ciliary body,** or **ciliary ring,** a ring of smooth muscle that is attached to the **lens** by the **suspensory ligament.** Contraction of the ciliary ring relieves tension on the suspensory ligament and causes the lens to *thicken* by its own elasticity. Thickening the lens focuses light from nearby objects on the retina (see p. 224). The ciliary body is also continuous with the **iris,** another smooth muscle structure; the iris determines the color of the eye and surrounds the pupil. It also contains circular muscle fibers that contract to constrict the **pupil,** and radial muscles that contract to open the pupil (see p. 226).

The **retina** covers only a part of the interior surface of the eyeball, the back portion. The retina contains the light-sensitive receptor cells as well as several kinds of nerve cells. It develops as an extension of the cerebral cortex of the brain and grows out from the brain on two large "stalks," the optic nerves, to invade the developing eyeballs. The retina therefore contains nerve cells and synapses in well-defined layers, as does the cerebral cortex. Much of its fine structure has recently been defined by the electron microscope.

The retina is arranged "inside out"; that is, the receptors lie nearest to the choroid coat, and light must pass through several layers of connecting nerve cells to reach the receptors (Fig. 11-2). The receptors, called **rods** and **cones,** form a distinct layer in the retina. The most distinct of the other layers of the retina are the **bipolar cell layer** and the **ganglion cell layer.** The rods and cones pass excitation to the bipolar cells when stimulated by light. The bipolar cells, in turn, pass excitation on to the ganglion cells. The axons of the ganglion cells form the optic nerve, the nerve that carries ex-

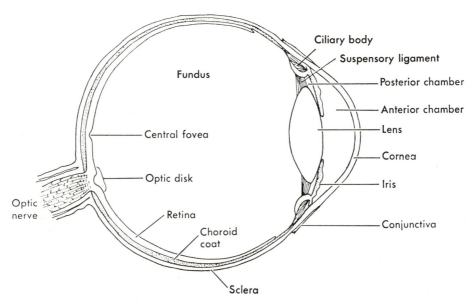

Fig. 11-1. Cross section of the eye in diagrammatic form, as seen from above.

citation from the eye to visual centers in the brain. In the retina itself there are interconnections between the receptors via **horizontal cells; amacrine cells** interconnect the bipolar cells. Excitation and inhibition can thereby spread from one point to surrounding areas of the retina. This mechanism will become important later, when its function in sharpening visual input is discussed. Finally, there are *efferent* fibers reaching the retina from the brain. These fibers probably synapse with amacrine and ganglion cells; their function appears to be inhibitory. The efferent fibers may act to sharpen vision by blocking off extraneous input from other parts of the retina, or they may reduce visual input generally, but this is still speculation. (Efferent inhibitory fibers were found in the somesthetic and auditory systems as well.)

The **fovea** is a pit, or depression, in the retina that is in line with the pupil of the eye when the eye is directed toward an object (Fig. 11-1). The fovea is the point of clearest vision and is densely packed with receptors. The receptors are arranged radially around the pit, with connecting bipolar and ganglion cells radially connected to them. Therefore light does not have to pass through the ganglion and bipolar cells to reach the receptors in the fovea. Only cones are found in the fovea, but they are packed so densely together that they take on the elongated shape of rods. Since light reaches foveal cones directly and since they are so numerous, foveal vision is clearer than peripheral vision from other parts of the retina. Light rays from objects are focused by the lens on the fovea in visual accommodation.

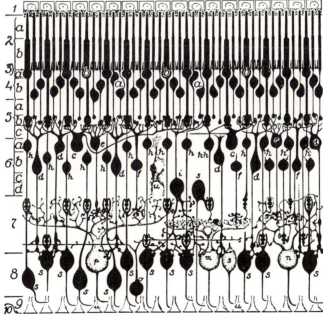

Fig. 11-2. Drawing of structure of retina as seen under microscope (Golgi stain). Rods **(a)** and cones **(b)** are seen at top, next to pigmented layer **(1)** of choroid coat (interior of eyeball is at bottom of figure). Bipolar cells **(d, e, f, h)** are the principal feature of the middle layers, but amacrine cells **(i, l)** and horizontal cells **(c)** can also be seen. Ganglion cells **(m, n, o, p, s)** dominate inner layers. (From Polyak, S. L.: The retina, Chicago, 1941, The University of Chicago Press.)

The cones are the hue-sensitive receptor cells of the retina. Stimulation of cones results in sensations of hue as well as brightness. Cones are most numerous in the fovea, but they rapidly become scarcer as one moves toward the periphery of the retina. So few cones are found in the peripheral part of the retina (beyond about 20 degrees from the fovea) that they have no known function in peripheral vision. The cone input has a relatively high threshold—cone vision is daylight vision. Light stimulates the cones by breaking down a chemical pigment called **iodopsin,** as well as related chemicals, into intermediate compounds; light further causes the intermediate compounds to break down into vitamin A and cone opsin (Fig. 11-3). Iodopsin is found in the sensory end of the cone, next to the pigmented epithelium of the choroid coat, which furnishes the vitamin A. Studies with the electron microscope show that the light-sensitive ends of both rods and cones have the appearance of a "stack of disks," like stacked poker chips. This appearance is caused by a regular infolding of the cell membrane. The probable function of the membrane's infolding is to increase the area of the membrane. Because this membrane contains the light-sensitive pigment, a larger supply of pigment is thereby ensured.

The rods are sensitive only to brightness and give sensations of varied shades of gray. Thus one does not have sensations of hue under conditions of night vision, when rod response predominates. At night there is often not enough light to stimulate cones. Instead of iodopsin the rods contain **rhodopsin.** Light breaks down rhodopsin into intermediate compounds, which stimulate rods; the intermediate compounds may further break down into rod opsin and vitamin A (Fig. 11-3).

Since visual response depends as much on the nature of the retinal pathways as on the receptors themselves, it is appropriate, at this point, to compare the rod system and the cone system. The threshold of the rod system is lower than the threshold of the cone system for three reasons: (1) cone pigments regenerate faster than rod pigments after exposure to light, and therefore are better suited to continue stimulating sensory input under conditions of high illumination, when the rod pigments are, for the most part, broken down; (2) there

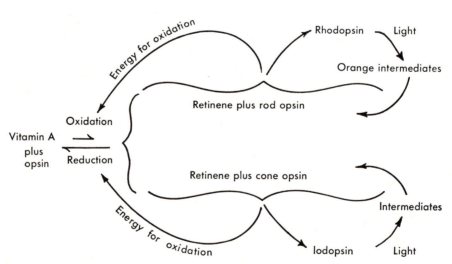

Fig. 11-3. Simplified synopsis of some of the major photochemical reactions in rod and cone vision.

is more convergence from a number of receptor cells onto a single optic nerve cell in the rod system than in the cone system, and thus the rod system is capable of more summation; and (3) the excitation of cones stimulates neural pathways that inhibit input at synapses of the rod system. Recent research suggests that the rods and cones themselves are of approximately equal sensitivity.

Rods and cones excite bipolar cells, which in turn stimulate ganglion cells. It is the ganglion cell axons that leave the eye to form the optic nerve. At the point where the axons leave the eye there are no receptors; this point (the optic disk) is called the blind spot because it is insensitive to light. The blind spot lies on the nasal (nose) side of the retina; since light travels in a straight line, there is a blind spot in the temporal (toward the temples) visual field in peripheral vision. One is ordinarily not aware of this small area of blindness. To demonstrate its presence, one can close the left eye, hold up a left finger at arm's length and focus on it with the right eye, and bring an upright right finger in from the periphery. When the right finger crosses the blind spot in the visual field, the right fingertip will seem to disappear.

Cavities and fluids of the eye (Fig. 11-1)

The **anterior chamber** of the eye lies between the cornea and the iris of the eye and communicates with the **posterior chamber** of the eye via the pupil. The posterior chamber lies between the iris on one hand and the ciliary ring, suspensory ligament, and lens on the other. Both anterior and posterior chambers are filled with **aqueous humor,** a watery fluid resembling the extracellular and lymph fluids of other parts of the body. Neither chamber communicates with the **fundus,** the large interior cavity of the eye, at least not directly. The fundus contains a jellylike substance, the **vitreous humor,** that is much more viscous than the aqueous humor. Both fluids absorb some light rays and scatter others, as do the lens and cornea. Despite its pigment coating, the interior of the eyeball scatters some light, and still more light leaks through the opaque outer covering (sclera) of the eyeball. Considering all these facts, it is a matter of some wonder that we see as well as we do.

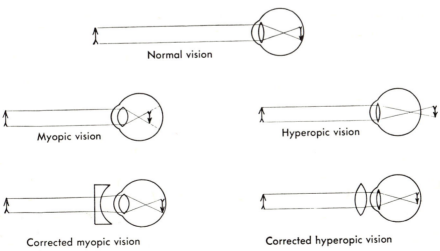

Fig. 11-4. Focus of light rays in normal, myopic, and hyperopic vision.

Mechanisms of accommodation

Light rays that reach the eye from objects more than 15 to 20 feet away are parallel, as compared to light rays from nearby objects that *diverge* noticeably in reaching the eye. The normal eye is arranged so that the parallel rays from distant objects are bent just enough by the cornea and lens to be focused on the retina (Fig. 11-4). Light rays travel in a straight line except as they are bent by the cornea and lens. The image focused on the retina is therefore upside down and reversed. (Rays from the lower half of the visual field stimulate the upper part of the retina, and vice versa; rays from the left visual field stimulate the right half of the retina, and vice versa.) If the object is closer than 15 to 20 feet away, light rays from it *diverge* noticeably on their way to the eye. Such diverging rays must be bent more than parallel rays to be focused on the retina. This is accomplished by *thickening* the lens, a process called **accommodation.** The ciliary muscle contracts to constrict the ciliary ring, drawing it forward and decreasing its diameter. This relieves tension on the suspensory ligament holding the lens. Under decreased tension the lens, because of its own elasticity, bulges to become thicker, causing increased bending of diverging light rays as an object is brought closer to the eye.

A **myopic,** or nearsighted, person has a lens that is too thick or an eyeball that is too "long" in the front-to-back dimension. Parallel rays of light from distant objects are therefore bent too much and are brought into focus before they reach the retina, where the receptors are found (Fig. 11-4). Rays reaching the retina are therefore scattered again and "blurred," and the myopic person cannot see distant objects clearly. Nearby objects can be brought into focus because their light rays diverge and require either a thickened lens or an elongated eyeball in order to be focused on the retina. Because the myopic individual

must focus on objects closer to his eyes than an individual with normal vision, the myopic person without glasses holds things "close to his nose." The condition is corrected by *concave* lenses, which make parallel light rays diverge and thus compensate for the tendency of the myopic eye to bend light rays too much; parallel rays become diverging rays that can be focused on the retina of the myopic individual.

A **hyperopic,** or farsighted, person has an eyeball that is too short or a lens that is too thin. In either case parallel rays of light from distant objects are not bent enough to be in focus when they reach the retina; these rays would focus "behind" the fovea if that were possible (Fig. 11-4). The hyperopic person can focus parallel rays of light from distant objects by thickening his lens in accommodation—the same response the normal eye makes to the diverging rays of nearby objects. The hyperopic eye is therefore accommodating all the time, whereas the normal eye accommodates only to nearby objects. Further, there is "disagreement" between the reflexes that converge ("cross") the eyes to focus on nearby objects and the reflexes that thicken the lens. Abnormal stresses in the extrinsic muscles that "point" the eyes can result in fatigue and headaches. The hyperopic person is unable to thicken his lens enough to focus on objects held close to his eyes; to read, he must hold a book at arm's length. The condition is corrected by convex lenses that partly bend the parallel rays from distant objects before the rays reach the lens. The lens completes the job of bringing the light into focus on the fovea.

Presbyopia is the lack of accommodation usually seen in older persons. Nearly everyone becomes less able to accommodate with age, from adolescence onward. The problem becomes acute for most people in their late forties or early fifties. The range of accommodation is reduced because the lens has less elasticity (with age) and does not thicken enough. The presbyopic person often must wear bifocals, spectacles that have thin lenses in their upper half, enabling him to see distant objects, and thick lenses in their lower half for viewing nearby objects.

In **astigmatism** the eye may be partly farsighted, partly nearsighted, or both. This anomalous condition usually occurs because the cornea has an unequal curvature. The correct curvature for one cross section accompanies another cross section that is too curved or not curved enough. For example, a horizontal line may be correctly focused because the horizontal section of the cornea has the correct cross section, whereas a vertical line may be blurred because the vertical section of the cornea is incorrect for focus. Lenses of opposite error in cross section correct the condition.

Cataracts result from a clouding of the lens because of disease or injury; the eventual outcome is blindness. The only cure is removal of the clouded lens and the use of spectacles with a thick lens that substitutes for the missing lens. If the cornea is scarred, a transplant can be made of a living cornea from a deceased donor. "Eye banks" of living corneal tissue bequeathed in wills form the main supply of corneal tissue.

Convergence and accommodation

The ciliary muscles of each eye contract to close the ciliary ring, allowing the lens to thicken because of its own elasticity and thus bringing diverging rays of light from nearby objects into focus on the retina, as explained previously. Ciliary contraction also serves as a cue to the distance of nearby objects, since the nearer the object, the greater is the ciliary contraction and the stronger is the sensation of muscle strain. One may experience these sensations by closing one eye, focusing on a fingertip held about a foot away, and then slowly bringing the finger as close to the eye as possible while keeping it in focus. If both eyes are used in this exercise, another set of muscle strain sensations will be experienced. In addition to the sensations from the *intrinsic* ciliary muscles, sensations from the *extrinsic* muscles that "point" the eyeballs will be felt. The closer the object, the more "cross-eyed" one must look at it to keep the fovea of each eye "pointed" in visual **convergence.** These two sets of muscle sensations serve as *cues* to the distance of objects up to several feet away. In the normal eye the two sets of reflexes are linked so that the correct amount of convergence of both eyes accompanies the correct amount of thickening of the lens of each eye. In the myopic or hyperopic individual, correct focus does not accompany correct convergence, because the lens or cornea of one eye or both is abnormal. In the hyperopic person, especially, one eye sees a blurred image because it is out of focus, or double images are seen because the eyes are not converged properly. As a result the brain learns to suppress the input from one eye and depend on the input from the other, a condition called **amblyopia.** It is especially common in children with undetected visual defects. If it is not discovered early enough, the input from one eye may be permanently suppressed, causing irreversible partial blindness in that eye as far as its use is concerned. If amblyopia is detected early, the impaired eye's function can be restored by forcing its use, which is accomplished by partly or completely blindfolding the other eye for part of each day.

Retinal development: dependence on stimulation

The studies of one prominent investigator (Riesen) show clearly how dependent the retina is on light stimulation for normal development *and* maintenance. The microscope reveals severe retinal degeneration after 16 weeks of complete light deprivation in the infant *or* adult chimpanzee; degeneration follows light deprivation at any age. The effect is less severe in lower animals (cats). Ninety minutes per day of diffuse light through a Plexiglass dome will protect the chimpanzee retina from degeneration, but the animals show severe deficiencies in pattern vision and the recognition of objects. Ninety minutes per day of normal visual experience results in chimpanzees whose pattern vision and object recognition are normal. If the chimpanzees receive normal visual experience with one eye and only diffuse light in the other eye, they show deficiencies in pattern vision and form recognition when the normal eye is blindfolded. Clearly, the retina requires visual pattern stimulation to develop its input relationships with the central nervous system.

Pupillary reflexes

The pupil, the opening by which light reaches the interior of the eye, is surrounded by the colored iris. The contraction of intrinsic muscle fibers in the iris determines the size of the pupil and therefore the amount of light that reaches the retina. Contraction of the **radial fibers** of the iris opens the pupil to admit more light in dim illumination. Contraction of **circular fibers** of the iris constricts the pupil to admit less light under conditions of bright illumination. These *reflex* reactions to light are mediated by the autonomic nervous system. They help explain how the eye can react to very small amounts of light and yet function under brightnesses of hundreds of candlepower without damage.

NERVOUS CONNECTIONS OF THE EYE

As already noted, the retina itself is an extension of the brain, and many intercon-

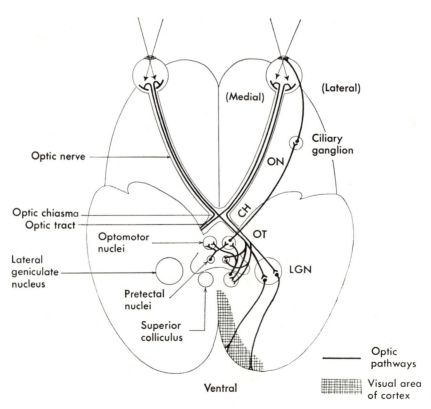

Fig. 11-5. Optic pathways as viewed from beneath brain.

nections between nerve cells are made there. The axons of ganglion cells of the innermost layer of the retina converge on the optic disk, or blind spot, and emerge from the eyeball as the **optic nerve** (Figs. 11-1 and 11-5). The optic nerves from the two eyeballs are really *tracts,* since they are part of the central rather than the peripheral nervous system. However, for convenience the ganglion cell axons are called the optic nerve before they reach the **optic chiasma** and are called the **optic tract** after they leave it, as can be seen in Fig. 11-5. When the ganglion cell axons reach the optic chiasma, a hemidecussation, or "half crossing," occurs in the ganglion cells (in higher mammals). Fibers from the *nasal* (toward the nose), or medial, halves of each retina cross, whereas fibers from the *temporal* (toward the temple) halves of each retina do not cross. As a result the crossing fibers from the nasal halves of the retina of each eye send excitation to the *opposite* cerebral hemispheres, whereas fibers from the temporal half of each retina, which do not cross, send excitation to the cerebral hemisphere of the *same* side. The right optic *tract,* for example, would contain fibers from the nasal half of the left retina and the temporal half of the right retina. Thus the nasal half of the left retina and the temporal half of the right retina "see" the *left* half of the visual *field.* Damage to the right optic tract would therefore impair vision in the left visual field. By contrast, cutting the right optic nerve would merely blind the right eye. Damage to the crossing fibers of the chiasma (as sometimes occurs from pituitary gland tumors) would destroy fibers from the nasal halves of both retinas, impairing peripheral vision from the temporal halves of both visual fields (tunnel vision).

The optic tract of each side terminates in the **lateral geniculate body,** or lateral geniculate nucleus (LGN). Like the sensory nuclei of the closely related thalamus, the lateral geniculate nucleus serves mainly as a relay station for the cortex and is topographically organized. The optic tract also sends fibers to the **superior colliculi** and **pretectal nuclei.** The superior colliculi mediate reflex movements of the eyeball in convergence and in other eye movements. These responses are handled by connections with the **optomotor nuclei** of the third, fourth, and sixth cranial nerves. The pretectal nuclei, on the other hand, are concerned with the intrinsic muscles of the eye, the ciliary muscles of lens accommodation, and the reflex regulation of the pupil by the iris. Intrinsic eye muscle reactions are controlled via the parasympathetic fibers of the third nerve and via sympathetic fibers that relay excitation from the spinal cord.

The major function of the lateral geniculate nucleus is to supply the **striate cortex,** the primary visual projection area in occipital lobes. This is the area called visual I, and it corresponds with Brodmann's area 17. (The lateral geniculate nucleus also sends fibers to the association nuclei of the thalamus.) Visual I is *topographically organized.* That is, each point on the retina that is excited by light causes excitation of a corresponding point in area I. (The same kind of organization was encountered in pressure sensitivity and audition.) The cerebral cortex has a visual II in the prestriate area (areas 18 and 19) and a visual III in parietal and temporal areas. The topographical organization of visual II is the mirror image of the organization of visual I. Visual II and visual III have been located mainly by recording from the cortex of anesthetized animals while the eye was stimulated with light. The exact anatomy of these pathways is not known. They are presumed to include the association nuclei of the thalamus (diffuse thalamic projection system) and the brainstem reticular formation (ascending reticular activating system).

Some of the functions of the three visual areas have been worked out in careful ablation experiments with monkeys. Removal of area I reduces visual function to brightness alone. Discrimination experiments show that the visual system is able to detect only the total amount of light entering the eye, like a photo cell. No form or pattern perception remains. When area I is intact but areas II and III are removed, a different sort of visual impairment follows. Visual pattern and form recognition are normal, but the monkey makes errors in spatial judgment and is confused by moving objects. (Visual recognition is impaired by lesions of the ventral part of the temporal lobe—infratemporal lesions. This impairment is a part of the Klüver-Bucy syndrome, which is discussed in Chapter 16.)

PHYSICS OF LIGHT

One should understand at least in elementary fashion, the physics of the light energy that stimulates the retina, before undertaking the study of the physiology and psychophysics of vision. Light is a complex form of energy that is part of the **electromagnetic spectrum** of energy. This spectrum is a different form of energy from the air pressure changes perceived as sound; unlike sound, electromagnetic energy travels readily through a vacuum and travels at a rate much higher than sound (the speed of light is about 186,272 miles per second). Light consists of individual particles of matter, each of which demonstrates the property of wavelike motion at a specific frequency. The "particles" are quanta, a quantum being the least measurable part of radiant energy. The wavelengths form a spectrum of wavelengths that are a part of the more extensive electromagnetic spectrum (Fig. 11-6). The electromagnetic spectrum includes radio waves (18 miles to 1-inch wavelengths), infrared waves (1 inch to 32 millionths of an inch), light (32 millionths to 16 millionths of an inch), and x rays and gamma rays (down to 4 ten-trillionths of an inch). One can see that visible light forms a small part of the electromagnetic spectrum and that its wavelengths are very short. The wavelengths are measured in **nanometers** (nm., millionths of a millimeter, billionths of a meter, or 10^{-9} meters). The term **lambda** (λ) is sometimes used as a symbol to designate wavelengths. The upper atmosphere acts like a filter in reducing the energy spectrum of

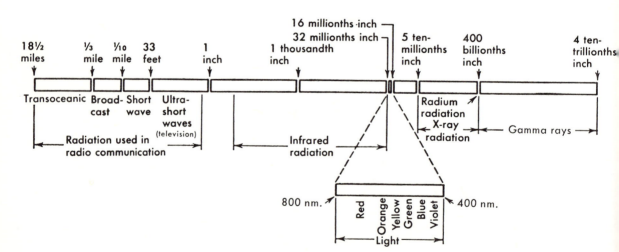

Fig. 11-6. Electromagnetic spectrum, showing range of wavelengths that stimulate visual receptors (light). (Modified from Dimmick, F. L. In Boring, E. G., Langfeld, H. S., and Weld, H. P., editors: Foundations of psychology, New York, 1948, John Wiley & Sons, Inc.)

electromagnetic radiation from the sun to a range of λ300 to λ760 nm. Our visual receptors have evolved to be most sensitive to this approximate range of frequencies.

Light reaching the eye from the sun is a mixture of all the visible wavelengths. If a small beam of sunlight from a point source is passed through a *prism,* the light will be bent, or refracted. A prism is a wedge-shaped block of glass that bends light rays as a function of their wavelengths. The longer wavelengths of light are bent less than the shorter wavelengths, so that an orderly array of wavelengths is produced by the prism (Fig. 11-7). The resulting **visible spectrum** will be seen as bands of different **hues,** from violet through blue, green, yellow, orange, and red, as shorter to longer wavelengths are separated. Any single wavelength is spectrally pure and fairly **saturated,** that is, distinct in hue. (Some mixtures of wavelengths produce gray-looking hues, or colors low in saturation.) Single wavelengths are **homogeneous;** mixtures of wavelengths are **heterogenous.** Increasing the *amplitude* of either a single wavelength of light or any mixture of wavelengths produces increases in **brightness.**

Light, then, varies in wavelengths, intensity (amplitude), and heterogeneity (wavelength mixture). Changes in wavelength are perceived by the eye as changes in hue; changes in amplitude, or intensity, are perceived as changes in brightness; changes in the homogeneity of light can result in saturation differences.

Measurements of light

Wavelengths are measured in **nanometers** (see above). A range of 400 to 750 nm. is commonly taken as the limits of the visible spectrum, although some intense stimuli outside these limits can be seen. Homogeneity or heterogeneity may be specified in terms of the proportion of each component wavelength in mixtures of light waves. Measurements of intensity are more complex and are based on the rate of flow of "particles" (quanta) of light rather than on the amplitude of a vibratory light wave.

Brightness of a source. The brightness of a light source is calibrated in terms of the flow of light from an international **candle,** a standard source about as bright as a

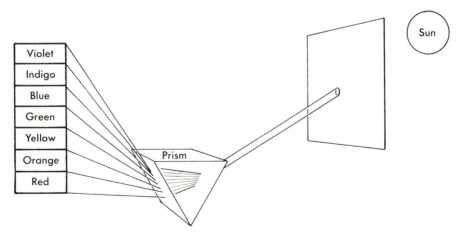

Fig. 11-7. Spectrum, as revealed through use of prism.

candle with a 1-inch flame. The candle radiates luminous **flux,** or flowing light particles, in all directions. The density of these particles—how close they are together—diminishes with increasing distance from the source, because light scatters with distance. (A standard candle radiates 4π [or 12.56] **lumens** of luminous flux.) One lumen of light would cover a square inch 1 inch from the candle or a square mile 1 mile from the candle.

Illuminance. Measurements of brightness for light falling on a surface differ from measurements of light coming from a surface. **Illuminance** is the name given to measurements of light falling on a surface. A **footcandle** of light (1 lumen) would fall on a square foot of surface placed 1 foot from a standard candle.

Luminance. **Luminance** is the brightness of a surface that is either emitting or reflecting light. The usual standard is the **lambert,** defined in lumens per square centimeter of area.

Light stimuli

Light reaching the eye from any point or surface varies in intensity, wavelength, and heterogeneity of wavelengths. The resulting sensation appears to vary in brightness, hue, and saturation, respectively. Light reaching the eye from the sun is uniform in brightness; sunlight lacks hue and saturation because it is a heterogeneous mixture of all visible wavelengths. Light reaching the eye from other objects has undergone changes in intensity and component wavelengths; therefore it is changed in brightness, hue, and saturation.

A physical object may **transmit, reflect, absorb, refract,** or **radiate** light. In each case it is the light reaching the eye that determines the hue, saturation, or brightness that is sensed. A color filter may be placed between the source and an observer; the filter will absorb some wavelengths and transmit others. For example, it may transmit only the longest wavelengths, resulting

in a red hue. The mixture of wavelengths transmitted determines saturation, whereas the amount of light transmitted determines brightness. A prism, on the other hand, refracts, or bends, the light it transmits, resulting in a spectrum of wavelengths, as already pointed out. A surface such as a painted wall may absorb some wavelengths and reflect others. The wavelengths that are reflected to the eye determine the hue and saturation; those that are absorbed are not seen. The amount of light of any wavelength that is reflected would determine brightness. An object may also radiate light of certain wavelengths because of heat (incandescence) or chemical reactions (luminescence). Short-wave radiation causes fluorescent materials to glow during activiation and luminescent materials (like the painted numbers on a watch face) to continue glowing after activation (phosphoresce). In all cases of light radiation, the wavelengths emitted are determined by the chemical properties of the object. Electricity passing through an ordinary light bulb heats a tungsten filament and causes it to give off more "yellow" wavelengths than others as a result. The hue of the luminescence of a "neon" light will depend on the type of gas used in it—different gases produce different wavelengths of light by chemical reactions. This property is often used in "neon" advertising signs.

VISUAL PHYSIOLOGY

Now that the anatomy of the eye, the visual pathways, and the physics of the stimulus have been discussed, the topic of visual physiology may be undertaken. Beginning with the reactions of the rods and cones to light, the known effects of visual stimulation can be traced to the highest parts of the brain.

Duplicity theory

The initial assumption made about the way in which rod and cone systems work assigns them different intensity ranges and reactions to hue. The rod system is supposed to be **achromatic,** or **scotopic;** that is, it has inputs that do not give sensations of hue and has very low thresholds for functioning in low illumination (night vision). The cone system is supposed to be **chromatic,** or **photopic;** it has a relatively high threshold (about 10 microlamberts) and functions under conditions of daylight vision. The evidence behind these statements can be summarized as follows:

1. Two different visual pigments in the eye, iodopsin and rhodopsin, have been discovered.

2. Relative sensitivity to individual wavelengths differs under high illumination as compared to low illumination; the cones seem most sensitive in the yellow-green region of the spectrum (555 nm.), whereas the rods seem most sensitive in the green region of the spectrum (511 nm.).

3. The curves for spectral sensitivity, or sensitivity to different wavelengths of light for rods and cones, look like curves measuring the amount of light of the same wavelengths that is absorbed by rhodopsin and iodopsin, respectively. Presumably, the more a given wavelength is absorbed to break down rhodopsin, for example, the more sensitive the rhodopsin-containing rods would be to that wavelength.

4. The central part of the retina—the fovea, which contains only cones—provides the most acute vision in high illumination; the periphery of the retina (peripheral vision), contains nearly all rods and is most sensitive in the dark-adapted eye.

5. When one is looking at a gray field, hues are seen only in the central part of the visual field, where the cones respond; spots of color in the periphery, where the rods respond, are seen as gray (see the discussion of color zones of the retina, below, in the section on visual phenomena).

6. Adaptation to darkness from daylight seems to occur in two stages. For approximately the first 5 minutes the eyes become more sensitive at a diminishing rate as more iodopsin is built up in the cones, but there is not enough light to break it all down. Later, enough rhodopsin begins to be built up in the rods so that they begin responding. Since rod input is more sensitive than cone input, the eyes again start increasing in sensitivity at a rapid rate, reaching maximum sensitivity after a half hour or so.

There is other evidence supporting the duplicity theory, but these points seem to be the main ones. The theory needs restatement, however. For instance, new evidence shows that there are three kinds of cones that respond differently to different hues, and perhaps another kind of cone, or a mixed reaction of the retina, that responds to brightness alone.

Electroretinogram

In stimulating the eye of an anesthetized animal the electrical responses of the retina are often used to indicate visual response to light. Some recording measures to be reported involve electrodes placed in the retina—in single ganglion cells of the retina or in their fibers in the optic nerve. A more gross measure of the overall response of the retina is used often enough to deserve mention, however. This measure is the **electroretinogram (ERG).** The ERG is usually recorded by placing one electrode on the cornea and another near the back of the eye. Four electrical waves are recorded when the eye is stimulated with light (Fig. 11-8); A, B, and C waves are recorded when the light is turned on, and a D wave is recorded when the light is turned off. Gross recordings of this kind are, of course, compounded of the electrical responses of many cells. The A and B waves are compounded of an early component that has been identified with photopic receptors (cones) and a late component that is identified with scotopic receptors (rods). As a result an arbitary amplitude of the A or B wave is often selected as a threshold measure for vision experiments.

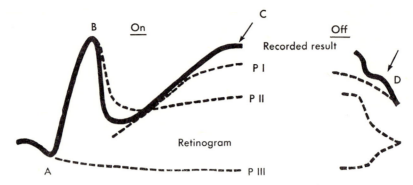

Fig. 11-8. Electroretinogram (ERG). Major **A, B, C,** and **D** waves (see text) recorded are presumably made up of the components **P I, P II,** and **P III.** (From Bartley, S. H.: Psychol. Rev. **46:**337-358, 1939.)

Early receptor potential

When a microelectrode is placed in the retina and the eye is stimulated by an intense flash of light, a brief electrical response is obtained (**early receptor potential, or ERP**), with no detectable latency (time lag after the stimulus). It is biphasic (positive and negative) and unlike more complex responses that follow. Its early appearance after the stimulus indicates that it is probably from the rods and cones themselves, rather than from elements farther along the neural pathway. Exploring parts of the retina that have only cones or only rods reveals a larger early receptor potential in the cone area. The early receptor potential is believed to be caused by the breakdown of iodopsin and rhodopsin in cones and rods, respectively.

Color vision theory

Over the last hundred years theories of color vision have been based on either a three-color or a four-color response of the eye. Three-color theorists (such as Young and Helmholz) have been impressed by the fact that three hues can be selected that mix to give white or gray; mixing these hues two at a time can reproduce all other hues. They proposed that the eye works the same way, having three kinds of cones that respond maximally to three different "primary" hues—a mixed response would signal other colors. Four-color theorists (such as Hering) were impresssed by the unitary nature of red, green, yellow, and blue. When other hues are mixed to give red, green, yellow, or blue, their presence cannot be detected. By contrast, red and yellow can be detected in an orange, or blue and green in an aqua. Four-color theorists also note that color-blind individuals are usually deficient in red *and* green vision, or blue *and* yellow vision, not other combinations. Since the red and green in question mix to give gray or white, as do the yellow and blue, they proposed a red-green (R-G) cone and a blue-yellow (B-Y) cone. Red light would polarize the R-G cone oppositely to green light; the same kind of reaction would occur in the B-Y cone to blue and yellow light. In this manner two kinds of cones could signal four primary visual responses to the brain.

Modern research suggests that both sets of theorists may have been right. To oversimplify the findings that will be reported, it appears that there are three kinds of cones: a "blue" receptor with maximum sensitivity near 450 nm., a "green" receptor with maximum sensitivity near 525 nm., and a "red" receptor with maximum sensitivity near 555 nm. On the other hand, recordings from the connecting cells of the retina suggest positive electrical reactions to red and yellow and negative reactions to green and blue. There is still another negative reaction of the retina in signaling the amount of light of any wavelength (brightness). It appears that the cones may react on a three-color basis, but the retina transforms the input into a four-color signal to the ganglion cells that lead to the brain. Such notions will become clearer as some of the experiments giving rise to them are explained.

Absorption spectrum of single rods and cones

The rods are stimulated when the rhodopsin they contain is affected by light; the cones are stimulated when their iodopsin is changed by light. However, neither rhodopsin nor iodopsin is equally sensitive to all wavelengths of light. It is reasonable to assume that rods in the dark-adapted eye would absorb more of the wavelengths that break down rhodopsin most readily; cones in the light-adapted eye should absorb more of the wavelengths that affect iodopsin most. In a general way experiments have shown this theory to be correct. The rhodopsin and iodopsin used were chemical extracts of the retina, however, and the tests of visual sensitivity involved the whole eye. Newer optical techniques permit the stimulation of *single* rods and cones in the freshly removed living human retina by using exactly controlled wavelengths. The proportion of light absorbed at each wavelength can be measured over the whole visible spectrum for each single rod or cone. Presumably the more a given wavelength is absorbed by a rod or cone, the more sensitive the receptor is to light of that wavelength. In Fig. 11-9 there is a diagram of some of the results obtained by this method under conditions given in the legend. Only a single kind of rod was found, and its absorption spectrum agrees rather well with sensitivity to various wavelengths in night vision; maximum absorp-

tion was at 505 nm., whereas night vision is most sensitive at 511 nm. The difference can probably be accounted for by the wavelengths absorbed by the fluids in the cavities of the normal eye, as well as light scattering, and so on, in normal vision (the excised retina was stimulated directly). The cone data are of greatest interest, however. Three kinds of cones were found, as predicted by the three-color theorists: a blue cone with an absorption peak at 450 nm., a green cone with an absorption peak at 525 nm., and a red cone with an absorption peak at 555 nm. These data compare well with some tests of human visual sensitivity that follow.

Sensitivity of human retina

If there are three kinds of cones, tests of sensitivity by a human observer to various wavelengths involve a mixed response —more than one kind of cone responds to each wavelength to some degree. However, if there are three kinds of cones—blue, green, and red—the response of one cone might be emphasized by selectively *adapting,* or "fatiguing," both of the others to make them less sensitive. If the eye were stimulated with yellow, the green and red receptors would respond until they lost some sensitivity, but the blue receptor would not react and would be "rested" and quite sensitive. If the sensitivity of the retina to various wavelengths were tested under these conditions, the reaction of blue receptors would be at a maximum, and blue would seem more intense when the green and red receptors were "fatigued." The experiment has been ingeniously performed; the conditions and results are presented in Fig. 11-10. The visual field was restricted to 1 degree to confine the image to the fovea, where only cones (color receptors) are found. When the eye was adapted to maximum cone sensitivity, a "dominator" curve of visual sensitivity by wavelength was found, with maximum sensitivity at 568 nm.; this curve represented the mixed

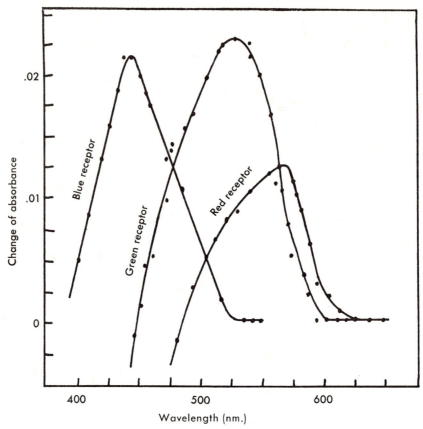

Fig. 11-9. Absorption spectrum of single cones. Freshly excised human retina, including the fovea, was placed in small container and axially exposed to light the width of a single cell from a recording spectrophotometer; absorption spectrum was measured while the cells were under ×2000 microscopically projected observation. Wavelengths were varied from 650 to 380 nm and back again, with recordings being taken after dark adaptation and after bleaching of receptors by exposure to a flashbulb. Curves are averages of the conditons. (Redrawn from Brown, P. K., and Wald, G.: Science **144:**46, copyright 1964 by the American Association for the Advancement of Science.)

response of all three kinds of cones. Then the red and green receptors were adapted with a "surround" patch of yellow, and the apparent brightness of this stimulus was compared with a central test patch of different wavelengths by the subject. This procedure brought out the relative sensitivity of blue cones, which showed peak sensitivity at 435 nm.—in good agreement with the 450 nm. absorption maximum for blue cones in the previous experiment. Adapting red and blue cones with purple light brought out a green cone modulator curve with a maximum at 550 nm., which compares with the absorption spectrum maximum of 525 nm. Finally, adapting blue cones brought out a red modulator peaking at 585 nm., which compares with the absorption peak of 555 nm. Differences in the two experiments can probably be accounted for by the way the intact eye absorbs and scatters light in this experiment, as compared with the excised retina of the previous experiment.

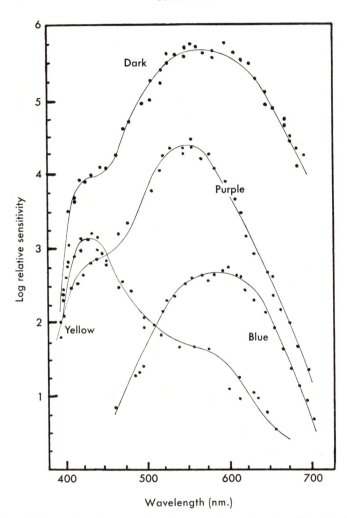

Fig. 11-10. Sensitivity of the human retina to spectral wavelengths. The curve labeled *dark* is for the dark-adapted eye, *yellow,* is yellow-adapted, *purple* is purple-adapted, and *blue* is blue-adapted, bringing out the response of blue, green, and red receptors, respectively. (Redrawn from Wald, G.: Science **145:**1009, copyright 1964 by the American Association for the Advancement of Science.)

Retinal responses

So far there appear to be three kinds of cones affected differently by different wavelengths. What happens when these cones stimulate the bioplar and ganglion cells of the retina to send nerve impulses to the brain? Briefly, it appears that the cones cause the bioplar (and horizontal and amacrine) connecting cells to increase or decrease their polarity without firing; the change in polarity changes the rate of firing of the ganglion cells going to the brain in the optic nerve. In this manner it appears that three-color cone signals are changed into four-color signals in the ganglion cells —a red-green signal and a blue-yellow signal. In addition, another signal depends on brightness rather than on wavelength alone.

Some of the color-coded cells fire when the visual stimulus is turned "on," representing excitation, and some fire when the stimulus is turned "off," representing inhibition (perhaps a "rebound effect" of firing that follows inhibition). Positive and negative responses of the retina to various hues may be represented by "on" and "off" types of responses that signal excitation and inhibition.

Microelectrode recordings

A technique has been developed (Granit) for recording from single ganglion cells in living animals of various species. The cornea and lens are removed from the eye and a microelectrode is lowered through the fundus of the eye until it impales a single cell in the retina. Since the retina is "inside out," the electrode encounters a ganglion cell first rather than the underlying connector or receptor cells. The eye is then stimulated with various wavelengths of light, and the responses of the single ganglion cell are recorded. Some arbitrary number of impulses—for example, four—is chosen as response threshold, and the sensitivity of response of the ganglion cell to various wavelengths is tested. Many ganglion cells can be tested in a single eye in this manner. The response of each cell represents the signal being sent to the brain in that ganglion cell, a signal that results from the stimulation of several rods or cones or both, the interaction in connecting cells, and the outcome in ganglion cell firing. The eyes of several species have been tested in this manner and the results compared

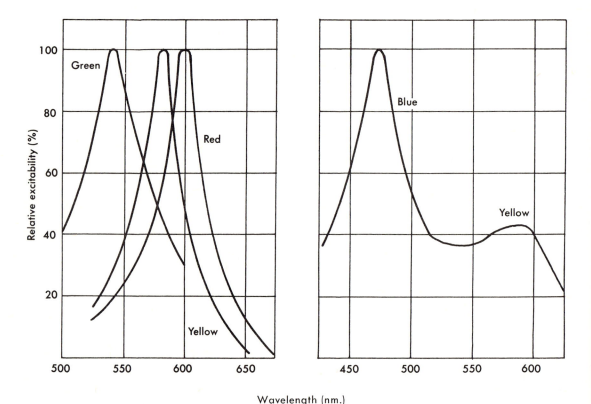

Fig. 11-11. Modulator and dominator curves in frog retina. (Redrawn from Granit, R.: Acta Physiol. Scand. **3:**137-151, 1941.)

with what is known of the rods and cones of the eye of each species.

Dominator and modulator curves. In retinas that resemble man's, ganglion cell units have been found that respond to a broad spectrum of wavelengths; the resulting "threshold" curve for various wavelengths is called a **dominator curve.** The sensitivity of these ganglion cell units to various wavelengths under light-adapted conditions is in good agreement with the threshold curve for human daylight (cone) vision; the threshold curve of other units under dark-adapted conditions resembles the sensitivity curve for night (rod) vision in man. Other ganglion cells have been found that respond to a narrower band of wavelengths. The resulting curves are called **modulator curves,** illustrated in Fig. 11-11. In the frog eye, four modulator curves have been recorded, peaking in the blue, green, yellow, and red regions of the spectrum at wavelengths close to the four that appear primary to man.

Coupled and uncoupled receptors. In these experiments the ganglion cell that is firing in response to light may be reacting to more than one kind of cone, or even to a rod and a cone, because of the many interconnections between the rods and cones and the ganglion cells that form the optic nerve (Fig. 11-2). If more than one receptor will fire the ganglion cell, the two receptors are said to be **coupled receptors.** If two cones of different sensitivities to different wavelengths control a ganglion cell, a modulator curve with two "humps" of ganglion cell response may be found (Fig. 11-11). For example, a blue-sensitive receptor and a yellow-sensitive receptor may each fire the ganglion cell. Its threshold modulator curve may then show two peaks of sensitivity, depending on which of the two receptors is controlling the ganglion cell. Coupling like this may explain why red and green or blue and yellow cancel each other out in human color vision, or why a person may be red-green color-blind

or blue-yellow color-blind, and not color-blind in some other fashion. Perhaps the three types of cones discussed previously are coupled to give results of this kind.

Retinal interactions. Microelectrode recordings from near the "connecting" cells (bipolar, horizontal, and amacrine) of the retina show **graded potentials** when excitation is transferred from the rods and cones to the ganglion cells. That is, the connecting cells increase or decrease their polarized condition to cause firing of ganglion cells, but they themselves do not fire. To simplify, it looks as though decreased polarization of the connecting cells causes the ganglion cells to fire at the onset of the visual stimulus; increased polarization of the connecting cells causes other ganglion cells to fire when the visual stimulus ceases, in a "rebound" effect. Still other ganglion cells are influenced by both "on" and "off" cells and fire briefly when the stimulus is turned on and briefly again when it is turned off. Whether a ganglion cells acts as an "on" cell, an "off" cell, or an "on-off" type depends on the conditions of stimulation at the minute. The interconnections between rods and cones on one hand and ganglion cells on the other are very diffuse, so that the response of the ganglion cell depends on the *pattern* of retinal stimulation at the moment.

Retinal zones. If one records from a single ganglion cell in the retina, and the stimulus light is directed toward receptors adjacent to it and farther from it, retinal "zones" of effect on the ganglion cell can be plotted (Fig. 11-12). The zone has a central area that is consistent in giving *either* an on or an off response, but not both. It is surrounded by an area consistently giving the opposite response; that is, if the central area gave a consistent on response, the peripheral area gives a consistent off response. In between the central and peripheral areas is an intermediate zone that gives *both* on and off responses. If the central area gave an on response, it was considered an *excitatory*

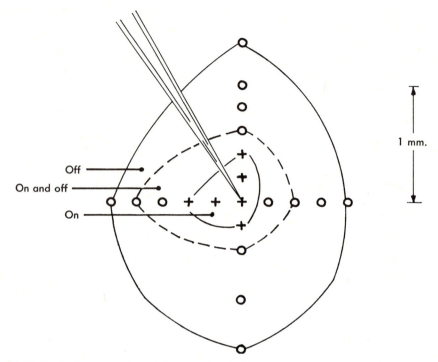

Fig. 11-12. Retinal zones, plotted by ganglion cell response at tip of electrode. (Redrawn from Küffler, S. W.: J. Neurophysiol. **49:**16, 1953.)

area, surrounded by a peripheral *inhibitory* area (off response), with an intermediate zone of interaction (on-off response) between excitation and inhibition.

Light and dark adaptation. Light adaptation has neural components as well as receptor components. The retinal zones just described are found in the light-adapted eye. These zones seem well adapted for the detection of contrasting borders and fine detail. As will be discussed later, the detection of a border requires different firing rates for ganglion cells that are close together but on opposite sides of the border in the visual field. Differences in discharge rates would be enhanced by the presence of excitatory "on" cells and inhibitory "off" cells in the same visual field. During dark adaptation, the organization of the retina changes, and the retinal zones of "on" and "off" ganglion cells disappear. All of the cells become "on" cells, and the retina is orga-

nized for summation and light-detection, at the expense of detail vision. The mechanism in the retina that changes the relationships between the receptors and the ganglion cells under light and dark adaptation is not understood.

Color coding. One important feature of the "on" and "off" responses is that some of them are color coded, whereas others depend only on brightness. The color-coded ganglion cells in goldfish give an on or off response, depending on the wavelength used as a stimulus to the receptors. The on response covers a band of wavelengths but is most sensitive at 650 nm., for example, whereas the off response covers an overlapping band of wavelengths and is most sensitive at 500 nm. Other color-coded cells with different on and off peaks have been found. Non–color-coded cells are also found, giving both on and off responses to a wide variety of wavelengths over most

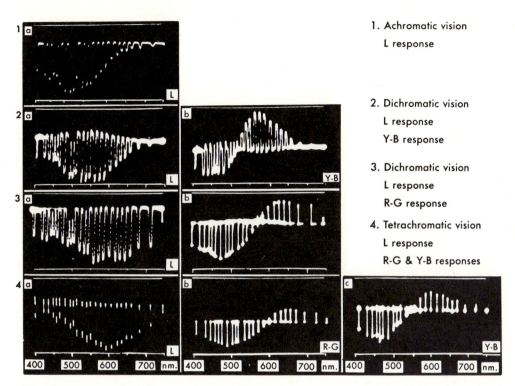

1. Achromatic vision
   L response

2. Dichromatic vision
   L response
   Y-B response

3. Dichromatic vision
   L response
   R-G response

4. Tetrachromatic vision
   L response
   R-G & Y-B responses

Fig. 11-13. Graded slow potentials recorded from retina as a function of wavelength of stimulus. (From Svaetichin, G., and MacNichol, E. F.: Ann. N. Y. Acad. Sci. **74:**388, 1958.)

of the visible spectrum. In these cells the wavelength giving peak sensitivity to the on response is the same as the wavelength giving the most sensitivity to the off response; these cells are therefore not color coded. In either color-coded or non–color-coded cells, the on response always has a lower threshold than the off response, as would be expected of an excitatory process, as compared to an inhibitory process. Color-coded on and off responses in ganglion cells may provide a way for the retina to signal hue to the brain, whereas non–color-coded ganglion cells may signal brightness. Recordings from near the cells that "connect" the rods and cones with the ganglion cells suggest that such may be the case.

Graded potentials

As previously reported, excitation of the rods and cones sets up *graded* potentials of increased or decreased polarization in the cells that transfer excitation from rods and cones to ganglion cells. It was formerly believed that these potentials came from glial cells—the supporting cells of the retina. It now appears more probable that horizontal cells produce the potentials. Under conditions of dark adaptation the decay from maximum of the graded potential is more rapid in response to intense stimuli than it is to near-threshold stimuli. This may indicate a difference in the response of the horizontal cells to cone stimulation as compared to rod stimulation. In any case, the cells show generator potentials (Chapter 4) that have been called S potentials (slow potentials). Their resting potentials are reduced in the dark (dark adaptation), and their response is of two main types, depending on the effect of the hue of the light. The type L (luminosity) response is the same depolarization of cells for all wavelengths of light. Only the *degree* of depolarization varies with wavelength in a way much like the sensitivity curve for brightness varies at different wavelengths (Fig. 11-13). This response may signal *brightness*. The type C (chromatic or hue) response, on the other hand, is a depolarization or a hyperpolarization of a cell that depends on wavelength. Type C responses seem coded to either yellow and blue or red and green wavelengths rather than to other combinations of wavelengths—a four-color signal. (Positive potentials in a single cell represent a depolarization effect and negative potentials a hyperpolarization effect because the electrode is *inside* the cell.) You will recall from Chapter 4 that the inside of the cell is normally negative with respect to the outside of the cell. If the inside of the cell becomes more positive, the cell is therefore less polarized in a positive to negative sense. If depolarization is excitatory, it may initiate an on response, and if hyperpolarization inhibits ganglion cells, it may initiate an off response. However, the experiments measure only the degree of response of each cell to each of the visible wavelengths.

Sometimes an attempt is made to adapt the eye to a band of wavelengths to see if adaptation changes the response of a cell. The subjects have usually been fish of various kinds believed to have color vision, but similar results have been found for the cat; the results can probably be generalized for many vertebrates. Three types of responses have been found: (1) an L (luminosity) response, (2) an R-G (red-green) response, and (3) a Y-B (yellow-blue) response. The L response is a change in cell polarization that depends on wavelength. It does not seem to be color-coded, however, since adaptation to specific wavelengths does not change the shape of the curve of polarization in a way that depends on wavelength; that is, if the cell becomes less sensitive to one wavelength stimulus, it adapts to all of them. The L response may signal bright-

ness to the ganglion cells; its curve is strikingly like that of sensitivity of the light-adapted eye to various wavelengths. The R-G and Y-B responses *are* color-coded and may signal hue to the brain. In each case the response at the shorter end of the spectrum (G or B) is negative, and the response at the longer end of the spectrum (R or Y) is positive. (Recall again that a positive response inside the cell means cell depolarization.) The G or B response will disappear after the eye selectively adapts to green or blue light; the R or Y response can be eliminated with red or yellow light. Different processes must therefore be involved; fatiguing the red process, for example, reduces the positive polarization response in the cells. If the positive (depolarization) Y or R responses are excitatory, they should cause "on" firing in ganglion cells, whereas the negative (polarization) G or B responses could cause "off" response in the ganglion cells. In this manner four-color signals could be sent to the brain.

As a practical matter, the student may ask how "off" firing to signal hue is possible when color-coded cells are polarized or inhibited and cannot fire until the stimulus is removed so that they can depolarize—the "rebound" effect. The answer may lie in the constant small (saccadic) movements of the eye that result in frequent stimulation and stimulus change for every point in the retina. Stimulus onset and stimulus removal (change) would be equally frequent under these conditions, allowing for as much "off" firing as "on" firing. Change in retinal stimulation appears necessary for retinal function. If a contact lens with a small mirror on the cornea to one side of the pupil is placed over the eye so as to reflect a tiny beam of light to a gray field, it will always stimulate the same small area of the retina; each time the eye moves, the spot in the visual field will move in a corresponding way. Under these conditions the image of the light spot will disappear in 3 to 6 seconds because of retinal adaptation. Eye movements are therefore necessary for the perception of both brightness (L, or luminosity response) and the on-off firing of color-coded cells.

Color vision responses of lateral geniculate cells

The lateral geniculate nucleus (LGN) is the only "relay" nucleus in the visual pathway from the retina to the striated cortex (Fig. 11-5). For every input ganglion cell to the LGN there is an output cell to the cerebral cortex; the ratio is 1:1 in man and 2:1 in the monkey, where some information condensing must go on. The responses of LGN cells can therefore add to our knowledge of color information processing in the visual system. One prominent investigator (DeValois) has shown that lateral geniculate neurons can be divided into **spectrally opponent cells,** which are differentially sensitive to different wavelengths of light (hues), and **broad-band cells,** which respond to all wavelengths. In the macaque monkey, 80% of the LGN cells excited by ganglion cells from the all-cone foveal area of the retina are spectrally opponent cells. They alter their rate of spontaneous firing as a function of wavelength. For example, a cell may increase its firing rate to green light and decrease its firing rate to red light. Adapting the retina to green light will leave only the red response, and vice versa.

Wiesel and Hubel have proposed three types of LGN cells. (Refer again to Fig. 11-12 and the discussion of retinal zones.) A stimulated area on the retina may cause firing in ganglion cells of the optic nerve at the onset of the stimulus—an "on" response. This area is often surrounded by an area that is excited when the stimulus ceases—an "off" response. Some of these ganglion cells appear to stimulate LGN cells that respond in the same way. Furthermore, the LGN cells respond in a color-coded fashion (Fig. 11-14). Three types of relationships between retinal cones and LGN cells have been proposed: (1) type

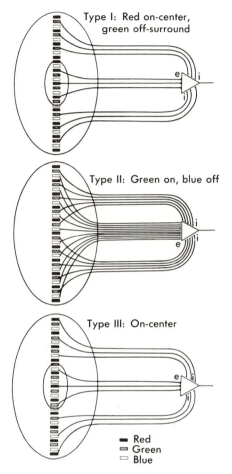

Fig. 11-14. Schematic diagram illustrating relationship between red, green, and blue cones and type I, type II, and type III LGN neurons. *e,* Excitation. *i,* Inhibition. Circles at left represent visual field for each of the three types of geniculate neurons. Red, green, and blue cones are represented by rectangles of different shading. (Redrawn from Wiesel, T. N., and Hubel, D. H.: J. Neurophysiol. **29:**1115, 1966; from Poggio, G. F.: In Mountcastle, V. B., editor: Medical physiology, ed. 13, vol. 1, St. Louis, 1974, The C. V. Mosby Co.)

I cells give a central hue response to retinal stimulation—an on response, surrounded by cells that give an off response to an antagonist hue; (2) type II cells are not formed into zones, but give an on response to one hue and an off response to another; (3) type III cells are not color-coded, but they give either an excitatory on response or an inhibitory off response to all wavelengths. These are "broad-band" cells, in contrast with the other two, "narrow-band" types (types I and II).

Response of cerebral cortex to visual information

Recall that the primary visual projection area of the cerebral cortex (area I) is topographically organized (each point in visual space excites a corresponding point on the cortex). It is surrounded by two visual association areas, one that is topographically organized (area II) and one that is not topographically organized (area III). The response of area I cells to retinal stimulation seems to be different from that of ganglion cells and LGN cells (Hubel and Wiesel). Instead of responding to a central excitatory "on" zone and a surrounding inhibitory "off" zone, cells in all three visual areas respond most readily to slits, edges, and lines—linear visual stimuli. The cells surrounding the linear receptive field of excited cells are inhibited, or else the excited cells are separated from inhibited cells along a linear margin. Furthermore, the linear stimulus must have a specific orientation to excite the cells—either vertical, horizontal, or oblique in specific cases. Moving lines are a more effective stimulus than stationary lines. Simple, complex, and hypercomplex neurons have been found in the information-processing complex of the visual cortex. Simple cells respond as just described only when the linear stimulus is in the part of the visual field that directly excites them. They are found in area I. Complex neurons in area I respond to linear stimulation of

specific orientation anywhere in a broad visual field. Their response forms a broad uniform pattern of excitation and inhibition rather than the simple linear opposition of excitation and inhibition. Complex neurons seem to represent the first stage of abstracting the information from simple neurons for form perception. Hypercomplex neurons are found in areas II and III. Their response is similar to that of some simple neurons, except that they respond only to lines of a specified *length*. This appears to represent a further step in the process of form perception. The importance of these studies cannot be overemphasized —they represent our first reliable information on how the central nervous system processes sensory information to form complex perceptions. Geometrical angles and lines that our brain sees as three-dimensional squares, rectangles, and objects that become smaller with distance may be based on this kind of information processing by the brain.

VISUAL PHENOMENA

This section is a consideration of the phenomenology of vision—that is, the way in which hue, saturation, and brightness appear to interact in laboratory tests of color mixing, visual adaptation, aftersensations, contrast, acuity, some complex phenomena such as flicker and apparent movement, the cues to depth and distance, and color blindness. Wherever possible, each visual phenomenon will be related to visual physiology on the one hand and everyday experience on the other.

Newton's laws of color

Many years ago Sir Isaac Newton produced a visible spectrum of hues by separating the wavelengths of light coming from the sun. Using a narrow beam of sunlight coming through a pinhole, he interposed a prism that bent, or refracted, the beam of light. Light refraction depends on wavelength; the shorter wavelengths were bent more than the longer wavelengths, producing an array of wavelengths—the visible spectrum. Different wavelengths are perceived by the eye as different hues, so that bands of different hues were seen from violet through blue, green, yellow, orange, and red, with shorter to longer wavelengths over the 400 to 750 nm. visible spectrum (Figs. 11-6 and 11-7). Any single wavelength is fairly saturated, that is, distinct in hue, and the spectrum produced in this manner is of intermediate brightness. Having separated the wavelengths to produce the hues of the spectrum, Newton recombined individual hues, a process often called "color mixing." His experiments led to Newton's three laws of color, which can be rephrased as follows:

1. **Law of complements.** For each hue there is another hue that will mix with it in some proportion to cancel both hues and give a gray or white color. (Whether gray or white is obtained depends on brightness.)

2. **Law of supplements.** Noncomplementary hues will mix to give a hue that lies between them on the spectrum. For example, a chartreuse (yellow-green) and an orange will mix to give a yellow. Hues from the ends of the spectrum—violets and reds—mix to give purples, which are not spectral hues.

3. **Law of resultants.** The same hue may be produced by several mixtures. Mixing two similar hues produced in different ways alters nothing; mixtures that match one another mix without change in hue. For example, a green could be obtained with a single wavelength or by mixing yellow-green and orange-red. If the two greens matched, their apparent hue would not change when they were combined.

Visual response

The eye perceives changes in the physical amplitude—the rate of flow (flux) of light—as a change in brightness, from black to gray to white, for example. Changes in the wavelength of light are perceived as changes in hue—reds, greens, blues and

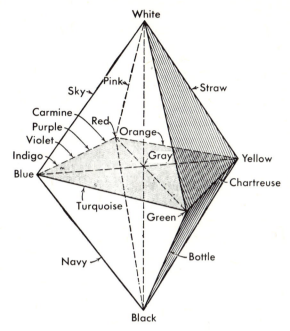

Fig. 11-15. Color pyramid. (From Dimick, F. L.: Color. In Boring, E. G., Langfield, H. S., and Weld, H. P.: Foundations of psychology, New York, 1948, John Wiley & Sons, Inc.)

yellows, for instance. But colors that are of the same hue and brightness may differ in saturation—a green may appear as green as it can be or it may be a grayish green—equally bright, of the same basic hue, but "not as colored." The last statement is a bit misleading since gray, black, and white are colors, although they lack hue or saturation. *Saturation is the amount by which a hue differs from the total lack of hue perceived in a gray of equal brightness.* A further complication arises because brightness and saturation *interact.* The hue, saturation, and brightness interactions of human visual response are diagrammed in the double pyramid of Fig. 11-15. (The dimensions are not psychophysically accurate.) The vertical dimension of the figure represents brightness differences and the horizontal dimensions represent saturation differences, with the outside surfaces at all vertical levels representing the maximum saturation response at a given brightness. The figure tells us that maximum saturation of any hue is possible only at intermediate levels of brightness. Thus a sky blue can never be as saturated as a blue or an indigo, but a blue can be desaturated (moved toward gray at the center) until it is no more saturated than the brighter sky blue of maximum saturation. The corners of the figure are labelled blue, red, yellow, green, white, and black, with gray at the center, since these seem to be unique colors (see below). This is why hues seem more saturated near sunset—in "bright" daylight, they seem "'washed out," and as dusk approaches they seem "too dark" to be appreciated. Although black represents absence of stimulation, it is not a true sensation. The retina never ceases signaling the brain and a kind of "brain gray" results—the dark gray sensation you have when you close your eyes.

Unique colors

It has been estimated that there can be about 7,295,000 discriminable colors (including grays), although industry uses only about 5,000 in the Natural Bureau of Standards compilation. A careful study of Chapanis (1965) suggests that the number of color names actually used by human subjects is 52 to 55. Some of these color names represent differences in brightness; others, differences in saturation; and still others, differences in hue. It is not necessary to have even this many color names, however, because colors can be classified by their resemblance to seven colors that are unique (in the Munsell system). A **unique color** is one that can be psychologically described only in terms of itself. This is true because the component colors making up a unique color cannot be perceived when the unique color is viewed. By this definition the seven unique colors are red, green, yellow, blue, white, black, and gray. A neutral gray may be composed of a mixture of black and white, but neither black nor white can be perceived by looking at gray. A green may be a mixture of a yellow-green and a blue-green, but neither the yellow nor

the blue can be perceived in the green. By contrast, a non-unique hue, such as orange, recognizably contains red and yellow. A whole series of oranges can be described by reference to the relative amount of unique red or yellow they appear to contain. The same can be said for the blue and green in aqua, the red and blue in purple, or the yellow and green in chartreuse. The three achromatic unique colors—black, white, and gray—represent differences in brightness. The four chromatic unique colors—red, green, blue, and yellow—represent differences in hue. Mixing gray with any of the four unique hues reduces saturation. The seven unique colors are the seven **primary qualities** of vision, the irreducible elements making up differences in visual hue, brightness, and saturation.

Color mixing

The four **unique hues** (red, green, yellow, and blue) can be used, two at a time, to reproduce any other hue. Just as unique red and green or unique yellow and blue mix to give gray (complementary colors), all four unique hues mix to give gray. These facts are in agreement with the four-color coding that the retina appears to use in signaling the brain. There are, however, only three kinds of hue-sensitive cones in the retina—a blue cone, a green cone, and a red cone; if all three were stimulated at once at the proper intensity, their response would probably "mix" to produce a visual sensation that *lacks* hue. It is therefore not surprising that three hues can be selected that are **primary hues** in the sense that (1) all three mix to give gray and (2) by mixing any two of these hues, any other hue can be produced. There are a large number of trios of primary hues. When one selects any hue made of any mixture, one has determined the composition of the other two hues that will mix with it to cancel hue response, leaving a gray or white. The three hues, thus determined, can be used two at a time to produce all the other hue responses. The relative brightness and saturation of each of the three components will have to be adjusted to obtain a gray. Reproducing some hues that lie between two of the primaries will also require adjustment of relative brightness and saturation. Within these limits, however, there are many sets of three primary hues, or primary colors, as they are often called.

Color mixing by addition. A method of mixing colors that usually increases the *brightness* of the mixture over the brightness of its components is color mixing by addition. One such method would involve overlapping spots of light from supplementary hues. If a spot of light from a red spotlight were shining on a white reflecting surface, a red circle would be seen—red wavelengths would be reflected off the surface to the eye. If a yellow spot of light were shown on the wall, yellow wavelengths would be reflected to the eye. If both spots of light were shown on the reflecting surface in such a way as to *overlap,* the overlapping area would look orange—a mixture of red and yellow. Furthermore, the orange area would be *brighter* than either the red or yellow areas since it would be reflecting light to the eye from *both* spotlights. Three spotlights could be used whose hues mixed to cancel each other out as a set of primary hues. In the area where all three spots overlapped, white would be seen rather than gray because of the increase in brightness; the brightness of all three spotlights would be mixed by addition. Of course the brightness of each spotlight could be reduced until the overlapping area looked gray.

Colors can be mixed by addition without increasing brightness if another method is used—the **color wheel.** If a red disk of paper is interleaved with a yellow disk of paper, a single disk can be produced that is half yellow and half red. If this disk is rotated rapidly by an electric motor, an orange disk will be seen. Red and yellow are, of course, supplementary hues that mix to give orange. The orange is no brighter than the red or the yellow, however, if the red

disk and the yellow disk reflect equal amounts of light. If three disks are selected that mix to cancel each other, they will mix on the color wheel to give a gray of the same brightness as the component hues. If two disks are used two at a time, other hues can be produced by varying the proportion of each hue on the disk. This is color mixing by addition without increasing brightness.

Color mixing by subtraction. Color mixing by subtraction always results in diminished brightness. Therefore, when three primary hues are mixed by subtraction, a very dark gray or black is usually seen. One method of mixing hues by subtraction is by overlapping colored filters. A color filter *absorbs* all wavelengths of "white" light, except those transmitted to the eye to be seen as a hue. Suppose that three primary hues were created by three filters: for example, a red of 650 nm., a green of 530 nm., and a blue of 460 nm. If these filters were perfect, each would absorb all wavelengths but the one named in each case. If any two of them were overlapped in front of a light source of all visible wavelengths, no light would reach the eye; the second filter would absorb all the wavelengths transmitted by the first filter. However, filters usually transmit a *band* of wavelengths, the amount of light that is transmitted decreasing on either side of the wavelength for which they are named. The green filter of 530 nm. in the example would transmit more light energy at 530 nm. than at any other wavelength. However, it would pass some of the light at wavelengths that might range from 480 to 620 nm., the amount transmitted being less and less in either direction from 530 nm. Therefore, if the red (650 nm.) filter and the green (530 nm.) filter were overlapped, *each* would pass *some* wavelengths in the 580 nm. range (yellow) while absorbing most other wavelengths. A yellow hue of diminished brightness would result. If the blue (460 nm.) filter were now placed in front of the other two, it would absorb the residual 580 nm. yellow wavelengths, so that no light could pass all three filters, and a black would be seen. Mixing paint pigments has the same effect as overlapping filters. A paint pigment has the hue of the wavelengths it *reflects* (does not absorb). Therefore, mixing two hues of paint will result in an intermediate hue of diminished brightness consisting of the wavelengths that neither pigment absorbs (or both reflect). Subtractive color mixing is somewhat more complex than this in practice, but the basic principles explained here govern the process. It explains why the amateur, mixing water colors, often winds up with a gray or dark brown instead of the hue he was attempting to produce.

Color classifications

Systematic and standardized methods for classifying colors that differ in hue, saturation, and brightness depend on characteristics of human visual response. For example, at optimum brightness, there are sixteen distinguishable saturation differences for yellow ($\lambda 575$ nm.) but twenty-three differing saturations for red or violet ($\lambda 680$ nm. and $\lambda 440$ nm.). There are 128 discriminable hues in the spectrum plus 28 purples (red and violet mixtures). Brightness can change from a glaring white where hue response is not possible to an intermediate brightness where saturation can vary the most to the "black" of absence of visual stimulation (Fig. 11-15). One way of bringing order out of this confusion is the Munsell system, upon which the previous section on unique colors was based. The Munsell system classifies colors according to the proportion of each of the seven unique colors present (red, green, yellow, blue, white, black, and gray). The ICI (International Commission on Illumination) has devised a system based on three "primary" hues, mixed by addition in the fashion just described. A wavelength mixture is chosen that resembles green ($\lambda 520$ nm.). Each wavelength in the green mixture is there in the same proportion as the retinal sensitivity to that wavelength for daylight vision. The green component thus describes the eye's sensitivity to various wavelengths. A reddish purple and a blue that mix with the green to cancel out the hue response are thereby determined. Hues are described in terms of the proportion of these primaries present in a matching hue. Finally, the ISCC (Intersociety Color Council)—a clearing house for color information—has devised a color designation system based on red, orange, green, blue, violet, purple, brown, pink, and olive, with modifying terms like light, vivid, weak, very, and so forth, that results in 267 color names. These examples of color classifications are given only to show that there is more than one way of organizing color information.

Color zones of retina

The phenomena of hue and the mixing of hues hold when the retina receives widespread stimulation, especially in the foveal (central) region. All areas of the retina are not equally sensitive to hue, and peripheral areas that lack enough color receptors (cones) do not see hue; thus peripheral vision is "color-blind." If one brings a small spot of a definite hue in from the periphery of a gray visual field, it is seen as gray until it reaches a point where it can stimulate the more centrally located color receptors of the retina. Blues can be seen most peripherally, then yellows, then reds, and then greens. The wavelengths involved do not exactly match those of the four unique hues, but the difference may be accounted for by the nervous connections of the peripheral retina. Oddly enough, a small patch of blue, the hue seen most peripherally, is not perceived as hue by the fovea, which appears to lack blue sensitivity.

Purkinje shift

According to the duplicity theory (see the discussion of visual physiology, above) the cones are chromatic, photopic receptors in a system that has a relatively high threshold. The rods are achromatic, scotopic receptors in a system that has a very low threshold. The absolute threshold of either system depends on wavelength. The rods "see only gray," but they are maximally sensitive at about 511 nm. (green region) and are less sensitive to other wavelengths. For example, they do not react to red wavelengths (above 680 nm.). The cones react to all wavelengths of the visible spectrum to some extent, but they are most sensitive at near 555 nm. (yellow-green region). The change in the relative brightness of various wavelengths in passing from photopic (daylight) to scotopic (night) vision and vice versa is called the **Purkinje** (poor'kin-yay) **shift.** For example, objects known to be green (such as grass) would appear as a brighter gray at night than objects known to be blue (such as a lake). For this reason, movie directors can shoot black and white moonlight scenes in the daytime by using a blue filter. The blue filter shifts the relative brightness of objects to the blue and green areas of the spectrum and produces the relative brightness one is used to seeing at night.

Adaptation

In common with other receptors the rods and cones of the eye become less sensitive with continued stimulation. The adaptation of rods differs from the adaptation of cones, however, because of differences in the brightness threshold of each system and in the *range* of brightness to which each responds.

Dark adaptation. During normal daylight vision few rods are responding. Their rhodopsin has been bleached into vitamin A by light, and there are few rods with enough rhodopsin left for light to affect. The cones are firing at intermediate sensitivity; their iodopsin is broken down by light to fire nerve impulses and is reconstituted in a continuous cycle. If the subject goes into a dark environment, both rods and cones increase their sensitivity by build-

ing up more visual pigment. The cones increase their sensitivity first by building up iodopsin in the absence of light—the more iodopsin that is built up, the more sensitive are the cones. The cone system reaches sensitivity in 5 to 10 minutes of darkness. It takes this long for the more sensitive rod system to build up enough rhodopsin from vitamin A so that it can begin to respond to light. As it begins to function, the threshold drops again, diminishing further over 20 minutes or so as rod vision increases in sensitivity. As a result there is a "break" in the threshold curve for dark adaptation; the first segment represents increased cone sensitivity to a limiting point; the second segment represents increasing rod sensitivity (Fig. 11-16). After a half hour in the dark, the retina's sensitivity increases 1 million times!

Light adaptation. Under conditions of darkness or dim illumination the cones are not stimulated; thus they build up a maximum supply of iodopsin because there is insufficient light to break it down. The rods may have a moderate supply of rhodopsin since it is being reconstituted as fast as it can be broken down by dim light. When a person suddenly comes into bright light, the threshold of most of the rods and cones is exceeded and most of the receptors of the retina fire, causing a "blinding" sensation of light. The pupil constricts in order to reduce the amount of light entering the eye and to protect the receptors from overstimulation. The rods cease to respond because all of their rhodopsin is broken down into vitamin A and because they are inhibited by the cone system. The cones reconstitute their iodopsin faster, however, and since their iodopsin continues to be broken down and reconstituted, these cells continue to respond with light sensations. Light adaptation, as measured in various ways, requires 20 to 30 minutes.

Hue adaptation. Continuous stimulation by a given hue appears to reduce the sensitivity of cones responding to that hue.

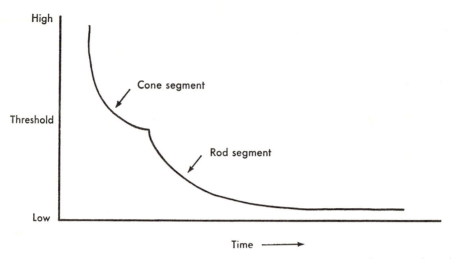

Fig. 11-16. Curve of dark adaptation. Two segments of the curve show first the adaptation of cones and then the adaptation of rods.

The result is a decrease in the apparent saturation of the hue—the color appears grayer. Adaptation is the basis for visual aftersensations.

Aftersensations

Aftersensations are sensations that are caused by a stimulus, but they begin after the stimulus is removed. Visual aftersensations may be positive or negative. After stimulation ceases, the eye may continue to react with the same sensation for a time—a **positive aftersensation.** Or the eye may react with a quality or an intensity opposite to that caused by the stimulus after the stimulus is removed—a **negative aftersensation.** Examples will be given below for aftersensations of brightness (intensity) and hue (quality). Meanwhile, a good rule to remember is that *brief, intense* stimulation usually causes positive aftersensations, whereas *prolonged, moderate* stimulation usually causes negative aftersensations.

Brightness aftersensations. Stare at the filament of an electric light bulb for a few seconds and then look at the wall. You will continue to see the filament for a time as a positive aftersensation. The receptors continue to respond for a time after they have been intensely stimulated. Prolonged moderate light stimulation raises the brightness threshold because of light adaptation, however (see above). As a result a room looks darker after coming in from the sunlight than it will later—a negative aftersensation of brightness.

Hue aftersensations. Aftersensations of hue are usually negative. If one stares at a patch of color for a minute and then looks at a neutral gray wall, a patch of color will appear that is the *complement* of the stimulus patch. This is a negative aftersensation. There appears to be a balance among the color receptors that has been upset by adaptation to the stimulus hue; a hue of opposite quality results when stimulation ceases. For example, one sees a patch of yellow on a gray surface after staring at blue. As a technical point, negative hue aftersensations are not exactly complementary to the stimulus. Hues near the ends of the color spectrum have aftersensations displaced farther toward the other end of the spectrum than expected.

Contrast

Contrast effects are caused by adaptation of *areas* of the retina. As a result neighboring areas become more sensitive to the opposite process—either a complementary hue (quality) or the opposite brightness (intensity). The effect of adaptation of one area of the retina on neighboring areas is called **simultaneous induction.** Red looks more saturated against a blue background, for example, and white looks brighter against a black background.

Brightness contrast. The darker one stimulus patch is, the lighter an adjacent one will seem. For example, the same light gray patch may appear white against a black background and dark gray against a white background. When the gray is on a black background, the receptors responding to it become more sensitive because of lack of activity in neighboring receptors from the black surrounding it (dark adaptation). This increased sensitivity makes the gray patch look brighter (whiter). When the surrounding receptors adapt to white (light adaptation), the more central receptors responding to the gray patch also become less sensitive, making the gray patch appear darker.

Hue contrast. A hue appears maximally saturated against a background of the *complementary* hue. Thus a red patch looks more saturated against a complementary green background than against a gray background. The green background prevents the central area of the retina from adapting to red and losing sensitivity because of simultaneous induction. If two complementary hues are placed side by side, the line at which they meet will appear gray; perhaps this is caused by retinal color mixing of the complementary hues. The area of each hue that is near the complementary hue will seem more saturated than outlying areas. Apparently the closer two oppositely stimulated areas lie on the retina, the greater is the simultaneous induction effect and the less is the resulting adaptation in either area. Hue is also capable of simultaneous induction. A saturated hue that adjoins a gray area will induce a de-

saturated ("faint") complementary hue (approximately) in the gray area. This kind of simultaneous hue contrast was used to great effect by French painters of the impressionist school in creating "colored" shadows that adjoined vivid hues in their paintings.

Brightness thresholds

The absolute threshold for light reaching the rods has been calculated in careful experiments to be 5 to 14 quanta—if a single quantum excites each rod, only one molecule of rhodopsin has excited each rod! This *is* visual sensitivity. However, the rod system is poorly organized to detect *differences* in brightness, because its brightness *range* is not great. The threshold of the cone system is 10,000 times greater than the threshold of the rod system, but it has 500 JNDs (just noticeable differences) of intensity difference compared to 30 for the rod system. Furthermore, ΔI (the difference threshold) decreases for the cone system as brightness increases; that is, the brighter the light, the smaller is the increase in brightness that can be detected. (The Weber ratio of $\Delta I / I$ varies from $1/1$ at low intensities to $1/167$ at high intensities.)

Visual acuity

Visual acuity is just a special sort of intensity discrimination that the cone system is better organized for than the rod system. Under daylight conditions it is the ability to distinguish the contours of an object from its background. Obviously the more the object and background differ in brightness, the easier this is to do. Given an equal brightness difference, smaller objects are more difficult to see than are larger ones, and larger objects may be seen at a greater distance than may smaller ones. With good brightness contrast, the only way to standardize a measure of acuity is in terms of the angle subtended by the light rays as they reach the eye from the object. A large object at a great distance may form the same

visual angle at the cornea of the eye as a small object a short distance away. Technically, acuity is usually defined as the reciprocal (upsidedown fraction) of the angle separating two just distinguishable contours. "Normal" acuity is the ability to discern 1′ (1 minute or 1/60 of a degree) of arc for a score of 1, but some individuals score as high as 3 (1/3 of 1′). Scores also vary widely with the method of measurement used from the Snellen test (see below) to the minimum separable angle (space between two lines), minimum visible angle (narrowest line seen), stereoscopic (depth) acuity, line movement, and so forth. The minimum separable angle is used in a rough fashion in the most common test of visual acuity, the **Snellen test.** This test uses rows of letters of diminishing size, displayed from a distance of 20 feet. The horizontal bars of the large **E** found at the top of the chart form a separable angle, for example. When the test is scored, the distance at which a normal eye sees a given row of letters forms the denominator of a fraction; the distance in feet at which the subject must stand to see the same letters forms the numerator. Thus 20/20 eyes are normal, 20/40 indicates subnormal acuity, and 20/10 is superior acuity. The Snellen test is far from the best test of visual acuity, but it is the one most comonly used. Almost anyone who has had a general physical examination or who has consulted an eye specialist has seen a Snellen chart.

Critical flicker frequency

Visual acuity is a test of spatial thresholds for the eye, but the eye has temporal (time) thresholds as well. One way of measuring a temporal threshold for the eye is to measure the **critical flicker frequency (CFF)** (sometimes also called the critical fusion frequency). The CFF refers to the rate at which a light must flicker on and off before the eye fails to perceive it as flickering and sees it as a steady light. The CFF

depends on the relative duration of the light and dark cycles as well as on the rate of flicker. The higher the CFF, the greater the temporal resolving power—the ability to detect rapid change. One can compare the CFF for the cone system to the CFF for the rod system by comparing foveal (cones) with peripheral (rod) vision. The CFF is higher at the fovea for small stimuli and higher at the periphery for large stimuli because of the greater temporal resolving power of the rod system and greater spatial resolving power of the cone system. The many overlapping cone pathways discharge too continuously for detection of a brief dark interval, but the cone system has greater visual acuity. Hue has little effect on cone CFF but does affect rod CFF. The CFF tends to decrease as subjects grow older, and large individual differences in CFF are found. For some reason there is a low positive correlation between the CFF and standard tests of intelligence.

Apparent movement

Another temporal threshold for the eye is that for movement as compared to displacement in space. If two lights spaced a few inches apart are slowly turned on and off, so that one light is on while the other is off, each light will be perceived as turning on and off at its true location. If the rate of alternating flicker of the lights is increased, a point will be reached at which a single light is perceived as moving back and forth between the two locations. This is the **apparent movement** that forms the basis for animated street signs and motion pictures. The rate at which the lights must be alternated to produce the illusion of apparent motion depends on the duration of the light cycle and dark cycle of each light, the intensity and size of each light, and the distance between them. At a still higher rate the CFF for each light will be exceeded, and two steady lights at different locations will be perceived.

Cues to depth and distance

The perception of the distance of an object from the observer, or depth perception, depends on a number of sensations from the eyes, some of them visual and some kinesthetic. Two kinesthetic cues of muscle sensation have already been mentioned in this chapter—convergence and accommodation. Convergence is a **binocular cue,** since sensations from the extrinsic muscles of both eyes must be compared to judge how much the eyes are "crossed" in training them on a nearby object. Accommodation is a **monocular cue,** since it depends on sensations of intrinsic muscle strain that are the same for each eye when the lens is thickened to focus on nearby objects.

Binocular cues. Convergence depends on strain sensations from the extrinsic muscles of the eyes when the eyes are "crossed" to focus nearby objects on corresponding points in the foveae of the two eyes. The closer the object, the greater is the sensation. The geometry of seeing is such that the strain is perceived only within a very few feet. Since the eyes are only about 2½ inches apart in the head, muscular convergence of the visual axes of the eyes is noticeable only when the object is close to the eyes. The visual geometry of binocular vision is called **binocular parallax,** and it has consequences in visual as well as in kinesthetic sensations. Since the eyes are about 2½ inches apart, the visual angle, or angle of regard of an object, will differ for the left eye as compared to the right eye. Thus the left eye will see more of the left side of a three-dimensional object, and the right eye will see more of the right side of the object. The difference between the image formed on the right retina and the image formed on the left retina is called **retinal disparity.** The closer the object, the greater the difference in what the two eyes see—the greater the retinal disparity. You can demonstrate this phenomenon for your-self by holding up an index finger about 6 inches from your nose, closing one eye, and then opening it and closing the other; observe how much the finger appears to "jump" back and forth against the background. Then repeat the experiment with the finger at arm's length; it will appear to move less because the retinal disparity is less. The principle of retinal disparity is used to lend an illusion of depth in the **stereoscope.** Two pictures are taken at once: the two cameras (or twin lenses) are about as far apart as the two eyes. The resulting pictures are presented in a stereoscope, which presents the left picture to the left eye and the right picture to the right eye. A startling illusion of a single three-dimensional, or stereoscopic, photograph is obtained.

Monocular cues. Monocular cues to depth and distance are those that do not depend on the displacement of the eyes in the head; they are as useful to a one-eyed person as to one with two eyes. Monocular depth perception is not nearly so accurate as binocular depth perception within 15 to 25 feet, as can be rapidly discovered by trying to park a car with one eye closed. Beyond this distance one relies on monocular cues exclusively, since no convergence is needed to focus on distant objects and since the images formed in the two eyes are essentially identical. The most important monocular distance cue is *size.* The farther an object from the observer, the smaller is the visual angle subtended at the eye and the smaller is the image on the retina. Since it is assumed that objects remain constant in size, the smaller the object looks, the more distant it is judged to be.

Defects of color vision

Color blindness may be in the form of **protanopia, deuteranopia,** or **tritanopia,** depending on whether the first (red), second (green), or third (blue) inputs are absent as hue inputs. (Less severe hue deficiences are known as protanomaly, or protanomalopia, for red weakness and deuteranomaly, or deuteranomalopia, for green weakness.) The defects in hue perception are not attributable to lack of receptors, because normal visual acuity is retained; there is no loss of detail vision aside from the hue deficiency. However, a case can be made for impairment of red, green, or blue perception on the following basis: both red and green receptors span most of the spectrum (Fig. 11-9). As a result, both protanopes and deuteranopes are deficient in detecting reds from greens, although the blue receptor covers the blues and yellows. Tritanopia could result from abnormal functioning of the blue input, with resulting confusion of blues and yellows. This disorder is quite rare. Both protanopia and deuteranopia are inherited as sex-linked recessive characteristics (Chapter 2) carried only by the female X chromosome. Therefore the defects are present to some degree in 8% of the male population but are found in only 0.5% of the female population.

Monochromatism is complete hue blindness. All hues appear as gray to the subject, and he cannot distinguish between any hue and a gray of equal subjective brightness. All colors that he sees lack hue and saturation because he responds only to differences in brightness. The disorder is rare and is sometimes caused by complete lack of cone vision, with the resulting foveal blindness and poor adaptation to daylight conditions that are the consequences of total dependence on rod vision.

SUMMARY

The eye, as a visual sense organ, is controlled or "pointed" by extrinsic muscles and is made up of specialized tissue in three layers—an outer sclerotic coat, an intermediate choroid coat, and an inner retina. The sclera is continuous with the cornea, and the choroid coat is continuous with the intrinsic muscles of the iris and the ciliary body, which holds the lens by the suspensory ligament. The retina contains several layers of nerve cells as well as the receptors (rods and cones) since it is an extension of the brain. Light must pass through the ganglion cell layer and the bipolar cell layer before reaching the rods and cones, except in the fovea. Horizontal and amacrine cells interconnect retinal areas; ganglion cells form the optic nerve as they leave the eyeball at the blind spot. After a hemidecussation the optic nerve forms the optic tract. Only the hue-sensitive, photopic, high-threshold cone system is found in the fovea; its photosensitive pigment is iodopsin. The more peripheral low-threshold rod system is scotopic and has rhodopsin for visual pigment. The anterior and posterior chambers of the eye contain aqueous humor; the fundus contains vitreous humor. In the normal eye parallel rays of light from distant objects are focused on the fovea by the cornea and lens; diverging rays from nearby objects are focused by thickening the lens in accommodation. The myopic eye has a lens that is too thick or an eyeball that is too long, errors that are corrected by concave lenses; the hyperopic eye has an abnormally thin lens or a short eyeball, requiring a convex correcting lens. Presbyopia is the reduced accommodation that results from aging; astigmatism usually results from unequal curvature of the cornea; and a clouded lens is the result of cataracts. Convergence and accommodation may become disassociated, causing amblyopia. Pupillary reflexes regulate pupil size in response to the amount of light reaching the eye.

Because of the hemidecussation that forms the optic tracts at the chiasma, damage to either tract causes loss of the opposite visual field, whereas damage to the crossing fibers causes "tunnel vision." The optic tracts terminate in the lateral geniculate nuclei (LGN), which send topographically organized fibers to cortical area 17, visual area I. Areas I and II are topographically organized. The optic tract also sends fibers to the superior colliculi for reflex eye movement, to the pretectal nuclei for the intrinsic eye muscles, ciliary muscles, and iris reflexes, and to the optomotor nuclei controlling eye movements. Other fibers reach visual areas II and III via association nuclei of the thalamus and brainstem reticular formation. Ablation of area I leaves only brightness discrimination; ablation of areas II and III impairs spatial judgment.

Light energy consists of wavelengths from 400 to 750 nm. on the electromagnetic spectrum. Changes in wavelength cause perceived hue changes; mixtures of wavelength cause saturation changes; and amplitude differences change brightness. Brightness is also measured in flux, or rate of flow, from a point source of a standard candle. Light falling on a surface is illuminance; light coming from a surface is luminance. A physical object may transmit, reflect, absorb, refract, or radiate light; in each case light reaching the eye determines hue, saturation, and brightness.

The duplicity theory states that the rod system is a low-threshold achromatic scotopic system for night vision and that the cone system is a high-threshold chromatic photopic system for day vision. The theory is based on differences between rods and cones in visual pigments, wavelength sensitivity, absorption spectra, foveal and peripheral sensitivity, and color zones, as well as the break in the dark adaptation curve.

The electroretinogram (ERG) shows the gross electrical response of the retina, recorded with electrodes on the cornea and near the back of the eye. The A and B waves have been identified with rod and cone system response, respectively, and are often used in threshold measures. Microelectrode recordings reveal an early receptor potential (ERP) preceding the ERG that is associated with the rod and cone receptor response to light.

Some color vision theory has assumed three color responses of the cones because sets of three primaries can be used to match all hues. Other theories assume opposing red-green and blue-yellow processes because of the psychological primary nature of these four hues, their paired opposition as complementary colors, and the usual red-green or blue-yellow color blindness. Research now suggests that there are three kinds of cones, but that their interactions in the retina result in a four-color signal to the brain.

Measurements of the absorption spectra of single rods and cones support the duplicity theory and the concept of blue-, green-, and red-sensitive cones. Tests of human foveal sensitivity after adaptation to yellow (adapting red and green cones), purple (adapting blue and green cones), and blue (for blue cones) brought out sensitivity peaks for blue, green, and red cones that agree with the absorption spectrum data. Microelectrode recordings from bipolar and ganglion cells of the retina show a four-color response, however. When the threshold of firing of ganglion cells is tested for various wavelengths, a dominator curve for rod or cone vision emerges, depending on brightness and on how the ganglion cells are coupled to rods and cones. Selective adaptation reveals modulator curves with sensitivity peaks in the blue, green, yellow, and red regions of the spectrum in several species. Man's three types of color cones may be coupled in a red-green and blue-yellow manner. Microelectrode recordings from horizontal cells reveal slow potentials from light stimulation: (1) a luminosity response (L response) of partial depolarization, which is like the cone sensitivity curve and is not color-coded, (2) a red-green (R-G) response, and (3) a blue-yellow (B-Y) response. The latter two responses are negative at the short end of the spectrum (G or B) and positive at the long end (R or Y); they are color-coded because either the positive or negative response can be abolished by selective adaptation. The responses probably come from horizontal cells in the retina. The R and G responses seem excitatory to the ganglion cells and the B and Y responses seem inhibitory. They may be related to the excitatory "on" responses of firing ganglion cells that accompany the onset of visual stimulation and to the "off" responses of other ganglion cells that occur when stimulation ceases. Some of these cells are color-coded, and the on response always has a lower threshold than the off response. When retinal zones are plotted by recording from ganglion cells, the central area stimulated by light may show an on (excitatory) response surrounded by a peripheral off (inhibitory) response, with cells in between that fire to both on and off signals. In other cases there is a central off and a peripheral on area. However, this organization holds only for photopic vision. Under scotopic conditions, and rod rather than cone stimulation, the whole retina is organized for on responses.

Exploration of the LGN with microelectrodes reveals spectrally opponent cells that change their rate of firing in response to different hues, and broad-band cells that respond to all visible wavelengths. Three types of LGN cells are also found that differ in "on" and "off" firing in response to hue. In area I of the cerebral cortex there are simple and complex cells that respond to lines in the visual field with a pattern of excitation and inhibition; hypercomplex cells of areas II and III respond to the length of the line.

Most visual phenomena agree with what is known of visual physiology. Newton's laws of color include (1) the law of complements, (2) the law of supplements, and (3) the law of resultants. These laws govern complementary colors, supplementary colors, and color mixing as far as hue is concerned. The dimensions of brightness and saturation must be added in addition to the psychologically unique hues—red,

green, yellow, and blue. Seven visual primary colors result—black and white for brightness, gray for saturation, and red, green, yellow, and blue for hue. However, brightness and saturation interact in that maximum saturation may occur only at intermediate brightness. Any hue may be reproduced by the mixture of two of any set of three primary hues that will combine as a trio of complements (brightness and saturation must be adjusted). Color mixing by addition may involve overlapping spots of light; where all three overlap, the result is a white of increased brightness. A color wheel may be used for additive color mixing without brightness change where complements give gray. Color mixing by subtraction involves overlapping color filters or mixing paints. This reduces brightness, and complements give dark gray or black. Colors are usually specified by reference to the Munsell, ICI, or ISCC systems.

All areas of the retina are not equally sensitive to hue, and color zones result. Most peripherally the retina is not sensitive to hue; moving centrally reveals the boundaries of zones sensitive to blues, yellows, reds, and greens, in that order. The Purkinje shift involves a change in sensitivity to wavelengths, daylight (cone) sensitivity is maximum at 555 nm. (yellow-green), whereas night (rod) sensitivity is maximum at 511 nm. (green). Dark adaptation involves increasing sensitivity of the cones for about 10 minutes as iodopsin is built up until the cones reach their minimum threshold to light; then the beginning and continued increase in rod sensitivity as rhodopsin is built up—the resulting threshold curve has cone and rod system segments. Light adaptation first involves incapacitating the rods as all their rhodopsin is bleached by light. The cone threshold is exceeded also, and the pupil constricts to limit light input to the range of optimum cone acuity. Adaptation to brightness, or hue, results in aftersensations that are positive if the same brightness, or hue, is seen, or negative if the opposite brightness, or complementary hue, is seen. Contrast effects occur when different *areas* of the retina are stimulated by contrasting brightnesses or complementary hues. The resulting simultaneous induction prevents adaptation. The cone system is more sensitive than the rod system to brightness differences, increasingly so with greater brightness. Visual acuity is measured in terms of the angle subtended by the light as it reaches the eye from a just-distinguishable object in various ways. One test of acuity is the Snellen test, scored as a ratio between the distances letters can be read by the subject and the normal eye. Temporal thresholds of the eye include the critical flicker (or fusion) frequency (CFF) and apparent movement. The CFF is the rate at which a light must flicker to be seen as constant. Apparent movement is caused by alternation of the light and dark cycles of two flashing lights placed near one another.

Cues to depth and distance are binocular within 15 to 20 feet and monocular at any distance. Convergence and the retinal disparity that results from binocular parallax are binocular cues.

Color vision defects affect both hue and brightness sensitivity. Monochromats are completely color-blind and may have only rod vision. Dichromats include red-green blind protanopes and deuteranopes.

READINGS

Alpern, M., Lawrence, M., and Wolsk, D.: Sensory processes, Belmont, Calif., 1967, Brooks-Cole Publishing Co., Division of Wadsworth Publishing Co.

Begbie, G. H.: Seeing and the eye, Garden City, N.Y., 1973, Anchor Books.

Botelho, S. Y.: Tears and the lacrimal gland, Sci. Am. **211**:78-86, Oct. 1964. (W. H. Freeman Reprint No. 194.)

Brindley, G. S.: Afterimages, Sci. Am. **209**:84-91, Oct. 1963.

Case, J.: Sensory mechanisms, New York, 1966, The Macmillan Co.

Dowling, J. E.: Night blindness, Sci. Am. **215**:78-84, Oct. 1966. (W. H. Freeman Reprint No. 1053.)

Epstein, J. P., and Casey, A.: The current status of the size-distance hypothesis, Psychol. Bull. **58**:491-514, 1961. (Bobbs-Merrill Reprint No. P-437.)

Ewert, J.: The neural basis of visually guided behavior, Sci. Am. **230**:12-93, March 1974.

Fantz, R. L.: The origin of form perception, Sci. Am. **204**:66-72, May 1961. (W. H. Freeman Reprint No. 459.)

Fatechand, R.: The cells that organize vision, New Scientist **24**:726-728, 1966.

Gesell, A.: Infant vision, Sci. Am. **182**:20-22, Feb. 1950. (W. H. Freeman Reprint No. 401.)

Granit, R.: Receptors and sensory perception, New Haven, Conn., 1955, Yale University Press.

Hubbard, R., and Kropf, A.: Molecular isomers in vision, Sci. Am. **216**:64-76, June 1967. (W. H. Freeman Reprint No. 1075.)

Hubel, D. H.: The visual cortex of the brain, Sci. Am. **209**:54-62, Nov. 1963. (W. H. Freeman Reprint No. 168.)

Ittelson, W. H., and Kilpatrick, F. P.: Experiments in perception, Sci. Am. **185**:50-55, Aug. 1951. (W. H. Freeman Reprint No. 405.)

Julesz, B.: Texture and visual perception, Sci. Am. **212**:38-48, Feb. 1965. (W. H. Freeman Reprint No. 318.)

Kennedy, D.: Inhibition in visual systems, Sci. Am. **209**:122-130, July 1963. (W. H. Freeman Reprint No. 162.)

Kolers, P. A.: The illusion of movement, Sci. Am. **211**:98-106, Oct. 1964. (W. H. Freeman Reprint No. 487.)

Luckiesh, M.: Visual illusions, New York, 1965, Dover Publications, Inc.

MacNichol, E. F.: Three-pigment color vision, Sci. Am. **211**:48-56, Dec. 1964. (W. H. Freeman Reprint No. 197.)

Michael, C. R.: Retinal processing of visual images, Sci. Am. **220**:105-114, Feb. 1969. (W. H. Freeman Reprint No. 1143.)

Mueller, C. G.: Sensory psychology, Englewood Cliffs, N.J., 1965, Prentice-Hall, Inc.

Muntz, W. R. A.: Vision in frogs, Sci. Am. **210**:110-119, March 1964. (W. H. Freeman Reprint No. 179.)

Neisser, U.: Visual search, Sci. Am. **210**:94-102, June 1964. (W. H. Freeman Reprint No. 486.)

Neisser, U.: The processes of vision, Sci. Am. **219**:204-214, Sept. 1968. (W. H. Freeman Reprint No. 519.)

Pettigrew, J. P.: The neurophysiology of binocular vision, Sci. Am. **231**:84-95, Sept. 1974.

Pritchard, R. M.: Stabilized images on the retina, Sci. Am. **204**:72-78, June 1961. (W. H. Freeman Reprint No. 466.)

Riesen, A. H.: Arrested vision, Sci. Am. **183**:16-

19, July 1950. (W. H. Freeman Reprint No. 408.)

Rock, J.: Vision and touch, Sci. Am. **216:**96-104, May 1967. (W. H. Freeman Reprint No. 507.)

Rushton, W. A.: Visual pigments in man, Sci. Am. **207:**120-132, Nov. 1962. (W. H. Freeman Reprint No. 139.)

Teeven, R. C., and Birney, R. C.: Color vision, Princeton, N.J., 1961, D. Van Nostrand Co., Inc.

Thomas, E. L.: Movements of the eye, Sci. Am. **219:**88-95, Aug. 1968. (W. H. Freeman Reprint No. 516.)

von Buddenbrock, W.: The senses, Ann Arbor, Mich., 1958, The University of Michigan Press.

Wald, G.: Eye and camera, Sci. Am. **184:**32-41, Aug. 1950. (W. H. Freeman Reprint No. 46.)

Wald, G.: Life and light, Sci. Am. **201:**92-108, Oct. 1959. (W. H. Freeman Reprint No. 61.)

Wallach, H.: The perception of motion, Sci. Am. **201:**56-60, July 1959. (W. H. Freeman Reprint No. 409.)

Wittreich, W. J.: Visual perception and personality, Sci. Am. **200:**56-60, April 1959. (W. H. Freeman Reprint No. 438.)

Young, R. W.: Visual cells, Sci. Am. **223:**80-91, Oct. 1970. (W. H. Freeman Reprint No. 1201.)

part four
Adaptive behavior

chapter 12

Motor organization

OVERVIEW

The book began with a survey of certain aspects of the anatomy and physiology of the nervous system in order to form a background for Part III, which covered the senses. This chapter begins a new section on adaptive behavior. In addition to discussing adaptive responses to outside sensory information, the section will cover central states of the body. The nature of this material is complex, and in order for the student to understand it, further background material on the nervous system will be presented, with emphasis on central motor mechanisms rather than on sensory input. At this point the student should reread Chapter 5 in order to make sure that the major subdivisions of the central and peripheral nervous systems are fresh in his mind. He will thus be prepared for this chapter, which surveys adaptive reflexes and their control by higher centers. Chapter 13, on brain dynamics, will show the way in which higher brain centers are organized in order to control adaptive behavior of a more complex nature. Finally, chapters on states of consciousness, motivation, emotion, learning, and stress will survey these kinds of complex adaptive behavior and describe their control by nervous and endocrine mechanisms.

This chapter begins with the reflex (see Chapter 5). Despite its relatively fixed pathways, response variability is seen because of the influence of higher centers; yet the reflex is under *stimulus control*. Various types of reflex preparations that isolate the reflex from different higher centers are described—spinal, decerebrate, and decorticate preparations. Spinal mechanisms in the reflex response are explained by comparison of a reflex with a muscle twitch (stimulation of a muscle by its motor nerve). The latent period, contraction time, and relaxation time of each are compared. The final common (nervous) path for a reflex movement will show facilitation or occlusion, depending on its inputs. These phenomena are also seen in reflex inhibition as well as in excitation. Varieties of reflexes and their mechanisms are discusssed—stretch, extensor thrust, flexion, crossed-extension, and long spinal reflexes, as well as higher-level reflexes. The higher levels of motor organization form the last section of this chapter. This organization is arbitrarily divided into the pyramidal, extrapyramidal, and cerebellar systems for study. Each system is studied in terms of (1) function, (2) pathways (in the nervous system), and (3) symptoms of damage.

NATURE OF A REFLEX

As explained in Chapter 5 the usual reflex has five categories of "elements": (1) receptors, (2) afferent, or sensory, neurons, (3) interneurons, or asssociation neurons, (4) efferent, or motor, neurons, and (5) effectors (muscles or glands). These are categories rather than single elements. In the simplest reflex, such as withdrawing the hand from a painful stimulus, many receptors, neurons, and effectors are involved. The pathways are relatively fixed from receptors to afferent neurons, interneurons, efferent neurons, and effectors and produce an automatic withdrawal response. The stimulation of pain receptors always leads to withdrawal; therefore the reflex response is under *stimulus control.* However, the exact movement involved in withdrawal will vary to some extent, depending on posture and on the position of the limb relative to the body. For example, the withdrawal movement will involve some different muscle groups when one burns the back of his hand on a stove as compared to burning the palm. Some different movements will follow, depending on whether one is leaning on that arm. The reflex reactions are *modified* by both spinal and higher centers in such a way as to withdraw the hand efficiently while balance and posture are maintained. Some different interneurons and therefore some different motor neurons and muscles are used, but the *form* of the reaction is determined by "fixed" pathways from the pain receptors through the central nervous system. To paraphrase Sherrington, the nervous system "thinks" in terms of movements rather than muscle contractions.

Stimulus control

The kind of stimulus that is used will determine the kind of reflex response that will occur. Different receptors are specialized to respond to different kinds of energy and activate specific kinds of reflexes. For example, the **flexion reflex,** already mentioned, involves contraction of the flexors of a limb in response to pain stimulation of the limb. The nervous "connections" between pain-specialized receptors and flexor muscles are "built into" the central nervous system. For this reason a person will always withdraw his hand from a painful stimulus, and a dog with an injured paw will hold that limb in a flexed (withdrawn) position, even if he has to walk on three legs. On the other hand, the **extensor thrust reflex,** the opposite movement to flexion, will result from the stimulation of pressure and proprioceptive receptors in the limb. Different afferent neurons are fired, and therefore different inter-

neurons, motor neurons, and effectors are activated. Pressure instead of pain stimuli to the sole of the foot, or spreading of the toes, increases contraction of extensor instead of flexor muscles in the limb. In standing or walking, the onset of foot pressure from the weight of the body extends the limb to support the body. The two reflexes are opposed, and if the stimuli for both are used at once, which response will occur? If both pain and pressure receptors in an animal's paw are stimulated, will he flex or extend the limb? This depends to some extent on the intensity of the pain stimulus as compared to that of the pressure stimulus, that is, on the number of receptors and therefore the number of other elements activated. In general, however, the flexion reflex will predominate. It overrides extension because it is a reflex of survival value to the animal.

REFLEX PREPARATION

As already explained, the exact form of a "fixed" reflex response, such as the flexion reflex, will depend on higher centers in the brain that respond to the posture and movements of the animal. Other movements may be set off by the reflex stimuli to higher centers. To keep the reflex as constant as possible while studying it and to prevent most other responses, one **transects** (cuts) the central nervous system above the level of the neurons involved in the reflex. An animal surgically prepared in this way is called a **reflex preparation.** For example, if a flexion reflex of the hindlimb is being studied, the spinal cord may be cut above the level of the sensory and motor roots involved in the reflex. This isolates the interneurons from higher centers. Input from the stimulus cannot cause widespread body movements via higher brain centers, and the reflex response will no longer be affected by higher centers that respond to position and movement. As a result the flexion response will be more consistent from one stimulation to the next. The effect of other variables on the reflex can be best studied when the response is consistent.

Spinal preparation

In the spinal preparation just described the spinal cord is severed above the level of the spinal cord involved in the reflex. Reflexes of the limbs are isolated from higher centers in this way. However, spinal preparations have severe practical disadvantages. It is more convenient for the physiologist to study **acute** preparations, that is, anesthetized animals kept alive only for the duration of the experiment (a day or two). Spinal animals cannot be studied as acute preparations because **spinal shock** ensues when the cord is severed, and the shock lasts for some time. All muscles supplied by motor neurons below the level of the lesion become flaccid (lose tone) and will not react to reflex stimulation. The recovery time involved depends on the development of the brain in the species being studied. Cat and dog—the usual subjects—require about 48 hours for all reflexes to recover, most monkeys about a week, and spinal **(paraplegic)** man about 2 to 3 weeks. Spinal shock is caused by the dependence of the motoneurons on constant excitation from the brainstem reticular formation (BSRF) and vestibular nuclei (Fig. 12-1). The vestibular nuclei normally bombard the spinal motoneurons with excitation through the vestibulospinal tract. This makes the motoneurons more excitable when incoming reflex stimuli are added. The brainstem

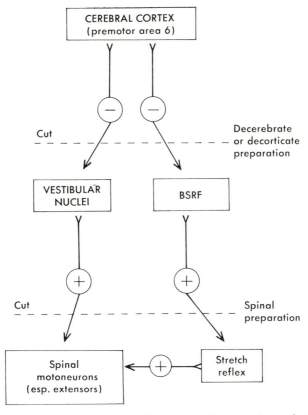

Fig. 12-1. Diagram showing the types of reflex preparation and the excitatory (+) and inhibitory (−) influences of various centers on each other and on the extensor motoneurons.

reticular formation (BSRF) excites moto-neurons by a different mechanism. The BSRF sends excitation to the gamma efferent neurons that contract the muscle spindles for stretch reflexes. Contraction of muscle spindles excites their annulospiral receptors, which in turn send reflex stimulation to the muscles (Chapter 8). The latter mechanism maintains the *tone,* or constant partial contraction, of healthy muscle. When spinal transection interrupts excitation of the muscle spindles, tone is lost and the muscles become flaccid. If the experimenter waits for the animal to recover from spinal shock, the wait is long enough for infection to develop (2 to 3 days). The original operation must therefore be carried out under troublesome aseptic, or sterile, conditions, the incisions carefully closed, and the animal allowed to recover. Such a **chronic** preparation can be maintained for a long time with careful nursing, but it is troublesome to keep and the animal must be operated on a second time to expose the nervous system for experimental manipulations.

Decerebrate preparation

Spinal shock can be avoided so that acute preparations can be studied if the neuraxis is cut at the level of the midbrain. This procedure does not isolate the cord from all higher centers, but it does cut off most of the brain. The cut lies above the vestibular nuclei and most of the BSRF, leaving them functionally "connected" to the motoneurons. The motoneurons continue to receive excitation from these centers to maintain reflex excitability (Fig. 12-1). The animal will, however, display **decerebrate rigidity,** a state of *exaggerated* extensor tone in which all four limbs are rigidly extended. Extensor tone is caused by stretch reflexes (see above), which depend on excitation from the vestibular nuclei and BSRF, particularly the latter. These two centers receive some constant inhibition from the cerebral cortex and basal ganglia.

A midbrain transection cuts off inhibition to the vestibular nuclei and BSRF. When the vestibular nuclei and BSRF are released from inhibition by higher centers, their excitatory effect on motoneurons is increased. The effect on extensor motoneurons is the most pronounced, and the limbs are rigidly extended. The **spastic** condition of the extensors is permanent and provides an abnormal background of muscle tension in the study of reflexes. The transection is usually made between the superior and inferior colliculi, but it may be made higher for some midbrain reflex studies or lower to reduce decerebrate rigidity a little.

Decorticate preparation

The decorticate preparation is made by removal of the cerebral cortex. The preparation is useful for studying reflexes of the diencephalon, or upper midbrain, since they are left intact. Examples could include reflexes of the hypothalamus or visual and auditory reflexes involving the colliculi. Decerebrate rigidity is present, of course, because cortical inhibition of the vestibular nuclei and BSRF is eliminated. The same decerebrate rigidity or spastic condition is seen in people who suffer from cerebral palsy. Damage to parts of the premotor cortex (Fig. 12-1) releases selected parts of the BSRF and vesticular nuclei from inhibition. The muscles excited by these parts of the brain are rigidly contracted to make the person's walk stiff and "jerky" while the hand and arm are often rigidly flexed (the arm and hand flexors resist the force of gravity; so they are "wired" like the antigravity extensors of the rest of the body).

CNS MECHANISMS IN THE REFLEX

The response of a muscle to direct electrical stimulation of its motor nerve is called a muscle twitch. If the muscle is a limb flexor, it will also respond to electrical stimulation of pain receptors in the limb. The reflex response of the muscle to pain stimulation differs in important ways from the muscle twitch because the central nervous system (CNS) is involved in the reflex response but not in the muscle twitch. Important CNS mechanisms were discovered in attempts to explain the differences.

Experimental arrangements

When the characteristics of a muscle response are studied independently of other muscles, the muscle under study is *excised,* or removed from the limb, with its nerve and blood supplies intact (Fig. 12-2). Strong stimulation at S_1 in Fig. 12-2 will fire all the motoneurons to the muscle and cause a muscle twitch—a full contraction of the muscle. If the muscle is a flexor, intense stimulation at S_2 will fire afferent pain fibers to cause reflex contraction in the same muscle. If one end of the muscle is fixed and the other is hooked to a lever, a

trace can be made on a revolving drum **(kymograph)** for both kinds of muscle response. The records shown in Fig. 12-2 for the muscle twitch and for the reflex response can be compared.

Latent period

The **latent period** is the time required for the muscle to *begin* to respond after the onset of the stimulus. It is the period that elapses between the stimulus and the onset of the muscle response. The muscle twitch may begin within $\frac{1}{100}$ second after the stimulus is applied; the reflex response does not begin until about $\frac{1}{5}$ second after the stimulus. There are two minor reasons and one major reason for the difference.

The *conduction time* for neurons involved in the reflex is obviously greater than for neurons in the muscle twitch. The im-

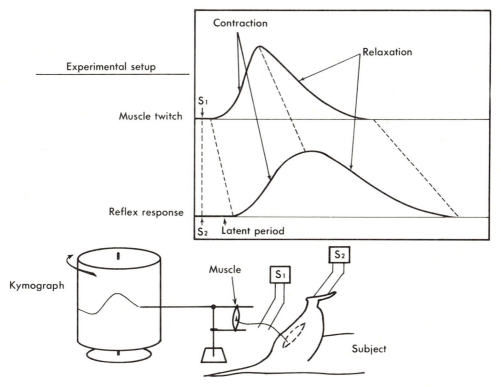

Fig. 12-2. Diagram of setup for recording from a reflex preparation and records obtained from muscle twitch and reflex stimulation.

pulse initiated at S_2 must traverse as much as 2 feet of nerve fibers before reaching the muscle; the impulse initiated at S_1 has only a few inches to go. Figuring that the conduction speeds involved range from 5 M./sec. in the fastest sensory pain neurons to 120 M./sec. in motoneurons, the difference in conduction time can amount to less than $\frac{1}{10}$ second. This does little toward explaining a difference of between $\frac{1}{5}$ and $\frac{1}{100}$ second in the two types of responses.

Synaptic delay is involved in the reflex but not in the muscle twitch. That is, excitation from the sensory neurons for the reflex must cross synapses between nerve cells in the spinal cord; this is not true of excitation for a muscle twitch. In Fig. 12-2 the nerve impulse from S_2 must cross spinal cord synapses to excite the motoneurons; S_1 stimulation directly excites the motoneurons. However, direct measurement of synaptic delay shows that one nerve cell excites another within 0.5 msec. (half of $\frac{1}{1000}$ second), so that synaptic delay *as such* is a negligible factor.

Summation is the most important factor. It is probably *not* true that a single neuron fires another single neuron through their synapses in a reflex. For each motoneuron to fire, excitation must *converge* on it from several interneurons, and many synapses are involved. When an interneuron acts on the cell body and dendrites of a motoneuron, the effect is over in 0.5 msec. or less. Since the interneuron has a refractory period of at least 1 msec., it will be that long before it fires again, and the effect of the first impulse will have died away before the second arrives to supply more excitation. This means that excitation must *converge* on the motoneuron from several interneurons and that these impulses must arrive within 0.5 msec. of each other in order to summate and fire the motoneuron. When these repetitive impulses arrive via pathways of different length, having crossed different numbers of synapses en route, they arrive at different intervals after stimulation. Time is required before enough of them arrive at a motoneuron within 0.5 msec. of each other to summate and fire the motoneuron. To use an analogy, it would require some time before ten men of different stride, walking together, all put their right foot down within a $\frac{1}{5}$-second interval.

Contraction time

Contraction time is the time required for the muscle to reach full contraction after it has begun to shorten. It is much longer for the reflex than the muscle twitch, as can be seen in Fig. 12-2. The reasons for the greater contraction time of the reflex are classified under the term **recruitment.** Stimulation to the motor nerve for a muscle twitch at S_1 fires all the motoneurons simultaneously, so that all motor units are excited at nearly the same time. As a result nearly all the muscle cells begin to contract at the same time. Contraction time for a muscle twitch, therefore, is largely the time required for the muscle cells to shorten when excited. Stimulation at S_2 for a reflex involves summation at synapses, conduction time in neurons, and muscle contraction time (see above). Even if all the pain impulses from S_2 arrive at the cord nearly together, interneurons will respond at different rates. Summation will require a longer time for some motoneurons than others, so that different motoneurons will begin firing at different time delays after the S_2 stimulus. As each motoneuron is added to the response, it is said to be recruited into the active **motoneuron pool** until all motor units are responding. As each motoneuron becomes active, its motor unit is added to the reflex response. The time required for this process increases the contraction time over that of the muscle twitch.

Relaxation time

Relaxation time is the time required for the muscle to reach its original length (that is, relax) after the maximum contraction is attained. After stimulation at S_1, the muscle cells all contract nearly simultaneously. This means that all the muscle cells begin to relax at once. Relaxation time for the muscle twitch is therefore only the time required for the muscle cells to reach their original length after the mechanical relaxation process begins in all of them. Relaxation time for the reflex response is longer than this. The longer relaxation time can only mean that some muscle cells remain contracted after others have begun to relax. Some motoneurons must still be firing after stimulation at S_2 has ceased and after maximum contraction has been reached. This phenomenon is called **afterdischarge.** It is caused by two kinds of "circuits" in the interneurons of the CNS that continue to stimulate motoneurons after input excitation is over. These are the loop and parallel circuits illustrated in Fig. 12-3.

The **parallel circuit** results when there are several interneuron pathways of dif-fering lengths and a number of synaptic interruptions that are interposed between the sensory neurons and motoneurons for a reflex. In Fig. 12-3 stimulation of sensory neuron A fires pathways *1, 2,* and *3.* Pathway *1* involves the fewest synaptic interruptions and less summation; thus it fires motoneuron X first. By the time excitation reaches neuron X by pathway *2,* the motoneuron has recovered and is fired a second time. It recovers again, and pathway *3,* with still more synapses, fires it a third time. In this over-simplified example three output impulses result from one input stimulus. In the CNS hundreds of interneurons diverge and converge to form many parallel pathways.

A **loop,** or **reverberatory, circuit,** or **closed chain,** involves reexcitation of an interneuron over and over by way of a circular pathway. In Fig. 12-3 the input pathway A fires interneuron B, which fires motoneuron X. But neuron B has a collateral that fires

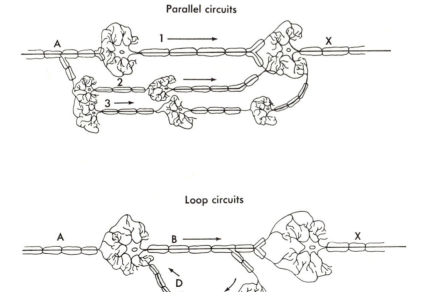

Fig. 12-3. Loop, or reverberating, and parallel circuits in the CNS. Semidiagrammatic.

neuron *C, C* fires *D,* and *D* fires *B,* which has recovered by now. Then *B* fires *X* and again reexcites the loop. In the example, one input impulse at *A* can follow this loop and continue to fire the reflex response via *X* until some element in the loop becomes involved in other CNS pathways; this might cause it to be refractory when the loop excitation reaches it. The example is simplified, of course. Many interneurons would be involved in a loop circuit, and loop and parallel circuits probably interact in the interneurons of the CNS. Both kinds of pathways have been seen under the microscope, and both pathways represent ways in which reflex motor units could continue to respond for a time after stimulus input and maximum reflex contraction are over.

Final common path

A given reflex response may be excited in several ways. No matter what the input, however, the motoneurons controlling the responding muscles constitute the **final common path** taken by any excitation that elicits the reflex. These motoneurons receive excitatory and inhibitory influences from all levels of the CNS. The algebraic sum of

the excitation and inhibition that reach the motoneurons of the final common path will determine whether the response will occur and what its extent will be. The extent of the response will also be determined by the manner in which interneurons from several inputs converge and "overlap" as they reach the motoneuron pool for a reflex response. The result of this convergence and overlapping is called facilitation if it results in a greater response than expected and occlusion if the response is less than expected.

Facilitation. When two different stimuli are simultaneously applied to a reflex, **facilitation** may occur, and the reflex contraction may be greater than the sum of the reflex contractions to each stimulus. Suppose that stimulating pain receptors in the paw causes a 1-gram contraction in a flexor muscle and that stimulating pain receptors in the lower leg causes a 1-gram response in the same muscle, but stimulating both sites at once causes a 3-gram response. A 3-gram response is greater than the sum of two 1-gram responses, and therefore facilitation has occurred. Fig. 12-4 shows how interneurons can converge on motoneurons

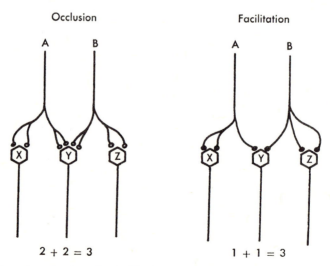

Occlusion

Facilitation

2 + 2 = 3

1 + 1 = 3

Fig. 12-4. Neural mechanisms for facilitation and occlusion. For explanation see text.

so that facilitation can occur. Suppose that motoneurons *X, Y,* and *Z* control different motor units in the reflex, each contributing 1 gram of muscle contraction. Suppose further that two of the synaptic "end-knobs" shown in Fig. 12-4 must be active to fire a motoneuron. This means that input *A* will fire motoneuron *X* for a 1-gram response, but it will only *facilitate* (not fire) neuron *Y.* Input *B* will cause a 1-gram response via motoneuron *Z,* but it will only facilitate *Y.* However, if inputs from *A* and *B* both arrive at once, motoneurons *X, Y,* and *Z* will fire for a 3-gram response.

Occlusion. When two different stimuli to a reflex are applied at once, **occlusion** may occur, and the reflex contraction may be *less* than the sum of the reflex contractions to each stimulus. Suppose an excised extensor muscle responds with a 2-gram contraction to either pressure on the footpad or spreading of the toes (extensor thrust reflex). Yet applying both stimuli results in only a 3-gram contraction—less than the sum of two 2-gram contractions. In this case the motoneurons might receive input as shown in Fig. 12-4 under occlusion. Each of motoneurons, *X, Y,* and *Z* controls different sets of muscle fibers, and each gives a 1-gram contraction. Two "synaptic knobs" are required to fire each motoneuron. Input *A* (paw pressure) fires neurons *X* and *Y* for a 2-gram response. Input *B* (spreading of digits) fires *Y* and *Z* for a 2-gram response. Inputs *A* and *B* "share," or both control, neuron *Y.* Thus when *A* and *B* fire together, only three motoneurons can respond—*X, Y,* and *Z.* This results in a 3-gram response, which is less than the sum of two 2-gram responses. The facilitation and occlusion diagrams are, of course, vast oversimplifications of the way that interneurons converge on the motoneuron pool of even the simplest reflex.

INHIBITION

Two reflexes may be opposed. This was true of the flexion and crossed-extension reflexes in the examples already given. If flexion in a limb is stimulated by a standard stimulus to pain fibers, a certain strength of flexion will occur. If, at the same time, extension is stimulated by spreading the toes of the same limb, flexion will still occur, but the strength or amount of flexor contraction may be reduced by the stimulus to extension. The amount by which flexion is reduced is the amount of **inhibition** of the flexor response caused by the extensor thrust stimulus. A more common example involves crossed extension. If flexion is stimulated in the right hindlimb, the left hindlimb will extend to support the weight of the animal **(crossed-extension reflex).** If pain fibers in both limbs are stimulated strongly, both hindlimbs will flex and the animal will fall, showing that flexion overrides crossed extension just as it overrides the extensor thrust reflex. However, a weak pain stimulus to the right hindlimb will cause enough crossed extension to reduce left flexor reaction to pain stimulation of the left limb. Again, the amount by which left hindlimb flexion is reduced is the amount of inhibition. Since flexion and extension cannot occur in the same limb at once, the interneurons for the two responses are "wired" so that reflex pathways that excite flexion inhibit extension, and vice versa, an arrangement called **reciprocal innervation.**

Phenomena

Inhibition is caused largely by inhibitory neurons, as will be explained shortly. Just as excitatory neurons converge on the motoneuron pool to excite a reflex response, so inhibitory neurons converge on the motoneuron pool of opposed muscles to inhibit them. The resulting inhibition can be measured as a reduction in the opposed response. Inhibition therefore shows all the reflex phenomena already discussed—latency, conduction time, synaptic delay, afterdischarge, summation, facilitation, and occlusion. The principles are the same in each instance, but the response measured is response reduction rather than response excitation.

Central inhibitory mechanisms

At all levels of the central nervous system, inhibition is just as important as excitation. Theoretically, any one of the billions of nerve cells in the CNS could excite any other cell by some indirect pathway of intervening neurons. This would logically mean that the first stimulus the CNS received would cause a spread of excitation from cell to cell until all the cells of the brain were firing in a complete and incapacitating seizure of all the muscles of the body. For the CNS to function in an organized and selective way, some groups of synaptic pathways must be excited while others are inhibited.

At the reflex level of the spinal cord, where inhibition is most easily studied, inhibition occurs when reflex response of the motoneurons is directly prevented via interneurons that are excited by an opposed reflex response. Inhibition may be **presynaptic** or **postsynaptic inhibition.** Postsynaptic inhibition occurs when the collaterals of interneurons for a reflex stimulate **Renshaw cells,** which in turn inhibit the motoneurons for the *opposed* reflex response. Renshaw cells are short Golgi II cells that release gamma-aminobutyric acid (GABA) to hyperpolarize the neurons and make them harder to excite (Chapter 4). The inhibitory influence occurs after the synapses and is therefore postsynaptic. Presynaptic inhibition occurs when the inhibitory neurons or their collaterals contact some of the *axon terminals* of cells that would otherwise excite the motoneurons. They may keep the axon terminals partly depolarized and the transmitter substance of these filaments exhausted so that they cannot participate in depolarizing postsynaptic motoneurons. Such synapses are called **axoaxonic synapses,** in contrast to the normal **axodendritic synapses** (synapses between axon filament

endings and dendrites or cell bodies). Inhibition occurs at centers, or groups of synapses, in all parts of the CNS.

VARIETIES OF SPINAL REFLEXES AND THEIR MECHANISMS

So far, the flexion, crossed-extension, and extensor thrust reflexes have been used as examples in explaining reflex mechanisms of excitation and inhibition. They are not the only examples of adaptive reflexes, and their utility will be further explained in the course of citing the adaptive reflexes that have received the most study.

Stretch reflex

The **stretch,** or **myotatic, reflex** was covered in some detail in Chapter 8. The muscles, especially the extensors, react in response to stretching with a partial contraction that maintains muscle *tone.* Annulospiral receptors in the intrafusal fibers react to stretching of the muscle by firing some motor units of the muscle in a monosynaptic, or single synapse, reflex, with the afferent neurons directly exciting the motor neurons. Sensitivity to stretching can be increased by contracting the muscle spindles themselves with excitation from the BSRF and gamma efferent fibers; intrafusal contraction causes its annulospiral receptors to fire just as muscle stretching does. In response to increased stretching, as when limb extensors are stretched by shifting weight to a limb to bend the knee, extensors react to straighten the limb and maintain an upright position. The reflex is therefore useful in postural adjustment as well as in maintaining muscle tone.

Extensor thrust reflex

The **extensor thrust reflex** has already been used as an example. This reflex also aids postural adjustment and reflex standing. Pressure receptors on the sole of the foot and proprioceptors that respond to spreading of the toes because of body weight reflexly contract extensor muscles in the limb. The extensor contraction stiffens the limb to support the weight being placed on it. The more pressure, the more extension there is, so that shifts in posture are accommodated.

Flexion reflex

The **flexion reflex** has also been cited. In response to pain stimulation to a limb, particularly the foot, flexor muscles withdraw the limb from the stimulus. The reflex is a powerful one, taking precedence over opposed reflexes in most circumstances. This reflex is also adaptive, because it removes the limb from injurious stimuli. It is therefore a reflex that has survival value for the animal.

Crossed-extension reflex

The **crossed-extension reflex** accompanies the flexion reflex and was used as an example when inhibition was discussed. Flexion of a limb is accompanied by extension of the contralateral limb. The contralateral limb thus supports the weight of the animal when a leg is withdrawn from an injurious stimulus. Limb flexion in walking is also accompanied by contralateral extension; the reflex is therefore adaptive for the alternating stepping movements required for walking.

Long spinal reflexes

The reflexes discussed so far have involved only one level of the spinal cord. Stimuli to a limb result in flexion or extension responses of that limb or the contralateral limb, all supplied by the same segments of the spinal cord. **Long spinal reflexes** involve excitation entering one level of the cord and traveling up and down the cord to result in limb and body movements at other levels. Such reflexes have both spatial and temporal characteristics. The **reflex figure** of Sherrington demonstrates the *spatial* characteristics of long spinal reflexes. Flexion of the right hindlimb will cause reflex extension of the left hindlimb in the crossed-extension reflex of the same spinal segments. But excitation will also ascend the cord to cause extension of the right forelimb and flexion of the left forelimb. In four-legged animals this long spinal reflex is useful in maintaining balance and in producing the alternating movements of forelimbs and hindlimbs in walking. The **scratch reflex** is a long spinal reflex that demonstrates *temporal* characteristics. Tickling the flank of a dog— even a spinal preparation—will result in scratching movements of the hindlimb on the same side. Scratching involves alternating flexion and extension of the limb, a temporal pattern of movement that is useful in walking as well.

HIGHER-LEVEL REFLEXES

Not all reflexes are mediated by the interneurons of the spinal cord alone. Many reflexes are organized by the interneurons of the brainstem or even the cerebral cortex. The sensory or the motor side of these reflexes, or both, may involve the cranial nerves. Most of the reflex centers are found in the medulla of the brain, since most of the cranial nerves originate in the medulla, but reflexes with centers at higher levels of the brain also occur. The higher-level reflexes are usually concerned with two kinds of adaptive behavior:

1. The "vital reflexes" maintain automatic adjustments of the visceral muscles and glands of the body in response to changes in internal states, such as changes in blood pressure and blood chemistry. The motor adjustments are largely accomplished by the autonomic nervous system; the reflexes maintain the consistency of the internal environment necessary for life.

2. Other higher-level reflexes involve postural adjustments and are superimposed on some of the postural spinal reflexes already mentioned. Reflexes of this kind adjust the whole posture of the body in response to movements of the head and limbs. Complex adjustments of this kind are controlled

by the extrapyramidal and cerebellar systems, to be discussed in the next section.

ORGANIZATION OF MOVEMENT

The brain integrates behavior in a very complex manner that is constantly modified by input from many sensory receptors. As behavior moves the animal about, the sensory input changes. This is a *feedback* situation—input modifies behavior and behavior modifies input. To consider all the sensory inputs that initiate or modify movement at the same time would unduly complicate this section. To simplify matters, all input except that from the proprioceptors will be ignored. Proprioceptive inputs from the semicircular canals, maculae, and kinesthetic receptors in the muscles are the most integral part of the feedback modifying movement. Such inputs must therefore be considered in motor organization. Ap-

propriate change in response to visual, auditory, tactile, and other sensory input will be assumed rather than discussed. To further make the section manageable, a more or less arbitrary distinction will be made between the following three "motor systems" of the body: (1) **pyramidal,** (2) **extrapyramidal,** and (3) **cerebellar.** Modern research shows that these categories are artificial ones since no one system can operate normally without the others and their major functions overlap so much. However, each system can be said to make a major contribution to behavior, and it is less confusing to discuss them one at a time. Considered in this light, the major contribution of the pyramidal system is the initiation of precise movement, whereas the extrapyramidal system provides for gross "background movements," and the cerebellar system supports balance and coordination.

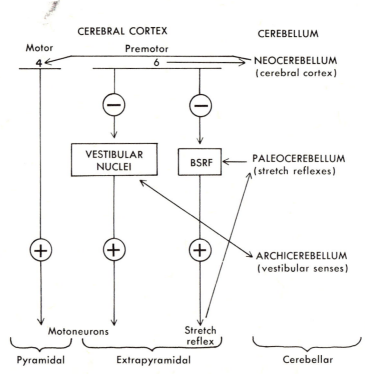

Fig. 12-5. Diagram of interactions between pyramidal, extrapyramidal, and cerebellar systems. *Arrows,* Direction of flow of excitation (+) or inhibition (−). Precise pathways are not given.

Before detail on the anatomy and function of the three systems is given, a broad look at how each contributes to the control of movement and how they interact is a useful approach. A block diagram that extends Fig. 12-1 is given in Fig. 12-5. Fig. 12-1 explained decerebrate rigidity and spinal shock in terms of damage to the extrapyramidal system, although it was not called that at the time. A comparison of the two figures will show that Fig. 12-5 merely adds the pyramidal and cerebellar systems to the extrapyramidal system.

The ultimate aim in control of movement is to make changes in muscle contractions. The pyramidal system does this *directly,* with pathways to the motoneurons of the limbs that excite muscles of precise control—the fingers and toes that execute "target" movements in such precise acts as picking up a pencil. These are movements of the *extremities*—the parts of the limbs most distant from the body trunk. The pathways originate in area 4, the motor area of the cerebral cortex. The extrapyramidal system originates in area 6, the premotor area of the cerebral cortex. It controls the more "axial" muscles of the body that adjust our posture—chiefly gross movements of the arms, legs, and body trunk—shifting our position in such a way as to adjust the body position. These movements form a background to the precise acts controlled by the pyramidal system. Adjustments in posture are primarily made by extensor or antigravity muscles that oppose limb and body flexion that would otherwise result from the force of gravity. Control over motoneurons for these muscles is largely *indirect* and consists of releasing excitatory pathways to the motoneurons from inhibition by area 6 in a patterned way. The vestibular nuclei receive a continuous flow of excitation from the receptors for head position and movement (vestibular senses) and send constant excitation to the extensor motoneurons. The excitation is suppressed in a patterned way by area 6. Body posture is shifted by the release of inhibition from area 6 to vestibular

nuclei. The vestibular neurons that are released excite the appropriate extensor motoneurons for an adjustment in posture. A second mechanism for postural adjustment results from releasing motor areas of the brainstem reticular formation (BSRF) from inhibition by area 6. The BSRF receives input from the stretch reflex receptors. The BSRF sends excitation to the gamma efferent fibers that increase muscle tone in the stretch reflex (Chapter 8). By releasing BSRF fibers that increase muscle tone in the appropriate extensor muscles, body position can be changed.

The cerebellum coordinates movement by (1) integrating input from the vestibular senses, (2) integrating input from the stretch reflexes, and (3) coordinating background movements controlled by area 6 with the precise movements of area 4. Each part of the cerebellum is cross connected with every other part, so that all three functions are continuously integrated. The part of the cerebellum that is oldest in evolutionary history was developed in fish that lacked a cortex and were not subject to gravity. The archicerebellum deals with vestibular information on position and movement and is in two-way communication with the extrapyramidal system by the vestibular nuclei. As land-dwelling species developed, stretch reflexes became necessary, and their receptor input developed the paleocerebellum to deal with information about gravitation influence on movement. The paleocerebellum sends its integrated information to the BSRF to make further adjustments in posture by use of the stretch reflex. Finally, when the cerebral cortex developed, the neocerebellum appeared to provide communication between the extrapryramidal and pyramidal systems so that precise movement could be adjusted to changes in body posture.

Pyramidal system

The pyramidal system contains most of the fibers that run directly from the motor projection areas of the cerebral cortex to excite the motoneurons of the cranial and spinal nerves. These fibers are found chiefly in the **pyramidal tract.** Pyramidal tract fibers that originate in the cerebral cortex pass to the brainstem and spinal cord via the medullary pyramids. The pyramids can be seen on the ventral side of the brainstem, emerging from under the temporal lobes as prominent ropelike strands, diving beneath the pons, and emerging on the ventral side of the medulla to either side of the midline (Fig. 5-8, cerebral peduncles). Fig. 12-6 shows the cortical areas originating pyramidal fibers, in contrast to extrapyramidal fibers. The *single* cortical area that supplies most fibers to the system (31%) is the motor projection area of the brain, area 4 in the Broadmann system (Fig. 5-9). However, all other cortical lobes but the occipital, prefrontal, and temporal contribute fibers to the pyramidal tract.

Topographical organization. The motor projection area of the bain, area 4, is topographically organized. Stimulation of the exposed brain in an anesthetized animal shows that each part of area 4 controls a selected set of the muscles controlling body movement. Starting from within the longitudinal fissure that divides the hemispheres in man, one can find movements of the toes, then ankles, and then knees when the cortex is stimulated (Fig. 12-7). Continuing downward in Fig. 12-7, the precentral gyrus elicits movements in a toes-to-head direction, except that the direction is reversed from the tongue upward. The illustration also shows that muscle groups requiring the most precise control, such as the lips and

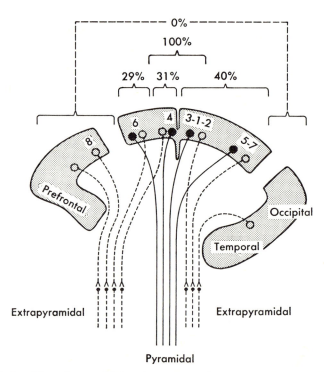

Fig. 12-6. Cortical origins of pyramidal and extrapyramidal tracts. (Based on data of Russell, J. R., and De Meyer, W.: Neurology **11:**96-108, 1961; from Ruch, T. C.: The cerebral cortex: its structure and motor functions. In Ruch, T. C., et al., editors: Neurophysiology, ed. 2, Philadelphia, 1965, W. B. Saunders Co.)

fingers, have a disproportionately large cortical area devoted to them. By contrast, the large muscles of the body trunk are represented by a rather small cortical area. To understand this phenomenon, one must realize that pyramidal neurons control spinal motoneurons rather directly and that each spinal motoneuron controls a *motor unit*. In Chapter 4 it was shown that muscles requiring precise control of movement had fewer muscle cells supplied by each nerve cell than muscles controlling gross body movement. Precise control involves many degrees of contraction, and therefore only a few muscle cells are

brought into contraction as each motor nerve cell is excited—a small innervation ratio. Such muscles require more motoneurons for their size than do muscles controlling gross movements. The motoneurons are stimulated via pyramidal neurons that originate in the cortex. Therefore more pyramidal neurons are found controlling the movement of muscles of precision than controlling muscles of gross movement. As a result a greater area of cortex is devoted to precisely controlled muscles, such as those of the lips and fingers, in comparison with muscles of the body trunk.

Anatomy. The pyramidal tracts are

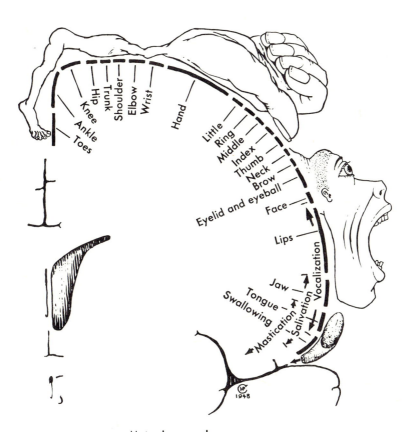

Motor homunculus

Fig. 12-7. Motor homunculus. Diagrammatic section of precentral gyrus. *Dark lines* represent relative proportion of cortical tissue controlling muscles of parts of the body on the labels. Surrounding the section is a caricature of the body in the same relative proportions. Compare with Fig. 7-6. (From Penfield, W., and Rasmussen, T.: The cerebral cortex of man, New York, 1950, The Macmillan Co.)

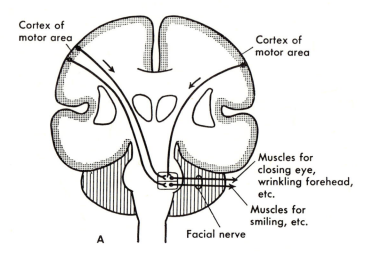

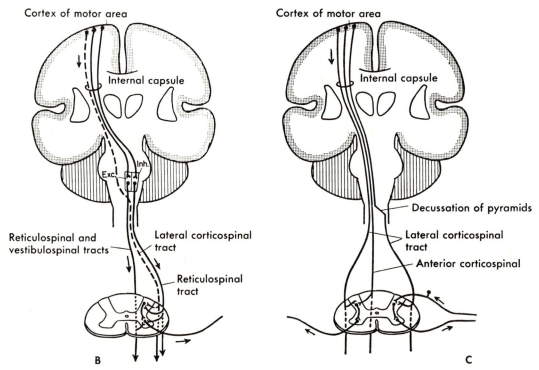

Fig. 12-8. Major motor tracts of brain in diagrammatic form. **A,** Corticobulbar tract. **B,** Reticulospinal and vestibulospinal tracts. **C,** Lateral and ventral (anterior) corticospinal tracts. (From Gardner, E. O.: Fundamentals of neurology, ed. 5, Philadelphia, 1968, W. B. Saunders Co.)

largely *crossed,* that is, the left hemisphere of the brain controls the right side of the body and vice versa. Three tracts are involved: (1) the **corticobulbar tract,** which supplies motor fibers of the cranial nerves, (2) the **lateral corticospinal tract,** a crossed tract of the lateral funiculus of the cord, and (3) the **ventral corticospinal tract,** an uncrossed tract of the ventral funiculus of the cord. In each case the fibers run from the cortex to the level of the motoneurons and excite them via interneurons, much like a reflex. All three tracts are shown in Fig. 12-8. The corticobulbar tract contains fibers that originate in the face area of the precentral gyrus. The fibers descend the brainstem of the same side (with few exceptions) and cross at the level of the cranial motoneurons they supply. The lateral corticospinal tract is formed by approximately 75% of the pyramidal fibers that cross at the decussation of the pyramids in the lower medulla. The remaining uncrossed fibers form the ventral corticospinal tract. Most of these fibers cross in the ventral white commissure of the spinal cord at the level of the motoneurons they excite via interneurons.

There is evidence that the pyramidal tract gives off collaterals to the gracile and cuneate nuclei of the medulla. The influence is both excitatory and inhibitory. Since the gracile and cuneate nuclei relay pressure and fine touch sensations, these inputs are directly altered by movements initiated by the pyramidal system.

Symptoms of damage. If area 4 is selectively damaged by surgery, without damage to other areas, a **flaccid paralysis** results in the muscles represented by the damaged area. The muscles retain normal tone, but their are poorly controlled. The paralysis is severe only in the muscles of precise movement (digits, lower limbs, lips, and so forth); the animal is still capable of gross movements. The nervous system is capable of considerable retraining, and some control of the affected muscles can be learned by remaining brain areas. The younger the animal, the more complete the retraining can be. Some loss of precise control of muscles, such as those of the fingers or lips, is permanent, however. Accidental brain damage is seldom restricted to area 4, so that flaccid paralysis is rarely seen without symptoms of extrapyramidal damage as well.

Extrapyramidal system

The extrapyramidal system seems largely organized for "background movement," the postural adjustments that accompany more precise movements. For example, when one picks up a pencil from a table, gross adjustments in the position of the body trunk, shoulder, and upper arm accompany the precise, pyramidally controlled movements of the lower arm and fingers. As one can see in Fig. 12-6, many of the cortical fibers of the extrapyramidal system originate in area 6, the **premotor area,** although fibers are supplied by many other areas of the cortex. Intense stimulation of area 6 will lead to gross body movements, although the threshold is higher than that for area 4. Body areas nearer the midline seem to be represented by area 6 as compared to area 4—muscles of the trunk, hip and shoulder. Topographically, moving from area 4 into area 6 is like moving from areas with more control of the extremities to areas with more control of the body trunk, shoulders, and thighs. However, the mechanisms of extrapyramidal control over the muscles are quite different from the mechanisms of pyramidal control.

Anatomy. The extrapyramidal system consists of an array of relatively short and branching neurons that descend through the brainstem to excite subcortical nuclei; it includes much of the brainstem reticular formation and the cerebellum. Some of the pathways—those leading from the cortex to the thalamus, from the cortex to the corpus striatum, from the cortex to the red nucleus (an important motor center in four-legged animals), and from the cortex to the cerebellum—are anatomically distinct.

Others can be followed only by the technique of stimulating the cortex and following the course of the resulting nerve impulses with implanted electrodes. All the extrapyramidal pathways that originate in the cortex form part of the **cortically originating extrapyramidal system (COEPS).** Other descending pathways of the extrapyramidal system originate in the nuclei named above as well as in other nuclei of the brainstem. Some of the pathways involved are shown in Figs. 12-8 and 12-9. These pathways control "background movements" by adjustment of extensor muscle tone, although this is an entirely different mechanism from the direct control of motoneurons exerted by the pyramidal system. The cortex and the caudate nucleus selectively inhibit a large excitatory area and a smaller inhibitory area in the brainstem reticular formation (BSRF). These two areas give rise to the **reticulospinal tract.** The reticulospinal tract supplies the gamma efferent motoneurons, which, in turn, excite the intrafusal fibers in extensor muscles. When the intrafusal fibers contract, their sensory endings (annulospiral endings) fire stretch reflexes in the extensors. The BSRF inhibitory area has an inhibitory effect on the gamma efferent motoneurons that stimulate stretch reflexes. The cortex and caudate nucleus selectively suppress these influences to cause a *pattern* of background movement. The BSRF inhibitory area also receives a pattern of inhibition from the cerebellum. In this general way the cortex, caudate nucleus, and cerebellum control the BSRF, which in turn regulates the extensor stretch reflexes. By the mechanism of reciprocal innervation, the contraction of extensor muscles is accompanied by the relaxation of their opposed flexor muscles and vice versa. As a result, the area of the BSRF that is labeled excitatory for extensors inhibits flexors, and the inhibitory BSRF excites the flexors while it inhibits extensors. However, the main influence of the BSRF is to excite extensor muscles via the reticulospinal tract. This is why a decerebrate animal shows decerebrate rigidity, or spastic paralysis. The large excitatory BSRF area is released from the inhibitory influence of the premotor cortex and caudate nucleus when these centers are cut away. Excitation to the extensor stretch reflexes through the reticulospinal tract is thereby increased. The extensors react with strong stretch reflex contractions, and the animal assumes a

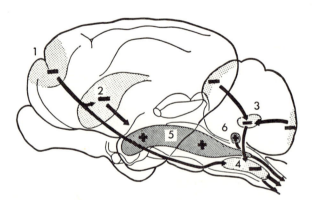

Fig. 12-9. Reconstruction of cat brain showing inhibitory and facilitatory interactions that relate to spasticity and decerebrate rigidity. Inhibitory pathways: *1,* corticobulboreticular; *2,* caudatospinal; *3,* cerebelloreticular; *4,* reticulospinal. Facilitatory pathways: *5,* reticulospinal; *6,* vestibulospinal. (From Lindsley, D. B., Schreiner, L. H., and Magoun, H. W.: J. Neurophysiol. **12:**197-205, 1949.)

posture in which all four limbs are rigidly extended.

The extensor motoneurons are subject to direct rather than to indirect excitation by another pathway of the extrapyramidal system. The **vestibular nuclei** of the eighth nerve send excitation directly to the extensor motoneurons by the **vestibulospinal tract** (Fig. 12-9). The vestibular nulei are normally subject to cortical inhibition. Their direct excitation of extensor motoneurons is therefore increased when the cortex is cut away in decerebration. This adds to the decerebrate rigidity caused by the BSRF. In the normal animal the vestibular nuclei receive a pattern of input from the semicircular canals and maculae, reporting on the position and movements of the head. In response the vestibular nuclei send a pattern of excitation to the extensor motoneurons by the vestibulospinal tract. The extensor muscles respond to adjust the posture of the animal to the position and movements of the head.

Some of the pathways of the extrapyramidal system are involved in a cortical feedback mechanism. Cortical feedback coordinates events in the premotor area and basal ganglia with initiation of movements from pyramidal area 4. Neurons leaving premotor area 6 relay in subcortical nuclei and feed back to area 4. In this manner the "background movements" initiated by the extrapyramidal system are coordinated with the more precise movements initiated by the pyramidal system. The circuit involved is shown in Fig. 12-10 and part of Fig. 12-5. Excitation from premotor area 6 goes to the **basal ganglia** (striatum or putamen, caudate nucleus, and globus pallidus). The basal ganglia send excitation to the thalamus (ventrolateral nucleus), and the thalamus feeds back to both area 6 and area 4. This is a case of *negative feedback* since area 6 and the basal ganglia largely *inhibit* area 4. However, selective inhibition can coordinate the pyramidal and extrapyramidal systems just as well as selective excitation could.

Symptoms of damage. Damage to premotor area 6 or other parts of the COEPS results in **spastic paralysis** of the affected extensor muscles. This is similar in principle to the decerebrate rigidity already discussed. The excitatory BSRF and vestibular nuclei are released from cortical and subcortical inhibition. As a result extensor muscle tone is increased, and the affected limbs are rigidly extended in four-legged animals.

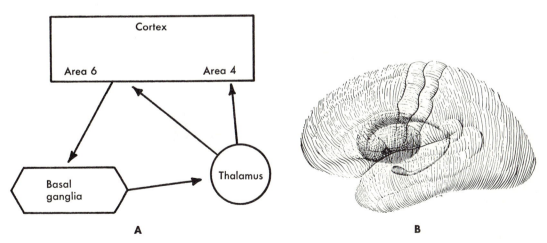

Fig. 12-10. A, Diagram showing some of the relationships between cortical and subcortical motor centers. **B,** Phantom of basal ganglia within cerebral hemisphere. (From Krieg, W. J. S.: Functional neuroanatomy, Evanston, Ill., 1972, Brain Books.)

Extensor muscles are antigravity muscles, as they bear the weight of the animal in reflex standing and prevent the limbs from flexing against the force of gravity. In two-legged primates (including man) the flexors of the arms and hands, rather than the extensors, resist gravity; bending the arm and fingers is done against the force of gravity. As a result the flexors of the arm and hand take on the antigravity role of extensors and are connected to the extrapyramidal system accordingly. Spastic paralysis of the arm and hand in man, therefore, involves a rigidly *flexed* arm, wrist, and hand. This position of arm, wrist, and hand is frequently seen in spastics when damage to the appropriate brain areas has occurred.

Damage to the cortical feedback loop or to its connections with extrapyramidal centers has a more complex and variable outcome. It is now believed that such pathways can be classified by chemical transmitter substances that the nerve cells release to excite other nerve cells of the pathway at synapses. Damage to pathways using acetylcholine as a transmitter ("cholinergic" pathways) are believed responsible for **chorea** (St. Vitus' dance), a disorder (in its most common form) characterized by spasmodic involuntary movements of the limbs or facial muscles. The cholinergic pathways appear to oppose, in a balancing way, pathways that use dopamine as a chemical transmitter. One of these "dopaminergic" pathways involves the *substantia nigra* (black body), a deeply pigmented nucleus of the midbrain. When this nucleus loses its ability to produce dopamine, the nucleus turns pale and **Parkinson's disease** results. Parkinsonianism involves tremor at rest (when movement is not attempted), a disabling limitation of voluntary movement (poverty of movement), and impaired facial expression (masklike face).

Minor damage to the extrapyramidal system from circulatory disorders often occurs in elderly persons, and continuous fine tremors, especially of the hand, are often seen. These tremors usually disappear when a voluntary movement is made. Thus tremors at rest can be suffered by an elderly watchmaker, for example, without unduly affecting the precise movements necessary to his work. Some believe that the feedback loop and connections to other subcortical motor centers suppress continued activity of centers that cause the alternating muscle contractions of tremor.

In the case of chorea, increasing the supply of acetylcholine for the cholinergic pathways is impractical because cholinergic pathways are so widespread in the brain that widespread and debilitating excitation would result. Muscle relaxants, sedatives, hypnotics, and tranquilizers all are drugs that give some symptomatic relief from the continuous movements of chorea. Increasing the dopamine output of the substantia nigra to treat parkinsonianism has been successful, however. The obvious treatment would be to supply the nuclei with dopamine by injecting it into the bloodstream. However, dopamine is too large a molecule to pass the blood-brain barrier (Chapter 5) that exists between the capillaries and the tissue fluid of the brain. The brain can make dopamine from a smaller molecule, called **L-dopa** (3,4-dihydroxyphenylalanine) or levodopa, that *will* pass the blood-brain barrier. Treatment of parkinsonian patients with large doses of L-dopa has resulted in a dramatic relief of the symptoms described above, in many instances. However, there are problems of dosage management and some interesting side effects. The drug often has mood-elevating effects that have relieved some elderly patients from depression and have relieved others from mania (a type of psychosis—see Chapter 18). (This may be the case because the brain can make epinephrine as well as dopamine from L-dopa. Epinephrine is a mood-elevating drug as well as a transmitter in the sympathetic nervous system.) Less frequently, an increase in the sex drive has been reported—perhaps the first true aphrodisiac has been discovered! The large doses of L-dopa required for successful treatment have been reduced in recent experiments by heating the brain slightly with radio-frequency waves or giving enzyme inhibitors that slow the metabolic destruction of L-dopa.

Cortical control of movement: supplementary motor areas

The distinction between the pyramidal and extrapyramidal systems in both origin and function has been overemphasized to simplify matters for the student. When the cortical origin of extrapyramidal fibers (COEPS) and the cortical origin of the pyramidal system were outlined (Fig. 12-6), extensive overlapping could be seen. The major cortical area where pyramidal fibers originate is area 4 on the precentral gyrus. The COEPS originates from premotor area 6 more than from many other areas. However, many neurons of both systems originate from the same areas and the frontal and parietal lobes contribute to both systems. The origin of COEPS fibers is still more extensive. It is therefore not surprising that movement can be elicited by stimulating widespread areas of the cerebral cortex.

This is especially true when the cortex retains its normal excitability and is not depressed by the drugs used to anesthetize the animal for study. Experiments on lightly anesthetized or paralyzed animals have shown that the primary motor area is more extensive than was previously believed (Fig. 12-11). This is the area of major origin for pyramidal fibers and may include part of area 6 as well as area 4. The topographical organization of muscle groups in the monkey is the same as that described for man, except that the head is inverted instead of upright. Tail and hindlimb representation begins deep in the longitudinal fissure. As the precentral gyrus is stimulated farther and farther down the side of the brain, movements occur more and more toward the "head end" of the animal. As mentioned before, stimulating cortical areas from the central fissure forward causes a change in movements from the limbs to the body trunk. A "map" of the body is represented from tail to head in one direction and from the extremities to the body axis in the other direction. As before, muscles of the lips and digits have a larger cortical area devoted to them than do muscles of the body trunk. The contribution of the pyramidal system

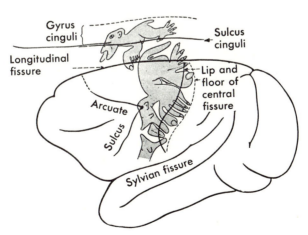

Fig. 12-11. Cortical representation of primary (classical), supplementary, and ipsilateral face motor areas in the monkey. Note that primary area extends beyond area 4 into area 6. (From Woolsey, C. N., et al.: Res. Publ. Assoc. Res. Nerv. Ment. Dis. **30:**238-264, 1951.)

to movement is probably greatest for the muscles of the extremities controlling precise movements. The COEPS contribution is greater as stimulation moves forward across areas 4 and 6 toward the frontal part of the cortex, eliciting postural movements of the body trunk.

A **second motor area** for the face has been discovered on the lateral surface of the precentral gyrus as it extends into the lateral fissure. The face is represented just above the lateral (sylvian) fissure, with the right side of the brain controlling the right side of the body and vice versa (ipsilateral face area). The topographical "map" of the movements obtained is opposite from that of the primary area, in the head-to-neck direction. Body muscle representation is buried in the lateral fissure. This area may be phylogenetically older than the motor projection area, and it receives sensory input as well.

A **supplementary motor area** has also been discovered and "mapped." This area lies in the cortex of both hemispheres and is buried in the longitudinal fissure (Fig. 12-11). Stimulation of the facial part of this area often causes coordinated acts such as yawning, vocalization, or coordinated head and eye movements. Body responses involve assuming and holding a posture that outlasts the stimulation by many seconds. The representation is bilateral—a stimulus to one hemisphere can cause movements of both sides of the body. The supplementary motor area has connections to the primary and the secondary motor areas. However, its control of movement is through the COEPS rather than pyramidal fibers.

Cerebellum

The cerebellum regulates the postural adjustments of the extrapyramidal system and governs certain interactions between extrapyramidal and pyramidal systems. The cerebellum brings kinesthetic and vestibular inputs to bear on both systems and plays an integral role in motor organization. It is treated separately in this chapter only for the sake of taking up topics one at a time; in the end, pyramidal, extrapyramidal, and cerebellar influences are part of one motor organization system. The cerebellar contribution to motor organization includes all proprioceptive and cortical input to the cerebellum and all cerebellar output to cortical and subcortical centers involved in movement. The cerebellum aids in the regulation of balance and coordination.

Anatomy. The cerebellar pathways involve three sets of inputs to the cerebellum and three sets of outputs. All inputs and outputs interconnect by neurons that crisscross the cortex of the cerebellum in both directions; therefore all inputs to the cerebellum affect all outputs from the cerebellum. However, one input and one output form a negative feedback loop from the premotor areas of the cerebral cortex to the cerebellum and back to the motor cortex. From the standpoint of evolution this feedback loop interconnects the newest part of the cerebrum with the newest part

Table 12-1. Organization of the cerebellum

Phylogenetic division	Anatomical division	Input	Output
Archicerebellum	Flocculonodular lobe	Vestibule, vestibular nuclei	Vestibular nuclei
Paleocerebellum	Vermal areas, anterior and posterior lobes	Vestibular nuclei, kinesthesis	BSRF, vestibular nuclei, midbrain thalamus
Neocerebellum	Cerebellar hemispheres	Premotor cortex, olive	Red nucleus (to area 4), thalamus, BSRF

of the cerebellum (neocerebellum). A second input from the stretch receptors in the extensor muscles (muscle spindles) stimulates an older part of the cerebellum, the paleocerebellum. This part of the cerebellum regulates extensor tone by its output to the BSRF and other nuclei of the brainstem. The oldest part of the cerebellum (archicerebellum) receives input from the position and movement receptors of the inner ear. Its output also regulates extensor tone, but by way of the vestibular nuclei instead of the BSRF. The subdivisions of the cerebellum are given in Table 12-1 in terms of cerebellar anatomy and evolutionary age (phylogenetic divisions). In Fig. 12-12 are shown some of the parts of the cerebellum in relation to parts of the brainstem.

The **archicerebellum** is the oldest part of the cerebellum and is found in fish, which have no gravity receptors or cerebral cortex. The input to the archicerebellum deals with head position and movement (plus the lateral-line canals that register changes in water pressure). The archicerebellum receives excitation from the inner ear, the semicircular canals signal head movement, and the maculae signal head position (Chapter 8). This input reaches the cerebellum from the eighth nerve, both directly and as relayed by the vestibular nuclei. The output of the archicerebellum feeds back to the vestibular nuclei. The archicerebellum regulates the excitatory output of the ventibular nuclei to extensor motoneurons (vestibulospinal tract). The resulting pattern of background postural movement depends on the position of the head. The archicerebellum helps to regulate these adjustments (of course the other two lobes of the cerebellum affect the vestibular nuclei through their interconnections with the archicerebellum). Anatomically, the archicerebellum consists of two small paired structures that overhang the brainstem beneath the main mass of the anterior cerebellum, the flocculi (sing., **flocculus**), and a medially placed structure that hangs down in the posterior part of the fourth ventricle, the **nodule.** The archicerebellum is identified with the **flocculonodular lobe.**

The **paleocerebellum** includes the medially placed **anterior** and **posterior lobes** of the **cerebellum** and the narrow central vermis that connects them. The paleocerebellum developed when animals left the sea to live on land. Living on land subjected their muscles to the pull of gravity

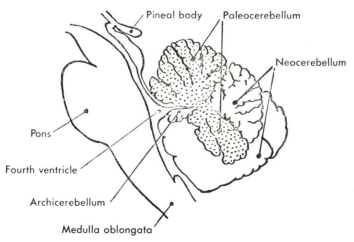

Fig. 12-12. Sketch of major phylogenetic divisions of cerebellum seen from midline. (From Gardner, E. O.: Fundamentals of neurology, ed. 5, Philadelphia, 1968, W. B. Saunders Co.)

in the absence of the supporting effect of the water. Antigravity muscles, the extensors, developed receptors that were sensitive to stretching in their intrafusal fibers. Reflexes aroused by stretching resulted to extend the limbs against the pull of gravity. (The monosynaptic stretch reflex has already been discussed.) The annulospiral sense organs that respond to muscle stretching also connect with tracts of the spinal cord that ascend to the cerebellum. These tracts are the **spinocerebellar tracts**, which carry excitation to the paleocerebellum. After integration with activity in other lobes of the cerebellum, the paleocerebellum acts on the BSRF inhibitory areas with a pattern of suppression from the anterior and posterior lobes (Figs. 12-5 and 12-9, 3). As previously explained, the BSRF regulates the excitability of extensor stretch reflexes, and stretch reflexes are responsible for postural adjustment. The paleocerebellum responds to muscle stretching and other inputs by regulating stretch reflex excitability through the BSRF. The paleocerebellum suppresses inhibitory areas of the BSRF in a patterned fashion so that the extensor tone is regulated in an organized way. Changes in posture result. The whole "circuit" is a patterned mechanism of positive feedback; the excitation of extensor stretch reflexes also arouses centers in the paleocerebellum that act to sensitize stretch receptors. In developing a pattern of stretch reflex excitability, the paleocerebellum also receives input from the vestibular nuclei and other lobes of the cerebellum; it acts on them, and on the midbrain and thalamus as well (Table 12-1).

The **neocerebellum** is the most recently developed part of the cerebellum in evolution. The development of the neocerebellum parallels the development of the motor areas of the cerebral cortex. As the great cerebral hemispheres began to cover most of the brain, the paired cerebellar hemispheres began to overlie the older areas of the cerebellum, forming the neocerebellum (Fig. 12-12). As the motor and premotor cortex assumed the task of integrating complex movements, interaction with the activity of the paleocerebellum and archicerebellum became necessary. The neocerebellum developed to provide this interaction, and two-way connections were established between cortical motor areas and the neocerebellum. The names of these tracts describe their connections. The **corticoponto-cerebellar tract** runs from the premotor cortex (area 6) to the cerebellar hemispheres via nuclei in the pons. Fibers leaving area 6 descend in the cerebral peduncles to the pons, where they synapse in nuclei of that area. Neurons from these nuclei cross to the opposite side of the brainstem and ascend to the opposite cerebellar hemisphere. The tract that returns from the neocerebellum to the motor cortex is also crossed, so that the left cerebral hemisphere has two-way connections to the right cerebellar hemisphere and vice versa. The returning tract is called the **dentato-rubrothalamic tract** for nuclei where it relays. It originates in the output nucleus of the cerebellar hemispheres, the **dentate nucleus.** The fibers cross, and the tract relays in the red nucleus and the thalamus before projecting to the motor area of the cortex (area 4). The two-way connections between cerebrum and cerebellum form a feedback loop that originates in the premotor cortex (area 6) and ends in the motor cortex (area 4). The premotor cortex is a major origin for the extrapyramidal system (COEPS), and the motor cortex is a major origin for the pyramidal system. The feedback loop takes "information" about the background movements initiated from area 6 of the COEPS, adds cerebellar inputs from kinesthetic and vestibular sources, and feeds back the result to area 4. By means of these pathways precise movements initiated by area 4 can be "programmed" by the cerebellum to agree with background movement from area 6 and with kinesthetic and vestibular input reaching the neocerebellum from other parts of the cerebellum. As Table 12-1 shows, the neocerebellum also receives inputs from the olive and sends outputs to the BSRF.

Symptoms of damage. Knowing the functions of the three major subdivisions of the cerebellum enables one to predict the consequences of damage to various parts of the cerebellum. The archicerebellum regulates postural extensor tone in response to the vestibular inputs that are governed by head position and movement. Damage to the flocculi or nodule, therefore, results in disturbances of balance. When the paleocerebellum is impaired by damage to the anterior or posterior cerebellar lobes, postural adjustments suffer with the lack of proprioceptive coordination, and a particular uncoordinated (ataxic) gait results, with exaggerated extensor muscle tone. Neocerebellar damage to the hemispheres causes **intention tremor** (tremor when a movement is begun) and overreaching or underreaching when grasping for an object. Some coordination between background movements and precise voluntary movements has been lost. The patient's hand may be steady until he makes a voluntary motion. Tremor then results, and he is unable to coordinate the position of his body in space with the precise motion needed to reach and grasp an object; he therefore overshoots or undershoots.

SUMMARY

Reflexes involve receptors, afferent neurons, interneurons, efferent neurons, and effectors. A reflex response, such as the flexion (withdrawal) reflex to pain, is under *stimulus control* because of the fixed nature of the connections between reflex elements, starting with the specialized receptors. Some response variability will occur, however, because of the influence of higher brain centers that coordinate the reaction with body posture. In opposed reflexes such as the flexion and extensor thrust reflexes, one reflex will dominate because of

the number of receptors activated, the influence of higher centers, or the built-in protective dominance of the flexion reflex over the extensor thrust reflex. To reduce reflex variability for study of spinal reflex mechanisms, one transects the central nervous system above the level of the input and output neurons for the reflex. The spinal preparation isolates spinal reflexes from higher central nervous system centers, but the resulting spinal shock reduces reflex sensitivity for several days, time enough for infection to set in. Chronic rather than acute preparations must be used, since the reflex must recover from dependence on BSRF and vestibular facilitation. Vestibular facilitation of flexors and extensors is direct; BSRF facilitation is caused by excitation of the intrafusal fibers, which stimulate their stretch receptors to reflexly increase extensor tone. The decerebrate preparation involves a cut above the level of the vestibular nuclei and BSRF. This releases both of them from cortical and subcortical inhibition to cause a spastic condition of decerebrate rigidity of the extensors. The decorticate preparation is also spastic, but such an animal is useful for studying cranial nerve reflexes. One may study reflex mechanisms by comparing the reflex response of a muscle to a muscle twitch response of the same muscle. The muscle twitch is obtained by stimulating the motor nerve to the muscle. The reflex shows a longer latent period, contraction time, and relaxation time. The longer latent period is caused mostly by summation rather than conduction time or synaptic delay. The longer reflex contraction time results from recruitment of motoneurons into the active motoneuron pool a few at a time; all the motoneurons are fired at once in the muscle twitch. The longer reflex relaxation time is caused by afterdischarge of the motoneurons; reflex excitation outlasts the stimulus in parallel and loop circuits in the central nervous system. The motoneurons exciting the muscle response are the final common path to that response; they are subject to excitatory and inhibitory influences from many levels of the central nervous system. Facilitation of a response occurs when two stimuli to a reflex cause a larger response than the sum of the reactions to each stimulus. The two inputs summate to fire some motoneurons that neither input can control alone. Occlusion is smaller than expected reflex response to two inputs. It occurs because both inputs excite some of the same motoneurons.

Reflex inhibition can be measured by the reduction in reflex response caused by stimulation of an opposed reflex. Inhibition shows all the phenomena cited for reflex excitation. Inhibition is just as important as excitation at all levels of the central nervous system because neural pathways must be selectively activated or deactivated. Inhibition may be presynaptic and caused by axoaxonic synapses, or it may be postsynaptic and caused by axodendritic Renshaw cell synapses.

Reflexes are adaptive behavior. The stretch, or myotatic, reflex adjusts extensor muscle tone as weight is placed on a limb. The extensor thrust reflex stiffens a limb when plantar pressure receptors are stimulated or the toes are spread by body weight. The flexion reflex protects against injury by withdrawing a limb, whereas the crossed-extension reflex supports the animal and aids walking. The reflex figure involves the opposite reaction of the other pair of limbs and is a long spinal reflex, as is the scratch reflex. Higher-level reflexes are mediated by the brain. The vital reflexes are autonomic responses to internal changes in the body that maintain the consistency of the internal environment. Higher-level postural reflexes involve the extrapyramidal and cerebellar systems in adjusting body posture to head and limb movements.

The organization of movement involves feedback, because sensory input causes behavior and behavior changes sensory input. The proprioceptors are most intimately in-

volved, but all receptors participate. The pyramidal system controls motoneurons of the extremities in precise "target" movements. The extrapyramidal system regulates "background" postural adjustments of the extensors directly when vestibular nuclei are released from cortical inhibition and indirectly when the BSRF excites stretch reflexes upon cortical inhibition release. The cerebellum integrates input from the vestibular senses, stretch reflexes, and cortex. The archicerebellum, paleocerebellum, and neocerebellum developed in evolution as the three inputs developed. The pyramidal system is most involved in precise movement. Pyramidal fibers originate predominantly in the motor cortex (area 4), where they are topographically organized to control the opposite side of the body, but other cortical areas are involved as well. Precisely controlled muscles with small motor units occupy the largest cortical areas. The pyramidal tracts include the lateral and ventral corticospinal tracts, which excite spinal motoneurons via interneurons, and the corticobullar tract, which controls cranial motoneurons. Damage restricted to the motor cortex results in flaccid paralysis of the affected muscles. The extrapyramidal system controls background postural movements and originates predominantly in the premotor cortex (area 6), although widespread cortical areas are involved in the cortically originating extrapyramidal system (COEPS); subcortical nuclei contribute to the extrapyramidal system as well. The pathways to the motoneurons involve synapses in many nuclei of the brainstem, with the output focusing on the BSRF and vestibular nuclei. The vestibular nuclei excite extensor motoneurons by the vestibulospinal tract. BSRF areas excite or inhibit gamma efferents to the extensor intrafusal fibers by the reticulospinal tract. Intrafusal receptors (annulospiral endings) react to interfusal fiber contraction, as they do to stretching, by increasing extensor muscle tone. Postural adjustments result from these two influences of the extrapyramidal system. Reciprocal innervation controls the opposite reaction of the flexors. The premotor cortex and caudate nucleus inhibit the BSRF excitatory areas; their removal therefore results in spasticity or decerebrate rigidity. The extrapyramidal system also includes a negative feedback pathway, from the premotor cortex via the basal ganglia and thalamus to the motor cortex. Damage to cholinergic pathways in this system results in chorea. Damage to opposed dopaminergic pathways involving the substantia nigra causes Parkinson's disease. Treatment of the latter involves giving the patient large doses of L-dopa, from which the nuclei involved can manufacture their depleted synaptic transmitter, dopamine.

In addition to the classic motor area of the cortex (the primary motor area), stimulation studies show a topographically organized second area on the lateral precentral cortex and a supplemental motor area in the longitudinal fissure.

The cerebellum regulates the extrapyramidal system and its interactions with the pyramidal system. The archicerebellum regulates balance and posture with inputs from the vestibular nuclei and outputs to the vestibulospinal tract for extensor muscle excitation. It includes the flocculus and nodule. The paleocerebellum includes the anterior and posterior lobes and the vermis. It receives inputs from the extensor stretch receptors through the spinocerebellar tracts and regulates their reflex contraction via the BSRF. The cerebellar hemispheres form the neocerebellum. Neocerebellar input is from the premotor cortex through the corticopontocerebellar tract. Its output goes to the motor cortex in the dentatorubrothalamic tract. This feedback pathway integrates extrapyramidal and pyramidal system activities. All lobes of the cerebellum interconnect diffusely. However, symptoms of cerebellar damage depend on the locus of the injury. Archicerebellar damage causes disturbances of balance. Paleocerebellar damage results in ataxia, impairs postural adjustments, and increases extensor tone. Neocerebellar damage causes intention tremor and overshooting or undershooting when reaching for an object.

READINGS

Gardner, E. D.: Fundamentals of neurology, ed. 5, Philadelphia, 1968, W. B. Saunders Co.

Lippold, O.: Physiological tremor, Sci. Am. **224:** 65-73, March 1971.

McGeer, P. L.: The chemistry of mind, Am. Scientist **59:**221-229, 1971. Also in Leukel, F.: Issues in physiological psychology, St. Louis, 1974, The C. V. Mosby Co.

Ochs, S.: Reflexes and reflex mechanism. In Selkurt, E. E., editor: Physiology, Boston, 1963, Little, Brown & Co.

Ochs, S.: Upper somatic and visceral control. In Selkurt, E. E., editor: Physiology, Boston, 1963, Little, Brown & Co.

Sherrington, C.: The integrative action of the nervous system, New Haven, Conn., 1961, Yale University Press.

chapter 13
Brain dynamics

OVERVIEW

In the second of the four parts of this book a reflex model of the CNS was presented. The model was based on a comparison of the association areas of the cortex and subcortical nuclei with the interneurons of a reflex. It was assumed that the association areas and subcortical nuclei related sensory input to motor output in a way that was similar to interneuron connections between sensory and motor nerves in a reflex. The major difference cited between a reflex and a complex response was that the complex response is variable, whereas the reflex is relatively fixed. Variable stimulus-response connections in the complex response allow for trial-and-errow behavior and for learning through new connections in the CNS. The reflex model was adequate for the discussion on sensation. This part of the book, however, deals with the more complex phenomena of motivation, emotion, learning, and stress. To deal with these phenomena, a more complex and complete understanding of brain function is required. The current chapter on brain dynamics presents a modern view of the organization of brain functions. The material is presented here rather than in the early chapter on the CNS (Chapter 5) so that it will be fresh in mind for the last five chapters on complex behavior (states of consciousness, motivation, emotion, learning, and stress).

This chapter begins by a restatement of the reflex model of CNS function and the presentation of its origins. The reflex work of Sherrington, presented in Chapter 12, was the main root of the so-called reflex model. This led to an overemphasis on the

cerebral cortex per se, since animals with more cortex show more complex behavior. Animals without a cortex can learn and show some complex behavior, but it was assumed that these functions were transferred to the cortex in higher animals through encephalization. The more developed the cortex in a species, the greater is the impairment to complex behavior from cortical damage, so that the idea of encephalization seemed valid. It was assumed that transcortical connections were made from one cortical area to another in variable and complex behavior.

This chapter then develops a new CNS model for complex behavior by showing the inadequacies of the old transcortical reflex model. Evidence from both evolution and anatomy will be presented. The result is a *vertical organization* model of CNS function. The new model gives little importance to direct connections from one part of the cortex to another. Vertical organization refers to connections between *subcortical nuclei* made *by way of* the cortex. This makes the subcortical nuclei pivotal in complex behavior. Subcortical nuclei dominate the connections between sensory input to the cortex and elsewhere and motor output from the cortex and subcortical nuclei that results in behavior. This makes the neocortex only part of a vertically organized system.

The system is first presented from an evolutionary point of view. The allocortex, or paleocortex, was the first to appear in the evolutionary development of olfaction (smell). Described first are its parts and their location, then the transitional cortex, and finally the neocortex (the last to appear in evolution). At this point the chapter outlines the functional organization of the brain in terms of the neocortex, the reticular and projection systems, and the limbic system and hypothalamus. A discussion of the functions of each of these parts of the brain in complex behavior follows. The chapter closes with a discussion on cerebral metabolism, which shows how the internal environment of the body acts on the CNS and vice versa. Maintaining consistency (homeostasis) in the internal environment is the basis for all behavior, complex or simple.

HISTORY OF THE TRANSCORTICAL REFLEX MODEL

The fundamental work of Sir Charles Sherrington on the reflex provided psychologists with a model for more complex behavior. Sherrington showed that the reflex response varied somewhat with the posture of the animal, even when the spinal cord was isolated from most of the higher nervous centers. As shown in Chapter 12, the variability in a reflex response depends on connections between interneurons. Pain stimulation always leads to a flexion (withdrawal) reflex, but the exact pattern of the movement depends on the posture of the animal. Interneurons bring the influence of posture sense organs (proprioceptors) to bear on the reflex response. The flexion is varied to maintain the animal's balance. The response varies with postural input because the interneuron pattern *varies* from one response to the next. The interneuron "connections" between the pain stimulus and the withdrawal response therefore change from one occasion to the next. This concept of changing stimulus-response connections seemed well suited to explain more complex behavior. Complex behavior is more variable than a reflex because more interneurons are involved, and their connections are not fixed. Higher parts of the brain are more involved in a complex response than in a simple spinal reflex, and higher brain centers contain millions of

"interneurons." The functional connections between these interneurons could change from one presentation of a stimulus to the next. As a result the response would vary from one stimulus presentation to the next. Complex and variable behavior would thereby occur. Repeated presentations of a stimulus would cause variable behavior in learning. The response could be followed by reward or punishment. The interneuron connections for responses that led to reward or avoided punishment would tend to become "fixed," like a reflex, so that other responses to the stimulus would drop out. Learning would then have occurred.

Research on learning has been important to many fields of psychology, including physiological psychology. Psychologists and physiologists observed that development of the neocortex seemed to parallel the development of more complex and variable behavior. Phylogenetically, complex animals with a more developed cortex are able to learn more difficult patterns of behavior. The cortex therefore seems to be the most important part of the brain in complex behavior, including learning. The cerebral cortex first developed as a sensory correlation center for smell. Some of the older ventral cortex still relates to smell, even in man. The more dorsal parts of the cortex have nothing to do with smell, however, and have been dubbed the neocortex, or "new cortex." It is the development of the neocortex that has been associated with more complex behavior and a greater ability to learn in some species of animals, including man. Following the reflex model for learning, the concept of transcortical association was developed to explain the function of the neocortex in learning. Sensory input has been traced to the sensory projection areas of the neocortex. Pathways for response originate in the motor projection area. The connections between sensory input and motor output were assumed to be in "association areas" of the neocortex, which lay between sensory and motor areas. These transcortical, or "across the cortex," connections should therefore "associate," or connect, input to sensory projection areas with motor output from the motor projection areas. Transcortical connections would therefore mediate stimulus-response associations of the highest level of the brain, the neocortex. Changes in transcortical connections should cause complex new responses to stimuli and therefore form a physical basis for learning.

Objections to transcortical association as a basis for most learning were soon pointed out. Animal species that do not have a neocortex can learn; from earthworms to alligators, the more primitive species can be trained. The problems they can solve for reward or avoidance of punishment are simpler than the problems mammals can solve, but they learn without a cortex.

The objection was answered with the concept of **encephalization.** As each new species evolved with a neocortex, the cortex "took over" some of the functions of the lower brain centers. Learning was one of the most complex functions carried out by lower brain centers in species without a cortex. Learning would therefore be taken over by the neocortex as it evolved, leaving simpler functions for lower brain centers. The more developed the neocortex in a species, the more it dominates the function of lower brain centers, and the less the lower brain centers can function without the neocortex. It was pointed out that the visual responses of a frog are little disturbed by removal of the cerebrum, whereas removal of the visual cortex in man leaves him blind. The more developed the species, the more profound are the effects of removing parts of the cortex. Removal of the motor cortex in man or monkey causes nearly total paralysis of the extremities (Chapter 12); animals with a less developed neocortex are less paralyzed by motor area decortication. Finally, the more developed the cortex, the greater is the effect of decortication on complex behavior. Decorti-

cating a rat has far less effect on its ability to learn than does decorticating a man.

However, it was decided that the transcortical connections involved in learning were widespread and variable. Lashley, in a series of pioneering studies, removed various cortical areas in rats. He studied the effect of this operation on the learning and retention of maze habits. No one cortical area seemed more important than another. The more cortex he removed, the greater was the impairment of learning or memory. Yet the location of the area he removed seemed to make little difference. He concluded that the cortex acted "as a whole" in learning and memory (mass action, Chapter 17) and that one part was as useful as another for learning (equipotentiality). Now that we know that the degree of specialization of specific cortical areas depends on (1) their relation to subcortical nuclei in a vertically organized system and (2) the degree to which the cortex has developed in area and vertical complexity—specific areas of the cortex are much more specialized in a man than in a rat.

Stereotaxic apparatus

Lesions of subcortical nuclei with minimal cortical damage are often made with a **stereotaxic apparatus.** This apparatus fixes the animal's head in a known position by means of tapered bars in the ears (in each external auditory meatus) and a bar under the upper front teeth (incisors). A needle, insulated except at its tip, is held in a rack over the animal's head. The rack is devised so that the needle can be moved in all three dimensions. There is a scale for each dimension so that the tip of the needle can be accurately positioned in each dimension. The skull is exposed and the needle positioned over the bregma—a suture, or intersection of bones, on about the middle of the dorsal surface of the skull. The bregma serves as a beginning landmark. Three-dimensional "maps" of the brain are available, so that moving the needle a given amount in the two horizontal dimensions places its tip over the desired position. A small hole is bored in the skull here, and the needle is lowered a known distance into the brain. Its tip is then in the desired position. Because the insulated needle is small, it causes little damage in passing through the cortex. A known current is then passed through the needle for a fixed period, causing bubbles at its tip (hydrolysis) or producing heat to kill cells at that point. The extent of the damage is determined by the current intensity and duration. In this manner subcortical nuclei can be destroyed with little damage to the cortex. The location and extent of the damage, however, must be confirmed after the experiment is over by sectioning and staining the brain tissue and studying it under a microscope. Lesions of this kind have impaired complex learning behavior as much as cortical lesions and in just as diffuse a fashion.

EVOLUTION OF NEOCORTEX
Sensory dominance of cortical development

The cerebral hemispheres began in fish and reptiles as input centers for the sense of smell and were little more complex at that stage of development than the primary "relay" nuclei that have been discussed in studying the special senses, such as the cochlear nuclei for hearing or the nucleus of the tractus solitarius for taste. As the sensory inputs for the special (head) senses became more complex in evolutionary history and as the general (whole body) senses began relaying their input to higher centers of the CNS, a vertically organized surface layer of cortical cells appeared to integrate this input. Only then did the motor organization discussed in the last chapter develop cortical levels of control.

The importance of all this to understanding the brain of man is to realize that cortical development took two different directions depending on the use made of the sensory information by the species involved.

The use made of the sensory information depended on the environmental demands for survival made upon the species. Many experiments on brain function require that we experiment with animals whose brains are not so complex at the cortical level as the brain of man. It is therefore important that we choose species whose brains are evolving in the same pattern of cortical development as that of man rather than in some other fashion.

One may trace this "main line" of cortical evolution by comparing a theoretical early reptile with a "living fossil" like the hedgehog whose brain has not changed for millions of years with a more developed but still primitive brain like the shrew and finally with a primate brain (Fig. 13-1). This development can be seen most clearly with respect to a single sensory input such as vision although other cortically organized inputs like hearing and somesthesis would show similar cortical development. In summary of the information given in the figure, it appears that what has been called visual area II, or visual association cortex ("visual belt") developed before and not after the "primary" projection area (striate cortex, "visual core," or visual area I) appeared. The two inputs overlapped at first, then developed separate input pathways from different parts of the thalamus (the lateral geniculate nucleus is functionally part of the thalamus). Only after these developments had taken place did other parts of the thalamus and cortex emerge that were not a part of this or any other sensory system. These "intrinsic" nuclei of the thalamus formed interconnections with "association" areas of neocortex (new cortex) in a fashion that allows integration of many sensory inputs.

By contrast, the cortex of more "stimulus-bound" species continued to develop along the same line as that in Fig. 13-1, *B,* with considerable overlap between primary and association sensory cortex, so that little develops in the way of intrinsic thalamic

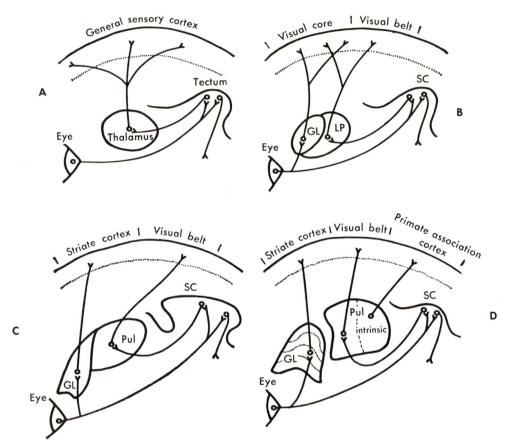

Fig. 13-1. Four main stages in evolution of visual pathways to thalamus and cerebral cortex. *GL,* Lateral geniculate nucleus (LGN); *intrinsic,* nuclei of pulvinar that project to cortex outside of visual sensory pathways; *LP,* lateral posterior nucleus of the thalamus; *Pul,* pulvinar, a nucleus of the thalamus; *SC,* superior colliculus; *Tectum,* roof of the midbrain, forerunner of the superior colliculus. **A,** An early reptile-like ancestor of the mammals with visual input to the tectum and then the thalamus, which diffusely projects into a general-purpose sensory cortex. **B,** Early mammals, represented by the hedgehog where a direct pathway from the optic tract to the thalamus and cortex has been added to **A;** the thalamus has differentiated into lateral geniculate and lateral posterior nuclei, whose projections to the cortex still overlap in the visual core (area I) and visual belt (area II). **C,** Later but still primitive mammals, represented by the tree shrew. Lateral posterior nucleus resembles the primate pulvinar and projects to the temporal lobe as well (not shown). The old and new pathways show no overlap in their projections to the visual core (now striate cortex, area I) and visual belt (area II). **D,** The primate cortex, represented by monkey species. A new part of the pulvinar, the "intrinsic" portion, sends input to association cortex that is not a part of the visual pathways. (From Diamond, I. T., and Hall, W. C.: Evolution of neocortex, Science **164:**251-262, copyright 1969 by the American Association for the Advancement of Science.)

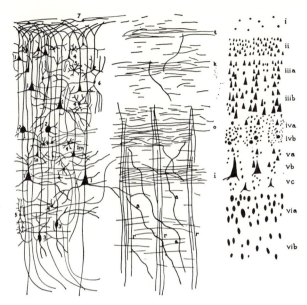

Fig. 13-2. Structure of cerebral cortex, drawn from microscopic observation. Staining procedures (from left to right) brought out some whole cells, fibers, or cell bodies. Numbered cells are as follows: *1,* pyramid; *2,* star pyramid; *3,* fusiform; *4,* star (stellate); *5,* spider; *6,* double bush; *7,* horizontal. *Right,* Six cortical layers. (From von Bonin, G.: Essay on the cerebral cortex, Springfield, Ill., 1950, Charles C Thomas, Publisher.)

nuclei and associated neocortex. The cat is one such species, yet the cat is frequently used in studies of cortical response to sensory input. Anatomical and physiological (stimulation and evoked potential) studies of the cat cortex demonstrate that cortical development is nearly all sensory or motor in nature, and little intrinsic cortex can be found.

Anatomical evidence

The cerebral cortex is a complex structure that has three to six layers of a variety of cell types with complex synaptic structures. The structure of the cortex, however, seems designed for conduction in a vertical direction rather than a horizontal direction (Figs. 13-2 and 13-3). Horizontal cells are found only in the most superficial layer, occur only in the more phylogenetically developed species, and then are found only in the neocortex. Cortical structure seems designed so as to concentrate incoming excitation from subcortical nuclei on a cortical focus, spread it to nearby areas, amplify it, and redirect it to subcortical nuclei. The development of cortex would, then, not increase transcortical connections as much as it would increase the number of ways that subcortical nuclei could be interconnected and increase the number of subcortical nuclei that could be involved at once. The anatomical model suggested for the cortex is a collection of loop and amplifier circuits that interconnect subcortical nuclei. Damage to the cortex would destroy certain of these pathways, but alternate routes could be found between subcortical nuclei. Damage to the subcortical nuclei, on the other hand, would destroy the centers to and from which excitation flows. This is why the subcortical nuclei have been called "pivotal" in brain function. Development of an increasingly elaborate cortex was the

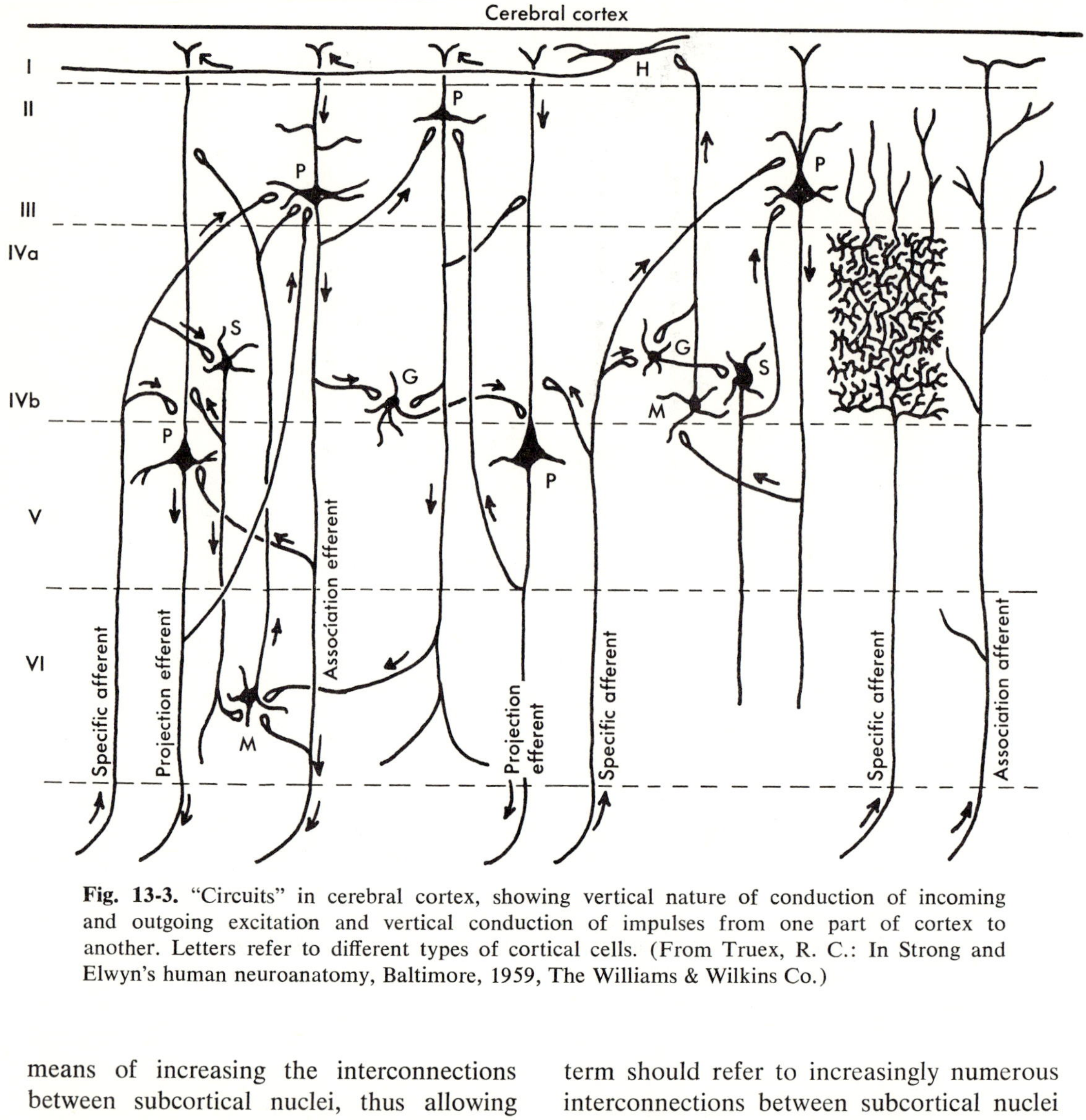

Fig. 13-3. "Circuits" in cerebral cortex, showing vertical nature of conduction of incoming and outgoing excitation and vertical conduction of impulses from one part of cortex to another. Letters refer to different types of cortical cells. (From Truex, R. C.: In Strong and Elwyn's human neuroanatomy, Baltimore, 1959, The Williams & Wilkins Co.)

means of increasing the interconnections between subcortical nuclei, thus allowing more variable and complex behavior in response to more and more complex stimulus patterns perceived by the brain. In the vertical model of brain organization the cortex amplifies the interconnections that are possible between subcortical nuclei rather than merely replacing the connections that exist in simpler animals without a cortex.

Encephalization

Thus encephalization is not the domination of lower centers by the neocortex; the

term should refer to increasingly numerous interconnections between subcortical nuclei made *by* the cortex. The neocortex must be considered as a part of a vertically organized system. The changes in interconnections in this system may lead to changes in response patterns to stimuli; these changes are called learning. Whether the changes occur at synapses in the cortex or at synapses in subcortical centers, or both, it is the organization of the system that has altered. Altering the organization of the system means altering the interconnections between subcortical nuclei. The more elaborate the cortex,

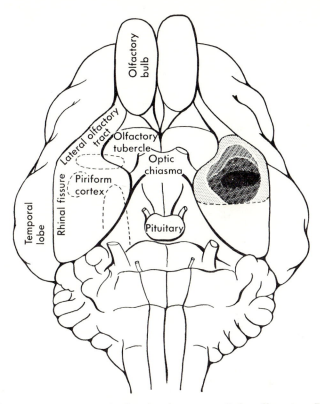

Fig. 13-4. Ventral view of the cat brain, showing parts of the allocortex. Removal of area marked on right resulted in hypersexuality (See Chapter 16). (From Green, J. D., Clemente, C. D., and deGroot, J.: J. Comp. Neurol. **108:**522, 1957.)

the more elaborate is the interconnection system—and the more complex and varied behavior can become.

PHYLOGENETIC ORGANIZATION OF THE CORTEX

Areas of the cortex can be divided into "old" cortex **(paleocortex, or allocortex), transitional cortex,** and **neocortex,** according to how recently they have developed in evolution. These three classifications of cortex differ in their anatomical structure and differ in the subcortical nuclei they interconnect; therefore the classification is a functional one. The allocortex may have as few as three recognizable layers of cells, whereas the neocortex has six layers of cells. The allocortex is related to subcortical nu-

clei once concerned with smell and is often lumped with these parts of the brain as the **rhinencephalon** (*rhis, rhin-,* 'nose'; *encephalon,* 'brain'), when certain parts of the transitional cortex are included. The neocortex is most closely related to the thalamus, geniculate bodies, and basal ganglia. Transitional cortex interrelates these two sets of centers.

Allocortex

The cerebrum originally developed as a correlation center for smell input, and the allocortex includes the parts originally devoted to smell. These parts of the brain can be seen in Figs. 13-4 and 13-5. Some parts of this cortex are still devoted to smell in higher mammals, including the **olfactory**

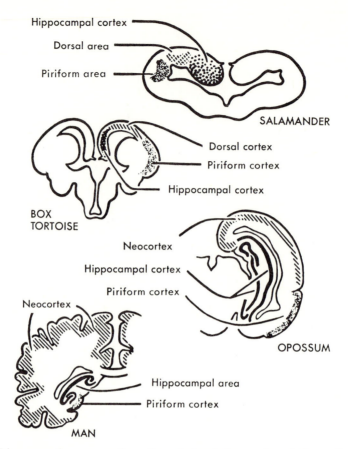

Fig. 13-5. Diagrammatic cross sections through hemispheres of a phylogenetic series of vertebrates, showing how hippocampal cortex has become buried in hemisphere and piriform cortex has been displaced to ventral surface. (Modified by McCleary, R. A.; from Herrick, C. J.: Proc. Nat. Acad. Sci. **19:**7-14, 1933. By permission of the publisher.)

bulbs and **tracts** and the **prepiriform area.** Other parts, such as the **piriform lobe** and **hippocampus,** have developed into cortical centers involved in complex reactions of emotion and motivation. The piriform cortex remains visible on the ventral surface of the brain, but the hippocampus is "rolled up" into the interior of the cerebrum with the extensive development of the neocortex (Fig. 13-5).

Transitional cortex

The transitional cortex is intermediate in age and structural complexity. It is sometimes called **juxta-allocortex.** Some parts of the transitional cortex are shown in Fig. 13-6. It includes the **cingulate gyrus,** which lies between the two hemispheres, deep in the longitudinal fissure and above the corpus callosum. The anterior part of this area is called the **septum.** The **presubiculum** lies in the fissure between the temporal lobes. Frontal and temporal lobe areas on the base of the brain are also included. Transitional cortex has connections with the piriform lobe and hippocampus (allocortex areas) by subcortical tracts on the one hand and connections with the anterior thalamus (related to frontal neocortex) on the other. The transitional cortex connects therefore with the part of the allocortex that is no longer devoted to smell and

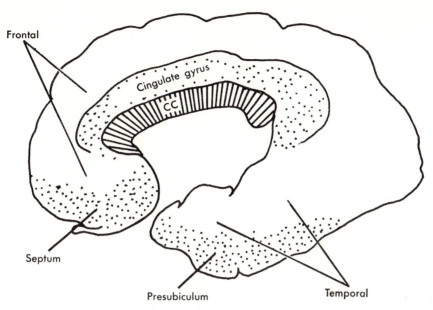

Fig. 13-6. Medial view of the brain, showing transitional cortex. *CC*, Corpus callosum connecting the hemispheres.

with a part of the thalamus that supplies frontal neocortex.

Neocortex

The neocortex includes the rest of the cerebral cortex and most of the frontal, parietal, temporal, and occipital lobes. The neocortex also includes the classical sensory and motor projection areas, as well as association areas. The sensory projection areas are in two-way connection with sensory nuclei of the thalamus and geniculate bodies. The motor projection area and premotor area have extensive two-way connections with the basal ganglia, as discussed in Chapter 12. Parietal, occipital, and temporal association areas are interrelated with certain posterior thalamic nuclei. These association areas seem to differ in function from the association areas of the frontal lobes, as will be seen later. The association areas of the frontal lobes interconnect with a cluster of nuclei in the anterior thalamus and, by way of these nuclei, relate to the rhinencephalon. The rhinencephalon has been mentioned only

slightly so far—it will be discussed later in the chapter.

FUNCTIONAL ORGANIZATION OF THE BRAIN
Neocortex

The neocortex is the site of intricate, vertical organizations between subsystems of subcortical nuclei. The parietal, occipital, and temporal lobes (POT areas) receive sensory input and seem involved, along with subcortical centers, in learning and memory. The frontal lobes, on the other hand, include the origins of the motor projection systems. In a very general way, the POT areas could be regarded as receptive and integrative in function, whereas the frontal cortex organization is expressive and related to brain output. The more anterior parts of the frontal lobes, the so-called **prefrontal lobes,** seem to function in more complex expressive ways. Animal experiments show that they affect the ability to delay response to a stimulus and distractibility. Human brain damage to these areas results in subtle personality disturbances, including increased impulsiveness. The frontal lobes show the greatest increase in size of all the cortical areas as one moves up the mammalian scale from rat to man. This has led some writers to speak of frontalization instead of encephalization. Not enough is known of the role of the frontal lobes in behavior to make such a distinction here. Further distinctions between frontal and POT functions in behavior will be discussed later.

Reticular and projection systems

The inputs to the cortex from lower brain centers involve conscious states of arousal, attention, and sleep, as well as the inputs governing simple sensation. The brainstem reticular formation (BSRF) is involved as an ascending reticular activating system (ARAS).

Specific thalamic projection system. The classic sensory pathways form a **specific thalamic projection system (STPS)** that results in topographically organized sensory input for vision, hearing, and somesthesis. The pathways involved were fully discussed in the chapters on those topics. The somesthetic sensory pathways form the medial lemniscus and relay in the ventrolateral thalamus before ending in the postcentral gyrus of the cortex. The topographically organized projection area includes Brod-

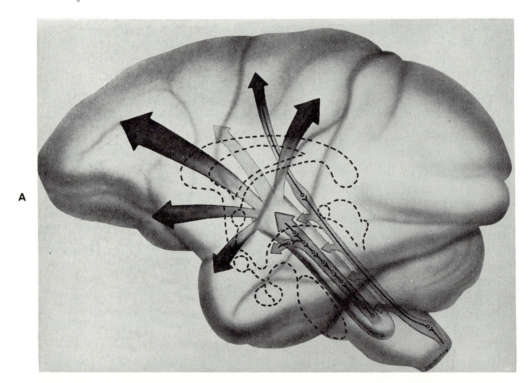

Fig. 13-7. A, Ascending reticular activating system *(ARAS)* schematically projected on a monkey brain. **B,** Schematic diagram showing sensory projection to cortex through specific thalamic projection system *(STPS),* diffuse thalamic projection system *(DTPS),* and ascending reticular activating system *(ARAS).* (**A** from Lindsley, D. B.: Attention, consciousness, sleep, and wakefulness. In Field, J., editor: Handbook of physiology, vol. 3, Baltimore, 1960, The Williams & Wilkins Co.)

mann areas 3, 1, and 2, sometimes called somesthetic area I. The auditory pathway relays in the medial geniculate body and ends on the superior temporal gyrus in area 41, or auditory area I. The visual pathway relays in the lateral geniculate body and ends in the occipital lobe along the calcarine fissure of the striate cortex in area 17, or visual area I. There are secondary sensory areas for all three senses, but they are phylogenetically older and are not a part of the STPS.

Diffuse thalamic projection system. The secondary sensory areas for somesthesis, vision, and audition were described in the chapters on those topics. These secondary areas are supplied partly by the **diffuse thalamic projection system (DTPS)** (Fig. 13-7). The DTPS has a more widespread distribution than does the STPS, represents an earlier form of sensory input, and is less "modality specific." Its arousal by auditory stimulation, for example, may result in a change in nerve impulses reaching widespread areas of the brain. The reaction of the cortex to the DTPS is brief compared to its reaction to the ascending reticular activating system (see below). The cortical responses observed have been called "recruiting responses" because the brain waves in areas supplied by the DTPS become more regular and synchronized and have

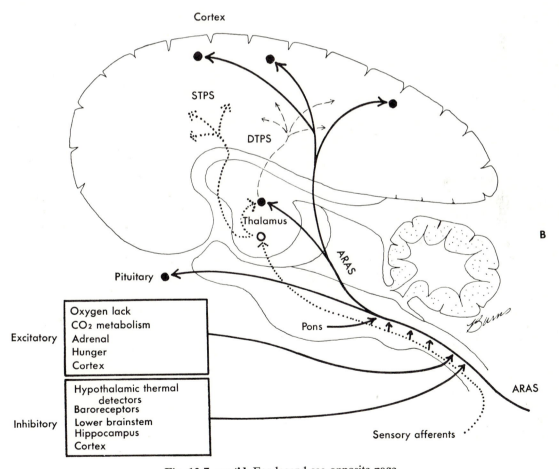

Fig. 13-7, cont'd. For legend see opposite page.

a larger amplitude. Recruiting responses are probably caused by excitation reverberating back and forth between the thalamus and cortex. The sensory pathways involved begin with the STPS, which has collaterals to diffuse anterior and midline nuclei of the thalamus. These nuclei in turn send fibers to the basal ganglia and to widespread cortical areas, including the secondary sensory areas. The effect of the DTPS on the secondary sensory areas in particular may serve as a mechanism for *selective attention*. Certain cells in the secondary areas may be active only when the animal is attending to that specific sensory input. This would form a "modality-specific" mechanism for attention.

Ascending reticular activating system. The **ascending reticular activating system (ARAS)** serves the whole cerebral cortex. The ARAS originates in the central parts of the medulla, midbrain, and diencephalon, as compared to the thalamic projection of the STPS and DTPS. The medulla, midbrain, and diencephalon are like the spinal cord in that the gray matter of nuclei and short interneurons lie in the central core, surrounded by the white matter of myelinated tracts. Much of this central gray matter is composed of short, many-branched, interconnecting cells, called the **brainstem reticular formation (BSRF).** Part of the BSRF forms the inhibitory and excitatory reticular activating systems for motor control, as discussed in Chapter 8. The role of this descending reticular activating system (DRAS) in cortical arousal by reflexes will be further discussed. Part of the BSRF makes up the ARAS (Fig. 13-7). The cells of the ARAS, like those of the DTPS, are fired by collaterals from the incoming sensory pathways of the STPS. The cells of the ARAS fire through many synapses; the relayed excitation being passed from cell to cell up through the central core of the brainstem reaches all areas of the cerebral cortex. The ARAS excites the cells of the cerebral cortex and lowers their threshold to

incoming stimuli from other sources. The main function of the ARAS is to "keep the brain awake." The more active the ARAS, the more aroused and alert is the animal. Quiescence of the ARAS results in a low level of cortical activity, a state of sleep, and a higher threshold for the cortex to incoming sensory stimulation.

Descending reticular activating system. As described in Chapter 12 on motor organization, the cells of the BSRF can regulate muscle tone by exciting or inhibiting extensor stretch reflexes. To coin a term, this can be called a **descending reticular activating system** (DRAS) because of the role of *sensory feedback* in maintaining states of wakefulness and attention. Perhaps you have noted that your neck muscles ache or your leg muscles are tired after a period of alert, concentrated study, although you have been sitting in a chair the entire time. When the BSRF is active and the cerebral cortex is stimulated by the ARAS, the DRAS increases extensor muscle tone. The more the extensor muscles are contracted in maintaining this tone, the greater is the stimulation of kinesthetic receptors—the receptors in muscles that are sensitive to muscle contraction. As discussed in Chapter 8, excitation from some of these receptors reaches the cerebral cortex and gives rise to sensations of muscle contraction. In states of alert attention, then, the BSRF activates the cortex via the ARAS and also increases muscle tone. Increased muscle tone fires kinesthetic receptors that feed back excitation to the cerebral cortex, further increasing cortical excitation. Thus the BSRF has both an ascending and a descending activating system.

Limbic system

Earlier it was pointed out that the cerebral cortex began in evolution as a correlating center for smell. The olfactory bulbs and tracts, and the prepiriform area are still closely related to smell, but the piriform lobe and hippocampus are not (Figs.

13-4 and 13-5). Nevertheless, all the allocortex and its related subcortical centers are sometimes called the rhinencephalon ('nose brain'). Those parts of the rhinencephalon that are no longer directly involved in smell have formed close connections with some of the transitional cortex to form the **limbic system.** It was pointed out previously that the transitional cortex is in two-way connection with the allocortex on one hand and with the neocortex on the other. So, therefore, is the limbic system. The limbic system was so named by Papez because it forms a ring (*limbus,* 'border') in the medial part of each cerebral hemisphere (Fig. 13-8). The limbic system includes the **hypothalamus, septal area** (septum), **cingulate gyrus, hippocampus** and **entorhinal cortex,** most of the **amygdala** (amygdaloid nuclei), and the anterior thalamus. The limbic system receives input from (1) parts of the rhinencephalon still concerned with smell (olfactory bulb and lobe, prepiriform area), (2) sensory areas of the neocortex, (3) the BSRF, and (4) the hypothalamus. The limbic system sends excitation to (1) many areas of the neocortex, (2) the BSRF, and (3) the hypothalamus. In Fig. 13-8, the original circuit of Papez is shown by the black arrows. The Papez circuit involves excitation in a closed reverberating loop, from the hippocampus to the mammillary bodies of the hypothalamus, from there to the anterior thalamus, thence to the cingulate gyrus and entorhinal cortex, and finally back to the hypothalamus via the hippocampus. Papez suggested that this circuit provides a neural basis for emotional behavior and experience. The suggestion has been a fruitful one as Chapter 16 will demonstrate. The limbic system has recently been involved in the learning research reported in Chapter 17. The hypothalamus governs the autonomic nervous system in

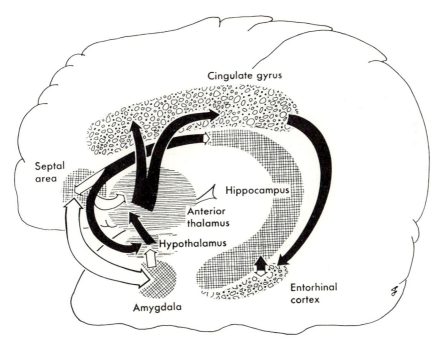

Fig. 13-8. Diagram of limbic system, projected on outline of brain. *Black arrows,* Neural connections referred to by Papez as the limbic pathways. *White arrows,* Connections discovered since that time. Compare with Fig. 16-1. (Modified from McCleary, R. A., and Moore, R. Y.: Subcortical mechanisms of behavior, New York, 1965, Basic Books, Inc.)

emotional states, and two of the most important tracts connecting it with other parts of the brain are found in the limbic system. These tracts are the **fornix,** which connects the hippocampus with the mammillary bodies, and the **medial forebrain bundle,** which interconnects the BSRF, hypothalamus, and rhinencephalon.

The limbic system communicates with the frontal lobes of the neocortex via the anterior thalamus. The frontal lobes play an important role in human personality, and damage to them often causes impulsivity and reduced affect (lack of emotionality). Limbic connections with the parietal, occipital, and temporal neocortex (POT "association areas") involve the limbic system in research on learning and memory.

Hypothalamus

The **hypothalamus** consists of a continuous group of nuclei occupying the walls and floor of the third ventricle of the diencephalon (Chapter 5). Research on the hypothalamus has shown that it plays a dominant role in (1) regulation of the motor activity of the autonomic nervous system, (2) homeostatic response to changes in the internal environment, either by sensitivity of its own cells to these changes or through input from internal receptors, (3) regulation of endocrine output through connections to the pituitary gland and hypothalamic releasing factors (Chapter 3), (4) drives, or the arousal and maintenance of behavior in states of hunger, thirst, sexual input, and so on, and (5) emotional responses in states of rage and fear. The hypothalamus seems to be the pivotal point between somatic and visceral sensory input and somatic and visceral motor output in the responses of the body to internal and external stress. The anterior hypothalamus has been called a **trophotropic** area by Hess because when it is stimulated it causes parasympathetic responses—slowed heart rate, dilation of blood vessels in the stomach and intestines, and drowsiness, as if

the animal were digesting a big meal. Responses of the parasympathetic nervous system are also dominant. He referred to the posterior hypothalamus as **ergotropic,** because stimulation there raised the heart rate and blood pressure, made the animal alert and aroused, and often caused him to attack nearby objects or the experimenter. Responses of the sympathetic nervous system were dominant. It is evident that the anterior (and medial) hypothalamus is trophotropic because it stimulates parasympathetic responses. The posterior (and lateral) hypothalamus is ergotropic because it stimulates the sympathetic nervous system.

BRAIN FUNCTIONS

This discussion will anticipate some of the material in Chapters 14 to 18. It will also review material already covered. In this way functions of the brain circuits just discussed can be understood while the circuits themselves are fresh in mind. No one circuit of the brain can be completely explained without involving others. However, this section will be organized like Chapter 12 for simplicity's sake: one part of the brain will be taken up at a time. The cortex, reticular formation, limbic system, and hypothalamus will be discussed in that order.

Cortex

The cortex is the highest level of the vertically organized connections between subcortical systems. Through study of the cortex one can learn as much about subcortical systems as one can learn about the way in which the cortex organizes them. On the sensory side the most direct input to the cortex arrives in the STPS. Even here the input for vision, audition, and somesthesis is integrated and topographically organized in the lateral and medial geniculate bodies and thalamus. The input from the DTPS initiates reverberatory activity back and forth between the cortex and thalamus, activity that seems important to attention for a specific sensory modality. Sensitivity to all inputs in states of wakefulness and alert attention is caused by the diffuse stimulation of the cortex by the ARAS. Once aroused, the cortex can "stimulate itself" in a feedback manner, exciting the ARAS, which reexcites the cortex. Feedback also comes from cortical excitation of the DRAS, with heightened reflex tone and kinesthetic feedback from the muscles, keeping the cortex awake. However, the brain cannot respond to all possible sensory inputs at once—some selective attention is necessary. The STPS seems involved in this selective attention. Also involved is **sensory gating,** a topic mentioned in Chapters 7, 10, and 11. In each of these sensory modalities efferent pathways leading from the brain have been found. These efferent pathways reach either the receptors, first relay nuclei, or higher centers in the sensory pathways. Some of these efferent pathways are inhibitory. They *block* excitation from a sensory modality so that the brain can deal with other inputs more effectively. In topographically organized inputs like hearing, inhibitory pathways may sharpen the "place cue" for pitch, allowing only signals from the most stimulated part of the receptor to get through to signal only one dominant pitch that depends on which part of the receptor receives the most stimulation.

On the motor side the cortex is stimulated to initiate movement and to control that movement by reverberation with subcortical centers. The motor area of the cortex initiates precise movement by the pyramidal system. At the same time the motor and premotor areas are interacting through subcortical nuclei and the extrapyramidal system to control position and "background movement." The two areas also interact through the cerebellum to control balance and coordination.

In associating sensory with motor cortical areas the cortex is also part of a vertically organized system. The so-called association areas of the cortex are merely nuclei and fibers that form feedback loops between subcortical centers. The POT (parietal, occipital, and temporal) association areas are in two-way connection with the limbic system, via the amygdala and hippocampus (Fig. 13-8). Reverberatory activity in the limbic system is set off by the ARAS. This activity seems to be integrated, as far as learning and memory are concerned, by the POT cortical areas. The limbic system is also connected to the prefrontal cortex by the anterior thalamic nuclei. The prefrontal cortex is involved in complex behaviors called personality, temperament, affect, and anticipation. These responses entail emotional reactions that include organized autonomic nervous system activity. The hypothalamus governs organized emotional behavior that involves both autonomic and somatic responses. The hypothalamus and prefrontal cortex are integrated through the limbic system.

The functioning of the prefrontal and POT cortex may be understood by contrasting what is known about each. In both cases most of the knowledge has come from ablation studies with animals or from accidental damage or "psychosurgery" in humans, when the cortical damage was more or less restricted to either the prefrontal cortex or the POT areas. The prefrontal cortex undergoes more development than do other areas of the cortex, as the phylogenetic series of brains from rat to man are compared ("frontalization"). For this reason it was long believed to govern "thinking," consciousness, and most intellectual functioning. Examination of the evidence does not bear out this idea. The story begins in the midnineteenth century when Phineas P. Gage, a railroad construction foreman, had a crowbar (tamping iron) blown through the frontal lobes of his brain by an explosion. Surviving the accident, he changed from an "efficient and capable, sober and industrious" foreman into a "fitful, irreverent, profane, impatient, obstinate, and vacillating" fellow, according to his physician. The changes observed were more in temperament and personality than in "intellect" per se. Subsequent cases of prefrontal damage revealed flattened affect, indifference to pain, and reduced anxiety.

Some of these changes were seen as desirable in the case of certain psychotic patients for whom other remedies had failed; therefore operations called "psychosurgery" were developed. The operations involved either prefrontal lobectomy, topectomy, or lobotomy. **Prefrontal lobectomy** involves removing all dorsal cortex anterior to the premotor areas and has the most profound effects of the three procedures. In **prefrontal topectomy,** selected areas of the prefrontal lobes are removed. **Prefrontal lobotomy** consists of severing the fibers connecting the prefrontal lobes with the thalamus (and limbic circuit). Clinical reports made after these operations indicate reduced anxiety, but it is accompanied by impulsiveness, flattened affect, lack of foresight, and increased distractibility. Topectomy of area 11 has been used for the relief of intractable pain, particularly in terminal cancer cases. The patient reports that it "still hurts" but that it "doesn't bother" him any more. His threshold for pain is unchanged, but pain has lost its "insistent" quality; it "hurts just as much" if he pays attention to it, but he can "ignore it most of the time," which may relate to his distractibility.

Other types of psychosurgery that involve destroying parts of the limbic system are a more recent development. These are noted in the section on the limbic system and in Chapters 16 and 17.

Before-and-after testing of intelligence is difficult with most prefrontal psychosurgery patients because their psychosis affects test performance. The studies that have been done suggest that the operation has little effect on performance in intelligence tests for otherwise normal patients. However, certain sorting tests that involve categorizing objects in various ways show impairment because the subject persists in using an incorrect category after he has discovered that it is wrong.

Animal experiments involving the effect of prefrontal lobectomy on monkeys have been done. The task that seems most affected by the operation is called **delayed reaction.** The monkey is shown food being placed under one of two or more cups. He is restrained from going to the food for intervals of a few seconds to several minutes, during which the cups may or may not be out of his sight. Then he is released to see if he selects the correct cup. The prefrontal monkey cannot correctly respond after as long an interval as can a normal monkey and makes more mistakes at most of the intervals tested. His performance deficit has been attributed to his "distractibility," or inability to keep his attention focused on the correct cup. Inability to "respond to an absent object" is another explanation. When the monkey cannot see the cups during the delay interval, he must respond to his "memory" of where the food was when he sees the cup again. The experiments show that both factors are probably involved.

Damage to POT cortical areas results in strikingly different symptoms in man when compared with the results of prefrontal lesions. Association areas in these parts of the cerebral cortex seem most involved in the synthesis of input arriving through several different sensory modalities, in memory, and in language. Damage in some of these areas can cause **agnosia,** the inability to recognize objects presented to one or another sensory modality. For example, a common object such as a hammer can be recognized visually but not by touch; the patient may report that it "feels rubbery" and that he "doesn't know what it is," but he will recognize and correctly name it as soon as he sees it. Language difficulties are called **aphasias;** for example, the patient may recognize words by seeing them but not by hearing them or vice versa. **Amnesia,** or loss of memory, may be present. In this case memory for recent events (just before the brain damage occurred) suffers more than older memories do. Such **retroactive amnesia** (RA) is a common result of concussions, strokes, and other brain traumas. Memory formation in particular seems related to temporal lobe function. Penfield reports two cases of damage to both temporal lobes and underlying (amygdaloid) nuclei. In both instances the individuals apparently had normal memory for events that preceded the damage, although some RA had occurred. They could also function well using "immediate memory," that is, recall over short periods, as one remembers a telephone number until after dialing it. However, the patients had difficulty learning anything new. If introduced to someone who then left the room and returned in 15 minutes or so, they would not recognize him nor remember having met him. Penfield also reports that stimulation of the temporal lobes in patients undergoing brain operations causes them to have a flight of images that recall past events in their lives.

Language functions also seem to have more or less specific foci within the POT area. In the first place disorders of language caused by brain damage must be designated as *expressive* or *receptive*. Expressive disorders (aphasias) involve inability to use the vocal cords, lips, and so forth (paralyses) or damage to a specific area of the frontal cortex where the sequencing and patterning of the motor expression of language is organized (Broca's area). Receptive aphasias involve damage to a specific temporal part of the POT cortex (Wernicke's area) that appears to organize the perception of language. In about 95% of the population, these areas are found in the left, or "dominant" hemisphere (especially for right-handed people). Most precise acts (including writing) are initiated by the pyramidal system and involve feedback from the kinesthetic receptors. If you are right-handed, the left hemisphere is dominant because it controls and receives feedback from the more skilled right hand by the "crossed" motor and kinesthetic sensory pathways. The right hemisphere is dominant in left-handed people, although the language areas are in the left hemisphere for most of them. (A minority of left-handed and ambidexterous people have the language areas in the right hemisphere or both hemispheres.) The hemisphere that controls language also appears to function more importantly in analytical, mathematical, and deductive tasks; the other hemisphere seems to be illiterate, skilled in space perception, form perception (like the recognition of a familiar face), music recognition, and synthetic and inductive nonverbal tasks. The vertically organized cortex appears to be two brains in one skull in some ways, as can be seen in the "split-brain" experiments described below.

The brain, like the rest of the body, is in duplicate. Just as one has two arms and two legs, one has two cerebral hemispheres, two thalami, pairs of brain tracts, and so on. This suggests the importance of the connections between the two hemispheres, especially the corpus callosum—the great sickle-shaped band of nerve fibers running from one hemisphere to the other (Fig. 5-5). Sometimes brain surgeons are forced to cut the corpus callosum to remove tumors deep in the brain. They find little sensory, motor, or intellectual impairment in their patients after recovery. It was also noted that epileptic seizures would not spread from one hemisphere to the other if the corpus callosum was cut. Therefore the operation was sometimes performed to reduce the spread of seizures in the brain.

The right side of the brain controls the left side of the body and vice versa, as previously noted. Similarly, most sensory input from the left side of the body goes to the right side of the brain and vice versa. In the event of brain damage to one hemisphere, however the other hemisphere can take over these sensory and motor functions by using the corpus callosum and other crossing commissural fibers between the hemispheres to control the input and output of the damaged hemisphere. This caused Sperry to wonder what would happen if sensory input to a split-brain animal were confined to one hemisphere. He operated on cats and monkeys, cutting the corpus callosum and other fibers going from one hemisphere to the other (anterior and posterior commissures, etc.). He also cut through the optic chiasma, so that input from the left eye went to the left hemisphere only and input from the right eye was restricted to the right hemisphere (Fig. 13-9). He then blindfolded the left eye and taught monkeys a visual discrimination habit. Presumably only the right half of the brain learned because sensory input was restricted to the right eye and right hemisphere. To test this theory the monkey's right eye was blindfolded and the discrimi-

nation problem was presented to the left eye (and left cerebral hemisphere). The monkey behaved as though he had "never seen" the discrimination problem before, and his left hemisphere had not, of course. The left hemisphere could even be taught a discrimination that conflicted with the one "stored" in the right hemisphere. For example, a monkey could be taught to look with his right eye (and hemisphere) for food under a cube rather than a pyramid. With the right eye blindfolded the left hemisphere could then be taught that the food was under the pyramid rather than the cube. What happens when the two hemispheres have been taught conflicting correct choices, and the monkey sees the discrimination with both eyes open? The answer seems to be that one hemisphere dominates, usually the one controlling the arm that the monkey uses to indicate his response. Dominance may shift back and forth from one hemisphere to the other,

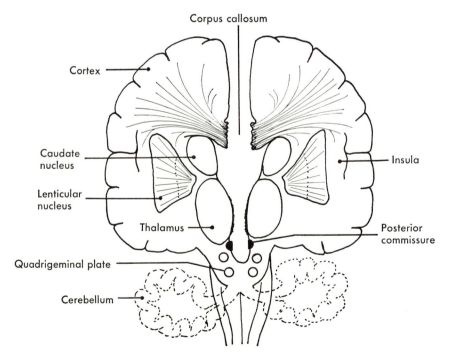

Fig. 13-9. Diagram of split-brain operation.

and each hemisphere may take its turn at controlling behavior, but there is no apparent conflict. When real handedness appears in some species of primates, however, they become specialized with regard to memory storage. Doty has shown that a normal monkey, taught a conditioned response or maze habit, stores the habit in one hemisphere only. The process of splitting the brain after learning and restricting sensory cues to the "ignorant" hemisphere results in failure to demonstrate the learned performance. The corpus callosum acts in this instance to prevent memory formation in both hemispheres at once—perhaps "doubling" the memory storage capacity of the brain!

Man's hemispheres are quite specialized for verbal (left hemisphere) and nonverbal (right hemisphere) function as noted above. Patients whose corpus callosum has been severed to prevent the spread of seizures have been tested. These patients cannot read in their left visual field (neurons from the right retina go to the right hemisphere—Fig. 11-5). Writing anything meaningful with the left hand was impossible though the patients could copy patterns. Verbal commands could not be carried out with the left hand because the crossed pyramidal tract control came from the nonverbal right hemisphere. However, the extrapyramidal system is not altogether crossed; so the left verbal hemisphere could communicate response to verbal commands for postural changes in body and whole arm and leg movements, such as "pose like a boxer" or "salute." On the other hand, the right hemisphere appears, in tests, to be more accomplished in space perception, form perception, music recognition, and so on. Experiments on hemispheric specialization will be described in Chapter 17.

Reticular formation

The reticular formation strongly influences the loop circuits interconnecting cortical and subcortical nuclei. The influence is most direct, lasting, and widespread when excitation reaches diffuse areas of the cortex through the ascending reticular activating system (ARAS), which "keeps the brain awake." The influence is briefer and less widespread when excitation reaches the cortex through the diffuse thalamic nuclei (DTPS). In either case electrodes can be implanted in the BSRF or thalamus, respectively. In anesthetized subjects these areas can be stimulated, and the electrical response of the exposed cortex can be recorded from various sites. A record can be made of a single cell with a microelectrode, or the summed responses of a number of cortical cells can be recorded with a larger electrode.

As in all nerve cells the cortical cell bodies do not reverse polarization, or "fire" (Chapter 4), but their partly depolarized state causes firing of the axons they send to subcortical centers. Stimulation of the ARAS or DTPS causes a change in the polarized condition of the cortical cell bodies and therefore a change in the rate of firing of their axons that lead to subcortical centers. Stimulation of the ARAS results in widespread partial depolarization of cortical cell bodies and increased firing of their axons. A larger electrode on the surface of the cortex records this state as a desynchronized negativity of widespread cortical cell bodies. (Some think the firing of dendrites leading to cell bodies contributes to electrical recordings from the cortex. Whatever the origin of the electrical changes recorded, the recording is called an **electrocorticogram.**) When ARAS stimulation ceases, regular fluctuations in cortical potential are recorded as brain waves. These brain waves can be recorded in humans or animals with electrodes glued to the surface of the scalp (the **electroencephalogram,** or **EEG**). An animal can have electrodes permanently implanted in the ARAS so that he can be "plugged in" for ARAS stimulation at any time, whether he is awake or asleep. The sleeping animal will show a large voltage fluctuation and a regular series of EEG waves. Stimulation of the ARAS will wake the animal to a state of alert attention. At the same time the EEG will show desynchronized negativity, indicating negativity of cortical dendrites and rapid firing of cortical axons to lower centers. The EEG in man likewise indicates the state of activity of widespread cortical neurons. In the relaxed but awake state, the potential of the cortex fluctuates in a regular way so that alpha waves of about 10 Hz are recorded, especially over the occipital lobes. If the subject is startled or is aroused by trying to actively solve problems in mental arithmetic, the alpha pattern disappears and desynchronized activity of the cortex is recorded. If the subject drops off to sleep, the reduced excitation of the cortex by the ARAS is shown in the EEG by larger and lower-frequency brain waves.

Various stages of sleep can be distinguished (Fig. 13-10). Light sleep is called stage 1 sleep. The alpha rhythm is desynchronized, and low-voltage waves of 4 to 6 Hz can be seen; sporadic slower high-voltage delta waves (0 to 3 Hz) are also present. Stage 2 sleep includes spindles, or bursts, of fast waves (14 Hz) against a background of delta waves with K com-

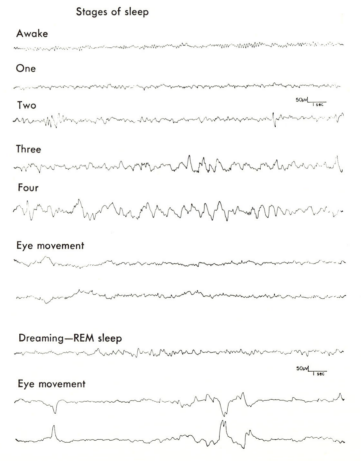

Fig. 13-10. EEG changes with sleep and dreaming in man, and simultaneous recordings of rapid eye movements (REM). (From Johnson, L. C.: U. S. Navy Report no. 66-9, San Diego, Calif., 1966, U. S. Navy Medical Neuropsychiatric Research Unit.)

plexes (a sharp negative variation followed by a positive wave). In stage 3 sleep the spindles disappear, delta is prominent, and some K complexes persist. In stage 4, high-voltage random delta waves dominate the record. Dreaming can be detected by a combintation of stage 1 sleep and rapid eye movements (REM). The eye movements are measured by electrodes placed near the eye muscles. Relations between the EEG and sleep will be discussed more extensively in Chapter 14.

Limbic system

The limbic system, along with the hypothalamus, has been a fruitful area for the study of the neural control of emotion. Parts of the limbic system have also been implicated in learning studies. Papez proposed that nerve impulses underlying emotional arousal originate in the hippocampus. From here they pass to the (hypothalamic) mammillary bodies via the fornix and thence to the anterior thalamic nuclei and cingulate gyrus of the cortex (Fig. 13-8). Early experiments showed that removal of the parts of the neocortex that stimulate this circuit resulted in a placid and docile animal. Lesions of the amygdala and overlying piriform cortex in monkeys and cats cause docility and hypersexuality. Dominance behavior in monkeys is abolished by removing the amygdala. On the other hand, destroying the septal cortex makes the rat very savage for a time. Limbic operations have been performed on man in attempts to reduce "uncontrollable" violence in man with far more variable and controversial results (Chapters 16 and 17). Destruction of the connections between anterior thalamic nuclei and the frontal cortex (prefrontal lobotomy) has already been cited as causing reduced anxiety and impulsiveness. Therefore limbic structures are definitely implicated in emotional behavior. The mechanisms involved will be discussed in Chapter 16.

Learning also involves activity in the limbic system. Kappa waves have been re-corded from the hippocampus as a symptom of successful learning, for example. Evidence has already been cited to show that temporal lobe destruction (including the amygdaloid nuclei) in man impairs the ability to form lasting memory traces. It has also been shown that septal damage impairs the rat's ability to learn passive avoidance habits, whereas hippocampal lesions interfere with the learning of active avoidance habits. Passive avoidance habits require that the animal refrain from a normal response to avoid punishment. A passive avoidance task might require the animal to refrain from stepping off a low platform to avoid shock. In active avoidance the animal performs a response to obtain a reward or to escape punishment. Experiments of this kind will be detailed in Chapter 17.

Hypothalamus

The hypothalamus has been described as closely related to the limbic system and as a focus of somatic and autonomic responses in emotion. The hypothalamus is also involved in *drives*—aroused and sustained external and internal responses to hunger, thirst, sex, and so on. Arousal in emotion or in drive states seems to depend on the posterior and lateral hypothalamic areas that are **ergotropic** in function. These areas stimulate the sympathetic nervous system, which mobilizes visceral responses (such as heart rate, blood glucose, and so on) to meet a crisis (Chapter 5). Glandular response to stress results from connections of the hypothalamus to the pituitary gland —either direct nervous connections or the influence of secretions from hypothalamic neurons (hypothalamic releasing factors). Ergotropic areas seem to organize stereotyped emotional behavior. Rage responses to moderate stimulation occur when the ergotropic centers are released from cortical inhibition by removal of the neocortex. Stimulation of ergotropic centers by implanted electrodes causes rage and attack behavior. The ergotropic centers seem involved in drives, and they arouse and sustain behavior in hungry, thirsty, or sexually deprived animals. The **trophotropic** centers in the anterior and medial hypothalamus, on the other hand, seem to cause parasympathetic activity in animals. The responses resulting are those of emotional quiescence, digestion, satiation, and so on. Lesions in certain trophotropic nuclei can cause an animal to eat and drink to excess, whereas lesions in certain ergotropic nuclei can cause the animal to die of thirst or stravation. This seems to show that ergotropic centers arouse these drives, whereas trophotropic centers signal satiation. General theories of this kind will be outlined in Chapter 15.

CEREBRAL METABOLISM

A review and extension of some of the material of Chapter 2 on cerebral metabolism is essential at this point. Many of the experiments to be recorded in Chapters 14 to 18 involve the effect of drugs on the CNS. Others suggest the role of various neural transmitter substances in complex behavior. To understand these experiments one must know a few principles of general CNS metabolism, the blood-brain barrier, and neural transmitters.

General CNS metabolism

The metabolic rate of any tissue may be measured by its oxygen consumption (Chapter 2). Using this standard, the metabolic rate of the CNS is many times that of any other tissue in the body. The metabolic rate is higher in the gray matter than in the white matter and higher in the brain than in the spinal cord. The ratio of CO_2 given off by a tissue to the uptake of oxygen is the respiratory quotient (RQ) of that tissue. The RQ of the tissue differs, depending on whether fat, protein, or carbohydrate is being utilized as a source of food by the tissue. The RQ of CNS tissue is near unity, which shows that the CNS depends almost solely on blood glucose (a carbo-

hydrate) as a source of food. Unlike other tissues the CNS is dependent on a constant supply of blood glucose and cannot depend on secondary sources of food energy. (This is not true of peripheral nerves, the RQ of which is about 0.8.) As a result of its high metabolic rate, O_2 and glucose are utilized in larger amounts by CNS tissue than by other tissues of the body. The high O_2 and glucose consumption of CNS tissue necessitates a more extensive blood supply than is required by other tissues of the body. The vascular (blood vessel) system of the brain and spinal cord is more extensive than that of any other organ in the body. In man the brain receives blood equal to its weight each minute. Although the brain constitutes only 2% of the total body weight, it receives one third of the total blood output of the heart to the body.

CNS circulation

The brain and spinal cord are covered by three layers of connective tissue (Chapter 5). The outermost layer is the tough fibrous dura mater. Just beneath that layer is the thicker and less dense arachnoid layer. A considerable space, the subarachnoid space, separates the arachnoid layer from the innermost layer, the pia mater. The pia mater is a thin and fragile layer that is closely applied to the brain and spinal cord. All the space beneath the dura and all the ventricles and canals of the brain and spinal cord are filled with cerebrospinal fluid. Cerebrospinal fluid is a clear, plasmalike fluid that is secreted by the circulatory system. It seems to function mainly to cushion the brain and spinal cord, although some believe it may serve a nutritive function as well. The cerebral arteries run in the subarachnoid space between arachnoid and pia layers until they enter the brain, where they branch and form capillaries (Fig. 13-11). Oxygen, carbon dioxide, and glucose exchange between the blood and brain cells takes place across the thin walls of the capillaries. The capillaries then rejoin to form veins that empty into **dural sinuses** formed within the dura mater. The dural sinuses, in turn, empty into major veins, which return to the heart.

The cerebrospinal fluid is formed in another way. There are dense networks of capillaries and supporting tissues, each called a **choroid plexus,** in the lateral, third, and fourth ventricles of the brain. These structures filter out clear cerebrospinal fluid from the brain under pressure (10 to 20 mm. Hg). The fluid circulates from the lateral ventricles into the third ventricle, thence to the fourth ventricle, and out into the subarachnoid space for circulation around the outside of the brain and spinal cord. The cerebrospinal fluid is reabsorbed by small tufts, or villi (sing., villus), of

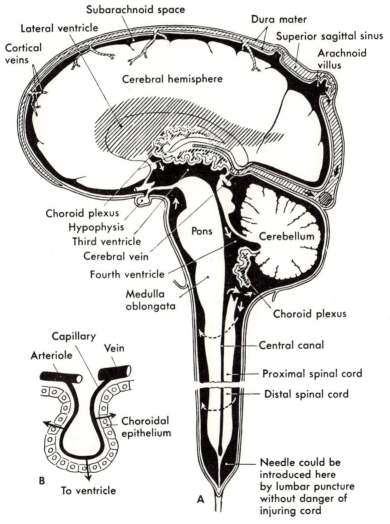

Fig. 13-11. A, Circulation of cerebrospinal fluid *(arrows)*. Note opening in fourth ventricle, where fluid reaches subarachnoid space. Note also one of the arachnoid villi that filters fluid out of the blood. **B,** Formation of cerebrospinal fluid from blood plasma in a choroid plexus. (From Gardner, E. O.: Fundamentals of neurology, ed. 5, Philadephia, 1968, W. B. Saunders Co.)

arachnoid tissue; the villi project into the dural venous sinuses and empty the cerebrospinal fluid into them. The cerebrospinal fluid differs from the blood plasma in that it contains little protein, less glucose, and more chloride and has a lower specific gravity. It is under 10 to 20 mm. Hg pressure and probably has more of a cushioning, protective function than a nutritive role.

Blood-brain barrier

Fluid is filtered from whole blood in two places in the brain: (1) at the choroid plexus, where cerebrospinal fluid is formed, and (2) through the walls of the capillaries throughout the brain, where the extracellular fluid of the brain is formed. For this reason some authors speak of two barriers: (1) a blood–cerebrospinal fluid barrier formed by the capillary walls and epithelium of the choroid plexuses (Fig. 13-11) and (2) a blood-brain barrier formed by the capillary walls and glial cells that surround the capillaries throughout the brain. Since the cerebrospinal fluid probably plays a minor part in brain cell nutrition and metabolism, only the blood-brain barrier will be considered here.

Unlike the capillaries of other tissues the capillaries of the brain are closely surrounded by **glial cells,** types of cells that seem to have both a nutritive and a supporting function for the fragile nerve cells. The blood plasma must pass through the walls of the capillaries in all tissue to form intercellular fluid. This process filters out red blood cells and the largest protein molecules. In the brain the blood plasma must also filter through the glial cells that adhere to the capillaries and pass through the thick masses of reticular fibers that surround the nerve cells. As a result large molecules never reach the fluid surrounding the nerve cells. This phenomenon, known as the blood-brain barrier, is important in several ways; for example, the adenohypophysis (anterior pituitary) puts out more ACTH under stress, which causes the adrenal

cortex to manufacture more corticosterone. Corticosterone reduces blood glucose utilization by other body tissues, but it cannot affect the brain because it does not pass the blood-brain barrier. The brain is thereby assured of a greater supply of blood glucose under stress because other cells are not using as much as they otherwise would use. This is important because brain tissue cannot store blood glucose like liver and muscle cells can; it must depend on a constant supply to function. Glutamic acid will not pass the blood-brain barrier; yet it is one of the essential amino acids required by all the other cells of the body and manufactured by none of them. It may pass the barrier in another form and be reconstituted because it critically affects nerve cell excitability. Despite the amount of filtration involved, extracellular fluid, and therefore extracellular space, occupies about 25% of brain volume, according to tests that depend on known differences in the concentration of certain ions in brain cells, extracellular fluid, and blood.

Neurosecretion

As seen in Chapter 4, nerve cells excite or inhibit one another at synapses by the release of chemical transmitters. Most of the nerve cells of the brain seem to excite one another by the release of acetylcholine (ACh) and are therefore called cholinergic cells. Others excite one another by the release of norepinephrine (noradrenaline) and are called adrenergic cells. Still other pathways use dopamine (dopaminergic) or serotonin. The distinction is especially important in the hypothalamus, where trophotropic cells seem to be cholinergic and ergotropic cells seem to be adrenergic. As pointed out before, anterior hypothalamic cells appear to be cholinergic and control parasympathetic functioning and satiation. Posterior ergotropic cells appear to govern sympathetic function and the arousal of drives. In some cases the difference seems to be one of cell chemistry rather than of location, as will be seen in the discussions on hunger and thirst. Finally, posterior adrenergic cells send fibers to the posterior pituitary gland to control its secretions. These cells also release their neurotransmitters into a portal system of blood vessels running from the posterior pituitary gland to the anterior pituitary gland. When the "neurohormone" secretions of nerve cells reaching the posterior hypothalamus flow to the anterior pituitary, they stimulate the anterior pituitary to release various hormones. Hypothalamic releasing factors also regulate the release of these neurohormones to control the anterior pituitary. The anterior pituitary secretions govern the output of several other endocrine glands. In this manner the functions of the hypothalamus, autonomic nervous system, and endocrine glands are interrelated.

SUMMARY

This chapter presents a model of brain function adequate to deal with the complex behavior to be described in Chapters 14 to 18. The model adds to the reflex model of CNS function given in Chapter 5. The reflex model was adequate for understanding the "simple" phenomena of sensation presented in Chapters 6 to 11 and for dealing with reflexes in Chapter 12. The history of the reflex model was given first. Sherrington's discovery that simple "spinal" reflexes varied somewhat with the posture of the animal showed that interneuron connections changed to modify the simplest behavior. The variability was caused by interneurons supplied by the proprioceptors—balance receptors of the inner ear and kinesthetic receptors of the joints and muscles. It was reasoned that the brain acted merely as a more complex and less fixed set of interneurons between stimulus and response.

The variable nature of these connections and the great number of interneurons would allow enough stimulus-response connections to account for the most complex and variable behavior. Repeated presentations of a stimulus would lead to variable responses in learning because of the many possible interneuron connections. Those connections causing responses that led to reward or avoidance of punishment would become fixed like those of a reflex. The ability to learn and exhibit more complex behavior seemed to parallel the development of the cerebral cortex in animal species. Sensory input and motor output had been traced to the cortex. It was assumed that learning occurred by transcortical association of neurons running from sensory to motor projection areas. To meet the objection that animals without a cortex could learn, it was assumed that the cortex took over this and other complex functions from lower centers (encephalization). The concept seemed valid since the more developed the cortex in a species, the more profound the effect of decortication on sensory, motor, or associative functions. It was decided that the transcortical associative connections must be diffuse ones, however. The affect of cortical lesions on maze learning and retention in rats seemed to depend on the amount of cortex removed rather than on the locus of the lesion. However, the cortex of man is much more specialized and complex than that of the rat. Yet lesions of subcortical nuclei with the stereotaxic apparatus produce as diffuse an impairment of learning behavior as do cortical lesions even in the rat.

Modern research has shown the transcortical association model to be inadequate. The cortex developed in evolution when a primary sensory nucleus for smell began receiving other sensory inputs; then cortical motor control appeared. The sensory cortex evolved in four main stages from reptile to primate. The "secondary" (cortical area II) sensory inputs through the midbrain and then thalamus came before the "classical" (area I) pathways from sense organ to thalamus to cortex. In primates, cortical "association" areas developed that relate "intrinsic" thalamic cortex to the thalamus in a way that is not bound to any given sensory input. The thalamus and cortex of other species (such as the cat) developed largely without intrinsic thalamic nuclei and related cortex. Drawing conclusions about cortical function in man from experiments done with a species whose cortex has evolved in a different way may be misleading. In any case, the correct model for brain function seems to be one of *vertically organized interaction* between cortical and subcortical centers. Anatomical study of the structure of the cerebral cortex bears this model out. The cortex appears to act as a complex set of amplifying interconnections between subcortical nuclei. Encephalization would merely mean an increase in the variety and complexity of this system.

Phylogenetically, the cortex is organized into the allocortex, the transitional cortex, and the neocortex. The allocortex is the oldest phylogenetically, being originally devoted to smell, and is the simplest anatomically. It includes the olfactory bulbs, piriform areas, and hippocampus. The neocortex is the newest and most complex cortex and includes most of the frontal, parietal, occipital, and temporal lobes. The transitional cortex includes the cingulate gyrus, septum, and presubiculum; it interconnects with the allocortex by subcortical nuclei and with the frontal lobes by the anterior thalamus.

Functionally, the neocortex is divided into the frontal lobes and POT areas. The POT areas can be regarded as receptive and integrative, whereas the frontal lobes seem expressive in function. The prefrontal areas mediate complex personality functions, and the POT areas are involved in learning and memory. The sensory inputs to projection areas for vision, audition, and somesthesis form the specific thalamic projection system (STPS). Collaterals of the STPS go to diffuse thalamic nuclei to contribute to the older diffuse thalamic projection system (DTPS) for more widespread cortical effects, including the secondary sensory projection areas. The DTPS may aid in attention to a specific

modality. Collaterals of the STPS also supply the BSRF, parts of which diffusely connect with all cortical areas to form an ascending reticular activating system (ARAS.) The ARAS activates the cortex in waking states of alertness and attention. BSRF cells also increase muscle tone, which feeds back excitatory sensations to the cortex in a descending reticular activating system (DRAS).

Some parts of the brain once devoted to smell (rhinencephalon) interconnect with the transitional cortex to form a loop circuit called the limbic system. The limbic system receives input from the rhinencephalon, neocortex, hypothalamus, and BSRF, and feeds back into all but the smell areas. It includes the septal area, cingulate gyrus, hippocampus, entorhinal cortex, amygdala, and anterior thalamus. The limbic system is involved in emotion, learning, and memory; it connects with the frontal lobes by the anterior thalamus and with the POT areas by the septum, hippocampus, and amygdala.

The hypothalamus is involved in the limbic system by the fornix from the hippocampus and the medial forebrain bundle from the BSRF and rhinencephalon. It regulates the autonomic nervous system, emotional responses, homeostasis, drives, and endocrine reactions (by affecting the pituitary gland). Anterior and medial parasympathetic activity in the hypothalamus is trophotropic, and responses are quiescence and satiation. Posterior and lateral sympathetic excitation is ergotropic, causing drive arousal and emotional responses. The medial hypothalamic area receives excitation from the rhinencephalon (by the fornix) and ARAS and connects to the pituitary and lateral hypothalamic zones. The lateral hypothalamic zones relate to the septum and rhinencephalon, and to the ARAS by the medial forebrain bundle (MFB).

Operations called prefrontal lobectomy, lobotomy, or topectomy result in reduced anxiety, impulsiveness, and indifference to pain, suggesting a complex role for these areas. POT temporal lobe damage results in impaired ability to form lasting memory in man. Frontal lesions disturb delayed reaction in monkeys. POT damage also results in aphasia, agnosia, and retroactive amnesia (RA). Language functions are nearly always found in the left hemisphere, especially in right-handed subjects. Brain damage to specific areas on the frontal cortex causes expressive aphasias. The right hemisphere seems more inductive and involved in space perception and form recognition. Split-brain experiments in cats and monkeys show that learning can be confined to one hemisphere by restricting sensory information to that hemisphere. With the appearance of handedness in primates, the corpus callosum appears to prevent the learning of some habits by both hemispheres. Special testing techniques with split-brain humans result in more evidence for hemispheric specialization.

Reticular influence on the cortex can be seen in the electroencephalogram (EEG) in man or animals. ARAS stimulation in animals desynchronizes the EEG as does alert attention in man. Alpha waves are typical of the relaxed state, and four stages of sleep can be distinguished by brain wave patterns. Dreaming is indicated by rapid eye movements (REM).

The Papaz circuit in the limbic system is implicated in emotion and learning. Amygdaloid lesions cause docility. Septal lesions interfere with passive avoidance, and hippocampal lesions interfere with active avoidance. Limbic psychosurgery in man has more unpredictable effects on emotional behavior.

The hypothalamus is involved in drives as well as in emotional behavior. Posterior ergotropic centers control drive arousal and rage, whereas anterior trophotropic centers stimulate satiation and quiescence.

Cerebral metabolism is important in complex behavior. The metabolic rate of the CNS is quite high and dependent on a constant glucose and oxygen supply. The cerebrospinal fluid is filtered from the blood in the choroid plexuses of the ventricles, is circulated through them and through the subdural and subarachnoid spaces, is absorbed by arachnoid villi, and is delivered to dural venous sinuses. The cerebrospinal fluid serves a cushioning protective function for the brain. The intercellular fluid of the brain is filtered through glial cells that surround the capillary walls as well as through the capillary walls themselves. This filtration forms a blood-brain barrier; thus the brain's extracellular fluid does not contain molecules as large as those in the extracellular fluid of other tissue. The blood-brain barrier keeps out corticosterone, which reduces blood glucose use by other cells, and the essential amino acid, glutamic acid, which excites brain cells.

Nerve cells are cholinergic or adrenergic, depending on whether their neural transmitters are acetylcholine (ACh) or norepinephrine (noradrenaline). Dopamine and serotonin are other transmitters. In the hypothalamus, trophotropic cells are probably cholinergic, and ergotropic cells are adrenergic. The hypothalamus stimulates the anterior pituitary by neurosecretions.

READINGS

Chauchard, P.: The brain, New York, 1962, Grove Press, Inc.

Gardner, E. O.: Fundamentals of neurology, ed. 5, Philadelphia, 1968, W. B. Saunders Co.

Gazzangia, M. S.: The split brain in man, Sci. Am. **217:**21-29, Aug. 1967. (W. H. Freeman Co. Reprint No. 508.)

Gazzangia, M. S.: One brain—two minds? Am. Scientist **60:**311-317, 1972.

Geshwind, N.: Language and the brain, Sci. Am. **226:**76-83, April 1972. (W. H. Freeman Co. Reprint No. 1246.)

Geshwind, N.: The aphraxias: Neural mechanisms of disorders of learned movement, Am. Scientist **63:**188-195, 1975.

Luria, A. R.: The functional organization of the brain, Sci. Am. **222:**66-78, March 1970. (W. H. Freeman Co. Reprint No. 526.)

McCleary, R. A., and Moore, R. Y.: Subcortical mechanisms in behavior, New York, 1965, Basic Books, Inc.

Milner, P., and Clickman, S., editors: Cognitive processes and the brain, New Work, 1965, D. Van Nostrand Co., Inc.

Moruzzi, G., and Magoun, H. W.: Brainstem reticular formation and activation of the EEG, Electroenceph. Clin. Neurophysiol. **1:**455-473, 1949. (Bobbs-Merrill Reprint No. P-256.)

Pfeiffer, J.: The human brain, New York, 1962, Pyramid Publications, Inc.

Sperry, R. W.: The great cerebral commissure, Sci. Am. **210:**42-52, Jan. 1964. (W. H. Freeman Reprint No. 174.)

Von Neumann, J.: The computer and the brain, New Haven, Conn., 1958, Yale University Press.

Walter, W. G.: The living brain, New York, 1963, W. W. Norton & Co., Inc.

chapter 14

States of consciousness

OVERVIEW

States of consciousness may be defined by physiological as well as psychological methods, at least in extent or intensity. Alert attention, resting wakefulness, "dreaming" sleep and "dreamless" sleep, and meditation will be treated in this chapter.

The sleep and arousal topic begins with Kleitman's evolutionary theory of sleep. The theory distinguishes between the wakefulness of necessity seen in human children and lower animals when they are hungry, thirsty, or uncomfortable and the wakefulness of choice found in adult humans and some adult animals. Wakefulness of choice involves a single sleep period and a single waking period during each day and is less dependent on the need state of the animal. Kleitman's ideas about the neural mechanisms underlying sleep and wakefulness are followed by modern theories and experiments on centers in the brain controlling sleep and wakefulness. Evidence has been obtained by use of the electroencephalograph (EEG, Chapter 13) and eye-movement recordings about the nature of human sleep patterns. Four stages of sleep are defined by the EEG patterns. A sleep stage that is often acompanied by rapid eye movements (REM) is associated with dream recall. The course of human sleep during the night is traced. Then certain phenomena of sleep disturbance that result from sleep deprivation are considered, as well as the effects on sleep of sedatives, biochemicals, alcoholism, and addiction. Evolutionary development, sleep disorders, electrosleep, sleep humors, and human growth hormone are other topics. Modern theories of the role

of REM sleep follow. The discussion closes with the topics of attention, vigilance, and meditation.

PHYSIOLOGICAL AND PSYCHOLOGICAL STATES

Psychological states of awareness (or the lack of awareness) result from physiological changes in the brain. This point of view takes no position on whether any particular state of awareness is necessary to the behavior or lack of behavior that follows or whether the psychological state is just a "by-product" of brain changes that govern behavior. In either case, research has shown that we can learn much about the state of awareness of the individual subject by recording the electrical and chemical changes going on in the brain.

States of awareness

Most of what we know about brain activity and states of awareness comes from monitoring EEG records in human subjects. Animal subjects cannot report states of awareness to compare with brain waves going on at the time. Clues provided by human research have, however, led to important animal experiments. These experiments concern biochemical changes at specific places in the brain that appear to govern states of awareness because they result in the same EEG changes found in man.

Changes in brain waves and the biochemical changes that underlie them tell us about the intensity or extent of awareness but do not reveal conscious content. We can determine whether the subject is alert and attentive or daydreaming, whether he is asleep and whether he is probably dreaming. A beginning has been made on finding out how brain activity may differ in the states of meditation practiced by eastern philosophies (Zen, Yoga, and transcendental meditation, for example). The utility of an alert and vigilant state to behavior is obvious when conditions demand it. The role of other states of awareness and the changes in the brain that underlie them are less obvious. We can assume that sleep and dreaming are necessary to brain function and play a role in behavior because they occur regularly in all normal subjects. The utility of these states of the brain for brain function and behavior is the subject of several interesting theories but a general theory of the role of states of brain awareness has not yet emerged.

SLEEP AND ACTIVATION

A motivated animal is not asleep. The more motivated an animal, the more *activated* he seems, as the high level of CNS activity is accompanied by much restless behavior. In this sense, sleep was once believed to be the lowest point on a scale of CNS activation that extends through waking activity to extreme arousal. Sleep is now known to be more complex. It is a biochemically different state of the brain, as compared to the waking state, and it differs from the waking state in qualitative as well as quantitative ways.

A certain amount of sleep is required for normal CNS functioning. Sleep deprivation studies show that short mental tasks, such as arithmetic, do not suffer from loss of sleep if the subject is well motivated; however, long-term alertness does suffer, and bodily discomfort is felt. Animal studies have revealed that forced and long-continued wakefulness results in death—thus sleep is required (a need) for existence, as is food or water. In this vein, investigators sought for years to find out why we sleep. Kleitman, on the other hand, learned much about sleep by asking the opposite question: Why do we stay awake?

Kleitman's evolutionary theory of sleep and wakefulness

In primitive animals and in children, sleep seems to be a more "natural," or homeostatic, state than waking activity. Infants and many lower animals sleep most of the time, unless they are aroused by bodily needs such as thirst, hunger, or discomfort. A human baby, for example, sleeps most of the day and night, waking at intervals when hunger or the discomfort of a wet diaper serves as a motivating stimulus to wakefulness. The wakefulness that results was called **wakefulness of necessity** by Kleitman, since it was necessary for the infant to awaken to satisfy his hunger or to remove the source of the discomfort. Wakefulness of necessity is **polyphasic,** that is, it occurs in several phases, or cycles, during the course of a 24-hour day. The infant awakens because of the stimulus of a bodily need and returns to a contented state of natural sleep soon after his needs are satisfied. With growth and development, however, the child sleeps for longer periods without waking and stays awake for still longer periods. When even the afternoon nap is abandoned, the youngster sleeps for a continuous 8- to 10-hour period at night and remains awake for a continuous daylight period, during which most of his bodily needs are satisfied. Kleitman called such a sleep cycle **monophasic,** since it consists of a single sleep and waking cycle each day. The continuous waking period he called **wakefulness of choice,** since it did not depend on the stimulus of an immediate need. He suggested that wakefulness of necessity depends on a primitive center in the diencephalon (see below) stimulated directly by bodily needs. With evolution the cerebral cortex developed, allowing an increase in learning ability that varied from species to species. Need satisfaction became associated with daylight (except for nocturnal animals), and there were more stimuli to arouse the animal during daylight hours. The cortex began to control the center governing sleep. Cortical activity as well as bodily needs stimulated the primitive "sleep center" (really a waking center). The animal *learned* to remain awake during daylight hours, when the cortex was stimulated by environmental events. With reduced stimulation at night the cortex ceased to arouse the "sleep center" (or, rather, the waking center), and the center failed to drive the cortex and other parts of the brain to keep the animal awake.

Neural mechanisms

Kleitman suspected the existence of a sleep center because of the symptoms shown by victims of sleeping sickness (encephalitis lethargica), when the disease damaged the diencephalon. (In parts of Africa, sleeping sickness is common; the spirochete is carried by the tsetse fly.) Victims of one variety of the disorder seemed to show only the primitive wakefulness of necessity, and Kleitman suggested that their "sleep center" (waking center) had been destroyed. The center was not aroused by cortical activity during daylight hours. As a result, the cortex, rather than the sleep center, "kept the brain awake," but only when it was directly stimulated by strong stimuli such as bodily discomfort, hunger, thirst, or other intense inputs. Dogs show a relatively monophasic sleep pattern in adulthood. If decorticated, however, they revert to the polyphasic sleep cycle of puppyhood. Wakefulness of necessity in this case is maintained by the subcortical center instead of the cortex.

Ranson was able to confirm the waking center in the posterior hypothalamus in the monkey. Lesions in this area produced somnambulant monkeys that slept except when aroused by intense stimulation. There appears to be a waking center in the posterior hypothalamus, which is an important part of the activating system of the BSRF (ascending reticular activating system, or ARAS).

The importance of the ARAS to states of alertness and attention can be seen in several ways. For instance, electrodes can be permanently implanted in the ARAS of a cat and used to stimulate the ARAS electrically. Such a stimulus will immediately rouse a sleeping cat to a state of alert attention. A similar stimulus delivered to areas located elsewhere in the brain has no such effect. When the ARAS is stimulated, the EEG of the sleeping cat is transformed immediately, from the high-voltage slow waves characteristic of sleep into the desynchronized low-voltage activity typical of alert attention. The ARAS seems much more important to attention and wakefulness than the sensory pathways of STPS. The pathways of the STPS are carried in the laterally placed white matter of the brainstem, whereas the ARAS occupies the central core of the brainstem. Cutting the lateral sensory (somesthetic and auditory) pathways in the midbrain of a cat has no obvious effect on behavior, surprisingly enough. The sleeping cat is aroused as readily as before by a sound stimulus, although the STPS is not carrying the sensory information to the cortex. Perhaps the ARAS serves in its stead. In any case the cat remains as alert as before, and the EEG shows the normal wakeful pattern. If the central core of the midbrain is severed, however, a different result follows, even when the lateral STPS pathways are left intact. The operation abolishes normal waking behavior (at least for a few days) and the desynchronized EEG pattern that accompanies it. The cat shows the slow-wave EEG pattern typical of sleep, and the most intense stimuli fail to wake it. Evidently the ARAS is necessary to wakefulness, although the part of the ARAS located in the posterior hypothalamus (waking center) may play a vital role in waking behavior and brain activity.

The ARAS (and associated DTPS) shows an inherent, or "spontaneous," 3 to 5 Hz rhythm of electrical activity, which seems important to its function in arousing the brain. Implanted electrodes show that this rhythm is intensified in alert states of arousal and suppressed during sleep. The spontaneous 3 to 5 Hz waves seem subject to both excitatory and inhibitory influences from other brain centers (including the cortex) and from sensory input. A scheme of the many influences on the inherent wakefulness rhythm of the BSRF can be seen in Fig. 14-1. Metabolic influences on the inherent BSRF waking rhythm can be excitatory or inhibitory. The excitatory influences come into play when the metabolism of the internal environment is upset by bodily needs of one kind or another. For example, an excess of carbon dioxide stimulates nerve cells in the medulla, which, in turn, stimulate the BSRF.

A stress-induced increase in norepinephrine can directly stimulate the BSRF. In either case the BSRF increases its 3 to 5 Hz inherent rhythm. Parts of the BSRF act as an ARAS in stimulating the cortex and other parts of the brain to arouse the animal to a state of vigilance and attention. This state represents wakefulness of necessity in Kleitman's terms. The BSRF, especially the hypothalamic reticular cells, arouse the animal because of bodily need or discomfort. In the same manner excitatory inputs from the sense organs can stimulate the ARAS by collateral afferents to

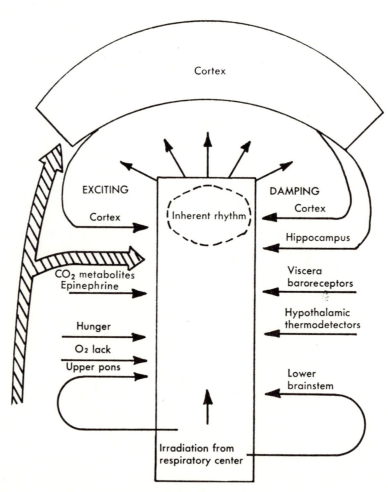

Fig. 14-1. Factors affecting brainstem reticular formation ARAS to influence sleep or wakefulness. *Large arrow on left* represents sensory input. (From Oswald, I.: Sleeping and waking, Amsterdam, 1962, Elsevier Publishing Co.)

cause wakefulness of necessity by the "waking centers" of the ARAS. Inhibitory influences from visceral and other internal receptors can reduce the activity of the BSRF when the animal's needs have been satisfied, terminating wakefulness of necessity by direct inhibition as well as by reduced excitation.

Wakefulness of choice is represented by the interactions of the cerebral cortex and the wakefulness centers of the BSRF. The cortex can excite or inhibit the inherent rhythms of the BSRF to arouse or not arouse the brain (Fig. 14-1). Action of the cortex on the BSRF depends partly on the sensory input to the cortex, which tends to be greater during the day than the night for most animals that develop a monophasic sleep pattern through conditioning.

EEG during sleep and wakefulness

The **electroencephalogram (EEG)** is a recording made by cementing small electrodes to the scalp and by picking up and amplifying gross electrical changes in potential from the surface of the cortex through the skull (Chapter 13). If the recording was taken from the surface of the cortex (**electrocorticogram, or ECG**), these potential changes would amount to about 1 mv. (1/1000 volt). As measured at the surface of the skull, the electrical changes are as small as 1 μv. (1/1,000,000 volt). The changes in potential are amplified and used to drive an ink-writing oscillograph. These changes wax and wane in a rhythmic fashion and may represent the moment-to-moment state of partial depolarization of nerve cells or the firing of dendrities in the more superficial layers of the cortex. In either case, the more depolarized the cells, the more rapidly their axons are firing and, roughly speaking, the more "active" is the cortex. In states of extreme arousal the EEG is desynchronized; many of the cells are partly depolarized (negative), and they fire their axons at a rapid rate. As the cortex becomes less excited, the cells appear to wax and wane in potential in a synchronous fashion, producing regular brain waves of voltage change. Generally speaking, the less excited the cortex, the lower is the frequency of the brain waves and the greater is their amplitude. In other words, a less excited cortex features brain cells whose potentials change at a slower and rhythmic rate with greater amplitude. These and other predictable changes occur in the EEG pattern with reduced excitation of the cortex, from aroused excitation through a state of resting wakefulness, dozing, and sleep. The brain waves during sleep can be compared to how much stimulation is required to wake the subject, and a scale of EEG changes with sleep has been constructed. The most widely used scale of this kind was pub-

Table 14-1. Scoring criteria for the EEG*

Stage W (wakefulness)	EEG containing alpha activity and/or low-voltage, mixed-frequency activity
Movement time (MT)	Scoring epoch during which polygraph record is obscured by movements of subject
Stage 1	Relatively low-voltage, mixed-frequency activity without rapid eye movements (REM)
Stage 2	Sleep spindles of 12 to 14 Hz and K complexes on a background of relatively low-voltage, mixed-frequency EEG activity
Stage 3	Moderate amounts of high-amplitude, slow-wave activity
Stage 4	Large amounts of high-amplitude, slow-wave activity
Stage NREM (non-REM)	Stages 1, 2, 3, and 4 combined
Stage REM	Relatively low-voltage, mixed-frequency EEG in conjunction with episodic REMs and low-amplitude electromyogram (EMG)

*Based on data from Rechtschaffen, A., and Kales, A., editors: A manual of standardized terminology, techniques, and scoring system for sleep stages of human subjects, Bethesda, Md., 1968, National Institutes of Health, Pub. no. 204, U.S. Department of Health, Education, and Welfare.

lished by Dement and Kleitman. It has been extended and standardized by others (Table 14-1).

In the scale four stages of sleep are added to the patterns that distinguish the aroused state from the resting but alert state. In the aroused state, as indicated above, the cortex is desynchronized, so that few regular rhythmic brain waves are seen. The **alpha rhythm** is dominant in the resting state of wakefulness of most human subjects. The alpha rhythm is a 10 to 14 Hz pattern of low and slightly irregular amplitude (Fig. 13-10). This pattern shows its greatest amplitude from electrodes in the occipital region. Some subjects show a slightly faster low-amplitude beta rhythm. As the subject goes to sleep, differences in the EEG pattern occur. Four stages of sleep can be distinguished in the EEG pattern. Stage 1 occurs when the subject is dozing and can be easily aroused. Its EEG pattern is dominated by a low-voltage, mixed-frequency pattern, mostly in the 2 to 7 Hz range. Sleep spindles and K complexes are absent. (Sleep spindles are brief bursts of 12 to 14 Hz activity; K complexes consist of a single sharp negative wave followed by a positive component.) Slow eye movements are present, but rapid eye movements (REMs, see below) are absent. Stage 2 sleep is defined by the presence of sleep spindles and K complexes. Stage 3 is defined by the presence of waves of 2 to 7 Hz or slower in 20% to 50% of the record. Slow high-amplitude waves are called **delta waves** when their frequency is 2 to 7 Hz. Stage 4 is defined by the presence of delta waves in over 50% of the record. A distinction between slow-wave sleep (stages 3 and 4, or SWS) and light sleep (stage 1) is sufficient for most investigations, however.

During the night the amount of time spent in each sleep stage varies with the subject. For example, some people never demonstrate stage 4 sleep. However, all subjects show *phasic* cycles in stages of sleep during the night, shifting back and forth from stage 3 or 4 to stage 1 or 2. Slow-wave sleep and REM sleep cycles total 90 to 100 minutes in length. When averaged out over the course of a night's sleep, the typical subject spends more time in slow-wave sleep stages than in stage 1 during the first 2 or 3 hours of sleep. In the last 2 or 3 hours of sleep increasing amounts of time are spent in stage 1, and REMs are more frequent. However, if one prevents slow-wave sleep for a night or two, by waking the subject each time he shows a stage 3 or 4 sleep pattern, the subject will spend a greater part of his sleep period in slow-wave sleep on the subsequent night.

Dreaming is often accompanied by rapid eye movements. If the subject is awakened during REM sleep, he is more likely to recall that he had been dreaming than if he had been awakened during non-REM sleep. If an electrode is placed near the "corner" of each eye, and another is placed at an indifferent point, such as the earlobe, eye movements will be detected as a change in the potential between the electrodes (because the eye is polarized between the front and back of the eyeball). In slow-wave sleep, the eyes are motionless or move slowly. As REM sleep begins, the eyes often begin to move rapidly, largely in a back-and-forth scanning motion. The recording of REMs is accompanied by a change in the EEG from other stages to stage 1. The change from other stages to stage 1 has been called an E-1, or emergent stage 1.

If REM and E-1 are taken as signs of dreaming, there is evidence that dreams can last as long as an hour. Nearly all subjects have three or four dreams during the night, whether they remember the dreams or not. Subjects have been prevented from dreaming by waking them every time they showed the E-1 and REM pattern, for three or four nights. Compared with subjects who were awakened equally often during slow-wave sleep, the REM-deprived subjects were reported to be more irritable and anxious during their waking hours. If REM-deprived subjects are permitted uninterrupted sleep on subsequent nights, they will dream more (by REM criteria) for a night or two. These observations have led some to speculate that REM sleep is a symptom of some metabolic activity of the brain that is necessary for its proper development or functioning during sleep. Infants spend more time in REM sleep than do adults (up to one half of sleep periods); as the polyphasic sleep cycle gives way progressively to the monophasic cycle, less time is spent in REM sleep. Observers have speculated that longer periods of REM sleep are necessary for the infant, who sleeps more than the adult and whose brain would not otherwise be active enough of the time for proper development.

Paradoxically, it is harder to wake a cat from REM sleep than from deeper stages of sleep. Cats showing REM sleep are harder to wake, even by ARAS stimulation. This is not the case for humans; man seems to be more alert after being awakened from REM sleep than from non-REM sleep. The brain of the cat seems to be more under the control of a center in the pons during REM sleep than subject to outside stimulation. In the BSRF of the rostral pons there is a nucleus (nucleus pontis caudalis) whose destruction abolishes REM sleep in cats. These cats show the other normal stages of sleep at first, but their condition progresses to insomnia and finally death. On the other hand, a decorticate cat shows nothing but slow-wave sleep; thus perhaps the cortex is necessary for REM sleep. (Normal cats do not display slow-wave sleep.)

Studies by Jouvet on cats have pointed to chemical differences in the brain between light (dreamless?) sleep and REM sleep and have helped identify nerve centers that may be responsible for each state. In cats, during paradoxical sleep (REM sleep), the neck muscles are completely relaxed

and the cat is hard to waken; yet the EEG shows E-1 stage activity and the cat shows movements (dreaming?). In non-REM (stage 2) sleep, the cat's neck muscles show some tension and the cat is easily awakened. Certain midline nuclei in the brainstem (raphe nuclei) produce serotonin, a hormonelike substance found throughout the brain. If most of these nuclei are destroyed, the cat becomes sleepless (less than 10% of the time spent in sleep compared to 66% in the normal cat). On the other hand, certain nuclei of the pons (locus ceruleus, output portion of the nucleus pontis caudalis—see preceding paragraph) produce epinephrine. When these nuclei are destroyed, paradoxical E-1 (REM) sleep is abolished. In the cat, then, serotonin produced by the raphe nuclei may stimulate non-REM sleep, whereas epinephrine produced by nuclei of the pons may result in REM sleep. It is interesting to note, however, that the slow-wave stages (3 and 4) of sleep in man (who sleeps much less) are not reported for the cat. Jouvet has also found that inhibiting the production of serotonin causes reversible insomnia, whereas destruction of the raphe nucleus leads to fatal insomnia (inability to sleep). In an important theory he proposes that production of serotonin by the raphe nuclei initiates stage 2 sleep. (In man, slow-wave sleep always occurs during the first part of the night, except in children.) The serotonin stimulates the locus ceruleus to produce epinephrine. Epinephrine production results in paradoxical sleep; then the whole cycle begins again. Jouvet finds that rat brain serotonin is increased during the day, the period of time when these animals normally sleep; however, serotonin is reduced in the brains of rats who have been deprived of REM sleep.

Sleep phenomena

It is evident from Jouvet's work that sleep involves more than one biochemical state of the brain. An examination of some normal and abnormal phenomena of sleep may aid our understanding of the way in which these states relate to one another and the way in which they interact with the waking state. More background of this sort will contribute to a critical examination of modern sleep theories—theories that concern the role of the states of sleep in man.

Patterns of sleep. In one English study of 240 subjects, 70% were found to sleep less than 8 hours a day. Men in the sample tended to sleep slightly longer than women. Age was also a factor: middle-aged people (40 to 59 years) slept longer than younger (20 to 39) or older (60 to 79) subjects. Duration of sleep was longer on weekends, indicating that some kind of "sleep debt" was accumulated during the workweek. This was particularly true for workers on rotating shifts—nurses, policemen, and the like—who have difficulty establishing regular sleep habits.

Sleep deprivation. Studies of sleep deprivation have generally been of three types: (1) total sleep deprivation, (2) deprivation of REM sleep, and (3) deprivation of slow-wave sleep.

Total sleep deprivation studies are typified by one experiment in which four men were kept awake for 205 hours. The subjects experienced a gradual increase in fatigue, as well as a decline in perceptual, cognitive, and psychomotor abilities, as shown by appropriate tests. After the fifth day they appeared to obtain a "second wind"; that is, their performances returned to normal after they were sufficiently aroused. Episodes of brief disorientation and of brief hallucinations were experienced by the subjects—one even went briefly berserk at 200 hours—but no evidence of psychosis was seen. Follow-up studies of the men after several months showed no evidence that the experience had had any permanent effects on them.

Experiments that deprive the subject of either REM sleep or slow-wave sleep have also been carried out. (As previously noted, REM sleep is associated with dream recall

and epinephrine activity in a nucleus of the pons; slow-wave sleep has been associated with serotonin activity in the raphe nuclei.) The usual procedure is to wake the subject every time his EEG record shows evidence of REM sleep, or every time the record shows slow (delta) wave activity. (Although the subject's sleep is interrupted, it is of normal duration.) In the REM-deprivation studies, REM "attempts" increase over as many as seven successive nights. On recovery nights of uninterrupted sleep the incidence of REM sleep increases by as much as 30% over normal, in a "rebound" effect that suggests that a "need" for REM sleep has been built up by the deprivation. Deprivation of stage 4 sleep for two nights also leads to a "rebound" of 60%, suggesting that stage 4 sleep may be more important to the brain than REM sleep. This idea is further supported by the results from experiments in which subjects are restricted to 3 hours of sleep per night. Their sleep profile of early slow-wave sleep and of REM sleep, which occurs later in the sleep period, does not change. As a result, they "lose" more REM sleep than slow-wave sleep. Despite this, stage 4 sleep dominates their EEG record on recovery nights, when they sleep as long as they wish.

A review of the sleep literature suggests that poor sleepers—those who awake often during the night—show records that are deficient in REM sleep. This is often true of people who work night shifts and sleep in the daytime. On the other hand, elderly people are frequently poor sleepers, and their records show deficiencies in stage 4 sleep. This is also true of many middle-aged people. Within limits the distribution of sleep between REM sleep and slow-wave sleep seems more important than sleep duration.

There also appears to be a relationship between sleep stages and body temperature. For most of us who sleep from 11 or 12 P.M. until 7 or 8 A.M., there is a regular daily cycle of body temperature change.

Body temperature is low early in the morning, rises to a plateau during the afternoon, rises still higher in the evening, and falls during the night. Daytime nap records show more REM sleep, and evening nap records show a greater incidence of delta waves. Thus REM sleep accompanies a lower body temperature than does delta sleep, and delta waves are found when the body temperature is higher. During normal sleeping hours more delta waves are found in the early hours of the night, when body temperature is high. More REM sleep is found later in the night, when body temperature is falling. Thus persons who travel by jet, from one time zone to another, often experience sleep disturbances. Their "biological clocks" of daily body temperature and sleep cycles have been set to the daily cycle of the time zone in which they live. They must readjust their circadian rhythms to a time that may be 6 or 8 hours different. If they use sedatives to get to sleep at a new hour, they may experience REM deprivation (see below). Further evidence that body temperature and sleep are related is found in an experiment using cats. A diathermy machine, similar to those which create heat in the deeper layers of muscles to relieve cramps, was employed. Diathermic warming of the preoptic and anterior hypothalamic areas induced relaxation and normal sleep in these animals. The areas thus warmed are important "centers" for the regulation of both body temperature and sleep.

The evolutionary development of REM sleep. REM sleep is absent in fish, probably absent in reptiles, present (but of brief duration) in birds, and present in all mammals studied, including the opossum, the elephant, and man. This suggests that the development of REM sleep parallels the development of the cerebral cortex in evolutionary history. Fish and reptiles have no cortex. The cortex in birds is limited to a small area that serves vision. Mammals, on the other hand, all have a complete cerebral cortex, although the extent of its development varies from species to species.

Autonomic activity and sleep. During non-REM (NREM, or slow-wave) sleep, the electromyograph (EMG) activity is suppressed, indicating muscle relaxation in man (muscle relaxation in the cat occurs during REM or paradoxical sleep). Reflexes are also suppressed, which would seem to indicate a less active nervous system. However, the autonomic nervous system shows more activity during sleep than it does in a relaxed waking state. Changes in heart rate, blood pressure, skin resistance (indicating sweat gland activity), and respiration are seen. The onset of autonomic activity is usually signaled by the spontaneous (unpredictable) appearance of K complexes in stage 2 sleep. Skin resistance fluctuations ("GSR storms") increase if the subject's sleep pattern then changes to SWS.

Drugs and REM deprivation. Barbiturates and most other sedatives suppress REM sleep. They appear to act by suppressing the activity of the brain and preventing the occurrence of the light sleep stage (stage 1) that always accompanies REM sleep. Alcohol also depresses neural activity, but it has different effects on sleep. Alcoholics frequently suffer night terrors and insomnia (inability to sleep). Both slow-wave sleep and REM sleep are reduced. Perhaps alcohol interferes with serotonin metabolism. As previously noted, an increase in the secretion of serotonin from the raphe nuclei is believed to be responsible for initiating the sleep cycle.

Sleep disorders. The most common sleep disorders are enuresis (bed-wetting), somnambulism (sleepwalking), night terrors (waking suddenly in a frightened state), and nightmares (bad dreams, technically called incubus). All four are commonly assumed to be caused or accompanied by dreaming as in the usual association of nightmares with bad dreams. EEG and eye movement recordings have now shown this assumption to be false (Broughton). All four disorders occur during rapid arousal from slow-wave sleep. Any REM sleep (dreaming) that occurs follows the end of the sleep-disorder episode. The response of bed-wetting may trigger a dream; then if the subject wakes he may have incorporated bed-wetting into the content of his dream. Sleepwalking occurs during slow-wave sleep; the subject is hard to wake during the episode and then seldom reports a coherent dream. The sleep terror (pavor nocturnus) is common in children and not unusual in adults—the child sits up screaming, emotional, and staring wide-eyed at something he imagines—dream recall is rare and fragmented. The nightmare (incubus and succubus) is more common in adults. All the signs of anxiety like sweating, trembling, and heavy breathing are present and the subject may cry out. If wakened, he reports a terrifying situation like being suffocated or crushed, rather than a sequence of events in a narrative dream. (This is not to deny terrifying dreams that occur during REM sleep but cause no respiratory symptoms of the sort described.) The subject seldom recalls the attack the following morning. The four disorders are classified together because the first three are more common in children, two or all three of the first three disorders may occur in the same subject, and one or more of the three often shows up in the subject's family history. Since all four result during rapid arousal from slow-wave sleep, they could be more properly termed *disorders of arousal,* although the question of what triggers the disorders remains unanswered.

Electrosleep. It has been known since the turn of the century that passing a low-voltage intermittent current through an animal's brain induces a state resembling sleep, although the brain structures affected by this treatment remain a mystery. During the last 20 years, the phenomenon has been intensely investigated in Russia; little work has been done outside of eastern Europe, although the equipment is commercially available here. Electrodes are placed over the eyes and behind the ears and a low-volt-

age intermittent direct current is used (pulse duration 0.1-1 msec., frequency 5 to 100 per second, intensity 0.4-8 milliamps, treatment duration 30 to 60 minutes, 5 to 10 daily treatments). The patients report a tingling sensation, but no discomfort. Sleep may or may not occur, depending on the current used; so electrosleep may be a misnomer. The treatment has received little experimental evaluation; the Russian studies are largely clinical reports of therapeutic effects in the treatment of sleep disorders, anxiety, brain disease, and a variety of symptoms from asthma to hypertension (high blood pressure).

Humoral factors. The search for a hormone or a natural hypnogenic chemical that induces sleep is an old one, with little in the way of reliable results until recently. Newer methods of separating brain chemicals according to their molecular weight (gel filtration) have renewed interest in research of this kind in Europe. Stimulation of a specific area in the thalamus of the rabbit induces continuous slow-wave sleep. A fraction of tissue fluid of defined chemical properties from the sleeping rabbits was injected continuously into the ventricles of the brain of normal rabbits for a period of about a half hour. Progressively over the first few minutes of this period, the recorded delta-wave activity nearly doubles; during the last part of the period, the animal shows all the behavioral signs of sleep. Control animals that were treated in a similar way with other chemical fractions from the sleeping rabbits showed none of these effects. The research is not yet extensive enough to evaluate in terms of normal sleep mechanisms.

Human growth hormone. The most recent and active field of sleep research concerns the release of somatotrophic hormone (STH, Chapter 3) from the anterior pituitary and during slow-wave sleep (EEG stages 3 and 4). (STH is called human growth hormone, or HGH in these studies.) Apparently HGH not only regulates normal growth, especially during adolescence. but also plays a role in day-to-day metabolism. HGH is released in response to stress, along with pituitary activation of the thyroid and adrenal glands. In the waking subject, HGH output is stimulated by low blood glucose (hypoglycemia) and suppressed by high blood glucose (hyperglycemia); the effect is reduced in obese subjects, but malnourished subjects respond even to glucose administration with HGH release. Apparently the CNS reacts to the nutritional state of the body by controlling HGH release in the waking state. During slow-wave sleep, however, hyperglycemia does not suppress the output of HGH; increased HGH output is a reliable response to slow-wave sleep. Research is now going on to clarify other endocrine gland responses to HGH release during slow-wave sleep; the results have not yet fallen into a theoretically understandable pattern, but the approach seems to be a promising one.

Modern sleep theories: role of REM sleep

Brain development. As previously noted, infants, as compared with adults, spend much more of their time in sleep. It is also true that they spend much more time in REM sleep than do adults. REM sleep time is greatest *before* birth, and the amount of REM sleep diminishes as the individual matures to adulthood and less and less total time is spent in sleep. This pattern of development has prompted some investigators (Roffwarg and associates) to propose that REM sleep plays a role in the development of the brain. They assert that during slow-wave sleep the brain is not active enough to establish the necessary sensory and motor pathways in the developing infant. Since the infant spends so much total time in sleep, the neural activity of REM sleep substitutes for waking activity, in this regard.

Dispersing excess activity. Another view of REM sleep (Iskander and Kaelbling) emphasizes inhibition rather than excitation. According to this view the cortex is active enough during stage 1 sleep to discriminate between stimuli. Discrimination requires inhibition of excess neural activity, which is "released" when each discrimination is over; this released activity causes REMs.

Protein synthesis. It has already been pointed out that morphine, barbiturates, and sedatives decrease the amount of REM sleep by decreasing the neural activity of the brain. After the individual has withdrawn from these drugs, the amount of REM sleep on subsequent nights is increased in a "rebound" phenomenon. Oswald has pointed out that REM sleep is above normal for as many as ten recovery nights. Recovery of this duration suggests to him a slow process, such as protein synthesis. Some of the brain's proteins, those which are affected by many of the drugs that depress REM sleep, are called monoamines—a family of chemicals, some of which are believed to be neural transmitters. REM sleep is suspected of being a symptom of the synthesis that replenishes depleted supplies of monoamines.

Appetitive instinct. Another prominent sleep theorist (Morruzzi) suggests that sleep is an "appetitive instinct" like hunger, thirst, or sexual behavior. The "appetitive phase" is drowsiness and the "consummatory phase" is sleep. He notes that the neural mechanisms of sleep are inherited and that sleep is quite different from coma (absence of recorded neural activity). REM depends on a critical level of neural activity in the brain-activating parts of the brain-stem reticular formation (ascending reticular activating system, or ARAS; Chapter 13), and deep sleep depends on another level of activity. The onset of sleep can be elicited by stimulation of certain nuclei in the thalamus; in a similar manner, hunger, thirst, and sexual behavior can all be aroused by brain stimulation.

A sentinel function for REM. Another view of the function of REM sleep has come from study of the opossum, one of the more primitive species of mammal. Snyder has found that the opossum sleeps as much as 85% of the time and spends a third of that time in REM sleep. He believes that REM sleep provides a "sentinel" function for the sleeping animal, periodically arousing the nervous system for action in case of attack by a predator. According to this view, REM sleep has played a vital role in the survival and evolution of mammals and appeared very early in the development of mammalian species, as shown by the primitive opossum. Accordingly, one might find a greater percentage of REM sleep among primitive people who have not lived through centuries of safety from predators.

REM as one of three brain states. In agreement with Jouvet, Johnson holds that there are three "states" of the brain, defined by accompanying neural activity—waking, REM sleep, and slow-wave sleep. However, he disagrees that EEG and autonomic activity data can be used to define three corresponding states of consciousness, such as thought, dreaming, and lack of consciousness. All states of consciousness have been found in all three sleep stages, and there appear to be exceptions to every "rule" relating to them that has so far been stated. In a later article he argues that no clear and reliable relationships have been established between REM and slow-wave sleep stages and waking behavior. He suggests directing research toward relating specific sleep stages to something other than waking behavior (such as endocrine changes) and relating the *timing* of sleep stages and the waking state to waking behavior. In this view, disruption of the sleep to waking cycle or the REM to slow-wave sleep cycle may be the significant variable for waking behavior.

Tonic versus phasic sleep. By contrast with the views of Jouvet and of Johnson, Grosser and Siegel propose that sleep should be classified into tonic and phasic stages rather than into REM and slow-wave sleep.

They use two categories developed by Morruzzi to describe REM sleep. The tonic phase endures throughout stage REM sleep, and the phasic events are superimposed on the tonic phenomena. The tonic phenomena include stage 1 sleep, hippocampal theta waves of 5 Hz, and reduced tone in the extensor muscles. The phasic events include neural activity in pathways from the pons to the visual cortex (ponto-geniculo-occipital, or PGO, spikes), brief changes in autonomic activity, and twitching muscles. The phasic events have also been found to occur during slow-wave sleep, although not as often as during REM sleep. They cite studies in which cats were deprived of *either* REM sleep *or* neural activity in the visual pathways. The condition resulting from the latter deprivation produced more subsequent increase in REM sleep than did REM deprivation. Furthermore, the REM sleep "rebound" in visual-activity deprivation showed more phasic activity than usual. Finally, if visual activity was permitted during slow-wave sleep in REM-deprived cats, there was no subsequent REM sleep rebound at all. Of course, Jouvet has pointed out the importance of nuclei in the pons to the initiation of REM sleep. Since eye movements are involved, activity in pathways from the pons to the visual cortex would be expected.

Conclusion. One emerges from a consideration of various theories of REM sleep with a sense of confusion. The theories frequently attempt to explain different aspects of REM sleep, often do not offer clear-cut alternatives for experimental attack, and are frequently vague in detail. Probably the theories of Jouvet on the states of the brain —wakefulness, REM sleep, and non-REM sleep—have the most supporting data at this time.

ATTENTION AND VIGILANCE

The distinction between the specific thalamic projection system (STPS), the diffuse thalamic projection system (DTPS), and the ascending reticular activating system (ARAS) has already been made in this chapter and in Chapter 13. To summarize again, the STPS seems to carry sensory information to the visual, auditory, and somesthetic projection areas of the cerebral cortex in the classical sensory pathways. Collaterals from the STPS go to diffuse thalamic nuclei to form a "parallel" pathway (DTPS) to secondary sensory areas (visual, auditory, and somesthetic), which are older in evolutionary history. The ARAS receives collaterals from sensory inputs and acts to arouse the whole brain in a nonspecific fashion.

Role of the DTPS. Both the ARAS and the DTPS are involved in states of arousal and attention. However, the DTPS and the secondary (areas II and III) sensory projection areas may be more modality-specific than the ARAS. Area I is served by area II as well as the STPS, and area II receives fibers from the DTPS. One investigator (Galambos) has found area I cortical cells in the cat that are active only when the animal is "paying attention" to that modality. The cats were prepared with implanted electrodes in single cells of the auditory projection area. These cells seem to be fired by the DTPS rather than the STPS; for example, if the animal was not orienting toward an auditory stimulus, the auditory "attention cells" in the auditory projection system would be silent. When a novel sound stimulus such as a squeaking toy mouse was introduced, the cat would orient toward the stimulus, and the "attention units" in the auditory cortex would fire. With repeated sound stimuli the cat would adapt to the sound and quit paying attention. At the same time the auditory attention units would stop firing.

Vigilance. The ARAS and DTPS seem to be involved in the attention required for an animal to make a rapid discrimination. If the animal is awake but inattentive, alpha rhythms are seen in the EEG. If the animal is aroused, the ARAS is activating the cortex and a desynchronized EEG pattern

is seen. This pattern, along with behavioral arousal, can be produced by stimulation of the ARAS with electrodes implanted in an otherwise normal cat. Two flashes of light, presented 50 msec. apart, produce only one potential in the visual cortex if the cat is inattentive, and the EEG shows mostly alpha rhythms. If a sound stimulus warns the cat that the light flashes are to follow, the EEG desynchronizes. The two light flashes then produce separate evoked potentials in the visual cortex. The more the alpha waves are blocked by a desynchronized EEG in man, the faster is his reaction time to a visual stimulus. Finally, both the reaction time and discrimination rate in monkeys can be improved by BSRF stimulation. If electrodes are implanted in the BSRF of an otherwise normal monkey, the ARAS can be stimulated before it is forced to choose between two objects for a food reward. Stimulating the ARAS reduces the time it must see the objects before it can discriminate between them. It also improves its reaction time to the stimuli—the speed with which it reaches for the correct object.

Sensory gating, habituation, and attention. It is evident that attention to one sensory modality often requires inattention to another. When a student is reading (attending to a complex visual input), he may have to be called several times before an auditory input shifts his attention. It is as if the auditory input were turned off, and some of the evidence from animal experiments supports this interpretation. On the other hand, a repeated, monotonous auditory stimulus such as a dripping faucet may arouse attention at first as a novel sound, and then no longer be "heard" if one is attending to other things.

Experiments with animals who have electrodes implanted in auditory or visual projection areas show large evoked potentials to a novel auditory or visual stimulus. As the stimulus grows repetitive and the animal appears to turn its attention elsewhere, the evoked potentials become smaller—

habituation has occurred. One neural mechanism believed to be responsible for this phenomenon is the *efferent control of afferent input.*

Efferent pathways that go to the cochlea and can inhibit auditory input have been discovered (the olivocochlear tract of Rasmussen—Chapter 10). Similar efferent inhibitory pathways have been found for vision and somesthesis. (In the case of somesthesis, input is blocked at the gracile and cuneate nuclei; visual input is altered at the retina.) The efferent pathways to the receptors probably serve to "tune" the "local sign" of these topographical senses—to improve pitch discrimination in hearing, contrast in vision, and localization for touch. All the "local signs" depend on neurons firing in a given location and a lack of firing in adjacent neurons. However, efferent excitatory and inhibitory pathways to higher-level "relay" centers can serve habituation—they can reduce the input from one sensory modality and increase the input from another. Efferent pathways to sensory input are not all inhibitory—the "gate" may be opened wider instead of being closed. There are both excitatory and inhibitory efferent pathways to the thalamus and geniculate bodies to affect the STPS and the DTPS. Efferent pathways from higher levels can more diffusely excite, sensitize, or inhibit the ARAS, as has already been seen. The general principle of *efferent control of afferent impulses* is important to general arousal and specific attention as well as to habituation. By blocking or sensitizing specific sensory inputs in the STPS and DTPS, the CNS can pay attention to one or two sensory modalities while minimizing the input of others. At the same time the general arousal of the CNS may be increased by excitation of the ARAS from higher centers, creating a state of **vigilance.** Higher centers not only *select* the sensory input attended to; they also excite themselves by stimulating increased input from the ARAS. Repetitive stimuli, on the other hand, result in at least partial inhibition of their sensory channel and may reduce activity in the ARAS as well.

MEDITATION

Research in several laboratories concerns whether there is a state of consciousness not previously studied from a physiological point of view. As organized in this chapter, we have defined four states of consciousness: (1) aroused attention, (2) quiet waking, (3) slow-wave sleep (or stages 3 and 4 NREM sleep—stage 2 may be transitional), and (4) REM sleep. The state in question involves a combination of psychological reports of awareness and physiological measures that do not appear to occur at the same time in the above four states of awareness. These are (1) reports of heightened awareness similar to aroused attention but not directed toward an arousing stimulus, (2) presence of a regular alpha rhythm of greater amplitude and regularity than is seen in quiet wakefulness, and (3) lowered metabolic activity and muscle relaxation similar to sleep stages that are not accompanied by increases in movement or autonomic activity.

Interest in the phenomenon began with EEG studies of meditation as practiced by devotees of the Indian philosophy of Yoga. With the introduction and widespread popularity of transcendental meditation (TM), physiological study has shifted to meditation as practiced by this group. Two questions appear to arise: (1) Is there a state of brain function and awareness not previously defined? (2) Is this state beneficial in the relief of anxiety and symptoms of anxiety such as high blood pressure? Although the initial studies look promising, questions remain. For example: (1) Are the various forms of meditation practiced—Zen, Yoga, TM, and so on—similar in their physiological and psychological attributes despite differences in the technique of meditation? (2) If the phenomenon is valid, can all subjects be taught to attain this state, or are there large individual differences in ability? (3) Are any benefits achieved from the practice of meditation transitory or lasting and do all subjects realize them to the same degree?

SUMMARY

A position defining states of consciousness physiologically as well as psychologically began the chapter and promised to treat the topics of aroused alertness, resting wakefulness, "dreamless" and "dreaming" sleep, and meditation. In treating sleep and wakefulness together, Kleitman's evolutionary theory came first. To Kleitman, sleep seemed a more homeostatically normal state than wakefulness, and therefore his theory attempted to explain wakefulness. In Kleitman's theory wakefulness of necessity in lower animals and children results from bodily needs or other discomforts and causes a polyphasic sleep cycle. As need satisfaction becomes conditioned to daylight, wakefulness of choice and a monophasic sleep cycle ensue. He postulated that a sleep center (really a waking center) in the diencephalon aroused the whole brain to wakefulness upon stimulation. The theory was supported by the somnambulance and wakefulness of necessity shown by some encephalitis victims with brain damage in that area. The sleep center in normal adults could be stimulated by the cortex during daylight hours to cause wakefulness of choice. A posterior waking center has been found in ablation studies on the monkey. The waking center is probably only a focal part of the ascending reticular activating system (ARAS) of the brainstem. The ARAS is aroused by collaterals from the classic sensory pathways (specific thalamic projection system, STPS) en route to the primary sensory projection areas. A diffuse thalamic projection system (DTPS) supplies secondary cortical projection areas, which also receive input from the primary areas. Stimulation of the ARAS by implanted electrodes in the cat arouses the sleeping animal to alert attention and changes the EEG from a sleeping to a waking pattern. Transecting the STPS pathways in the brainstem has no gross effect on the animal, but cutting the ARAS pathways makes it somnambulant. The inherent EEG rhythm of 3 to 5 Hz in the brainstem reticular formation (BSRF) is intensified during arousal and suppressed during sleep. Many influences, sensory and metabolic, act to excite or suppress this wakefulness rhythm, and higher brain centers can excite it during "voluntary" wakefulness.

Changes in the EEG parallel states of arousal from deep sleep to vigilance. EEG waves are believed to be synchronous changes in the depolarization of cortical dendrites or cells that reflect the rate of firing in their fibers. During arousal the cells are largely depolarized and fire rapidly, producing a desynchronized EEG. With increasing quiescence and sleep, brain waves generally become synchronized and of lower frequency.

When brain wave patterns are used as a measure, four stages of sleep can be distinguished, each with its characteristic EEG pattern, whereas the alpha rhythm is often characteristic of the relaxed waking state. Sleeping subjects show cyclic shifts between the sleep stages every 30 to 90 minutes during the night, but generally spend more time in the slow-wave stages 3 or 4 during the second through the third or fourth hours. If deprived of slow-wave stages by being awakened from them during one night, the subject will compensate with longer slow-wave periods the next night. Dreaming can be detected by emergence of the EEG from a sleeping pattern to stage 1 (E-1) and the appearance of rapid eye movements (REM). When deprived of E-1 and REM sleep by being awakened, subjects become irritable and anxious, and spend more time showing these patterns on the subsequent night. Infants and other polyphasic animals spend more time in REM sleep than do adults. It is harder to wake animal subjects from REM sleep than from deeper sleep stages. Slow-wave sleep is stimulated by serotonin production in the raphe nuclei, according to Jouvet. REM sleep results from epinephrine production by nuclei of the pons.

There are differences in the duration of sleep stages among normal people, depending on age, sex, and work habits. Sleep deprivation affects orientation and efficiency but does not cause psychosis. Deprivation of either REM or slow-wave sleep will cause an increase in the deprived pattern on recovery nights. Slow-wave sleep "rebounds" more than REM sleep, and REM sleep accompanies a lower body temperature than does slow-wave sleep. Only mammals show much REM sleep and have a developed cortex. Autonomic changes often accompany stage 2 sleep when K complexes are seen. Most sedatives depress REM sleep. The sleep disorders of enuresis, somnambulism, night terrors, and nightmare are disorders of arousal from slow-wave sleep. Electrosleep is of interest but little studied outside of Russia and eastern Europe. A natural hypnogenic chemical has been isolated from the brains of sleeping rabbits. The release of human growth hormone (HGH) with the onset of slow-wave sleep has led to an increased interest in endocrine factors in sleep.

Theories that explain the role of REM sleep include brain development, dispersal of suppressed neural excitation after cortical discrimination, REM sleep as a symptom of protein synthesis of neural transmitters, an appetitive instinct, a sentinel function, one of three brain states, and a tonic-phasic theory.

During the waking state, "attention" cells have been found in the visual and auditory projection areas of the cat cortex, which fire only when the animal is "paying attention" to those modalities. Vigilance, as indicated by a desynchronized EEG from ARAS stimulation, "separates" the cortically evoked potentials produced by two light

flashes 50 msec. apart. The same stimulation in a monkey reduces the time it must see two objects to discriminate between them, as well as reducing its reaction time. Efferent inhibitory output to nuclei of the STPS from higher centers reduces or blocks sensory input in habituation; efferent excitatory output sensitizes these channels. Both types of output, known as sensory gating, provide efferent control of afferent input in states of attention. The ARAS and DTPS are under similar control. Questions were raised concerning the validity and usefulness of the physiological role of a fifth state of consciousness: meditation.

READINGS

Allison, T., and van Tuyver, H.: The evolution of sleep, Nat. History **79**:56-75, Feb. 1970. Also in Leukel, F.: Issues in physiological phychology, St. Louis, 1974, The C. V. Mosby Co.

Berger, R. J.: Morpheus descending, Psychol. Today **4**:33-35, 70, June 1970.

Broughton, R. J.: Sleep disorders: Disorders of arousal? Science **159**:1070-1078, 1968. Also in Leukel, F.: Issues in physiological psychology, St. Louis, 1974, The C. V. Mosby Co.

Dement, W., and Kleitman, N.: The relation of eye movements during sleep to dream activity: An objective method for the study of dreaming, J. Exp. Psychol. **53**:339-346, 1957. (Bobbs-Merrill Reprint No. P-87.)

Johnson, L.: Are stages of sleep related to waking behavior? Am. Scientist **61**:326-338, 1973.

Jouvet, M.: The states of sleep, Sci. Am. **216**: 62-72, Feb. 1967. (W. H. Freeman Reprint No. 504.)

Jouvet, M.: Biogenic amines and the states of sleep, Science **163**:32-41, 1969. Also in Leukel, F.: Issues in physiolological psychology, St. Louis, 1974, The C. V. Mosby Co.

Kleitman, N.: Sleep, Sci. Am. **187**:34-38, Nov. 1952. (W. H. Freeman Reprint No. 431.)

Kleitman, N.: Patterns of dreaming, Sci. Am. **203**:82-88, Nov. 1960. (W. H. Freeman Reprint No. 460.)

Kripper, S., and Hughes, W.: Genius at work, Psychol. Today **4**:40-43, June 1970.

Malmo, R. S.: Activation: A neuropsychological dimension, Psychol. Rev. **66**:367-386, 1959. (Bobbs-Merrill Reprint No. P-507.)

Oswald, J.: Sleep, Baltimore, 1966, Penguin Books, Inc.

Sharpless, S., and Jasper, H.: Habituation of the

arousal reaction, Brain **79:**655-680, 1956. (Bobbs-Merrill Reprint No. P-558.)

Snyder, F.: The physiology of dreaming. In Kramer, M., editor: Dream psychology and the new biology of dreaming, Springfield, Ill., 1969, Charles C Thomas, Publisher. Also in Leukel, F.: Issues in physiological psychology, St. Louis, 1974, The C. V. Mosby Co.

Tune, G. S.: The human sleep debt, Sci. J. **21:**67-71, Dec. 1968.

van de Castle, R. L.: His, hers, and the children's, Psychol. Today **4:**37-40, June 1970.

Wallace, R., and Benson, H.: The physiology of meditation, Sci. Am. **228:**84-90, Feb. 1972. (W. H. Freeman Co. Reprint No. 1242.)

Webb, W. B.: Sleep: an experimental approach, New York, 1968, The Macmillan Co.

chapter 15

Motivation

OVERVIEW

The chapter on motives begins with some definitions and a conceptual framework. The terms used in the study of motivation often have varied meanings for the reader; thus a single meaning for each must be decided on before proceeding. Terms are defined in a conceptual framework that distinguishes between what is going on in the animal and what is going on in the environment. The definitions distinguish between changes in the external environment that stimulate the animal and the resulting behavior that follows from the altered body conditions in the internal environment. The distinctions assist in understanding the characteristics of drives and motives—hunger, thirst, and sex being used as examples. The roles of more or less *local states* that accompany these motives are considered first—the dryness of the mouth in thirst or the sensations of stomach contractions in hunger, for example. When these states prove inadequate to explain motivated behavior, the *self-regulatory* characteristics of motives are added; for example, central factors control eating and drinking behavior so that we eat and drink enough, but not too much, in maintaining the consistency of the internal environment. These behaviors are controlled by *multiple factors,* no one of which dominates behavior. The role of the *hypothalamus* is central to motivated behavior, however. The specific mechanisms governing the thirst, hunger, and sex drives are then taken up in detail. Other drives such as pain, activity, and curiosity, are more briefly treated. Finally, some central neural mechanisms of reward and punishment are surveyed. Cen-

ters in the brain have been found whose stimulation is so "rewarding" that the animal (or human) will work to stimulate himself. Conversely, others have been found whose stimulation the animal will avoid even though it takes considerable work to do so.

SPECIFIC MOTIVES

The neural mechanisms of specific motives will be discussed in this chapter—thirst, hunger, and sex motivation serving as the primary examples. Before these topics are discussed, there must be agreement on the terms to be used in describing stimulus events preceding motivated behavior, the resulting events in the internal environment of the animal, and the consequent observed behavior. Much of the difficulty experienced in early studies of motivation came from confusion in regard to terminology. In using the term "need," for example, some would be referring to a lack, or absence, in the external environment, whereas others would be referring to a change in the animal's (internal) *state*. The statement that "the dog needs water" could refer to an empty water dish or be an inference about the animal's internal condition when it was panting in hot weather and probably dehydrated. In other instances an attempt would be made to explain behavior by merely naming it. "The dog inherits a 'water need' (internal state)." How does one know? "He drinks water every day (external behavior)." Similar difficulties led to the controversy over instincts, or complex motivation, which was presumed to be inherited. Women were assumed to inherit a "maternal instinct" defined as behavior involving child care.

"Women inherit a love for children." How does one know this? "They love children." All these statements ignore the complex of internal conditions, external stimuli, and rewarding or punishing effects of the resulting behavior.

Terminology

In the definitions and the schema to be used here, an attempt will be made to *predict* behavior as a *consequence* of predetermined external stimulus events and known internal conditions of the organism. Stimulus events interact with preexisting conditions in the internal environment of the organism; stimulus events also result in further changes in the internal environment. From this interaction of external and internal events, behavior results. The behavior changes the external stimulus conditions and the internal state of the animal, which results in further behavior.

Both external and internal stimuli result in behavior, whether or not the stimuli are "known" to the organism and whether or not the stimuli can be seen by an outside observer. The organism may respond to an external stimulus that is not evident to an-

other observer, as when a dog barks in response to a high-pitched whistle that is outside the frequency limits audible to a human observer. (The observer, of course, may use instruments to detect the sound and eventually discover that it is usually followed by a barking response.) The animal may react to some change in his internal environment that results from lack of water, an aspect that affects some center or system in the CNS. Only tedious and ingenious research can detect (1) what changes in the internal environment result from lack of water, (2) which of these changes affect the CNS, (3) how and where they affect the CNS, and (4) what kind of CNS activity leads to the behavior that usually follows lack of water.

Table 15-1 summarizes the order of events in motivated behavior and the terms to be used in the remainder of the chapter. A **need condition** is any state of affairs in the *external environment* that disturbs equilibrium, or homeostasis, in the internal environment. The need condition is often *inherent* if it is required for individual or species survival; otherwise it is *acquired,* or learned. Thus a condition of adequate water

Table 15-1. Schema for motivated behavior

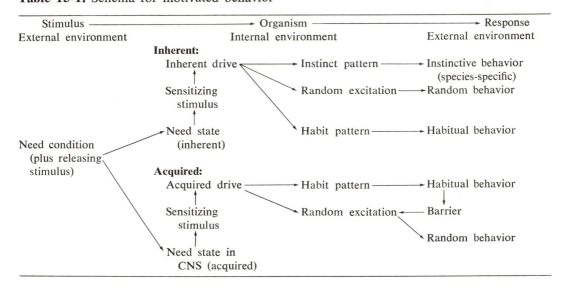

would be required for the individual to survive, or the presence of the opposite sex would be needed for the species to survive. Higher animals, especially man, acquire the need for many conditions not originally related to survival—approval by others, status symbols, and so forth—and his internal equilibrium is upset in the absence of these conditions. Whether inherent or acquired, a need condition leads to a **need state,** the complex of resulting *inherent* or *acquired* changes in *internal* equilibrium. A **sensitizing stimulus** is the aspect of a need state that sets off a drive mechanism in the CNS. A **drive** is a CNS mechanism for arousing and sustaining behavior when the need state has a sensitizing stimulus. The lack of water (need condition), for example, causes many changes in the tissues (need state). The CNS is sensitive to some of these changes (sensitizing stimuli), and parts of the CNS (drive) arouse and sustain behavior. Of course there are acquired drives as well—behavior can be aroused and sustained for many learned reasons, from pay to patriotism—and all acquired drives must have sensitizing stimuli whether or not one is aware of his upset condition. Not all inherent need states have sensitizing stimuli, however. Vitamin B_1 is required for survival, and a lack of this vitamin severely disturbs internal equilibrium. Yet aroused behavior does *not* result directly from vitamin B_1 deficiency (although an animal can *learn* to choose B_1-rich foods because of the rewarding effects on his internal condition).

A drive arouses and sustains behavior; it does not direct, or channel, behavior. Behavior appropriate to the drive occurs only in the presence of a **releasing stimulus** that is somehow related to the **incentive.** The incentive is the external stimulus that changes the need condition and therefore the need state, drive, and sensitizing stimulus. Water, for example, would be the incentive for the thirst drive. It is also a releasing stimulus for thirst since it releases

behavior appropriate to the drive, that is, drinking. Other stimuli that serve as *cues* to the presence of water are also releasing stimuli for behavior appropriate to thirst. For a thirsty man a water fountain leads to complex behavior that is appropriate to thirst; the water fountain is a releasing stimulus but not the incentive per se, because a water fountain cannot relieve thirst. The water fountain leads to thirst-related behavior only as a result of learning.

Inherent need states and inherent drives arouse behavior. In the case of some lower animals, behavior appropriate to the drive is "built into" the nervous system, and this behavior is the same for all members of the species (species-specific). In this case one speaks of an **instinct,** consisting of an inherent drive and inherited CNS systems for complex behavior. The behavior may or may not require releasing stimuli. For example, nest-building is an instinct in many species. For certain wasps the only need condition required is absence of a nest; the wasp produces its own nest-building material and will usually build a nest whenever a nest is lacking. The rat, however, builds a nest only in the presence of nest-building materials (releasing stimuli) *and* certain internal conditions (sensitizing stimuli) such as cold or the hormonal changes of pregnancy.

The primates, including man, do not seem to inherit CNS patterns for complex organized behavior in response to inherent drives. Primates appear to lack instincts. Drive arousal results in random behavior until the incentive is reached. Behavior becomes less random and variable with learning, and the animal develops a **habit**—behavior patterns appropriate to the drive under the conditions in which he lives. The existence of a drive *and* a habit is referred to as a **motive.** Organized and learned behavior follows an aroused hunger drive in adult man, so that the adult has a hunger motive. An infant responds to the hunger drive with random behavior since he has no hunger motive prior to learning how to obtain food. If hunger-motivated behavior does not lead to food, however, it will become more variable and random until new and successful habits have been learned. Finally, there are certain habits that lead to changes in the internal environment and thus cause **addiction.** The habitual use of certain drugs can change the internal equilibrium of the body so that the CNS no longer functions well in the absence of the drug. Strong need states and sensitizing stimuli result from withdrawal of the drug, and the CNS reacts as it does to an inherent drive.

It should be stressed at this point that no explanation of motivated behavior has been given so far. Definitions of terms have been made explicit to avoid confusion later on. The schema in Table 15-1 is not explanatory because it is essentially "circular"—a need condition leading to a need state, drive, motive or instinct, behavior related to an incentive, and removal of the need condition. The explanation of drives and motives will require proof of what conditions terminate motivated behavior as well as what conditions initiate it. Nearly all references to thirst, hunger, and sexual behavior will refer to inherent needs and drives, because the neural mechanisms underlying acquired drives are complex and largely unknown. The terms "need" and "drive" will refer to inherent needs and drives unless otherwise specified. However, the role of learning in developing motivated behavior must be recognized as one goes along; therefore terms that are relevant to learning are necessary.

Characteristics of drives and motives: local states

Early approaches to the thirst, hunger, and sex drives were made with the assumption that man was *aware* of their sensitizing stimuli. In this view, need states in the body resulted in consciously perceived stimuli that were restricted to local sensory areas of the body—hence the term "local states." In thirst one is aware of dryness of the mouth and throat. When one is extremely hungry, powerful stomach contractions may be perceived as "hunger pangs." In the male it was assumed that accumulation of seminal fluid in the vesicles made the penis more sensitive to stimulation, arousing the sex drive. All these stimulus sites are "peripheral" to most of the internal environment, although the stimulation *results* from changes in the internal environment. Local-state drive theories have been called "peripheral theories" for that reason, in contrast to theories about the direct effect of internal changes on the brain. To prove that "local states" are the sensitizing stimuli for drives, they must be shown to be both *necessary* and *sufficient* to the arousal of appropriate motivated behavior.

Thirst. When the body is dehydrated, or low on water, salivation is reduced as one way of reducing loss of water in the tissues. This results in the dry mouth sensations one experiences when thirsty. Cannon suggested that dryness of the mouth and throat arouses and sustains thirst-drive behavior when an animal is thirsty. This means that mouth and throat dryness is the sensitizing stimulus for the thirst drive. Is mouth and throat dryness a necessary and sufficient condition to arouse and sustain the thirst drive? The evidence suggests that it is not. In the first place, the first swallow of water when one is thirsty abolishes these sensations; yet drinking behavior continues for some time before one is satiated. Dryness of the mouth and throat could therefore arouse the first swallow, but what sustains subsequent drinking behavior? Experimenters have tied off the ducts of salivary glands in animals to make them permanently "dry mouthed." Such animals drink more frequently, but they do not consume more water in the course of the day than do normal animals. The same has been found true of humans born without functional salivary glands. It is evident that mouth and throat dryness has something to do with the *initiation* of drinking behavior, but it has little to do with the *regulation* of how long drinking behavior is sustained or the amount of water drunk. The evidence does not show that mouth and throat dryness is *necessary* to the initiation of drinking behavior, although the sensation may contribute to initiation of drinking. (Other experiments have induced mouth dryness by blocking salivation with atropine, with much the same results. These experiments must be cautiously interpreted, however, because atropine has widespread effects on the nervous system.)

Hunger. Another local stimulus that could arouse a drive comes from stomach contractions that may accompany hunger and are sensed by the subject as hunger pangs. Sensations of stomach distention usually accompany satiation and could terminate eating behavior. A low blood glucose level induced by insulin injections can cause stomach contractions, but whether blood glucose gets that low during ordinary hunger is not clear. Cannon suggested that hunger was caused by stomach contractions, after he performed an experiment in which he abstained from food for several days and then swallowed a balloon that was connected by a tube to a pressure-measuring device. When the stomach contracted, it squeezed the balloon, and increased pressure was indicated. Without seeing the pressure measurements, he signaled when he sensed a hunger pang. The sensations corresponded with stomach contractions. Subsequent studies have cast some doubt on this famous experiment. It has been shown that the presence of the balloon in the stomach stimulates stomach contractions, for example. However, powerful stomach contractions and hunger pangs do occur during starvation, although they are reported to last for only 3 to 5 days. None of this tells us whether stomach contractions, as a sensitizing stimulus, are necessary and sufficient to arouse and sustain the hunger drive. Other evidence suggests that stomach contractions are unnecessary to the hunger drive, although they may contribute to the aroused and sustained behavior for a time. (Certainly the starving man is still hungry for days after the contractions cease!)

Some of the evidence comes from operations performed on people with stomach ulcers. In some cases nerves leading to the stomach were cut to block parasympathetic facilitation of automatic stomach contractions and stop the stimulation of acid secretion by the stomach. Denervating the stomach also cuts sensory nerves and eliminates sensations caused by stomach contractions. It does not alter the arousal or regulation of eating behavior in these patients. In other ulcer operations all or part of the stomach is removed without interference with eating behavior, except that less can be eaten at one time (until the small intestine enlarges to store food as the stomach once did). Although these patients eat less, they eat more frequently, and food intake is thus regulated as before. (Nausea is a chronic condition in some patients, but others adjust well.) Removing the stomach of animals produces the same general effects. Animals without a stomach show aroused and sustained behavior when deprived of food, and they will learn complex habits to obtain a food reward. Therefore stomach contractions as a sensitizing stimulus are neither necessary nor sufficient to arouse or sustain the hunger drive—although they may contribute to the regulation of normal food intake.

Sex. In the mature male, semen is stored in the seminal vesicles after being produced by the gonads. If the accumulation is not drawn off by intercourse, nocturnal emissions occur at fairly regular intervals. In the absence of regular copulation and ejaculation, the accumulation of unspent semen in the vesicles might act as a sensitizing stimulus that arouses the sex drive in males. No similar mechanism was proposed for females. Research on the function of the endocrine glands has now shown that both the sex drive and the production of germ plasm are under the control of the endocrine glands in vertebrate species (Chapter 3). In man the sex drive becomes dominated by learning, and sensitizing stimuli are more a function of past experience than hormone levels. As a result the female sex drive becomes largely independent of the regular monthly changes in hormone level caused by the estrus cycle, and sexual behavior continues after germ plasm and sex hormone production ceases in both sexes with aging. This is not to say that the strength of the sex drive or the frequency of intercourse is independent of sex hormone level in the human. However, sex hormones are neither necessary nor sufficient to arouse and sustain sexual behavior, at least in the human adult with past sexual experience.

Characteristics of drives and motives: self-regulation

In general, motivated behavior is organized to maintain the consistency of the internal environment. Evidence will be presented to show that animals, including man, can estimate their need for food or water very closely after a given amount of deprivation. Experiments show that normal animals drink or eat the amount necessary to replace a loss from deprivation, and very little more or less. The time required to replace the lost food or water is not enough to enable the body to restore internal equilibrium. An animal will drink enough to restore body water level (within 0.5% of body weight) within a few minutes and *stop,* even though the body has not had time to distribute the water to most of the tissues. This means that there must be shut-off stimuli to signal satiation as well as sensitizing stimuli to signal need. Furthermore, behavior that satisfies one need of the body can create others. For example, perspiring to keep the body temperature down in hot weather results in dehydration and consequent thirst. Continuous adjustment is necessary to keep the body's needs in balance. There are, however, inherent drives, or "appetites," that seem independent of the body's needs. They are externally controlled by releasing stimuli instead of being initiated by internal changes (for example, in animals and children, the taste for nonnutritive sweet substances such as saccharin). On the other hand, there are need states that threaten survival but appear to have no sensitizing stimuli because they do not arouse and sustain behavior. Certain vitamin deficiencies are examples. Finally, the self-regulation of drives and motives extends beyond the energy requirements (caloric needs) of the body for food, to its requirements for specific amounts of fats, proteins, and so on (specific as well as general hungers).

Hierarchy of need states. The need states of the body are not independent of one another. They compete or cooperate for behavior priority when their drives are aroused by need conditions in the environment and need states in the body. In general, the priority of a need state that arouses a drive depends on how long that internal imbalance can be tolerated by the body. For example, needs for breathing, heat regulation, thirst, and hunger coexist in that order of priority in the body. Breathing must be regulated from moment to moment because the body stores little oxygen. Yet breathing may be interrupted momentarily to permit the swallowing of water. Heat regulation has more "inertia" of gain or loss —errors may be corrected over periods of many minutes without an undue change in body temperature. Body heat is continuously lost in breathing, whatever the body temperature. A change in body temperature has more immediate effects than water loss; therefore water may be sacrificed for cooling (as in a perspiring man or panting dog), since a water deficit can be tolerated for 2 or 3 days. Food intake and energy output can be out of balance for even longer, and a thirsty animal eats little because water is required for digestion and waste elimination. The behavior that results from drives and regulates drives depends on other drives and the effect of the behavior on the internal environment.

Satiation. Experiments have shown over and over again that deprived animals are able to estimate their food and water deficiencies quite accurately. A dog will begin to drink when it has lost only 0.5% of its body weight in water. If deprived of water for a period of time, the amount of water it drinks will correct the deficit it has undergone. Furthermore, it will drink this amount within 5 minutes. Five minutes is almost surely too short a time for water to be absorbed from the stomach and change the dehydrated state of the other tissues of the internal environment. The state of the tissues that initiated the thirst drive has not changed—the sensitizing stimulus is still there. Therefore, one must look for satiation, or stop, stimuli that halt drinking behavior when enough has been ingested to eventually restore internal balance (even though the balance has not yet been restored).

Hunger seems to act in much the same way. Animals seem to estimate their caloric needs and respond accordingly. Animals, including man (not always!), maintain their weight at a constant level by varying their intake according to the caloric value of a changing diet—less will be eaten of high-calorie than low-calorie foods to maintain body weight within narrow limits. An animal will stop eating when it has "had enough," even though the food it has eaten is not utilized until after digestion has taken place. Since animals eat at intervals, some state of the body arouses eating behavior and serves as a sensitizing stimulus. But animals stop eating before digestion has taken place; therefore, satiating stimuli must be found that tell the organism when enough calories have been ingested. If the customary diet of a dog or a rat is "diluted" with a nonnutritive bland substance, the animal will increase its intake accordingly, up to the limit of stomach capacity. If offered diluted alcohol, rats (like some people!) will prefer a certain amount of alcohol to pure water. They will, however, reduce their caloric intake of food enough to compensate for the calories gained from the alcohol. Most convincing of all is the fact that rats will restore their normal body weight by reduced caloric intake after having been artificially fattened.

Insulin is required in certain amounts to utilize the blood glucose obtained from food. If too much insulin is present, the animal either must eat more or suffer insulin shock—fainting and possible death—because the blood glucose has been used up by other tissues and does not reach the brain, where a constant supply is necessary for brain function. Injections of insulin will cause an animal to eat more to keep up blood glucose supplies to the brain. The extra calories form fat deposits, and the animal gains weight and becomes obese. As soon as the injections are stopped, however, the rat will reduce his caloric intake for 20 days or so, losing weight until his normal body weight is reached. When the rat is overweight, either the sensitizing stimulus loses potency, or (more probably) satiation stimuli are more readily aroused.

Drives controlled by releasing stimuli: "appetites," and palatability. Both the initiation and the cessation of eating or drinking behavior are influenced by the palatability of the substances ingested, although not beyond the bounds of keeping water and food intake in balance with each other and with the need states of the body. If water or food is made bitter with quinine, it is avoided by the animal when other sources of water or food are available. If not, the animal will eat or drink just enough of most quinine concentrations to maintain itself. On the other hand, it will prefer water sweetened with saccharin to natural water, even though saccharin has no nutritive value. Here is a case of an "appetite"—a drive controlled by the releasing stimulus in the absence of an internal sensitizing stimulus. Rats prefer the taste of saccharin to many nutritive solutions, even when they are deprived of food, and will choose saccharin-flavored water over pure water when satiated for food.

Inherent need states without sensitizing stimuli or drive mechanisms. In some instances, need states of the body that imperil survival have no apparent way of arousing and sustaining behavior. The body requires minimum amounts of vitamins A and D for survival, but the complete absence of either or both will not arouse and sustain behavior. Breathing is almost completely regulated by the CO_2 level of the blood. In a closed room a lack of oxygen is accompanied by an increased CO_2 level. But a lack of O_2, not accompanied by increased CO_2 (as at high altitudes), causes no aroused and sustained behavior and no symptoms of suffocation (though some intoxication may result). Other need states of the body without effective sensitizing stimuli to the CNS could be cited.

Multiple-factor control of motivated behavior. Both external (releasing) and internal (sensitizing) stimuli control the arousal of motivated behavior in a complex fashion. There may be several releasing stimuli for thirst, hunger, or sexual behavior because the cues vary from one situation to another. As a result, even instinctive behavior, such as sexual behavior in the rat, is complex and variable rather than stereotyped and falls under the control of a variety of releasing stimuli. Smell, taste, touch, visual, and other stimuli combine to release sexual behavior in the rat. Experiments that eliminate these sensory inputs, singly or in combination, show that several sensory channels must be lost before the sexual response of the male rat to the female is eliminated. Furthermore, the number of sensory inputs that must be eliminated to abolish sexual behavior depends on the internal level of sex hormones. The higher the hormone level, the more sensory imputs must be eliminated to abolish male sexual behavior. Since the sex hormones act as sensitizing stimuli for sexual behavior in the male, it is evident that the effectiveness of releasing stimuli depends on the level of sensitizing stimuli. (Sexual behavior in the female is harder to eliminate by depriving her of sensory input, but the responses required of the female are less complex and less subject to varied stimulus control. All she has to do is "relax and enjoy it," aside from reflex responses. This point will be more fully discussed later.) Thirst and hunger behavior are also jointly under the control of sensitizing and releasing stimuli. The effectiveness of cues (releasing stimuli) in a learning situation, to a food or water reward, depends on how deprived the animal is. Up to a point, greater deprivation means stronger sensitizing stimulation, higher drive level, more effective releasing stimuli, and more rapid learning.

Hypothalamic centers

The hypothalamus contains important "centers" that arouse drives. The hypothalamus receives nervous input from higher centers that regulate its activity (particularly the limbic system), but it is also aroused by, and forms a part of, the ARAS. The discussion of sleep (Chapter 14) emphasized the role of the posterior hypothalamus in mobilizing the brain's activity in states of alertness and attention—states that are important to drive-aroused and sustained behavior. Many pathways for sensory input pass near and possibly stimulate the hypothalamus on the way to the thalamus and cerebral cortex. The sensory input is aroused by sensations from taste, smell, and eating or drinking behavior, as well as from the stomach and intestines, which react to their contents. On the motor side the hypothalamus governs the activity of the sympathetic and parasympathetic nervous systems. Sympathetic activity is increased when the animal mobilizes to meet the threat of deprivation. The parasympathetic system is more active in states of quiescence and satiation. Finally, cell groups in the hypothalamus are *directly sensitive* to conditions in the internal environment (extracellular tissue fluid). The internal changes that accompany thirst, hunger, sexual deprivation, and possibly loss of sleep affect different centers in the hypothalamus. As a result, behavior is aroused and sustained. In some cases (for example, thirst) we know which tissue fluid changes affect which centers in the hypothalamus. In other cases we only suspect that the centers exist because removing the areas where they are believed to be located abolishes the drive in question, and stimulating these areas initiates specific motivated behavior. Therefore, these areas are termed "excitatory" hunger, thirst, or sexual centers. In some drives (for example, hunger and possibly sleep) *inhibitory* centers have been found. Stimulating these centers *abolishes* the motivated behavior. The inhibitory area may respond to sensory input from the nervous system or to changes in the internal environment to tell the animal when it has "had enough." Therefore, the inhibitory area for a given drive may act as a satiation, or stop, center. The excitatory area would respond to sensitizing stimuli as the "start" center for motivated behavior. In other cases, destroying part of the hypothalamus may involve the destruction of nearby pathways carrying sensory input that signals behavior (for example, eating) and the consequences of that behavior in sensations of "fullness" of the stomach—the hypothalamus may not be directly involved at all.

Some authors (Valenstein, Cox, and Kakolewski, for example) put less emphasis on the hypothalamic "centers" that seem to arouse motivated behavior, and more emphasis on the role of the releasing stimuli that elicit motivated behavior. They point out that electrical stimulation of hypothalamic "centers" that elicits eating in the presence of food will also elicit drinking in the presence of water, or gnawing, if there is something to gnaw on. They propose that the hypothalamus or nearby sensory pathways can arouse several overlapping behavior patterns that are "stimulus-bound," that are specific to a given species, and that involve many other areas of the brain. For example, object-carrying in the rat does not require learning, and it serves several motivated behaviors, such as hoarding, or retrieving pups. In their view the simple carrying out of the response is rewarding to the animal.

Regulation of thirst, hunger, and sex drives

In studying the thirst, hunger, and sex drives, one needs to know (1) what internal sensitizing stimuli are necessary to arouse the behavior, (2) how these stimuli act on the hypothalamus or other parts of the brain, (3) what stimuli terminate motivated behavior, that is, what is satiation, and (4) how these stimuli act on the brain. Evidence in regard to thirst, hunger, and sexual behavior will be discussed.

Regulation of the thirst drive. As pointed out previously, the body is continually losing water through (1) respiration, (2) perspiration, and (3) formation of urine. The body has little control over water loss from breathing or sweating; neither process can be interrupted long enough to prevent significant water loss. However, the kidney can reabsorb about one third of the water it uses to flush wastes from the blood. The kidney acts to reabsorb water when it is stimulated to do so by the antidiuretic effect of vasopressin (ADH, or antidiuretic hormone, effect) of the posterior pituitary gland (Chapter 3). The posterior pituitary releases ADH in response to excitation from nerve fibers that originate in the anterior hypothalamus (supraoptic nucleus). The fibers release **neurosecretions** in the pathway to the posterior pituitary. Perhaps these neurosecretions are transmitter substances that stimulate gland cells to release ADH. What stimulates the anterior hypothalamus to begin this chain of events when the water supply of the body is low? Apparently it is the change in osmotic pressure (viscosity) of the blood that normally occurs when the fluid level of the body falls. Most of the solid particles in the blood and tissue fluids (except for wastes) are retained by the kidney; therefore, as the water level is reduced, the blood and tissue fluids become more concentrated. As a result, fluid is drawn from the cells, including cells in the anterior hypothalamus (osmotic thirst). In response the hypothalamic cells seem to stimulate the posterior pituitary to release ADH. A minute amount of salt deposited in the anterior pituitary by an implanted tube will cause water-satiated goats to drink. (Not enough salt is used to affect other areas of the brain.) Therefore dehydration of these cells can initiate drinking behavior as well as kidney regulation; the behavior is probably initiated by connections between the hypothalamus and other parts of the brain.

A more important factor in regulating thirst is the volume of extracellular fluid, that is, fluid outside of the cells. Because of the reduced (extracellular) fluid volume, this is called volemic thirst, or, more accurately, hypovolia. Although some cells in the lateral and anterior hypothalamus are sensitive to dehydration, other anterior cells are sensitive to a hormone that is activated by the kidney when the blood pressure falls. When fluid volume of the body is decreased because of dehydration, so is the amount of circulating blood. Reduced blood volume results in reduced blood pressure. Reduced blood pressure affects pressure receptors in the arteries and veins (see Fig. 15-1). The pressure receptors affect the hypothalamic thirst centers in two ways: (1) directly by

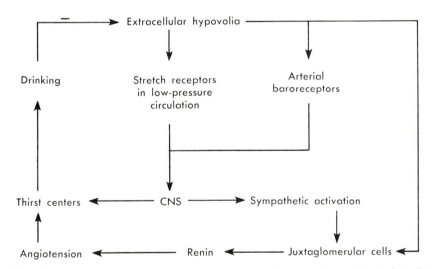

Fig. 15-1. Proposed mechanism for drinking caused by extracellular dehydration. Reduced blood pressure attributable to reduced blood volume stimulates the kidney (juxtaglomerular cells) both directly and indirectly by way of pressure receptors in the arteries and veins (the low-pressure circulation of the veins returning blood to the heart is more sensitive to changes in blood pressure than the high-pressure circulation of arteries). Input from the pressure receptors to the CNS reflexly stimulates the thirst centers and the kidney. The juxtaglomerular cells react by producing renin. Renin activates blood plasma angiotensinogen into a form that stimulates thirst centers in the hypothalamus (see text). There is also a delayed increase in sodium appetite not shown in the figure. (From Fitzsimons, J. T.: The renin-angiotensinogen system in the control of drinking. In Martini, L., Motta, M., and Fraschini, F., editors: The hypothalamus, New York, 1970, Academic Press Inc.)

way of the CNS and (2) indirectly by sympathetic fibers to the kidney. The kidney itself also responds to low blood pressure. In reaction to both sympathetic stimulation and to low blood pressure, certain kidney cells (juxtaglomerular cells, Fig. 15-1) release an enzyme called **renin.** The renin converts one of the normal blood proteins **(angiotensinogen)** into a form (angiotensinogen II) that stimulates thirst centers in the hypothalamus. Both the antidiuretic effect of vasopressin release (see p. 340) and drinking behavior are aroused.

Satiation stimuli. All this says something about the sensitizing stimuli for thirst but nothing about satiation stimuli. How does the CNS know when the animal has had enough water? In the first place, water intake is dependent on food intake, because water is required to digest food. A second factor appears to be the act of drinking itself—consummatory behavior. In dogs the esophagus can be cut and the upper and lower ends brought to the surface. When the animal drinks, the water passes through the throat and out the upper end of the esophagus, never reaching the stomach ("sham drinking"). A thirsty dog, prepared in this way, will drink enough water to replace the deficit in about 5 minutes and then stop, almost as if it had a water meter in its throat or had been counting the swallows. If the water balance is not restored, however, the dog will go back and drink again in a few minutes; thus consummatory behavior is not the only factor regulating the thirst drive. If water is placed in the lower end of the esophagus, the thirsty dog can be "preloaded" with water and released to see if it will drink. If released immediately, it will sham drink as before. If 15 minutes elapse after "preloading," it will not drink at all. This period of time is probably enough for water to reach the tissues via the stomach and intestinal walls and reduce stimulation to cells in the hypothalamus. Regulation of intake by water reaching the stomach may be more precise,

however. Rats can be prepared with tubes inserted into the stomach so that all water intake bypasses the mouth and throat and enters the stomach directly. Rats prepared in this fashion can be trained to press a lever to receive a squirt of water directly into the stomach. After initial training they can regulate their water intake solely by this means over a long period of time—and they do it about as well as normal animals do, although their body weight is reduced.

Although animals can be taught to press a lever in order to have food delivered directly into the stomach by a tube, experiments have shown that *both* an oral stimulus (for example, saccharin) and intragastric injections are necessary to maintain the response. Humans can be trained to press a lever that causes liquid diet food to be injected directly into the stomach by a tube. When either one meal (Stellar) or all three (Jordan) were consumed in this fashion, the subjects regulated their caloric intake rather well. However, when they fed themselves, both orally and intragastrically at the same time, they tended to overeat. Obviously, both oral and gastric factors are involved in the control of food intake.

Finally, the osmotic pressure of the fluid consumed may be a factor in regulating the amount that a thirsty animal will drink. It takes more slightly salty water than pure water to reduce the osmotic pressure of the cells because the sodium ion remains outside the cells. A thirsty animal will drink more slightly salty water than "pure" water (up to salt water of the same concentration as the body fluid). In Chapter 9, fibers (in the nerves originating in the tongue) that fire in response to salt solutions were described. They have a resting rate of firing, probably in response to the salt content of the salvia (about the same as other body fluids). Pure water reduces this rate of firing. Therefore, the rate of firing in some taste nerves depends on the salt content of the water ingested. The "salt fibers" may excite additional drinking by initiating impulses that reach the hypothalamus, so that enough salt water is ingested to balance the body fluids. Even when sham drinking is used in rats, and the fluid never reaches the stomach, animals will drink more salt water than pure water (up to the point at which the water has the same salt content as the body fluids). A reduced rate of firing from salt fibers, when the animal is drinking pure water, may reduce the excitation of the hypothalamic drinking centers.

Regulation of the hunger drive. As in the case of the thirst drive, food intake depends on water intake. It will be seen that regulation of hunger as well as thirst is determined by several factors. However, regulation of the hunger drive is more complex, and more factors are involved. In thirst, arousal of the drive has little to do with oral factors such as dryness of the mouth and throat—hypothalamic cells govern arousal. In hunger, sensitizing stimuli probably act to arouse activity, but the oral releasing stimuli of taste (and smell) are more important in determining whether the animal will eat—water is water, but there are many tastes to food. Oral factors also determine *what* foods are eaten according to the animal's dietary needs, but that is a subject for a later section. Here the interest is in whether the animal eats and how much. Thirst satiation can be regulated by oral factors in sham drinking, but an animal can also learn to control the amount of water directly delivered to his stomach, so that both oral and gastric cues *can* be used. (Of course, animals without a stomach can control both food and water intake.) In hunger, many factors can influence satiation, although they seem to act through a mechanism that "counts calories." Earlier it was seen that animals could regulate their intake according to the caloric value of the diet available and their caloric needs— forced exercise such as swimming to exhaustion will cause rats to increase their caloric intake to meet the demand.

Sham feeding. One way of determining the importance of oral factors in arousal and satiation is sham feeding. A dog with the esophagus severed and stitched to the surface will eat, but the food never reaches the stomach. Experimenters agree that a hungry animal prepared in this way will work to obtain food that passes only through the mouth; thus oral taste (and smell) stimuli serve as effective releasing stimuli. There is disagreement about whether oral factors— taste and the act of eating and swallowing— have anything to do with satiation. It has been reported that a hungry animal will sham feed to exhaustion, an indication that oral stimuli are not a major factor in satiation. However, milk taken by mouth (that reaches the stomach) reduces intake more than direct gastric (stomach) injection does, indicating that oral factors may have an influence in satiation. Gastric factors seem more important, however. Just as in thirst, rats can be prepared with tubes leading directly to the stomach and can learn to feed themselves through these tubes by pressing a lever that controls injections of liquid food directly into the stomach. The animals can maintain their normal weight for a long time with this apparatus. Furthermore, they will regulate the amount they feed themselves according to how much the diet is diluted with tap water. Quinine added to the diet in concentrations that caused normal animals to reduce their intake had no effect on intragastric feeding because oral factors of taste were not involved. All this control of the diet by intragastric factors is puzzling in view of the fact that animals (and humans) *without* stomachs can regulate their food intake. However, since food absorption takes place in the intestine, perhaps the control site lies there; liquid food reaches the intestine quite rapidly.

Osmotic pressure. Whether gastric or intestinal, the *osmotic pressure* of ingested food seems important to satiation. In one experiment two kinds of sugar solutions (glucose and sucrose) were presented (at the same time) to rats to determine their preference. (Presumably, the animals would select the sugar that tasted sweeter.) At concentrations in which glucose and sucrose were matched in preference (drunk in equal amounts), the glucose was more concentrated than the sucrose. This meant that the glucose had a higher osmotic pressure. The rate of drinking was tested for the two sugar solutions. The rate was equal at first, but the animals slowed down their rate of glucose intake before they slowed down on sucrose intake. The animals showed satiation effects sooner when drinking the sugar solution with the higher osmotic pressure. Therefore, osmotic pressure of the contents of the stomach (or intestine?) is a factor in satiation. The presence of a high-viscosity fluid in the stomach could draw other body fluid into the stomach in order to reduce the osmotic pressure therein. This additional fluid could distend the stomach and "fill it up." On the other hand, osmotic changes could directly signal the hypothalamus by hormonal or other means.

Satiation factors. Many factors are involved in satiation; however, it is not known what they have in common or how they signal what parts of the nervous system. The intake of food causes a variety of changes in the internal environment (Fig. 15-2). Gastric distention occurs. Water is lost to the gastrointestinal (GI) tract, where it is attracted by the high osmotic pressure of the food, causing dehydration of other tissues. Any existing hypoglycemia (low blood glucose) is relieved. The metabolic activity involved in digestion increases the "heat

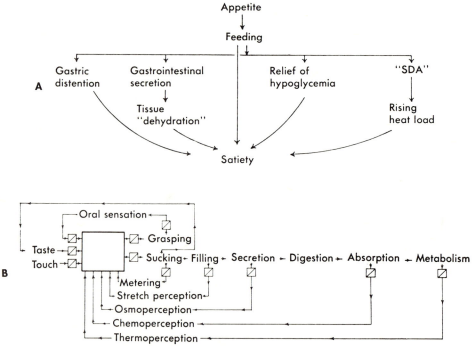

Fig. 15-2. **A,** Simplified outline of a multifactor concept of satiation. **B,** Schema of sensory feedback relationships involved in regulation of feeding. (**A** from Brobeck, J. R.: Regulation of feeding and drinking. In Field, J., editor: Handbook of physiology, vol. 2, Baltimore, 1960, The Williams & Wilkins Co.; **B** from Brobeck, J. R.: Review and synthesis. In Brazier, M. A. B., editor: Brain and behavior, vol. 2, Washington, D. C., 1962, American Institute of Biological Sciences.)

load" on the body. It has been shown that body temperature affects neural activity in the same areas whose stimulation leads to eating behavior. Other changes could be cited, but these serve to show how many factors *could* affect satiation. It is not known which are the most important normally, much less which ones are *necessary* to signal that enough has been eaten.

Glucostatic theory. One theory, the **glucostatic theory,** proposed that the level of blood glucose affects cells that arouse eating when the blood glucose level is low. This view has been largely abandoned for a number of reasons, chiefly the lack of evidence of a relationship between normal fluctuations in blood glucose and the hunger drive. This leaves us with the suspicion that some change or changes in the tissue fluids, osmotic or otherwise, affect hunger and satiation centers in the hypothalamus, but this conclusion does not tell us what the changes are or how they are affected by food or lack of food.

Lipostatic theory. There is also a hypothesis that the level of fatty acids in the blood can serve as an arousal or a satiation stimulus for hunger mechanisms. This idea encounters the same difficulties as did the glucostatic theory, in that there is little evidence that normal fluctuations in the fatty acid content of the blood and tissue fluid affect eating behavior.

Plasma amino acids. Since neither carbohydrate level (glucostatic theory) nor fat level (lipostatic theory) can clearly be shown to govern eating behavior, other investigators (Leung and Rogers) have turned to protein. Their interest was aroused by the fact that animals who were given a surplus of all but one of the amino acids on a low-protein diet showed a depression of their food intake in 5 to 12 hours. They infused rats through the carotid artery (an artery going to the brain) with a surplus of all of the amino acids except a growth-limiting one (either threonine or isoleucine). Other rats ate the same diet in a normal way.

Both groups showed a 40% to 50% reduction of food intake, thus proving that oral factors were not responsible for the lack of appetite. Restoring the missing amino acid led to a normal food intake. The data suggest that a food intake regulation mechanism somewhere in the brain is sensitive to the amount of amino acids in the blood.

Hypothalamus and the hunger drive. Many parts of the brain are involved in the hunger drive, particularly parts of the brain described in Chapter 13 as the limbic system. However, certain focal centers in the hypothalamus seemed to have the most to do with hunger drive arousal and with satiation. Two centers seemed to be involved. The first center is the **ventromedial nucleus** of the hypothalamus. This nucleus appeared to function as a **satiation,** or **satiety, center,** reacting to changes in the tissue fluid that signal when the body has had enough food. The second center is made up of a pair of nuclei, located in the lateral hypothalamus on both sides and overlapping with centers controlling thirst behavior. These nuclei are more scattered than is the ventromedial nucleus, but their location is well known. The **lateral hypothalamic nuclei** appeared to react to sensitizing stimuli—changes in the tissue fluid that occur when the animal's food reserves are low. For this reason they have often been called the **feeding center.** Their activity was assumed to set off the widespread CNS and behavior changes of the aroused hunger drive. More recent experiments suggest that lesions of the ventromedial hypothalamus (VMH) damage nearby pathways leading to the forebrain, especially to the limbic system from the brainstem sensory nuclei (chiefly trigeminal). The brainstem nuclei receive fibers from the mouth, pharynx, stomach, and intestine that pass input from eating behavior and the presence of food in the stomach and gut. These pathways are adrenergic—norepinephrine is probably the transmitter substance for the cells involved. Lateral hypothalamic (LH) lesions appear to damage descending pathways from the anterior (pre-optic) thirst centers and ascending pathways from the mouth, pharynx, stomach, and so on. These pathways seem to be cholinergic, utilizing acetylcholine as a synaptic transmitter. There are several reasons for this point of view. In the first place, lesions adequate to produce either hyperphagia or the LH syndrome must be large enough to damage nerve tracts passing through nearby areas of the hypothalamus —lesions strictly confined to these nuclei do not seem to produce significant changes in eating or drinking behavior. When chemical stimulation is used (Grossman) carbachol (which mimics acetylcholine) produces drinking, not eating, whereas norepinepherine produces eating and not drinking. Finally, lesions and chemical stimulation of several limbic areas reproduce some of the symptoms of lesions and stimulation of the ventromedial hypothalamus and lateral hypothalamus.

Hypothalamic hyperphagia. Lesions in various parts of the limbic system will cause rats to overeat and become quite obese (fat). Lesions near the ventromedial hypothalamus seem most effective in this regard. After the area is destroyed, the animals double or triple their normal food intake within a few days and continue eating at this rate until their weight is two or three times normal. Then their intake drops to the amount necessary to maintain their obese condition and remains at that level. The syndrome is called **hypothalamic hyperphagia.** The most reasonable explanation is that pathways involved in the shut-off mechanism for hunger have been destroyed.

Several lines of evidence support this view. In the first place, hyperphagic rats that are fed a liquid diet of low bulk eat no more often, while they are gaining weight, than do normal rats. They just eat for longer periods of time. Second, hyperphagic rats are more sensitive to the palatability of their food than are normal rats— they seem more finicky about what they

eat. Normal rats will tolerate considerable "bitterness" (caused by adulterating the food with quinine) without reducing their food intake; small amounts of quinine will reduce the hyperphagic rats' intake drastically. Third, normal rats will eat more when the caloric value of their food is reduced by mixing it with nonnutritive kaolin (clay) or cellulose; hyperphagic rats will not. Since hyperphagic rats are more finicky about their food than are normal rats, their overeating cannot be caused by increased avidity. They just stop eating less readily. If required to press a bar to obtain food, they will not work so hard or so long as normal rats; if required to cross a shocking grid to obtain food, they will not tolerate as much shock as will a normal animal. Because their metabolism is otherwise normal, it is reasoned that they are less sensitive to bodily changes that result from overeating; because an essential part of the stop mechanism has been removed, they have a *higher threshold* of satiation.

Hyperphagics regulate their weight just as do normal animals, by reducing their food intake *after* they have become obese; they just maintain their weight at a higher level, being less sensitive to the internal changes that accompany obesity and excess fat storage. It seems to make no difference whether the animal is made obese before or after the operation—he will still level off at the same weight. As previously noted, normal rats can be made obese by injecting them with insulin since they must eat more to keep the brain supplied with blood glucose. Normal rats fattened in this manner become almost as obese as hyperphagic rats. If they are operated on *after* being fattened in this way, they will increase their food intake only enough to reach the same weight as that of the control animals, who are already hyperphagic. The hyperphagic rat, then, just has a higher threshold to the bodily changes that accompany overeating or obesity. Whatever these changes are, they seem to be present in the hyperphagic as much as in the normal rat, and some are carried in the bloodstream like a hormone.

Experiments on **parabiotic** rats provide the evidence for the "hormone" statement. Parabiotic rats are pairs of rats that are operated on to connect their circulatory systems so that they have a common blood supply. Whatever is in the bloodstream of one animal is therefore found in the bloodstream of the other. If the ventromedial area of one of the two animals is removed, that rat becomes hyperphagic, but its "Siamese twin" does not. As a matter of fact, the control rat becomes quite thin. This suggests that fat deposits cause a biochemical change in the blood, a change that makes the control rat stop eating sooner. The rat operated upon is less sensitive to this change than normal and becomes hyperphagic; its parabiotic twin is *normally* sensitive and stimulated by blood from *excess* fat deposits in its twin, and therefore eats *less* than normal. At least this explanation of the results seems to be the best one, so far.

Stimulation. If the ventromedial area contains satiation pathways, one would expect a feeding animal to stop eating when it is stimulated, and this is just what happens. Furthermore, there is a rebound effect, and the animal resumes eating more rapidly after the stimulus ceases, or if the animal was not eating before the stimulus, it often begins to eat. Animals that have learned a response to obtain food will not perform the response during stimulation; they will not cross a shocking grid to obtain food during stimulation but will do so either before or after stimulation. Of course electrical stimulation of the hypothalamus may be aversive or may inhibit all behavior. But if cannulas (tubes) are implanted in the ventromedial area, the same results can be obtained with chemical stimuli. Anesthetics injected into the same area act like ventromedial lesions by causing overeating until the anesthetic wears off.

One investigator (Schacter) has made a number of interesting comparisons between hyperphagic rats and obese (fat) people. It is his contention that both kinds of subjects are less sensitive to the cues that accompany satiation than are their leaner counterparts. In the case of humans it may be that they have insensitive satiation receptors or that they do not associate these stimuli or more local stimuli, such as stomach distention, with satiation. In other words, they do not know when they have "had enough." Their eating behavior seems to be determined by the external cues of palatable food, whereas that of normal subjects appears to be determined more by internal cues of satiation. In comparing hyperphagic rats and obese humans to their normal counterparts, in a series of experiments, it was found that both obese rats and obese humans were more finicky about the taste of food, were less active, ate fewer but larger meals, ate more rapidly, were more emotional, ate less when food was difficult to obtain, and reacted less to distant stimuli as opposed to more prominent stimuli. In view of the external control of eating behavior in the obese, it may be that environmental control would do more to help them lose weight than would dieting—the cues to eating, as well as the food itself, could be removed, less palatable food could be eaten, and the like.

If the ventromedial pathways signal satiation, a question arises concerning the neural pathways from this region to other brain areas concerned in feeding behavior. Margules has traced pathways from the ventromedial hypothalamus to areas of the medial forebrain bundle near the fornix. Anatomical methods have defined the pathways, and lesions of the pathway have produced overeating. The neurons involved appear to use norepinephrine as a transmitter. Injection of chemicals that increase the availability of norepinephrine in the brain suppresses eating behavior. A norepinephrine-blocking chemical delivered to the medial forebrain bundle increases eating behavior, and norepinephrine delivered to this site decreases eating behavior. (The norepinephrine involved is a specific form—levorotatory norepinephrine.)

Lateral hypothalamic syndrome. If the ventromedial pathways signal satiation, hunger-arousal pathways should be found at a different location in the hypothalamus. Hunger-arousal input should respond to changes in the internal environment (sensitizing stimuli) caused by lack of food intake by arousing hunger-drive behavior. If the hunger-arousal fibers are destroyed, the animal should be insensitive to body changes in hunger, and **aphagia** (lack of appetite) should result. These areas have been found on both sides of the *lateral hypothalamus* in the rat; destruction results in sudden and continued refusal to eat, and the animal starves to death. The aphagia is accompanied by *adipsia;* the rat refuses liquids as well as food. There are three probable reasons for the lateral hypothalamic symptoms: (1) There is a metabolic association of food and water intake. A food-deprived animal drinks less and a water-deprived animal eats less. Presumably, disruption of a hunger-arousal system would impair drinking behavior and vice versa. (2) Descending pathways from the previously described anterior hypothalamic nuclei that are involved with water regulation have been interrupted. The anterior control nuclei have lost pathways exerting control over behavior. (3) Ascending pathways from brainstem sensory nuclei to the thalamus have been severed. These inputs along these pathways carry sensations from the mouth (taste, eating, and drinking behavior), pharynx (smell), and stomach. Teitelbaum notes a lack of response to touch of the snout or smell that he calls *sensory inattention.* Poor motor control of eating during recovery results in much spilled food.

Certain methods of reintroducing food and water can result in recovery from the effects of lateral hypothalamic lesions. There are four definite steps in the recovery process, which are described as the **lateral hypothalamic syndrome.** In the first stage the animals refuse food and water and must be tube-fed; they are aphagic and adipsic. After several days the animals will eat moist and palatable food but will continue to refuse water. In the second stage they still will not eat enough to maintain body weight, and supplemental tube feedings are required. In the third stage the animals regulate their own food intake normally (even on dry foods) if fluid intake is artificially maintained; they will not drink "pure" water, however, and if they become dehydrated, their food intake drops below maintenance level. They will drink water only if it is sweetened with sugar or saccharin. The fourth stage constitutes recovery—the animals maintain themselves on dry food and "pure" water. They are still finicky about their food, however. Like hyperphagic rats, they will not tolerate as much "bitter" quinine in their food as will normal rats.

Recovery by stages suggests relief from the effects of the lesions, relief that is attributable to the recovery of a few undamaged cells. The symptoms also suggest that the hunger and thirst mechanisms overlap anatomically. As expected, one can make satiated animals eat by stimulating the lateral hypothalamus electrically or with local injections of epinephrine. It is interesting to note that the lateral hypothalamic feeding areas are among the ones whose stimulation is rewarding to the rat—at least the animal will work hard to obtain electrical stimulation in the lateral hypothalamus. (The reward areas will be discussed later.)

In experiments of this kind, two questions always rise: (1) What kind of relationship do the hypothalamic pathways have with the other parts of the brain? (2) Have we found a "natural" system for sensitizing stimuli? Attempts have been made to deal with at least one aspect of each of these questions.

In partial answer to the first question, it appears that the cerebral cortex has much to do with stimulating the lateral hypothalamic zones. The cerebral cortex can be reversibly anesthetized in the rat by the application of potassium chloride (KCl) through small holes in the skull. When this is done to animals who have recovered from the lateral hypothalamic syndrome, the symptoms reappear. Apparently the cortex has much to do with the recovery of remaining lateral hypothalamic cells after the lesion. In the normal animal, this means that the cortex can excite the hypothalamic pathways that arouse appetite, a state of affairs that we should expect, considering the earlier discussion of the effect of food perception on the obese.

Other investigators (Blatt and Lyon) have discovered two other pathways involved in feeding behavior. One is a descending path from the basal ganglia, or neocortex, and the other is an ascending pathway leading to the posterior hypothalamus; both are in the brainstem reticular formation. Lesions of both pathways severely depress eating behavior; a lesion occurring in only one pathway has a less pronounced effect. Although neither pathway has extensive connections with the lateral hypothalamus, they are advanced as important to the lateral hypothalamic syndrome. Alternatively, two different "feeding systems" may be involved.

A study of the development of feeding behavior in newborn rats suggests that the lateral hypothalamic areas are the "natural appetite arousal pathways." Behavior development in newborn rats can be slowed by removal of part of the thyroid gland at 1 or 2 days of age. When this procedure is done, the development of eating and drinking behavior resembles the four stages of recovery from lesions of the lateral hypothalamus previously described. A parallel between recovery and development of the nervous system is suggested.

Specific hungers

The body requires *qualitative* regulation of food intake as well as adequate calories to meet its energy requirements. Minimum intakes of fats (for fatty acids), proteins

(for amino acids), essential fatty and amino acids (that the body does not manufacture), and trace amounts of vitamins and minerals are required (Chapter 2). The neural mechanisms underlying **specific hungers** are not well understood, but naïve children and laboratory rats seem to be able to maintain a *balanced* diet that includes all these essentials when offered their choice of a selection of natural foods. With their intake averaged over a period of time, young children maintain themselves on a balanced diet and grow normally when they select from a variety of natural foods, each containing some of the essentials of a balanced diet. As they grow older, dietary habits seem to interfere with this ability, and older children frequently will not eat foods that are "good for them." Different strains of laboratory rats vary in their ability to self-select an adequate diet, and maturational level, as indexed by age, seems important to this ability. As with humans, they can develop maladaptive eating habits under artificial laboratory conditions. Specific changes in food preferences with changes in body needs can be seen in pregnancy and lactation (nursing)—pregnant and nursing rats usually prefer foods rich in sodium, phosphorus, calcium, fats, and proteins. Removal of the parathyroid glands causes rats to increase their calcium intake, removal of the adrenals causes great avidity for salt, and removal of the pancreases reduces the rats' sugar intake. All of these reactions are adaptive (Chapter 3).

Regulation of sex drive

To make a long story short, sexual behavior seems to be under joint hormone and nervous control, and the major site of interaction of these factors is the hypothalamus and its connections with the pituitary gland. Hormonal factors (Chapter 3) will be briefly reviewed first. Then neural factors will be considered. A review of the effect of sensory input on the system will conclude this section.

Hormonal factors. In adolescence the

increased output of gonadal hormones causes the appearance of secondary sexual characteristics (Chapter 3). The sex hormone level also governs the sex drive in lower animals. The constant level of androgen output by the testes in most adult male species (except seasonal mating species) maintains the sex drive in males. The fluctuating estrogen level of the monthly cycle in females causes them to come into heat during ovulation, when the female egg, or ovum, is produced to be fertilized by copulation with the male. In lower species, removal of the gonads, either before or after puberty, often abolishes sexual behavior as soon as the hormone level drops enough. Normal sexual behavior in adult castrates of either sex can be restored by injections of sex hormones. Early puberty can be induced in man or lower animals, of either sex, by injection of sex hormones before the gonads have begun to produce them. In lower animals the effects of senility on the sex drive (when the gonads cease producing hormones) can be overcome by injections of sex hormones. As the nervous system develops in higher species, it becomes as important as the hormones to the sex drive in primates and more important than the hormones in man. The increased influence of the CNS on the sex drive is caused by the enormous effect of learning on sexual behavior. In subhuman primates castration before puberty prevents the appearance of most normal sexual behavior in both male and female (though fragments of sexual responses may survive). Castration before puberty may prevent adult sexual behavior in man. If castration occurs after puberty and sexual experience, sexual behavior takes some time to disappear in lower species—longer than hormone levels would predict. The effect of castration, however, is more severe in the female than in the male. In higher primates, such as chimpanzees, sexual behavior may survive castration in the adult and may be unaffected in the male. In man, adult castration has

little effect on the male and a variable effect on the female. Both sexes seem to show little reduction in sexual behavior after sexual senility has abolished hormonal effects. The general picture is one of decreased importance of the hormones and increased importance of learning as the brain develops through evolution.

Important as they are, the gonadal hormones are governed by pituitary hormones, which are controlled in turn by the hypothalamus. As explained in Chapter 3, the anterior pituitary controls the output of germ tissue (ova or sperm) by the gonads by its production of FSH; it governs the output of sex hormones (and thus the onset of puberty) by its output of LH. The fluctuating sexual cycle and sex drive of females and the maintained sex drive of males of most species are governed by the output of anterior pituitary LH. LH production, in turn, is under the influence of the hypothalamus. Ablation of the pituitary may abolish sexual behavior, just as castration does (the production of sex hormones falls off because of loss of LH), but hormone injections restore the sex drive.

Neural factors. At the lowest levels of nervous organization, erection and ejaculation are spinal reflexes and can be elicited by genital stimulation, even in men who have a severed spinal cord. Erection is largely governed by the parasympathetic nervous system and ejaculation by the sympathetic nervous system. As such, these reflexes come under the control of the hypothalamus, which largely controls the autonomic nervous system. It is probable that the hypothalamus also governs the output of LH and FSH. The output of these hormones from the anterior pituitary seems controlled by nerve fibers from the hypothalamus to the posterior pituitary. These fibers release **neurohumors** that are carried by a portal system of blood vessels from the stalk of the posterior pituitary to the anterior pituitary, to affect hormone output there.

The hypothalamus is also sensitive to the level of sex hormones in the internal environment and regulates the sex drive accordingly. Studies show that estrogen crystals implanted in the hypothalamus of female rats do not dissolve for up to 2 months, and during all that time the female remains in heat. The sensitivity of the hypothalamus to hormone level may be destroyed when lesions are made in ventral and anterior areas of the hypothalamus. The gonads do not atrophy, and yet sexual behavior is abolished and not restored by hormone injections. The normal condition of the gonads suggests that they still receive normal LH and FSH stimulation from the pituitary and produce a normal supply of gonadal hormones. The damaged hypothalamus is just not sensitive to the hormones. On the other hand, destruction of the mammillary bodies of the hypothalamus probably abolishes its ability to stimulate the output of pituitary FSH and LH. As a result, the gonads atrophy, and sexual behavior is impaired—the gonads are not being stimulated to produce sex hormones. Injection of sex hormones reverses the condition and restores normal sexual behavior. Therefore, a feedback relationship seems to exist between the hypothalamus and the gonads. The hypothalamus stimulates sex hormone output by the gonads through pituitary LH, and the sex hormone level arouses the sex drive by stimulating the hypothalamus. More extensive neural structures are involved, of course, but the hypothalamus appears to play a pivotal role.

Other drives

The list of need states of the body that arouse and sustain behavior is very lengthy, and the neural mechanisms involved vary from simple reflexes such as breathing to complex behaviors such as nest-building and migration. Hunger, thirst, and the sex drive have been used as examples in this chapter because more research has been done on them than on other drives and be-cause they are more complex than homeostatic reflexes. Other drive-related phenomena such as pain, activity level, "curiosity" behavior, and the homeostatic reflexes and drives deserve mention, however.

Pain stimulation acts like a drive in that it arouses and sustains behavior—the sensations act as releasing stimuli that control the drive mechanism.

Another drive with a more complex basis is the activity drive. Food taken in by the organism is stored as fat and glycogen or released as energy for metabolic activities, including behavior. The activity level of an animal is thus related to its food intake in a complex fashion that aids in energy storage and expenditure. The neural regulation of activity level is quite complex, and little is known about how activity is regulated by the metabolic requirements of the body.

Little is known about curiosity behavior in monkeys and higher primates, a kind of behavior that is controlled by the releasing stimulus. A monkey in a small, featureless room will perform work to open a window, the only reward being the opportunity to see another monkey, a moving toy, or some other complex visual stimulus. It will take apart simple latch puzzles for hours with the experimenter putting them back together.

At the other end of the continuum of behavior complexity, there are relatively simple homeostatic drives that arouse and sustain reflexes and behavior in order to maintain the consistency of the internal environment. The hypothalamus or medulla seems to be sensitive to many changes in the internal environment that act as sensitizing stimuli for these homeostatic drives. Changes in body temperature, acid-base balance, CO_2 content, and so on, reflexly cause changes in respiration, heart rate, blood distribution, and so on. These changes also arouse behavior, from shivering, muscle tension, or sweating, to complex behaviors —from general activity levels to specific learned adjustments to bodily discomfort.

NEURAL MECHANISMS
OF REWARD OR PUNISHMENT
Reward centers

Sites in the brain of the rat have been discovered where electrical stimulation by implanted electrodes has the effect of reward. A physiological psychologist (Olds) was investigating the effect of stimulating the brainstem ascending reticular arousal system (ARAS) in healthy and active rats with permanently implanted electrodes. One of the electrodes was misplaced, and he made the serendipitous discovery that the rat seemed to "like" being stimulated there —at least the animal would return often to that part of the table where he had received the brain stimulation. It was then discovered that the rat would learn a T maze for a reward of brain stimulation, or press a lever in a Skinner box when the lever was wired to the stimulator so that the rat could stimulate himself.

Systematic studies were made, and a variety of reward centers were discovered, some more effective than others. In order to receive brain stimulation in the most effective centers, rats would cross a shocking grid at currents they would not endure for food when hungry, water when thirsty, or copulation with another rat when stimulated by sex hormones. Reward areas have been found in the septal areas, cingulate gyrus, dorsal thalamus, tectum, anterior hypothalamus, and medial forebrain bundle (Chapter 13 and Fig. 13-8). Some of these centers are related to other drives. For example, the lateral hypothalamic "feeding pathways" (see lateral hypothalamic syndrome, p. 348) presumably arouse the hunger drive. It is an effective reward center, but it is more effective when the animal is hungry than when it is satiated by food, or when the ventromedial satiety pathways are stimulated. Psychiatrists have tried implanting electrodes in reward areas in the brains of psychotic patients in an attempt to improve their condition by effectively rewarding more normal behavior. The reports of these patients on their sensations when stimulated are open to some question because of their disorganized condition, but more rational epileptics have been tested in a similar way. Some sites of stimulation resulted in vague sensations of "well-being" or "pleasure." Others gave rise to sexual fantasies.

"Punishment" centers

The work of several investigators (Olds, Delgado, Miller, and others) has led to the locating of punishment centers in the brain of the cat and rat. Stimulation of these brain centers will serve as a negative reinforcement in the learning of escape or avoidance habits, as does painful electric shock. Cats will learn to turn a wheel to end or avoid stimulation in these areas of the brain, or they will learn to escape a compartment where they had been stimulated previously. Some of these areas lie in the medial lemniscus and posteroventral nuclei of the thalamus and are part of the pain sensation pathways from pain receptors to the brain. Stimulation in these areas should affect the cat in the same way as does the stimulation of pain receptors. However, other areas of the posterior parts of the brain have elicited reactions in animals that look more like "fear" responses, and these negative reinforcement centers are also effective in teaching cats avoidance or escape habits. Implanted electrodes in human psychotics and epileptics have produced aversive sensations as well as pleasurable ones. Reports indicate fright, a feeling of being sick, or apprehension. A more extensive and intricate system than that of pain stimulation seems indicated.

Other investigators (Stein and Margules) have "mapped" the "reward" and "punishment" areas in the brain of rats in a clever series of experiments using chemical stimulation and analysis. Cannulas (small tubes) were implanted in known neural systems in the brainstem reticular formation and the limbic areas. During brain stimulation, chemicals were used to block conduction in either the ascending or descending systems; radioactive tracer chemicals were used to analyze the chemical transmitters normally utilized by the nerve cells involved. As a result of these experiments, two systems that control reinforcement in the brain have been proposed (Fig. 15-3). The median forebrain bundle (MFB) is believed to be the reward system, and the periventricular system (PVS) is thought to be the principle punishment system. The medial forebrain bundle is primarily an ascending system whose chemical transmitter is norepinephrine. The periventricular system is primarily a descending system whose chemical transmitter is acetylcholine. Interactions between the two systems are

held to be largely a function of the limbic system at sites in the thalamus, hypothalamus, and amygdala. The principal site of interaction is held to be the amygdala, a behavior-suppressing part of the periventricular system that inhibits behavior in response to punishment (learning what not to do). Behavior is released from inhibition when the median forebrain bundle inhibits the behavior-suppressing amygdala to explain the reinforcing effect of reward (learning what to do). The theory is a complex one, but it shows considerable promise.

There has been considerable controversy over whether "reward" and "punishment" systems of the brain are involved in natural reinforcement events, or whether they are

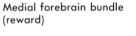

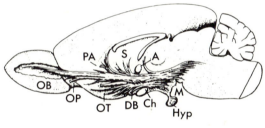

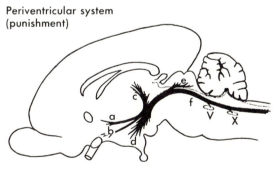

Fig. 15-3. Midline view of medial forebrain bundle (MFB), or reward system, and periventricular system (PVS) for punishment, in a generalized and primitive mammalian brain. **Upper:** *A,* Anterior commissure; *DB,* nucleus of the diagonal band; *M,* mammillary body; *OP,* olfactory peduncle; *PA,* paraolfactory area; *S,* septum. **Lower:** *a,* Periventricular nucleus; *b,* supraoptical nucleus; *c,* dorsomedial thalamus; *d,* posterior hypothalamus; *e,* tectum of midbrain; *f,* motor nuclei of cranial nerves. (From Le Gros Clark, W. E., et al.: The hypothalamus, Edinburgh, 1938, Oliver & Boyd, Ltd.)

merely a laboratory curiosity. Some (for example, Trowill) hold that electrical stimulation of the brain (ESB) has the same properties as natural incentives. They hold that stimuli that *arouse* a drive cannot be rewarding. Others (for example, Valenstein and associates) challenge the view that discrete drive states are aroused by ESB, pointing to the "stimulus-bound" properties of behavior referred to earlier. Others (Wurtz and Olds) have found discrete sites in the amygdala where ESB elicits escape behavior and other sites where ESB elicits approach behavior. Roberts trained rats to push one of two pedals to turn ESB on or off in stimulating the hypothalamus. He found that the rats used the "on" pedal to maintain a series of stimuli of short duration and the "off" pedal to rid themselves of long duration stimuli all applied at the same "rewarding" location— apparently the rewarding stimulus turned aversive with time. The whole research area of ESB is in a state of rapid change, and no general theory of the relationship between ESB and drive states has been clearly stated.

SUMMARY

Precisely defined terminology is needed to distinguish between events in the environment and events in the organism before specific motives can be discussed. A need condition in the environment sets up a need state in the organism; some aspect of the need state may serve as a sensitizing stimulus to arouse a drive in the CNS. The drives discussed are inherent, but there are acquired need conditions, states, and drives. If the behavior that results from an inherent drive is caused by "built-in" nervous patterns, the whole is an instinct; a drive and learned behavior that lead to the incentive constitute a motive.

The incentive or the cues to its presence are releasing stimuli for motivated (goal-directed) behavior. Addiction results when drugs alter the CNS so that their absence causes a need state. Thirst, hunger, and sex deprivation cause local states such as mouth dryness, stomach contractions, and full seminal vesicles (in the male). These states are neither necessary nor sufficient to arouse drives. In the case of hunger and thirst, local states are abolished immediately by eating and drinking and therefore cannot tell the animal when it has had enough. In adult man the sex drive is more a function of learning than either local states or hormone levels. Furthermore, need states affect one another, one need state being increased to satisfy another. In general, a hierarchy is established, and the need state, or internal imbalance, that can be tolerated for the shortest time is given priority. Mechanisms for signaling satiation to the CNS must also be sought for each drive—an animal stops eating or drinking before the need state of its tissues has time to change, and an animal regulates its food and water intake accurately.

Some drives, however, are controlled by their releasing stimuli; these drives are called appetites or aversions. There are need states, such as those for certain vitamins, that do not arouse drives (have no sensitizing stimuli). Most motivated behavior is controlled by many factors that serve as releasing stimuli once the drive is aroused, and their effectiveness depends on the degree of drive arousal by sensitizing stimuli. Sensitizing stimuli to drives often act on the hypothalamus, which is sensitive to internal need states, carries need-related sensory input from the brainstem, is a part of the ARAS, and controls the autonomic nervous system. Stimulation and ablation studies have shown excitatory and inhibitory areas for several drives in the hypothalamus; these areas are responsive to sensitizing and satiation stimuli, respectively. However, the behavior aroused by electrical stimulation of some areas depends on the incentive stimuli that are present at the time.

In thirst, the body conserves water by

the release of antidiuretic vasopressin from the posterior pituitary gland, which has been excited by neurosecretions from the hypothalamus. Intercellular dehydration appears to stimulate this process as well as to arouse the thirst drive. A more important mechanism for the thirst drive seems to be extracellular (volemic) dehydration, which reduces blood pressure to stimulate anterior hypothalamic thirst cells by a blood-pressure reflex and by kidney release of renin, activating an angiotensinogen to stimulate the hypothalamus.

The thirst and hunger drive cells in the hypothalamus differ chemically, the former being adrenergic and the latter cholinergic. Experiments in sham drinking show that consummatory behavior alone serves as a temporary satiation stimulus—the animal stops drinking for a few minutes after it has "replaced" the lost water, even though none of it reaches the stomach. "Salt fibers" in taste may act to control drinking, since rats drink more salt water than pure water, as is required for cellular hydration. A rat can, however, learn to control its water balance by pressing a lever for intragastric injections of water.

Food intake depends on water intake, since water is required for digestion. Animals accurately regulate their caloric intake, but this ability depends more on gastrointestinal factors than on oral factors, since a hungry sham-fed animal eats to exhaustion. Animals that press a lever for intragastric squirts of food can regulate their intake according to their needs and the caloric value of the food. Foods of higher osmotic pressure cause quicker satiation. Water loss, relief of hypoglycemia, increased metabolic heat load, and other factors can affect satiation. The glucostatic theory proposes that blood glucose level controls the hypothalamically regulated hunger drive, but reliable relationships have not been found. The lipostatic theory holds that the hunger drive is controlled by the level of fatty acid in tissue fluid; another hypothesis cites certain essential amino acids as the controlling factor. The ventromedial area of the hypothalamus seems to carry pathways from the brainstem giving sensory information concerning satiation; its ablation causes hypothalamic hyperphagia, and chemical or electrical stimulation of this center stops eating behavior. Several lines of evidence show that hyperphagic rats are more finicky about their food than are normal rats, and therefore the hunger arousal mechanisms are not involved; rather, the satiation threshold is higher. A part of whatever stimulates satiation is carried in the bloodstream since the normal parabiotic partner of a hyperphagic rat becomes thin, perhaps because of some factor carried in the blood from excess fat deposits in the hyperphagic animal. Both hyperphagic rats and obese humans seem less sensitive to internal cues that signal satiation. The lateral hypothalamus seems to contain hunger pathways because ablation of these areas makes a rat aphagic. The animal shows adipsia as well, and four separate stages, called the lateral hypothalamic syndrome, are found in recovery. Recovery probably results from the restored function of injured cells in the lesion area. Recovery seems to require a normally excitable cerebral cortex, and the stages of recovery parallel the development of eating behavior in newborn rats. Electrical or epinephrine stimuli to the lateral hypothalamus cause eating behavior. However, hunger is specific as well as general, and animals and small children can maintain a balanced diet when allowed free access to an array of *natural* foods. Maladaptive feeding habits, or "tastes," can develop with later learning. Dietary changes in pregnancy and lactation, or after adrenalectomy, reflect changed bodily needs.

The sex drive, on the other hand, seems to be under both nervous and hormonal control. Male androgen and female estrogen output by the gonads is stimulated by anterior pituitary LH and FSH at puberty, and the anterior pituitary is stimulated by neurosecretions from hypothalamic fibers en route to the posterior pituitary. The maintained hormone level and sex drive of the male, as well as the estrous fluctuations of both in the female, are under the control of the anterior pituitary by FSH and LH. In higher animals the sex drive is controlled by learning, and the drive survives castration or senility in adults (more effectively in the male than in the female). In lower animals, ablation of the pituitary, like castration, abolishes most sexual behavior, but hormone injections restore it. Estrogen crystals in the hypothalamus of females maintain estrus, or heat. Ventral and anterior hypothalamic lesions can abolish sex behavior without change in hormone levels; thus these lesions may indicate drive arousal areas. Mammillary body destruction probably destroys anterior pituitary output, since the gonads atrophy.

Other drives vary from homeostatic reflexes to those that arouse very complex behavior patterns. Pain acts like a drive in arousing and sustaining behavior—a drive controlled by the relasing stimulus. The activity level of animals is regulated to meet their metabolic conditions. Primates show curiosity behavior controlled by novel stimuli, the basis of which is unknown.

Reward centers have been found in the rat brain—stimulation of these centers serves as reinforcement for maze learning, and a rat will rapidly learn to stimulate itself with a Skinner box lever. Some of these centers seem related to those for hunger and sex. Punishment centers have been found in more posterior brain areas, some in the pain pathways, but others are found in areas that appear unrelated to pain. In both instances a complex and interrelated neural system is probably involved. The reward system appears to be organized as an adrenergic medial forebrain bundle and the punishment system as a cholinergic periventricular system. They interact at the amygdala, where the medial forebrain bundle inhibits behavior suppression by the periventricular system. There is considerable controversy over whether electrical stimulation of the brain acts like normal incentives.

READINGS

Andersson, B.: The effect of hypertonic NaCl solutions into different parts of the hypothalamus of goats, Acta Physiol. Scand. 28:188-201, 1953. (Bobbs-Merrill Reprint No. P-9.)

Andersson, B.: Thirst—and brain control of water balance, Am. Scientist 59:408-415, July-Aug. 1971.

Beach, F. A.: Evolutionary changes in the physiological control of mating behavior in mammals, Psychol. Rev. 54:297-315, 1947. (Bobbs-Merrill Reprint No. P-27.)

Bermant, G.: Copulation in rats, Psychol. Today 1:53-60, July 1967.

Butler, R. A.: Curiosity in monkeys, Sci. Am. 190:70-75, Feb. 1954. (W. H. Freeman Reprint No. 426.)

Cannon, W. B.: The wisdom of the body, New York, 1963, W. W. Norton & Co., Inc.

Carlton, P. L.: Cholinergic mechanisms in the control of behavior by the brain, Psychol. Rev. 70:19-39, 1963. (Bobbs-Merrill Reprint No. P-416.)

Cicala, G. A.: Animal drives, Princeton, N.J., 1965, D. Van Nostrand Co., Inc.

Delgado, J.: ESB, Psychol. Today 3:49-54, April 1970.

Deutsch, J. A., and Howarth, C. I.: Some tests of a theory of intracranial self-stimulation, Psychol. Rev. 70:444-460, 1963. (Bobbs-Merrill Reprint No. P-427.)

Deutsch, J.: Brain reward/ESB and ecstasy, Psychol. Today 7:46-48, July 1972.

Fernston, J. D.: Nutrition and the brain, Sci. Am. 230:84-91, Feb. 1974.

Fischer, A. E.: Maternal and sexual behavior induced by intracranial self-stimulation, Science 124:228-229, 1956. (Bobbs-Merrill Reprint No. P-113.)

Fischer, A. E.: Chemical stimulation of the brain, Sci. Am. 210:60-68, June 1964. (W. H. Freeman Reprint No. 485.)

Fuller, J. L.: Motivation: A biological perspective, New York, 1964, Random House, Inc.

Hebb, D. O.: Drives and the CNS (conceptual nervous system), Psychol. Rev. 62:243-254, 1955. (Bobbs-Merrill Reprint No. P-151.)

Hess, E. H.: Attitude and pupil size, Sci. Am.

212:46-54, April 1965. (W. H. Freeman Reprint No. 493.)

Holst, E. von, and Saint Paul, U. von: Electrically controlled behavior, Sci. Am. **206:**50-59, March 1962. (W. H. Freeman Reprint No. 464.)

Levine, S.: Sex differences in the brain, Sci. Am. **214:**84-90, April 1966. (W. H. Freeman Reprint No. 498.)

Margules, D. L., and Olds, J.: Identical feeding and rewarding systems in the hypothalamus of rats, Science **135:**374-377, 1962. (Bobbs-Merrill Reprint No. P-508.)

Olds, J.: Pleasure centers in the brain, Sci. Am. **195:**105-116, Oct. 1956. (W. H. Freeman Reprint No. 30.)

Olds, J.: Self-stimulation of the brain, Science **127:** 315-324, 1958. (Bobbs-Merrill Reprint No. P-264.)

Pribram, K. H., editor: Brain and behavior. I. Mood, states, and mind, Middlesex, England, 1969, Penguin Books, Ltd.

Richell, M.: Biological clocks, Psychol. Today **3:** 33-60, May 1970.

Schacter, S.: Eat, eat, Psychol. Today **4:**45-50, April 1971.

Schacter, S.: Some extraordinary facts about obese humans and rats, Am. Psychol. **26:**129-144, 1970. Also in Leukel, F.: Issues in physiological psychology, St. Louis, 1974, The C. V. Mosby Co.

Stein, L.: The chemistry of reward and punishment. In Efron, D., Cole, J., Levine, J., and Wittenborn, J., editors: Psychopharmacology: A review of progress, 1957-67, USPHS Publication No. 1836, Washington, D.C., 1968, U.S. Government Printing Office, pp. 105-123. Also in Leukel, F.: Issues in physiological psychology, St. Louis, 1974, The C. V. Mosby Co.

Teevan, R. C., and Smith, B. D.: Motivation, New York, 1967. McGraw-Hill Book Co.

Thomas, D., and Meyer, J.: The search for the secret of fat, Psychol. Today **7:**74-79, Sept. 1973.

chapter 16
Emotion

OVERVIEW

At first glance this chapter may seem to have been written in reverse. Although it begins with historical and definitional problems, it continues with theories of emotion, and examines the evidence only after the theories have been discussed. There are reasons for this approach. In the first place, definitions of emotion vary so widely that one must understand an investigator's theoretical approach before one can understand why he designed his experiment and what his results contribute to the understanding of emotion. Second, studies on the role of parts of the nervous system in emotion produce such variable and conflicting results that they can be understood only in terms of a widespread nervous circuit that governs emotional behavior—and proposing such a circuit involves theory. Thus the chapter begins with definitional problems in distinguishing emotion from other kinds of motivated behavior and experience. Then the criteria for useful theory in emotion are established. The phenomena to be explained are set forth—conscious states, behavior, and physiological events. The phenomena explained determine the position the theorist adopts and whether he believes that emotion organizes or disorganizes behavior. Theories of emotion, each contributing to the understanding of emotional phenomena, are taken up in historical order so that they increase gradually in complexity and generality. When the known factors contributing to emotion are understood, the evidence can be studied in a meaningful context. Therefore neural mechanism in emotion follow. The topic begins

with the effect of somatic and visceral feedback on emotion and then proceeds to the role of the autonomic nervous system, the hypothalamus, and finally the limbic system. The uniquely human emotional area of sexual behavior forms the final section. Human sexual development and adult sexual behavior, both "normal" and "abnormal," are considered. Sexual therapies conclude the section.

APPROACHES TO EMOTION

The first problem encountered in the study of emotion results from habits of language and thought inherited from the seventeenth and eighteenth century rationalist philosophers. Especially as seen by Descartes and others, *reason* was *the* unique attribute responsible for man's artistic and scientific accomplishments. Man's intelligence governed his actions in a rational way only as long as emotion did not *interfere* with the process. Emotional arousal was seen as a regrettable feature of physical existence that disrupted intelligent behavior. When Darwin revolutionized scientific theory in biology by classifying man as only one of many species that evolved from other animals, he pointed out that emotion would not exist unless it was adaptive, that is, useful for the survival of humans as well as other animals. Rationalistic thought persisted, however, in treating emotion as a regrettable inheritance from "lower" animals that disrupted intelligent and rational behavior in humans. (This view will be encountered later on when the behavior disorganization theory of emotion is considered.) A change in approach has done as much toward understanding emotion as improved methods for studying emotion. This approach recognizes *emotion as a special case of motivation.* Animals, including humans, are emotional when they are extremely motivated or aroused and when no adaptive habit or instinct can immediately solve the problem. Fear occurs when immediate escape is not assured; anger is aroused when mastery of the situation is not easy. Sexual arousal is a different case of extreme motivation to be treated later in this chapter, but frustration in this regard often leads to the further arousal of emotion.

Another problem encountered in the study of emotion is definitional—what is being studied? Earlier writers on the topic were attempting to explain emotional *experience,* the conscious events accompanying the highly motivated states of anger, fear, joy, and so on. Others, both long ago and recently, have attempted to explain emotional *behavior*—why one snarls, runs, or laughs. Still other students of emotion have tried to understand the *physiological events* accompanying emotion, from the responses of the autonomic nervous system to activity in various centers of the brain. The nature of any investigation of emotion will depend on which of these phenomena the investigator is trying to "explain," and his theory, or explanation, will, for the most part, involve these limited phenomena. To assert a theory of emotion is to state what emotion *is* or what emotions are—conscious states, behavior, or physiological events. A theory should state the conditions that are both *necessary* and *sufficient* for the emotional state.

Definitions

What is an emotion? Although no two authorities seem to agree completely, an emotion may be characterized as a highly motivated state, usually accompanied by heightened awareness (in man), often recognizable approach or withdrawal behavior, much autonomic activity, and widespread activation in the central nervous system. Consider the classic emotional states of fear, anger, and joy. All involve a high degree of motivation. Changes in conscious content are evident. Fear involves withdrawal behavior, whereas anger or joy implies approach, aggressive or peaceful. In all three states, increases in heart rate, rapid breathing, and "butterflies in the stomach" signal heightened autonomic activity. Finally, none of these conditions can be maintained without widespread increases in CNS activity.

Conscious states. Novelists, many philosophers, and early psychologists tried to classify emotion as a "conscious state." They believed that different kinds of awareness resulting from the perception of external events "caused" different conscious states. These conscious states *were* emotions, each in turn causing a different kind of emotional behavior. This position asserts that conscious events are *necessary* to emotional behavior and *sufficient* to cause emotional behavior. Because so much behavior (emotional or otherwise) is not accompanied by awareness, such assumptions seem unfounded. Much emotional behavior is "unconscious"; that is, the "cause" of the behavior cannot be verbalized. It is a common occurrence to encounter hostile behavior from persons who insist they are not angry; timidity and anxiety from persons with (objectively) nothing to fear; and exhilarant behavior for "no good reason," perceived or experienced. A given conscious state seems neither necessary nor sufficient for a given kind of emotional behavior. However, conscious states can serve as *clues* to the presence of emotion *if* one recognizes that these clues are not always reliable.

Behavior. Other writers have asserted that emotion *is* behavior of one kind or another. Anger *is* aggressive behavior, fear *is* flight or withdrawal, joy *is* laughter, and so on. This approach ignores many instances when the defined overt behavior does *not* accompany conscious states nor physiological events that strongly indicate the presence of emotion. A well-controlled individual can avoid emotional behavior, exhibiting a "poker face" or calm and unhurried normal movements, when he is angry, frightened, or happily excited. The internal physiological responses may be present—the pounding heart, etc.—but an external observer can sense no change in his demeanor. This may be true only of man, however. Some forms of emotional behavior, such as the rage-attack pattern in animals, seem to be controlled by some of the same CNS systems that govern autonomic arousal in emotion.

Physiological events. Emotional behavior and emotional awareness are accompanied by physiological events, many of which are mediated by the autonomic nervous system. In aroused emotion the heart beats faster, blood pressure may rise, blood may drain from the stomach, causing "butterflies," "goose pimples" form because of the erection of body hair, and so on. Both these events and somatic responses, such as striking out or running, are caused by physiological events in the central nervous system. The necessary and sufficient conditions for emotion may therefore be certain kinds of autonomic activity or events in certain brain systems that control *both* autonomic activity and behavior. Those who assert that autonomic arousal is the necessary and sufficient condition for emotion must explain different emotions by different patterns of autonomic arousal. In autonomic activity some differences have been found between rage and fear and between either of these emotions and "positive" emotions such as joy or sexual arousal (Arnold). As far as is known, however, there are not enough differences in the patterns of autonomic arousal to account for the variety of emotions experienced and acted out by man. Furthermore, simple exercise causes autonomic arousal. Most theorists would

not call the bodily changes in exercise an "emotional state." On the other hand, centers or systems can be found in the central nervous systems that control *both* the patterns of autonomic response *and* the overt behavior in emotion. "Centers" have been found for rage, fear, and pleasure, but they exist in bewildering variety. More subtle emotions, moreover, seem to depend on learning and involve widespread CNS activity. A *system* interrelating emotional "centers" seems necessary if emotion is to be understood in terms of CNS activity. Such a system should include all brain centers whose stimulation or removal directly alters emotional behavior and (in humans) emotional experience. The interrelationships among these centers are far from understood, but some attempts have been made to systematize them as a "limbic system," to be discussed later.

Behavior organization and disorganization in emotion

Much of the early interest of psychologists in emotion came from the apparent effect of emotion on learning behavior in both humans and laboratory animals. The "goal-seeking" activity of a highly motivated rat in a maze became disorganized when the animal encountered a barrier in its accustomed path. Error behavior increased, and emotion was seen as a "disorganized" state that resulted from interference with highly motivated behavior. The behavior of a highly motivated student often becomes similarly disorganized when he encounters a question he cannot answer on an examination, and he then misses subsequent questions that he would otherwise have answered correctly. P. T. Young and others have proposed, therefore, that emotion is the disorganization that results from the blocking of highly motivated goal-oriented behavior. Later theorists (Duffy, Leeper, Webb, Bindra, and others) have taken issue with this point of view. In the first place, the disruption is necessary if "blocked" or unsuccessful behavior is to change so that adaptation may occur; if the behavior is highly motivated, extreme changes will occur that are not typical of less motivated behavior. They point out that autonomic emotional responses and the overt behavior patterns of rage, fear, and so on would not have developed in the course of evolution if such internal and external responses did not have survival value for the organism. It is further evident that autonomic responses in rage and fear are highly organized and support highly organized overt behavior. Darwin was the first to compare the expression of emotion in animals and men to show that emotional expression was useful for survival—a biological adaptation. Cannon's emergency theory (Chapter 5) states that the sympathetic nervous system responses in rage and fear prepare an animal for fight or flight, and in a general way this seems to be the case. Fight and flight are both highly motivated and very organized responses, and sympathetic arousal helps prepare an animal for the exertion required in either case. Neither type of behavior, however, is appropriate for a rat learning a maze or a student taking an examination. But neither maze-running nor exam-taking was important to survival in the primitive world in which emotional behavior evolved; fighting and fleeing *were* important survival mechanisms. The conclusion follows that emotional responses, autonomic and somatic, are highly organized and serve as a primitive mechanism for *motivation,* arousing and sustaining behavior appropriate to a primitive emergency. The fact that such behavior is not appropriate to highly artificial situations such as maze-running for the rat or exam-taking for the student seems beside the point.

THEORIES OF EMOTION

As suggested earlier, attempts to explain emotion often differed widely because theorists were trying to explain different phenomena, each considered to *be* emotion. Attempts to explain the conscious events accompanying emotion will be quite different from attempts to explain observed emotional behavior, autonomic responses in emotion, or brain function in emotion. From this point of view, none of the theories to be considered is right or wrong, and each contributes something to the understanding of emotional phenomena. On the other hand, one can better examine which of these phenomena—conscious, behavioral, autonomic, or CNS activity—is a necessary and sufficient condition for emotion after one sees how each could theoretically control emotional states.

James and Lange theories

For William James, emotion was a *conscious state* that resulted from sensed emotional behavior and visceral reactions. He sought the causes of this conscious state in the reactions of the body to stimuli that called forth anger, fear, or joy. His famous dictum that we do not run because we are afraid, we are afraid because we run, summarizes his position. To James a perceived stimulus became a consciously emotional stimulus *after* reaction to the stimulus began. When a threatening stimulus resulted in flight, it also resulted in sensations of running and sensations from the visceral reactions of the autonomic nervous system. The somatic sensations of running and the sympathetically aroused sensations of rapid heartbeat, panting, "gooseflesh," and so on were *added to* the initial perception of the threatening stimulus. Adding the somatic sensations of running to the visceral sensations from the autonomic reactions resulted in a perception of fear. The stimulus was therefore feared after the reaction to it began. A simple example might be your own reaction to an emergency while driving an automobile at high speed. Another car pulls out in front of you, you react quickly to avoid it, and only after the incident is over do you begin to tremble, sweat, and feel frightened. Anger, as another emotion, would include some of the same and other sensations of autonomic arousal, but it would also include somatic sensations of overt or suppressed attack behavior. Joy would involve more parasympathetic arousal, perhaps, and sensations of approach reactions; sexual arousal would involve a different autonomic sensation pattern, feedback from copulation responses, and so on. (Lange proposed the same kind of theory, except that he restricted the sensations to those that come from the blood vessels.)

Behavioristic theory of emotion

Several decades ago the famous behaviorist John B. Watson rejected consciousness as a cause of behavior. He believed that stimuli caused behavior as a direct result of their action on the sense organs and nervous system, and consciousness did not belong in this sequence of events.

For Watson rage *was* attack, fear *was* flight, and lust *was* sexual behavior. He sought to determine which of these and other emotional responses were "inherited," in what form they began, and what stimuli controlled them. His experiments with 6-month-old children convinced him that there were three inherited patterns of emotional behavior controlled by four stimuli. Pattern X, tentatively identified as "fear," consisted of withdrawal responses and wailing cries in response to either a loud noise or sudden loss of support when being held (falling). Pattern Y, assumed to be "rage," was aroused by restraining an infant's movements, which resulted in strident crying and a flushed face. Pattern Z, called "lust," resulted in the inhibition of active behavior and was accompanied by gurgling, smiling, and sometimes erection of the penis. The stimulus was stroking of the skin, especially near the genitals. To Watson the more complex emotional behavior of adults in response to more varied

stimuli resulted from conditioning. If the child was frightened by a loud noise while he was petting a rabbit, he would "attach" the fear response to the rabbit. Furthermore, he would show the fear response to objects resembling the rabbit in any important way; he would *generalize* his fear, and contact with any furry object would result in the fear response. With learning, the fear response would also become more varied, and the withdrawal response would include running and other means of avoiding the feared stimulus. Although these notions may seem oversimplified today, physiologists have found "centers" in the brain that seem to control both visceral and somatic reactions of flight and attack. Other centers that control sexual behavior have been found. Certain responses, such as smiling, seem to have inherited neural mechanisms. In this sense, perhaps Watson was correct in his assumptions about the inheritance of mechanisms for emotional behavior.

Autonomic response theories of emotion

Many writers have identified autonomic nervous system responses with emotion. Most of them state that parasympathetic nervous system reactions, or PNS dominance, are necessary (at least at first) to positive, or pleasurable, emotions. Sympathetic nervous system reactions are necessary to rage or fear, with a different SNS pattern of response for rage, as compared to fear. Some assert a different autonomic pattern acquired through learning for each of the more subtle emotions. Others have said that different autonomic patterns are inherited as a few beginning emotional reactions —PNS dominance for elation or joy, and SNS patterns for rage, fear, and perhaps a few others such as "disgust" or "apathy." In some cases it is suggested that the autonomic reaction *is* the emotion and is always necessary to it. Other writers believe it is necessary only at first—after learning has occurred, only activity in the brain systems that normally control the autonomic nervous system is necessary. Some have suggested inherited autonomic patterns that *are* simple emotional reactions such as lust, rage, and fear; the more subtle and varied emotions are one or more of these patterns plus varied somatic responses. Jealousy, for example, could be a mixture of rage and fear of a given degree, along with both approach and avoidance reactions. In any case all assert that the ANS reactions *are* emotion, at least at first.

Cannon-Bard theory of emotion

The Cannon-Bard theory originated as an attempt to explain the behavior of decorticate cats. After removal of the cerebral cortex the animals do not respond, except in a reflex fashion, to vision, audition, or smell. However, they are capable of reflex standing, and their response to somesthetic input from the skin is attack. Stimuli such as pinching the skin or pulling the tail merely cause moving away in normal cats. In decorticates an immediate and integrated rage-attack behavior pattern results. The response was called **sham rage** because the animal lacked the sensory and nervous equipment to direct and maintain the attack behavior. The animal attacked in whatever direction it happend to be "pointed" at the moment, without attacking the source of the stimulation. Furthermore, the attack behavior stopped as soon as the stimulus was removed—rage behavior did not continue for a time, as in the normal animal. However, the rage response was integrated; both organized overt behavior *and* a generalized autonomic nervous system reaction were present. In further experiments more and more of the higher nervous system areas were removed. As long as the posterior third of the hypothalamus was intact, the sham rage pattern was present. When this area was removed, the sham rage behavior disintegrated into isolated "part responses" of somatic and visceral reactions. Snarling

might occur, or some autonomic change, but the organized rage reaction had disappeared. The experimenters suggested, therefore, that centers in the posterior part of the hypothalamus organized *both* the ANS responses in rage *and* the behavior pattern in rage. (An early version of the theory placed these "centers" in the thalamus.) Extending this idea, others assumed that the hypothalamus contained centers responsible for both behavior and autonomic reactions in each of the major emotional states. They also proposed that activity in the same centers stimulated the cerebral cortex to give rise to the "conscious state" appropriate to the emotion. Overt behavior, autonomic responses, and conscious states in emotion were assumed to be aroused by stimuli from the sense organs that reached appropriate centers in the hypothalamus. Other emotions could of course be added by learning—conditioning of the hypothalamic centers to new stimuli and elaboration of the response patterns initiated there.

Subsequent experiments on sham rage have shown that partial decortication that spares the cingulate gyrus and ventral paleocortex, or allocortex (Chapter 13), makes cats *placid,* raising their rage threshold rather than lowering it. Yet either cingulate lesions or lesions in the ventral complex (amygdala, piriform cortex, and hippocampus) make these placid animals ferocious! It is evident that a more widespread neural "circuit" than the hypothalamus is involved in the control of rage and perhaps other emotions as well. There is little doubt that rage-attack behavior and autonomic responses are *organized* at a subcortical level. Posterior hypothalamic lesions produce somnambulant animals (Chapter 13) that are unemotional, and medial and ventromedial lesions of the hypothalamus make cats ferocious. With the rest of their nervous system intact, however, the ferocity of the lesioned cats is well directed and outlasts the stimulus—they are difficult and dangerous to handle. However well the hypothalamus organizes the rage-attack pattern and perhaps other emotional responses, more widespread areas of the nervous system are involved in its *control*. For example, selective lesions in the piriform areas, amygdala, or hippocampus make animals ferocious, beginning several weeks *after* the operation. Other investigators report placidity after lesions in some of these same areas. Stimulation of one part of the amygdala causes rage responses, whereas stimulation of another part causes fearlike responses; stimulation of the latter site can suppress rage behavior from hypothalamic stimulation. Lesions of the septal

area lower the rage threshold, but removal of the amygdala reverses this effect, and so on. Even changing the stimulus parameters, such as voltage or frequency, can elicit fright behavior or rage behavior from the same stimulus site. Obviously, widespread systems *control* the expression of emotional responses, even if there is a focus of organization. Even the stimulation of still *lower* centers in the midbrain can suppress rage behavior that was brought on by hypothalamic stimulation; these sites are often more effective in suppressing rage behavior than are the higher centers. Others (Freeman and Arnold) have proposed that emotional behavior and experience are *initiated*

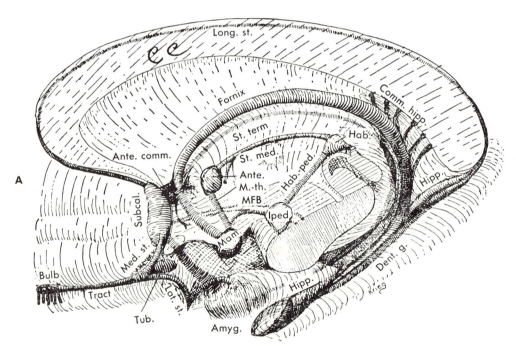

Fig. 16-1. A, Reconstruction of a medial view of human rhinencephalon. **B,** Reconstruction of rhinencephalon as seen from above. *Amyg.,* amygdala; *Ante. comm., A.C.,* anterior commissure; *Ante.,* anterior nucleus of thalamus; *Bulb,* olfactory bulb; *C.C.,* corpus callosum; *Comm. hipp.,* hippocampal commissure; *Dent. g.,* dentate gyrus; *Diag. bd.,* diagonal band; *Hab.,* habenula; *Hab.-ped.,* habenulopeduncular tract; *Hipp.,* hippocampus; *Iped.,* interpeduncular nucleus; *Lat. st.,* lateral olfactory stria; *Long st.,* longitudinal stria; *Mam.,* mammillary body; *Med. st.,* medial olfactory stria; *MFB,* medial forebrain bundle; *M.-th.,* mammillothalamic tract; *St. med.,* stria medullaris; *St. term.,* stria terminalis; *Subcal.,* subcallosal gyrus; *Tract,* olfactory tract; *Tub.,* olfactory tubercle. Compare both **A** and **B** with Fig. 13-8. (From Krieg, W. J. S.: Functional neuroanatomy, Evanston, Ill., Brain Books, Inc.)

by the cortex, and merely carried out by the hypothalamus and other subcortical centers.

Finally, the role of sensitivity to stimulation must be considered. Cannon and Bard assumed that intact animals do not show a low threshold to rage because the cerebral cortex normally inhibits the rage centers in the hypothalamus. An alternate hypothesis has been suggested. Perhaps the decorticate animals were made hyperalgesic (abnormally sensitive to pain) by the operation. Since the stimuli to sham rage were tactile (pinching, hair pulling, tail twisting), these stimuli could arouse pain centers in the decorticate cat—pain centers

whose activity was suppressed by the cortex in the normal cat.

Papez-MacLean theory

The Papez-MacLean theory is a gradually evolving set of notions about a system of nervous centers that perhaps *control,* rather than organize, emotional behavior (and perhaps emotional experience). The centers and pathways involved were described in Chapter 13 as the limbic system (Figs. 13-8 and 16-1). The septal area of the cortex, the cortical cingulate and entorhinal areas, the hippocampus, and most of the amygdaloid nuclei are involved. Papez suggested a circuit from the entorhinal cor-

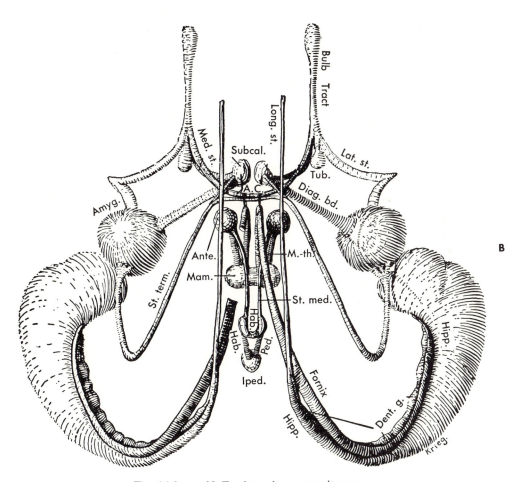

Fig. 16-1, cont'd. For legend see opposite page.

tex to the hippocampus, thence to the hypothalamus via the fornix, from there to the anterior thalamus, and finally to the cingulate gyrus. Most of these structures had been associated with smell input, but Papez suggested that they were involved in emotional experience. MacLean elaborated on Papez' ideas, and the additional circuits shown in Fig. 13-8 have been traced by subsequent work. Since then the work of many scientists has shown the involvement of many of these structures in emotional *behavior,* whereas stimulation of and surgery on human epileptics and psychotic patients have shown some of these structures to be involved in emotional *experience.* The "connections" of Fig. 13-8 are supposed to integrate perception by higher centers with emotional behavior that is organized by the diencephalon (chiefly the hypothalamus) and perhaps midbrain structures.

Lindsley activation theory

The ARAS and DTPS were described in some detail in Chapter 13. The ARAS extends throughout the scattered gray matter cells of the medulla, pons, midbrain, and diencephalon, including much of the hypothalamus. The ARAS receives collateral input from many sensory pathways, and its intrinsic rhythm in turn keeps the brain "awake" by stimulating higher centers. The extensive invasion of the hypothalamus by the ARAS assures that activation will reach any emotional "centers" in the hypothalamus. These connections, as well as the thalamic interconnections of the DTPS, involve the limbic system. The role of the ARAS and DTPS in motivation was surveyed in Chapter 15, and emotion is certainly a highly motivated state. Lindsley points out that (1) the EEG in emotion has an "activation pattern," including depressed alpha rhythms and much low-voltage fast activity; (2) the same EEG pattern can be reproduced by electrical stimulation of the BSRF (ARAS areas), which extends into

the basal diencephalon (including the hypothalamus) and by these pathways reaches the thalamus; (3) if the basal diencephalon is destroyed (the anterior parts of the ARAS), an activated EEG cannot be obtained, and synchronized rhythmic discharges between thalamus and cortex are dominant; (4) the behavior resulting from point 3 includes apathy, lethargy, somnolence, catalepsy (rigid posture), hypokinesis (little movement), and so on; and therefore (5) the BSRF mechanism, which includes outflow to behavior termed emotion, "is either identical with, or overlaps, the EEG activating mechanism, described under point 2, which arouses the cortex."* In other words, the neural mechanisms controlling emotional behavior are to be sought in the BSRF.

NEURAL MECHANISMS IN EMOTION
Somatic and visceral feedback

To what extent are somatic and visceral reactions essential to emotion as it has been defined? To what extent do visceral reactions vary for different emotions, and are they essential for emotional experiences? Rage and fear involve the diffuse reactions of the sympathetic nervous system as well as fight or flight behavior. In one early experiment Cannon removed the sympathetic chain ganglia and collateral ganglia from cats, which abolished most sympathetic responses. After recovery these cats appeared normal, except that their tolerance for cold and stress was reduced. Their reaction to a dog showed normal "emotionality," including the baring of teeth and claws, arched back, spitting, and hissing.

It could be argued that the brain centers controlling sympathetic response had already been conditioned to "emotional" stimuli and that these centers were intact and were sufficient for the emotional be-

---

*From Lindsley, D. B.: Emotion. In Stevens, S. S., editor: Handbook of experimental psychology, New York, 1951, John Wiley & Sons, Inc.

havior, now that learning had taken place. Yet it is evident that major sympathetic *reactions* are unnecessary to emotional behavior, at least in the adult animal. In man, who can tell us about emotional experience, visceral sensations seem to have more to do with emotional experience than emotional behavior. **Paraplegic** patients, with the spinal cord severed as high as at the neck level, have become a common casualty of war and traffic accidents. Some of these patients are paralyzed from the neck down, and facial expression is their only somatic

expression of emotion aside from verbal responses. Diffuse sympathetic arousal cannot be organized by the brain. Furthermore, sensations from the body cannot reach the brain; thus any isolated autonomic reflexes that *do* occur cause no sensations. Of course, the extent to which paraplegic patients receive visceral sensations depends on the level at which the spinal cord is severed. At the neck level, no somatic or visceral sensations are possible save for facial expression (somatic) or oral (visceral) input. As the cut becomes as low as the level of the lowest

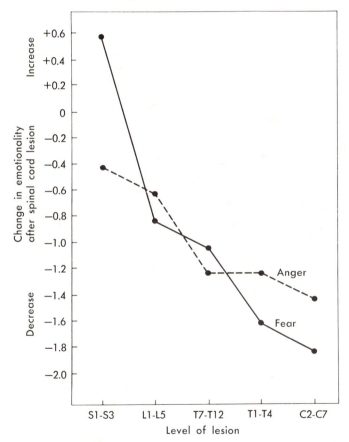

Fig. 16-2. Changes in rated emotional feeling before and after lesions of the spinal cord for patients with lesions at different levels. Compare this figure with Figs. 5-1 and 5-2 to clarify the level at which the spinal cord has been severed. (From Schacter, S.: Emotion, obesity, and crime, New York, 1971, Academic Press Inc. Adapted from the data of Hohman, G.: Some effects of spinal cord lesions on experienced emotional feelings, Psychophysiology **3**:143-156, 1966.)

attachment of the ribs (C7, see Fig. 5-1), sensations of rapid heartbeat, "butterflies" in the stomach, and some lower somatic inputs become possible. Schacter reports a study by Hohman of changes in rated emotional feeling for 15 subjects before and after spinal lesions at various levels (Fig. 16-2). The higher the level of the break in the cord, the fewer the somatic and visceral sensations, and the less intense the reported emotional experience in the case of either anger or fear. However, the patients often *behave* in an appropriate way even though they may report only a "mental sort of anger." Except for the group with the lowest level of section (the group with the most somatic and visceral sensations) an increase in "sentimentality" as evinced by more frequent crying or tears in the eyes was reported.

Evidently, autonomic *reactions* are not *necessary to* emotional *behavior.* There is little doubt, on the other hand, that autonomic and somatic reactions *contribute to* emotional experience and behavior. An injection of epinephrine, which mimics the effect of mass sympathetic response, will cause the subject to experience a "cold emotion"—sensations such as a pounding heart, empty stomach, and so on. Unless the subject *perceives* these inputs as resulting from emotional upset, no emotional behavior will result. In one experiment by Schacter, subjects were given injections of epinephrine under another name or a placebo (fake drug) and were either informed of the effects of epinephrine or told the drug would have no side effects at all. (Epinephrine causes a rapid heartbeat, "butterflies" in the stomach, and other internal sensations usually associated with emotion.) Both groups of subjects believed the experiment involved drug effects on a visual acuity test. While supposedly waiting in a room for the vision test, each subject was accompanied by a stooge of the experimenter acting like another waiting subject. Under one set of conditions—

euphoria—the stooge began acting in an exuberant way by flying paper airplanes, dancing, and keeping up a happy patter while asking the subject to join him. The other set of conditions—anger—involved filling out an extremely personal and insulting questionnaire, which asked, for example, how many extramarital affairs the subject's mother had had. While filling out the same questionnaire, the stooge increasingly expressed rage and finally tore up the offending questionnaire and left in a huff. The experimenters observed the action through a one-way screen and systematically rated how much the subject's behavior resembled the stooge's behavior. After the stooges left, the experimenters, giving a plausible reason, had the subject fill out a standard rating scale to assess the intensity of anger or euphoria. Both the behavior observations and rating scales came out as expected. Subjects who had a placebo or who knew their inner sensations resulted from the drug were relatively indifferent to either kind of stooge and rated their emotions as neither angry or euphoric. Subjects who did not know the reason for their inner turmoil became angry or euphoric in both behavior and rating scale, depending on which stooge they were with.

In another experiment, injections of a tranquilizer that reduces autonomic activity also reduced the laughter and reported amusement to a slapstick movie, whereas epinephrine had the opposite effect when the subjects were not informed of the effects of the drugs. Although autonomic reactions may be *unnecessary* to emotional experience and behavior, they *can* initiate both, depending on how the subject interprets them.

ANS and emotion

According to Cannon's emergency theory, diffuse sympathetic discharge prepares an animal for fight or flight, both highly emotional responses. Both responses are highly organized and motivated, as already pointed out. Are different emotional behavior patterns, such as rage and fear, accompanied by different ANS reactions? Do the different ANS reactions influence typical emotional "experience" in man? It appears that there *are* different autonomic response patterns for rage, fear, and sexual arousal, and perhaps for other emotions, such as apathy. Studies of psychotic patients suggest that their predominant autonomic pattern strongly influences their reported "mood," as well as their behavior. As far as the more pleasant emotions are concerned, many of them appear to be accompanied by widespread but discrete parasympathetic responses, which are cholinergic and governed from the anterior and medial hypothalamus. Such parasympathetic reactions include sexual excitement and dilation of blood vessels supplying the viscera and the skin. Rage and fear, on the other hand, are accompanied by diffuse sympathetic discharge, reinforced by hormones from the adrenal medulla.

The adrenal gland produces two hormones: epinephrine and norepinephrine. Epinephrine is sympatheticomimetic (has the same effect as SNS discharge), whereas in some respects norepinephrine is not. Epinephrine raises the blood pressure by cardioacceleration (increasing the rate of beating of the heart). Norepinephrine raises the blood pressure by constricting blood vessels leading to the skin and viscera. It appears that more epinephrine is released in fear reactions, and that greater norepinephrine release accompanies anger. Parasympathetic stimulation would therefore lower the blood pressure more in fear than in anger because it slows the heart and combats the effect of epinephrine more directly. This can be tested by injecting a drug (methacholine [Mecholyl]) that mimics parasympathetic stimulation. The drug rapidly lowers the blood pressure of depressed psychotics or of normal people experiencing fright because it slows their rapid heartbeat. A smaller effect on blood pressure is

typical of a high norepinephrine response in rage because the drug has no effect on constricted blood vessels that raise the blood pressure. This response is found in paranoid psychotics and normal subjects experiencing anger. The tests show that predatory animals such as lions have a higher norepinephrine level in the blood whereas animals that survive by flight, such as the rabbit, produce more epinephrine. Funkenstein suggests that sympathetically aroused animals exhibit only rage and fear, but man experiences self-directed anger, which leads to depression. Depression, like anxiety or fear, is accompanied by a high epinephrine output. Since the visceral blood flow is not reduced in fear, the stomach is flushed, making a large hydrochlorc acid output possible, which can cause ulcers. If physiological development parallels psychological development, one would expect the young child to demonstrate more anger than fear and produce more norepinephrine than epinephrine. With training—"development of a conscience"—more self-directed anger and anxiety should be accompanied by a higher epinephrine output. As far as the adrenal output is concerned, the ratio of norepinephrine to epinephrine *is* higher in infants than in older children.

Endocrine glands and emotion

Under the stress of emotion, sympathetic stimulation often increases epinephrine output by the adrenal medulla, which in turn elicits ACTH output by the anterior pituitary. ACTH increases corticoid output by the adrenal cortex to improve carbohydrate metabolism and nervous excitability (Chapter 3). Output of the thyroid glands is also increased to raise the metabolic rate. If the emotional stress is frequent or of a long duration, these glands hypertrophy (increase in size) to keep up with the demand for their secretions (Chapter 18). One way to intervene in this chain of events is to inject ACTH to increase the stress effect and see if differences in emotional learning or other emotional responses result. The problem is that an increased ACTH level increases the adrenal steroid output. This in turn reduces hypothalamic stimulation of ACTH output by the anterior pituitary (corticotrophin releasing factor [CRF], see Chapter 3). Removing the adrenal cortex first will enable the experimenter to keep the ACTH level high without increasing natural adrenal steroids. This was done, and animals were taught an avoidance habit—running to avoid shock in response to a light and a tone. When the shock was omitted during extinction trials, the running response dropped out, or became extinguished among control animals in a few days. The ACTH rats never exhibited extinction during the 2 weeks of tests (deWied). To show the effect of decreased ACTH on emotional behavior, habituation can be used as a test (Levine). Rats will jump measurably to a sudden loud sound—repeat the sound at regular intervals and the jumping behavior is reduced until it drops out (habituation). A crystal of a corticosteroid hormone placed in the hypothalamus will reduce its CRF stimulation of ACTH output by the anterior pituitary. Rats with the resulting low ACTH level habituate much faster than normal rats. Finally, the blood level of ACTH increases as rats acquire an avoidance response similar to the one described above (Levine and Brush). Apparently, ACTH level has something to contribute to the amount of emotional arousal.

Hypothalamus and emotion

Removal of the brain anterior to the posterior third of the hypothalamus leaves a cat able to display sham rage—integrated attack behavior, however brief, accompanied by the autonomic responses of typical rage. Subsequent removal of this area reduces the rage behavior to fragments of the original response. Posterior hypothalamic lesions of the rage area in an otherwise intact animal results in placidity and somnambulance. These observations led many researchers to conclude that the hypothalamus was the seat of integration of the somatic and visceral responses in rage and perhaps in other emotions as well. Subsequent studies with implanted electrodes seemed to confirm these conclusions, although the locations differ, since stimulation of the anterior hypothalamus and related areas (basal septal nuclei, preoptic area, lateral hypothalamus, basal medial thalamus) produces organized and lasting rage behavior. Furthermore, stimulation of the posterior hypothalamus produces fear-escape responses (Hess), and self-stimulation "reward" areas (Chapter 15) lie in the anterior medial hypothalamus. It appears that there are "centers" in the hypothalamus that are important to pathways for rage, fear, and pleasure whose stimulation produces both the autonomic and somatic reactions of these emotions.

Hess and Akert found that stimulation of the cat hypothalamus often resulted in all of the symptoms of rage (erect hair, arched back, spitting, and hissing) and a directed attack on the experimenter might occur if he moved suddenly. This phenomenon has been examined in more detail by Flynn and his colleagues. They found that attack behavior was of two kinds, depending on where the hypothalamus was stimulated. Stimulation of the *medial* hypothalamus resulted in *affective* attack (rage) of the kind described by Hess, in which the cat attacked any convenient object, especially if it moved, as when a rat is placed in the cage. The cat begins by hissing and lashing out with its claws and bites the rat later on. If the *lateral* hypothalamus is stimulated, a *quiet biting* attack occurs—the cat stalks the rat in an effective and more *directed* fashion, using the paws to hold the rat to direct biting at the throat. This sort of behavior is believed related to the animal's normal predatory hunting behavior.

The lateral "predator" response can be

further analyzed chemically. Cats can be classified as killers or nonkillers, depending on whether they execute a predatory quiet biting attack when a rat is placed in the same cage with them (no brain stimulation is used at this stage of the experiment). Hoebel et al. implanted small cannulas (tubes) in the lateral hypothalamus of both killers and nonkillers for delivering chemical stimulation. When carbachol (a chemical that mimics the neural transmitter acetylcholine) was used, it stimulated nonkillers to kill. Atropine blocks the action of acetylcholine and would make the killer rats stop killing. Apparently the pathways involved in the predatory attack use acetylcholine as a neural transmitter (cholinergic pathways).

A question remains: How dependent are these stimulus areas on the input of other centers at higher and lower levels, and to what extent do these cells dominate the activity of other parts of the brain at higher and lower levels? Stimulation of a hypothalamic area may be merely exciting a pathway to another part or parts of the brain where the somatic and visceral responses are actually integrated. And ablation of an area in the hypothalamus may be merely interrupting a major pathway going to a more important integrating center elsewhere in the brain. Important as the hypothalamus is to the integration of the somatic and visceral responses of emotion, it appears to be part of a larger system, involving higher and lower centers, that organizes emotional response and perhaps emotional experience as well.

Limbic system and emotion

In more primitive animals the cerebral cortex began as a set of centers for correlating smell input. As a result, many of the older cortical structures such as the hippocampus and prepiriform areas (Figs. 13-8 and 16-1) were classified along with the olfactory bulbs as **rhinencephalon** ('nose brain'). Papez, in a theory elaborated by MacLean, proposed that some of these cortical centers and certain subcortical structures serve to integrate perception by higher centers with emotional expression that originates in the diencephalon (primarily the hypothalamus). As previously explained, he proposed a "circuit" (Fig. 13-8) from the hippocampus and amygdala to the hypothalamus via the fornix and thence to the anterior thalamus and gyrus cinguli. Subsequent studies have added other pathways to the system as indicated in Fig. 13-8.

Pribram and Kruger, taking a phylogenetic approach to the development of cortical and associated subcortical structures, have traced the evolutionary development of cortical and subcortical centers from their origin in smell. They classify as "nose brain" the olfactory bulb connections with the prepiriform areas on the base of the brain and parts of the amygdaloid nuclei. Connections exist from these areas, but not the olfactory bulb, to areas beneath the corpus callosum (subcallosal), the presubiculum, and the frontotemporal areas. Connections from here go to the third system of hippocampus and cingulate gyrus. In terms of the evolutionary age of the cortical parts of this system, the hippocampus, piriform lobe, and olfactory bulb are the oldest, and constitute the **paleocortex.** The cingulate gyrus, presubiculum, and frontotemporal areas are intermediate, or **transitional, cortex.** The remainder of the cerebral cortex is the **neocortex** ('new cortex').

Papez' original speculations were fruitful ones, leading to experiments on what has been called the **Klüver-Bucy syndrome,** after its discoverers. They found that bilateral ('both sides') temporal lobe ablations made rhesus monkeys docile, oral (mouthing things), indiscriminative (putting anything in their mouths), and hypersexed. The changes in emotional behavior were profound and obvious. The ablations involved included, along with the temporal lobes, the frontotemporal cortex, piriform lobe, amygdala, presubiculum, and hippocampus. These areas are involved in Papez' circuit and in the second and third systems, which Pribram and Kruger believe to have evolved from the olfactory brain.

Subsequent experiments have shown that various parts of the areas destroyed in the Klüver-Bucy surgery are important to different aspects of the syndrome. Hypersexuality, for example, can be produced by piriform lesions alone. It is abolished by castration and returns with hormone therapy. Lesions of the amygdala alone seem related to the taming effects of the Klüver-Bucy syndrome. If a boss monkey in a cage group suffers amygdaloid lesions, he falls to the bottom position in the "social hierarchy" more frequently than not. A follow-up study by Mirsky produced the suggestion that circuits involved in learning social dominance had been interrupted by the operation. If the adult monkeys that were operated on were placed in a cage with easily dominated young monkeys, they seemed to relearn dominance behavior. Once the dominance behavior was reestablished, each operated monkey could be put back into its original adult colony where he assumed more or less his original position in the "pecking order." Other species seem to respond to amygdaloid lesions in the same way. Even the wild agouti and the lynx of the cat family can be tamed by removing the amygdala and piriform cortex. None of these effects seems directly related to the olfactory origin of the limbic system since the Klüver-Bucy syndrome appears even if the olfactory tracts are severed prior to the Klüver-Bucy type of surgery.

More selective stimulation or lesions of *parts* of the amygdala reveal a less evident area that inhibits aggression as well as the Klüver-Bucy area does. (The Klüver-Bucy area seems to excite aggression because its removal has a taming effect.) Stimulation of one set of nuclei (basolateral) yields aggressive behavior in cats (Kaada et al.).

Cutting the pathways from these nuclei to the (lateral) hypothalamus abolishes the response to stimulation. After the amygdala was removed, stimulation of the tract to the hypothalamus still caused aggression, so the amygdala stimulates aggression systems involving the hypothalamus. Another area of the amygdala has the opposite effect (corticomedial nuclei). Lesions of this area decrease hypothalamic aggression in the cat. Decreased aggression is also seen when tracts from the corticomedial area to the hypothalamus (ventromedial and medial area) are cut. The corticomedial nuclei must inhibit "hypothalamic aggression"— they may excite flight behavior.

Recently, the relationships between the limbic system and the cortex (which is assumed to guide and direct behavior) have been traced by a rather novel method. Horseradish peroxidase was injected into different parts of the frontal and parietal cortex in a number of monkeys (Kievit and Kuypers). The enzyme was transported by the nerve cells that reach these areas back to their origin in the lateral hypothalamus, other basal forebrain areas (substantia innominata), and the thalamus.

Until the role of each part of the limbic system is known, as well as the manner in which it interacts and affects other parts of the brain, few conclusions are possible.

Cerebral cortex and emotion

Septal area. The septal area is a part of the transitional cortex that forms a part of the limbic circuit (Figs. 13-6 and 13-8). Lesions in this area produce the type of savageness in rats that results from stimulation of certain hypothalamic and amygdala nuclei that were previously described (Brady and Nauta). A striking difference is that the animals *can* be tamed, if handled, within a couple of weeks; recovery does not occur if the animals are isolated. An explanation of the phenomenon has not appeared. Presumably pathways involved in the inhibition of rage behavior have been destroyed, but other sources of inhibition are available.

Frontal lobes. A major output of the limbic system seems to project to the frontal areas of the cerebral cortex from the anterior nuclei of the thalamus. These cortical areas are anterior to the motor and premotor areas; so they are sometimes known as the **prefrontal lobes** (Fulton and Jacobsen). In studies on the ability of primates in a learning task involving a delay between stimulus presentation and discrimination (delayed reaction, Chapter 13), the effects of removing the prefrontal areas were tested. A side observation noted was that the animals were less "excited" (emotional) in response to errors and were more generally docile.

Psychosurgery

With all of the research involving the effects of brain stimulation and lesions on emotional behavior in animals, it should come as no surprise to find that these procedures have been attempted to relieve emotional disorders in man. The legal and ethical issues involved in perhaps changing permanently the emotional behavior of another human being are outside the scope of a simple textbook. It can be said that the effects are complex and profound and the procedures are susceptible to misuse, unless careful social control is exercised. Even then, the emotional behavior of humans is so much more complex than that of other animals—even other primates—that unpredictable results may follow the most careful diagnosis and surgery. The procedures have been used to relieve severe pain in terminal cancer, terrifying anxiety that is not relieved by psychotherapy, psychosis (Chapter 18), and severe assaultive behavior. Some fear their use in controlling anger that has legitimate cause in social deprivation or in "socializing" criminals whose crimes have social rather than neurological

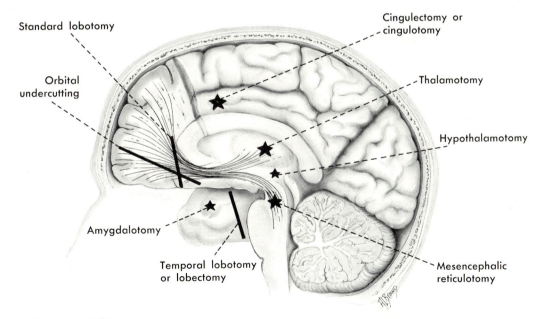

Fig. 16-3. Medial (cut down the center) view of human brain, showing different sites for destroying tissue in psychosurgery. *Bars,* Cutting tracts (lobotomy, orbital undercutting, temporal lobotomy) or removing a lobe (temporal lobectomy). *Stars,* Focal brain sites destroyed by current at the tip of a precisely placed electrode (stereotaxic surgery). (From Hitchcock, E.: Psychosurgery today, Ann. Clin. Res. **3:**187-198, 1971.)

causes. The debate can be left to relevant readings at the end of the chapter, should the student wish to pursue it.

Prefrontal lobectomy. These cases result in most instances from accidental brain damage although surgery to remove tumors may remove prefrontal areas. The consequences are similar to prefrontal lobotomy (see below) and are more severe if most of the prefrontal areas are removed.

Prefrontal lobotomy. This operation was perfected by Moniz in response to animal experiments reported on by Jacobsen (see Fulton and Jacobsen in the discussion on frontal lobes, p. 373). The surgery involves severing some or all of the fibers connecting the anterior thalamus and prefrontal cortex (similar to standard lobotomy, Fig. 16-3). It is estimated that over 70,000 of these operations were performed between 1935 and the mid-1950s. The early operations were done primarily on institutionalized psychotics and extreme-anxiety neurotics (Freeman and Watts) where side effects beyond the relief of anxiety and fear were not obvious because their behavior was so abnormal to begin with. With more widespread use of the technique for anxiety, side effects like apathy, impulsiveness, possible loss of intelligence (not usually on standard tests), asocial behavior, and impaired judgment became more evident. (The operation was also used to relieve pain in cases of terminal cancer, with patients reporting that pain had lost its insistent quality—it didn't bother them because they didn't have to pay attention to it.) More careful and selected lesions of the prefrontal lobes were made in conjunction with a careful program of testing at Greystone Hospital by Columbia University scientists in the 1950s with some degree of success in the treatment of anxiety, but the results were still quite variable (Mettler). The advent of tranquilizers and electroshock treatment led to near-abandonment of the treatment by the 1960s.

Limbic operations. With the many animal experiments on changes in emotional behavior that result from lesions of the limbic system, attention turned to these areas of the brain. It was pointed out that interrupting excitation to and from the frontal lobes via the thalamus to the amygdala could be responsible for the behavior changes seen in prefrontal lobotomy. More recently, frontal and parietal areas have been found to receive fibers from the hypothalamus. Research of this kind raised hopes that precise lesions of the limbic system and related cortical areas could change emotional behavior in a desired way without undesirable side effects. The most carefully documented cases are those of Mark and Irwin (see readings); most of the literature, however, is based on subjective observations of small numbers of cases.

Mark and Irwin tried to reduce violent assaultive behavior that seemed associated with temporal lobe epilepsy in a number of cases with a fair degree of success. They performed lesions (amygdalotomy, Fig. 16-3) in areas where abnormal seizure discharges were recorded with depth electrodes, hoping to obtain the "calming" effect demonstrated in animals, but only after noting that they could induce the initial symptoms of aggression by stimulating at these sites. The whole temporal lobe has been removed from one or both sides of the brain in tumor operations or to relieve epilepsy. Reports of a calming effect also reported disturbances of memory (see Chapter 17). Cingulate lesions have been performed for aggression and obsessive behavior. Orbital undercutting has been tried for anxiety and depression. Thalamic lesions were an attempt to destroy the source of the fibers involved in lobotomies (with less extensive damage). Lateral hypothalamic lesions are supposed to relieve anxiety, aggression, and so on. Most of the reports, as previously noted, are subjective reports of a small number of cases where the results are quite variable.

SEXUAL BEHAVIOR IN HUMANS

The hormones controlling the reproductive cycles of subprimate species were explained in Chapter 3. It was noted in Chapter 15 that primates, especially man, were more strongly influenced by learning in the development, expression, and decline of sexual behavior than other mammals. This results in a greater variety of sexual behavior, with more frequent occurrence of "deviant" sexual behavior. At the same time, sexual motivation in humans as in other animals is a highly motivated state subject to frustration and therefore an emotion.

Fetal development

The **genetic sex** of the embryo is determined at fertilization, being female (XX) if both female chromosomes are joined, or male (XY) if one male chromosome is inherited (see Chapter 3). In either case, the embryo has the pregenital structures to be either male (wolffian) or female (müllerian), as shown in Fig. 16-4, *A,* where male and female are identical. Although both hormones will be present in later life, the embryo will be male only if androgen is present in the embryo, otherwise the female structures develop. As seen in Fig. 16-4, when the female structures develop, the male structures degenerate, and vice versa. This process can be interfered with before birth, by injection of androgens into the mother who is pregnant with a female (XX) embryo—a genetic female offspring will be born with a well-developed penis (but no testes, thus a pseudohermaphrodite). Normally, however, genetic sex determines the **gonadal sex** at birth—the appearance of the external genitals. Hormone imbalances in the mother may result in the birth of a **hermaphrodite,** with a genetic female looking like a male without testes or a genetic male having the external genitals of a female.

Development before puberty

At birth, the influence of learning begins to be evident, as the child is assigned a sex role according to the appearance of the external genitals. Male and female babies are assigned sex roles at birth, and children assigned sex roles usually behave accordingly even if the assigned gender role contradicts genetic, gonadal, or genital sex (Money and Ehrhardt).

Puberty

Somewhere between 12 and 15 years of age, the hypothalamus reacts to unknown influences to initiate the onset of puberty, as defined by the appearance of the **secondary sexual characteristics.** In the male, the voice takes a lower pitch, the muscles develop (especially in the chest), and facial and chest hair appears and darkens. In the female, a slight change in voice quality results, and the hips, breasts, vulva, and vagina enlarge. In both sexes underarm and pubic hair appear. As explained in Chapter 3, the hypothalamus stimulates the anterior pituitary gland to release luteinizing hormone (LH), which stimulates production of androgens by the male testes and estrogens by the female ovaries to cause the appearance of secondary sexual characteristics. At the same time, the hypothalamus stimulates anterior pituitary release of follicle stimulating hormone (FSH), resulting in the production of sperm in the male and ova in the female.

Adult sexual behavior

It was not until the pioneering survey work of the biologist Alfred C. Kinsey and his colleagues in the late 1940s and early 1950s that the variety of human sexual behavior became known in any scientific fashion. As social taboos in research with human sexual behavior gradually became less formidable, the research of William H. Masters and Virginia E. Johnson became possible. Out of their work on physiological responses during sexual intercourse, meaningful methods of treating sexual frustrations emerged in the Reproductive Biology Research Foundation in St. Louis. Others

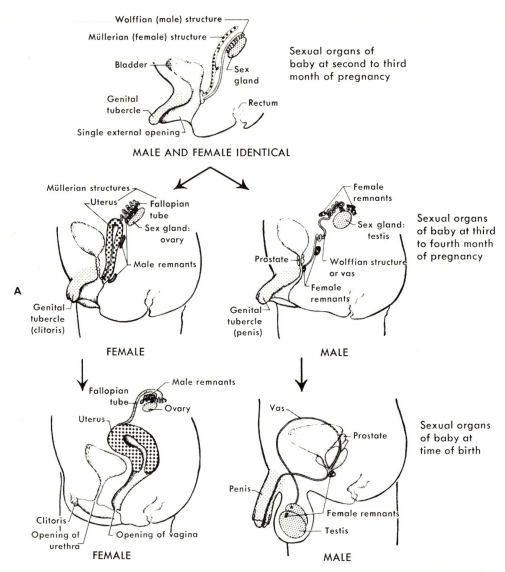

Fig. 16-4. Development of internal and external genitals in the human embryo and fetus. (From Money, J., Hampson, J. G., and Hampson, J. L.: Hermaphroditism: Recommendations concerning assignment of sex, change of sex, and psychologic management, Bull. Johns Hopkins Hosp. **97:**284-300, 1955. Reprinted by permission of The Johns Hopkins Medical Journal.)

have taken up their approaches (Kaplan, for example), and courses on human sexuality are finding their way into the curriculum of many colleages and universities. The general picture that emerges is one of four stages of a normal sex cycle, important differences in recovery characteristics between the male and female, and methods

for treating sexual dysfunction with a high degree of success. The treatment of these topics in this chapter can only be cursory at best; the student should consult the readings and references for a more extensive treatment.

Normal sexual behavior. Masters and Johnson define four phases in the sexual

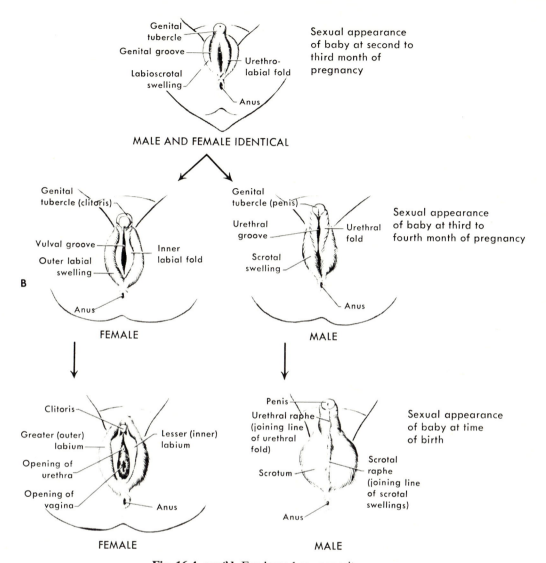

Fig. 16-4, cont'd. For legend see opposite page.

response cycle (before, during, and after sexual intercourse): (1) excitement, (2) plateau, (3) orgasm, and (4) resolution (see Fig. 16-5). In the male, the *excitement phase* is characterized by erection and enlargement of the penis caused by engorgement with blood because more blood flows into the organ than out of it as a result of a spinal reflex action. The early excitement phase of the female is the moistening of the vagina with a lubricating fluid that occurs within seconds of the onset of sexual excitement in the "sweating reaction" of the walls of the vagina, also caused by vascular engorgement, of the vagina in this case. The increase in local blood pressure causes a "seepage" of plasma from the engorged blood vessels into the vagina. As the excitement phase in the female continues, the clitoris (Fig. 16-4) enlarges, the nipples of the breasts swell, and later on the breasts themselves increase in size. (The nipple

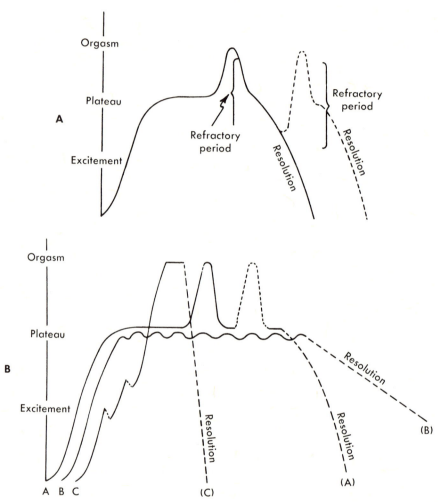

Fig. 16-5. Male, **A,** and female, **B,** sexual response cycles. Four successive phases during sexual intercourse are excitement, plateau, orgasm, and resolution. Note that only the male has a refractory period after orgasm when erection declines even though sexual excitement is otherwise present. Rearousal and a second orgasm is shown after a refractory period, *dotted line. Solid line,* Resolution without a second excitation and orgasm. **B,** Reactions of three females. Female *A* has a second orgasm after returning only to the plateau phase after the first orgasm. Female *B* does not reach orgasm; resolution occurs after a period spent in the plateau phase. Female *C,* with no plateau, reaches resolution after a single orgasm. (From Masters, W. H., and Johnson, V. E.: Human sexual response, Boston, 1966, Little, Brown & Co.)

change occurs to a minor degree in the male.) Then the inner and outer lips of the vagina swell and the vaginal "barrel" expands. There is an increase in heart rate and blood pressure in both sexes, and a flushing (vasodilation) of the skin that begins in the abdomen and spreads over the upper body. The excitement phase blends into the *plateau phase*. The male testes double in size and are pulled higher into the scrotum and the ridge at the base of the glans of the penis enlarges. In females, the swelling of the outer third of the vagina reduces its diameter by half and increases the frictional stimulation of the penis; the inner vagina enlarges and the clitoris becomes more erect, while a darkening of the inner lips of the vagina signals imminent orgasm. The *orgasm* in the female is distinguished by rhythmic muscular contractions (at intervals of four-fifths of a second) of the outer third of the vaginal barrel and surrounding tissues, usually 3 to 12 in number. The uterus also contracts in a rhythmic way. The male orgasm is also distinguished by a series of muscular contractions at the same intervals during which the semen is ejected. The semen has collected in the seminal vesicles and the connected bulblike ampullae. The latter contract to force their contents into the urethra (duct of the penis) while the prostate gland contracts to add its fluids. A bulb in the urethra near the base of the penis enlarges to receive these fluids, which produce the first sensations of ejaculation. Contractions of this bulb and the penis eject the semen with considerable force. In both sexes, muscles of the neck, abdomen, buttocks, and limbs contract, and vigorous grasping occurs. *Resolution* in females is first seen in return to normal of tissues around the nipples, disappearance of the sex flush, and widespread perspiration. In seconds, the clitoris relaxes, the outer vaginal barrel increases in diameter, the uterus shrinks, and the passage from vagina to uterus (cervix) enlarges, permitting easier entrance

of sperm. Total resolution may require as long as a half hour. The male resolution is quickly seen in loss of erection of the penis and return to its normal size. The sex flush disappears and the testes descend. Breathing and heart rate return to normal in both sexes.

Males and females differ most in the "refractory period" that follows the male resolution but not the female resolution (Fig. 16-5). During this period, the male cannot be aroused to an erection. This period lasts several minutes in most men and increases in duration with age. By contrast, continued sexual stimulation can result in a series of orgasms in females, during which their sexual excitement does not fall below the plateau phase.

Sexual dysfunction. Human sexual behavior is so variable that what is "normal" becomes difficult to define. Male homosexuality or female homosexuality (lesbianism) can apparently result from a difference between genetic sex and gonadal sex. This can result from hormone disturbances of the individual's mother during pregnancy—see previous discussion. There have been widely publicized cases where the gonads have been surgically altered to agree with the individual's desired sex role. I am not aware of any reliable large-sample studies of homosexuality that assess the relative influence of genetic sex, gonadal sex, development of secondary sex characteristics, or assigned gender role and experience. The majority of medical opinion seems to indicate that homosexuality results from sexual experience. The most common sorts of human sexual dysfunctions appear to be in the heterosexual area, where the individual desires a "normal" sex life.

Sex therapy. Through the work of Masters and Johnson, Kaplan, and others, six heterosexual malfunctions have been defined (Kaplan). These are (1) male impotence—inability to produce or mantain an erection, (2) male premature ejaculation—inability to control orgasm, (3) male retarded ejaculation—inability to trigger orgasm, (4) female sexual dysfunction—lack of erotic response to sexual stimulation, or frigidity, (5) female orgasmic dysfunction—difficulty in reaching orgasm, and (6) vaginismus—spasm of the muscles at the entrance to the vagina, preventing penetration of the penis. Preliminary results in attempted treatment of these disorders show that they can be helped in a surprisingly brief period of time (a few weeks) by a combined program of counseling and sexual exercises by the couples involved, in the privacy of their home.

Male disorders. Male impotence, inability to produce or maintain an erection even when sexually excited, appears to happen occasionally to about half of the male population on the basis of informal surveys. (Most men report the experience as very humiliating.) If it happens frequently (secondary impotence) or has always been the case (primary impotence), the sufferer is likely to seek help. Primary impotence is reported to be rare and difficult to treat and more likely to be attributable to physical disorders than to so-called mental problems. Secondary impotence is reported by Masters and Johnson to be relieved by counseling sexual anxieties and sexual exercises at home in 70% of the cases they have treated. The general technique, once the couple is convinced that there is nothing wrong with it, involves mutual sex play of any kind that will arouse either to climax. Once convinced that the male's failure to reach orgasm is becoming less frequent, the couple can stimulate each other by masturbation of clitoris and penis and gradually approach sexual intercourse.

Premature ejaculation appears to be both the most common complaint among men and the easiest one to correct. The strategy is that of learning control over the ejaculation reflex. If the individual has always had the problem, there is not likely to be a physical cause; sudden development of the problem may indicate a disorder of the urethra or spinal reflex. If organic causes are ruled out, premature ejaculation usually disappears when the male learns to detect the symptoms that precede ejaculation soon enough. The wife stimulates the husband's penis with her hand until he first detects symptoms of ejaculation; he directs her to stop until he regains control and then directs her to start again. After control improves, the same stop-start method is used in intercourse.

Physical disorders seem rarely to be the cause of retarded ejaculation. Anxiety about sex because of strict early training or a traumatic sexual experience are the most frequently suspected causes of this problem. Most reported cases can achieve ejaculation by masturbating themselves or having their wife masturbate them. Some form of systematic desensitization seems to help—a step-by-step approach to the threatening sexual encounter. For example, the male may be able to learn to masturbate while his wife observes, and then she can do it for him; they can masturbate each other; he can learn to enter just before ejaculation and then sooner before ejaculation, and so on.

Female disorders. Female disorders are less well understood than male disorders. "Frigidity" has been used to refer to both lack of erotic feelings and inability to achieve orgasm, and these may be two different complaints. A woman may be able to achieve orgasm by other means, but not during sexual intercourse. Only a small percentage of females are reported never to have achieved orgasm, whereas a large percentage of those who have, do not achieve it consistently during intercourse. There is also debate over whether inability to achieve orgasm during sexual intercourse is a dysfunction if mutual orgasm can be achieved in some other way. Finally, it is stimulation of the clitoris that triggers orgasm in women, but they *perceive* orgasm primarily from the strong contractions of the vagina that result.

Female sexual dysfunction, or "frigidity,"

is the most difficult female problem to over-come. Those with primary frigidity have never experienced erotic sensations; second-ary dysfunction usually occurs among women who were aroused by "petting" be-fore marriage but could not respond when sexual intercourse was the object of sex play. Frank counseling to bring out an exchange of sexual feelings and fears is followed by private exercises conducted by the couple. The female caresses her hus-band's body first; this is reported to relieve her anxieties more than the reverse pro-cedure; the reverse procedure follows until she experiences erotic sensations. Mutual genital stimulation is the next step under the wife's guidance. If he has an orgasm, he is instructed to continue genital stimula-tion of the wife. These experiences proceed to intercourse gradually with the wife as-suming the superior position and controlling events. The majority of cases are reported to respond to this procedure.

Female orgasmic dysfunction—failure to reach orgasm—involves women who reach a strong plateau phase during intercourse but never achieve orgasm (primary orgas-mic dysfunction) or lose the ability (second-ary orgasmic dysfunction). These are probably the most common sexual com-plaints among women. Some women can achieve orgasm during masturbation, but not intercourse; others experience it under neither circumstance. A primary case can often be helped by the intense stimulation of an electric vibrator, transfer to mastur-bation, and then attempt intercourse until her husband has an orgasm, after which he stimulates her to orgasm.

Vaginismus—contraction of the vaginal entrance muscles to prevent penetration of the penis—is reported to be relatively rare. Though anatomically normal, the muscles contract, even during a vaginal examination by a physician. Yet many of these women are reported to be sexually responsive otherwise and able to achieve orgasm by masturbating their own clitoris. Pain associ-ated with penetration of the vagina in the past is inferred to be the major factor responsible. An experience of this sort could be caused by a rigid hymen (the membrane covering part of the vagina in a virgin), inflammation, tumor, hemorrhoids ("piles"), and so forth. Other causes may have been psychological, such as rape, the husband's impotence, and guilt. After counseling to bring out possible reasons for the disorder, deconditioning of the reaction is attempted. The husband examines the vagina in private. Then the wife attempts to gently thrust her own or her husband's finger into it. When discomfort gradually disappears, gentle back and forth movement is attempted, with the woman in control to prevent discomfort, and then rotating two fingers is attempted. Penetration by the penis follows, but thrust-ing is attempted only later at the wife's signal. He withdraws and starts over if she signals discomfort. The procedure is re-ported to be successful in nearly all cases.

The report by Masters and Johnson on "normal" human sexual response is based on scientifically conducted physiological measurements during sexual intercourse. Their information on sex therapy and the therapy reports of Kaplan are necessarily based on second-hand reports of the sub-jects being treated and are therefore less reliable, even though the sample size ap-pears to be large. Given human learning ability compared to that of other species, it should not be surprising that the greater variability of human sexual behavior is also accompanied by ability to unlearn undesired behavior and learn desired behavior. The techniques involved do not differ in principle from the behavior therapy discussed in Chapter 18.

SUMMARY

Language habits resulting from rational-istic philosophy treat emotion as disruptive when emotion should be considered as a special case of motivation that occurs when adaptive behavior is blocked. Students of emotion have also been variously concerned with emotional experience (conscious events), overt emotional behavior, or the internal physiological events accompanying emotion. Individual differences in emphasis determine the way emotion is defined and theoretically explained.

The most useful definition includes all three aspects of emotion and how they are organized by the CNS. Theories emphasizing conscious states fail because awareness is neither necessary nor sufficient for emotional behavior. Theories emphasizing emotional behavior ignore instances of physiological and conscious signs of emotion without evidence of overt emotional responses. Theories emphasizing autonomic response fail because ANS response does not differ for each emotion; furthermore, emotion occurs when the ANS response is blocked by drugs or surgery, and simple exercise causes ANS response changes without emotion. Because emotion disrupts complex learning behavior, it was once defined as a disorganized response; the evolutionary development of emotion suggests that it is a highly organized, primitive CNS mechanism for motivation in an emergency. James believed that conscious emotional events were sensations aroused by visceral and somatic emotional responses. For Watson, emotion *was* overt behavior—inherited fear, rage, and lust responses to specific stimuli; the responses were made more variable and the stimuli eliciting them increased through conditioning and generalization. ANS response has been identified with emotion by other writers who believe that the ANS responses are necessary to emotion, at least until some learning has occurred.

The Cannon-Bard theory of emotion originated as an attempt to explain the sham rage behavior of decorticate cats by assuming that centers in the hypothalamus organized overt and autonomic emotional responses on the one hand and caused the perception of emotions by higher centers on the other. However, more widespread areas in the CNS that control emotion have been discovered since the Cannon-Bard work. The Papez-MacLean theory proposed that a more widespread system formed a circuit in the rhinencephalon that included the entorhinal cortex, hippocampus, hypothalamus, anterior thalamus, and cingulate gyrus. Subsequent work has shown some of these areas to be involved in both emotional behavior and experience. Lindsley's activation theory of emotion, however, identifies emotion with states of activation in the ARAS.

Somatic and visceral feedback contributes to emotion, but this feedback seems unessential to emotion in the adult animal because sympathectomized cats show emotional behavior and so do paraplegic humans although the extent of human emotional "feelings" depends on the extent of their somatic and visceral input (level of spinal cord section). However, ANS responses can cause emotion. If human subjects are aware that the internal ANS responses they perceive are caused by a drug, they do not become emotional; if they are unaware of the cause of the internal upset, they often think they are emotional and behave accordingly. Although ANS responses are not varied enough to account for all emotions, pleasure seems to be accompanied by parasympathetic responses, whereas rage and fear involve widespread sympathetic response.

In fear the adrenal medulla produces mostly epinephrine, which raises the blood pressure by increasing the heart rate. In rage it produces more norepinephrine, which raises blood pressure by constricting the arteries supplying the viscera and skin. Man is capable of learning the self-directed anger and depression that lead to epinephrine output just as fear responses do. Epinephrine causes increased ACTH output, which stimulates corticoid production by the adrenal medulla. Stress therefore results in hypertrophy of the pituitary and adrenal glands. If the adrenal cortex is removed, ACTH level can be maintained by injection without a compensating reaction by the hypothalamus. Increased ACTH delays extinction of a running response to shock in rats, and decreased ACTH causes more rapid habituation to a loud sound, whereas ACTH level increases during avoidance learning.

It seems that there are areas in the hypothalamus that are important to the autonomic reactions of rage, fear, and pleasure and that stimulation of these areas produces both the autonomic and somatic reactions of these emotions. Medial hypothalamic stimulation results in an effective (rage) attack on rats by cats, whereas lateral stimulation causes a quiet biting (predatory) attack. The former is adrenergically mediated and the latter is cholinergic. Hypothalamic areas seem dependent on lower midbrain centers for rage behavior and dependent on rhinencephalic centers of the Papez-MacLean variety for emotional responses. For example, bitemporal lobectomies, including the amygdala and hippocampus, make monkeys docile, hypersexed, indiscriminative, and oral in their behavior (the Klüver-Bucy syndrome). The hypersexual symptom seems to be caused by piriform cortex lesions and the docility by loss of the amygdala. Removal of the amygdala reduces a monkey's position in the dominance hierarchy unless he has an opportunity to dominate young monkeys before returning to the adult colony. In cats, pathways from one set of nuclei in the amygdala to the hypothalamus stimulate aggression, whereas another set of nuclei or pathways decrease aggression. Pathways from the hypothalamus and other basal areas to the frontal and parietal cortex have been traced. Septal lesions cause savagery in rats, yet they can be tamed. Prefrontal lobectomy reduces emotionality in monkeys.

Psychosurgery is an attempt to relieve emotional disorders in man with variable results. Prefrontal lobectomy and lobotomy relieve intractable pain and reduce anxiety but often result in irresponsible behavior. Limbic surgery, especially of the amygdala has some effectiveness in relieving assaultive behavior.

In humans, the genetic sex is determined by chromosomes, although embryonic androgen is necessary to produce a male. Endocrine disturbances in the mother can produce a hermaphrodite. Gonadal sex determines gender role after birth and learning that largely determines future sexual behavior results. The hypothalamus stimulates the anterior pituitary to initiate changes in gonadal hormones that result in the secondary sex characteristics of puberty.

The early survey work by Kinsey et al. revealed the variety of human sexual behavior. Masters and Johnson defined the phases of excitement, plateau, orgasm, and resolution in sexual intercourse and described physiological changes that accompany each phase. Only the male has a refractory period after orgasm.

Human sexual dysfunction is difficult to define. Homosexuality in both sexes (called lesbianism in women) can be caused by disparate gonadal and genetic sex, but it is probably learned in most cases. Sex therapies have been devised for male impotence, premature ejaculation, and retarded ejaculation, as well as female frigidity, orgasmic dysfunction, and vaginismus. Descriptions of the four phases of sexual intercourse are based on physiological measurement. Sex therapy information is less reliable, but agrees with what is known about behavior therapy.

READINGS

Andrew, R. J.: The origins of facial expressions, Sci. Am. **213**:88-94, Oct. 1965. (W. H. Freeman Reprint No. 627.)

Arnold, M. B., editor: The nature of emotion, Baltimore, 1968, Penguin Books, Inc.

Ax, A. F.: The physiological differentiation between anger and fear in humans, Psychosom. Med. **15**:433-442, 1953. (Bobbs-Merrill Reprint No. P-16.)

Brady, J. V., and Nauta, W. J. H.: Subcortical mechanisms in emotional behavior: Affective changes following septal forebrain lesions in the albino rat, J. Comp. Physiol. Psychol. **46**:339-346, 1953. (Bobbs-Merrill Reprint No. P-46.)

Brecher, R., and Brecher, E., editors: An analysis of *Human sexual response,* Boston, 1966, Little, Brown & Co.

Candland, D. K., editor: Emotion: Bodily change, New York, 1962, D. Van Nostrand Co., Inc.

Cannon, W. B.: Bodily changes in pain, hunger, fear and rage, New York, 1963, Harper & Row, Publishers.

Charover, S.: The pacification of the brain, Psychol. Today **7**:59-69, May 1974.

Darwin, C.: The expression of the emotions in man and animal, Chicago, 1965, The University of Chicago Press.

Denenberg, V. H., and Zarrow, M. X.: Rat pax, Psychol. Today **3**:45-68, April 1970.

Funkenstein, D. H.: The physiology of fear and anger, Sci. Am. **192**:74-80, May 1955. (W. H. Freeman Reprint No. 428.)

Grastyán, E.: Towards a better understanding of human emotion, Impact of Science on Society **18**:187-205, 1968. Also In Leukel, F. (editor): Issues in physiological psychology, St. Louis, 1974, The C. V. Mosby Co.

Harlow, H. F.: The heterosexual affectional system in monkeys, Am. Psychol. **17**:1-9, 1962. (Bobbs-Merrill Reprint No. P-470.)

Harlow, H. F., and Zimmerman, R. R.: Affectional responses in infant monkeys, Science **130**:421-432, 1959. (Bobbs-Merrill Reprint No. P-145.)

Hunt, H. F., and Brady, J. V.: Some effects of electro-convulsive shock on a conditioned emotional response ("anxiety"), J. Comp. Physiol. Psychol. **44**:88-98, 1951. (Bobbs-Merrill Reprint No. P-170.)

Kaplan, H.: No-nonsense therapy for six sexual malfunctions, Psychol. Today **8**:77-86, Oct. 1974.

Katchadorian, H.: Fundamentals of human sexuality: Sense and nonsense, San Francisco, 1974, W. H. Freeman Co.

Klüver, H., and Bucy, P. C.: Preliminary analysis of functions of the temporal lobes in monkeys.

In Isaacson, R. L., editor: Basic readings in neuropsychology, New York, 1964, Harper & Row, Publishers.

Liddell, H. S.: Conditioning and emotions, Sci. Am. **190**:48-57, Jan. 1954. (W. H. Freeman Reprint No. 418.)

Lykken, D. T.: The GSR in the detection of guilt, J. Appl. Psychol. **43**:385-388, 1959. (Bobbs-Merrill Reprint No. P-218.)

McCary, J.: Sexual myths and fallacies, New York, 1973, Schocken Books, Inc.

McCleary, R. A., Moore, R. Y.: Subcortical mechanism in behavior, New York, 1965, Basic Books, Inc., Publishers.

Malmo, R.: Emotions and muscle tension, Psychol. Today **3**:64-83, March 1970.

Mark, V.: A psychosurgeon's case for psychotherapy, Psychol. Today **8**:28-38, July 1974.

Mark, V., and Irwin, F.: Violence and the brain, New York, 1970, Harper & Row, Publishers.

Moyer, K.: The physiology of violence, Psychol. Today **7**:35-38, July 1973.

Pomeroy, W. B.: Dr. Kinsey and the Institute for sex research, New York, 1973, The New American Library, Inc.

Pribram, K.: The new neurology and biology of emotion: A structural approach, Am. Psychol. **22**:830-838, 1967. Also in Leukel, F., editor: Issues in physiological psychology, St. Louis, 1974, The C. V. Mosby Co.

Rosvold, H. E., Mirsky, A. F., and Pribram, K.: Influence of amygdaloidectomy on social behavior in monkeys, J. Comp. Physiol. Psychol. **47**:173-178, 1954. (Bobbs-Merrill Reprint No. P-296.)

Schacter, S., and Singer, J. E.: Cognitive, social and physiological determinants of emotional state, Psychol. Rev. **69**:379-399, 1962. (Bobbs-Merrill Reprint No. P-553.)

Smith, B. M.: The polygraph, Sci. Am. **216**:25-31, Jan. 1967. (W. H. Freeman Reprint No. 503.)

Watson, J. B., and Rayner, R.: Conditioned emotional reactions, J. Exp. Psychol. **3**:1-13, 1920. (Bobbs-Merrill Reprint No. P-360.)

chapter 17

Learning

OVERVIEW

This chapter is divided into seven sections. The first section is concerned with the anatomical location of changes in the brain that could occur with learning. This is the oldest problem in the physiological psychology of learning, and its consideration gives perspective for the discussion of other aspects that follows. Anatomical studies lead to some understanding of brain mechanisms in language, the second section. The third section on other aspects of learning and memory broaden the learning topic, including brain reinforcement centers, brain stimulation, and nerve cell approaches. A brief discussion on biofeedback and learning visceral and glandular responses forms the fourth section. The fifth section questions the time course of changes in the brain that occur with learning because most of the internal changes called learning take place *after* practice is over. In the sixth section a theoretical system is presented to explain brain function. Finally, after showing that learning changes probably occur at synapses between nerve cells, the last section deals with the nature of this change. Gross biochemical and anatomical changes in the brain are first surveyed in a "molar" approach. The chapter closes with a discussion of the "molecular" approach, which is concerned with what happens in each single nerve cell involved in the learning process.

LOCUS OF THE MEMORY TRACE
Historical background: search for the engram

Two principles seemed to guide early investigators who studied the physiological basis of learning and memory. The first principle was the "reflex model" of the nervous system, which was presented in Chapter 5 as a first approximation of how the brain mediates responses to stimuli. In this model, simple connections are made at synapses between incoming sensory neurons association neurons, and outgoing motoneurons. Such connections in the brain are variable; thus responses to stimuli vary. An action would follow a sensory stimulus by chance, and the action would be rewarded. The rewarded response would be repeated when the stimulus appeared, and the synaptic connections between stimulus and response would be improved through *use* until the stimulus-response relation became automatic, like a reflex. The model does not say, however, how reward affects synaptic connections in the first place. This problem will be encountered later in a more sophisticated form.

The second principle that seemed obvious to early researchers was **encephalization.** As newer parts of the brain developed through evolution, they came to dominate the activity of older parts of the brain. In mammals such as man, the newest part of the brain is the cerebral cortex. The most distinctive feature of animals with complex brains like man is their superior ability to learn complex behavior. It was therefore assumed that the cerebral cortex had taken over the newest kind of complex brain function—the formation of new connections between stimulus and response at synapses. If these synaptic connections were to be found in the cerebral cortex, they would be found in the association areas rather than in the sensory projection areas for incoming stimuli or in the motor projection areas for outgoing responses; the synaptic connections of the association areas would link the sensory and motor projection areas.

Of course it is known now that there are two or three sensory projection areas for some senses as well as two or three motor projection areas, and many cortical connections are made via lower brain centers rather than directly with other cortical areas. However, the simple model of the early investigators explains why they sought the **engram**—the physical synaptic changes of learning—in the cerebral cortex. They used the method of **ablation,** taking out parts of the cortex and observing the effect on learning and memory. If removing a given part of the cortex impaired learning and memory, it was assumed that the stimulus-response connections for the habit being studied were ordinarily made in the part of the cortex that had been removed.

Cortical ablation effects on maze learning and retention. Lashley studied the effects of ablating cortical tissue in rats. He studied their ability to learn and remember mazes of three levels of difficulty (based on the number of blind alleys) by operating on them either before or after they had learned. The results of his pioneering experiments can be summarized, in an oversimplified way, by three conclusions:

1. Cortical ablation had more effect on retention of a given maze habit than on ability to learn mazes; that is, if the rat was operated on before he learned, his ability to learn was impaired in comparison with control rats. However, if he learned a maze, was operated on, and was then tested on the same maze, his retention was affected more than his ability to learn new mazes.

2. The more difficult the maze (that is, the more blind alleys), the greater was the effect of removing a given amount of cortex on *either* learning or retention. Removing

10% of the cortex would affect learning or memory for complex mazes more than for simple ones.

3. It did not seem to matter which areas of the cortex were damaged, but the *amount* of cortex removed was critical. Removing 10% of the frontal area had about the same effect as removing 10% of the parietal area, but removing 50% of any area would have a greater effect on learning and memory. From these results Lashley evolved the principles of **mass action** and **equipotentiality,** each a corollary of the other. The principle of mass action states that the cortex acts *as a whole* in learning—that all areas of the cortex are involved at once. Equipotentiality therefore means that one cortical area is as good as another for learning the maze habit; if a rat has 75% of the cortex left, it does not matter where the 75% is located as far as the rat's ability to learn or retain the maze habit is concerned.

Cortical connections. It was originally assumed that learning consisted of establishing synaptic connections between (incoming) sensory projection areas and (outgoing) motor areas through the neurons of the association areas of the cortex. It was believed that perhaps these connections could be cut to affect learning and retention, even if they differed from one rat to another. However, thin cuts made in the cortex in such a way as to isolate small squares of cortex had no effect on learning or retention (Lashley). Even electrically insulating these squares from one another by the placement of small strips of mica in the cuts had no effect (Sperry). Cortical cells seem to conduct vertically rather than horizontally. On the other hand, cuts of this kind do not sever fibers that "loop" down through the interior white matter to connect one cortical area with another, nor do they sever the crossing fibers (**commissural fibers**) that connect corresponding areas of the two hemispheres. More will be explained later about the effects of cutting the fibers that connect the two hemispheres.

Subcortical centers. The cortex is "vertically organized"; that is, most cells connect with others above or below them, and one part of the cortex connects with another mostly by subcortical routes, including the thalamus. Accordingly, thalamic areas were damaged in rats (Gheselli and Brown), with minimum cortical damage, by use of the stereotaxic instrument (Chapter 13). The effects on learning and retention resembled mass action.

Lashley's paradox. The work of Lashley and others who attempted to locate the engram, or trace of memory, leads to a paradox. If memory is impaired by the destruction of nerve cells in many cortical and subcortical locations, it must mean that many millions of cortical and subcortical cells participate in the memory in some fashion and are altered by learning in some way. One conclusion that follows is that single individual cells must participate in each of the thousands of memories we accumulate in a lifetime! How can a single cell contain this much information? We will return to this question near the end of the chapter when we consider molecular biochemical changes in learning. However, considerations of this kind led Lashley to say in 1950: "I sometimes feel in reviewing the evidence on the localization of the memory trace, that the necessary conclusion is that learning is just not possible."[*]

Extent of recorded brain changes in learning. In an attempt to simplify the problem of neural changes in learning, James Olds has recorded changes in the response of cells of the auditory pathway while training rats to associate a tone with delivery of food to a food dish in their cage. He recorded cell activity to the tone at the following five "stations" along the auditory

pathway: (1) cochlear nucleus, (2) nucleus of the lateral lemniscus, (3) inferior colliculus, (4) medial geniculate body, and (5) auditory cortex (see Chapter 10 and Fig. 10-7). Other electrodes recorded what was going on in other parts of the brain—the hypothalamus, reticular formation, extrapyramidal motor system, and cerebral cortex. In terms of behavior, the rats seemed to learn nothing at all during the first 10 to 20 trials, learned to go to the food box when the tone sounded during the next 10 trials, and learned to move more rapidly and smoothly during later trials. For each block of 10 trials a "map" of cell response changes were made for each of the five sensory stations in the auditory pathway and at the other brain locations. The sensory message initiated by the tone moved through the five stations of the sensory pathway at about two milliseconds per station, accelerating the firing of cells as it passed each location. With learning, the change in the pattern of firing was largest at the thalamus (medial geniculate body) and next largest at the inferior colliculus (note what was said about old and new sensory pathways to the cortex in Chapter 13), but all stations changed their firing pattern. The surprising aspect of the changes is that they occurred at *every* station about 10 milliseconds after the tone. However, the changes did not have a common source because changes at the inferior colliculuus occurred at the beginning of training, whereas those at the medial geniculate body began after about 20 trials. Other recordings showed changes in the pattern of firing with learning. The hypothalamus "learned" during the first 20 trials when no behavioral changes were seen (drive mechanism?). The reticular formation (ARAS, Chapter 13) learned during the next 10 trials while the animal began to orient toward the source of the tone. The extrapyramidal system learned as the animal began to move toward the food in response to the tone. The sensory cortex

[*]Lashley, K.: In search of the engram, Symp. Soc. Exp. Biol. **4:**425-482, 1950.

learned as the movement became more co-ordinated, but the frontal cortex only after the movement became rapid and smooth. The reticular formation seemed important to the changes at other locations; large changes occurred here two milliseconds before they appeared in the auditory pathway.

Equipotentiality quantified. Although many cells in the brain participate in learning, some locations seem more important than others. E. Roy John and his associates, Bartlett, Hudspeth, and others, have recorded and computer-averaged evoked potentials from many parts of the brains of animals while the animals learn. The computer analysis enables them to determine the difference between evoked potentials attributable to simple sensory input ("exogenous") and those that occur only after the animals have learned ("endogenous"). With the "endogenous" changes being representative of brain changes during learning, the changes are found to be widely distributed throughout the brain. However, the greater the response of an area to the initial (exogenous) sensory input, the greater the change with learning. The relationship is a logarithmic one. This represents a compromise between a strict localization view of the engram and the ideas of mass action and equipotentiality.

Split-brain and spreading depression approaches

Split-brain techniques. The two hemispheres of the brain, and therefore the cortex of those hemispheres, are connected by **commissural fibers,** particularly the **corpus callosum** (Chapter 5 and Fig. 5-10), although the anterior and posterior commissures participate as well. Neurosurgeons were puzzled for years by the absence of any gross behavioral or perceptual abnormalities in human patients after the corpus callosum had been severed. In some instances the operation was necessary to remove brain tumors in the third ventricle. When no apparent consequences were seen, one prominent investigator facetiously remarked that the only apparent function of the corpus callosum was mechanical—to keep the hemispheres from sagging apart! Another reason for the operation was to keep epileptic seizures from spreading from one hemisphere to the other—which prompted the remark that the function of the corpus callosum was to spread seizures! However, during subsequent careful investigation a technique was developed for confining visual and somesthetic input to one hemisphere of the brain, and for separating one hemisphere of the brain from the other (Sperry). The initial experiments using the technique asked the following questions:

1. If sensory input is restricted to one hemisphere of the brain in training, will the other hemisphere learn too (with the two hemispheres still connected)?

2. If the sensory input requires the cerebral cortex for discrimination, and if the connections between the two hemispheres are cut, can the training be restricted to one hemisphere?

Pattern discrimination requires the cerebral cortex. Each eye supplies both hemispheres, the left visual field (right half of both retinas) stimulating the right visual cortex, and the right visual field (left half of both retinas) stimulating the left visual cortex (Fig. 11-5). Thus it is not surprising that a cat that has been taught a visual discrimination with the left eye blindfolded can perform the discrimination with the right eye blindfolded; both sides of the cortex receive information from each eye, and both sides learn the habit at once. If the crossing fibers of the optic chiasma are cut, however, only fibers from the temporal halves of the retina will survive (Fig 11-5). The cat will have "tunnel" vision, and the right eye will supply only the visual cortex of the right hemisphere, whereas the left eye supplies only the left visual cortex. If such a cat is trained in a visual discrimination with the right eye only (left eye blindfolded) and then tested with the left eye only, he will perform perfectly. Obviously, the trace laid down in the right visual cortex has been transferred to the left visual cortex through the parts of the corpus callosum that connect them.

What happens if the corpus callosum and other commissural fibers are severed prior to training under the above conditions? If the corpus callosum and other commissural fibers are severed, the two hemispheres are no longer in communication. The operation severs the anterior and posterior commissures, thalamic connections, and midbrain tectum, so that no crossing fibers exist above the hindbrain (Fig. 13-9). If such cats are trained in a pattern discrimination with one eye only and then tested with the other eye only, they show no evidence of learning. The memory trace has been confined to the cortex of one hemisphere. To obtain food, split-brain cats can be taught to go to a door with a cross on it when one eye is blindfolded and to go to the adjoining door with a circle on it when the other eye is blindfolded. The two hemispheres have learned contradictory habits. Furthermore, contradictory training can occur on alternate trials, by the blindfolding of one eye and then the other. Finally, polarized glasses can be fitted to these cats so that the left door has a cross and the right door a circle as seen by one eye, whereas the left has a cross and the right a circle as seen by the other eye. As training proceeds, one hemisphere learns to go to the cross and the other hemisphere learns to go to the circle on the same trials. The effect is not confined to vision. Roughness discrimination requires the somesthetic cortex, and the sensory input from one paw goes to somesthetic sensory projection areas in the opposite hemisphere (the fibers cross in the hindbrain, below the split-brain section— Figs. 7-7 and 7-8). Split-brain cats cannot perform a roughness discrimination with the left paw if they are trained with the right, and vice versa; the memory trace has been confined to one hemisphere.

Spreading depression. According to Leao and Bures, animals without cortical convolutions (fissures, gyri, and sulci), such as the rat, are useful in a technique that depresses the activity of one hemisphere at a time. Potassium chloride (KCl) solution can be administered to the cortex of one hemisphere through a small hole in the skull. This causes a depression of electrical activity in the cortex that spreads over the entire hemisphere, "anesthetizing" it, so to speak. The spreading depression should not cross the fissure dividing the two hemispheres; thus the effect is confined to one hemisphere of the brain. Furthermore, because the cortex recovers after a period of time, the technique allows a reversible decortication of one hemisphere at a time. If a rat is trained in a visual pattern discrimination while one hemisphere is depressed, allowed to recover, and then tested while the other hemisphere is depressed, the untrained hemisphere will show no results of the training. Only one hemisphere learned when the other was inactive, and the inactive hemisphere could not "copy" the trace. However, only a few trials are needed while both hemispheres are active for the untrained hemisphere to copy the trace; depressing the originally trained hemisphere will not impair performance thereafter.

More recently, doubts have been raised about the technique of spreading depression. The following points have been made: (1) hypoesthesia (loss of sensitivity) has been used as a criterion for spreading depression, although brain wave recordings show that hypoesthesia does not always result from spreading depression; (2) saline flushing of the cortex, used to abolish spreading depression, does not always do so; (3) KCl applied to one hemisphere sometimes causes spreading depression in in both hemispheres; (4) KCl can cause irreversible cortical damage; and (5) the spreading depression that results from KCl is sometimes of shorter duration than expected. It appears from these findings that one should always monitor the spreading depression that results from the application of KCl by recording neural activity from several sites in the cortex, to ensure that cortical activity is being depressed in the expected manner. Allowance should also be made for cortical damage, and cortical tissue should be examined under a microscope after the experiment is over.

All these experiments suggest that rats and cats can learn as well with the cortex of the right hemisphere as with the cortex of the left hemisphere. Is the same true of man? In humans the left side of the brain controls the right hand and vice versa, and they exhibit right- or left-handedness far more frequently than do animals, especially where language skills such as writing are concerned. Many years of brain surgery have convinced Penfield that language habits are confined to the left ("dominant") hemisphere in normal humans, and that the right hemisphere "specializes" in nonverbal memory and space perception. (Left-handed people sometimes have a right dominant hemisphere containing the speech areas.) Perhaps in this manner, man has "doubled" his cranial capacity in a way not possible for other mammals, and this has enabled him to learn the immensely complex skills of language. Patients who have undergone spit-brain surgery have difficulty in responding to verbal commands with their left hand. The right hemisphere controls the left hand, and it does not have access to verbal information stored in the left hemisphere. These patients also cannot recognize written words presented in their left visual field (input to the nonverbal right hemisphere). However, the right hemisphere is more skilled in nonverbal memory and space perception problems presented to the left visual field. Penfield believes that the speech areas of the dominant hemisphere are fully established by the age of about 12 years. In an aside to educators, he suggests that unless a child has learned a second language by that age, he never will be truly bilingual—as facile with one language as with the other.

Role of corpus callosum. Doty proposes that for primates, the corpus callosum has two major roles in memory: (1) controlling the formation of memory traces so that they are laid down in only one hemisphere instead of both and (2) providing access by each hemisphere to memory traces stored in the other. He suggests that the anterior commissure, but not the corpus callosum, can transfer an engram from one hemisphere to the other. Finally, the posterior part of the corpus callosum (splenium) serves in a pathway from the visual system of one hemisphere to the amygdala of the other hemisphere. The amygdala, in this case, serves in an emotional role because its removal has a "taming" effect on the monkey. These conclusions are based on evidence from split-brain humans (see Bogen, next section) that nonlanguage spatial memories are stored in the right hemisphere and that visual pattern discrimination in the split-brain monkey is confined to one hemisphere (Gazzaniga), and they are based on a series of his own experiments with an ingenious technique. The technique allows him to split the brain of a monkey without surgical aftereffects that would confuse the experimental results. Either the anterior commissure or the posterior corpus callosum is "ensnared" or surrounded by a ligature (length of surgical thread) that is led to a small hole in the bone flap (which allowed access to the brain during surgery) and left just below the skin. After recovery from the operation, the skin can be locally anesthetized and cut in a conscious monkey, and pulling the ligature splits the brain—the only reaction is a slight blink! In one experiment the optic tract of one hemisphere was cut to make it blind, the amygdala of the opposite hemisphere was removed, and the splenium was ensnared. After recovery, as long as the hemisphere with sight was in communication with the amygdala of the other hemisphere, the monkey would flee at the approach of a human, when the human was "seen." When the snare was pulled to interrupt these connections, the monkey would not flee unless touched (nonvisual information for the blind hemisphere that has an amygdala). In another experiment the optic chiasma was cut (to restrict visual information from each eye to the hemisphere of the same side) and the splenium was snared. One hemisphere was taught a five-choice maze. The monkey could perform perfectly after that with either eye (hemisphere). The "naïve" hemisphere was getting its information from the trained hemisphere because the monkey could not perform with the naïve eye (and hemisphere) after the snare was pulled. These experiments were extended in teaching a monkey to press a lever for food in response to electrical stimulation of the visual cortex of one hemisphere or the other. As long as the splenium was intact, stimulation of the "untrained" hemisphere resulted in lever pressing—after the snare was pulled, the response was abolished permanently. If the splenium was cut *before* the training and the anterior commissure was snared, the untrained hemisphere could respond after the snare was pulled. The engram had been transferred from one hemisphere to the other by the anterior commissure. (The splenium was not there to restrict visual training to one hemisphere.) Doty suggests that ". . . achievement of unilateral engrams with bihemispheric transcallosal access to them effectively doubles the mnemonic storage capacity of the brain" (Doty, 1973, p. 726).

LANGUAGE AND THE BRAIN

The study of brain functions in language is over 100 years old, and information has accumulated very slowly because man is the only really useful subject (see Geshwind, 1969, for a historical review). Until recently, most of the information has come from tumors that distort the brain to cause errors, from penetrating head wounds when there were few examinations after death to locate the injury, or from strokes (bursting blood vessels in the brain). The last source was the best because postmortem dissections were common, because the "weak point" where the blood vessels burst was frequently near the cortical areas serving language in one hemisphere, and because language behavior was frequently observed before death. Recently, however, the split-brain operation involving the corpus callosum and anterior commissure has become a practice for human epileptics so that brain seizure activity can be prevented from spreading from one hemisphere to the other in attempts to control epileptic "fits" that will not respond to other treatments. Careful testing of these subjects shows the extent of hemispheric specialization in man, as an extension of Doty's work on monkeys in the preceding section. Then we can examine the older work that shows the typical organization of the language areas within one hemisphere.

Split brain in man

The topic could have been reviewed in Chapter 14 on conscious awareness because the human split-brain subject has a disrupted unity of consciousness, with a verbally aware left hemisphere (usually) and a non–verbally aware right hemisphere—in effect, two minds in one brain (Gazzaniga). However, both hemispheres normally receive the same sensory input; so the disunity can only be demonstrated by special testing techniques. Further, nonverbal learning procedures are necessary to communicate with the right hemisphere.

Special learning and testing techniques show that two different value systems can compete for the same response mechanisms (Gazzaniga). Information presented to the left visual field goes only to the right hemisphere and vice versa (Figs. 11-5 and 17-1). In the split-brain patient, the information is not available to the unstimulated

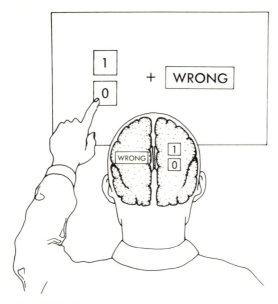

Fig. 17-1. Stimulus input for split-brain subjects learning a discrimination task. (From Gazzaniga, M.: One brain—two minds?, Am. Sci. **60:**311-317, 1972. Reprinted by permission of American Scientist, journal of Sigma Xi, The Scientific Research Society of North America.)

hemisphere through the corpus callosum and anterior commissure. If a discrimination between 0 and 1 is presented to the right hemisphere and reward or punishment—the word "right" or "wrong"—is presented to the left hemisphere, no learning occurs in over thirty trials (normals require one or two trials). If reprimanded for errors, however, quick learning occurred. The patient would respond to the reprimand with a sigh or exclamation or gesture or disgust, whereupon the other hemisphere would "catch on" to which symbol was incorrect (therefore which symbol was correct).

I should not leave the impression that the right (nonverbal) hemisphere is incapable of symbolic thought. Various tests show that it is. When the language areas of the left hemisphere are completely destroyed by a stroke, a patient can be taught a language based on cut-out paper symbols with

concepts like "same" or "different" for other symbols. Sodium amobarbital (Sodium Amytal) can be injected into a major blood vessel (the carotid artery) going to one hemisphere or the other in tests (the Wada test) that involve anesthetizing of one hemisphere of the brain at a time. When the left (language) hemisphere of the brain is "asleep," the patient cannot speak or use language but will perceive a spoon placed in his left hand (sensory input to the right hemisphere, Chapter 7). After recovery, he cannot say what was placed in his left hand but will point out the spoon with his left hand from among a series of objects.

Hemispheric specialization in normal subjects

If a device (a tachistoscope) is used to flash visual information to one visual field fast enough, the input will go to only one hemisphere in the normal subject. If the information is verbal, the response will take longer if it is flashed to the right (nonverbal) hemisphere than to the left (verbal) hemisphere—communication through the corpus callosum requires several milliseconds. The right hemisphere is faster, however, in space-perception problems. Other tests have shown the right hemisphere to be superior in recognizing faces, remembering music, and so on. EEG recordings of the normal resting alpha rhythm can be taken from each hemisphere (Chapter 13) to show that the rhythm is blocked when each hemisphere is active. The alpha rhythm of the left hemisphere is blocked when language, mathematical, or analytical problems are presented; the alpha waves of the right hemisphere are blocked for spatial and nonverbal inductive tasks. People tend to glance to the right (left hemisphere field) when solving verbal or math problems and to the left (right hemisphere field) when solving spatial recognition problems. The normal subject seems to have two specialized hemispheres, and

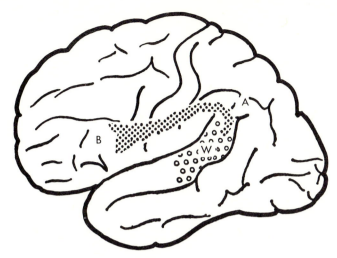

Fig. 17-2. Lateral surface of left hemisphere of human brain. *B*, Broca's area, which lies anterior to the lower end of the motor cortex. *W (open circles)*, Wernicke's area. *A (closed circles)*, Arcuate fasciculus, which connects Wernicke's to Broca's area. (From Geschwind, N.: The organization of language and the brain, Science **170:**940-944, copyright 1970 by The American Association for the Advancement of Science.)

unity in conscious awareness is contributed by the corpus callosum and commissures.

Language areas of the brain

There is evidence that the language areas are restricted to the left hemisphere in nearly all right-handed people and in the majority of those who are left-handed or ambidextrous. Using the sodium amobarbital Wada test and anesthetizing one hemisphere at a time on 95 right-handed subjects, researchers found only seven right-hemisphere and one bilateral speech areas. For 74 left-handed or ambidextrous people, there were 13 right hemisphere and 10 bilateral areas (Milner, Branch, and Rasmussen). Geshwind has examined over 100 normal brains and found one left-hemisphere language area (Wernicke's area, see Fig. 17-2 and p. 394) about one third larger than the corresponding area of the right hemisphere. Wada has found this to be true of human infants who died shortly after birth; so the left hemisphere language specialization would seem to be an inherent and inherited condition.

The term **aphasia** refers to disorders of language of several varieties that result from brain damage. These are not disorders of *speech* caused by lack of control over the muscles of speech, but are disorders of *language,* because the verbal output is incorrect. The term includes disorders of verbal comprehension or understanding as well. The subject may be unable to understand written or spoken language even though his vision and hearing are normal. Paul Broca was the first to relate difficulties of spoken language to specific areas of damage in the left hemisphere of the brain in the 1860s. Carl Wernicke in the 1870s extended this study to other areas of damage that result in impaired comprehension of language. He also related the functions of the two areas.

Broca's aphasia results from damage to a specific area of the left frontal lobe, just anterior to the lower end (face area) of the motor cortex (Fig. 17-2, *B*). These patients speak with great effort and poor articulation, omitting small grammatical words and endings. They cannot even repeat aloud a correct sentence that they read or that is spoken to them. Geshwind reports that if asked about the weather, a patient might say, "Overcast"; asked to produce a sentence, he might manage, "Weather . . . overcast."

Wernicke's aphasia results from damage to a different area of the left temporal lobe (Fig. 17-2, *W*). Since no motor or premotor areas are involved, speech is rapid and effortless, but remarkably free of meaningful information. Geshwind reports many errors in word usage like "spoot" for "spoon" or word substitutions such as "fork" for "spoon." He quotes a patient as saying: "I was over in the other one, and then after they had been in the department, I was in this one." The written output is of the same variety. In addition the patient does not understand written or spoken language although he is free of sensory defects in vision or hearing.

Wernicke established that Broca's area contained the complex code for turning perceived language into speech. Broca's area lies just in front of the cortical motor areas controlling the tongue, lips, and vocal cords and is in close communication with these areas. Wernicke's area is next to the sensory projection area for hearing and is responsible for the complex code ruling the recognition of the patterns of spoken language. He showed that the two areas were connected by a band of fibers (the arcuate fasciculus, Fig. 17-2, *A*). Spoken language is learned first, and the complex code is established in Wernicke's area. (Written language is learned in terms of perceived speech; so destruction of Wernicke's area impairs the perception of both.) The decoded perception is then transferred to Broca's area through the arcuate fasciculus. Broca's area then organizes the verbal response.

More complex aphasias can be understood in terms of damage to the band of fibers connecting Wernicke's area to Broca's area and in terms of damage to the corpus callosum that interconnects the verbal and nonverbal hemispheres. In pure word deafness, the patient with normal hearing cannot understand the spoken word, although his own speech is normal and he can read and write. Here, the auditory pathway to the verbal hemisphere is destroyed and the part of the corpus callosum carying hearing input from the auditory area of the nonverbal to the verbal hemisphere is destroyed. Wernicke's area is intact, but has no auditory input. In conduction aphasia, speech is deranged as it is in Wernicke's aphasia, but there is no impairment in the understanding of the writen or spoken word. However, the subject cannot repeat a sentence he sees or hears. The symptoms result from damage that impairs conduction from Wernicke's to Broca's area (Fig. 17-2, *A*). Wernicke's area is normal; so language comprehension is preserved. Broca's area is intact; so speech is fluent. However, there is no language relationship between comprehension and verbal output. If the left visual cortex is destroyed, visual information can reach only the right (nonverbal) hemisphere. If the part of the corpus callosum interconnecting the two visual hemispheres (splenium) is also destroyed, visual information cannot reach the verbal hemisphere from the nonverbal hemisphere. The result will be loss of the ability to comprehend written language without loss of the ability to write or understand spoken language. Memory disorders are associated with damage to the hippocampus, and verbal memory is involved if the left hippocampus is destroyed. Other complexities could be cited, but these should show the basic mechanisms involved.

OTHER ASPECTS OF LEARNING AND MEMORY
Reinforcement centers of the brain

As pointed out in Chapters 13 and 15, brain systems for reward and punishment have been found—systems that must be included in any account of the physiological psychology of learning. Experiments have been cited that show that a rat will work to stimulate itself via electrodes implanted in the limbic, anterior midbrain, and anterior (parasympathetic) hypothalamic areas, which form a medial forebrain bundle system. Within these areas hunger reward centers have been discovered, but they work only when the rat is hungry. Sexual reward centers have been found that will work with normal males, or with castrates who have been injected with male sex hormones; but these centers will not work with castrated rats unless they receive hormone therapy. Human patients have reported erotic sensation and daydreams from stimulation in some of these areas and more generalized pleasure from stimulation in others. Rats will learn complex tasks if rewarded with such brain stimulation. On the other hand, centers found in the thalamus, midbrain, and limbic areas are punishment centers; they form the periventricular system. Some of these centers are involved in the pain pathways, but others are not; human patients report feelings of anxiety and panic from stimulation in certain sites included in the punishment group. Stimulation of these sites in animals leads to all the responses typical of fear. A cat will learn a wheel-turning avoidance conditioned response when a light or tone signals the onset of brain stimulation unless the cat turns the wheel within a few seconds. This conditioned response is very resistant to extinction.

Brain stimulation and memory

Operations for brain tumors are often carried out under local anesthesia; the patient is conscious but experiences no pain. Under these conditions the surgeon can stimulate the brain electrically, and the patient can report the sensations he experiences as a result. (The procedure is done so that the surgeon can "map" the brain to avoid damaging sensory projection areas when removing a tumor, for example.) If the patient has a tumor in the temporal lobe, the temporal lobe will have

a low threshold to brain stimulation and will give a large electrical response to stimulation. Vivid reenacted memories are reported by such patients during temporal lobe stimulation. They will "see" a friend walking across the room toward them or "hear" a familiar piece of music. This is of interest to the physiological psychology of learning because of the close connections of the temporal lobes with the limbic system via the amygdaloid nucleus.

Nerve cells and behavior

The cellular connection approach has been one of the most useful strategies in the study of learning. Assuming the plasticity of interconnections between neurons is basic to that strategy—even if the anatomical connections between neurons may develop according to a rigid plan—the effectiveness of synaptic "connections" can vary with experience. Both excitatory and inhibitory synapses would have to be involved. An early demonstration of synaptic plasticity involved the single-synapse pathway through the stellate ganglion of the autonomic nervous system (Chapter 5). When neurons leading to the ganglion are repetitively stimulated at a high frequency (tetanizing), the responsiveness of the single synapse pathway is enhanced for several minutes—**posttetanic potentiation.** Other monosynaptic pathways demonstrate a posttetanic depression in synaptic conductivity. Kandel and Tauc, in working with marine snails because of their simple nervous system, were able to show that synaptic conductivity, as measured by the excitatory postsynaptic potential (EPSP, Chapter 4), could be facilitated by activity in a nearby pathway. They proposed that the nearby pathway had axon terminals that ended on the axon terminals of the other cells (axoaxonic synapses, Chapter 4); thus such activity stimulates them to release more transmitter substance.

Habituation to a novel stimulus can be studied in the snail and was chosen because it is a form of behavior that resembles learning. Recovery from habituation results from withholding the stimulus to which the snail has been habituated or from changing the stimulus pattern. The snail was chosen for its large neurons (up to 1 mm. in diameter), which can easily be impaled with a microelectrode. In addition, individual neurons can be visually identified while recording is going on. A defensive gill-withdrawal reflex response to a touch was chosen for study. Both the motor and sensory neurons of this reflex were mapped with double-barreled microelectrodes—one "barrel" for stimulation and the other for recording. Habituation was accompanied by a decrease in the EPSP of motor neurons controlling the reflex; recovery from inhibition was accompanied by an increase in the EPSP. Neither of these changes resulted in a change in the measured resistance across the cell membrane of the motor neurons. Therefore it is likely that the presynaptic neurons were releasing less synaptic transmitter substance during habituation and more during recovery.

BIOFEEDBACK

Biofeedback is a term that has come to mean learning "voluntary" control over what was previously an "involuntary" response. The approach assumes that voluntary control becomes possible when the subject receives information or "feedback" about the biological response. Learning to control the rate of one's heartbeat becomes possible when the subject knows when it changes in the desired way—information not ordinarily available to the subject. In experiments with human subjects, the only reward necessary to learn the response is knowledge of success. In animal experiments, other kinds of reinforcements are used in conditioning techniques.

Types of conditioning

A technique called "bell shock" conditioning can be described. A bell (conditioned stimulus) is sounded, followed by a shock to the paw (unconditioned stimulus), which forces leg flexion. After a number of trials, the bell alone will elicit a leg withdrawal—a conditioned response has been formed. This is an example of a type of conditioning often called *classical conditioning*. Reward as well as punishment can be used to force the response. For example, food may be used to condition salivation to a conditioned stimulus. Much everyday learning takes place in a different way, however. In a trial-and-error learning situation the subject hits on the correct (or incorrect) response by accident and is immediately rewarded (or punished). In this situation the subject, rather than the experimenter, is in control of the behavior. This is an example of *operant conditioning*. The question then arises, How do you induce the subject to make the response that you wish to reward? The most effective method lies in a technique called **shaping.** Any movement approximating the desired response is rewarded. Then closer and closer approximations to the desired response are required for subsequent rewards until the desired response emerges. Escape from punishment can be used as a reinforcement in the same way.

Somatic versus visceral and glandular learning

For many years it has been the conventional wisdom in psychology that visceral and glandular responses are capable of classical conditioning only, and that only somatic responses can be operantly conditioned. Visceral and glandular responses were believed to be "involuntary"—not under the control of the subject, as are somatic responses. The experimenter would therefore have to "force" the response he wished to reward with a reflex stimulus before he could reward it. Many theorists held that classical and instrumental conditioning are different kinds of learning, rather than merely different learning procedures. However, in a series of important experiments, Neal Miller and his associates at Rockefeller University have shown that the so-called involuntary visceral and glandular responses can be operantly conditioned. The consequences of their findings will be noted after a survey of some of the experiments involved.

Visceral and glandular conditioning

The initial study involved conditioned salivation for a water reward in thirsty dogs. (Water has no effect on bursts of spontaneous salivation.) One group of dogs was conditioned through shaping techniques to increase salivation frequency, and the other group was taught to decrease salivation frequency. This procedure eliminated the possibility of the water's forcing either salivation or lack of salivation. The group conditioned to increase salivation seemed more active than the other group; thus the possibility that somatic motor activity resulted in salivation had to be eliminated. Because curare, used to paralyze the animals, resulted in increased salivation, another response was chosen. (Curare blocks the junction between nerves and muscles, necessitating artificial respiration; curare has no effect on the heart rate.) Because it is difficult to reward paralyzed animals in the usual manner, rewarding brain stimulation was used. Rats were conditioned to either increase their heart rate or decrease it. Furthermore, a discrimination response was conditioned —a light indicated when reward was available, and the rats learned to increase or decrease their heart rates only when the light was on. Memory for the training survived a 3-month retention interval. Heart rate conditioning could be shaped to avoidance of a punishing shock as well, when heart rate change in the first 10 seconds after the light turned on prevented a shock to the tail. Heart rate conditioning that was carried on in the curarized state appeared in the normal state, and no differences in activity were seen between rats trained to increase heart rate and those trained to decrease heart rate. Choosing a response less related to activity than heart rate, the investigators trained curarized rats to either increase or decrease the frequency of intestinal contractions (recorded by a balloon inserted in the anus) for a rewarding brain stimulation. Heart rate did not change significantly in either group. Catheterized rats (a tube to the bladder) have been trained to either increase or decrease their rate of urine formation. Tests showed that the rats changed their blood flow through the kidney to control the response. Both vasoconstriction (constriction of blood vessels) and vasodilation in the tail have been conditioned, and rats have been trained to show these responses in one ear and not in the other. Finally, the investigators showed that operant control of visceral responses could be initiated by the animal to balance an abnormal homeostatic condition. Rats "preloaded" with water learned to choose the arm of a Y maze that led to a saline injection rather than one that led to an injection of antidiuretic hormone (ADH results in water retention by the kidney).

There has been some recent difficulty in repeating these careful experiments in other laboratories. Whether the conflicting results are caused by technical problems or by some artifact in the procedures used, only time and much work will tell. However, the basic principles of visceral conditioning and biofeedback seem to be established.

Implications for man

Evidence for the instrumental, or operant, learning of visceral responses has profound implications for so-called "psychosomatic" disorders in man (Chapter 18). Many disorders, such as asthma, stomach ulcers, piles, and hives, may occur as a result of psychological stress, in the absence of disease or other trauma. However, the particular symptom that results may depend as much on learning as on any "weakness" in the organ itself. As Miller points out in an example, a child may fear going to school to face an examination for which he is unprepared, and this fear can result in a variety of fluctuating autonomic symptoms, including perhaps pallor and faintness, as well as stomach upset. The mother may decide the child is sick and must stay at home. If she makes her decision on the basis of the faintness, she is rewarding one symptom, and if she makes it on the basis of the stomach upset, she is rewarding another symptom.

On the more positive side, operant conditioning of visceral responses in man may be used to control, if not cure, a variety of disorders. Patients with high blood pressure could be taught to control their heart rate. Similiar benefits could occur for spastic colitis, asthma, acid stomach, and so on.

EEG experiments have shown that some subjects can learn to control the appearance of their own alpha rhythms. All that seems to be required is a reliable signal that tells the subject when he is displaying alpha rhythms—a light or a buzzer will suffice. The signal is always on when the subject's EEG is displaying alpha waves and never on when the EEG does not contain alpha waves. Some subjects learn to control alpha waves more readily than do others, but none of the subjects are able to report how they do it. Interest in the technique arises because the subject must be in a relaxed state in order to display alpha waves. Thus if a subject can be conditioned to display alpha waves, then he is being conditioned to relax. The phenomenon has obvious applications in cases of hypertension (high blood pressure) and anxiety. Interest among less scientific circles has been aroused by the finding that yogis show extremely stable alpha rhythms while meditating. This has led some enthusiasts to learn how to control their own alpha rhythms as a shortcut to learning how to meditate, although there is no proof that alpha control is the only element in meditation. The appearance of alpha-signaling electronic devices on the open market has been one result.

TIME COURSE OF BRAIN ACTIVITY IN LEARNING: PERSEVERATION AND CONSOLIDATION
Two-phase hypothesis

Another approach to events in the brain accompanying learning concerns the time course of these events, irrespective of their location. Activity in many brain centers, both cortical and subcortical, accompanies learning and memory. Experiments have shown that the brain activity accompanying learning lasts for a longer time than was previously suspected. It may outlast the practice experience by as much as a half hour or more. A **two-phase hypothesis** of learning and memory has gained wide acceptance, a hypothesis that further distinguishes between immediate memory and long-term memory. During the brain activity that occurs immediately after practice, the subject remembers perfectly; thus one may dial a telephone number without error just after having read it. However, unless the brain activity continues for a time without interruption, no "permanent" trace will be formed in the brain (memory). Brain activity that occurs after practice is called **perseveration,** and the consequent formation of a learning trace is called **consolidation.** Perseveration is believed to be the basis for immediate memory and is perhaps necessary for consolidation of the memory trace. Whether ordinary environmental events can interrupt perseveration and thereby prevent consolidation is a moot question to be taken up later.

Development of the hypothesis. The two-stage, or perseveration-consolidation, hypothesis was invented to explain **retroactive inhibition** (Müller and Pilzecker). It was found that subjects could not remember a list of nonsense syllables well if they had learned a subsequent list. It was proposed that learning the second list interrupted perseveration of the first list before consolidation of a permanent trace of the first list was complete. Later experiments showed, however, that most of the forgetting was caused by confusion between the syllables of the two similar lists. In the same way one might have difficulty remembering two telephone numbers that were very much alike—digits from one phone number might appear in one's attempt to recall the other. Furthermore, the second list was learned more than an hour after the first, and it is doubtful that perseveration of the first list would last that long. More recently, another writer (Hebb) was speculating about perceptual learning. He proposed that the stimuli of learning initiated activity in reverberating circuits of the associative cortex, self-reexciting "loop circuits" of nerve cells (Chapter 12). This activity constitutes the basis for immediate memory and could last for up to an hour. The activity spreads to **cell assemblies,** whose synapses are changed by their activity; therefore they are more likely to excite each other the next time. When a series of cell assemblies are excited in order in a perception, such as when the corners of a triangle are viewed successfully, a **phase sequence** is built up, with the cells that unite the cell assemblies being the basis for the permanent memory of the perception.

Interruption of consolidation

At about the same time the above hypothesis was proposed, another investigator (Duncan) was studying the effects of **electroconvulsive shock (ECS)** on learning and memory in rats. ECS is a strong electrical current stimulus to the brain, usually delivered by electrodes attached to the head. The massive brain stimulation that results causes a convulsion that resembles an epileptic seizure or the seizures that result from insulin shock or overdoses of stimulating drugs. ECS, insulin, and drugs, have been used to induce seizures as a form of treatment for mental patients.

Side effects on memory were noted that were the same as those occurring after other trauma or damage to the brain—retroactive amnesia (RA, Chapter 13). Memory for events that occurred immediately before the treatment was impaired more than were older memories.

In the investigation of retroactive amnesia at short time intervals, the amnesia effect in rats for a just-practiced habit was profound, even though a simple habit was used. (Retroactive amnesia for complex habits, such as a maze, can occur, even when treatments follow practice by several hours.) In Duncan's pioneering study, rats were trained to jump a barrier to avoid electric shock. If they jumped from the black side of a box to the white side of the box within 10 seconds after being placed in the apparatus, they avoided shock to the feet. If ECS occurred after each trial by 20 seconds, 40 seconds, 4 minutes, or 15 minutes, the rats learned more slowly than did those given no ECS. ECS given 2 to 14 hours after each trial did not affect learning of this simple response; therefore brain trauma could not have been the reason for the impairment (as may be the case for ECS effects on more complex habits, such as maze learning). The amount of brain trauma would not depend on the interval between practice and ECS; yet the shorter this time interval, the more poorly the animals performed. The rats could have hesitated to jump the barrier if the ECS treatment that followed was painful. The effect of punishment on learning the response was checked with control groups. It was found that punishment (foot shock with the ECS apparatus) had to be given within 2 minutes after each trial to impair performance, whereas ECS was effective at much longer intervals. Duncan reasoned that the massive brain stimulation of ECS caused a convulsive "storm" of neural activity in the brain, which interrupted the perseveration of the habit in the brain after each trial if ECS was given while perseveration was still going on. The longer that perseveration was allowed to go on after each trial before interruption of it with ECS, the greater was the consolidation of the memory trace and the better was the performance on subsequent trials.

Since this pioneering study, it has been found that less traumatic treatments can be used to interrupt perseveration and thereby impair consolidation. For example, anesthetizing rats (sodium thiopental [Pentothal]) within 5 minutes after each trial in a maze slows learning. Furthermore, both anesthesia and convulsions impair one-trial learning of a conditioned avoidance response (CAR) if given within a few minutes of the trial. The animal was shocked while bar pressing in a Skinner box for water and then was given a convulsive or drug treatment to interrupt subsequent consolidation of the experience. If it did not learn, it would continue to bar-press for water the next day. This proved to be the case for many of the treated animals. If the treatment had been punishing, the animals would have avoided bar pressing because they would have anticipated shock for doing so, as well as a painful treatment afterward. Other agents have proved useful in interrupting the consolidation process—hypoxia in rats through simulated altitude or carbon dioxide, or heat narcosis in goldfish, for example. Finally, human patients under deep surgical anesthesia often report retroactive amnesia for the events just preceding onset of anesthesia.

Stimulating consolidation

Another group of experiments (McGaugh and others) has shown that brain stimulants (such as strychnine), administered within a few minutes *after* each practice trial has ended, can improve the rate of maze acquisition in rats. Presumably, the neural processes underlying consolidation are more effective when the brain is most active. A variety of stimulants have been used (pentylenetetrazol [Metrazol], caffeine, picrotoxin, 1757 I.S., and so forth), so that the effect is not specific to any one drug. The treatment is more effective for rats bred to be poor maze learners (maze-dull rats) than for maze-bright rats. Other experiments seem to show that the maze-bright rats consolidate faster after each trial than do the maze-dull rats. Consolidation can be interrupted, or at least learning is impaired, when ECS is administered at a longer interval after each trial for the maze-dull rats than for the maze-bright rats. The "bright" rats appear to finish consolidation within 45 minutes, but the "dull" rats do not. These experiments are exciting because of their implications for improving the learning rate in subnormal people.

Alternative explanations

No alternative explanations have been offered for improved learning when drug *stimulants* are administered *after* practice. Other explanations have been proposed, however, for impaired learning resulting from ECS treatment after practice. Some investigators (Coons and Miller) have shown that repeated trials, each followed by ECS in an avoidance box or in a runway-to-food situation, can impair the animal's performance in a way that suggests fear of the treatment. Other experimenters (Hudspeth and others) have used a passive avoidance task to analyze this fear conditioning. If a rat is placed on an elevated platform, it will naturally step down onto a grid floor. If the animal is shocked through the grid floor for doing so, it will avoid stepping down on subsequent trials. If ECS given immediately after each trial prevents it from learning its lesson, the animal will step down on each following trial. If it "remembers" and is afraid of the ECS, foot shock followed by ECS has been even more effective than foot shock alone in keeping it on the platform. However, the results show that the rat begins to avoid stepping down when the daily trial is followed by

ECS, but only after 4 to 8 days, whereas 1 or 2 days is enough to train a control rat, who receives only foot shock. Repeated ECS does cause avoidance. However, a single ECS treatment can impair a habit ordinarily learned in *one* trial, as has already been seen.

A moot point remains. Even if drugs or ECS can affect consolidation to improve or impair learning, these are extreme conditions. There is no clear evidence that everyday experiences interfere with consolidation. The superior recall that occurs when sleep rather than waking activity follows learning or when practice trials follow each other by hours rather than by minutes has been cited as an example of improved learning caused by less stimulus interference with consolidation. Interference explanations that depend on confusion at the time of recall, caused by stimulus similarity, are also offered. Similar events can become confused because they occurred one after the other rather than because one event interfered with consolidation of a previous one. On the other hand, differences in sleep *stages* seem to affect memory. In Chapter 14, slow-wave sleep stages were distinguished from rapid eye-movement (REM) sleep, called paradoxical sleep in animals. Reports of dreaming frequently accompany REM sleep awakenings. It may be that the neural activity that accompanies REM and paradoxical sleep has something to do with rearousing perseveration and thereby improving consolidation. Rats and mice can be deprived of paradoxical sleep by forcing them to sleep on a pedestal above a pool of water—if the muscles relax, as they do in paradoxical (but not slow-wave) sleep, the animal falls off the pedestal into the water (this was called the "flower pot" technique in some experiments because upside-down flower pots were used as pedestals!). In passive-avoidance tasks, Y mazes, brightness discriminations, and other experiments, depriving the animal of paradoxical sleep by this technique impairs memory.

Locus of consolidation

Hudspeth has given evidence on the question of the locus of consolidation. By permanently implanting electrodes in the anterior limbic field of mice, he was able to make lesions in that area at any time he wished. Control animals had electrodes at other cortical locations. The animals were taught a simple avoidance habit that could be learned in one trial. Lesions were made 24 hours before the trial, immediately after the trial, 10 minutes after the trial, or after a 45-minute interval. Only the groups in which lesions were made in the limbic field immediately after or 10 minutes after the trial failed the retention tests. The other lesions had no effect. This experiment suggests that the limbic system is involved in the consolidation process. How did the animals that had been given limbic lesions *before* practice manage to learn? Later studies showed that learning may have been an artifact of the apparatus familiarization procedure used. In these later studies, the animals who were given limbic lesions *prior* to training did not learn.

Short- and long-term memory and the hippocampus

It has already been reported that stimulation of the temporal lobes causes vivid reenacted memories in patients being operated on for brain tumors. The same investigator (Penfield) has reported two cases of penetrating brain injury that damaged the temporal lobes and underlying parts of the hippocampus in both hemispheres. These patients seemed unable to form new memories, even though their recall for events prior to their accidents seemed normal for brain-damaged individuals. Yet they were not able to recall anything new over an interval longer than 10 minutes. Perhaps some of the connections between the hippocampus and temporal cortex that were destroyed in these patients are essential to the process of forming permanent memories —the process called consolidation. As an overstatement, the patients seemed able to operate on perseverating neural traces only, but the perseveration left no permanent traces, or "memory." Upon meeting someone new, for example, they could converse with him and use his name. If the person left for an hour and returned, they were unable to recall ever having met him.

Memory storage processes

As work of the nature described in this section continues, theories of the relationship between memory storage and retrieval begin to emerge. One of the most prominent theorists in the field is James L. McGaugh. After extensively reviewing the literature, he concludes that consolidation is a "time-dependent" process that is essential to the formation of long-term memory. Although the evidence is indirect, he suggests that "immediate memory" depends on neural activity, whereas the formation of long-term memory depends on a slower process that probably involves protein synthesis. As will be seen in a later section, protein synthesis is involved in memory phenomena. His ingenious hypotheses and those of others are summarized in Fig. 17-3. Incoming sensory information is "held" in a sensory buffer. This is to prevent our being overwhelmed by sensory information; feedback to the inputs allows selection or rejection of inputs for immediate action (like dialing a telephone number) and those for later storage. One example of the action of such a perceptual buffer can be seen when you are a part of one of two conversational groups of friends. You are paying attention only to your own group until you name is mentioned in the other conversation. This commands your attention and you find that you can immediately recall not only the mention of your name, but several preceding words from the other conversation that were being "held" in the sensory buffer. Once items are selected from the sensory buffer, they enter short-term memory for action and or storage. Short-term memory is immediate memory and is believed to be based on the neural activity of perseveration. Feedback from short-term memory to the sensory input continues to select items for attention from the sensory buffer. Reverberating items from short-term memory may be acted on and forgotten, or perseveration can last long enough so that the information enters long-term memory. Long-term memory is be-

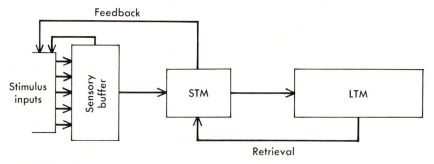

Fig. 17-3. Model for information selection, storage, and retrieval. A number of stimulus inputs that do not exceed the information-processing capacity of the organism are selected by feedback from a sensory buffer that determines the selection process. Selected inputs reach short-term memory, *STM*, for immediate action, changes of attention by feedback, or continuing activity that leads to long-term memory, *LTM*. Remembering (retrieval) is a process of rearousing some part of the original STM by LTM patterns.

lieved to be based on some protein change in the nerve cells, as will be seen later on. When you "remember" the information later on ("retrieval"), the changed nerve cells initiate a version of the perseverating activity that initiated short-term memory.

Old and new memories

Although many variables control how well one remembers things, an old memory is frequently recalled with more clarity than a recent event. When an event becomes a part of the array of memories that can be recalled on demand, an older memory can often be recalled more readily than a newer one. Some suggest that this is because it has been recalled more often. In line with such an idea, one writer (Russell) has suggested that the underlying trace of a memory in the nervous system is a pattern of excitation that is more readily aroused by random activity than is a new pattern. If so, a pattern would have been stimulated more often by random brain activity the longer it had existed—there would have been a series of many perseverations and consolidations. Perhaps for this reason, old memories are less susceptible than newer memories to the brain trauma of ECS, strokes, concussions, and so on—their neural traces have been activated more often, have become more numerous and fixed, and thus are less susceptible to severe disruption.

HOLOGRAM MODEL

Suppose that we accept the idea that short-term memory is based on a pattern of neural activity and that long-term memory results from a protein change in this pattern of cells (see molecular biochemical changes). We are still faced with Lashley's paradox because the nerve cell changes involved in learning are so widespread that each cell must be involved in many memories. What is the "code" that would enable a single cell to carry so many "bits" of in-

formation, and how could each "bit" be expressed differently? We will consider later on, that the DNA molecules that contain the "blueprint" in each cell for an entire organism have the information-carrying capacity to enable one cell to contain the code for many memories. But how can the information be impressed and retrieved? What kinds of interaction among many cells could differ for each memory? The discovery and development of the hologram by Dennis Gabor from 1948 to 1971 provides a model. A model is a plan or mechanism that fits the facts—it could do all the things that the nervous system does with information. We have little direct evidence that the nervous system receives and retrieves information the way a hologram does. However, the model fits the facts of Lashley's paradox.

The input changes in learning must be impressed and expressed at synapses because these are the only places where nerve cells interact with one another by electrochemical change. Rate of firing of axons or dendrites, or patterns of slow potential change in cell bodies that cause axon firing are all symptoms of the release of the transmitter chemicals that allow one cell to influence other cells. The hologram model proposes that *interference patterns* among the firing or slow potentials of many cells forms the mechanism by means of which memories are impressed and expressed.

The model begins as a photographic one, but it is a different kind of photograph. The usual photograph is an impression of many wavelengths of light from an object, each part of the object being represented on a corresponding part of the picture. Consider what can happen if a single coherent wavelength of high intensity is used (Fig. 17-4), such as a laser beam. A beam splitter divides the laser beam into two sources. One is directed by a prism and lens to the subject and is reflected by the subject onto the holographic plate. The lens so scatters the beam that every part of the subject is re-

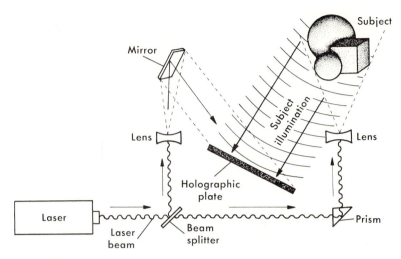

Fig. 17-4. Processes involved in forming and recording interference patterns of hologram.

flected to every part of the plate, and the resulting picture would be a blur. The other half of the beam splitter is directed by a lens and mirror onto the same holographic plate without being reflected by the object. The two beams *interfere* with one another because the reflected and direct light waves are *out of phase*. In terms of the wave form of the single-wave light rays, the "peaks" and "valleys" of the two groups of light rays alternately agree to form bigger peaks and valleys (bright spots) and disagree to cancel out (dark spots). Thus an *interference pattern* is created that does not look like an image. This interference pattern forms the "photograph." Now, if the developed holographic plate is reilluminated by the same interfering beam from the same angle and distance, the image will reappear. Furthermore, it will be three-dimensional; that is, by viewing the plate from different angles, you can see "around the corners" to see different parts of the object! You may also cut the holographic plate in half, reilluminate each half as described, and have two pictures, because each part of the plate registered light waves reflected from each part of the subject! Finally, you can use the same plate

for a laser hologram of another subject, which will have a different interference pattern. Then depending on the angle and position of the interference beam, you can view either of two different subjects on the same plate. Gabor reports storing 300 pages of printed matter in the area of an ordinary photograph! That would appear to be an incredible memory storage capacity, but in a different form of holography, 10 billion bits of information have been stored in 1 cubic centimeter.

If holography were confined to light rays, it would be a poor model for memory in the nervous system. However, any wave form of energy that will form interference patterns of the kind described can be used to store information. Perhaps, as noted near the beginning of this section, chemical changes at many synapses during learning form holographic interference patterns of electrical activity as their symptom.

CHANGES AT THE SYNAPSE IN LEARNING
Molar biochemical changes

Learning involves a change in response to stimuli. Many writers believe that memory is caused by some physical change, or "memory trace," in the nervous system that results from learning. Whatever parts of the brain are involved in learning, any physical changes should logically occur at synapses—the anatomical sites where one neuron excites another neuron. Synapses appear to be the only places in the central nervous system where pathways between stimulus and response can be changed, however complex the pathways. This section concerns the nature of the change at synapses during learning, without regard to where the synapses are located.

Biochemical and anatomical changes in the rat brain. Synapses in which one neuron stimulates another by the release of **acetylcholine (ACh)** have been demonstrated in autonomic ganglia, the spinal cord, and some centers of the brain. The ACh acts only briefly because it is hydrolized (chemically removed), a reaction speeded by the enzyme **acetylcholine esterase (AChE),** which is present at all cholinergic synapses. Such cholinergic synapses may be involved in learning. Repeated synaptic "use" during learning could increase the efficiency of synapses by leading to the release of more ACh. The difference between fast and slow learners could be caused by a biochemical difference in the Ach/AChE ratio rather than by anatomical differences in their brains. Either high ACh or low AChE could make synapses more excitable.

Such speculations have led to a fascinating series of experiments under the direction of Krech, Rosensweig, and Bennett. The earlier studies in the series demonstrated chemical differences in the brains of rats selectively bred to be maze-bright or maze-dull, according to their ability to learn a complex maze. The maze-bright rats had a greater brain AChE content than did the maze-dull rats. Later studies showed that this difference was largely confined to the cortex and that in different strains of rats it was the ACh/AChE *ratio* that seemed most closely related to learning ability.

ACh and AChE content appeared to be independently determined, genetically. Breeding for AChE content in the brain, for example, can lead to high-AChE, maze-dull animals and low-AChE, maze-bright animals, provided that the ACh content varies only randomly.

Having established that hereditary differences in brain chemistry could affect learning ability, this Berkeley group asked whether environmental stimulation could affect brain chemistry and, perhaps, the anatomy of the brain as well. In those experiments one group of rats was raised in solitary confinement (isolated controls, or IC rats). Their littermates were raised in groups and given training in several tasks as well as having frequently changed toys in their cages (ladders, wheels, etc.) for stimulation (environmental complexity and training, or ECT). Animals given ECT for 30 days after weaning were compared with those suffering IC for a similar period. In over seven strains that were tested, the ECT animals had less cortical and more subcortical AChE in their brains than did the IC rats when sacrificed. In other experiments the ECT animals were found to have thicker and heavier cortical tissue, better blood supply to the brain, and biochemical changes (in proteins, hexokinase, and serotonin) expected of a more active brain. In more recent experiments, it has been shown that as little as 2 hours a day of ECT protects rats from some degenerative changes in the brain that result from isolation. Finally, it has been found that rats in a semi-natural environment showed greater brain development than did the ECT rats. Despite generations of laboratory conditions, the natural conditions under which rats have evolved proved to be the most enriching of all.

The effects do not seem restricted to early growth and development; similar results have been obtained when the difference in treatment began at 105 days of age (young adult rats). Considering the attention being given today to human mental deficiency and to "head start" preschool programs for environmentally deprived children, the Berkeley experiments may have far-reaching implications. Biochemical and anatomical differences in the brain may be effected in man in the same general way as in the rat— by differences in environmental stimulation.

Molecular biochemical changes

As explained in Chapter 2, the cell reproduces itself and repairs its parts according to patterns contained in the DNA molecules of the chromosomes in its nucleus. In cell reproduction by cell division each DNA molecule is reproduced in the nucleus of each of the two daughter cells. In repairing parts of the cell, sections of the DNA molecules assemble simpler RNA molecules, with the form of the DNA section serving as a pattern. The messenger RNA, so assembled, migrates from the nucleus to the cytoplasm of the cell. There it assembles transfer RNA by a similar process. The transfer RNA, in turn, assembles enzymes to speed the needed chemical reactions of cell metabolism. Some theorists believe that changes in the DNA molecules, the RNA molecules, or the enzymes they form, produce changes in nerve cell excitability that accompany learning. DNA, RNA, or enzymes could change the structure of a nerve cell. Changes in the structure of the nerve cell membrane could make the cell more excitable or cause it to release more transmitter substance at synapses. It is pointed out that nerve cells in mammals do not reproduce themselves. Perhaps part of the DNA-RNA mechanism involved in cell repair and cell reproduction is used for learning instead. (Such changes would not be passed on to the animal's progeny—inheritance of acquired characteristics—because the reproductive cells in the gonads would not be affected. Only the nerve cells would change, and these would die with the animal.) If the DNA mechanism can store the blueprint for assembling an entire organism in cell reproduction, it certainly

should have enough information capacity to store the memories of a lifetime, especially if relieved of the reproductive task.

Most of the evidence for this view comes from experiments by McConnell, of the University of Michigan, with flatworms **(planarians),** small primitive invertebrates with a "nerve net" nervous system, a primitive ganglion type of "brain" in the head end, and visual receptors in the head. Unlike vertebrates, they reproduce asexually as well as sexually and can reproduce missing parts after amputation, *including nervous tissue,* to the extent that two complete planarians are regenerated if one is cut in two. The head end grows a new tail, and the tail end grows a new head. McConnell and his colleagues wondered if changes in the nerve cells caused by learning would be passed on to new nerve cells as the new nerve cells were formed to regenerate amputated parts of the worm. The DNA-RNA-enzyme mechanism is involved in cell reproduction. Any change in nerve cells caused by learning might involve the same mechanism. If so, the change resulting from learning would be reproduced when new nerve cells were "copied" from old ones in cell division. To test these notions, flatworms were trained, cut in two, and tested after regeneration. Flatworms respond to electric shock by curling into an S shape. The response was conditioned to a flash of light. The worms were then cut in two, and the head ends grew new tails, and the tails grew new heads. Both groups of regenerated flatworms learned the habit faster than did the "naïve" worms.

The next question concerned the role of the nerve ganglion in the head, which serves as a flatworm's brain. If the head is split so that the ganglion is cut in half longitudinally, each half of the head creates a matching half, and a two-headed worm results. The two-headed worm learns the CR faster than does a normal worm. Two heads seem better than one, at least for this purpose, and the head ganglion seems to dominate the nervous system of the flatworm.

A further test of the head dominance hypothesis was made in the following way. An enzyme, RNAase, interferes with the regeneration process and would presumably interfere with learning patterns being passed on to regenerating tissue. After learning the conditioned response the worms were cut in two, and their missing parts were regenerated in RNAase solution. The trained heads were thus prevented, at least partly, from passing on the learning change and developed "naïve" tails; the trained tails developed "naïve" heads. If the head dominates, the worms with experienced heads should show the results of training, whereas those with "naïve" heads should not. In a general way this is what happened.

These experiments have been extended at the University of California at Los Angeles by Jacobson. The general plan of his experiments involves teaching rats a simple habit, such as lever pressing in a Skinner box, or a simple discrimination. The rat's brain is then removed and the RNA is extracted from it. The extract is then injected (intraperitoneally) into a second "naïve" rat, which is then taught the same habit. The learning of the second rat is compared with the learning of rats that have been injected with RNA extracts from rats that have had no learning experience. Jacobson's results indicate that rats that have received extract from "experienced" rat brains learn faster than rats that have received extract from "naïve" rat brains. These "memory transfer" experiments have led to much controversy, and many attempts have been made to replicate Jacobson's results. Both failures and successes have been reported. Some investigators suggest that RNA is too large a molecule to cross the blood-brain barrier (Chapter 13) and therefore cannot reach the brain from the blood. The RNA extraction procedure is a complex one, and mistakes in the procedure could account for differing results.

Ungar, of Baylor University, has recently reported a series of even more controversial experiments. Rats are normally noctur-nal—they prefer a dark compartment to a lighted one. The Baylor scientists taught over 4000 rats to avoid the darkest of three compartments by shocking them if they entered it. A peptide composed of fourteen amino acids was extracted from the brains of these rats and injected directly into the brains of 3000 "naïve" rats. Before the injections, these rats had spent most of their time in the dark compartment. After the injections, they spent only a few seconds there, and many of them would not enter the dark compartment. Most recently, Ungar has reported synthesizing all of the amino acids in correct sequence for the extracted peptide. He reports that brain injections of the synthetic molecule have the same kind of "fear of the dark" effect as did the extract (called "scotophobin" for 'fear of darkness'). Results of this kind are mind-boggling for most scientists and will generate much debate and experimentation before they can be validated.

Another line of evidence for the DNA-RNA-enzyme-protein synthesis idea comes from the effects of the drug puromycin. Puromycin inhibits protein synthesis in the cell. It must be injected directly into the brain to affect learning because it does not pass the blood-brain barrier (Chapter 5). Strangely enough, the injection must follow learning (a Y maze) in the rat by 3 to 6 days to be effective. Under these conditions it blots out the habit, leaving intact the responses learned before or after this period.

When the DNA-RNA hypothesis is applied to humans, it has been found that administering RNA (but not DNA) to elderly individuals improves their memory. However, the improvement does not outlast the treatment and may have merely overcome a nutritional deficiency. Still, it *has* been found that the supply of nerve cell RNA increases in humans from ages 3 to 40, is constant to 60, and decreases rapidly thereafter. This roughly parallels changes in the ability to learn new material (intelligence).

SUMMARY

Using a reflex model and assuming encephalization, early investigators sought to locate the "trace" left in the brain by learning. They removed parts of the cortex of rats and observed the effect on learning and memory for mazes of differing difficulty. The lesions had more effect on memory than on new learning, and impaired performance in difficult mazes the most; the effects depended on the size rather than on the locus of the lesion. The latter finding led to the mass action and equipotentiality principles. Cortical connections made in learning seem to be vertically organized interactions with subcortical centers because thin cuts that isolate sections of rat cortex from one another impair neither learning nor memory. Damage to the thalamus affects learning, but again the size rather than the locus of the lesion determines the effect. This leads to Lashley's paradox: When many cells are involved in each memory trace, each *single* cell must carry many memory traces. Recordings show electrical changes at several "stations" along the acoustic pathway when rats learn an avoidance response to a tone; different parts of the brain also "learn" at a different rate. Some changes are more important than others as revealed by computer-averaged EEGs, with areas that show greater response showing more change as well. If evoked potentials are averaged in animals, exogenous changes attributable to sensory input can be distinguished from endogenous changes attributable to learning.

If the commissural fibers connecting the two cerebral hemispheres are cut, little difference is seen in the behavior of man. Animal experiments show, however, that visual input from one eye can be restricted to the hemisphere of the same side if the crossing fibers of the optic chiasma are cut, as seen in split-brain cats and monkeys. Somesthetic input and motor control are restricted to the opposite hemisphere in split-brain animals. The traces of visual or somesthetic learning can be restricted to the one hemisphere by the split-brain technique, and contradictory habits can be taught to the two hemispheres. "Temporary decortication" of one hemisphere in rats can be caused by a spreading depression of neural activity that follows application of potassium chloride to that hemisphere. (This technique appears to be valid only when the brain waves are monitored so that one can be certain that depression has actually occurred.) Discrimination learning in rats can be confined to one hemisphere in this manner. Only a few trials are necessary after recovery for the untrained hemisphere to "copy" the trace in the trained hemisphere. In humans, however, language habits seem restricted to the dominant hemisphere (the left hemisphere in right-handed people). The other hemisphere appears to be more specialized for nonverbal memory and space perception. The corpus callosum in primates appears to permit the formation of memory traces in one hemisphere only. Only the anterior commissure can transfer the trace from one hemisphere to another. The testing of split-brain humans reveals that they have two minds in one brain: a verbally aware left hemisphere and a nonverbal right hemisphere that can form different value systems and compete for the same response mechanism. The language areas in the left hemisphere are Broca's area for carrying the code for articulating language and Wernicke's area for perceiving language; damage to these and related areas result in aphasias of various kinds.

Reward centers in the brain seem important to learning; some are generalized but others are closely related to hunger or sexual behavior in animals and human patients. Fear or punishment centers are found in both humans and animals in sites that have no known relation to the pain pathways. Stimulation of the temporal lobes in patients undergoing brain surgery leads them to report vivid memories.

Experiments with simple neural structures aid in the understanding of plastic changes at synapses that resemble learning. Repeated stimulation of the stellate ganglion increases conductivity for several minutes (posttetanic potentiation). Habituation in the sea snail can be traced to chemical changes at isolated synapses.

Biofeedback experiments show that animals and humans can learn voluntary control over involuntary responses if reinforcement informs them when they are successful. In contradiction to former beliefs, it has been shown that operant, as well as classical, conditioning is possible with visceral and glandular responses. Rewarding brain stimulation and shaping techniques have been used with paralyzed and normal animals to teach control of salivation, heart rate, intestinal contractions, and urine output. Humans can learn to control their own alpha rhythms if they are given a signal when alpha waves are present in their EEGs. Human control of psychosomatic symptoms therefore appears possible.

It appears that neural activity that outlasts practice (perseveration) is necessary to the formation of a "permanent" memory trace (consolidation). Perseverative activity may link cell assemblies into a "phase sequence" in a perceptual task such as successively viewing the corners of a triangle. This two-phase hypothesis of learning and memory is supported by experiments that show that the longer posttrial perseveration is permitted to go on before interruption by ECS, the faster an avoidance habit is learned by the rat. Drugs can also be used to interrupt perseveration, with similar effects on maze learning or on a one-trial conditioned avoidance response (CAR). Stimulating drugs seem to potentiate perseveration and consolidation to improve learning when administered *after* practice in a maze. The effect is greater for maze-dull than for maze-bright animals. The latter appear to consolidate faster because ECS given 45 minutes after practice does not impair their learning, but it does affect the maze-dull rats. Punishment hypotheses have been offered as alternative explanations to account for ECS effects on learning; these hypotheses do not explain the drug experiments. Deprivation of paradoxical sleep seems to impair consolidation. Consolidation has been somewhat localized by the interruption of the process with timed limbic lesions in mice. It is still not known whether everyday stimuli can interrupt the consolidation process.

Human patients with bilateral damage to the temporal lobes, amygdala, and hippocampus have normal memories but seem unable to learn anything new. It appears that a sensory buffer selects stimuli for action by short-term memory; short-term memory may be stored in long-term memory for recall. Over longer periods of time older memories seem less susceptible to trauma than newer memories, perhaps because they have been recalled more often, thereby becoming more fixed and less subject to impairment. It does appear that consolidation is necessary for the formation of long-term memory.

The hologram model attempts a solution to Lashley's paradox. Interference patterns can be formed by combining single wavelength light reflected from a subject with the same light from a direct source (interference beam). Illuminating the plate that records the pattern with the interference beam results in a three-dimensional picture. Many pictures can be formed on a single plate; each part of every picture contains the whole image. Memory traces may be stored as interference patterns that result from the electrochemical activity of cells at many synapses.

Wherever learning occurs, changes in the excitability of nerve cells at synapses may be involved. Such changes may involve the chemical transmitter, ACh, or the enzyme that speeds its removal, AChE. Rats selectively bred to be maze-bright have a higher ACh/AChE ratio in their cortex than do rats bred to be maze-dull; ACh and AChE are under separate genetic control in different strains of rats. Rats isolated for 30 days after weaning (isolated control, or IC, group) were compared with their littermates raised in groups with maximum "play" and learning opportunities (environmental complexity and training, or ECT, group). The ECT rats had less cortical and more subcortical AChE, thicker cortical tissues, and superior cortical circulation and biochemical activity. The results are the same if the experiment is done with young adult rats. ECT for only 2 hours a day helps to prevent IC changes in the brain. A seminatural environment results in more brain improvement than does the ECT condition.

The nerve cell changes in learning may also be molecular, involving the DNA-RNA-protein-enzyme mechanism, for cell repair and alteration. DNA and RNA are involved in cell reproduction (including nerve cells) in flatworms that have the ability to regenerate missing parts. A simple flexion response to shock is conditioned to a light stimulus in these animals. After learning the conditioned response (CR), flatworms were cut in two and they regenerated. The regenerated subjects "relearned" the CR faster than did "naïve" worms. The conclusion that the head ganglion dominates the CR was arrived at after experimentation showed that (1) two-headed flatworms (produced by regeneration) learn the CR faster than do normal planarians and (2) trained flatworms, cut in two and regenerated in RNAase (which interferes with DNA-RNA processes in cell reproduction), retain the habit only if the tail end (not the head) is the regenerated part. The RNA aspect has been extended to rats in memory-transfer experiments in which RNA extract from the brain of trained rats has been injected into "naïve" rats. A peptide has been extracted from the brains of rats who had been taught to fear the dark; when it was injected into the brains of "naïve" rats, they too feared the dark. The compound has been synthesized

from amino acids. Puromycin, which interferes with protein synthesis, may be injected into the brain to affect retention of the learning of a Y maze in rats. The effect appears only if the habit is 3 to 6 days old. In man the supply of nerve cell RNA increases from 3 to 40 years, is constant to 60, and then declines. This curve parallels that for the ability to learn new material (intelligence).

READINGS

Agranoff, B. W.: Memory and protein synthesis, Sci. Am. **216:**115-122, June 1967. (W. H. Freeman Reprint No. 1077.)

Bakam, P.: The eyes have it, Psychol. Today **4:** 64-96, April 1971.

Bennett, E. L., Diamon, M. C., Krech, D., and Rosensweig, M. R.: Chemical and anatomical plasticity of brain, Science **146:**610-619, 1964. (Bobbs-Merrill Reprint No. P-400.)

Best, J. G.: Protopsychology, Sci. Am. **208:**54-62, Feb. 1963. (W. H. Freeman Reprint No. 149.)

Bitterman, M. E.: The evolution of intelligence, Sci. Am. **212:**92-100, Jan. 1965. (W. H. Freeman Reprint No. 490.)

Boycott, B. B.: Learning in the octopus, Sci. Am. **212:**42-50, March 1965. (W. H. Freeman Reprint No. 1006.)

Breen, R. A., and McGaugh, J. L.: Facilitation of maze learning with post-trial injections of picrotoxin, J. Comp. Physiol. Psychol. **54:**498-501, 1961. (Bobbs-Merrill Reprint No. P-591.)

Brogden, W. J.: Sensory pre-conditioning, J. Exp. Psychol. **25:**323-332, 1939. (Bobbs-Merrill Reprint No. P-51.)

Bures, J., and Buresova, O.: The use of Leao's spreading depression in the study of interhemispheric transfer of memory traces, J. Comp. Physiol. Psychol. **53:**558-563, 1961. (Bobbs-Merrill Reprint No. P-412.)

Butter, C. M.: Neuropsychology: the study of brain and behavior, Belmont, Calif., 1968, Brooks-Cole Publishing Co., Division of Wadsworth Publishing Co.

Chauchard, P.: The brain, New York, 1962, Grove Press, Inc.

Deutsch, J. A.: Neural basis of memory, Psychol. Today **2:**56-61, May 1968.

DiCara, L. V.: Learning in the autonomic nervous system, Sci. Am. **122:**31-39, Jan. 1970.

Dyal, J.: Transfer of behavorial bias and learning enhancement: A critique of specificity experiments. In Adam, G., editor: Biology of memory, Budapest, 1971, Akadémiai Kiadó.

Also in Leukel, F., editor: Issues in physiological psychology, St. Louis, 1974, The C. V. Mosby Co.

Gazzaniga, M. S.: The bisected brain, New York, 1970, Appleton-Century-Crofts.

Gerard, R. W.: What is memory? Sci. Am. **189:** 118-126, Sept. 1953. (W. H. Freeman Reprint No. 11.)

Glickman, S. E.: Perseverative neural processes and consolidation of the memory trace, Psychol. Bull. **58:**218-233, 1961. (Bobbs-Merrill Reprint No. P-459.)

Golub, A., Masiarz, F., Villars, T., and McConnell, J.: Incubation effects in behavior induction in rats, Science **168:**392-395, 1970. Also in Leukel, F., editor: Issues in physiological psychology, St. Louis, 1974, The C. V. Mosby Co.

Gurowitz, E. M.: The molecular basis of memory, Englewood Cliffs, N.J., 1969, Prentice-Hall, Inc.

Halstead, W. C., and Rucker, W. B.: Memory: A molecular maze, Psychol. Today **2:**38-41; 66-67, May 1968.

Learning and memory. Part I. In Gross, C. G., and Zeigler, H. P., editors: Readings in physiological psychology, New York, 1969, Harper & Row, Publishers.

Hudspeth, W. J., McGaugh, J. L., and Thompson, C. W.: Aversive and amnesic effects of electroconvulsive shock, J. Comp. Physiol. Psychol. **57:**61-64, 1964. (Bobbs-Merrill Reprint No. P-591.)

Hyden, H.: Satellite cells in the nervous system, Sci. Am. **205:**62-70, Dec. 1961. (W. H. Freeman Reprint No. 134.)

Kandel, E. R.: Nerve cells and behavior, Sci. Am. **223:**57-67, July 1970.

Kennedy, D.: Small systems of nerve cells, Sci. Am. **216:**44-52, 1967. (W. H. Freeman Reprint No. 1073.)

Kimble, D. P., editor: The anatomy of memory, vol. 1, Palo Alto, Calif., 1965, Science & Behavior Books, Inc.

Landauer, T. K.: Two hypotheses concerning the biochemical basis of memory, Psychol. Rev. **71:**167-179, 1964. (Bobbs-Merrill Reprint No. P-499.)

Lang, P. J.: Learning to play the internal organs, Psychol. Today **4:**37-41; 86, Oct. 1970.

Lashley, K. S.: Brain mechanisms and intelligence, New York, 1963, Dover Publications, Inc.

Louttit, R. T., editor: Advancing psychological science, vol. 4, Belmont, Calif., 1965, Wadsworth Publishing Co.

McConnell, J. V.: Confessions of a scientific humorist, Impact Sci. Soc. **19:**241-252, 1969. Also in Leukel, F., editor: Issues in physiologi-

cal psychology, St. Louis, 1974, The C. V. Mosby Co.

McConnell, J. V., Jacobson, A. L., and Kimble, D. P.: The effects of regeneration upon retention of a conditioned response in the planarian, J. Comp. Physiol. Psychol. **52:**1-5, 1959. (Bobbs-Merrill Reprint No. P-222.)

McGaugh, J.: Facilitation of memory storage processes. In The future of the brain sciences, New York, 1969, Plenum Publishing Corp. Also in Leukel, F., editor: Issues in physiological psychology, St. Louis, 1974, The C. V. Mosby Co.

Miller, N.: Learning of visceral and glandular responses, Science **163:**434-455, 1969. In Leukel, F., editor: Issues in physiological psychology, St. Louis, 1974, The C. V. Mosby Co.

Milner, P. M., and Glickman, S. E., editors: Cognitive processes and the brain, Princeton, N.J., 1965, D. Van Nostrand Co., Inc.

Olds, J.: Ten milliseconds into the brain, Psychol. Today **8:**45-48, 1975.

Overton, R. K.: Thought and action, New York, 1959, Random House, Inc.

Peterson, L. R.: Short-term memory, Sci. Am. **215:**90-95, July 1966. (W. H. Freeman Reprint No. 499.)

Pfeiffer, J.: The human brain, New York, 1965, Pyramid Publications, Inc.

Pribram, K.: The brain, Psychol. Today **5:**44-48, 88-90, Sept. 1971.

Pribram, K. H.: The neurophysiology of remembering, Sci. Am. **220:**73-85, Jan. 1969. (W. H. Freeman Reprint No. 520.)

Pribram, K. H., editor: On the biology of learning, New York, 1969, Harcourt, Brace & Jovanovich, Inc.

Schwartz, G.: Biofeedback, self-regulation, and the patterning of physiological processes, Am. Scientist **63:**314-324, May-June 1975.

Skinner, B. F.: How to teach animals, Sci. Am. **185:**26-29, Dec. 1951. (W. H. Freeman Reprint No. 423.)

Sperry, R. W.: The great cerebral commissure, Sci. Am. **210:**42-52, Jan. 1964. (W. H. Freeman Reprint No. 174.)

Talland, G.: Amnesia: A world without continuity, Psychol. Today **1:**43-50, May 1967.

Ungar, G.: Molecular approaches to neural coding, Int. J. Neuroscience **3:**193-199, 1972. In Leukel, F., editor: Issues in physiological psychology, St. Louis, 1974, The C. V. Mosby Co.

Warden, C.: Animal intelligence, Sci. Am. **84:** 64-68, June 1951. (W. H. Freeman Reprint No. 424.)

Willows, A. O. D.: Giant brain cells in mollusks, Sci. Am. **224:**68-76, Feb. 1971.

chapter 18
Stress and psychosomatic relationships

OVERVIEW

This chapter is concerned with the effects of stress on the human organism. The stresses discussed range from those common to everyone and easily tolerated to those that result in metabolic disorders, disease, abnormalities of personality, drug addiction, neuroses, psychoses, and feeblemindedness. Much of the evidence comes from clinical studies of individual cases; therefore the information is not so reliable as information from well-controlled experiments. A book on physiological psychology should not end, however, without an attempt to survey the effects of stress on man.

The chapter opens by considering the relationships between stress, conscious states such as anxiety, and physical symptoms. Individual differences in tolerance for stress and the syndrome (set of symptoms) that follows stress that has gone beyond tolerance limits are considered. The balance of the chapter is in four parts: (1) normal stressors and metabolic activity, (2) abnormal stressors and functional disorders, (3) brain injury, and (4) mental deficiency. These categories overlap, but they seem as effective a way as any to organize the material.

The "normal" stress conditions that are met every day include variations in diet, hormone production, exercise, hypoxia, aging, and sleep. Adjustments to small variations are considered, and the effects on behavior of extreme stresses resulting from greater variations are outlined. "Abnormal"

stressors—those that often result in functional disorders of brain activity and behavior—are then discussed. Isolation, drugs, and epilepsy, as well as neurosis and psychosis, are included. Some physical therapies for psychosis and behavior therapy for neurosis are discussed. Brain injury effects are considered next. The results of traumatic injury, diseases, and senility on brain activity and behavior organization are included. Finally, the causes and consequences of mental deficiency are briefly discussed. The chapter concludes with some general observations on how the kind of stress that causes lasting impairment may be avoided.

STRESS AND THE MIND-BODY PROBLEM

According to many philosophers of science, conscious events are not ligitimate scientific data because conscious events are *directly* observed by only one person. The content of his conscious experience can be reported by that individual, but the accuracy of his report cannot be verified by the *direct* observation, of others; others cannot "look into his head," so to speak. However the presence or absence of conscious activity and its "intensity" *can* be verified by publicly observed means. The presence of conscious activity in man is accompanied by activity in certain parts of the brain, notably the brainstem reticular formation (ARAS areas) and cerebral cortex. Activity in the cerebral cortex that accompanies various levels of conscious awareness—from sleep to aroused vigilance —can be publicly monitored with the electroencephalograph. Experts observing the EEG can agree on whether a subject is asleep or awake, whether his sleep is light or deep, whether he is "daydreaming" or in a state of aroused vigilance, and so on. From one point of view conscious events can be considered as a *symptom* or "by-product" of certain levels of cortical activity that are measurable. From this point of view consciousness is not a cause of behavior but a symptom of activity in the cerebral cortex, activity that is necessary to some kinds of complex behavior. Other varieties of complex behavior may not be accompanied by conscious events or corresponding EEG changes at all.

Psychosomatic disorders

The term **psychosomatic** originates with the notion that certain mental, or psychic, states can cause somatic, or bodily, disorders, as in the case of continuous anxiety

that results in stomach ulcers. The term is too well embedded in the literature to discard, although the premise implied seems to be a false one. Environmental stress that results in a physical symptom is not always accompanied by conscious (that is, reportable) anxiety. The individual may not be aware of being under stress and may not feel anxious, whatever physical symptoms he shows—irritability, muscle tension, and so on. It *can* be shown that enough environmental stress will reliably produce physical disorders—psychosomatic disorders, if you will. It *cannot* be reliably shown that psychic states, such as sensed anxiety, always produce physical disorders. It is therefore well to look for the conditions underlying psychosomatic disorders among environmental stresses and to use reports of psychic states such as anxiety only as clues to the possible existence of stress.

Stress

Stress can be defined as any stimulus, internal or external, that disturbs the dy-

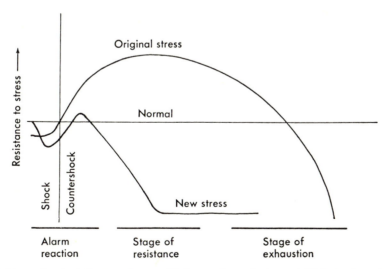

Fig. 18-1. General adaptation syndrome. Under prolonged stress, initial shock and countershock reactions may be followed by a stage of resistance and then a stage of exhaustion that culminates in death. Adding a new stress to the original stress will accelerate the process. (From Selye, H.: The physiology and pathology of exposure to stress, Montreal, 1950, Acta, Inc.)

namic equilibrium (changing balance) of the systems of the body (homeostasis, Chapter 2). In these terms any stimulus is a **stressor,** but it is considered to cause stress only to the degree and for the time that homeostasis is disturbed. The body is continually encountering stressful stimuli, or stressors, as a condition of life and of adjusting to a variety of environmental changes—heat or cold, the consequences of exercise, food deprivation, and so on. Stressors also include impediments to, or frustrations of, highly motivated behavior of very complex varieties in man. Frustration in attempts to perform well in an executive position can disturb the body's equilibrium as much as exposure to severe cold. Stress is more or less severe, depending on how successful the body is in restoring homeostasis, or the internal equilibrium necessary to sustain life over a long period. Restoration of equilibrium will depend on the severity of the stress, on the stress tolerance or the adaptability of the individual, and on the period of time the stress is continued.

Stress tolerance. Individuals differ in their ability to resist or adjust to many varieties of stress—temperature change, disease organisms, strenuous physical exercise, or the work and social demands of a complex society. An individual may have a high **stress tolerance** for one variety of stress and a low stress tolerance for another variety, depending on age, physical conditioning, learned behavior adjustments, and many other factors. The tolerance for some kinds of stress can be increased by physical conditioning or the learning of more effective modes of behavior. These statements may seem self-evident, but one must keep them in mind in evaluating the complex consequences of stress.

Stress syndrome. If the severity of a stressor is well within an individual's stress tolerance, he can adjust to the stress over a long period of time. The more a particular type of stress exceeds an individual's stress tolerance, the shorter will be the period

before the resources of the body are exhausted and physical deterioration sets in. The sequence of events is a predictable one (Selye). The shock of the initial stress is followed by initial countershock response in the **alarm reaction;** then a **period of adjustment** and apparent tolerance of the stress will be followed by a period of disorganization, physical disorders, a **stage of exhaustion,** and, finally, death (Fig. 18-1). The adjustments of rats to stress and their eventual failure can be seen in rats kept in freezing temperatures. Their metabolism will increase to produce body heat with the aid of enlarged pituitary, thyroid, and adrenal glands during the period of adjustment. As the resources of the body are exhausted, however, physical deficiencies such as loss of weight, decreased activity, and stomach ulcers will result. Finally, the loss of homeostasis will exceed the limits that support life, and death will ensue. This sequence of events is remarkably similar when rats are intolerably stressed by means varying from daily swimming to exhaustion to continued exposure to unpredictable electric shocks. Presumably, the same things happen to humans who are exposed to intense stress of many varieties.

NORMAL STRESSORS AND METABOLIC ACTIVITY

Normal stressors are those that fall within the range of conditions to which the body adjusts easily—those conditions encountered in everyday life. Changes in diet, exercise, hypoxia, aging, and sleep are included as examples. The effects of these changes are most easily understood in terms of the "metabolic equation" of Chapter 2—the balance between the intake of food and oxygen on one hand, and the output of work, carbon dioxide, and waste on the other. The effect of extreme deficiencies or excesses in any factors is considered only to illustrate the more normal variations. Those effects on the CNS that influence behavior will be emphasized.

Diet

The body requires carbohydrates, fats, and proteins, although the first can be manufactured from the other two. In addition, certain vitamins, traces of certain minerals, and several essential fatty acids and amino acids that the body cannot reconstruct from fats and proteins, respectively, are required. The diet, or food intake, may therefore be deficient or excessive in either a quantitative or a qualitative fashion. An individual on a balanced diet—one containing all the essentials just mentioned—may eat too much or too little. The diet would then contain too many or too few calories of food intake for that individual's work output. On the other hand, the diet may contain adequate calories but an oversupply or an undersupply of one of the essentials previously listed. Quantitatively, excess intake of calories results in excess fat deposits in the body, but fat acts as a stressor only because of the excess load put on the heart and circulatory system in supplying the excess tissue. The efficiency of the nervous system seems unimpaired, and a fat man is as intelligent as a thin man—even if getting fat seems to be a stupid thing to do. Qualitative excesses also have little effect; the body rids itself of excess vitamins, amino acids, and minerals. Starvation, however, puts greater stress on the nervous system than does obesity whether the starvation is selective or general.

General starvation. Insufficient caloric intake may or may not be accompanied by vitamin or mineral deficiencies or by inadequate protein or fat. In most areas of the world where malnutrition is common, general starvation is accompanied by selective starvation, particularly for vitamins and protein. So far as general starvation is concerned, however, there is no clear evidence that postnatal (after birth) malnutrition affects the nervous system, although it may have severe and lasting effects on other systems of the body. Metabolism seems organized to supply the CNS at the expense of the other tissues of the body when there are not enough dietary essentials to go around. Prolonged infant or adult malnutrition does not appear to affect intelligence, provided that certain amino acids and vitamins do not drop below critical levels (see below). Motivational effects are profound, however, and many may impair test performance. Starving individuals are motivated by little but food, show extreme lassitude, and sleep much of the time to conserve energy.

Selective starvation. Severe deprivation of vitamin B_1 in infancy or lack of certain amino acids (lysine, cystine) at any age impairs learning ability. Diets deficient in iodine lower the metabolic rate, and those deficient in calcium or magnesium may cause CNS irritability and seizures. If any of these elements are available, however, the nervous system seems to be supplied at the expense of other tissues.

Endocrine factors

Hormones are necessary to control the metabolic processes of the body and to integrate activity in differently specialized tissues. Deficiencies or excesses in the hormone output of the various endocrine glands can cause profound changes in the body, with important consequences for behavior (Chapter 3). Vigor and sexual behavior, for example, are influenced by the output of the anterior pituitary, adrenal cortex, thyroids, and gonads. Growth and body development depend on the anterior pituitary and thyroid. Major effects on the CNS seem to result only from thyroid insufficiency, and then the effects are most severe during growth (cretinism). Insufficiency of the other hormones appears to affect the CNS only if it is long-continued and severe. However, the effects on personality of dwarfism, giantism, abnormal or absent secondary sexual characteristics, and so on cannot be ignored. Physical abnormalities profoundly affect human behavior, even when the nervous system is untouched, because of the way other persons react to abnormal physical appearance.

Exercise

Physical exercise increases the metabolic rate and consumes blood glucose stored in the liver and muscles as glycogen. These stores are replaced by increased food intake or by the conversion of stored fat into glucose for consumption by the cells. In reacting to the stress of vigorous regular exercise, the heart and circulatory system become more efficient, the contractile efficiency of muscle tissue is improved, the lung capacity is increased, and the body becomes able to tolerate increased exercise for longer periods. Regular exercise has also been found to prevent artificially induced ulcers in animals. On the other hand, continuous or repeated exercise to exhaustion may permanently impair these systems.

Fatigue

Physiological fatigue results from an insufficient oxygen supply to the muscles, when they consume oxygen faster than the lungs, heart, and circulatory system can provide it. An **oxygen debt** of the amount of oxygen needed to restore equilibrium accumulates. At the same time the waste products of muscle metabolism—CO_2 and lactic acid—accumulate faster than the circulatory system can remove them. Accumulated lactic acid can result in cramps, or contractures of the muscles (contractions without nerve cell excitation), and nerve endings for pain are stimulated. **Impairment** of the muscles' ability to do work results, and a **work decrement** follows. The CNS, however, seems immune to oxygen debt under most conditions. Work decrement resulting from long periods of mental work can usually be ascribed to boredom or conflict of motives. An office worker, for example, would show no physical impairment at the end of a long day, despite reports of fatigue. Factory workers seldom show impairment, either. Studies of their output often show an end spurt of increased output near the end of each work period, before a coffee break, lunch, or the end of the day. Their output increases at the end of a work period, at a time when one would expect more fatigue and a work decrement. Such end spurts probably reflect increased motivation at the prospect of stopping a monotonous task. Their increased level of performance "spills over" into increased work output.

Hypoxia

Hypoxia is a condition in which the tissues are not receiving enough oxygen from the lungs through the circulatory system to sustain metabolic activity. The tissues therefore accumulate an oxygen debt. Sensations of suffocation and hard breathing result only if carbon dioxide accumulates in the tissues at the same time; the nervous system is sensitive to increases in carbon dioxide but does not respond in many ways to decreases in oxygen. As already explained, hypoxia can result from physiological fatigue. It can also result from impairment of the lungs or circulatory system, as in cases of emphysema (a lung disorder) or reduced cardiac output (heart failure). **Anemia,** or lack of enough red blood corpuscles to carry oxygen from the lungs to the tissues, can cause hypoxia. In all these cases capacity for physical work is reduced (impairment), an oxygen debt is acquired with less work, and sensations of suffocation and fatigue result. Hypoxia can result from reduced air pressure at high altitudes. The increased air pressure experienced in diving has opposite effects, which raise their own problems for the body.

Altitude effects. Air consists of a mixture of about 20% oxygen and 80% nitrogen. Air pressure is the amount of these gases per cubic foot of air. With increases in altitude there is less air per cubic foot, and, whereas the *proportion* of oxygen in the air remains constant, its *partial pressure* (20% of the total pressure) decreases along with the total air pressure. Oxygen diffuses into the blood from the lungs because the partial pressure of oxygen in the air of the lungs is greater than the partial pressure of oxygen in the blood returned by the heart from the tissues. As the partial pressure of oxygen falls, there is less difference between the concentration of lung oxygen and the concentration of blood oxygen. As a result, less oxygen diffuses from the lungs into the blood for distribution to the tissues. The outside pressure can be so low that one can breathe pure oxygen at that pressure and still not absorb enough oxygen for the tissues. Aircraft or manned satellites at high altitudes must be pressurized at about 5 pounds per square inch of oxygen pressure to provide for enough absorption of oxygen by the blood (sea level air pressure is about 15 pounds per square inch). Alternatively, a pressure suit and helmet may be worn. When the lungs are exposed to a vacuum, the blood "boils" as all its absorbed gases come out of solution, and immediate and total anoxia (loss of all oxygen) results, accompanied by widespread tissue damage (explosive decompression). When the blood oxygen drops sufficiently at high altitudes, the cerebral cortex ceases functioning, and sleepiness, followed by unconsciousness, results. Continued oxygen lack results in brain damage, coma, and death. No sensations of suffocation result because carbon dioxide is readily diffused and does not accumulate to stimulate the CNS.

Diving effects. In deep-sea diving, air must be delivered to the lungs at a pressure equal to the outside water pressure, or else the diver is unable to expand his chest to inflate his lungs. In a diving bell or diving suit, air is delivered to the diver from the surface by a hose until enough air has accumulated to equal the outside water pressure. In scuba diving (self-contained underwater breathing apparatus), a valve from tanks attached to the diver's back senses the water pressure and delivers air at the

same pressure to a mouthpiece in the diver's mouth. In either case water weighs much more than air, the pressure on the diver's chest increases as he descends, and air must be delivered to him at increasing pressures. More and more air (oxygen and nitrogen gases) is forced into solution in the blood. Much more nitrogen (80%) than oxygen (20%) goes into solution in the blood. At great depths enough dissolved nitrogen accumulates to cause nitrogen narcosis of the CNS, sometimes romantically called the "rapture of the deep." Disorientation, euphoria, disturbances in judgment, bizarre behavior, coma, and death may result. In returning to the surface—decompression—another difficulty is encountered. The deeper a diver has been, and the longer he has been down, the more nitrogen gas is dissolved in his body tissues and blood. If he returns toward the surface too rapidly, water pressure and the competing air pressure are reduced too fast. The lungs cannot rid the body of dissolved nitrogen fast enough, and bubbles of nitrogen gas come out of solution in the bloodstream. These bubbles cause intense pain (the bends) when they accumulate at body joints. They burst capillaries in the brain, causing permanent brain damage. The only cure is rapid return to high air pressures (recompression) in a tank or beneath the water. The only prevention seems to be slow decompression if normal air is breathed, giving the lungs time to rid the body of accumulated nitrogen. Strangely enough, helium gas, as inert as nitrogen, does not cause narcosis and comes out of solution in the body much more readily than nitrogen. Experts have been experimenting with mixtures of oxygen and helium to avoid nitrogen narcosis and reduce decompression time.

Sleep

The topic of sleep was covered in detail in Chapters 13 and 14. Attention was paid to the role of sleep as the absence of arousal; the function of the ARAS in sleep and waking; the evolutionary theory of sleep; and non-REM and REM sleep as two different biochemical states of the brain controlled by nuclei in the midbrain and in the pons. At the same time, it was pointed out that sleep is a bodily need, like hunger or thirst; if special brain operations or continuous stimulation keeps an animal awake for several days, the result is death. The role of sleep is an unknown one in the metabolic equation of food and air intake, energy, carbon dioxide, and waste disposal. The usual diet contains enough calories to sustain 24-hour waking activity. Yet sleep is a known requirement that seems especially essential to the CNS. In man those functions most related to higher CNS activity—alertness, problem-solving, etc.—demonstrate most clearly the effects of loss of sleep. Yet experiments on the effect of prolonged wakefulness in man show no evident tissue damage, and complex mental tasks *can* be performed normally if the subject is sufficiently motivated and aroused.

It has been suggested that the high level of CNS activity in the waking state results in the accumulation of some waste product of nervous metabolism, a **hypnotoxin.** If the hypnotoxin accumulates faster than it can be eliminated during waking periods of CNS activity, it drugs the CNS, and sleep results. During sleep the production of hypnotoxin is reduced, and it is gradually disposed of by the circulation until waking levels of CNS metabolism can again be sustained. A suggestion was made in Chapter 14 that a chemical causing sleep has been isolated from the cerebrospinal fluid of rabbits. However, the neural mechanisms underlying the waking state have been found in the ascending reticular activating system. The ARAS is profoundly depressed by some drugs and could be affected in a similar way by a hypnotoxin. It has been suggested that dreaming is a symptom of metabolic activity in the CNS that accom-

panies disposal of hypnotoxins. If dreaming (often detected by rapid eye movements during sleep, or REM sleep) is prevented by waking the subject, he will dream more on subsequent nights. This may suggest accumulation of hypnotoxin caused by preventing its removal, since the subject is awakened when he dreams. On the other hand, depriving the subject of EEG-detected NREM (non-REM) stages of sleep will cause more NREM sleep on subsequent nights. The role of sleep in metabolism, and how lack of sleep acts as a stressor, are important and unsolved problems.

Aging

As progress is made in the prevention and control of fatal diseases in modern society, more and more people are living longer. As the elderly population has increased, interest in the study of the aging process has resulted in expanded research in the science of **gerontology** (sometimes called **geriatrics**). The object of this research is to understand the aging process well enough to retard aging and to increase the life-span, vigor, and health of the aged.

Some theories of aging propose that the reason for aging lies in the DNA-RNA-enzyme process that is the basis of cell reproduction (Chapter 2). According to this view, cells can divide only so often before the DNA "templates" that control all normal cell division and all the chemical reactions of life "wear out." Others suggest that this is what happens to the pattern controlling the frequency of cell division to cause the uncontrolled growth in number of cancerous cells. One consequence of this theory would be that we would all die of cancer if we lived long enough. Some theorists believe that aging has no specific cause—that hormones and numerous other factors play decisive roles.

Nonetheless, the physiological changes of aging reduce the body's resistance to many kinds of stress and are themselves stressful to the individual. The reduced efficiency of the heart and circulatory system impairs physical adjustment to exercise. As the arteries of the brain harden and blood pressure rises, blood vessels burst in the brain (stroke) and neural tissue is damaged—particularly in the cerebral cortex. Other degenerative changes that occur with aging impair CNS function. The most common result is disturbance of recent memory—the retroactive amnesia discussed in Chapter 17. Sensory mechanisms deteriorate, particularly vision and hearing. Finally, motor degeneration is seen in tremor and, occasionally, in paralysis.

ABNORMAL STRESSORS AND FUNCTIONAL DISORDERS

Stress imposed on the nervous system by a variety of factors, such as isolation or persistent conflict, can cause disorders of the *functioning* of the CNS—**functional disorders.** Long-continued functional disorders of the CNS can damage the *structure* of various organs of the body whose activities are controlled by the CNS. Damage to body organs caused by functional disorders of the nervous system *are* the psychosomatic symptoms already discussed. Many psychosomatic symptoms can result from functional disorders as well as from diseases or allergies—asthma, hives, stomach ulcers, colitis (irritation of the colon), and piles (hemorrhoids) are a few examples. More specific agents such as drugs and toxic agents can likewise disturb the functioning of the CNS; they can also damage nerve tissue, which cannot be replaced in man.

Isolation

The brain seems to require a minimum level of sensory input to maintain normal functioning. Human subjects, deprived of sensory stimulation, develop bizarre hallucinations ("seeing things" or "hearing things") after a period of time. The length of time required for the effects depends on the extent of the **sensory deprivation.** In extreme cases the subject may be blindfolded (visual deprivation), have his ears plugged (auditory deprivation), and be lowered into a bath of tepid water (deprivation of temperature sensations and kinesthetic input from the muscles stretched by gravity). And initial period of sleep ensues, followed by disembodied *feelings;* then bizarre hallucinations develop within 24 to 48 hours. Some have speculated that sensory input is so necessary to organization of the brain's activities that the brain hallucinates sensations when they are not provided by the sense organs. Some of the symptoms resemble those of psychosis (see p. 426), and psychiatrists have subjected themselves to sensory deprivation in an attempt to understand the experiences of psychotics.

Drug effects

As would be expected from its high rate of metabolism, the CNS is more sensitive to drugs than are other cells of the body. The specific effects of various drugs on the CNS vary widely, however, and neither the site of their action nor how they affect nerve cells is known in many cases. Some drugs may *stimulate* activity in the CNS, preventing sleep when they affect the cortex either directly or through the ARAS. Other drugs may *depress* the cortex or ARAS, causing drowsiness, unconsciousness, or coma. Still other drugs are *selective* in their effects for largely unknown reasons, interfering with the perception of pain or with sympathetic nervous system arousal, for example. Some drugs *disorganize* CNS activity, causing distorted perceptions or hallucinations. Finally, some drugs may alter the functioning of the CNS, if they are taken habitually over a period of time, so that the CNS cannot function normally in their absence—this is **addiction.** Table 18-1 gives a classification of some of the major drugs and their properties and indicates which drugs appear to be addicting. A drug may be found in more than one category when it

Table 18-1. Classification of some major drugs*

Drug class	Group	Example	Trade or common name	Natural or synthetic	Usage	How taken	First used	Evidence of addiction
Psychotherapeutics These drugs typical of many used in treatment of psychological and psychiatric disorders								
Antipsychotic drugs used primarily to treat major psychoses such as schizophrenia and manic-depressive and senile psychoses	Antipsychotic Rauwolfia alkaloids	Reserpine	Serpasil	Nat.	Greatly diminished	Injected Ingested	1949	No
	Phenothiazines	Chlorpromazine	Thorazine	Syn.	Widespread	Injected Ingested	1950	No
Antianxiety drugs used to combat insomnia, induce muscle relaxation, treat neurotic conditions, and reduce psychological stress	Propanediols	Meprobamate	Miltown	Syn.	Widespread	Ingested	1954	Yes
	Benzodiazepines	Chlordiazepoxide	Librium	Syn.	Widespread	Ingested	1933	Yes
	Barbiturates	Phenobarbital	See *Sedatives,* below					
Antidepressant drugs effective in treatment of psychiatric depression and phobic-anxiety states	MAO inhibitors	Tranylcypromine	Parnate	Syn.	Diminished	Ingested	1958	No
	Dibenzazepines	Imipramine	Tofranil	Syn.	Widespread	Ingested Injected	1948	No
Stimulants (see *Stimulants,* below)	Stimulant	Amphetamine	See *Stimulants,* below					
Psychotogenics These drugs produce changes in mood, thinking, and behavior; resultant drug state may resemble a psychotic state, with delusions, hallucinations, and distorted perceptions; little therapeutic value	Ergot derivative	Lysergic acid diethylamide	LSD, lysergide	Syn.	Widespread?	Ingested	1943	No
	Cannabis sativa	Marijuana	Hemp, hashish	Nat.	Widespread	Smoked	?	No
	Lophophora williamsii	Mescaline	Peyote button	Nat.	Localized	Ingested	?	No
	Psilocybe mexicana	Psilocybin		Nat.	Rare	Ingested	?	No
Stimulants These drugs elevate mood, increase confidence and alertness, and prevent fatigue; analeptics stimulate central nervous system and can reverse depressant effects of an anesthetic drug	Sympathomimetics	Amphetamine	Benzedrine	Syn.	Widespread	Ingested Injected	1935	Yes
	Analeptics	Pentylenetetrazol	Metrazol	Syn.	Rare	Ingested Injected	1935	No
	Psychotogenics	Lysergic acid diethylamide	See *Psychotogenics,* above					

Description	Class	Drug	Common name	Nat./Syn.	Prevalence	Administration	Year	Addicting
Caffeine and nicotine, found in beverages and tobacco, are mild stimulants	Nicotinics	Nicotine		Nat.	Widespread	Smoked / Ingested	?	Yes
	Xanthines	Caffeine		Nat.	Widespread	Ingested	?	Yes
Sedatives and hypnotics Most of these drugs produce general depression (sedation) in low doses and sleep (hypnosis) in larger doses; used to treat mental stress, insomnia, and anxiety	Bromides	Potassium bromide		Syn.	Widespread	Ingested	1857	No
	Barbiturates	Phenobarbital	Luminal	Syn.	Widespread	Ingested / Injected	1912	Yes
	Chloral derivatives	Chloral hydrate		Syn.	Rare	Ingested	1875	Yes
	General	Alcohol		Nat.	Widespread	Ingested	?	Yes
Anesthetics, analgesics, and paralytics These drugs are widely used in field of medicine								
General anesthetics act centrally to cause a loss in consciousness	General anesthetics	Nitrous oxide	"Laughing gas"	Syn.	Rare	Inhaled	1799	No
		Diethyl ether		Syn.	Greatly diminished	Inhaled	1846	No
Local anesthetics act only at or near site of application	Local anesthetics	Chloroform		Syn.	Rare	Inhaled	1831	No
		Cocaine	Coca	Nat.	Widespread	Applied / Ingested	?	Yes
		Procaine	Novocain	Syn.	Widespread	Injected	1905	No
Analgesic drugs, many of them addicting, typically produce euphoria and stupor; effective pain relievers	Analgesics	Opium derivatives	Morphine, heroin	Nat.	Widespread	Injected / Smoked	?	Yes
Paralytic drugs act primarily at neuromuscular junction to produce motor (muscular) paralysis; commonly used by anesthesiologists	Paralytics	d-Tubocurarine	Curare	Nat.	Widespread	Injected	?	No
Neurohumors (neurotransmitters) Adrenergic and cholinergic compounds known to be synaptic transmitters in nervous system; other natural compounds (e.g., 5-HT, aminobutyric acid, substance P) may also be neurotransmitters	Cholinergic	Acetylcholine		Nat. Syn.	Laboratory	Injected	1926	No
	Adrenergic	Norepinephrine		Nat. Syn.	Laboratory	Injected	1946	No
	Others (?)	5-Hydroxy-tryptamine	5-HT, serotonin	Nat. Syn.	Laboratory	Injected	1948	No

*From Jarvik, M. E.: The psychopharmacological revolution, Psychol. Today **1:**51-59, 1967.

seems to have more than one kind of effect. For example, lysergic acid diethylamide (LSD) is a stimulant, but also a psychotogenic drug (one that produces delusions and hallucinations, like a psychosis). Only drugs that are likely to be of greatest interest to the student will be discussed. The psychotherapeutic drugs will be considered in a later section on physical treatments for psychosis.

Stimulants. Stimulants increase the metabolic rate of cells of the CNS and increase their excitability. Some stimulants affect the whole CNS, whereas others have their greatest effect at selected sites in the brain. Some act directly on the ARAS or cortex; others excite sympathetic nervous system arousal by their influence on the hypothalamus. A few stimulants reset the "thermostats" regulating the level of SNS arousal, presumably in the hypothalamus or ARAS. The body adapts to the latter drugs, so that their removal results in a lower-than-normal level of CNS activity. A craving for, or an addiction to, these drugs results because the CNS is no longer able to function normally without them.

Caffeine is an example of a mildly addicting cortical stimulant present in coffee, tea, cocoa, and some soft drinks. The effect on the user depends on the *tolerance* he may or may not have for the drug. Tolerance is increased by habitual usage. Small doses of caffeine seem to improve performance in psychomotor tasks such as typing. However, doses that exceed individual tolerance levels can result in indigestion, nervousness, and inability to sleep.

Nicotine is not the only drug in tobacco, and the action of all the various drugs taken by smoking is not understood. Tobacco smoking acts as a selective stimulant, leading to increased SNS activity. This results in increased heart rate, peripheral vasoconstriction, release of blood glucose from the liver and muscles, and so on. The extent and intensity of these effects depend on how much tolerance the individual has developed through habitual smoking and how much he inhales. (Inhaling enables the drugs in tobacco smoke to reach the bloodstream rapidly through the lungs.) In addition to drugs that cause the above effects, such as nicotine and pyridine, tobacco smoke contains **carcinogens**—agents such as "tars" that irritate tissue and seem thereby to predispose the tissue to **cancer.** Cigarette smokers are probably predisposed to cancer of the lungs and pipe smokers to cancer of the mouth. For reasons not clearly understood, cigarette smokers seem to be predisposed to circulatory disorders, including heart disease. Habitual tobacco smoking is addicting for most persons, altering physiological equilibrium so that abnormal sensations and irritability occur after withdrawal. Most of these people need 1 to 3 weeks of abstinence before the physiological withdrawal symptoms disappear. Some studies suggest that adjustment to exercise is impaired for about a half hour after smoking; other studies detect no effect.

Benzedrine is the trade name and a common term for **amphetamine,** a kind of drug that mimics some of the SNS arousal effects such as peripheral vasoconstriction. For this reason it was introduced into nasal inhalers as a decongestant; it shrinks the mucous tissue by constricting its blood vessels to increase the size of the nasal passages for freer breathing when they are clogged by a head cold. It is also a cerebral stimulant that combats sensations of drowsiness and fatigue and may lead to feelings of euphoria in larger doses. It has been widely used by military personnel, truck drivers who are driving at night, and students cramming for examinations, but toxic side effects have led to deafness and nervous disorders, and its use has been restricted. Because it raises the metabolic rate and diminishes appetite for food, it is employed as an aid to losing weight by reducing food intake while "burning up" stored fat deposits at a more rapid rate. As a stimulant, amphetamine and its derivatives have been used to combat psychotic depression or the low metabolic rate caused by thyroid insufficiency. In large doses, amphetamine has been used to elicit or intensify the symptoms of schizophrenia (see p. 430) in research on psychosis. In an attempt to reduce undesirable side effects, researchers have developed drugs that are derived from, or are similar to amphetamine, such as Dexedrine and Dexamyl. Amphetamines probably are addicting, and "bennies" are often taken among potential drug addicts for "kicks" (euphoria from large doses). Large doses are called "speed" by addicts.

Cocaine is a drug obtained from the leaves of the coca shrub of South America. Peruvian Indians chew coca leaves to alleviate symptoms of hunger and fatigue from hard work at high altitudes (where some hypoxia is inevitable). Cocaine is used medically as a local anesthetic for mucous tissue. Addicts take cocaine through the mucous tissue of the nose by sniffing it in the same way as tobacco was commonly taken as snuff long ago. Cocaine is a powerful CNS stimulant that causes "mood swings" from euphoria to depression, epinephrine-like effects on the CNS, insomnia, weight loss, and sensory hallucinations of "bugs" crawling on the skin. There is conflicting evidence on whether cocaine is addicting.

Psychotogenic drugs are also called hallucinogens because they distort perception and cause hallucinations. Overdoses of several drugs (bromides, cocaine, and so forth) can have this effect. The major hallucinogens, however, cause hallucinations at any effective dosage and are called **psychotomimetic,** or psychotogenic, drugs because they mimic the effect of psychosis in producing hallucinations. They are also called **psychedelic** (Gr., 'mind-revealing') drugs. Marijuana, LSD-25 (lysergic acid diethylamide), and mescaline (peyote) are examples. Peyote is used in some American Indians' religious ceremonies.

Depressing drugs. Drugs that depress the activity of the CNS may act in several ways. Sedatives and hypnotics produce a general lowering of CNS activity for general

depression and sleep, respectively. The general anesthetics such as ether reach the brain almost directly by the bloodstream as they are inhaled. The resulting coma leaves the individual insensitive to pain so that surgery can be performed. Local anesthetics work only at their site of application for local surgery. Analgesic drugs relieve more general pain without causing unconsciousness. Little is known of their mode of selective action on pain. Analgesics range from aspirin (acetylsalicylic acid) to the opium derivatives such as heroin and morphine, and include any depressing drug in a dosage that relieves pain without causing unconsciousness. Unfortunately, many of them are addicting (aspirin is not). Paralytic drugs do not act on the CNS at all; they merely block neuromuscular transmission, producing complete relaxation of all the muscles of the body. Some of the depressing drugs are of interest because they are used socially (alcohol), as sleeping pills (barbiturates), as anesthetics (ether), or as addicting drugs (opium). An initial sensation of euphoria may be experienced after taking these drugs as the CNS combats their effects with overexcitation, but the result of increased dosage in every case is unconsciousness. Intake of enough of any depressing drug disorganizes coordination and abstract thinking because depressing drugs usually affect the highest centers of the brain first.

Ethyl **alcohol** is contained in beer, wine, and whiskey. It is usually produced by the effects of living organisms in yeast on the sugars contained in grapes or grain (fermentation). The alcohol content of beer and wine is measured in percentage of total volume, being 3% to 6% in most beer and up to 12% in naturally fermented wine. Some wines, principally ports and sherries, which may contain up to 20% alcohol, are fortified by the addition of ethyl alcohol obtained by distillation. Whiskeys, by contrast are all distilled. After natural fermentation their alcohol content is increased by boiling; the alcohol boils first and is condensed, and water is left behind. The alcohol content of whiskey is measured in *proof*—200 proof is pure ethyl alcohol. A 100-proof bourbon is therefore half alcohol, and 86-proof scotch is 43% alcohol.

The effects of alcohol on the CNS depend on the concentration of alcohol in the blood and tissue fluid. As little as 0.1% to 0.2% alcohol impairs reaction time and complex behavior such as driving an automobile, as well as impairing most accurate tests of judgment and depth perception. About 0.5% results in coma. Blood alcohol content depends, in turn, on (1) rate of intake, (2) rate of elimination, and (3) size of the individual (since the human body is 96% fluid, larger individuals must ingest more alcohol to reach a given fluid percentage of alcohol). Rate of intake depends on the percentage of alcohol content of drinks, the rate of consumption, and, at first, stomach contents (alcohol is absorbed through the stomach wall like water, and the presence of food, especially greasy food, retards this process). The rate of elimination depends largely on metabolic rate, especially as it is increased by exercise, since alcohol is converted into blood glucose, which is used up in metabolism. Coffee and most other common stimulants do not "sober" a drunk very much because they do not increase the metabolic rate enough. Stimulants do more toward combating the depressing effects of alcohol on the CNS so that the drunk is a wide-awake drunk rather than a sleepy drunk!

Aside from body size and its effects on the percentage of alcohol content, some persons appear to "hold their liquor" better than others. In large measure the reason is that learned reactions such as habits of speech, walk, and self-arousal compensate superficially for the effects of alcohol on behavior. Alcohol does not seem to be addicting, as addiction has been defined, unless it is used consistently over a period of years. Some studies report that alcoholics seem less able to tolerate anxiety than nonalcoholics can and depend on the relief from anxiety that alcohol gives them. In addition, alcohol taken for the symptoms of a hangover can result in continuous drinking, whose cumulative effects on the CNS can eventually result in hallucinations known as delirium tremens (the "dt's"). Alcoholism often results in dietary deficiencies (especially vitamin B_1), since it reduces appetite by providing immediately available blood glucose without providing needed fats, proteins, and vitamins. Alcohol affects the highest levels of the CNS first, impairing cortical functions while the vital functions of the medulla (breathing, heart rate, and so forth) remain unimpaired, even after the individual has "passed out." Continuous overindulgence in alcohol for many years can cause cortical damage leading to psychotic symptoms (Korsakoff's syndrome).

Recent research has revealed a possible mechanism of the addiction that results from the long-term use of alcohol. One of the compounds that results from the breakdown of alcohol into blood glucose by the liver is acetaldehyde. This compound also results from the destruction of dopamine—one of the neural transmitters of the brain. When an excessive amount of acetaldehyde is present, dopamine destruction is incomplete. The incompletely destroyed dopamine combines with the acetaldehyde to form a compound with the awesome name of tetrahydropapaveroline (THP). THP is one of the central ingredients in morphine, a highly addicting narcotic drug. Thus it may be that alcoholism and morphine addiction have something in common. There is evidence, however, that morphine also affects other transmitters. An additional side effect of alcohol is that it reduces REM sleep (Chapter 14). Perhaps that is why alcoholics sleep poorly.

Opium (heroin is a close relative), extract of the opium poppy, is one of a class of alkaloids whose active ingredient is **morphine.** The action of the drug is narcotic, whether smoked as opium or injected as heroin or morphine. With daily usage addiction results within 3 weeks, secondary to the development of increasing tolerance for the drug. Its use as an analgesic is therefore limited. Withdrawal symptoms for the addict are severe, including vomiting, incessant yawning, sweating, and sometimes collapse and death.

Psychotogenic drugs. **LSD** is a synthesized drug that is effective in minute doses. It produces bizarre perceptions, hallucinations, and a state that often resembles catatonic schizophrenia, a psychosis. For this reason it has been used experimentally to study psychotic disorders. Research is under way on its effects on alcoholism and drug addiction. There are indications that some forms of LSD may cause brain damage. There have also been reports of chromosome damage. Its effects seem to depend on the personality of the user; there have been reports of individuals becoming actively psychotic after taking LSD and not recovering. There are also reports of delayed effects, in which symptoms have returned after weeks or months.

Marijuana, on the other hand, barely qualifies as a psychotogenic drug because its chief effects are mild distortions of perception, particularly time perception. It comes from the leaves of a plant (Indian hemp) that grows wild over most of the country. The leaves are dried, crumpled, and made into cigarettes by users in the same way that tobacco leaves are made into cigarettes. Inhaling the smoke from one or two marijuana cigarettes is enough to make the user "high." The initial sensations are usually those of euphoria and feelings of "floating," and events seem to occur very slowly. Feelings of depression frequently follow. The effects of marijuana depend on the concentration of its most active ingredient, Δ^1-3,4-*trans*-tetrahydrocannabinol, or THC. The upper leaves of the plant are "stronger" in this regard and exude a yellow sap that is even more concentrated. THC concentration varies with the climate and soil where the plant is grown. As a result, the illegal marijuana sold on the street varies widely in its effects.

Research on whether marijuana is addicting and has harmful side effects is still ongoing, and opinions vary widely in the absence of sufficient facts. However, tests made on users while they were under its influence reveal disordered time perception and disturbances of recent memory. Chemical tests show that the body does not clear itself completely of the drug for as long as 8 days. Perhaps it is for this reason that habitual users receive more of a "high" from the drug than do novices. Research has not continued long enough to reveal any long-term effects from habitual use of the drug, except for reports that long-term male users develop female breast characteristics. There are clinical reports that habitual users "drop out," become listless, disoriented, and unable to concentrate. However, because there were no control groups, such reports do not prove that these effects were caused by the drug rather than to personality problems.

Neurohumors are drugs that act as neurochemical transmitters at synapses or that are suspected of acting in this fashion. Their chief use is in research on the way the nervous system functions; other applications are rare except for the use of epinephrine as a stimulant.

Epilepsy

Epilepsy is considered here because it is a disorder in the functioning of the brain and therefore an abnormal stress caused by a functional disorder. It may have an organic cause in a brain tumor, or it may be caused by an unknown and widespread overexcitability of the brain cells, with no structural abnormality that can be detected. Epilepsy does not usually result in brain damage, nor does it cause psychotic symptoms. Epileptic symptoms are the result of abnormally increased brain cell excitability, detectable by a peculiar spike and slow-wave pattern in the EEG of the victim. Epileptic seizures vary from momentary loss of awareness (petit mal) to convulsions of the whole body (grand mal). Grand mal is caused by massive excitation of most of the brain cells, which causes a rigid extension of the body (tonic phase), followed by convulsive movements (clonic phase), and then coma. The seizures are similar to those caused by electroconvulsive shock (ECS), pentylenetetrazol (Metrazol) injections, or the extremely low blood glucose caused by insulin injections—all treatments that massively stimulate brain cells. Seizures induced by the latter methods are used in treating mental patients (see p. 431); however, they cause greater tissue damage and disturbances of memory than epilepsy does because the seizures are usually induced daily or every other day—epileptics seldom have more than one seizure a month. Epilepsy that is caused by a brain tumor can often be cured by surgical removal of the tumor. Epilepsy of all varieties can usually be controlled by small doses of drugs that reduce brain activity (anticonvulsive drugs) and thus prevent the seizures. In extreme cases, the fibers connecting the two cerebral hemispheres are severed to prevent the spread of seizure activity from one hemisphere to the other (see split-brain techniques, Chapter 17).

Neurosis

The term **neurosis** has become a catchall category for persistent maladaptive behavior, accompanied by reports of anxiety and physical symptoms of muscle tension, digestive disorders, "fatigue," and lassitude, as well as other psychosomatic symptoms. **Hysteria** is a variety of neurosis in which the individual becomes functionally blind, lacks skin sensations in a limb, or is functionally paralyzed in a limb. Many other emotional symptoms result, but disturbances of sensation and movement raise the question of nervous system damage. Sensory and motor disturbances of this kind have no

known cause in disease or damage, often disappear under hypnosis, and are often susceptible to psychotherapy of one kind or another. The usual report is that they result from self-punishment to relieve guilt feelings. The origins of the maladjustive behavior of the neurotic seem to lie in stress beyond the individual's tolerance, and in early and highly developed learning of inadequate behavioral adjustments to stressful situations. No physical damage can be found in the nervous system, but the persistent autonomic arousal that accompanies constant anxiety leads to stomach ulcers, colitis (irritation of the lower intestine), hemorrhoids (piles), allergies, and many other physical disorders. The physical disorders are no less debilitating because they have functional rather than organic (disease or brain damage) causes. In general, neuroses and some psychoses are termed "functional" for two reasons: (1) they have no known organic causes and (2) they are relieved by psychotherapy or improve without treatment (spontaneous remission).

Psychoses

A **psychotic** individual is one who suffers from unrealistic and illogical **delusions** (false beliefs) and bizarre hallucinations, and whose behavior is so disorganized that he is unable to care for himself in society, although there are many borderline cases who manage, especially in low-stress occupations. These disorders seem to differ in a qualitative way from neuroses, since organic causal factors seem involved even in the so-called functional psychoses and since the psychotic individual shows symptoms that the neurotic person does not have—delusions, hallucinations, and frequent lack of response to the "outside world." The psychotic in a low-stress situation may be free of these symptoms much of the time, but they often recur in an unpredictable way. "Organic" psychosis can result from brain damge (see p. 431), but many psychotics are termed "functional' because even an autopsy reveals no abnormalities in the brain.

If a hereditary predisposition to a specific psychosis moves the disorder from the functional to the organic category, schizophrenia and manic-depressive psychoses might be termed "organic." A higher proportion of these psychoses appears among offspring and siblings of those with the same disorder than appears in the normal population. Schizophrenics appear to beget schizophrenics, and manic-depressives pass their susceptibility to the disorder on to their offspring. Furthermore, protein metabolism in schizophrenics appears to differ from that in the normal population; the output of adrenal steroids in response to stress is subnormal, and the autonomic balance is abnormal. Which among these factors underlie the disorder and which *result* from it, is difficult to say. However, metabolic factors may underlie both schizophrenia and manic-depressive psychosis, and the most promising research leads may be found in the study of brain metabolism. Schizophrenia and manic-depressive psychosis do differ clearly from one another and seem to offer the most promising categories for research of this kind. Varied symptoms accompany schizophrenia, but the most prominent are delusions, hallucinations, withdrawal, and apparent lack of affect (feeling tone). By contrast, manic-depressive psychosis involves, besides delusions and hallucinations, alternating periods of extreme euphoria and depression that may last days, weeks or months. There are other kinds of psychosis and many other symptom patterns, but no one has come up with a classification system on which the majority of psychologists and psychiatrists can agree. Some experts believe that all psychosis has an organic basis, probably in disorders of brain metabolism. Other experts suggest that rejection and traumatic childhood experiences can result in functional psychoses—the so-called psychogenic theory of psychosis. As is usual in the area of behavior disorders, the specialists disagree.

There is one class of behavior abnormality that has recently been found to be related to genetic characteristics. It occurs in male individuals who have inherited an extra sex chromosome, making their pattern either XYY or XXY (Chapter 2). Statistically speaking, both groups are subnormal mentally and may have criminal tendencies because they are found in prisons at a rate over ten times their incidence in the population-at-large. The percentages involved are too small for social concern, but these cases may yet teach us something about genetic influences in abnormal behavior.

Therapies

Various forms of psychotherapy are the most common treatment for neuroses. Most psychologists and psychiatrists agree that neurotic behavior disorders are *learned,* and some kind of learning experience—psychotherapy—is therefore required to rid the patient of his anxiety and other symptoms. Disagreement is found on the nature of the most effective kind of psychotherapy, dividing the experts into two general schools of thought, as will be seen later. Psychoses, on the other hand, are usually treated with physical therapies of one kind or another, although psychotherapy may be used as well. Physical therapies seem to be the treatment of choice for psychoses because many believe they have an organic basis and because physical therapies can alter the withdrawn or violent behavior of the psychotic, making him accessible to psychotherapy. Physical therapies include drug treatments, brain operations, induced seizures, and so on. Evaluating the effectiveness of the various therapies is difficult because an unknown number of patients recover without treatment (spontaneous remission). Untreated groups are often not compared with treated groups, and a before-and-after comparison does not allow for spontaneous remission. In addition, treatment effects are seldom systematically compared by disorders.

Psychotherapy. Psychotherapists can be very roughly classified in two theoretical groups: (1) neofreudian therapists and (2) behavior therapists. Freudian theory holds that neurosis begins in early childhood, when some experience results in more fear and anxiety than the child can bear. The experience is therefore *repressed* and becomes inaccessible to recall. Later, however, some stimulus associated with the repressed experience rearouses the original anxiety, causing otherwise unexplained emotional behavior. A man may show an irrational fear of trains—a phobia—because of the repressed memory of his parents' having abandoned him in a railroad station. A woman may become a lesbian (female homosexual) because she is terrified of men, a fear attributable to a repressed childhood sexual experience. Freudian therapists believe that such neuroses can be cured only through many sessions of painstakingly probing the patient's memory for the original traumatic experience so that its relationship to the patient's present plight can be revealed. Unless this procedure is followed, they believe that the patient will develop new symptoms as fast as the therapist counsels him regarding the old ones, as new stimuli arouse the original emotion. Behavior therapists, on the other hand, hold that the symptoms *are* the disorder, and that the disorder can be cured by simple conditioning techniques such as those described in Chapter 17.

One investigator (Wolpe, see Grossberg) has been attempting to cure neurotic fears, or phobias, by conditioning. One technique is *desensitization.* A patient is trained first in a procedure called "progressive relaxation" (Jacobsen), a method of relaxing the muscles of the body a few at a time, and extending the relaxation from one part of the body to another. He is then asked to visualize or imagine some aspect of the feared stimulus, an aspect previously reported as arousing only mild anxiety. Then he is told to relax progressively. The anxiety is reported to disappear after the patient has thoroughly relaxed; the imagined stimulus has become *conditioned* to relaxation, a response incompatible with anxiety. Imagining the stimulus now gives rise to relaxation rather than to anxiety. Next, more anxiety-arousing stimuli are conditioned to relaxation, and the procedure is continued until the patient can imagine every aspect of the feared object without anxiety. The man with the fear of trains, for example, might begin by relaxing while imagining a toy train, then a real train at a distance, then a train coming toward him, and so on.

Aversion therapy is another behavior therapy technique. The female homosexual described previously might be given painful electric shocks (aversive stimuli) while looking at pictures of naked females, but the shocks are terminated (pleasant stimulus) when the picture of a naked male appears. *Instrumental conditioning,* in which the patient's behavior is instrumental in obtaining a reward or avoiding punishment, is also used. In one case a woman with paranoid delusions (delusions of persecution) was treated in this manner. She continually voiced the idea that communists were following her in an attempt to kill her. The therapist fitted her with earphones and pressed a button delivering an unpleasant noise through the earphones every time she mentioned her paranoid ideas. She gradually dropped the topic, not only in the therapist's presence, but in her hospital ward as well.

Which approach is more effective—traditional freudian psychotherapy or behavior therapy? The evidence is only beginning to accumulate, but much of it favors behavior therapy for neurosis. Some studies show that the spontaneous remission rate (relief of symptoms without treatment) approaches 90% over a period of 5 years or so. The behavior therapist would predict this state of affairs, and the freudian therapist would not. The freudian therapist would predict that the neurotic would develop new symptoms unless he understood the relation between his original traumatic experience and his present anxieties. The behavior therapist would predict that feared objects and situations would be encountered in the absence of traumatic consequences more and more often as the years went by. In the absence of painful consequences, or negative *reinforcement,* the anxiety response to feared stimuli would gradually be extinguished like any other conditioned response. Some studies that plot the relief of symptoms during the course of freudian psychotherapy show that the rate of such relief parallels the rate of spontaneous remission! Other studies favor the freudian treatment in rate of symptom relief, showing that learning is going on. Some experiments use objective measures of emotion such as heart rate and palmar sweating (GSR, Chapter 5) in the presence of a feared object, as well as subjective symptom appraisal. A number of these experiments compare behavior therapy with conventional psychotherapy or with no treatment at all. The majority of the results report that only behavior therapy was effective. Behavior therapy is usually briefer (nine sessions over 18 weeks versus twenty-one sessions of conventional therapy over 31 weeks in one study) and seems as effective in treating several patients at once as in treating one at a time in some studies, and the simple, monotonous training procedures are sometimes as effective when presented by programmed tape recorder as when presented by a bored psychotherapist. These points are important—there are so many more neurotics than therapists that there appear not to be enough of the latter to treat the former! The comparative evaluation of freudian psychotherapy and behavior therapy has just begun, however, and any sweeping conclusions are inappropriate at this time.

Drug therapies. Tranquilizers are used to calm neurotics and psychotics who show extreme anxiety, and "energizers" (stimulants) are used to arouse patients who evince depression and withdrawal. The tranquilizers appear to relieve anxiety and to make psychotic patients easier to manage, although wide individual differences in reaction occur. Drug therapies are reported to be most successful when combined with psychotherapy, but, again, systematic and well-controlled studies are few. Some of the psychotherapeutic drugs are shown in Table 18-1. Reserpine and chlorpromazine were the original drugs used to calm neurotic anxiety reactions and psychotic agitation. Both were therefore classified as tranquilizers, and they replaced the restraints and straitjackets that were used to keep agitated mental patients from injuring themselves or others. Many new tranquilizers with fewer side effects have been synthesized in recent years. The tranquilizing drugs have made it possible for a large proportion of these patients to be treated at home, rather than in mental hospitals. The action of these drugs on the CNS is far from being understood; the drugs seem to reduce the level of sympathetic arousal without depressing the CNS in general, at least not as much as do sedatives and hypnotics. The antianxiety drugs (Table 18-1) are most often used as tranquilizers for neurotic patients and others undergoing temporary stresses such as bereavement or illness. Antidepressant drugs are better understood than are the tranquilizers. One theory holds that feelings of well-being depend on adrenergic stimulation of brain receptors by catecholamines such as norepinephrine or dopamine. A compound called monoamine oxidase (MAO) destroys catecholamines. Therefore anything that inhibits MAO (MAO inhibitors) increases the supply of norepinephrine and produces feelings of well-being. Anything that depletes the supply of brain catecholamines would induce a state of depression. Reserpine, one of the antipsychotic tranquilizers, is believed to have this effect, and its use has been limited as a result. The theory has not been thoroughly tested, but it seems to be holding up well, so far.

More recently, organic theories of psychosis have resulted from biochemical treatments that have proved to be effective in a large percentage of cases involving mania and depression. According to one theory, mood depends in part on the balance between serotonin and epinephrine in the brain—the same two neurotransmitters that control non-REM and REM sleep, respectively. (This is an extension of the theory cited in the preceding paragraph.) As a matter of fact, the early cues that mania and depression might result from imbalances in brain biochemistry came from studies of sleep abnormalities in these two psychoses. The basic strategy is based on the hypothesis that brain biochemistry is unbalanced in favor of serotonin in depression, and in favor of epinephrine in mania. A large percentage of mania sufferers are helped by large doses of lithium, which is believed to alter the serotonin-norepinephrine balance in favor of serotonin. MAO inhibitors (see p. 429) and tricyclic antidepressants are believed to have the opposite effect and have been used with success in a large percentage of depressive cases.

One of the greatest difficulties in developing an organic theory of schizophrenia comes in diagnosis—the disorder has many bewildering symptoms so that experts disagree whether it is a distinct entity or a conglomeration of disorders. More agreement is found in "classic" schizophrenia as defined by Bleuler: (1) a particular thought disorder, (2) a disturbance of emotional or affective responses to the environment, and (3) autism, a withdrawal from interactions with other people. He felt that hallucinations and delusions were secondary symptoms, not always present. If neural transmitters are involved in mania and de-

pression, they may be involved in schizophrenia as well. A strategy evolved by Snyder and his colleagues at Johns Hopkins University consists of examining the effect on neural transmitters of drugs that (1) alleviate the three basic symptoms of schizophrenia, (2) elicit "model" psychosis in normal people, and (3) intensify the symptoms of schizophrenia. Following this strategy, they have found that the phenothiazines and butyrophenone tranquilizers are the most effective in relieving schizophrenic symptoms and that the amphetamines are more effective (in large doses) than LSD in eliciting a model psychosis in normal subjects. In small doses, amphetamines intensify the symptoms of schizophrenic patients. The chief effect of the phenothiazines and butyrophenone drugs is the blocking of dopamine receptors in the brain—an antidopamine action that sometimes has side effects like Parkinson's disease. Amphetamines seem to increase the brain's dopamine supply, and amphetamine psychosis responds well to the phenothiazines and butyrophenones. Overactivity in pathways of the brain that use dopamine as a transmitter looks like a promising lead in attempts to discover the cause and cure of schizophrenia.

Psychosurgery. Prefrontal lobotomy has been mentioned before (Chapters 13, 16, and 17). In extreme cases, especially in cases of psychotics with debilitating anxiety, the fibers connecting the anterior part of the frontal lobes with lower brain centers may be cut surgically. Individual reaction to the operation differs widely, but reduced anxiety is common. Personality changes also occur, however, including irresponsibility, indifference to consequences, disturbances in attention, and possible impairment of abstract intelligence. More restricted topectomy (ablation) of selected cortical areas in the frontal lobes seem to relieve anxiety with fewer side effects in personality changes. The use of tranquilizers has largely replaced these procedures. More recently, stereotaxic lesions of sites in the limbic system have been tried to calm assaultive behavior as they do in animal experiments. The results have been quite variable and need further evaluation.

Shock therapies. Various treatments massively stimulate the brain to cause a convulsive seizure that resembles an epileptic convulsion. A stimulant drug such as pentylenetetrazol may be used (Metrazol shock), the blood glucose may be reduced with insulin (insulin shock), or an electrical current may be passed briefly through the brain from electrodes on the temples (electroconvulsive shock, or ECS). A series of twenty-five treatments or more may be given daily or on alternate days. Disturbances of memory follow, the retroactive amnesia (RA) being greatest for recent events. Theorists have proposed that the amnesia (forgetting) of stressful events precipitating the disorder may account for any beneficial effects of the treatment. Hypertrophy of the pituitary and adrenal glands occurs, in the pattern previously described as part of the stress syndrome. Some claim that this mobilization of the body in response to the stress of the treatment is useful to the patient in combating psychological stress or recovering from apathy and depression. As usual, the shock therapies have had widespread use with little systematic evaluation.

Electrosleep. Over the past 20 years, a technique known as **electrosleep** has been developed in Russia; it has been little used in other parts of the world. Two electrodes are placed over the eyes and two just behind the ears. A low-intensity alternating current (100 Hz) is passed between the two sets, with the intensity level being set below the level of discomfort for the patient. The treatment lasts 30 to 60 minutes, and five to ten daily treatments are given. (The term electrosleep is a misnomer—some patients never lose consciousness.) Initial clinical trials outside Russia have been promising with patients who have chronic anxiety, depressive symptoms, and associated insomnia (inability to sleep). The

treatments appear to be relaxing, and insomnia and other symptoms are relieved. However, because few controlled and systematic studies of the technique have been published, it is difficult to evaluate its effect on specific disorders.

BRAIN INJURY

Brain injury can result in derangement of any or all the brain functions, described in Chapter 13, in addition to more complex disorders resulting from the impairment of the interaction of parts of the brain with different functions. Damage to the motor projection areas or the premotor areas of the cortex or to subcortical motor centers results in paralysis, spasticity, tremors, and incoordination (sometimes called cerebral palsy). Damage to the sensory projection areas or to the subcortical thalamic and related nuclei that project to them produces sensory impairment. Damage to parietal, occipital, and temporal cortex impairs memory and learning ability and causes language disorders (aphasia, agnosia, and aphrasia). Damage to the frontal lobes results in widespread personality changes and impaired abstract behavior. Finally, damage to the limbic system can cause irritability or rage behavior or extreme apathy. Temporal lobe damage can result in docility as well as memory disorders. Any or all of these symptoms can be seen singly or in combination, depending on the location and extent of the brain damage. Reeducation in cases of motor impairment and some sensory impairment is possible, healthy cortical areas substituting for the damaged ones. Focal lesions are often more easily compensated for than are widespread and diffuse ones. If the damage is sufficiently widespread, the whole functional organization of the brain is upset, and psychosis may result.

Traumatic brain injury

Damage to the brain can result from tumors, blows to the head, hypoxia, and long-standing alcoholism. The symptoms that result depend on the extent of the brain damage, or on its location if it is focal. Tumors, for example, cause focal lesions. Subcortically, therefore, they may cause sensory or motor disorders or disturbances of emotional behavior. A cortical tumor can cause a specific impairment that depends on its location. In addition, cortical tumors frequently serve as an irritative stimulus to brain tissue, resulting in focal epilepsy. Penetrating injuries to the brain made by a blow from a sharp object that penetrated the skull will cause localized damage, with effects similar to those of a tumor, and may cause focal epilepsy.

More diffuse and widespread damage to the brain is caused by blows to the head that slam the brain against the skull despite its surrounding liquid cushion. Frequent blows to the head that occur in body contact sports such as boxing, football, or ice hockey often kill widespread brain cells by mechanical damage or by bursting small blood vessels to cause hemorrhage. An event of this kind is called a **concussion.** A large number of concussions result in symptoms that are commonly seen in the person described as "punch drunk"—sensory impairment, motor incoordination, loss of intelligence, and psychotic irrationality, which are the symptoms of extreme drunkenness. Brain hemorrhages result from the bursting of blood vessels in the brain, a so-called "stroke." Strokes can result from high blood pressure in the small capillaries in the brain. They burst from the pressure, and the cells they nurture die. The damage is most likely to be cumulative and widespread, with the resulting symptoms increasing over a period of time, but focal damage can occur. Sometimes many little strokes occur over weeks and months, but a recognizable stroke means more massive damage. Sometimes the damage is confined to one hemisphere of the brain, resulting in paralysis of one side of the body. The symptoms of brain damage that result from anoxia differ from those just described in that the cells of the cortex succumb first, and the damage is total and extensive. If anoxia is severe enough, the individual never recovers from coma. The cortical cells are largely destroyed, whereas the lower centers survive to maintain the automatic (homeostatic) activities of the body. Patients of this sort may "live" for years in a coma with or without the support of devices that supply the bloodstream with nutrition and eliminate body waste. One consequence is recent legal controversy over the definition of death as lack of "vital signs" such as heart action or permanent coma by brain-wave criteria. Alcoholism of long standing diffusely impairs the brain, although some symptoms can be reversed after withdrawal and improved diet. Korsakoff's syndrome includes amnesia, irresponsibility, impaired intellect, delusions, and euphoria.

Disease

Certain disease organisms attack the brain directly, whereas others impair its circulatory and protective structures. In either case the effects on behavior can be profound. For example, syphilis begins to attack brain tissue within 5 years of the original primary infection. It seems to impair frontal lobe function more than the functions of other parts of the brain. The symptoms therefore include listlessness, irritability, lack of social concern, indifference to consequences, and, eventually, delusions.

Cerebrospinal meningitis, as the name implies, attacks the meninges, or covering tissue, of the brain and spinal cord. Unless it is arrested, neurological symptoms follow. Cord damage results, of course, in crippling and in somesthetic sensory impairment. The damage to higher centers shows up in impairment of memory, concentration, and emotional stability.

Encephalitis often has more focal effects. This disorder was discussed in Chapter 14 because one form of the disorder damages brain centers that seem to control activation of other parts of the brain. Encephalitis, literally speaking, means only 'brain inflammation.' But encephalitis lethargica, or sleeping sickness, results from an organism carried by flies and was common at one time in Africa. This form of the disease attacks centers in the diencephalon that form part of the ARAS, and the victim sleeps much of the time. Inflammation of the hypothalamus, in another form of the disorder, results in emotionality, restlessness, irritability, and sometimes seizures. The victim is subject to extreme mood changes, from euphoria to depression, and to some indifference to the consequences of his hehavior. There are also occasional movement disorders. Children seem especially susceptible to various kinds of encephalitis. **Rheumatic fever,** a variety of the disorder, is more common among children than adults and can leave behind the symptoms noted above.

Senile psychosis

Sooner or later, degenerative changes in the brain seem to occur with old age in the majority of the population. Whether these changes result in personality disorders seems to depend on how extensive they are and whether circulatory disorders (principally arteriosclerosis) are a complicating factor. Losses in brain weight and volume that are not accompanied by arteriosclerosis are common findings in postmortem examinations of the elderly. These changes are related to varied and diffuse symptoms, the most common being disturbances of recent memory (RA), emotional apathy, and lapses of attention. (The symptoms are difficult to distinguish from changes in morale and motivation that are often seen in the elderly, as they react to their diminishing physical ability to cope with the world around them.) Mild incoordination and tremors are usual. Arteriosclerosis and the strokes that result cause more specific symptoms as more specific brain areas are damaged.

MENTAL DEFICIENCY

Severe mental deficiency can often be detected at birth or in early childhood, suggesting that prenatal (before birth) or he-reditary factors are involved in various kinds of mental deficiency. In some cases the factors responsible are known, and in other cases sets of well-known symptoms have been classified. Many mentally deficient children are born, however, to normal parents after apparently normal prenatal development.

Prenatal factors

Any of a number of factors may cause failure of the brain to develop normally and result in a mentally deficient child. Although the nervous system seems less susceptible to damage before birth than later, it is subject to trauma despite its protected environment and early stage of development. Food and waste material are exchanged between the blood of the mother and the embryo in the placenta; extreme malnutrition of the mother, toxins (poisons), or drugs, in the mother's blood may therefore affect the developing nervous system of the embryo. Disease organisms may reach the embryo by the same route if they are not effectively neutralized by the leukocytes of the mother. One common example is measles. Excessive use of roentgen rays (x rays) may cause genetic changes in the cell nuclei of the infant (mutations), resulting in abnormalities of nervous system development.

Mechanical damage

Mechanical damage to the brain of the fetus usually occurs at birth, although the mother may suffer internal injuries caused by accidents that can damage the unborn child's brain. When instruments are required to help the mother expel the fetus at birth, they may damage the brain of the infant because the physician cannot always see to place them accurately, or he may have to apply too much pressure to the soft skull of the infant. Hemorrhage or mechanical damage to the brain may result. During a long and difficult delivery, the umbilical cord may become twisted, or the infant may not begin to breathe soon enough after birth, depriving the brain of oxygen for a period long enough to asphyxiate brain cells. All these factors affect the brain more than they affect other tissue, and brain cells cannot replace themselves to overcome the effects of impairment.

Hereditary factors

Hereditary factors certainly underlie much mental deficiency. **Mongolism,** a type of feeblemindedness named for the mongoloid facial features of these children, is caused by an excess chromosome in the germ tissue of one parent, a chromosome that has been identified. Less specifically classified mental deficiency may also be caused by hereditary factors. Many studies show that mentally deficient parents produce mentally deficient children at a high rate of probability.

Specific disorders

Mongolism has already been identified. **Phenylpyruvic oligophrenia** is a metabolic disorder that impairs brain development and often results in feeblemindedness. It is caused by the individual's inability to metabolize a specific amino acid (phenylpyruvic acid).

A **microcephalic** child, as the term implies, is born with an undersized brain and head and is usually mentally deficient. Hydrocephalus (water on the brain) is caused by an imbalance in the production and drainage of cerebrospinal fluid. Excess cerebrospinal fluid collects in the ventricles and beneath the meninges of the brain. The resulting fluid pressure can cause mechanical damage to the brain, which results in mental deficiency if the pressure is not relieved in time. Since the sutures, or "joints," between the cranial bones of the infant have not yet hardened, the skull becomes large and domelike as it expands under this pressure. On the other hand, premature hardening of the cranial sutures can cause pressure on the developing brain of the infant, retarding his development and causing mental retardation.

Cretinism should be mentioned here, as it was in Chapter 3. Cretinism results from thyroid deficiency or lack of stimulation of the thyroid gland by the anterior pituitary. Unless the disorder is diagnosed early and treated with thyroxin or some other drug that will raise the metabolic rate, mental deficiency follows.

Infantile autism is a disorder that has received increased attention in recent years. There is some controversy over whether it is a variety of feeblemindedness or a defect in mechanisms of attention and sensory processing, but the outcome is the same. It has been found that the blood platelets of these children contain abnormally large amounts of 5-hydroxytryptamine (5-HT), one of the catecholamines believed to be a synaptic transmitter. Lovaas, of the University of California at Los Angeles, has had some success in training these children, using operant conditioning techniques with immediate reward and punishment. Dr. Bernard Rimland, of San Diego, has founded an institute to study the causes of the disorder with the hope of devising physical therapies in the future.

CONCLUSION

This chapter has concerned, in a general way, the relationships encountered by man between the stresses of life, his mental state, and his physical well-being. This chapter also concludes the book. It might therefore be permissible to draw a few conclusions about how knowledge of psychosomatic relationships might be useful in everyday life. For example, rather severe stress can affect behavior and reduce effectiveness without the individual's being aware of its presence, although the effect of the stress is obvious to others. Thus it seems useful to accept the opinions of others on occasion, rather than trusting one's own introspection, regarding the effects our rather complex civilization is having on our physical well-being. Tolerance for stress differs widely among individuals, and certain individuals may be less able to tolerate one kind of stress than another. An accurate knowledge of one's limitations in this regard is not easily acquired, but it seems well worth making the effort, in consideration of the severe physical debilities that can ensue. On the other hand, resistance to physical stress and psychological stress can be improved by physical conditioning and development of more effective modes of behavior. Such physical and psychological conditioning requires exposure to stress that is within one's individual limits of coping. Useful conclusions are equally obvious from the facts surveyed on the effects of diet, endocrine imbalance, sleep, isolation, drugs (including alcohol and tobacco), neurosis, psychosis, and disease and of prenatal, dietary, and hereditary factors in mental deficiency. Simple self-interest, rather than moralistic considerations, seems to compel moderation in all things, including moderation itself!

SUMMARY

Since one can be under stress without being aware of it, and since the level of awareness can be objectively measured by the EEG, it appears that stress, rather than conscious events such as anxiety, should be investigated as the origin of psychosomatic disorders. Any stimulus can upset homeostasis, and therefore any stimulus can be a stressor, but only to the degree and for the time that it creates internal imbalance. Individuals differ in their tolerance of various kinds of physical and psychological stress; tolerance may be improved by physical and psychological exposure to stress within tolerance limits. Exposure beyond those limits leads to the stress syndrome, which includes the alarm reaction (shock and countershock), a period of adjustment with glandular and other changes, a stage of exhaustion, and death. Neither quantitative nor qualitative excesses in diet seem to affect the brain unduly, nor does starvation affect it if certain

dietary essentials are provided. Deprivation of vitamin B_1 in infancy or of certain amino acids, calcium, or magnesium impairs brain function. Glandular abnormalities impair vigor, sexual behavior, growth, and body development; the reactions of others to abnormality are stressful. Exercise within tolerance limits improves tolerance for exercise; beyond these limits physical impairment results. Physiological fatigue results from an oxygen debt in the muscles, but a work decrement can follow motivational changes as well. Hypoxia can result from impairment to the lungs, heart, or circulatory system (including anemia), or from reduced air pressure at high altitudes, when the partial pressure of oxygen is insufficient for diffusion from the lungs to blood in the capillaries. In the near-vacuum of space the blood boils as the gases of air come out of solution. The increased air pressure required for diving can put enough nitrogen from the air into the blood to cause nitrogen narcosis. Decompression must be slow, or else the nitrogen will form bubbles in the blood.

Sleep seems to be a necessity for CNS functioning. Sleep results from the absence of arousal and is part of the day-night cycle in man and some adult animals, but not in infants. A hypnotoxin could accumulate from the metabolism of the waking brain to drug the brain to sleep.

Study of the effects of aging is called gerontology, or geriatrics. Such study aims to relieve the stressful effects of aging, as well as to prolong human life.

Functional disorders of the nervous system cause no observable damage to the brain, but they may cause psychosomatic damage to many organs of the body that malfunction as a result. The sensory deprivation resulting from isolation disorganizes brain function, as shown by the hallucinations that follow this treatment. The CNS is susceptible to stimulating, depressing, and disorganizing drugs. Caffeine is a mild and nonaddicting stimulant. The drugs in tobacco are addicting and some of them can irritate tissue enough for cancer to result. Benzedrine is an addicting cortical stimulant used for wakefulness and to raise the metabolic rate. Cocaine is a stimulant that causes extreme mood swings. Ethyl alcohol is a depressant, measured in proof or in percentage, whose effects depend on intake rate, body size, and elimination rate through exercise. It is not addicting unless it is used regularly for a long time. The addictive effects of alcoholism may have something in common with morphine because they both increase THP in the brain. REM sleep deprivation also results from alcoholism. Marijuana is intoxicating but not addicting. Opium and its derivatives (heroin and morphine) are addicting narcotics. Analgesics such as aspirin relieve pain without causing sleep. Tranquilizers such as chlorpromazine or reserpine affect ARAS or SNS activity more selectively, to relieve anxiety and reduce muscle tension. Hallucinogens, psychotomimetics, or psychedelic drugs such as LSD and peyote cause distorted perceptions and hallucinations in small doses.

Epilepsy is caused by a focal tumor or injury or by widespread brain excitability, is detectable by means of the EEG, and results in seizures similar to those produced by stimulant drugs or ECS. The seizures are too infrequent to cause brain damage and can usually be controlled with anticonvulsant drugs.

Neurosis is a vague term that refers to anxiety and persistent maladaptive behavior. Hysterical neurotics develop functional anesthesias and paralyses. Neuroses have no known organic causes, seem to be functional disorders resulting from stresses, and are relieved by psychotherapy or spontaneous remission. Psychoses may be functional or organic, are manifested by delusions and hallucinations, and usually require institutional care. Schizophrenia and manic-depressive psychosis have hereditary components. Forms of criminal behavior

are statistically associated with men who inherit an extra X or Y chromosome.

Neurosis and psychosis have been treated by various therapies. The evidence favors behavior therapy for neurosis and physical therapies for psychosis, particularly drug therapy. The tranquilizers seem particularly effective in calming agitated psychotics. The antidepressant drugs may act by controlling the level of brain catecholamines. Depression and mania can be treated with drugs that alter the balance between serotonin and epinephrine in the brain. Schizophrenia seems to respond to drugs in a way that suggests overactivity in brain pathways that use dopamine as a transmitter. Other physical therapies include prefrontal lobotomy, topectomy, or limbic lesions, shock therapies, and electrosleep therapy, but little systematic evaluation of the effects of these therapies has been made.

Brain injury can cause sensory or motor disorders, disturbances of emotion or memory, or even psychosis, depending on the site or extent of the injury. Focal tumors and penetrating injuries often cause epilepsy. Repeated concussions can result in a "punch-drunk" syndrome that includes mild psychosis. Strokes (hemorrhage) can be focal or widespread in effect. Long-standing alcoholism damages the brain, and psychosis results.

Disease organisms cause syphilis and cerebrospinal meningitis by attacking the brain; psychotic symptoms often folllow. One form of encephalitis attacks the ARAS, causing stupor, and another the hypothalamus, causing emotional symptoms. Senile psychosis results from changes in the brain with age, including shrinkage and, sometimes, arteriosclerosis. Defects in recent memory and attention follow, together with a state of apathy

Mental deficiency can result from hereditary, prenatal, or traumatic causes. Prenatal malnutrition, toxins, and disease are included. The use of instruments at birth can cause mechanical damage to the brain.

Mongolism, caused by an abnormal chromosome, is hereditary. Less specific mental deficiency can also be hereditary. Phenylpyruvic oligophrenia is the result of a metabolic disorder. The causes of microcephaly are not known, but hydrocephalus results from excess cerebrospinal fluid. Cretinism is caused by subnormal thyroid output. Infantile autism may be a disorder of sensory or attentional mechanisms. It is accompanied by excessive 5-HT in the blood platelets.

READINGS

Bandura, A.: Behavioral psychotherapy, Sci. Am. **216**:78-86, March 1967. (W. H. Freeman Reprint No. 505.)

Barron, F., Jarvik, M. E., and Bunnell, S.: The hallucinogenic drugs, Sci. Am. **210**:38-49, April 1964. (W. H. Freeman Reprint No. 483.)

Brady, J. V.: Ulcers in "executive" monkeys, Sci. Am. **199**:95-100, Oct. 1958. (W. H. Freeman Reprint No. 425.)

Chapman, C. B., and Mitchell, J. H.: The physiology of exercise, Sci. Am. **212**:88-96, May 1965. (W. H. Freeman Reprint No. 1011.)

Clark, W. H., and Funkhouser, G. R.: Physicians and researchers disagree on psychedelic drugs, Psychol. Today **3**:48-73, April 1970.

Collier, H. O.: Aspirin, Sci. Am. **209**:96-108, Nov. 1963. (W. H. Freeman Reprint No. 169.)

Constantinades, P. C., and Carey, N.: The alarm reaction, Sci. Am. **180**:20-23, March 1949. (W. H. Freeman Reprint No. 4.)

De Ropp, R. S.: Drugs and the mind, New York, 1957, Grove Press, Inc.

Ebin, D., editor: The drug experience, New York, 1961, Grove Press, Inc.

Eysenck, H. J.: New ways in psychotherapy, Psychol. Today **1**:39-47, June 1967.

Eysenck, H. J.: A technology for mental disorder, Sci. J. **5**:3, June 1969.

Gates, M.: Analgesic drugs, Sci. Am. **215**:131-136, Nov. 1966.

Goldstein, K.: Prefrontal lobotomy: Analysis and warning, Sci. Am. **182**:44-47, Feb. 1950. (W. H. Freeman Reprint No. 445.)

Gray, G. W.: Cortisone and ACTH, Sci. Am. **182**:30-36, March 1950. (W. H. Freeman Reprint No. 14.)

Hammond, E. C.: The effects of smoking, Sci. Am. **207**:39-51, July 1962. (W. H. Freeman Reprint No. 126.)

Harlow, H. F.: Love in infant monkeys, Sci. Am **200**:68-74, June 1959. (W. H. Freeman Reprint No. 429.)

Harlow, H. F., and Harlow, M. K.: Social deprivation in monkeys, Sci. Am. **207**:137-146, Nov. 1962, (W. H. Freeman Reprint No. 473.)

Heron, W.: The pathology of boredom, Sci. Am. **196**:52-56, Jan. 1957. (W. H. Freeman Reprint No. 430.)

Himvich, H. E.: The new psychiatric drugs, Sci. Am. **193**:80-86, Oct. 1955. (W. H. Freeman Reprint No. 446.)

Isaacson, R. L.: When brains are damaged, Psychol. Today **4**:38-42, Jan. 1970.

Jackson, D. D.: Schizophrenia, Sci. Am. **207**:65-74, Aug. 1962. (W. H. Freeman Reprint No. 468.)

Jaffe, J.: Whatever turns you off, Psychol. Today **3**:43-62, April 1970.

Jarvik, M. E.: The psychopharmacological revolution, Psychol. Today **1**:51-59, May 1967.

Levine, S.: Stimulation in infancy, Sci. Am. **202**:80-86, May 1960. (W. H. Freeman Reprint No. 436.)

Levine, S.: Stress and behavior, Sci. Am. **224**:26-31, Jan. 1971.

Mark, V. H., and Ervin, F. R.: Violence and the brain, New York, 1970, Harper & Row, Publishers.

Masserman, J. H.: Experimental neuroses, Sci. Am. **182**:38-43, March 1950. (W. H. Freeman Reprint No. 443.)

Melzack, R., and Thompson, W. R.: Early environment, Sci. Am. **194**:38-42, Jan. 1956. (W. H. Freeman Reprint No. 469.)

Nichols, J. R.: How opiates change behavior, Sci. Am. **212**:80-88, Feb. 1965. (W. H. Freeman Reprint No. 491.)

Roueche, B.: Alcohol, New York, 1960, Grove Press, Inc.

Selye, H.: The stress of life, New York, 1956, McGraw-Hill Book Co., Inc.

Selye, H.: It's a G. A. S., Psychol. Today **3**:24-26, Sept. 1969.

Selye, H.: Stress without distress, New York, 1974, J. B. Lippincott Co.

Stewart, M. A.: Hyperactive children, Sci. Am. **222**:94-98, April 1970.

Weeks, J. R.: Experimental narcotic addiction, Sci. Am. **210**:46-52, March 1964. (W. H. Freeman Reprint No. 178.)

Weil, A. T.: Cannabis, Sci. J. **5A**:36-42, Sept. 1969.

Windle, W. F.: Brain damage by asphyxia at birth, Sci. Am. **216**:79-84, March 1967. (W. H. Freeman Reprint No. 1158.)

*Glossary**

ablation Removal of part of the brain or part of the body by surgical means.

absolute refractory period The period accompanying the *spike potential;* during this period the nerve cell cannot be excited.

absolute threshold Minimum physical energy that stimulates a receptor 50% of the time; a statistical average of receptor sensitivity.

absorb To take in, as light absorbed by a surface or by a color filter.

accommodation Process of thickening the lens of the eye to focus diverging rays of light from nearby objects on the *fovea* of the retina; visual focusing on nearby objects.

acetylcholine (ACh) A chemical transmitter substance released at *synapses* by the *synaptic knobs* of one neuron to excite other neurons.

acetylcholine esterase (AChE) An *enzyme* that speeds the destruction of *acetylcholine (ACh)* after ACh release at the *synapse.* The presence of acetylcholine esterase limits the response of a neuron to the chemical transmitter released at synapses.

ACh See *acetylcholine.*

AChE See *acetylcholine esterase.*

achromatic Without *hue,* as grays, blacks, and whites.

acoustical Rapid variations in air pressure (sound). especially as they result in hearing.

acromegaly A disproportioned body caused by hypersecretion of *somatotrophic hormone* by the *adenohypophysis* after normal growth has ceased. Lengthwise growth in the bones is no longer possible, and the body and features become misshapen.

ACTH See *adrenocorticotrophic hormone.*

action potential Complete sequence of electrical events accompanying and following the nerve impulse; changes in the potential of the nerve cell membrane that result from conduction.

active avoidance A learning situation in which the subject must perform a specific act to avoid punishment.

acute Immediate, as when an animal is operated on and kept alive and anesthetized only for the duration of a physiological experiment.

acute preparation See *acute.*

adaptation Decrease in the response of a receptor and in the perceived intensity of a stimulus resulting from a constant rate of stimulation; loss of receptor sensitivity caused by stimulation.

addiction Physiological dependence on a drug.

adenohypophysis Anterior part of the *hypophysis* (pituitary gland) that secretes the *somatotrophic, thyrotrophic, adrenocorticotrophic,* and *gonadotrophic hormones.*

adequate stimulus An energy change that activates a receptor and is the form of energy to which the receptor is most sensitive, such as light for the eye or sound for the ear.

ADH See *antidiuretic hormone, vasopressin.*

adipsia Lack of a thirst *drive;* absence of drinking behavior when the body water supply is low.

adrenal cortex Covering or outer cells of the adrenal glands that produce *corticoids.*

adrenal medulla The core, or central portion, of the adrenal glands that produces the hormones *epinephrine* and *norepinephrine.*

adrenaline See *epinephrine.*

adrenergic Pertaining to *epinephrine (adrenaline)* as a nerve cell transmitter. A nerve cell that stimulates other nerve cells by release of epinephrine is an adrenergic cell.

adrenocorticotrophic hormone (ACTH) The hormone of the *adenohypophysis* (anterior pituitary gland) that stimulates the *adrenal cortex* to produce *corticoids;* secreted by the anterior pituitary gland to control the hormone output of the adrenal cortex.

afferent Carrying impulses toward a *center,* as when sensory nerves carry nerve impulses toward the brain or spinal cord.

afterdischarge Firing of the motoneurons of a reflex after the reflex stimulus has ceased to act. As a result of afterdischarge, the reflex response continues for a time after the reflex stimulus ends.

afterimages Sensations that occur after stimulation has ended. The sensation to the stimulus may continue or change.

ageusia Lack of taste sensitivity—taste blindness.

---

*Italicized words in definitions are included in the glossary.

agnosia Inability to recognize objects presented through a given sensory modality; for example, a subject may recognize an object by seeing it but not by feeling its outlines.

agonist muscles Muscles that perform a given movement.

alarm reaction The initial response to *stress,* consisting of a shock to *homeostasis,* followed by the countershock reaction of the body.

alcohol An addicting depressant drug contained in wine, beer, and whiskey.

allocortex In evolutionary terms, the oldest areas of the cerebral cortex, originally devoted to smell.

all-or-none law The statement that the nerve cell responds with the maximum polarization change that its electrical and chemical conditions permit, if it responds at all.

alpha block Desynchronization of *alpha rhythm* shown by the *EEG* (brain waves) caused by a flashing light, concentration, or arousal. Low-voltage desynchronized brain waves replace the regular ten-per-second alpha waves.

alpha block conditioning Conditioning of the *alpha block* to a stimulus that does not ordinarily produce the alpha block response.

alpha cells Endocrine cells of the *pancreas* that secrete the hormone *glucagon,* a hormone that stimulates the storage of blood glucose in the liver and muscles.

alpha rhythm A 10 to 14 hertz rhythm often seen in the *EEG* of a resting but awake subject.

alpha wave driving Changing of the frequency of *EEG* alpha waves by using a dim flashing light of desired frequency; the alpha waves follow the frequency of the flashing light.

amacrine cells Cells of the *retina* that interconnect retinal *bipolar neurons* with one another.

amblyopia Impaired vision that does not result from detectable defects in the eye; often caused by suppression of the input from one eye by the brain to avoid double vision caused by conflicting images from the two eyes.

amino acid Type of organic acid that is the major ingredient of protein molecules, which are an essential part of the structure of the cell.

amnesia Partial or complete loss of memory.

ampere A measure of the rate of flow of current (electrons). A potential difference of 1 volt will cause a flow of 1 ampere of current through 1 ohm of resistance in a conductor.

amphetamine A nonaddicting type of drug that stimulates the *SNS,* causes peripheral vasoconstriction, and promotes wakefulness and arousal.

amplitude In physics, the difference between extreme limits of an oscillation or vibration, such as limits of the air pressure change in a sound wave.

ampulla A bulblike swelling on the end of each *semicircular canal,* where it contacts the *utriculus.* Contains the *crista,* a receptor that responds to head movements.

amygdala A nuclear complex buried in the temporal lobe that is important in the organization of emotion by the *limbic system.*

anabolism A metabolic reaction that requires energy input in order to proceed.

analgesic Any drug that relieves pain without causing unconsciousness; also, an area of the body that does not respond to pain stimuli.

anastomosis In neurology, a network of interlaced nerves and nerve fibers.

anatomist One who studies *anatomy.*

anatomy Structural relationship of parts of the body.

androgens Male sex hormones, produced by the *testes* (testicles) of the male.

anemia Lack of red blood corpuscles.

angiotensinogen A normal blood protein that is converted by *renin* from the kidney during thirst into angiotensinogen II that stimulates thirst centers in the hypothalamus to release vasopressin for an antidiuretic effect (ADH) and arouse drinking behavior.

anion A negatively charged ion (element or molecule in solution) that is attracted to the positively charged *anode.*

annulospiral endings Sensory endings in specialized *muscle spindle* cells that initiate the *stretch reflex.*

anode A positively charged electrode, that is, one that lacks *electrons.*

anosmia Lack of smell sensitivity—smell-blindness.

ANS See *autonomic nervous system.*

antagonist muscles Muscles that would oppose a given movement if not relaxed; for example, the *extensor muscles* of the arm are the antagonist muscles for arm flexion.

anterior Toward the head end of a four-legged animal or the embryo; toward the front in man (standing erect).

anterior chamber The cavity of the eyeball that lies between the *cornea* and the *iris.*

anterior lobe of cerebellum See *paleocerebellum.*

anterior pituitary gland See *adenohypophysis.*

anterior vertical canal The anterior vertical one of the three *semicircular canals* of the *inner ear.* (The semicircular canals are part of the receptor mechanism that responds to head movement.)

antidiuretic Any influence that reduces the loss of body water that results from the formation of urine in the kidney.

antidiuretic hormone (ADH) Refers to the antidiuretic effect of vasopressin, a hormone of the *posterior pituitary gland.*

antienzyme See *enzyme inhibitor.*

aperiodic Pertaining to a change that does not

repeat itself, such as the aperiodic air pressure changes of *noise.*

aphagia Lack of a hunger *drive;* absence of eating behavior sufficient to the needs of the body.

aphasia Impairment in language skills, usually caused by brain damage; inability to recognize words by sight (word blindness) or by sound (word deafness), for example.

apparent movement Perceived motion as a result of successively presenting two similar stimuli, displaced in space, at critical intervals and durations (basis of animated signs and motion pictures).

aqueous humor Fluid that fills the *anterior* and *posterior chambers* of the eyeball.

arachnoid layer *Vascular* middle layer of the *meninges,* which cover the brain and spinal cord.

ARAS See *ascending reticular activating system.*

archicerebellum In terms of evolution, the oldest part of the cerebellum. See *flocculonodular lobe.*

arcuate nucleus That part of the *ventrolateral nucleus* of the *thalamus* where *second-order neurons* excited by sensory nerves from the tongue and face terminate; a part of the nerve pathways serving taste and *somesthesis.*

arteries Blood vessels running from the heart to the tissues.

ascending reticular activating system (ARAS) A system of many short fibers of the central gray matter of the brainstem that is excited by collaterals of the afferent *spinothalamic system* and that activates or arouses activity in the whole brain, particularly the cortex.

association areas Those parts of the *cerebral cortex* that are neither *sensory projection areas* nor *motor projection areas.* Originally presumed to be the parts of the cortex that associated sensory input with motor output.

association neuron A nerve cell of the *CNS* that is neither sensory nor motor in function.

astigmatism An eye condition in which the lens or cornea has an uneven curvature.

audiogram A graph of the results of *audiometry,* or testing of the sensitivity of the ear to various frequencies (pitches) of sound.

audiometry Measurement of the *absolute threshold* of the ear for loudness over a range of frequencies.

audition Hearing.

auditory projection area Area 41 of the *temporal lobe* of the *cerebrum,* where fibers of the classical auditory pathway terminate; the sensory projection area of the cortex for audition.

aural harmonics Overtones added to a sound by resonant vibrations of the *cochlea.*

autonomic balance (A) Relative amount of *SNS* activity compared to *PNS* activity; degree of sympathetic versus parasympathetic control of visceral activity.

autonomic nervous system (ANS) Motor nerve supply to the viscera; the efferent fibers of the peripheral nervous system that supply the viscera with a dual innervation of two divisions, the *sympathetic* and *parasympathetic.*

axoaxonic synapses Synapses between the axon terminals *(end feet)* of one axon and the *axon filaments* of another.

axodendritic synapses Synapses between the axon terminals *(end feet)* of one axon and the *dendrites* and *cell body* of another.

axon An extension from the cell body of the neuron that carries nerve impulses away from the cell body and to other neurons.

axon filaments Fine threadlike extensions of the end of an *axon.*

axon hillock Area of the cell body from which the *axon* arises.

basal ganglia Certain subcortical nuclei of the *endbrain,* including the putamen, caudate nucleus, and globus pallidus.

basal metabolic rate (BMR) A measure of the metabolic rate taken with the subject fasting and at rest. The oxygen consumed in breathing under these conditions indicates the minimum rate of chemical reactions in the body.

basilar membrane The membrane forming part of the division between the *scala media* and *scala tympani* of the *cochlea.* The *organ of Corti* rests on the basilar membrane, part of the auditory apparatus.

basket endings *Afferent* nerve endings that surround roots of body hair and respond to touch (pressure) on the hair.

beats Variations in loudness that occur when the *fundamental* frequencies of two tones come in and out of *phase.* Beats occur at the same rate as the difference in frequency of the two tones.

behavior Any observable act of a living organism.

behavior genetics The study of the relative contributions of genetic and environmental influences on individual differences in behavior.

bel Unit on a logarithmic scale of sound intensity. The number of bels form the exponent of 10; the resulting number is multiplied by 0.0002 dyne/cm.^{2}, a zero point approximating the human hearing threshold.

Benzedrine See *amphetamine.*

beta cells Endocrine cells of the pancreas that secrete the hormone *insulin,* which stimulates the utilization of blood *glucose* by the cells.

bilaterally symmetrical The corresponding sides are the same.

binocular cue Any cue to depth or distance that depends on sensations from both eyes.

binocular parallax Difference in the angle of regard for the two eyes viewing nearby objects. Parallax results from the position of the eyes in the head.

biochemistry The study of chemical reactions in living organisms.

bipolar cell layer A layer of cells in the *retina* that transfer excitation from the *rods* and *cones* to the *ganglion cells* of the *optic nerve*.

bipolar neuron A neuron with a single *axon* and a single *dendrite,* each of which arises from different points on the *cell body*.

blood-brain barrier A physiological mechanism that filters the *extracellular fluid* of the brain from blood in a manner that makes it chemically different from other extracellular fluids of the body.

BMR See *basal metabolic rate.*

brain (encephalon) A large soft mass of nervous and supporting tissue contained within the skull.

brainstem All of the *brain* except the *cerebral* and *cerebellar hemispheres.*

brainstem reticular formation (BSRF) Mass of gray matter of the *brainstem* made up chiefly of short, branching *Golgi type II* cells. The BSRF arouses the brain to activity and stimulates or inhibits extensor motoneurons.

brightness Visual sensation that results from light intensity.

brightness constancy An assumption that objects remain constant in brightness and that changes in apparent brightness result from changes in the amount of light falling on the object.

broad-band cells Cells of the lateral geniculate nucleus that respond to all wavelengths of light that stimulate the retina.

Brodmann system A system for identifying different areas of the *cerebral cortex* by the relative thickness of the six cortical layers, assigning each such area an arbitrary number.

BSRF See *brainstem reticular formation.*

buffer A chemical compound that reacts with either hydrogen or hydroxyl ions to bind them so as to neutralize either an acid or a basic solution.

caffeine A mild but addicting cortical stimulant present in coffee, tea, and some soft drinks.

calorie A unit of heat. As commonly used in diets, it is the amount of heat necessary to raise the temperature of 1 gram of water by 1 degree Celsius at a pressure of 1 atmosphere.

camphoraceous One of the seven primary qualities of *stereochemical* smell *theory* whose receptor site is shaped like a hemispherical basin.

cancer An abnormal tissue growth (tumor) caused by uncontrolled cell multiplication.

candle A standard measure of the brightness of a light source. One candle emits 4π, or 12.56, *lumens* of luminous *flux.*

capillaries Thin-walled tiny blood vessels, through whose walls oxygen, carbon dioxide, and waste are exchanged with the *extracellular fluid.*

CAR See *conditioned avoidance response.*

carbohydrates Sugars and starches of various kinds from which the body derives glucose, the essential food of specialized cells.

carcinogen An agent that can cause *cancer.*

cardiac muscle The muscle that forms the heart; intermediate in structural and functional characteristics between *striated* and *smooth muscle.*

cardioaccelerator center A center in the *medulla* that excites the heart to beat faster.

cardioinhibitory center A center in the medulla that acts to slow the heart rate.

carotid sinus A dilated area, in either of the two carotid arteries supplying the brain, that is sensitive to blood pressure and stimulates a reflex that regulates heart rate.

carrier In genetics, an individual whose germ tissue contains genes for a given physical characteristic, whether or not that individual has the characteristic.

catabolism A metabolic reaction that releases energy.

catalyst A chemical that speeds the rate of a chemical reaction without being used up by the reaction.

cataracts Clouding of the *cornea* of the eye that results in partial or complete blindness.

cathode A negatively charged electrode, that is, one that has surplus electrons.

cathode-ray oscilloscope A device for measuring rapid voltage changes using a glowing trace left on the face of an evacuated tube by the rapid elevation of a stream of electrons that sweeps across the tube face at a known rate.

cation A positively charged ion (element or molecule in solution) that is attracted to the negatively charged *cathode.*

cell A protoplasmic body that is the unit of life. A cell can be an independent living organism or a specialized unit of a complex many-celled organism.

cell assemblies Groups of interconnected cortical cells supposed to excite one another over and over again. Cell assemblies are involved in the *phase sequence* hypothesis of perceptual learning.

cell body The part of the nerve cell that contains its *nucleus.*

cell colony A cluster of otherwise independent cells.

cell membrane The membrane that separates the cytoplasm of a cell from the environment of the cell.

cell metabolism Chemical reactions of a cell that are required for life.

center A group of nerve cell bodies where many *synapses* are found. See *nucleus.*

central nervous system (CNS) The brain and spinal cord.

central sulcus The *sulcus* that divides each *cerebral hemisphere* into an anterior one third and posterior two thirds; it separates the *somesthetic* sensory and *motor projection areas.*

CER See *condition emotional response.*

cerebellar hemispheres See *cerebellum.*

cerebellar system All proprioceptive and cortical input to the cerebellum and all cerebellar output to cortical and subcortical centers involved in movement.

cerebellum A large paired suprasegmental structure of the hindbrain, consisting of two hemispheres connected by a central vermis, and mediating postural responses to input from the *vestibular senses, muscle spindles,* and *cerebral cortex.*

cerebral aqueduct The tubular passage inside the midbrain that connects the *third* and *fourth ventricles.*

cerebral cortex Gray matter covering the *cerebral hemispheres.*

cerebral hemispheres Large twin *suprasegmental* masses of the brain of higher mammals that develop embryologically from the *endbrain* and overlie most lower parts of the brain.

cerebrospinal fluid The tissue fluid surrounding the brain and spinal cord and filling the *ventricles.*

cerebrospinal meningitis A disease that attacks the *meninges* (covering) of the brain tissue and causes brain damage.

cerebrum See *cerebral hemispheres.*

cervical Pertaining to the neck.

cervix The neck of the uterus; it contains an opening between the *uterus* and the *vagina.*

CFF See *critical flicker frequency.*

chemical The atomic or molecular structure of matter.

chemoreceptor A receptor that responds to chemical change, such as those of the carotid sinus that react to blood acidity that is caused by high carbon dioxide content.

chlorine ion (Cl-) An element that moves freely across the nerve cell membranes. See *ion.*

cholinergic Pertaining to nerve fibers that release *acetylcholine (ACh)* as a transmitter substance at their synapses with other nerve cells.

chorea (St. Vitus' dance) A disorder characterized by spasmodic involuntary movements of the limbs or facial muscles, or both.

chorionic hormone A hormone of the placenta that inhibits the *estrus cycle* during pregnancy.

choroid coat The vascular pigmented middle layer of eye tissue that lies beneath the *sclerotic coat.*

choroid plexus Vascular structures that secrete *cerebrospinal fluid* in the brain.

chromatic Having the characteristic of *hue,* such as reds, greens, yellows, and blues.

chromosomes Microscopic rod-shaped bodies in the cell nucleus. Chromosomes contain the DNA molecules that govern hereditary characteristics, cell specialization, and cell function.

chronic Of long standing, as when an animal is kept alive for a period of weeks after an experimental operation, or when a disease is of long duration.

ciliary body A ring of muscle tissues that surrounds the lens of the eye, is attached to the lens by the *suspensory ligament,* and contracts in *accommodation* to thicken the lens for focus on nearby objects.

ciliary ring See *ciliary body.*

cingulate gyrus The *gyrus* just dorsal to the *corpus callosum* on the medical surface of the *cerebral hemispheres* in the *longitudinal fissure.*

circular fibers Smooth muscle fibers that circle a visceral tube or the pupil, and that constrict when contracted.

circulatory system The system of heart, arteries, capillaries, and veins that carries blood to all parts of the body.

classical conditioning *Conditioned response.* The *CR* is similar to the *UR,* and training follows a procedure wherein the *US* always follows the *CS,* whether or not the CR occurs; for example, training a dog to salivate to a bell (CS) by feeding him (US) each time the bell is rung.

closed chain See *reverberatory circuit.*

CNS See *central nervous system.*

CO₂ Carbon dioxide.

cocaine A powerful stimulant drug usually absorbed through the mucous membranes.

coccygeal Pertaining to the fused *vertebrae* that form the rudiment of a tail in man.

cochlea The coiled, fluid-filled structure of the *inner ear.* The cochlea contains the structures that transduce sound vibrations into nerve impulses in hearing.

cochlear duct See *scala media.*

cochlear microphonic An electrical response of the *organ of Corti* to sound. It follows the form of the sound wave as does a microphone.

COEPS See *cortically originating extrapyramidal system.*

cold A decrease in temperature (molecular motion), especially as it stimulates the cold receptors to result in cold sensations.

collateral ganglia *Ganglia* of the *SNS* found in the body cavity and neck; formed by *cell bodies* and *synapses* of *postganglionic* sympathetic neurons.

colliculi Four visual and auditory reflex centers that form four pea-shaped enlargements on the roof of the *midbrain.*

color Any visible mixture of wavelengths of light.

color wheel A device for color mixing by rapidly rotating a wheel, segments of which differ in *hue.*

commissural fibers Refers to fibers connecting the *cerebral hemispheres,* such as those of the *corpus callosum* and anterior and posterior commissures.

common chemical sense Pain sensitivity of the mucous membranes, particularly of the eyes, nose, and mouth, when stimulated by substances in solution.

compensation Lack of sensation caused by the simultaneous stimulation of different (opposed) qualities.

complex periodic wave Graph of a complex change that repeats itself, such as the pressure changes of a *complex tone.*

complex tone A tone made up of several *simple tones* produced by a complex vibrating body.

concentration gradient Difference in concentration of an element or molecule in a solution, taken between two points in the solution or on each side of a membrane dividing the solution.

concussion A blow on the head that damages brain cells or impairs their function.

conditioned avoidance response (CAR) Any learned response performed to avoid punishment.

conditioned emotional response (CER) Fear-induced behavior such as "freezing" or crouching to a signal that precedes unavoidable punishment (shock).

conditioned response (CR) A response that results from repeated presentation of a *conditioned stimulus* followed by an *unconditioned stimulus (reinforcement).* A simple learned response to a stimulus.

conditioned stimulus (CS) A stimulus that results in a *conditioned response* only after being paired with an *unconditioned stimulus.*

conduction The property of a cell membrane that involves transmitting excitation from one part of the cell to another.

conduction time Time required for excitation to be transmitted from one part of the nervous system to another.

conductor A material in which ion or electron movement is relatively unimpeded. A good conductor offers little resistance to the flow of electrical *current.*

cones High-threshold *chromatic* visual receptors containing *iodopsin* and found in the central area of the *retina;* most active in daylight.

consolidation According to the *two-phase hypothesis,* the process of laying down a permanent memory trace that is caused by *perseveration* of neural activity after practice.

consonance Degree to which two or more sound stimuli have *consonant frequencies.*

consonant frequencies Frequencies whose pitches fuse or blend well together.

constancy An unconscious assumption that objects remain constant in size, shape, and brightness, despite changes in their location and brightness.

contraction Ability of a cell to change shape. A property especially developed in muscle cells.

contraction time Time required for a muscle to reach full contraction after it has begun to shorten.

contralateral Opposite side.

contrast In sensory psychology, when stimulation by one sensory quality enhances sensitivity to another sensory quality.

convergence In vision, extent to which the two eyes are crossed so as to focus a nearby object on the *fovea* of each eye.

coordination Divergence of many (motor) outputs from a single *center* or group of centers in the nervous system.

cornea The transparent outer tissue in the front of the eyeball that light first encounters when entering the eye.

corpus callosum Sickle-shaped band of crossing nerve fibers that connect the *cerebral hemispheres.*

corpus luteum Endocrine structure that develops from the *follicle* after *ovulation* in the female and secretes *progesterone* to maintain pregnancy.

corpus striatum Striped bodies; subcortical *centers* within the *cerebral hemispheres,* consisting of alternating layers of *gray* and *white matter.*

correlation Convergence of many inputs on a single area of the nervous system.

cortex The surface gray matter of either the *cerebral* or *cerebellar hemispheres,* usually the former.

cortically originating extrapyramidal system (COEPS) Neurons of the *extrapyramidal system* that originate in the cortex and descend the *brainstem* and *spinal cord* to the *motoneurons.*

corticobulbar tract Fibers that run from the *motor projection area* and excite the cranial *motoneurons.*

corticoids Hormones of the adrenal cortex that

govern the sodium and potassium balance of the body.

corticopontocerebellar tract A tract running from the *premotor cortex* to the pons and thence to the cerebellar hemispheres *(neocerebellum)*.

coupled receptor A *receptor* that shares an *afferent* (sensory) neuron with another receptor, particularly in vision. Either receptor can excite the sensory neuron.

CR See *conditioned response*.

cranial nerves The twelve pairs (in man) of *nerves* that connect the brain directly with the *receptors* and *effectors* of the head.

cretinism A variety of mental deficiency caused by hypothyroidism (insufficient thyroid secretion) in childhood.

cribriform plate The bone that forms the roof of the nasal passages and part of the floor of the brain case and contains holes through which the fibers of the olfactory neurons pass en route to the *olfactory bulb*.

crista A ridge of sensory cells inside the *ampulla* that thrust hair endings into the *cupula*. The cells respond to rotary acceleration and deceleration of the head.

critical flicker frequency (CFF) The rate at which a light is flashing when a subject just begins to perceive it as a steady light; a temporal visual *threshold*. Sometimes also called critical fusion frequency.

cross-extension reflex Extension of a limb caused by pain stimulation of the *contralateral* (opposite) limb.

crossovers Twisting of pairs of chromosomes. As a result the final cell division, which produces reproductive cells, may contain genes from both chromosomes of a pair.

CS See *conditioned stimulus*.

cuneate nucleus A nucleus of the *medulla* containing synapses between *first-* and *second-order neurons* serving *kinesthesis* and pressure impulses ascending from the *spinal cord*. See *gracile nucleus*.

cupula The gelatinous mass that crowns the *crista;* a part of the receptor mechanism for head movement.

current Movement of *electrons* or *ions* in a *conductor* that constitutes electricity.

cutaneous Pertaining to the skin.

cutaneous senses Receptors located just beneath the surface of the skin, serving sensations of pressure, warmth, cold, and pain.

cytoplasm The protoplasm of the cell external to the nucleus.

decerebrate rigidity A posture of rigid extension of the limbs (in a four-legged animal) caused by release of the *BSRF* and *vestibular nuclei* from cortical inhibition by removal of *cortex* or *cerebrum*.

decibel scale A physical scale of sound intensity, designed to match the response characteristics of the human ear. The zero point is a pressure energy of 0.0002 dyne/cm.^{2}. Each unit is an exponent to the base 10, multiplied by the zero point; thus 15 decibels would be $10^{1.5} \times 0.0002$ dyne/cm.^{2}, and so on.

delayed reaction A learning task in which the subject sees where a reward is concealed but is prevented from approaching it for a measured period of time so that it must react to the memory of the reward's location.

delta waves Large waves of 2 to 7 *hertz* often seen in the *EEG* of sleeping subjects.

delusions False beliefs.

dendrites Extensions of the cell body of a nerve cell that receive excitation or inhibition from other nerve cells.

density The psychologically scaled hardness of a tone, as a function of *pitch* and *loudness*.

dentate nucleus Output nucleus of the cerebellar hemisphere *(neocerebellum)*.

dentatorubrothalamic tract A tract from the dentate nucleus of the cerebellar hemispheres to the red nucleus, *thalamus,* and *motor projection area*.

dermatone An area, especially on the skin, that sends somesthetic input in a single dorsal spinal root.

dermis Inner layer of the skin that lies beneath the *epidermis*.

descending reticular activating system (DRAS) The outflow from the BSRF that increases muscle tone and thereby increases the sensory feedback that mobilizes the brain in an aroused state.

deuteranopia Red-green hue blindness in which reds and greens are confused with bluish and yellowish grays.

diabetes insipidus Water loss and excess urination caused by a lack of *antidiuretic hormone* from the posterior pituitary gland *(neurohypophysis)*.

diabetes mellitus Failure of the *beta cells* of the *pancreas* to produce enough *insulin*. Insulin is necessary for blood *glucose* utilization by the cells of the body.

diabetic coma A coma that results from *diabetes mellitus;* lack of *insulin* from the pancreas results in an oversupply of *glucose* to the brain cells.

dichromatism Inability to distinguish between either red and green or blue and yellow.

diencephalon Posterior part of the *forebrain* from which the *thalamus* and *hypothalamus* develop.

difference threshold The least difference between two stimuli in a given direction that can be detected 50% of the time.

difference tone A perceived tone, created by *aural harmonics* (resonant vibrations in the *cochlea*) when two *sine-wave* tones are sounded. The frequency of the difference tone is the difference between the frequencies of the sine-wave tones.

differential limen (DL) See *difference threshold*.

diffuse thalamic projection system (DTPS) Sensory projection to the cortex via the nonspecific association nuclei of the thalamus, excited by collaterals of the sensory pathways (STPS).

diffusion The process by which gases such as oxygen and carbon dioxide are exchanged between lungs and blood and tissue fluid as a function of their relative partial pressures (concentrations).

diplacusis An imbalance in pitch perception that results when input from the two ears differs in apparent pitch for the same tone.

dissonant frequencies Frequencies whose *pitches* sound harsh or discordant when sounded together.

DL (differential limen) See *differential threshold*.

DNA (deoxyribonucleic acid) Complex helical molecule found in the *chromosomes* of all cells; the sequence of *amino acids* in these molecules determines the inherited characteristics *(genes)* of the individual and regulates the *metabolism* of each cell.

dominant In heredity, pertaining to a *gene* that determines a physical characteristic of the individual, whether or not a paired *recessive* gene is present.

dominator curve A graph of the threshold of individual *ganglion cell* response to light of a range of wavelengths stimulating the *retina*.

dorsal Toward the back.

dorsal cochlear nucleus One of the two sensory nuclei of the *acoustical* branch of the *statoacoustical nerve*. See *ventral cochlear nucleus*.

dorsal columns The *dorsal funiculus* (of both sides of the cord) that carries kinesthetic and pressure input from the spinal cord to the brain.

dorsal funiculus The part of the peripheral *white matter* of the *spinal cord* that lies between the *dorsal roots* and the midline on both sides of the cord.

dorsal horns See *dorsal columns*.

dorsal ramus In the *spinal cord*, the *dorsal* branch of the paired *spinal nerves* that arises from the junction of the *dorsal* and *ventral roots* and carries sensory and motor fibers to the back.

dorsal root In the spinal cord, the *dorsal* termination of the paired *spinal nerves* at the *spinal cord*.

dorsal root ganglion The *ganglion* (collection of *cell bodies*) formed on each *dorsal root* of the *spinal cord* by the cell bodies of the *unipolar* sensory *neurons*.

DRAS See *descending reticular activating system*.

drive A CNS mechanism for arousing and sustaining behavior in the presence of a *need state*.

DTPS See *diffuse thalamic projection system*.

duct glands Glands that have ducts or pipelines that carry their secretions to its site of action.

ductless glands See *endocrine glands*.

dura mater The tough, fibrous outermost layer of the *meninges* (connective tissue layers covering the *brain* and *spinal cord*).

dural sinuses Reservoirs, beneath the *dura mater* covering the dorsal *cerebrum*, into which the venous circulation of the brain empties.

early receptor potential (ERP) A brief biphasic electrical response of the retina to an intense flash of light, a response that has no observable latency and that can be detected by microelectrodes. It is believed to be caused by chemical activity of the *rods* and *cones* in response to light.

ECG See *electrocorticogram*.

ECS See *electroconvulsive shock*.

EEG See *electroencephalogram*.

effector A muscle or a gland. Any organ of response.

efferent Carrying impulses away from a *center*, as when motor nerves carry nerve impulses from the brain and spinal cord to an *effector*.

electroconvulsive shock (ECS) An electrical current stimulus to the brain that results in massive stimulation and an epileptiform convulsion.

electrocorticogram (ECG) A recording of the electrical activity of the *cerebral cortex*, taken from electrodes placed directly on the cortex.

electrode Any conductor carrying an electrical charge that is used to transfer that charge to a solution or to animal tissue.

electroencephalogram (EEG) A recording of the electrical activity of the brain, particularly the *cortex*, taken from electrodes placed on the scalp.

electrolyte A molecule that breaks up, in a water solution, into positively and negatively charged *ions*.

electromagnetic spectrum The energy spectrum that includes radio waves, light, roentgen rays, and so on.

electron A negative particle in an atom of matter.

electron microscope A device for magnifying the image of submicroscopic structures by passing electrons through them and focusing the electrons with electromagnets.

electroretinogram (ERG) A gross electrical record of the response of the eye to light; usually one electrode is placed on or near the cornea and the other near the back of the eye.

electrosleep Electrical stimulation of the brain

through electrodes placed on the head at an intensity level that does not cause convulsions and does not cause discomfort.

elimination The process by which cells and multicellular organisms rid themselves of waste material.

embryo The immature organism from conception to 3 months of prenatal (before birth) development.

embryological A term that refers to study of the development of the individual from a single fertilized cell to birth.

encapsulated Surrounded by a specialized-looking capsule structure, as in *specialized nerve cells.*

encephalitis Literally, 'brain inflammation'; usually refers to encephalitis lethargica (sleeping sickness), an infectious disease that destroys the arousal centers of the brain; the patient sleeps much of the time unless outside stimuli arouse him.

encephalization The concept that phylogenetically newer and more complex parts of the brain take over, or dominate, the functioning of older parts of the brain.

end-feet Small bulblike endings on the *axon filaments.*

endbrain The anterior part of the forebrain from which the *cerebral hemispheres* and *corpus striatum* develop.

endocrine glands Glands that deposit their secretions into the bloodstream through the extracellular fluid and capillaries.

endolymph The fluid contained in part of the membranous labyrinth of the inner ear; fluid of the *semicircular canals* and *sacs* and the *scala media* of the *cochlea.*

end plate The thickened indentations of muscle *sarcolemma* that form part of the *myoneural junction;* the site of transfer of excitation from nerve cells to muscle cells.

end-plate potential (epp) Electrical potential induced at the *myoneural junction* by motoneurons. The epp results in the muscle action potential that stimulates contraction of the muscle cell.

energy Light, sound, temperature, mechanical deformation, and other physical events, especially as they affect the senses.

energy-rich phosphate bond A chemical bond between compounds that is made up of a phosphate; in a cell, breaking the bond releases energy and making the bond stores energy for chemical reactions.

engram Physical changes in the brain that are presumed to result from learning—the memory trace.

entorhinal area The cortical area posterior and ventral to the *corpus callosum* in the *longitudinal fissure.*

entorhinal cortex See *entorhinal area.*

enzyme An organic *catalyst* that increases the rate of specific chemical reactions in the cell.

epidermis The outermost layer of the skin, consisting of an outer layer of dead cells and an inner layer of living cells to replace them.

epilepsy Seizures caused by an abnormal amount of activity in brain cells.

epinephrine A hormone secreted by the *adrenal medulla* whose effects mimic *sympathetic nervous system* arousal, including an increase in heart rate. Also a transmitter at the nerve endings of the *SNS.* See also *norepinephrine.*

epp See *end-plate potential.*

EPSP See *excitatory postsynaptic potential.*

equipotentiality The principle that any part of the cortex can serve as well as any other part in learning. See *mass action.*

ERG See *electroretinogram.*

ergotropic Having to do with drive or arousal, such as the centers controlling the *sympathetic nervous system* in the *hypothalamus.*

ERP See *early receptor potential.*

essential amino acid One of the ten *amino acids* required by the body, but which the body cannot manufacture.

essential fatty acid One of the three *fatty acids* required by the body, but which the body cannot manufacture.

estrogens Female sex *hormones* produced by the *follicles* of the *ovary.*

estrus cycle In female mammals, the periodic cycle of *hormone* changes and their effect on the reproductive apparatus, culminating in estrus, the period of greatest sexual receptivity in the female.

ethereal One of the seven primary smell qualities of *stereochemical* smell *theory;* it appears to have a slot-shaped receptor site.

eustachian tube The tube that connects the *middle ear* with the throat.

evolution The process by which new species arise in nature over long periods of time, according to the principles of random variation and natural selection.

excitatory postsynaptic potential (EPSP) Partial depolarization of cell bodies and dendrites in response to the release of excitatory transmitter substance by *synaptic knobs.*

expiratory center A reflex center in the medulla that excites forced exhalation during hard breathing.

exposure deafness An auditory defect for certain frequency ranges that is caused by overstimulation of the auditory mechanism by loud sounds at those frequencies.

extensor muscles Muscles that extend the limbs or body.

extensor thrust reflex Reflex extension of a limb in response to either pressure on the sole of the foot or spreading of the digits.

extent The sensed size of a sensation caused by the extent of the perceptual field for that sensation aroused by the stimulus.

external auditory meatus The opening leading from the *pinna* to the *tympanum* (eardrum) in the ear. The pressure waves of sound reach the eardrum through this passage.

exteroceptors Receptors located at or near the surface of the body that respond to physical events in the environment.

extinguish To eliminate a *CR* by repeated *CS* presentations without *US reinforcement;* loss of a simple learned response caused by lack of punishment or reward.

extracellular fluid The fluid (plasma) inside the body that surrounds all cells.

extrapyramidal system A system of many short branching cells connecting the *premotor area* of the cortex with subcortical nuclei and with the motoneurons.

extrinsic Outside of, particularly with reference to the muscles attached to the eye that move the eyeball.

facilitation When two stimuli to a reflex cause a response greater than the sum of the reflex contractions to each stimulus alone.

fallopian tubes (oviducts) The ducts leading from the *ovaries* to the *uterus.* The *ova* (egg cells) produced by the ovaries reach the uterus through these tubes.

fast component The more rapid of the back and forth eye movements of *rotational* or *postrotational nystagmus* (reflex eye movements).

fat A compound made up of a glycerol and a *fatty acid.* Fats, along with *proteins* and *carbohydrates,* are essential for life.

fatty acid An acid compound that forms the basis of *fats.*

feeding center Centers in the *hypothalamus* whose stimulation by internal changes of hunger arouse the *CNS* in a hunger *drive.*

fetus The immature organism from 3 months after conception until birth.

fibrils See *myofibrils* or *neurofibrils.*

final common path Motoneurons to a given reflex response whatever stimulus is used to elicit the response.

first harmonic See *fundamental.*

first overtone The *sine-wave* component of a

complex *tone* that is twice the *frequency* of the *fundamental.*

first-order neuron A sensory neuron that runs from *receptors* to the *CNS.*

fissure A large *sulcus.*

flaccid paralysis Lack of motor control accompanied by muscle relaxation; usually caused by damage in the *pyramidal system.*

flexion reflex The reflex flexion of a limb in response to pain stimulation of that limb.

flexor muscles Muscles that flex the limbs or body.

flocculonodular lobe The two flocculi (sing., *flocculus*) and the *nodule* of the cerebellum. These structures receive input from the *vestibular senses.*

flocculus A paired cerebellar structure that receives input from the *vestibular senses.*

floral One of the seven primary qualities of *stereochemical* smell *theory* whose receptor site is probably shaped like a keyhole.

flower-spray endings Sensory endings in the *muscle spindle* that inhibit muscle contraction, probably in response to pressure from the contraction of surrounding muscle fibers.

flux Rate of flow.

follicles Tissue formations in the *ovaries* that produce *ova* (egg cells) and secrete *estrogens* (female sex hormones).

follicle-stimulating hormone (FSH) A hormone of the *adenohypophysis* (anterior pituitary gland) that stimulates the *gonads* to produce reproductive cells (*sperm* or *ova*).

footcandle The amount of light reaching a surface everywhere 1 foot from a standard candle. A measure of *illuminance,* or the light falling on a surface.

fornix A tract that leads from the *hippocampus* in each hemisphere to the *mammillary bodies* of the *hypothalamus.*

Fourier's law In any *complex tone* with a *fundamental* frequency n, the *overtone* frequencies are 2 n, 3 n, and so on.

fourth ventricle The *ventricle* (central cavity) of the *hindbrain.*

fovea Point of clearest vision in the *retina,* formed by a depression that is in line with the pupil of the eye when vision is directed toward an object.

free nerve endings Unspecialized-looking sensory nerve endings profusely distributed in skin and muscles and present in viscera.

frequency The number of times an event happens per second, such as the number of air pressure variations per second in a tone of a given frequency.

frontal lobe That part of each *cerebral hemisphere* anterior to the *central sulcus.*

FSH See *follicle-stimulating hormone.*

functional disorders Disturbances in the functioning of the *CNS*, resulting from *stress*, that cause physical symptoms and behavior abnormalities.

functional integrity The ability of any living cell to carry out the internal changes required by the cell to survive.

fundamental The lowest *frequency* of the *sine-wave* components of a *complex tone;* the component having greatest *amplitude* that determines the *pitch* of a complex tone.

fundus The large interior cavity of the eyeball that extends from the *lens* and *ciliary ring* to the *retina.*

funiculus A bundle of nerve fibers in the *spinal cord* or *brainstem.*

fusion The sensation that results when two different sensory qualities fuse to give a third quality, such as the fusion of red and yellow into orange.

galvanic skin response (GSR) Change in the resistance of the skin to a minute flow of current; a measure of sweat gland response to *SNS* activity.

gamma efferents Motor nerve fibers of a small size classification, particularly the *motoneurons* to the *muscle spindle* fibers.

ganglia (sing., **ganglion**) A collection of nerve cell bodies that lie outside the brain and spinal cord (whether or not synapses occur).

ganglion cell Type of cell making up the optic nerve.

ganglion cell layer The layer of cells in the *retina* that receive excitation from the *bipolar neurons* and whose axons make up the *optic nerve.*

gas chromatograph theory A theory that, in smell, the receptor surface responds to different odorous molecules to provide a pattern of nerve impulses in space and time as a code for odor detection and discrimination.

gastrula The stage in embryonic development when the *embryo* develops two layers.

gene A complex chemical structure in the cell *nucleus* that determines a unitary hereditary characteristic such as eye color.

gene linkage Refers to the fact that all the genes (*DNA* molecules) of a given chromosome are inherited together.

general senses Sensory *receptors* found at locations over the entire body.

generator potential The partially depolarized state of a *receptor* that results from receptor excitation and fires sensory *nerve impulses.*

genetic sex The sex of the individual as determined at conception by the presence of an XX chromosome pair (female) or an XY chromosome pair (male).

geriatrics See *gerontology.*

germ cells *Sperm* or *ova.*

germ tissue See *germ cells.*

gerontology The study of aging in animals, including man.

GI tract Gastrointestinal tract; the stomach and intestines taken as a unit.

gland A secretory organ or structure that manufactures and discharges a secretion that affects some other part of the body.

glial cells Supporting cells of the central nervous system that may also have a nutritive function.

glomeruli Complex synapses in the *olfactory bulbs* where the sensory nerve fibers from olfactory receptors end.

glucagon The hormone of the *alpha cells* of the *pancreas* that stimulates the liver and muscles to release stored blood glucose to body cells.

glucose The form of foodstuff best utilized by the specialized cells of the body; colloquially "blood sugar."

glucostatic theory The theory that the level of blood glucose affects hypothalamic cells to arouse eating behavior when the blood glucose level is low.

glycogen The compound into which blood *glucose* is transformed for storage in the liver and muscles.

goiter Swelling in the neck region caused by hypertrophy (increase in size) of the *thyroid gland.*

Golgi tendon organ A high-threshold receptor that responds to a pull on a muscle tendon by reflexly inhibiting the muscle. The pull may be externally applied, initiated by the muscle, or both.

Golgi type I neuron A *multipolar neuron* with a long axon that carries excitation from one part of the CNS to another.

Golgi type II neuron A *multipolar neuron* with a short branching *axon* that spreads excitation to nearby neurons.

gonadal sex The sex of the individual as determined by the appearance of the external genitals at birth.

gonadotrophic hormones (GTH) The *follicle-stimulating (FSH), luteinizing (LH),* and *lactogenic (prolactin)* hormones of the *adenohypophysis* (anterior pituitary gland) that stimulate the *gonads* to produce hormones and reproductive cells, and regulate the female *estrus cycle.*

gonads Structures (male or female) containing endocrine cells are reproductive tissue that produce sex hormones and cells (*sperm* or *ova*) necessary for reproduction.

gracile nucleus A nucleus of the *medulla* containing synapses between *first-* and *second-order neurons* serving *kinesthesis* and pressure impulses ascending from the spinal cord. See *cuneate nucleus.*

graded potential A partly depolarized state, as in a *receptor* or a nerve *cell body* and *dendrites,* that fires nerve impulses in the *axon.*

gray commissure In the *spinal cord,* the gray matter that connects the *dorsal* and *ventral columns* on both sides of the cord across the midline.

gray matter Parts of the CNS containing many *cell bodies* and *synapses.*

gray ramus The branch carrying *postganglionic* neurons of the SNS from a sympathetic chain ganglion to the spinal nerves in the *thoracic* and *lumbar* cord.

growth Increase in size of a single-cell organism or increase in the number of cells (therefore the size) of a many-celled organism.

GSR See *galvanic skin response.*

GTH See *gonadotrophic hormones.*

gustation Taste sensitivity of the tongue to sweet, sour, salt, and bitter.

gut Gastrointestinal tract. See *GI tract.*

gyrus The surface area between two sulci (sing., *sulcus*) in the *cerebral cortex.*

habit A learned pattern of behavior.

habituation Loss of attention to a stimulus caused by repetition, or lack of novelty.

hair cells Receptor cells ending in hairlike processes, such as those of the *organ of Corti, vestibular senses,* or *olfactory epithelium.*

hallucination A bizarre or self-induced *perception* without a known objective cause. "Seeing things" or "hearing things."

helicotrema The opening at the apex of the *cochlea* that connects the *scala vestibuli* with the *scala tympani.*

hermaphrodite A genetic female with a penis but no testes, or a genetic male with the external genitals of a female.

hertz (Hz) Cycles per second.

heterogeneous Containing varied components.

hindbrain The posterior one of the three primitive enlargements in the developing brain of the *embryo.*

HIOMT An enzyme, blocked by *SNS* response to light, necessary for manufacture of the hormone *melatonin* by the *pineal gland.*

hippocampus *Allocortex* that was "rolled into" the center of the cerebral hemispheres in phylogenetic development; phylogenetically older cortical tissue that is "buried" in the *cerebral hemispheres.*

homeostasis Maintenance of a dynamic equilibrium (changing balance) of the internal environment of the body, keeping the environment of the cells within the physical and chemical limits that support life.

homeostats Centers of the hypothalamus sensitive to conditions in the *internal environment* and involved in *drives;* abnormal internal conditions stimulate these centers and arouse behavior.

homogeneous Containing only one type of component.

horizontal canal The horizontal one of the three *semicircular canals* of the *inner ear* that react to rotary head movements.

horizontal cells In the *cerebral cortex,* cells of the most superficial layer. In the *retina,* cells that interconnect the visual receptors.

hormones Secretions of the ductless, or *endocrine, glands* carried by the circulation to affect metabolic reactions in selected *target tissue* over the entire body.

hue Response of the eye to the wavelength of light.

hyperalgesic pain A very painful burning sensation that results from pressure stimulation near an injured area.

hyperglycemia Abnormally high blood *glucose.*

hyperopia An eye condition in which the lens is too thin or the eyeball too "short" (in an anteroposterior dimension). The patient cannot focus distant objects on the retina without *accommodation.*

hypersecretion Oversecretion.

hyperthyroidism Overproduction of *thyroxin* by the *thyroid gland.* The condition results in an abnormally high metabolic rate.

hypnotoxin A hypothetical fatigue by-product of nervous activity that accumulates in the brain during waking hours and causes sleep until disposed of by *metabolism.*

hypoglycemia Abnormally low blood *glucose.*

hypophysis The pituitary gland, which hangs from the base of the brain. See *adenohypophysis* and *neurohypophysis.*

hypothalamic hyperphagia A syndrome of overeating, obesity, and ferocity that results from destruction of the *ventromedial nucleus* of the *hypothalamus.*

hypothalamus An area of the brain in the walls and floor of the *third ventricle* that controls reactions of the *hypophysis* and *ANS* and is sensitive to internal changes in the body *(need state).*

hypothyroidism Undersecretion of *thyroxin* by the *thyroid gland.* Causes *cretinism* and *myxedema.*

hypoxia A condition in which the tissues are not receiving enough oxygen from the lungs or the circulatory system, or both, to sustain their metabolic activity. The condition usually results from insufficient oxygenation of the blood by the lungs.

hysteria A neurosis in which the individual becomes functionally paralyzed in one or more limbs or shows sensory anesthesias. No damage to the nervous system can be found, and the symptoms often disappear under hypnosis.

Hz See *hertz.*

illuminance The amount of light falling on a surface.

impairment Impaired function of a tissue, usually caused by the *oxygen debt* that accompanies fatigue.

inadequate stimulus An energy change that activates a *receptor* but is not the form of energy for which the receptor is specialized to respond.

incentive A reward. More technically, the external stimulus that changes the *need condition* and therefore reduces the *need state, drive,* and *sensitizing stimulus* in motivated behavior.

inclusions An approximate and inclusive term for the many specialized structures found in the cell's *cytoplasm.*

incus The *ossicle* that conducts sound vibrations from the *malleus* to the *stapes* in the middle ear.

infantile autism A disorder of attention in young children that has the effect of making them mentally retarded.

inferior colliculi (sing., **colliculus**) A pair of auditory reflex centers found in the tectum (roof) of the midbrain.

inhibition Prevention of a response. Use of the term ranges from nerve conduction at the synapse to observable behavior.

inhibitory postsynaptic potential (IPSP) The increase in polarization (and increased threshold) of *cell body* and *dendrites* that follows release of an inhibitory transmitter substance at the *synapses.*

inner ear *Cochlea* and the *vestibular senses.*

innervate To supply with nerve fibers or to stimulate excitation through those nerve fibers.

innervation ratio Ratio between the number of nerve cells in the nerve to a muscle and the number of muscle cells in that muscle, expressed as 1:N or 1/N.

inspiratory center A reflex center in the *medulla* that causes inhalation.

instinct A *drive* plus inherited patterns in the *CNS* that arouse behavior appropriate to that drive, such as nest-building behavior in the rat as a response to low temperatures.

instinctive reactions Responses governed by inherited patterns of activity in the nervous system.

instrumental conditioning The learning of a re-

sponse *(CR)* to a stimulus *(CS)* when the response is followed by reward or punishment avoidance *(CAR)* and when the subject must respond before such *reinforcement* can occur (that is, the response is instrumental in obtaining reward or punishment).

insulin The hormone of the *beta cells* of the *pancreas* that inhibits blood *glucose* release by the liver and muscles and stimulates blood *glucose* utilization by the cells of the body.

insulin shock Convulsions resulting from an oversupply of *insulin* and the consequent low blood *glucose* that excites the *CNS.*

intensity Change in sensation that results from an increase in stimulation.

intention tremor Trembling of a limb that occurs only when movement is attempted.

intermediary metabolism Chemical reactions that go on outside the cells, supply the cells with glucose and oxygen, and eliminate carbon dioxide and waste.

internal environment Chemical, physical, and other conditions inside the body, surrounding the individual cells.

interneuron See *association neuron.*

interoceptors Receptors located in the *viscera* but respond to physical events inside the body.

interstitial tissue The tissue of the testes that produces *androgens,* or male sex hormones.

intracellular fluid The fluid inside the cells.

intrafusal fiber A specialized muscle cell within the *muscle spindle* that is sensitive to the stretch of the muscle. See *stretch reflex.*

intrinsic Included wholly within an organ.

introspection Observation of conscious events and reporting on them.

iodopsin The photochemical visual pigment of the *cones.*

ion An element or molecule that lacks *electrons* or has surplus electrons and therefore carries a charge; bioelectricity is caused by the movement of ions.

ipsilateral Same side.

IPSP See *inhibitory postsynaptic potential.*

iris A smooth muscle structure whose contractions open or close the *pupil* to regulate the amount of light entering the eye; its pigment determines the color of the eyes.

irritability Excitability. See *stimulus.*

juxta-allocortex See *transitional cortex.*

kinesthesis Sensations of position and movement from the limbs, neck, and body trunk.

kinesthetic senses Receptors in the joints, tendons, and muscles that give rise to sensations of limb and body position and movement.

Klüver-Bucy syndrome Docile, oral, undiscriminative, and hypersexed behavior in monkeys that results from bilateral removal of the *temporal lobes* of the brain.

Krause's end bulbs *Encapsulated* endings of afferent neurons in the skin, which are found in cold-sensitive areas.

kymograph A paper-covered drum that rotates at a controlled speed. A pen, connected to a physiological instrument, records physiological events on the kymograph as a moving line.

labyrinth Membranous sensory structures, for both *audition* and *proprioception,* in the *inner ear.*

lactogenic hormone A hormone of the *adenohypophysis* (anterior pituitary gland) that brings the *corpus luteum* to maturity, stimulates *progesterone* output by the *ovaries,* and stimulates the mammary glands.

lambert A measure of *luminance* (emitted or reflected brightness) in terms of *lumens* per square centimeter of area.

lambda (λ) A term and symbol (from the Greek letter) used as a prefix to designate wavelengths, especially in light measurements.

latent period The time elapsing between the stimulus to a response and response initiation, especially in a *muscle twitch* or a *reflex.*

lateral corticospinal tract A crossed motor tract of the *lateral funiculus* of the spinal cord. The tract originates in the *motor projection area,* and the axons terminate near the *motoneurons* of the cord.

lateral fissure The fissure between the *temporal* and *parietal lobes* of each *cerebral hemisphere.*

lateral funiculus The part of the peripheral *white matter* of the *spinal cord* that lies between the *dorsal roots* and *ventral roots* on both sides of the cord.

lateral geniculate body (LGN) The terminus of *ganglion cell* axons from the eye and the origin of fibers going to the *visual projection area* of the *cerebral cortex.*

lateral hypothalamic nuclei Paired nuclei in the *hypothalamus* that appear to act as a *feeding center.*

lateral hypothalamic syndrome Four stages of recovery from the *aphagia* (absence of feeding behavior) and *adipsia* (absence of drinking behavior) that follow ablation of the *lateral hypothalamus nuclei.*

lateral hypothalamic zone A part of the *hypothalamus* located in the walls of the *third ventricle* lateral to the *medial hypothalamic area.*

lateral inhibition Improving localization in a *topographical modality* by inhibiting receptors surrounding the area of maximum stimulation.

lateral lemniscus The auditory pathway that ascends the brainstem to the *medial geniculate body.*

lateral spinothalamic tract Fibers that originate in neuronal synapses and that carry pain and temperature input to the cord; they ascend the *lateral funiculus* of the cord and join the *medial lemniscus* to end the *thalamus.*

lateral ventricles *Ventricles* of the *cerebral hemispheres.*

law of complements For each *hue* there is another hue that will mix with it to give a gray, white, or black.

law of resultants Mixed *hues* that match will mix without changing hue, irrespective of their components.

law of specific nerve energies The generalization that the chemical and electrical characteristics of the nerve impulse do not depend on the receptor or nerve stimulated; all nerve impulses have the same general characteristics.

law of supplements Noncomplementary hues mix to give an intermediate *hue.*

L-dopa The chemical 3,4-dihydroxyphenylalanine or levodopa. A precursor of the neural transmitters dopamine and epinephrine used in the treatment of *Parkinson's disease,* a disorder believed to be caused by lack of dopamines in the substantia nigra (a nucleus of the midbrain).

learned reactions Responses that have been changed as a result of practice or experience.

lens The crystalline structure behind the *pupil* of the eye that focuses light rays on the *retina.*

LGN See *lateral geniculate body.*

LH See *luteinizing hormone.*

limbic system The "ring" of interconnecting pathways and centers that includes the *septum, cingulate gyrus, hippocampus, entorhinal area, amygdala,* and anterior *thalamus.*

local excitatory state The bioelectrical change that precedes the *spike potential;* a partial depolarization of the nerve cell membrane that occurs just prior to the nerve impulse.

long spinal reflex A *reflex* involving several segments of the *spinal cord.*

longitudinal fissure The *fissure* that divides the right and left *cerebral hemispheres.*

loop circuit See *reverberatory circuit.*

loudness The sensation that results from changes in the intensity of sound.

LSD Lysergic acid diethylamide, a *psychotomimetic drug.*

lumbar Pertaining to the unsupported vertebrae between the ribs and pelvis (hips).

lumen A standard measure of density of light; one *candle* radiates 4π lumens (12.56 lumens).

luminance *Brightness* of a surface that is reflecting or radiating light.

luteinizing hormone (LH) A hormone of the *adenohypophysis* (anterior pituitary gland) that stimulates the gonads to produce sex hormones (*androgens* or *estrogens.*)

lymph vessels Auxiliary circulatory vessels that return excess tissue fluid to the heart to be added to the blood. The lymph carried by the vessels is more dilute than the blood and contains no *red blood cells.*

lymphocyte A representative type of white blood cell (erythrocyte) that combats disease organisms and other foreign proteins in the body.

macula The patch of sensory tissue, including *otoliths, hair cells,* and gelatinous mass inside the *sacs* of the *inner ear.* The cells respond to linear acceleration and deceleration and to head position.

macula sacculi *Macula* of the *sacculus.* The sacculus is one of the two structures containing a macula.

macula utricula *Macula* of the *utriculus,* which is one of the two sensory structures containing a macula.

MAF See *minimum audible field.*

main sensory nucleus of fifth nerve The nucleus of termination for the sensory fibers of cranial nerves serving pressure.

malleus One of a chain of three bones that conduct sound vibrations from the eardrum to the cochlea. The bony *ossicle* is connected to the *tympanum,* which conducts sound vibrations to the *incus.*

mammillary bodies Paired nuclei that protrude on the ventral side of the brainstem in the posterior *hypothalamus.*

marijuana A nonaddicting depressant drug from the leaves of a common plant; it is usually smoked like tobacco.

masking When a tone of higher intensity makes a low-intensity tone inaudible.

mass action A principle that asserts that all parts of the cortex act as a whole in learning. See *equipotentiality.*

mechanical Forms of physical energy that deform tissue to stimulate, such as pressure stimulation on the skin.

medial forebrain bundle (MFB) A tract running through each *lateral hypothalamic zone* to interconnect it with the *septum, ARAS,* and *rhinencephalon.*

medial geniculate body A nucleus of the auditory nervous pathways; the terminus of the auditory fibers of the *lateral lemniscus* that relays excitation to the cortex.

medial hypothalamic area Densely packed cells closely surrounding the walls and floor of the *third ventricle.*

medial lemniscal system The afferent system of tracts that serve *kinesthesis* and the more sensitive pressure receptors.

medial lemniscus A tract of the *brainstem* serving the somesthetic senses of pressure, pain, and temperature. It terminates in the *posteroventral nucleus* of the *thalamus,* which relays excitation to the *cerebral cortex.*

medial longitudinal fasciculus A tract of the brainstem that interconnects the *vestibular nuclei* with the cranial nerve nuclei controlling eye and head movements.

mediolus A bony shelf in the *cochlea* of the inner ear that forms part of the division between the *scala media* and *scala tympani.*

medulla The posterior part of the *hindbrain.*

Meissner's corpuscles *Encapsulated* sensory endings of nerve cells in touch-sensitive hairless skin areas; these endings seem to be pressure receptors.

melatonin A hormone of the *pineal gland* that inhibits output of sex hormones by the *gonads.*

meninges The three layers of connective tissue covering the *brain* and *spinal cord.*

mesencephalic nucleus of fifth nerve The nucleus of termination for the sensory fibers of cranial nerves serving *kinesthesis.*

messenger RNA The ribonucleic acid molecule that is assembled on the *DNA* molecules in the nucleus of the cell, migrates to the *ribosomes* of the cell cytoplasm, and forms a pattern for *transfer RNA.*

metabolism Chemical reactions of life that change foodstuff into energy and waste.

MFB See *medial forebrain bundle.*

microcephalic A feebleminded child born with an abnormally small head and brain.

microelectrode An electrode of 0.5 to 5 microns in diameter, usually made by stretching a heated glass tube until it breaks, leaving a fine point, and then filling it with a potassium chloride solution.

micron (μ) A millionth of a meter; also called micrometer (which is rarely used).

microscope A device for optically magnifying the image of thin slices of tissue. Light is passed through the tissue, and the resulting image is magnified by a system of lenses.

microtome A precision instrument for cutting tissue into thin transparent slices for attachment to a glass slide and observation with the *microscope.*

midbrain The middle of the three primitive enlargements of the developing brain in the *embryo.*

middle ear The cavity in the skull bounded by the *tympanum* on one side and the *inner ear* on the other, and connect to the oral cavity by the *eustachian tube.*

millimicron (m$_\mu$) A thousandth of a millionth of a meter, one millionth of one millimeter, one *nanometer,* or one billionth of a meter.

mineral Any element or compound that results form natural inorganic reactions; some minerals, such as sodium, potassium, calcium, and phosphorus, are essential to life.

minimum audible field (MAF) The minimum air pressure change at 1000 *Hz* that is just sensed as sound in an echo-free open face.

minty One of the seven primary qualities of *stereochemical* smell *theory;* its receptor site seems to be wedge shaped.

miotic division The final cell division in reproductive tissue that produces the sperm or ova.

mitosis Cell division, a form of cell reproduction.

mitotic division Normal cell reproduction by cell division, or *mitosis.*

mixing olfactometer A device for mixing odorous vapors of known concentrations to test the sensations that result.

modulator curve A graph of the threshold of individual *ganglion cell* response to light of certain wavelengths; the measures are taken after some of the *rods* and *cones* are adapted with other wavelengths.

mongolism A type of hereditary feeblemindedness caused by an excess *chromosome* in the germinal material.

monochromatism Complete *hue*-blindness.

monocular cue Any cue to depth or distance that depends on sensations from only one eye.

monophasic Having only one change of condition. In sleep, a cycle consisting of a single waking period and a single sleeping period each 24-hour day.

monosynaptic Pertaining to a reflex pathway having only one set of synapses between *afferent* (sensory) neurons and *efferent* (motor) neurons, with no *interneurons* being involved.

morphine A powerful, addicting, narcotic drug.

motive A *drive* plus a *habit* appropriate to that drive, such as hunger accompanied by learned behavior leading to satiation.

motoneuron A single nerve cell connecting the *CNS* with an *effector.*

motoneuron pool Group of motoneurons participating in a response.

motor nerve A bundle of independently conducting nerve fibers connecting the *central nervous system* with the *effectors* (muscles and glands).

motor neuron See *motorneuron.*

motor projection areas Those parts of the *cerebral cortex* where nerve pathways to the *striated muscles* originate.

motor unit A single motor, or *efferent,* neuron and the several *striated muscle* cells it *innervates* (excites to contraction).

m$_\mu$ See *millimicron*

multicellular organism Any living organism that is made up of many specialized cells.

multinuclear cell Any cell with more than one nucleus, such as *striated muscle* cells or *neurolemma* (Schwann) cells.

multipolar neuron A nerve cell with several *dendrites* and an *axon* arising from the *cell body.*

muscle action potential Polarization reversal of the muscle cell *sarcolemma* (membrane) that excites contraction of the cell.

muscle spindle A sheath of connective tissue that contains two to twelve *intrafusal fibers,* which are sensitive to muscle stretch. See *stretch reflex.*

muscle tone Continuous contraction of some motor units in relaxed healthy muscle caused by the *stretch reflex.*

muscle twitch In a nerve-muscle preparation, a single contraction of the muscle caused by electrical stimulation of the *motor nerve* to the muscle.

muscular Pertaining to the *striated muscles.*

musky One of the seven primary qualities of *stereochemical* smell *theory;* its receptor site probably resembles an elliptical flat-bottomed pan.

mutation Change in the physical characteristics of an individual caused by the effects of radiation or other agents on the genetic material from which he developed.

myelin sheath A fatty covering of *axons* believed to be secreted by the *neurolemma (Schwann cell)* in the *peripheral nervous system* and by the *glial cells* in the *CNS.*

myofibrils Threadlike structures that run the length of the interior of the muscle cell and are the contractile mechanism of the cell.

myoneural junction Junction between each ending of the motor nerve cell and each striated muscle cell.

myopia An eye condition in which the lens is too thick or the eyeball too "long" in an anteroposterior dimension. The patient cannot focus the image of distant objects on the retina.

myotatic reflex See *stretch reflex.*

myxedema Adult *hypothyroidism,* which results in lowered metabolic rate, sluggishness, and increased sleep.

nanometer (nm.) A billionth of a meter (10^{-9} meter).

nasal septum The cartilage, covered with mucous membrane, that divides the two nostrils and nasal passages from one another.

nasopharynx Nasal passages, mouth, and upper throat.

natural selection The process by which members of a species perpetuate the physical characteristics that increase their chance of survival, through breeding until they dominate the species.

need A change in the *internal environment* that disturbs *homeostasis,* the internal balance of conditions necessary for survival.

need condition Any state of affairs in the external environment that disturbs equilibrium in the *internal environment.*

need state The disturbance in the equilibrium of the *internal environment* caused by a *need condition.*

negative afterimage A visual sensation of opposite *hue* or *brightness* that follows prolonged visual sensation of a given hue or brightness.

negative afterpotential The partly depolarized state of the *neuron* during recovery from the *spike potential* (nerve impulse).

negative aftersensation Appearance of an opposite sensation after a continuous stimulus ceases to act. See *negative afterimage.*

neocerebellum In evolutionary terms, the newest part of the cerebellum, the cerebellar hemispheres, which is in two-way communication with the cerebral cortex.

neocortex The phylogenetically newest part of the *cerebral cortex,* including all but the cortex lining the fissure between the hemispheres, the cortex covering ventral parts of the hemispheres, and the *hippocampus.*

nerve deafness Auditory defects resulting from damage to the hair cells or to the sensory nerve cells that *innervate* them.

nerve impulse See *action potential.*

nerve membrane Membrane of the *neuron,* or nerve cell.

nerves Bundles of independently conducting nerve fibers that make up the *peripheral nervous system.*

nervous system The system of microscopic cells that are specialized for conduction and contained in the *brain* and *spinal cord (central nervous system)* and peripheral *nerves (peripheral nervous system).*

neurofibrils Fine hairlike structures that extend the length of the *axon* inside a nerve cell.

neuroglia A singular noun (colloquially used as a plural noun) for neutral supporting tissue. See *glial cells.*

neurohumors Transmitter chemicals, secreted by nerve cell endings, that excite or inhibit nerve, gland, and muscle cells.

neurohypophysis the posterior portion of the *hypophysis* (pituitary gland) that is supplied with nerve cells from the hypothalamus and that secretes *oxytocin* and *vasopressin (antidiuretic hormone).*

neurokinin A chemical substance that is released by injured tissue and is believed to be the adequate chemical stimulus for pain receptors. See *adequate stimulus.*

neurolemma (Schwann cell) A multinuclear supporting cell that covers axons of the *peripheral nervous system,* and sometimes secretes a *myelin sheath* that covers the axon.

neuromyal junction See *myoneural junction.*

neuron A nerve cell.

neurosecretion A transmitter substance released by *neurons* at *synapses* and at junctions with muscle and gland cells.

neurosis Persistent maladaptive behavior accompanied by reports of anxiety and *psychosomatic* symptoms.

nicotine A drug found in tobacco that is an *SNS* stimulant.

nm. See *nanometer.*

nodes of Ranvier Regular interruptions in the *myelin sheath* covering an *axon.*

nodule A centrally located cerebellar structure that receives input from the *vestibular senses.* See *flocculus.*

noise Sounds made up of *aperiodic* air pressure changes with many high-frequency components.

nontopographic modality A sensory modality whose individual receptors and sensory neurons respond to a wide range of stimulus change by changing their rate of firing. A stimulus change is thus signaled to the brain by a change in the relative rate of firing of specific neurons. See *topographic modality.*

noradrenaline See *norepinephrine.*

norepinephrine A hormone secreted by the *adrenal medulla,* whose effects mimic *sympathetic nervous system* arousal and cause peripheral vasoconstriction; also a transmitter substance at *postganglionic* endings of the SNS. See *epinephrine.*

nucleus The central body within a cell that contains the basic mechanisms for cell growth, repair, and reproduction. Also a collection of nerve cells where many *synapses* are made.

O₂ Oxygen.

occipital lobe The part of each *cerebral hemisphere* that is posterior to the *parietal lobe;* the most posterior lobe of the cerebral hemisphere.

occlusion When two stimuli to a reflex cause a response that is less than the sum of the reflex contractions to each stimulus alone.

ogive A graph of the accumulated frequency or percentage of events or individuals included with increases in a quantitative measure.

ohm A unit of electrical resistance in a conductor. One *volt* of potential difference will result in 1 *ampere* of current if the resistance of the conductor is 1 *ohm*.

olfaction The sense of smell.

olfactometer A crude device for measuring smell threshold by an odorus hard-rubber tube that slides over a graduated glass cylinder, whose other end is inserted into the nostril.

olfactory bulbs Enlargements of the ends of the *olfactory tracts* on the base of the brain, where the olfactory neurons terminate.

olfactory cleft See *olfactory epithelium*.

olfactory epithelium Smell-sensitive area on the roof of the nasal passages to both sides of the *nasal septum*.

olfactory tracts Extensions on the base of the brain formed by tracts that run between the *olfactory bulbs* and the *prepiriform area*.

olive An important nucleus of the auditory pathway in the *medulla* and an accessory nucleus to the *cerebellum*.

opium A variety of *morphine* that is smoked by addicts; an addicting drug.

optic chiasma The hemidecussation (half-crossing) of the *ganglion cells* from the *retina* of the eye in the *diencephalon*.

optic nerve The visual *ganglion cell* axons that run from the eyeball to the *optic chiasma*.

optic tract *Ganglion cell* axons that run between the *optic chiasma* and the *lateral geniculate bodies*.

optomotor nuclei Nuclei of the third, fourth, and sixth cranial nerves that regulate eye movements.

organ An organization of differently specialized cells *(tissues)* that are arranged in a cooperative way to perform a function; for example, the stomach is an organ of muscular, connective, glandular, and other tissue for digesting food.

organ of Corti Auditory receptor structure of the *inner ear* that rests on the *basilar membrane* and transduces fluid movements in the *cochlea* of the *inner ear* into nerve impulses.

organic compounds A class of compounds made up of carbon atoms to which oxygen, hydrogen, nitrogen, or sulfur is chemically linked. Living organisms are made of organic compounds.

organic pain receptors Pain receptors in the *viscera*.

organic senses Receptors in the *viscera* for pressure, cold, warmth, and pain.

organism Any form of life, from a virus or a single cell to a complex many-celled animal such as man.

orienting reflex Response made by an animal to a novel stimulus, such as pricking up the ears or sniffing.

ossicles The three bony levers in the middle ear that connect the *tympanum* with the *oval window* of the *inner ear*; The ossicles conduct sound vibrations from the tympanum to the oval window.

otoliths Particles of calcium carbonate that are embedded in the gelatinous material of the *macula*.

outer ear *Pinna, tympanum,* and *external auditory meatus*.

ova See singular form *ovum*.

oval window The membrane-covered opening to the fluid-filled *inner ear*; sound vibrations are carried by the *ossicles* to the oval window, which communicates with the *scala vestibuli*.

ovaries Female *gonads*, or reproductive organs.

overtone In a *complex tone*, frequencies showing *resonance* of parts of the vibrating body to simple multiples of the fundamental frequency. See *Fourier's law*.

ovulation Release of an *ovum* by the *follicles* of the *ovaries*.

ovum Female reproductive egg cell.

oxidation A class of chemical reactions that includes the reaction of a chemical substance (such as a food) with oxygen to give off heat and energy.

oxidize See *oxidation*.

oxygen debt The amount of oxygen necessary to restore a tissue to equilibrium after its metabolic need for oxygen has exceeded the available supply.

oxytocin A hormone of the *neurohypophysis* (posterior pituitary gland) that contracts *smooth muscle* and stimulates the mammary glands to produce milk.

pacinian corpuscles Large encapsulated pressure receptors found in subcutaneous fat, in the joints, and in the mesenteries that support the viscera.

pain Any stimulation of free nerve endings that gives rise to pain sensations.

paleocerebellum A phylogenetically older part of the cerebellum that consists of the *anterior* and *posterior lobe,* receives input from muscle spindles, and regulates postural extensor tone.

paleocortex See *allocortex*.

pancreas A gland that lies between the stomach and the small intestine (duodenum) and contains the endocrine *alpha* and *beta cells* that secrete *glucagon* and *insulin*.

parabiosis Sharing of a common organ or system

between two animals, such as interconnected circulatory systems.

paradoxical cold Inadequate stimulation of cold receptors by an intense warm stimulus. Compare *inadequate stimulus.*

paradoxical warmth Inadequate stimulation of warmth receptors by an intense cold stimulus. Compare *inadequate stimulus.*

parallel circuit Several nervous pathways, usually of different length, beginning and ending at the same points in the nervous system.

paraplegic An individual whose spinal cord has been severed. Parts of the body below the separation are paralyzed and anesthetic as a result.

parasympathetic division A division of the *autonomic nervous system (ANS)*; an efferent nerve supply that innervates the *viscera* and discretely stimulates digestive functions as well as forming part of certain reflexes of the smooth muscles.

parasympathetic ganglia Collections of cell bodies of the *postganglionic PNS* nerve fibers; the ganglia lie near the smooth muscles and glands, which the postganglionic fibers *innervate.*

parasympathetic nervous system (PNS) See *parasympathetic division.*

parasympathetic overcompensation When the *PNS* is aroused by *SNS* activity and becomes dominant over some phase of *SNS* activity, so that *PNS* responses occur.

parathormone The hormone of the *parathyroid glands* that governs calcium and phosphate levels of the body.

parathyroid glands Four small *endocrine glands* embedded in the *thyroid glands* of the neck; they produce *parathormone* to control the calcium and phosphorus levels in the body.

parietal lobe That part of each *cerebral hemisphere* that lies between the *occipital lobe* and the *central sulcus.*

Parkinson's disease A disorder characterized by tremors at rest, muscle rigidity, and lack of facial expression, all caused by damage of the *basal ganglia.*

passive avoidance response A learned response of immobility or the stopping of some kind of ongoing behavior to avoid punishment.

penis Part of the external genitals of the male, exclusive of the *gonads* and *scrotum;* the organ of copulation.

perception A conscious event, initiated by *sensation,* but including memory, classification, and integration of the input from several sense organs.

perilymph The fluid of the *labyrinth* that surrounds it; it is also contained in the *scala vestibuli* and *scala tympani* of the *cochlea.*

period of adjustment The period during which an

organism successfully copes with an abnormal *stress.* See *stress syndrome.*

period of latent addition In a nerve cell, the period of lowered threshold to excitation that accompanies the *local excitatory state* preceding a *nerve impulse* or that results from subthreshold excitation.

periodic Repeated regularly.

peripheral nervous system *Nerves* that lie outside the *brain* and *spinal cord* and connect the latter with *receptors* and *effectors.*

peripheral somatic nervous system (PSNS) The *peripheral nervous system,* exclusive of the *autonomic nervous system,* that connects the *CNS* with *receptors* and *striated muscles.*

peristalsis Regular contractions of the intestine that aid in digestion.

perseveration Brain activity that follows practice, is the basis for immediate memory, and lays down the permanent memory trace *(consolidation)* in the *two-phase hypothesis* of learning and memory.

phase Each cycle of a periodic event is divided into 360 degrees. A phase is the point the periodic event has reached in this cycle at any instant in time.

phase sequence A number of *cell assemblies,* repeatedly excited in order by a perceptual act, such as in successive viewing of the corners of a triangle.

phenylpyruvic oligophrenia An inability to metabolize an essential amino acid that results in feeblemindedness.

photic Pertaining to electromagnetic energy in the wavelength range of 400 to 750 nm. that stimulates the eye.

photopic See *chromatic.*

physiological fatigue The *oxygen debt* incurred by muscles when they are exercised beyond the capacity of the body to supply them with oxygen.

physiological psychology Study of the relationships between physiology and behavior.

physiological zero The range of skin temperatures at which neither warmth nor cold is sensed.

physiologist One who studies the function of the tissue, organs, and systems of the body.

physiology Study of the functioning of tissues, organs, and systems of the body.

pia mater The fragile innermost layer of the *meninges,* which cover the *CNS.*

pineal gland (pronounced pin'e-al) An *endocrine gland* atop the posterior third ventricle that secretes *melatonin* to inhibit sex hormone output by the *gonads.*

pinna The "ear"—the convoluted structure on each side of the head that channels the pressure waves of sound to the *external auditory meatus.*

piriform lobe Projection area for smell on the ventral surface of the *temporal lobe* of the cerebral cortex.

pitch The single quality of hearing; the sensation that changes with changes in the *frequency* of a tone as in the musical scale.

pituitary dwarf An individual who is dwarfed by undersecretion of *somatotrophic hormone* from the *adenohypophysis* (anterior pituitary gland).

pituitary giant Giantism resulting from oversecretion of *somatotrophic hormone* by the *adenohypophysis* in childhood.

placenta Site of the interchange of carbon dioxide, oxygen, food, and waste between the embryo or fetus and the pregnant mother's circulation.

planarian Small primitive invertebrate with a nerve-net nervous system and the ability to regenerate missing parts; used in experiments on the role of *DNA* and *RNA* in learning.

plexus (plural, **plexuses**) A network of *nerves.*

pneumograph An instrument for measuring and recording the rate and depth of breathing as a record on a moving paper tape.

pneumotaxic center A reflex center in the pons involved in control of the *inspiratory center* and the *expiratory center* during hard breathing.

PNS See *parasympathetic division.*

PNS compensation An increase in *PNS* activity caused by an increase in *SNS* activity.

polarized condition A difference in voltage across a poor conductor, such as the difference in charge, positive to negative, on the outside and inside of the cell membrane.

polygraph An instrument that measures several responses controlled by the *ANS,* such as the *GSR,* breathing, heart rate, and blood pressure; results are recorded as line movements on a paper tape.

polyphasic Pertaining to many alterations between two states; usually refers to a sleep cycle consisting of several periods of sleep and several periods of wakefulness each day.

pons The ventral surface enlargement on the anterior part of the *hindbrain* formed by crossing tracts from higher parts of the brain en route to the *cerebellum.*

population genetics A study of the proportionate incidence of inherited characteristics in a population, as a means of detecting genetic control mechanisms.

portal system A system of blood vessels that carries a secretion from a limited site of production directly to a limited site of action.

positive afterimage A visual sensation that continues after the stimulus initiating it ceases to act.

positive afterpotential The overpolarized condition of the *axon* that follows the *negative afterpotential* of the *nerve impulse.*

positive aftersensation Continuance of a sensation after the stimulus initiating it ceases to act. See *positive afterimage.*

postcentral gyrus The *gyrus* of the cerebral cortex just posterior to the *central sulcus.*

posterior Toward the tail end of a four-legged animal or of an *embryo;* toward the back in man (standing erect).

posterior chamber The cavity of the eyeball that lies between the *iris* and the *lens.*

posterior lobe of cerebellum See *paleocerebellum.*

posterior pituitary gland See *neurohypophysis.*

posterior vertical canal The posterior vertical one of the three *semicircular canals* of the *inner ear.*

posteroventral nucleus A *nucleus* of the *thalamus* that receives input from *somesthesis* and projects this input to the cerebral cortex.

postganglionic Refers to neurons of the *ANS* that run from *ganglia* that are outside the *CNS* to *effectors.*

postrotational nystagmus Reflex eye movements that result from rotational deceleration and are seen after rotation ceases.

postsynaptic inhibition *Direct inhibition* such as occurs when *Renshaw cells* hyperpolarize a neuron.

posttetanic potentiation Enhanced conduction in a monosynaptic pathway as a result of a period of high-frequency stimulation. The effect lasts for several minutes.

POT areas Parietal, occipital, and temporal cortex.

potassium ion (K⁺) An element found inside nerve cells. See *ion.*

precentral gyrus The gyrus of the cerebral cortex that lies just anterior to the *central sulcus.*

prefrontal lobe Area of the cerebral hemispheres that is anterior to the *premotor area.*

prefrontal lobectomy Removal of the *prefrontal lobes* of the *cerebral cortex* (anterior to area 6).

prefrontal lobotomy Severing of the fibers connecting the thalamus with the prefrontal areas of the cerebral cortex.

prefrontal topectomy Removal of selected areas of the *prefrontal lobes* of the cerebral cortex.

preganglionic Pertaining to neurons of the *ANS* that run from the *CNS* to *ganglia,* where they synapse with *postganglionic* neurons going to the effectors.

premotor area Area 6 of the cerebral cortex in the Brodmann system; the original of most cortical fibers participating in the *extrapyramidal-system* regulation of background movements, and the origin of fibers going to the *cerebellum.*

premotor cortex See *premotor area.*

prepiriform area The projection area for smell located at the base of the brain; terminus of the *olfactory tracts.*

presbyopia Restricted *accommodation* of the lens that occurs in the elderly. It results in diminished acuity and increases distance to the nearest point at which the eyes can be focused.

pressure Mechanical deformation of the skin, muscles, or viscera, especially as it results in sensations.

presubiculum The cortical area medial to the temporal lobes.

presynaptic inhibition *Direct inhibition* by *axoaxonic synapses* that blocks effective excitation of presynaptic endings.

pretectal nuclei Visual reflex centers of the *diencephalon* that regulate the *iris* and *ciliary body.*

primary endings See *annulospiral endings.*

primary hues See *unique hues.*

primary qualities Irreducible attributes of a sensory modality such as primary hues in vision or primary tastes; sensory qualities whose component sensations cannot be detected.

progesterone A hormone of the *corpus luteum* of the *ovary* that inhibits production of *follicle-stimulating hormone* by the *adenohypophysis.* Progesterone prepares the female organs for pregnancy.

projection fibers Nerve fibers reaching or leaving a *center* of the brain, especially the *cerebral cortex.*

prolactin See *lactogenic hormone.*

proprioception Sensations of position and movement, including *kinesthesis* and the *vestibular senses.*

proprioceptors The general *kinesthetic* receptors of the joints and muscles and the special *vestibular senses* of the inner ear, both of which give rise to sensations of position and movement.

protanopia Red-green hue blindness with a shortened visible spectrum at the red end.

protein A large organic compound that is primarily composed of amino acids; it is both an essential food and an essential part of the structure of cells.

protoplasm The primitive organic material of which cells are made.

pseudopod False foot; an extension of the cell caused by protoplasm flow that thrusts out a process for cell movement.

PSNS See *peripheral somatic nervous system.*

psychedelic drugs See *psychotomimetic drugs.*

psychophysics The science concerned with measurable relationships between changes in physical energy and changes in the attributes of sensation.

psychosis See *psychotic.*

psychosomatic *Stress*-induced malfunction of the organs of the body.

psychotic An individual who has unrealistic and illogical *delusion,* bizarre *hallucinations,* and disorganized behavior.

psychotomimetic drugs Drugs that mimic the effect of *psychosis* by producing *hallucinations* and bizarre sensations.

PTC Phenylthiocarbamide, a substance to which some individuals inherit a high taste threshold; used in studies of taste and heredity.

pulmonary circulation The system of blood vessels that carry blood from the heart to the lungs and back for gas exchange with the air in the lungs.

pungent One of the seven primary qualities of smell, according to the *stereochemical* smell *theory;* a quality determined by a positive charge of the substance smelled.

pupil Opening in the *iris of the eye* through which light enters the eye.

Purkinje shift (poor′kin-yay) The change in apparent brightness of various wavelengths with the change from daylight *(cone)* to night *(rod)* vision or the reverse.

putrid One of the seven primary qualities of smell according to the *stereochemical* smell *theory;* a quality determined by a negative charge on the molecule smelled.

pyramidal system Fibers that run from the *motor projection area* to the level of the motoneurons and are carried in the pyramids of the brain and pyramidal tracts of the spinal cord.

pyramidal tract See *pyramidal system.*

pyriform lobe See *piriform lobe.*

quality The attribute that distinguishes one sensory modality from another and that distinguishes sensation differences within a modality that are not caused by *intensity, extent,* or duration.

RA See *retroactive amnesia.*

radial fibers Smooth muscle fibers that radiate from an opening such as the *pupil;* their contraction increases the size of the opening.

radiate To give off or emit, as light is radiated by a luminous source. See *luminance.*

random variation Variation in the characteristics of individual members of a species that occurs by chance or as a result of *mutation.*

rapid eye movements (REM) Eye movements that accompany dreaming during stage 1 sleep, recorded as muscle activity from electrodes placed near the *extrinsic* eye muscles.

receptors Structures specialized for irritability in

response to various forms of energy, such as light, heat, cold, sound, or mechanical deformation.

recessive In heredity, pertaining to a *gene* that will not determine a physical characteristic of the individual unless paired with another recessive gene for the same characteristic.

reciprocal innervation Excitation arrangements in the *CNS* that inhibit an *antagonist muscle* when the paired *agonist muscle* contracts.

recruitment The addition of active motoneurons to a response, a few at a time.

recurrent collateral A branch of a nerve fiber that turns back toward the origin of the fiber.

red blood cells The cells that, through chemical reaction, bind oxygen or carbon dioxide for gas exchange between the lungs, blood, and tissue fluid.

reflect To bounce off, as light reflected from a surface.

reflex An automatic and predetermined response to a stimulus, determined by interneuron *synapses* in the *CNS* and including *receptor, afferent* neuron, *association neuron, efferent* neuron, and *effector* elements.

reflex figure Opposite positions of the forelimbs and hindlimbs that result from a *flexion* and *crossed-extension reflex* in one pair of limbs.

reflex preparation An animal whose brain or spinal cord has been severed to isolate a reflex for study from nerve impulses that originate above the level of the cut.

refract To bend, as light is refracted by a lens or prism.

reinforcement Reward or punishment used to alter behavior.

Reissner's membrane The membrane between the *scala vestibuli* and the *scala media* in the *cochlea* of the *inner ear.*

relative refractory period The period during the early part of the *negative afterpotential* when the *axon* is harder to stimulate than normally.

relaxation time The time required for a muscle to reach its original length after full contraction has been attained.

releasing stimulus An *incentive,* or a cue to an incentive, that releases behavior appropriate to an active drive such as hunger or thirst.

REM See *rapid eye movements.*

renin A substance released by the kidney in thirst that converts *angiotensinogen* into a form that stimulates the hypothalamus to initiate drinking behavior and release *vasopressin* for an *antidiuretic* effect on the kidney.

Renshaw cells Short *Golgi type II neurons* that release GABA at synapses to hyperpolarize and thereby inhibit other neurons.

reproduction The production of two cells from one in cell *mitosis,* or the production of a new cell by the joining of egg and sperm cells to form a multicellular organism.

resonance The tendency of an object to vibrate at a characteristic frequency. In a complex instrument of several parts, this produces *overtones* as well as a *fundamental* frequency.

resonate See *resonance.*

respiratory quotient (RQ) Ratio between the carbon dioxide given off by the body and the oxygen intake, CO_2/O_2; a measure of *metabolism.*

resting discharge The firing of a neuron that occurs in the absence of stimulation.

resting potential The difference in charge, positive to negative, across the membranes of cells when they are not stimulated.

reticulospinal tract A *tract* of the spinal cord that originates in the *brainstem reticular formation* and terminates on spinal *motoneurons.*

retina An extension of the brain that contains the visual receptors; found in the posterior part of the *fundus* of the eyeball.

retinal disparity The difference between the images produced on the *retinas* of the two eyes by a nearby object.

retroactive amnesia (RA) Loss of memory for recent events when older memories remain unimpaired.

retroactive inhibition Forgetting of an event because of the occurrence of an intervening event.

reverberatory circuit A circular nervous pathway that can reexcite itself over and over.

rheumatic fever Inflammation of joints caused by bacteria that sometimes destroy tissue in the brain and spinal cord.

rhinencephalon Hippocampus, amygdala, cingulate gyrus, and piriform area; brain structures once believed to be integrating centers for smell.

rhodopsin Photochemical visual pigment of the *rods* that is chemically changed by light to stimulate optic nerve impulses.

ribosome A type of cell inclusion in which *enzymes* are assembled that determine the metabolic reactions of the cell.

righting reflexes A series of reflexes that stimulate one another to right the animal's position, beginning with vestibular stimulation and continuing with reflexes that twist the body into an upright position.

rods Low-threshold *achromatic* visual receptors containing *rhodopsin,* found in the periphery of the *retina;* night vision receptors.

rotational nystagmus Reflex eye movements that result from rotational acceleration of the head.

round window The membrane-covered window that

relieves the pressure changes of cochlear fluid caused by sound vibrations.

RQ See *respiratory quotient.*

Ruffini's endings *Encapsulated* endings of *afferent* neurons found in the skin of warmth-sensitive areas.

sacculus A sensory apparatus of the *inner ear* that responds to head position and linear acceleration. See *utriculus.*

sacral Pertaining to the vertebrae (sing., *vertebra*) of the pelvis (hips).

sacs See *sacculus* and *utriculus.*

satiation center See *satiety center.*

satiety center A center in the *hypothalamus,* probably the *ventromedial nucleus,* whose stimulation by the internal changes that result from feeding stops eating behavior.

saturated Pertaining to colors that contain maximum *hue* (contain little gray).

saturation Degree of *hue* response of the eye to a color; lack of gray in a color.

scala media The middle chamber of the *cochlea* that lies between the *scala vestibuli* and *scala tympani* and contains the *organ of Corti.*

scala tympani The fluid-filled lower chamber of the *cochlea* that receives sound vibration from the *scala media* through the *basilar membrane;* pressure changes are relieved by the *round window.*

scala vestibuli The fluid-filled upper chamber of the *cochlea* that receives vibrations from the *oval window* through the *ossicles.*

Schwann cells See *neurolemma.*

sclera See *sclerotic coat.*

sclerotic coat The tough opaque white outer fibrous tissue that forms the white of the eyeball.

scotopic See *achromatic.*

scratch reflex Alternate flexion and extension of a hindlimb in scratching movements, stimulated by tickling the flank of an animal.

scrotum The sac that contains the testes, or *gonads,* in the male.

second harmonic See *first overtone.*

second motor area A topographically organized cortical motor area on the lateral surface of the precentral gyrus of the cerebral cortex.

secondary endings See *flower-spray endings.*

secondary qualities Mixtures of *primary qualities* within a sensory modality to produce a different sensation; such as, in vision, the mixture of red and yellow for an orange sensation.

second-order neuron The neuron that runs from the *first-order neuron (sensory neuron)* to a subcortical center such as the *thalamus.*

secretion The ability of a cell to manufacture a needed substance and supply it to the cell itself or to other cells; especially developed in *endocrine glands* and exocrine glands.

segment One section of any serially repeated structure.

selective permeability A property of the cell membrane that permits passage of some types of *ions* and molecules (chemicals) but not others because of their properties of size, charge, and so on.

semen Fluid output of the male sexual apparatus, containing *sperm* and glandular secretions.

semicircular canals The three semicircular membranous structures of the nonauditory *labyrinth* of each *inner ear;* a sensory apparatus for detecting rotary movements of the head.

seminal duct A structure that carries sperm from the *seminiferous tubules* to the prostate gland in the male sexual apparatus.

seminal vesicle A tube carrying *semen* to the *urethra* of the *penis* in the male.

seminiferous tubules Tubes in which *sperm* develop.

sensation The immediate impression that senses make on the brain as detected by the method of *introspection.*

sense organs *Organs* that are specialized to be irritable to a specific form of physical energy.

sensitizing stimulus Any aspect of a *need state* that arouses a *drive* in the *CNS.*

sensory appropriation Alteration of a cell into a *specialized receptor cell* because of its invasion by a sensory nerve fiber.

sensory deprivation Severe reduction in sensory input by experimental techniques.

sensory gating *Efferent* control of *afferent* sensory input.

sensory nerve A bundle of independently conducting nerve fibers connecting *receptors* with the *central nervous system.*

sensory neuron A single nerve cell connecting a *receptor* with the *CNS.*

sensory projection area Those parts of the *cerebral cortex* where pathways from the *receptors* terminate.

septal area See *septum.*

septum The anterior part of the *cingulate gyrus* that lies on the medial surface of each cerebral hemisphere in the longitudinal fissure.

sex linkage Pertaining to *genes,* contained in the *chromosomes,* that determine sex; physical characteristics of the individual and the genes he carries are determined by the same chromosomes that determine his sex.

sham rage Violent but brief attack responses in decorticate animals that are caused by the release of hypothalamic rage centers from cortical inhibition.

shape constancy The assumption that objects remain constant in shape and that apparent changes in shape are caused by a changed angle of regard.

shaping The rewarding of increasingly accurate approximations to the desired response in an operant conditioning situation. Escape from punishment can be used in a similar manner.

silent period The brief period of muscle relaxation that follows the *tendon jerk* reflex.

simple tone A tone whose pressure variations can be graphed as a *sine wave*.

simultaneous contrast Increase in the perceived intensity of a sensation of one *quality* caused by the simultaneous stimulation of another quality.

simultaneous induction Mutual enhancement of sensitivity to two sensory *qualities* that are stimulated simultaneously.

sine wave A function, similar to a horizontal s, that describes *periodic* phenomena such as the air pressure changes produced by a *simple tone*.

size constancy The assumption that objects remain constant in size and that any apparent size changes are caused by changes in the distance of the object from the observer.

slow component The slower of the back and forth eye movements of *rotational* or *postrotational nystagmus*.

smooth muscle The muscle that lines the walls of all hollow viscera except the heart—the arteries, intestines, stomach, and so on.

Snellen's test A test of visual acuity that determines the subject's ability to read letters of diminishing size at a distance of 20 feet.

SNS See *sympathetic division*.

SNS reactivity How readily the *SNS* is aroused by environmental stimuli; a measure of mobilization or general activation.

sodium ion (Na⁺) An element excluded from nerve cells. See *ion*.

somatic muscle See *striated muscle*.

somatotrophic hormone (STH) A hormone of the *adenohypophysis* (anterior pituitary gland) that controls body growth.

somesthesis Sensations from the skin and viscera of pressure, warmth, cold, and pain.

somesthetic projection area Area of the *cerebral cortex* that is the terminus of the nerve pathways for skin sensations.

sound pressure level (SPL) The minimum air pressure change at 1000 *Hz* that is just sensed as sound when the stimulus is presented by earphones.

spastic See *spastic paralysis*.

spastic paralysis Loss of motor control accompanied by exaggerated extensor tone; usually caused by damage to the *extrapyramidal system*.

special senses Receptors found only in the head.

specialized nerve cell A sensory neuron whose endings form a specialized sensory structure.

specialized receptor cell A cell, specialized for irritability to a particular form of physical energy, that stimulates a separate *sensory neuron*.

specific hunger Avidity for a specific substance needed by the body.

specific thalamic projection system (STPS) Classical and anatomically distinct sensory pathways for vision, hearing, and somesthesis.

spectrally opponent cells Cells of the lateral geniculate nucleus that are differentially sensitive to different wavelengths of light that stimulate the retina.

sperm Male reproductive cells.

sphincters Muscles that close off segments of the tubular viscera, as at the lower ends of the stomach, rectum, and bladder.

sphygmomanometer An instrument for measuring heart rate and blood pressure.

spike potential Explosive polarization reversal that carries the nerve impulse down the *axon* of the nerve cell.

spinal cord Ovoid mass of soft nervous and supporting tissue contained within the vertebral canal.

spinal nerves *Nerves* that originate in the *spinal cord*.

spinal nucleus of fifth nerve The nucleus of termination for sensory fibers of the *cranial nerves* serving temperature and pain.

spinal reflex A *reflex* mediated by the *spinal cord*.

spinal shock A syndrome (set of symptoms) that ensues when the *spinal cord* is severed; for example, all muscles receiving innervation from below the lesion lose tone and become flaccid because of lack of excitation from higher centers.

spinal tract of fifth nerve Tract of descending pain and temperature fibers from the *cranial nerves* that terminate in the *spinal nucleus of fifth nerve*.

spinocerebellar tracts Tracts that run from the *spinal cord* to the *cerebellum*.

spinothalamic system The afferent system of spinal *tracts* that serve pain, temperature, and crude pressure sensitivity.

spiral ganglion The *ganglion* near the cochlea that contains the cell bodies of *bipolar neurons,* which form the acoustic branch of the *statoacoustic nerve* (nerve VIII).

SPL See *sound pressure level*.

stage of exhaustion That period of the *stress syndrome* during which the animal's adjustment to the stress fails.

stapedius A muscle that pulls on the *stapes,* limiting the response of the middle ear bones to loud sounds in a *reflex* that prevents damage to the auditory apparatus.

stapes The *ossicle* of the chain of middle ear bones that conducts sound vibrations from the *incus* to the *oval window*.

statoacoustic nerve The *cranial nerve* serving the *organ of Corti* and the *vestibular senses* for hearing and balance, respectively.

stereochemical theory A theory about the effects of molecular shape; in olfaction, the theory that *primary* odor *qualities* depend on the shape or charge of the odorous molecules.

stereoscope A device for simulating a three-dimensional view by presenting to the two eyes pictures taken from different angles.

stereotaxic apparatus An instrument for stereotaxically placing the tip of an electrode in a known position in an animal's brain. The electrode is positioned by referral to a three-dimensional atlas of the brain.

STH See *somatotrophic hormone*.

stimulation Activation of *sense organs* or nervous tissue by any form of physical energy—mechanical, chemical, acoustical, photic, or electrical.

stimulus Any physical energy change that activates a *receptor*.

STPS See *specific thalamic projection system*.

stress Any stimulus, internal or external, that disturbs the dynamic equilibrium of the systems of the body.

stress syndrome Sequence of events that follows application of severe *stress* to an organism.

stress tolerance Individual ability to withstand *stress* without disability.

stressor A stimulus that causes *stress*.

stretch reflex Reflex contraction of a muscle to stretch of that muscle; a *monosynaptic* reflex induced by the *annulospiral endings* of the *muscle spindle*.

striated cortex See *visual projection area*.

striated muscles Muscles that move the body and limbs.

subcutaneous fat A layer of fat that lies just beneath the skin in mammals.

subnormal period The period of decreased sensitivity of the *axon* to stimulation; it accompanies the *positive afterpotential*, which follows the nerve impulse.

substrate Element(s) or molecule(s) that an *enzyme* interacts with in a chemical reaction.

successive contrast Increase in the perceived intensity of a *quality* caused by the prior stimulation of an opposite quality, such as increased sensitivity to a red hue after prolonged exposure to green.

successive induction When stimulation of one quality enhances sensitivity to a second quality,

presented after the first stimulus is removed; see *successive contrast*.

sulcus (plural, **sulci**) Surface folds that are found in the *cerebral cortex*.

summation The accumulative effects that occur when two stimuli produce a greater response than one, or when two or more stimuli give rise to an effective response in a receptor or nerve cell when one stimulus will not.

summation tone A perceived tone, created by *aural harmonics* when two *sine-wave* tones are sounded. The frequency of the summation tone is the sum of the frequencies of the two sine-wave tones.

superior colliculi (sing., **colliculus**) A pair of visual reflex centers found in the tectum (roof) of the midbrain.

supernormal period The period during the last part of the *negative afterpotential*, when the threshold of the *axon* is lower than normal.

supplementary motor area A topographically organized motor area of the *cerebral cortex*; it is buried in the *longitudinal fissure*.

suprasegmental Above the segmented portion of the *CNS*.

suspensory ligament The structure that attaches the *ciliary body* to the *lens* in the eye.

sympathetic chain ganglia Interconnected *ganglia* that lie on the bony vertebral column and receive excitation from the *spinal nerves*, send excitation to the *viscera*, and form part of the *sympathetic division* of the *ANS*.

sympathetic division A division of the *autonomic nervous system (ANS)* that innervates the *viscera* and diffusely prepares it for vigorous body arousal in emotional states.

sympathetic nervous system (SNS) See *sympathetic division*.

sympatheticoadrenal Involving the *SNS* and the *adrenal cortex* and *adrenal medulla*.

synapse Where the *terminal arborization* of one *neuron* meets the *dendrites* and *cell body* of another to transfer excitation from one nerve cell to another.

synaptic delay The time required for one neuron to stimulate another at a *synapse*.

synaptic knob The terminal knob on an *axon filament* that comes close to a *cell body* or *dendrite* to form a *synapse*.

synaptic vesicles Small globules in the *synaptic knobs* of *axon filaments* at *synapses*; they are believed to release a chemical transmitter in synaptic condition of excitation between nerve cells.

system A number of *organs*, anatomically and functionally arranged for the performance of a generalized function, such as the organs of the digestive system—stomach, intestines, and so on.

systemic circulation The system of blood vessels that carry blood to and from the heart and all tissues of the body except the lungs.

tactile disks Disk-shaped endings on sensory nerve filaments in the skin that seem to serve touch (light pressure).

target tissue Similarly specialized cells that are affected in a specific way by *hormones* of the *endocrine glands*.

taste bud A "moat and island" structure on the tongue that contains receptor cells for taste.

tectorial membrane The overlying membrane in which the *hair cell* endings of the *organ of Corti* are embedded.

temperature Change in the molecular activity of matter; sensed as warmth or cold.

temporal lobe The part of each *cerebral hemisphere* that lies below the *lateral fissure*.

tendon jerk A rapid muscle contraction (caused by the *stretch reflex* response) in response to a blow to the muscle's tendon.

tensor tympani A muscle that pulls on the *malleus* to tighten the *tympanum* in a protective reflex that limits the response of the middle ear bones to loud sounds.

terminal arborization Endings on the *axon* of a nerve cell.

terminal threshold That intensity of receptor stimulation in which the increase of stimulus intensity results in a change in sensation only 50% of the time; a statistical measure of the maximum response of a *receptor,* or *sense organ.*

testes Male *gonads* that produce reproductive cells and sex *hormones.*

tetany Muscle spasm.

thalamus A pair of egg-shaped masses of *nuclei* on the walls of the *diencephalon;* an integrating center that relays excitation to the sensory projection areas of the cerebral cortex.

thermal Pertaining to a change in heat or rate of molecular motion, especially as it affects temperature receptors to produce warmth and cold sensations.

third ventricle *Ventricle* of the *diencephalon.*

third-order neuron Any neuron that runs from subcortical centers such as the *thalamus* to a *sensory projection area,* usually in the cortex.

thoracic Pertaining to the area of the chest, thorax, or ribs.

threshold The least change in physical energy that will, on the average, affect the response of a receptor. Without a modifier, it usually refers to the *absolute threshold.*

thymus gland An organ behind the sternum whose function is the manufacturing of *lymphocytes* (white blood cells).

thyroid gland A paired endocrine gland in the neck, whose hormone, *thyroxin,* governs the metabolic rate of the body.

thyrotrophic hormone (TTH) The hormone of the *adenohypophysis* (anterior pituitary gland) that stimulates the *thyroid gland* to produce *thyroxin.*

thyroxin The hormone of the *thyroid gland* that determines the metabolic rate of all cells of the body.

timbre (pronounced tam′ber) Complex of *overtones* in a *complex tone* that enables the listener to recognize the source, such as the difference between a trumpet and a violin playing the same *fundamental* tone.

tinnitus A continuous ringing, tinkling, or buzzing sound in the ear caused by infections or other disorders of the auditory mechanism; not caused by an external stimulus.

tissue A collection of cells specialized for a common function, such as nervous tissue or muscle tissue.

tonal gap An auditory defect restricted to a certain *frequency* range.

tonal island A *frequency* range of relatively normal hearing surrounded by *tonal gaps.*

tonotopic See *tonotopic organization.*

tonotopic organization The organization of various nuclei of the auditory pathway so that points along the length of the *organ of Corti* that respond to tones of different *pitch* are spatially represented in an organized way.

topographic modality A sensory modality in which individual receptors and sensory neurons respond to a narrow range of stimuli. Stimulus change is signaled to the brain according to which receptors are responding; the inputs at the receptor, sensory pathways, and projection area are organized in an orderly spatial arrangement. See *nontopographic modality.*

topographical organization In neuroanatomy, an arrangement whereby stimulus inputs from different parts of the body arrive at corresponding points in brain centers, such as the *cerebral cortex.*

TOTE Test, operate, test, exit; according to one theory, the sequence of events occurring in recognition, in which sensory input is compared to memory content, and response (exit) follows recognition.

tract A bundle of axons carrying excitation from one part of the *CNS* to another.

tractus solitarius A *tract* of the brainstem that carries *first-order neurons* from the receptors serving taste.

tranquilizer Any drug that reduces arousal (anxiety) without a major anesthetic effect.

transcortical association The concept that areas of the *cerebral cortex* are interconnected in learning without involving subcortical nuclei.

transducer A structure, living or nonliving, that transforms one form of energy into another; *receptors* are transducers because they transform physical energy into nerve impulses.

transected Cut completely through.

transfer RNA Ribonucleic acid, patterned by *messenger RNA* in the ribosomes, that assembles amino acids into the enzymes necessary for cell specialization and repair.

transistor amplifier An electronic device for amplifying voltage changes, including those that can be detected in human tissue. The device uses transistors instead of vacuum tubes.

transitional cortex Areas of the cerebral cortex in the *longitudinal fissure* and elsewhere that are phylogenetically younger than *allocortex* but older than *neocortex*.

transmission deafness Defects in hearing caused by failure of the middle ear bones to accurately conduct to the *cochlea* the vibrations of the eardrum in response to sound.

transmit To pass through, as light is transmitted by a color filter.

trichromatism Normal or near-normal hue vision.

tritanopia An absence of perception of yellow and green hues.

trophotropic Pertaining to functions having to do with digestion, satiation, cell maintenance, and so on, controlled largely by the *PNS* centers of the *hypothalamus*.

TTH See *thyrotrophic hormone*.

tumor A mass of tissue formed by overproduction of cells in a specific location. Brain tumors are masses of tissue in the brain formed by overproduction of *glial cells*.

tuning fork A device, shaped like a two-tined fork, that produces a *simple tone* when struck.

turbinate bones Baffle-shaped formations in the nasal passages that cause eddy currents in inspired air.

two-phase hypothesis The hypothesis that learning occurs in two stages, such that immediate memory depends on *perseveration* of neural activity that lays down a permanent *engram (consolidation)*.

two-point threshold The closest together two points may be placed on the skin and still be distinguished by a subject as separate; used as an indicator of receptor density in the skin when sensitivity to pressure is being tested.

tympanum The eardrum; the membrane that closes off the inner end of the *external auditory meatus* and vibrates in response to the air pressure variations of sound.

unconditioned response (UR) A response reliably produced by an *unconditioned stimulus*.

unconditioned stimulus (US) A stimulus that reliably results in an *unconditioned response*.

unipolar neuron A nerve cell with both *axon* and *dendrite* arising from a single process of the *cell body*.

unique color One whose components cannot be visually detected (red, green, yellow, blue, black, white, or gray).

unique hues The four *chromatic primary qualities* of vision (red, green, yellow, and blue).

unspecialized nerve cell A sensory neuron whose receptor endings are an *anastomosis* of *free nerve endings*.

UR See *unconditioned response*.

urethra The output tube, leading from the bladder, that carries off the urine; it also serves as a genital duct in the male.

US See *unconditioned stimulus*.

uterus That part of the female reproductive apparatus in which the *embryo* develops.

utriculus A sensory apparatus of the *inner ear* that responds to head position and linear acceleration. See *sacculus*.

vacuum-tube amplifer An electronic device for amplifying voltage changes, including those detected in living tissue.

vagina Muscular tube that is penetrated in sexual intercourse and forms a passage between the *uterus* and the external orifice.

vago-insulin Involving stimulation of *insulin* output from the pancreas by the *vagus nerve;* used in referring to the *PNS*.

vagus nerve Tenth *cranial nerve,* which contains many fibers of the *autonomic nervous system*.

vascular Containing many blood vessels.

vasoconstrictor center A center in the *medulla* that excites constriction of arteries, thus raising blood pressure.

vasodilator center A center in the *medulla* that stimulates dilation of arteries to lower the blood pressure.

vasopressin A presumed hormone of the *neurohypophysis* (posterior pituitary gland) that raises the blood pressure by causing peripheral vasoconstriction; synonymous with *antidiuretic hormone*.

veins Blood vessels that return blood from the tissues to the heart.

ventral In man, toward the front, or "belly" side.

ventral cochlear nucleus One of two sensory nuclei

of the acoustic branch of the *statoacoustic nerve.* See *dorsal cochlear nucleus.*

ventral columns The *ventral* extension of the central *gray matter* of the *spinal cord* on each side of the midline.

ventral corticospinal tract A tract of the *ventral funiculus* of the spinal cord that originates in the *motor projection area* and terminates near the *motoneurons* of the cord.

ventral funiculus The part of the peripheral *white matter* of the *spinal cord* that lies between the *ventral roots* and the midline on each side of the cord.

ventral horns See *ventral columns.*

ventral ramus In the spinal cord, the ventral branch of the paired spinal nerves that arises from the junction of the *dorsal* and *ventral roots* and carries sensory and motor fibers to the front, ventral, or anterior (in man) part of the body.

ventral root In the spinal cord, the *ventral* termination of the paired *spinal nerves* at the spinal cord.

ventral spinothalamic tract Fibers that originate in the *spinal cord* form synapses with sensory fibers serving pressure, ascend the cord in the *ventral funiculus,* and join the *medial lemniscus* to end in the *thalamus.*

ventricle A large hollow area inside the brain.

ventrolateral nucleus A nucleus of the *thalamus* that integrates somesthetic input and distributes it to the somesthetic projection area of the cerebral cortex.

ventromedial nucleus A pair of *nuclei* in the hypothalamus that act as *satiety centers* to reduce eating behavior; destruction of these nuclei results in *hypothalamic hyperphagia.*

vertebra One of the individual jointed bones of the *vertebral column.*

vertebral column Jointed bony vertebrae (sing., *vertebra*) extending down the middorsal line of vertebrate animals, including man; the backbone.

vesicles Small globular inclusions, especially those in nerve endings at the *synapse* and *myoneural junction,* that are believed to contain a transmitter substance for exciting or inhibiting nerve and muscle cells.

vestibular nuclei Nuclei of the vestibular branch of the *statoacoustic nerve* (VIII); they excite extensor motoneurons and are inhibited by higher centers.

vestibular senses Sensory structures in the *labyrinth* of the *inner ear* that respond to head position and movement.

vestibular sensitivity Sensitivity of the balance, position, and movement receptors of the *inner ear.*

vestibulospinal tract A tract of the spinal cord that originates in the *vestibular nuclei* and ends on the extensor *motoneurons* of the cord.

vigilance A state of arousal.

villi Tufts of tissue in the *arachnoid layer* of the *meninges* extending into *dural sinuses* of the brain to reabsorb *cerebrospinal fluid* into the blood.

viscera Stomach, intestines, heart, bladder, arteries, and so on—the internal organs.

visceral Pertaining to the *viscera.*

visceral muscles Muscles that line the walls of the *viscera.*

visible spectrum Light; the visible part of the *electromagnetic spectrum* composed of seven colors.

vision Stimulation of the eye by light.

visual angle The angle subtended at the eye by light rays coming from an object.

visual projection area Area of the *cerebral cortex* that is the terminus of the nerve pathways for vision.

vitamin Any of a group of organic compounds whose accessory actions are necessary to the chemical reactions that support life.

vitamin D A *vitamin* that regulates calcium and phosphorus levels of the body.

vitreous humor The jellylike substance that fills the *fundus* of the eyeball.

volley theory A statement that the frequency of auditory nerve impulses follows the frequency of sound waves by means of nerve cells firing in alternation.

volt Amount of electrical charge (potential difference) that will result in a current of 1 ampere passing through a conductor with a resistance of 1 ohm.

volume The perceived size of a tone as a function of *pitch* and *loudness;* a measure of auditory *extent.*

wakefulness of choice The wakefulness of a *monophasic* sleep cycle that results from conditioning; a single waking period each day.

wakefulness of necessity Wakefulness resulting from bodily need or discomfort.

warmth An increase in temperature (molecular motion), especially as it stimulates the warmth receptors to result in sensations of warmth.

wavelength The measured length of a complete cycle of change in a periodic (repeated) phenomenon, such as the wavelength of the pressure variation of a tone or of the *electromagnetic spectrum* of a given light *frequency.*

Weber's law The generalization that there is a constant relation between the increase in stimulus intensity required to reach the *differential* *threshold* and the stimulus intensity from which the increase originates ($\Delta I/I = C$).

white matter Parts of the CNS containing nerve *tracts* with many myelinated *axons* (see *myelin sheath*). The fatty myelin sheath covering on axons gives a whitish appearance to the tissue.

white ramus The branch through which *pre-ganglionic* axons of the *SNS* leave the *spinal nerves.*

work decrement Reduction in work output.

Z line Krause's lines; connective tissue that invades *striated muscle* cells, thereby dividing each cell into segments.

References

Some references cover large areas of physiological psychology and were written by a single author or by multiple authors. These are listed initially as general references; their appropriateness to areas within physiological psychology will be evident from their titles. After this list, by chapter heading, appear secondary sources in which references to the original literature may be found. Such references include review articles, individually authored chapters in edited books, and books useful only in narrow areas of physiological psychology. Originally articles appear when they are of particular importance or are not mentioned in secondary sources.

GENERAL REFERENCES

Altman, J.: Organic foundations of animal behavior, New York, 1966, Holt, Rinehart & Winston, Inc.

Deutsch, J. A., and Deutsch, D.: Physiological psychology, Homewood, Ill., 1966, The Dorsey Press, Inc.

Geldard, F. A.: The human senses, ed. 2, New York, 1972, John Wiley & Sons, Inc.

Grossman, S. P.: A textbook of physiological psychology, New York, 1967, John Wiley & Sons, Inc.

Milner, P. M.: Physiological psychology, New York, 1970, Holt, Rinehart & Winston, Inc.

Thompson, R. F.: Foundations of physiological psychology, New York, 1967, Harper & Row, Publishers.

Wyburn, G. M.: The nervous system: An outline of the structure and function of the human nervous system and sense organs, New York, 1960, Academic Press Inc.

CHAPTER REFERENCES
Chapter 1

Bures, J., Petrán, M., and Zachar, J.: Electrophysiological methods in biological research, ed. 3, New York, 1967, Academic Press Inc.

Sidowski, J. B.: Experimental methods and instrumentation in psychology, New York, 1956, McGraw-Hill Book Co., Inc.

Suckling, E. E.: Bioelectricity, New York, 1961, McGraw-Hill Book Co., Inc.

Chapter 2

Barrai, I.: Human genetics and public health, WHO Chron. **24:**1-7, 1968.

Britten, R. J., and Davidson, E. H.: Gene regulation for higher cells: A theory, Science **165:**349-356, 1969.

Christian, J. J.: Social subordination, population density, and mammalian evolution, Science **168:**84-90, 1970.

Doty, P.: Translating the genetic code, J. Polymer Sci. **12:**235-248, 1966.

Glass, D. C., editor: Genetics, New York, 1968, The Rockefeller University Press.

Kessler, S., and Moos, R. H.: The XYY karyotype and criminality: A review, J. Psychiat. Res. **7:**153-170, 1970.

King, J. L., and Jukes, T. H.: Non-Darwinian evolution, Science **164:**788-798, 1969.

Ling, G. N.: A new model for the living cell: A summary of the theory and recent experimental evidence in its support, Int. Rev. Cytol. **26:**1-61, 1969.

Lorenz, K.: Evolution and modification of behavior, Chicago, 1965, University of Chicago Press.

Motulsky, A. G.: Human genetics, society, and medicine, J. Hered. **59:**329-336, 1968.

Nielsen, J., Tsuboi, T., Tuver, B., Jensen, J., and Sachs, J.: Prevalence and incidence of the XYY syndrome and Klinefelter's syndrome in an institution for criminal psychopaths, Acta Psychiat. Scand. **45:**402-424, 1969.

Oppenheimer, J. M.: Cells and organizers, Am. Zool. **10:**75-88, 1970.

Phillips, A. P.: Unwinding models for double-helical DNA during its replication and transcription, J. Theor. Biol. **24:**273-278, 1969.

Romer, A. S.: Major steps in vertebrate evolution, Science **158:**1629-1637, 1967.

Siegel, P. B.: Behavior-genetics, BioScience **20:**605-608, 1970.

Sinsheimer, R. L.: The prospect for designed genetic change, Am. Sci. **57:**134-142, 1969.

Spiess, E. B.: Experimental population genetics, Annu. Rev. Genet. **2:**165-208, 1968.

Spuhler, J. N., editor: Genetic diversity and human behavior, Chicago, 1967, Aldine Publishing Co.

Tomkins, G. M., Geleherter, T. D., Granner, D. M., Samuels, H. H. and Thompson, E. B.: Control of specific gene expression in higher organisms, Science **166:**1474-1480, 1969.

Chapter 3

Axelrod, J.: The pineal gland: A neurochemical transducer, Science **184:**1341-1348, 1974.

Bretscher, P., and Cohn, M.: A theory of self-nonself discrimination, Science **169:**1042-1049, 1970.

Diassi, P. A., and Horovitz, Z. P.: Endocrine hormones, Annu. Rev. Pharmacol. **10:**219-236, 1970.

Feder, H. H., and Whalen, R. E.: Feminine behavior in neonatally castrated and estrogen-treated male rats, Science **147:**306-307, 1965.

Gittes, R. F., and Irwin, G. L.: Thyroid and parathyroid roles in hypercalcemia: Evidence for a thyrocalcitron-releasing factor, Science **148:**737-739, 1965.

Gruenstein, E., and Wynn, J.: A molecular mechanism of action of thyroxin: Modification of membrane phospholipid by iodine, J. Theor. Biol. **26:**343-363, 1970.

Henzl, M. R., and Serge, E. J.: Physiology of human menstrual cycle and early pregnancy, a review of recent investigations, Contraception **1:**315-338, 1970.

Hoffman, R. A., and Ritter, R. J.: Pineal gland: Influence on gonads of male hamsters, Science **148:**1609-1611, 1965.

Hurwitz, S., Stacey, R. E., and Bronner, F.: Role of vitamin D in plasma calcium regulation, Am. J. Physiol. **216:**254-262, 1969.

Lee, J., and Knowles, F. G. W.: Animal hormones, London, 1965, Hutchinson & Co.

Lissak, K., and Edröczi, E.: Neuroendocrine interrelationships and behavioral processes. In Bajusz, E., and Jasmin, G., editors: Major problems in neuroendocrinology, New York, 1964, The Williams & Wilkins Co.

Loomis, W. F.: Skin-pigment regulation of vitamin-D biosynthesis in man, Science **157:**501-506, 1967.

Martini, L.: Action of hormones on the central nervous system, Gen. Comp. Endocrinol. supp. 2, pp. 214-226, 1969.

Mayhew, D. A., Wright, P. H., and Ashmore, J.: Regulation of insulin secretion, Pharmacol. Rev. **21:**183-212, 1969.

Moore, W. W.: General endocrinology: Hypophysis; endocrine functions of the pancreas; functions of the parathyroid glands; thyroidal physiology; the adrenal cortex; the endocrinology or reproduction. In Selkurt, E. E., editor: Physiology, Boston, 1963, Little, Brown & Co.

Nocenti, M. R.: Endocrine glands. In Mountcastle, V., editor: Medical physiology, vol. 1, part VI, ed. 12, St. Louis, 1968, The C. V. Mosby Co.

Quay, W. B.: Evidence for a pineal contribution in the regulation of vertebrate reproductive systems, Gen. Comp. Endocrinol., supp. 2, pp. 101-110, 1969.

Quay, W. B.: Endocrine effects of the mammalian pineal, Am. Zool. **10:**237-246, 1970.

Reiter, R. J., Hoffman, R. A., and Hester, R. J.: The role of the pineal gland and of environmental lighting in the regulation of the endocrine and reproductive systems of rodents, Edgewood Arsenal Techn. Rep. **4032:**1-51, 1966.

Reiter, R. J., and Sorrentino, S.: Reproductive effects of the mammalian pineal, Am. Zool. **10:** 247-258, 1970.

Smelik, P. G.: The regulation of ACTH secretion, Acta Physiol. Pharmacol. Neerl. **15:**123-135, June 1969.

Tepperman, J.: Metabolic and endocrine physiology, Chicago, 1962, Year Book Medical Publishers, Inc.

Turner, C. D., and Bagnara, J. T.: General endocrinology, ed. 5, Philadelphia, 1971, W. B. Saunders Co.

Chapter 4

Anden, N. E., Carlsson, A., and Häggendal, J.: Adrenergic mechanisms, Annu. Rev. Pharmacol. **9:**119-134, 1969.

Axelrod, J.: Noradrenaline: Fate and control of its biosynthesis, Science **173:**598-606, 1971.

Bajusz, E.: "Red" skeletal muscle fibers: Relative independence of neural control, Science **145:** 938-939, 1964.

Bodian, D.: Neurons, circuits, and neuroglia. In Quarton, G. C., Melnechuk, T., and Schmitt, F. O., editors: The neurosciences, a study program, New York, 1967, The Rockefeller University Press.

Brazier, M. A.: The electrical activity of the nervous system, ed. 2, London, 1960, Pitman Medical Publishing Co., Ltd.

Cook, W. A., and Cangiano, A.: Presynaptic inhibition of spinal motoneurons, Brain Res. **24:** 521-524, 1970.

Eccles, J. C.: Neuron physiology: Introduction. In Field, J., editor: Handbook of physiology, vol. 1, Baltimore, 1960, The Williams & Wilkins Co.

Eccles, J. C.: Ionic mechanism of postsynaptic inhibition, Science **145:**1140-1147, 1964.

Eccles, J. C.: The physiology of synapses, New York, 1964, Academic Press Inc.

Eccles, J. C.: Postsynaptic inhibition in the central nervous system. In Quarton, G. C., Melnechuk, T., and Schmitt, F. O., editors: The neurosciences, a study program, New York, 1967, The Rockefeller University Press.

Grossberg, S.: On the production and release of chemical transmitters and related topics in cellular control, J. Theor. Biol. **22:**325-364, 1969.

Guth, L.: "Trophic" influences of nerve on muscle, Physiol. Rev. **48:**645-687, 1968.

Hodgkin, A. L.: The conduction of the nervous impulse, Springfield, Ill., 1964, Charles C Thomas, Publisher.

Hodgkin, A. L.: The ionic basis of nervous conduction, Science **145:**1148-1154, 1964.

Huxley, A. F.: Excitation and conduction in nerve: Quantitative analysis, Science **145:**1154-1159, 1964.

Huxley, H. E.: The mechanism of muscular contraction, Science **164:**1356-1366, 1969.

Katz, B.: Quantal mechanism of neutral transmitter release, Science **173:**123-126, 1971.

Kopin, I. J.: The adrenergic synapse. In Quarton, G. C., Melnechuk, T., Schmitt, F. O., editors: The neurosciences, a study program, New York, 1967, The Rockfeller University Press.

Kravitz, E. A.: Acetylcholine, gamma-aminobutyric acid and glutamic acid: Physiological and chemical studies related to their roles as transmitter agents. In Quarton, G. C. Melnechuk, T., and Schmitt, F. O., editors: The neurosciences, a study program, New York, 1967, The Rockefeller University Press.

Lorente de No, R.: Continuous conduction of action potentials by peripheral myelineated fibers, Science **140:**383, 1963.

McLennan, H.: Synaptic transmission, ed. 2, Philadelphia, 1970, W. B. Saunders Co.

Nachmanson, D.: Proteins in excitable membranes, Science **168:**1059-1066, 1970.

Patton, H. D.: Spinal reflexes and synaptic transmission. In Ruch, T. C., Patton, H. D., Woodbury, J. W., and Towe, A. L., editors: Neurophysiology, ed. 2, Philadelphia, 1965, W. B. Saunders Co.

Roberts, E. D., Salganikoff, L., Zeiher, L. M., and Araiz, G. R.: Acetycholine and cholinacetylase content of synaptic vesicles, Science **140:**300-301, 1963.

Roberts, E. D.: Molecular biology of synaptic receptors, Science **171:**963-971, 1971.

Stevens, C. F.: Neurophysiology: A primer, New York, 1966, John Wiley & Sons, Inc.

Suckling, E. E.: Bioelectricity, New York, 1961, McGraw-Hill Book Co., Inc.

von Euler, U. S.: Adrenergic neurotransmitter function, Science **173:**202-206, 1971.

Woodbury, W. J., and Ruch, T. C.: Muscle. In Ruch, T. C., Patton, H. D., Woodbury, J. W., and Towe, A. L., editors: Neurophysiology, ed. 2, Philadelphia, 1965, W. B. Saunders Co.

Chapter 5

Brazier, M. A.: The growth of concepts relating to brain mechanisms, J. Hist. Behav. Sci. **1:**218-234, 1965.

Chusid, J. C., and McDonald, J. J.: Correlative neuroanatomy and functional neurology, ed. 13, Los Altos, Calif., 1967, Lange Medical Publications.

Hochwald, G. M., Wallenstein, M. C., and Mathews, E. S.: Exchange of proteins between blood and spinal subarachnoid fluid, Am. J. Physiol. **217:**348-353, 1969.

Kobayashi, H., and Libit, B.: Actions of noradrenalin and acetylcholine on sympathetic ganglion cells, J. Physiol. (London) **208:**353-372, 1970.

Kreig, W. J. S.: Functional neuroanatomy, ed. 2, New York, 1953, Blackiston Co.

Levin, E., and Scicli, G.: Brain barrier phenomena, Brain Res. **13:**1-12, March 1969.

Macchi, G.: Introductory statement about the thalamocortical connections, Arch. Ital. Biol. **107:**547-569, 1969.

Minckler, J.: Introduction to neuroscience, 1972, St. Louis, 1972, The C. V. Mosby Co.

Mountcastle, V. B., and Poggio, G. F.: Structural organization and general physiology of thalamotelencephalic systems. In Mountcastle, V. B., editor: Medical physiology, vol. 2, ed. 12, St. Louis, 1968, The C. V. Mosby Co.

Pappas, G. D.: Some morphological considerations of the blood-brain barrier, J. Neurol. Sci. **10:**241-246, 1970.

Quarton, G. C., Melnechuk, T., and Schmitt, F. O., editors: The neurosciences: A study program, New York, 1967, Rockefeller University Press.

Ranson, S. W., and Clark, S. L.: The anatomy of the nervous system: Its development and function, ed. 10, Philadelphia, 1959, W. B. Saunders Co.

Sanides, F.: Comparative architectonics of the neocortex of mammals and their evolutionary interpretation, Ann. N. Y. Acad. Sci. **167:**404-423, 1969.

Schmitt, F. O., editor: The neurosciences: Second study program, New York, 1970, Rockefeller University Press.

Truex, R. C., and Carpenter, M. B.: Strong

and Elwyn's Human neuroanatomy, ed. 6, Baltimore, 1969, The Williams & Wilkins Co.

Zimmerman, H. M.: Brain tumors: Their incidence and classification in man and their experimental production, Ann. N. Y. Acad. Sci. **159**:337-359, 1969.

Chapter 6

Broadbent, D. E.: Information processing in the nervous system, Science **150**:457-462, 1965.

Erickson, R. P.: Stimulus coding in topographic and nontopographic efferent modalities, Psychol. Rev. **75**:447-465, 1968.

Held, R., and Freedman, S. J.: Plasticity in human sensorimotor control, Science **142**:455-462, 1963.

Stevens, S. S.: Mathematics, measurement, and psychophysics. In Stevens, S. S., editor: Handbook of experimental psychology, New York, 1951, John Wiley & Sons, Inc.

Stevens, S. S.: Neural events and the psychophysical law, Science **170**:1043-1050, 1970.

Stevens, S. S.: The surprising simplicity of sensory metrics, Am. Psychol. **17**:29-39, 1962.

Uttal, W. R.: Emerging principles of sensory coding, Prospect. Biol. Med. **12**:344-368, 1969.

von Békésy, G.: Some similarities in sensory perception of fish and man. In Cahn, P., editor: Lateral line detectors, Bloomington, Ind., 1967, Indiana University Press.

von Békésy, G.: Mach band type lateral inhibition in different sense organs, Gen. Physiol. **50**:519-532, 1967.

von Békésy, G.: Location of maxima and minima in sensation patterns influence by lateral inhibition, J. Applied Physiol. **25**:200-206, 1968.

von Békésy, G.: Similarities of inhibition in the different sense organs, Am. Psychol. **24**:707-719, 1969.

von Békésy, G.: Inhibition as an important part of sensory perception, Laryngoscope **69**:1366-1386, 1969.

Woodworth, R. S., and Schlosberg, H.: Experimental psychology, rev. ed., New York, 1954, Henry Holt & Co., Inc.

Chapter 7

Able-Fessard, D.: Organization of central somatic projections. In Neff, W. D., editor: Contributions to sensory physiology, vol. 2, New York, 1967, Academic Press Inc.

Barber, T. H.: Toward a theory of pain, Psychol. Bull. **56**:430-460, 1959.

Becker, D. P., Gluck, H., Nelsen, F. E., and Jane, J. A.: An inquiry into the neurophysiological basis for pain, J. Neurosurg. **30**:1-13, Jan. 1969.

Bundinger, T. F., Bichsel, H., and Tobias, C. A.: Shock-induced pain and its reduction by concurrent tactile stimulation, Science **172**:866-870, 1971.

Corkin, S., Milner, B., and Rasmussen, T.: Somatosensory thresholds, Arch. Neurol. **23**:41-58, 1970.

Felix, D., and Wiesendanger, M.: Cortically induced inhibition in the dorsal column nuclei in monkeys, Pfluegers Arch. **320**:285-288, 1970.

Geldard, F. A.: Cutaneous channels of communication. In Rosenblith, W. A., editor: Symposium on principles of sensory communication, Cambridge, Mass., 1961, The Technology Press of the Massachusetts Institute of Technology.

Harrington, T., and Marzenich, M. M.: Neural coding in the sense of touch: Human sensations of skin indentation compared with the responses of slowly adapting mechano-receptive afferents innervating the hairy skin of monkeys, Exp. Brain Res. **10**:251-264, 1970.

Kenshalo, D. R., and Scott, H. A., Jr.: Temporal course of thermal adaptation, Science **151**:1095-1096, 1966.

Lim, R. S.: Pain mechanisms, Anesthesiology **28**:106-110, 1967.

Lindsley, D. F., Ranf, S. K., and Barton, R. J.: Corticifugal influences on reticular evoked activity in cats, Exp. Neurol. **34**:511-521, 1972.

Manfredi, M.: Modulation of sensory projections in anterolateral column of cat spinal cord by peripheral afferents of different size, Arch. Ital. Biol. **108**:72-105, 1970.

Mellon, D.: The physiology of sense organs, San Francisco, 1968, W. H. Freeman & Co., Publishers.

Melzack, R.: Effects of early experience on behavior: Experimental and conceptual considerations. In Psychopathology of perception, New York, 1965, Grune & Stratton, Inc.

Melzack, R., and Schecter, B.: Itch and vibration, Science **147**:1047-1048, 1965.

Melzack, R., and Wall, P.: Pain mechanism: A new theory, Science **150**:971-979, 1965.

Merzenich, M. M., and Harrington, T. H.: The sense of flutter-vibration evoked by stimulation of the hairy skin of primates: Comparison of human sensory capacity with the responses of mechanoreceptive afferents innervating the hairy skin of monkeys, Exp. Brain Res. **9**:236-260, 1969.

Mountcastle, V. B.: Physiology of sensory receptors: Introduction to sensory processes. In Mountcastle, V. B., editor: Medical physiology, vol. 2, ed. 12, St. Louis, 1968, The C. V. Mosby Co.

Mountcastle, V. B., and Darian-Smith, I.: Neural mechanisms in somesthesia. In Mountcastle, V.

B., editor: Medical physiology, vol. 2, ed. 12, St. Louis, 1968, The C. V. Mosby Co.

Price, D. D., and Wagman, I. H.: Physiological roles of A and C fiber inputs to the spinal dorsal horn of *Macaca mulatta,* Exp. Neurol. **29:**383-399, 1970.

Rose, J. E., and Mountcastle, V. B.: Touch and kinesthesis. In Field, J., editor: Handbook of physiology, vol. 1, Baltimore, 1960, The Williams & Wilkins Co.

Ruch, T. C.: Neural basis of somatic sensation. In Ruch, T. C., Patton, H. D., Woodbury, J. W., and Towe, A. L., editors: Neurophysiology, ed. 2, Philadelphia, 1965, W. B. Saunders Co.

Rushmer, R. F., Buettner, K. J., Short, J. M., and Odland, G. F.: The skin, Science **154:**343-348, 1966.

Schwartzman, R. J., and Bogdonoff, M. D.: Proprioception and vibration sensibility discrimination in the absence of the posterior columns, Arch. Neurol. **20:**349-353, 1969.

Simmel, M. L., and Shapiro, A.: The localization of nontactile thermal sensations, Psychophysiology **5:**415-425, 1969.

Sternbach, R. A.: Pain: A psychophysiological analysis, New York, 1968, Academic Press Inc.

Straile, W. E.: Vertical cutaneous organization, J. Theor. Biol. **24:**203-215, 1969.

Sweet, W. H.: Pain. In Field, J., editor: Handbook of physiology, vol. 1, Baltimore, 1960, The Williams & Wilkins Co.

Vierck, C. J., Jr., and Jones, M. B.: Size discrimination on the skin, Science **163:**488-489, 1969.

Wall, P. D., and Sweet, W. H.: Temporary abolition of pain in man, Science **155:**108-109, 1967.

Woolsey, C. N., and Fairman, D.: Contralateral, ipsilateral, and bilateral representation of cutaneous receptors in somatic areas I and II of the cerebral cortex of pig, sheep, and other mammals, Surgery **19:**684-702, 1946.

Zotterman, Y.: Thermal sensations. In Field, J., editor: Handbook of physiology, vol. 1, Baltimore, 1960, The Williams & Wilkins Co.

Chapter 8

Banker, B. Q., and Guron, J. P.: The ultrastructure features of the mammalian muscle spindle, J. Neuropath. Exp. Neurol. **30:**155-195, 1971.

Bard, P.: Postural coordination and locomotion and their central control. In Mountcastle, V. B., editor: Medical physiology, vol. 2, ed. 12, St. Louis, 1968, The C. V. Mosby Co.

Bridgeman, C. F., and Eldred, E.: Hypothesis for a pressure-sensitive mechanism in muscle spindles, Science **143:**481-482, 1964.

Buchwald, J. S., Standish, M., Eldred, E., and Halas, E. S.: Contribution of muscle spindle

circuits to learning as suggested by training under Flaxedil, Electroencephalogr. Clin. Neurophysiol. **16:**582-594, 1964.

Gernandt, B. E.: Vestibular mechanisms. In Field, J., editor: Handbook of physiology, vol. 1, Baltimore, 1960, The Williams & Wilkins Co.

Gottlieb, G. L., and Agarwal, G. C.: The role of the myotatic reflex in the voluntary control of movements, Brain Res. **40:**139-143, 1972.

Grillner, S., Hongo, T., and Lund, S.: Descending monosynaptic and reflex control of gamma motoneurons, Acta Physiol. Scand. **75:**592-613, 1969.

Guedry, F. E.: Psychophysiological studies of vestibular function. In Neff, W. D.: Contributions to sensory physiology, vol. 1, New York, 1965, Academic Press Inc.

Henneman, E.: Peripheral mechanisms involved in the control of muscles. In Mountcastle, V. B., editor: Medical physiology, vol. 2, ed. 12, St. Louis, 1968, The C. V. Mosby Co.

Ruch, T. C.: Pontobulbar control of posture and orientation in space. In Ruch, T. C., Patton, H. D., Woodbury, J. W., and Towe, A. L., editors: Neurophysiology, Philadelphia, 1965, W. B. Saunders Co.

Stuart, D. G., Goslow, G. E., Mosher, C. G., and Reinking, R. M.: Stretch control of Golgi tendon organs, Exp. Brain Res. **10:**463-476, 1970.

Wersall, J., and Flock, A.: Functional anatomy of the vestibular and lateral line organs. In Neff, W. D., editor: Contributions to sensory physiology, vol. 1, New York, 1965, Academic Press Inc.

Chapter 9

Adey, W. R.: The sense of smell. In Field, J., editor: Handbook of physiology, vol. 1, Baltimore, 1960, The Williams & Wilkins Co.

Amoore, J. E.: Current status of the stereochemical theory of odor, Ann. N. Y. Acad. Sci. **116:**457-476, 1964.

Anderson, H. T., and Hartmann, A. O.: A fifth modality of taste, Acta Physiol. Scand. **82:**447-452, 1971.

Brush, A. D., and Halpern, B. P.: Centrifugal control of gustatory responses, Physiol. Behav. **5:**743-746, 1970.

de Lorenzo, A. J. D.: The chemical senses: taste and olfaction. In Mountcastle, V. B., editor: Medical physiology, vol. 2, ed. 12, St. Louis, 1968, The C. V. Mosby Co.

Doetsch, G. S., and Erickson, R. P.: Synaptic processing of taste-quality information in the nucleus tractus solitarius of the rat, J. Neurophysiol. **33:**490-507, 1970.

Frank, M., and Pfaffman, C.: Taste nerve fibers:

A random distribution of sensitives to four tastes, Science **164:**1183-1185, 1969.

Gorman, W.: Flavor, taste, and the psychology of smell, Springfield, Ill., 1964, Charles C Thomas, Publisher.

Kalmus, H., and Hubbard, S. J.: The chemical senses in health and disease, Springfield, Ill., 1960, Charles C Thomas, Publisher.

Moncreiff, R. W.: The chemical senses, Cleveland, 1967, Chemical Rubber Co.

Mozell, M. M.: Evidence for a chromatographic model of olfaction, J. Gen. Physiol. **55:**46-73, 1970.

Patton, H. D.: Taste, olfaction and visceral sensation. In Ruch, T. C., Patton, H. D., Woodbury, J. W., and Towe, A. L., editors: Neurophysiology, ed. 2, Philadelphia, 1965, W. B. Saunders Co.

Pfaffman, C.: The sense of taste. In Field, J., editor: Handbook of physiology, vol. 1, Baltimore, 1960, The Williams & Wilkins Co.

Pfaffman, C.: Taste: Its sensory and motivating properties, Am. Sci. **52:**187-206, 1964.

Pfaffman, C.: De gustibus, Am. Psychol. **20:**21-33, 1965.

Sato, M.: Gustatory response as a temperature-dependent process. In Neff, W. D., editor: Contributions to sensory physiology, vol. 2, New York, 1967, Academic Press Inc.

Tucker, D., and Smith, J. C.: The chemical senses, Annu. Rev. Psychol. **20:**129-158, 1969.

von Békésy, G.: Duplexity theory of taste, Science **145:**834-835, 1964.

Wang, M. B., and Bernard, R. A.: Adaptation of neural taste responses in cat, Brain Res. **20:**277-282, 1970.

Chapter 10

Ades, H. W.: Central auditory mechanisms. In Field, J., editor: Handbook of physiology, vol. 1, Baltimore, 1960, The Williams & Wilkins Co.

Boudreau, J. C., and Tsuchitani, C.: Cat superior olive S-segment cell discharge to tonal stimulation. In Neff, W. D., editor: Contributions to sensory physiology, vol. 4, New York, 1970, Academic Press Inc.

Clopton, B. M., Winfield, J. A., and Flammio, F. J.: Tonotopic organization: Review and analysis, Brain Res. **24:**1-20, 1974.

Davis, H.: Excitation of auditory receptors. In Field, J., editor: Handbook of physiology, vol. 1, Baltimore, 1960, The Williams & Wilkins Co.

Davis, H., and Silverman, S. R., editors: Hearing and deafness, rev. ed., New York, 1962, Holt, Rinehart & Winston, Inc.

Eldredge, D. E., and Miller, J. D.: Physiology of hearing, Annu. Rev. Physiol. **33:**281-310, 1971.

Goldstein, M. H.: The auditory periphery. In

Mountcastle, V. B., editor: Medical physiology, vol. 2, ed. 12, St. Louis, 1968, The C. V. Mosby Co.

Green, D. M.: Audition, Annu. Rev. Psychol. **20:**105-128, 1969.

Harris, J. D., editor: Forty germinal papers in human hearing, J. Aud. Res., 1969.

Harrison, J. M., and Irving, R.: Visual and non-visual auditory systems in mammals, Science **154:**738-743, 1966.

Jeffers, L. A.: Detection and lateralization of binaural signals, Audiology **10:**77-84, 1971.

Lipscomb, D. M.: The increase in prevalence of high-frequency hearing impairment among college students, Audiology **11:**231-237, 1972.

Marsh, J. T., Wordon, F. G., and Smith, J. C.: Auditory frequency-following response: Neural or artifact? Science **169:**1222-1223, 1970.

Mountcastle, V. B.: Central neural mechanisms in hearing. In Mountcastle, V. B., editor: Medical physiology, vol. 2, ed. 12, St. Louis, 1968, The C. V. Mosby Co.

Rose, J. E., Brugge, J. F., Anderson, D. J., and Hind, J. E.: Phase-locked response to low-frequency tones in single auditory nerve fibers of the squirrel monkey, J. Neurophysiol. **30:**769-793, 1967.

Towe, A. L.: Audition and the auditory receptors. In Ruch, T. C., Patton, H. D., Woodbury, J. W., and Towe, A. L., editors: Neurophysiology, ed. 2, Philadelphia, 1965, W. B. Saunders Co.

von Békésy, G.: Traveling waves as frequency analyzers in the cochlea, Nature **225:**1207-1209, 1970.

Ward, W. D.: Susceptibility to auditory fatigue. In Neff, W. D., editor: Contributions to sensory physiology, vol. 3, New York, 1968, Academic Press Inc.

Webster, W. E., Dunlop, C. W., Simons, L. A., and Aitkin, L. M.: Auditory habituation: A test of a centrifugal and a peripheral theory, Science **148:**654-656, 1965.

Chapter 11

Arden, G. B.: Receptor potentials, Br. Med. Bull. **26:**125-129, May 1970.

Bartley, S. H.: Central mechanisms of vision. In Field, J., editor: Handbook of physiology, vol. 1, Baltimore, 1960, The Williams & Wilkins Co.

Bishop, P. O., and Henry, G. H.: Striate neurons: Receptive field concepts, Invest. Ophthalmol. **11:**346-354, 1972.

Brown, K. T.: Physiology of the retina. In Mountcastle, V. B.: editor: Medical physiology, vol. 2, ed. 12, St. Louis, 1968, The C. V. Mosby Co.

Brown, P. K., and Wald, G.: Visual pigments in single rods and cones of the human retina, Science **155:**273-279, 1967.

Chapanis, A.: Color names for color space, Am. Sci. **53:**327-346, 1965.

DeValois, R. L.: Behavioral and electrophysiological studies of primate vision. In Neff, W. D.: Contributions to sensory physiology, vol. 1, New York, 1965, Academic Press Inc.

DeValois, R. L.: Processing of intensity and wavelength information by the visual system, Invest. Ophthalmol. **11:**417-427, 1972.

Dimmik, F. L.: Color specification based on just noticeable differences of hue, Vision Res. **5:**679-694, 1965.

Dowling, J. E.: The site of visual adaptation, Science **155:**273-279, 1967.

Fatehchand, R., Laufer, M., and Svaetichin, G.: Retinal receptor potentials and their linear relationship to light intensity, Science **137:**666-667, 1962.

Fisher, K. D., Carr, J. E., and Huber, T. E.: Dark adaptation and night vision, Fed. Proc. **29:**1605-1638, 1970.

Glickstein, M.: Organization of the visual pathways, Science **164:**917-926, 1969.

Goldstein, E. B., and Berson, E. L.: Rod and cone contributions to the early receptor potential, Vision Res. **10:**207-218, 1970.

Gouras, P.: Color opponency from fovea to striate cortex, Invest. Ophthalmol. **11:**427-432, 1972.

Gouras, P.: Electroretinography: Some basic principles, Invest. Ophthalmol. **9:**557-569, 1970.

Granit, R.: Neural activity in the retina. In Field, J., editor: Handbook of physiology, vol. 1, Baltimore, 1960, The Williams & Wilkins Co.

Granit, R.: The development of retinal neurophysiology, Science **160:**1192-1196, 1968.

Hartline, H. K.: Vision-introduction. In Field, J., editor: Handbook of physiology, vol. 1, Baltimore, 1960, The Williams & Wilkins Co.

Hartline, H. K.: Visual receptors and retinal interaction, Science **164:**270-278, 1969.

Henry, G. H., and Bishop, P. O.: Striate neurons: Receptive field organization, Invest. Ophthalmol. **11:**554-368, 1972.

Humphrey, N. K.: What the frog's eye tells the monkey's brain, Brain Behav. Evol. **3:**324-337, 1970.

Ingling, C. R.: A tetrachromatic hypothesis for human color vision, Vision Res. **9:**1131-1148, 1969.

Lakowski, R.: Theory and practice of color vision testing, Br. J. Ind. Med. **26:**173-189, 1969.

Levinson, J. Z.: Flicker fusion phenomena, Science **160:**21-28, 1968.

Marks, W. B., Dobelle, W. H., and MacNichol, E. F.: Visual pigments in single primate cones, Science **143:**1181-1183, 1964.

Poggio, G. F.: Central nervous mechanisms in vision. In Mountcastle, V. B., editor: Medical physiology, vol. 2, ed. 12, St. Louis, 1968, The C. V. Mosby Co.

Ruch, T. C.: Vision. In Ruch, T. C., Patton, H. D., Woodbury, J. W., and Towe, A. L., editors: Neurophysiology, ed. 2, Philadelphia, 1965, W. B. Saunders Co.

Rypps, H.: Color vision, Annu. Rev. Psychol. **20:**193-215, 1969.

Schneider, G. E.: Two visual systems, Science **163:**895-902, 1969.

Steinberg, R. H.: Rod and cone distributions to S-potentials from the cat retina, Vision Res. **9:**1319-1329, 1969.

Steinberg, R. H.: Rod-cone interactions in S-potentials from the cat retina, Vision Res. **9:**1331-1344, 1969.

Steinberg, R. H., and Schmidt, R.: Identification of horizontal cells as S-potential generators in the cat retina by intracellular dye injection, Vision Res. **10:**817-820, 1970.

Svaetichin, G., and MacNichol, E. F.: Retinal mechanisms for chromatic and achromatic vision, Ann. N. Y. Acad. Sci. **74:**385-404, 1958.

Svaetichin, G., Negishi, K., and Fatehchand, R.: Cellular mechanisms of a Young-Hering visual system. In Wolstenholme, G. E., and Knight, J., editors: Ciba Foundation Symposium on physiology and psychology of color vision, London, 1965, J. & A. Churchill, Ltd.

Svaetichin, G., Negishi, K., Fatehchand, R., Drujan, B. D., and DeTesta, A. S.: Nervous function based on interaction between neuronal and nonneuronal elements. In DeRobertis, E. D. P., and Carrea, R., editors: Progress in brain research, vol. 15, New York, 1965, American Elsevier Publishing Co., Inc.

Wald, G.: The photoreceptor process. In Field, J., editor: Handbook of physiology, vol. 1, Baltimore, 1960, The Williams & Wilkins Co.

Wald, G.: The receptors of human color vision, Science **144:**1007-1016, 1964.

Wald, G.: Molecular basis of visual excitation, Science **162:**230-240, 1968.

Westheimer, G.: The eye. In Mountcastle, V. B., editor: Medical physiology, vol. 2, ed. 12, St. Louis, 1968, The C. V. Mosby Co.

Weymouth, F. W.: The eye as an optical instrument. In Ruch, T. C., Patton, H. D., Woodbury, J. W., and Towe, A. L., editors: Neurophysiology, ed. 2, Philadelphia, 1965, W. B. Saunders Co.

Chapter 12

Angel, R. W., Garland, H., and Alston, W.: Interaction of spinal and supraspinal mechanisms during voluntary innervation of human muscle, Exp. Neurol. **28:**230-242, 1970.

Barbeau, A.: Dopamine and disease, Can. Med. Assoc. J. **103:**824-832, 1970.

Cheifetz, D. I., Garron, D. C., Leavitt, F., Klawans, J. S., and Garvin, J. S.: Emotional disturbance accompanying the treatment of parkinsonism with L-dopa, Clin. Pharmacol. Ther. **12:** 56-61, 1971.

Coyle, J. T., and Snyder, S. H.: Antiparkinsonian drugs: Inhibition of dopamine uptake in the corpus striatum as a possible mechanism of action, Science **166:**899-901, 1969.

Delgado, J. M. R.: Sequential behavior induced repeatedly by stimulation of the red nucleus in free monkeys, Science **148:**1361-1363, 1965.

Eccles, J. C.: The development of the cerebellum in relation to the control of movement, Naturwissenschaften **56:**525-534, 1969.

Fuxe, K., Goldstein, M., and Ljungdahl, A.: Antiparkinsonian drugs and central dopamine neurons, Life Sci. **9:**811-824, 1970.

Gottlieb, G. L., Agarwal, G. C., and Stark, L.: Interaction between voluntary and postural mechanisms of the human motor system, J. Neurophysiol. **33:**365-381, 1970.

Grillner, S., Hongo, T., and Lund, S.: Descending monosynaptic and reflex control of gamma motoneurons, Acta Physiol. Scand. **75:**592-613, 1969.

Ioku, M., Ribera, V. A., Cooper, I. S., and Matsuoka, S.: Parkinsonism: Electromyographic studies of monosynaptic reflex, Science **150:** 1472-1475, 1965.

Krieg, W. J. S.: Functional neuroanatomy, ed. 2, New York, 1953, Blackiston Co.

Lawrence, D. G., and Henricus, D. G.: Pyramidal and nonpyramidal pathways in monkeys: Anatomical and functional correlation, Science **148:** 973-975, 1965.

Mendell, L. M., and Wall, P. D.: Presynaptic hyperpolarization: A role for fine afferent fibers, J. Physiol. **172:**274-294, 1964.

O'Malley, W. E., editor: Pharmacologic and clinical experiences with levodopa: A symposium, Neurology **20:**1-66, 1970.

Patton, H. D.: Reflex regulation of movement and posture. In Ruch, T. C., Patton, H. D., Woodbury, J. W., and Towe, A. L., editors: Neurophysiology, ed. 2, Philadelphia, 1965, W. B. Saunders Co.

Poppele, R. E., and Terzuolo, C. A.: Myotatic reflex: Its input-output relation, Science **159:** 743-745, 1968.

Ruch, T. C.: Basal ganglia and cerebellum. In Ruch, T. C., Patton, H. D., Woodbury, J. W., and Towe, A. L., editors: Neurophysiology, ed. 2, Philadelphia, 1965, W. B. Saunders Co.

Ruch, T. C.: The cerebral cortex: Its structure and motor functions. In Ruch, T. C., Patton, H. D., Woodbury, J. W., and Towe, A. L., editors:

Neurophysiology, ed. 2, Philadelphia, 1965, W. B. Saunders Co.

Ruch, T. C.: Pontobulbar control of posture and orientation in space. In Ruch, T. C., Patton, H. D., Woodbury, J. W., and Towe, A. L., editors: Neurophysiology, ed. 2, Philadelphia, 1965, W. B. Saunders Co.

Chapter 13

Geshwind, N.: The organization of language and the brain, Science **170:**940-944, 1969.

Isaacson, R. L.: The limbic system, New York, 1974, Plenum Press.

Lindsley, D. B.: Attention, consciousness, sleep and wakefulness. In Field, J., editor: Handbook of physiology, vol. 3, Baltimore, 1960, The Williams & Wilkins Co.

McCleary, R. A., and Moore, R. Y.: Subcortical mechanisms of behavior, New York, 1965, Basic Books, Inc., Publishers.

Magoun, H. W.: The waking brain, ed. 2, Springfield, Ill., 1963, Charles C Thomas, Publisher.

Papez, J. W.: Comparative neurology, New York, 1929, Hafner Publishing Co.

Patton, H. D.: Reflex regulation of movement and posture. In Ruch, T. C., Patton, H. D., Woodbury, J. W., and Towe, A. L., editors: Neurophysiology, ed. 2, Philadelphia, 1965, W. B. Saunders Co.

Pribram, K. H., and Kruger, L.: Functions of the "olfactory brain." In Isaacson, R. L., editor: Basic readings in neuropsychology, New York, 1964, Harper & Row, Publishers.

Ruch, T. C.: The basal ganglia and cerebellum. In Ruch, T. C., Patton, H. D., Woodbury, J. W., and Towe, A. L., editors: Neurophysiology, ed. 2, Philadelphia, 1965, W. B. Saunders Co.

Ruch, T. C.: The cerebral cortex: Its structure and motor function. In Ruch, T. C., Patton, H. D., Woodbury, J. W., and Towe, A. L., editors: Neurophysiology, ed. 2, Philadelphia, 1965, W. B. Saunders Co.

Ruch, T. C.: Pontobulbar control of posture and orientation in space. In Ruch, T. C., Patton, H. D., Woodbury, J. W., and Towe, A. L., editors: Neurophysiology, ed. 2, Philadelphia, 1965, W. B. Saunders Co.

Smythies, J. R.: The neurological foundations of psychiatry, New York, 1966, Academic Press Inc.

von Bonin, G.: Essay on the cerebral cortex, Springfield, Ill., 1950, Charles C Thomas, Publisher.

Warren, J. M., and Alsert, K., editors: The frontal granular cortex and behavior, New York, 1964, McGraw-Hill Book Co.

Chapter 14

Aserinsky, E.: Drugs and dreams, a synthesis, Exp. Med. Surg. **25**:131-138, 1967.

Banquet, J. P.: Spectral analysis of the EEG in meditation, Electroencephalogr. Clin. Neurol. **35**:143-151, 1973.

Beh, H. C., and Barratt, P. E. H.: Discrimination and conditioning during sleep as indicated by the electroencephalograph, Science **147**:1470-1471, 1965.

Broughton, R. J.: Sleep disorders: Disorders of arousal? Science **159**:1070-1078, 1968.

Gellhorn, E., and Kiely, W.: Mystical states of consciousness: Neurophysiological and clinical aspects, J. Nerv. Ment. Dis. **154**:339-405, 1972.

Grosser, G. S., and Siegel, A. W.: Emergence of a tonic-phasic model for sleep and dreaming: Behavioral and physiological observations, Psychol. Bull. **75**:60-72, 1971.

Hösli, L.: Dialysis of sleep and waking factors in blood of the rabbit, Science **146**:796-798, 1964.

Iskander, T. N., and Kaelbling, R.: Catecholamines, a dream sleep model, and depression, Am. J. Psychiat. **127**:43-50, 1970.

Johnson, L. C: A psychophysiology for all states, Psychophysiology **6**:501-516, 1970.

Johnson, L. C., Burdick, J. A., and Smith, J.: Sleep during alcohol intake and withdrawal in the chronic alcoholic, Arch. Gen. Psychiat. **22**:406-418, 1970.

Jouvet, M.: Neurophysiology of the states of sleep, Physiol. Rev. **47**:117-177, 1967.

Jouvet, M.: Biogenic amines and the states of sleep, Science **163**:32-41, 1969.

Karczmar, A. G., Longo, V. G., and de Carolis, A. S.: A pharmacological model of paradoxical sleep: The role of cholinergic and monoamine systems, Physiol. Behav. **5**:175-182, 1970.

Kleitman, N.: Sleep and wakefulness, Chicago, 1963, University of Chicago Press.

Kollar, E. J., Pasnau, R. O., Rubin, R. T., Naitoh, P., Slater, G. G., and Kales, A.: Psychological, psychophysiological, and biochemical correlates of prolonged sleep deprivation, Am. J. Psychiat. **126**:488-497, 1969.

Lenard, H. G.: Sleep studies in infancy, Acta Paediatr. Scand. **59**:572-581, 1970.

Malmo, R. B.: Activation: A neuropsychological dimension, Psychol. Rev. **66**:367-386, 1959.

Mandell, A. J., and Mandell, M. P.: Peripheral hormonal and metabolic correlates of rapid eye movement sleep, Exp. Med. Surg. **27**:224-236, 1969.

Monnier, M., Hatt, A., Cueni, L., and Schoenenberger, G.: Humoral transmission of sleep, Pfluegers Arch. **331**:257-265, 1972.

Morruzzi, G.: Sleep and instinctive behavior, Arch. Ital. Biol. **107**:175-216, 1969.

Murray, E. J.: Sleep, dreams and arousal, New York, 1965, Appleton-Century-Crofts.

Orme-Johnson, D.: Autonomic stability and transcendental meditation, Psychosom. Med. **35**:341-349, 1973.

Oswald, I.: Human brain protein, drugs, and dreams, Nature **223**:893-897, 1969.

Pasnau, R. O., Naitoh, P., Stier, S., and Kollar, E. J.: The psychological effects of 205 hours of sleep deprivation, Arch. Gen. Psychiat. **18**:496-505, 1968.

Pivik, T., and Dement, W. C.: Phasic changes in muscular and reflex activity during non-REM sleep, Exp. Neurol. **27**:115-124, 1970.

Roberts, W. W., and Robinson, T. C.: Relaxation and sleep induced by warming of preoptic region and anterior hypothalamus in cats, Exp. Neurol. **25**:282-293, 1969.

Roffwarg, H. P., Muzio, J. N., and Dement, W. C.: Ontogenetic development of the human sleep-dream cycle, Science **152**:604-619, 1966.

Siegel, P. V., Gerathewohl, S. J., and Mohler, S. R.: Time-zone effects, Science **164**:1249-1255, 1969.

Vanderlaan, W., Parker, D., Rossman, L., and Vanderlaan, E.: Implications of growth hormone release in sleep, Metabolism **19**:891-897, 1970.

Wallace, R. K.: Physiological effects of transcendental meditation, Science **167**:1751-1754, 1970.

Wallace, R., Benson, H., and Wilson, A.: A wakeful hypometabolic physiologic state, Am. J. Physiol. **221**:795-799, 1971.

Weitzman, E. D., Kripke, D. F., Goldmacher, D., McGregor, P., and Nogeire, C.: Acute reversal of the sleep-walking cycle in man. Effect on sleep stage patterns, Arch. Neurol. **22**:483-489, 1970.

Williams, H. L.: The new biology of sleep, J. Psychiatr. Res. **8**:445-478, 1971.

Chapter 15

Albert, D. J., Storlien, L. H., Wood, D. J., and Ehman, G.: Further evidence for a complex system controlling feeding behavior, Physiol. Behav. **5**:1075-1082, 1970.

Blatt, B., and Lyon, M.: The interrelationship of forebrain and midbrain structures involved in feeding behavior, Acta Neurol. Scand. **44**:576-595, 1968.

Epstein, A., Kissileff, H., and Stellar, E., editors: The neuropsychology of thirst, New York, 1973, Halsted Press, John Wiley & Sons.

Heath, R. G.: Electrical self-stimulation of the

brain in man, Am. J. Psychiat. **120**:571-577, 1963.

Hebb, D. O.: Drives and the C.N.S. (conceptual nervous system), Psychol. Rev. **62**:243-254, 1955.

Hetherington, A. W., and Ranson, S. W.: Hypothalamic lesions and adiposity in the rat. In Isaacson, R. L., editor: Basic readings in neuropsychology, New York, 1964, Harper & Row, Publishers.

Hoebel, B.: Feeding: Neural control of intake, Annu. Rev. Psychol. **33**:533-568, 1971.

Holman, G. L.: Intragastric reinforcement effect, J. Comp. Physiol. Psychol. **69**:432-441, 1969.

Jordan, H. A.: Voluntary intragastric feeding: Oral and gastric contributions to food intake and hunger in man, J. Comp. Physiol. Psychol. **68**:498-506, 1969.

Leung, P. M., and Rogers, Q. R.: Food intake: Regulation by plasma amino acid pattern, Life Sci. **8**:1-9, 1969.

Margules, D. L.: Noradrenergic basis of inhibition between reward and punishment in amygdala, J. Comp. Physiol. Psychol. **66**:329-334, 1968.

Margules, D. L.: L-Norepinephrine: A possible synaptic transmitter for the suppression of feeding behavior by satiety. Proceedings of the seventy-seventh American Psychological Association Convention, pp. 205-206, 1969.

Margules, D. L., and Steir, L.: Cholinergic synapses of a perventricular punishment system in the lateral hypothalamus, Am. J. Physiol. **217**:475-480, 1969.

Miller, N. E.: Chemical coding of behavior in the brain, Science **148**:328-338, 1965.

Olds, J., and Milner, P.: Positive reinforcement produced by electrical stimulation of septal area and other regions of rat brain. In Isaacson, R. L., editor: Neuropsychology, New York, 1964, Harper & Row, Publishers.

Olds, J., Travis, R. P., and Schwing, R. C.: Topographical organization of self-stimulation functions, J. Comp. Physiol. Psychol. **53**:23-32, 1960.

Reynolds, R. W.: Hypothalamic lesions and disinhibition of feeding, Science **150**:1322, 1965.

Saint-Laurent, J., and Beaugrand, J.: Brain stimulation, reinforcement, and behavior, Rev. Can. Biol. **31**(supp.):193-213, 1972.

Samuels, I.: Reticular mechanisms and behavior, Psychol. Bull. **56**:1-25, 1959.

Schacter, S.: Obese humans and rats, New York, 1974, Halsted Press, John Wiley & Sons.

Schacter, S.: Some extraordinary facts about obese humans and rats, Am. Psychol. **26**:129-143, 1970.

Smith, O. A.: The physiologic basis of motivation. In Ruch, T. C., Patton, H. D., Woodbury, J. W., and Towe, A. L., editors: Neurophysiology, ed. 2, Philadelphia, 1965, W. B. Saunders Co.

Stein, L.: Chemistry of reward and punishment, Psychopharmacologia **8**:105-123, 1970.

Stellar, E.: Drive and motivation. In Field, J., editor: Handbook of physiology, vol. 3, Baltimore, 1960, The Williams & Wilkins Co.

Stellar, E.: The physiology of motivation. In Isaacson, R. L., editor: Neuropsychology, New York, 1964, Harper & Row, Publishers.

Stellar, E.: Hunger in man: Comparative and physiological studies, Am. Psychol. **22**:105-117, 1967.

Teitelbaum, P., Cheng, M., and Rozin, P.: Development of feeding parallels its recovery after hypothalamic damage, J. Comp. Physiol. Psychol. **67**:430-441, 1969.

Teitelbaum, P., and Cytawa, J.: Spreading depression and recovery from lateral hypothalamic damage, Science **147**:61-63, 1965.

Teitelbaum, P., and Epstein, A.: The lateral hypothalamic syndrome, Psychol. Rev. **69**:74-90, 1962.

Tralor, R. A., and Blackburn, J. G.: Effects of temperature on the electrical activity of hypothalamic feeding centers, Exp. Neurol. **23**:91-101, 1969.

Trowill, J. A., Panksepp, J., and Gandelman, R.: An incentive model of rewarding brain stimulation, Psychol. Rev. **76**:264-281, 1969.

Valenstein, E. S., Cox, V. C., and Kakolewski, J. W.: Reexamination of the role of the hypothalamus in motivation, Psychol. Rev. **77**:16-31, 1970.

Wurtz, R. H., and Olds, J.: Amygdaloid stimulation and operant reinforcement in the rat, J. Comp. Physiol. Psychol. **56**:941-949, 1963.

Chapter 16

Arnold, M. B.: Physiological differentiation of emotional states, Psychol. Rev. **52**:35-48, 1945.

Arnold, M. B.: In defense of Arnold's theory of emotion, Psychol. Bull. **70**:283-284, 1968.

Arnold, M. B.: Emotion, motivation, and the limbic system, Ann. N. Y. Acad. Sci. **159**:1041-1058, 1969.

Bard, P., and Mountcastle, V. B.: Some forebrain mechanisms involved in expression of rage with special reference to suppression of angry behavior. In Isaacson, R. L., editor: Neuropsychology, New York, 1964, Harper & Row, Publishers.

Bindra, D.: A unified interpretation of emotion and motivation, Ann. N. Y. Acad. Sci. **159**:1071-1083, 1969.

Brady, J. V.: Emotional behavior. In Field, J.,

editor: Handbook of psychology, vol. 3, Baltimore, 1960, The Williams & Wilkins Co.

Brady, J., and Nauta, W.: Subcortical mechanisms in emotional behavior: Affective changes following septal forebrain lesions in the albino rat, J. Comp. Physiol. Psychol. **46:**339-346, 1953.

Fehr, F. S., and Stern, J. A.: Peripheral physiological variables and emotion: the James-Lange theory revisited, Psychol. Bull. **74:**411-424, 1970.

Flynn, J.: The neural basis of aggression in cats. In Glass, D., editor: Neurophysiology and emotion, New York, 1967, Rockefeller University Press.

Flynn, J., Venegas, H., Foot, W., and Edwards, S.: Neural mechanisms involved in a cat's attack on a rat. In Whalen, R. T., Thompson, R., Verezano, M., and Weinberger, M., editors: The neural control of behavior, New York, 1970, Academic Press Inc.

Freeman, G. L.: Physiological psychology, New York, 1948, D. Van Nostrand Co., Inc.

Freeman, W., and Watts, J.: Psychosurgery, Springfield, Ill., 1942, Charles C Thomas, Publishers.

Fulton, J., and Jacobsen, C.: The functions of the frontal lobes: A comparative study in monkeys, chimpanzees, and man, Adv. Mod. Biol. **4:**113-123, 1935.

Gellhorn, E.: Prolegomena to a theory of the emotions, Perspect. Biol. Med. **4:**403-436, 1961.

Gellhorn, E.: Motion and emotion: The role of perception in the physiology and pathology of the emotions, Psychol. Rev. **71:**457-472, 1964.

Gellhorn, E.: The neurophysiological basis of anxiety: A hypothesis, Perspect. Biol. Med. **8:**488-515, 1965.

Goddard, G. V.: Functions of the amygdala, Psychol. Bull. **62:**89-109, 1964.

Goldstein, M. L.: Physiological theories of emotion: A critical historical review from the standpoint of behavior theory, Psychol. Bull. **69:**23-40, 1968.

Grastyán, E.: Towards a better understanding of human emotion, Impact Sci. Soc. **18:**187-204, 1968.

Hess, W., and Akart, K.: Experimental data on the role of the hypothalamus in mechanisms of emotional behavior, Arch. Neurol. Psychiatry **73:**127-129, 1955.

Hohman, G.: Some effects of spinal cord lesions on experienced emotional feelings, Psychophysiology **3:**143-156, 1966.

Isaacson, R.: Hippocampal destruction in man and other animals, Neuropsychologia **10:**47-64, 1972.

Kaada, B., Anderson, P., and Jansen, J.: Stimulation of amygdaloid nuclear complex in unanesthetized cats, Neurology **4:**48-64, 1954.

Kaplan, H.: The new sex therapy, New York, 1974, Bruner/Mazel, Inc.

Kievet, J., and Kuypers, H.: Basal forebrain and hypothalamic connection to frontal and parietal cortex in the Rhesus monkey, Science **187:**660-662, 1975.

Kinsey, A., Pomeroy, W., and Martin, C.: Sexual behavior in the male, Philadelphia, 1948, W. B. Saunders Co.

Kinsey, A., Pomeroy, W., Martin, C., and Gebhard, P.: Sexual behavior in the female, Philadelphia, 1953, W. B. Saunders Co.

Levine, S., and Brush, R.: Adrenocortical activity and avoidance learning as a function of time after avoidance training, Physiol. Behav. **2:**385-388, 1967.

Lindsley, D. B.: Emotion. In Stevens, S. S., editor: Handbook of experimental psychology, New York, 1951, John Wiley & Sons, Inc.

McCleary, R. A.: Response-modulating functions of the limbic system: Initiation and suppression. In Stellar, E., and Sprague, J. M., editors: Progress in physiological psychology, vol. 1, New York, 1966, Academic Press Inc.

MacLean, P. D.: Psychosomatic disease and the visceral brain: Recent developments bearing on the Papez theory of emotion. In Isaacson, R. L., editor: Neuropsychology, New York, 1964, Harper & Row, Publishers.

Masters, W., and Johnson, V.: Human sexual response, Boston, 1966, Little, Brown & Co.

Melzack, R.: The role of early experience in emotional arousal, Ann. N. Y. Acad. Sci. **159:**721-730, 1969.

Mettler, F. A., editor: Psychosurgical problems, New York, 1952, The Blackiston Co.

Money, J., and Ehrhardt, A.: Man and woman, boy and girl, Baltimore, 1972, Johns Hopkins Press.

Olds, J.: Emotional centers in the brain, Science **156:**87-92, 1967.

Papez, J. W.: A proposed mechanism of emotion. In Isaacson, R. L., editor: Neuropsychology, New York, 1964, Harper & Row, Publishers.

Pribram, K. H.: The new neurology and the biology of emotion: A structural approach, Am. Psychol. **22:**830-838, 1967.

Pribram, K. H., and Krüger, L.: Functions of the olfactory brain. In Isaacson, R. L., editor: Neuropsychology, New York, 1964, Harper & Row, Publishers.

Reis, D., and Lars-Magnus, G.: Brain catecholamines: Relation to the defense reaction evoked by amygdaloid stimulation in cat, Science **149:**450-451, 1965.

Ruch, T. C.: Neurophysiology of emotion. In Ruch, T. C., Patton, H. D., Woodbury, J. W., and Towe, A. L., editors: Neurophysiology, ed. 2, Philadelphia, 1965, W. B. Saunders Co.

Schlosberg, H.: Three dimensions of emotion, Psychol. Bull. **62**:89-109, 1964.

Schreiner, L., and Kling, A.: Behavioral changes following rhinencephalic injury in the cat. In Isaacson, R. L., editor: Neuropsychology, New York, 1964, Harper & Row, Publishers.

Simon, A., Herbert, C. C., and Strauss, R., editors: The physiology of emotions, Springfield, Ill., 1961, Charles C Thomas, Publisher.

Terzian, H., and Ore, G.: Syndrome of Klüver and Bucy reproduced in man by bilateral removal of the temporal lobes, Neurology **5**:373-380, 1955.

Webb, W. B.: A motivational theory of emotions, Psychol. Rev. **55**:329-335, 1948.

Wenger, M. A.: Emotion as visceral activation: An extension of Lange's theory. In Reymert, M. L., editor: Feelings and emotions: The Moosehart symposium, New York, 1950, McGraw-Hill Book Co., Inc.

Wenger, M. A.: Studies of autonomic balance: A summary, Psychophysiology **2**:173-186, 1966.

Chapter 17

Asrantian, E. A.: Compensatory adaptations, reflex activity, and the brain, New York, 1965, Pergamon Press, Inc.

Bartlett, F., and John, E.: Equipotentiality quantified: The anatomical distribution of the engram, Science **181**:764-767, 1973.

Bennett, E. L., Diamond, M. C., Krech, D., and Rosensweig, M. R.: Chemical and anatomical plasticity of brain, Science **146**:610-619, 1964.

Black, A. H.: The direct control of neural processes by reward and punishment, Am. Sci. **59**:236-245, 1971.

Bogoch, S.: The biochemistry of memory, New York, 1968, Oxford University Press, Inc.

Briggs, M. H., and Kitto, G. B.: The molecular basis of learning and memory, Psychol. Rev. **69**:537-541, 1962.

Byrne, W. L.: Molecular approaches to learning and memory, New York, 1970, Academic Press Inc.

Carew, T. J., Crow, T. J., and Petrinovich, L. F.: Some problems with the technique of cortical spreading depression. Paper presented at the 1970 Western Psychological Association Convention, Los Angeles, Calif., Dec. 30, 1970.

Deutsch, J. A.: The physiological basis of memory, Annu. Rev. Psychol. **20**:85-104, 1969.

Deutsch, J. A., Hamburg, M. D., and Dahl, H.: Acetylcholinesterase-induced amnesia and its temporal aspects, Science **151**:221-223, 1966.

Doty, R., Negras, N., and Yamaga, K.: The unilateral engram, Acta Neurobiol. Exp. **33**:711-728, 1973.

Duncan, C. P.: The retroactive effects of shock on learning, J. Comp. Physiol. Psychol. **42**:32-34, 1949.

Fishbein, W.: Interference with conversion from short-term to long-term storage by partial sleep deprivation Comm. Behav. Biol. **5**:171-175, 1970.

Fishbein, W., McGaugh, J. L., and Swarz, J. R.: Retrograde amnesia: Electroconvulsive shock effects after termination of rapid eye movement sleep deprivation, Science **172**:80-82, 1971.

Gabor, D.: Holography, 1948-1971, Science **177**:299-313, 1972.

Gaito, J.: A biochemical approach to learning and memory, Psychol. Rev. **68**:285-292, 1961.

Gaito, J.: DNA and RNA as memory molecules, Psychol. Rev. **70**:471-480, 1963.

Gaito, J., editor: Macromolecules and behavior, New York, 1966, Appleton-Century-Crofts.

Gaito, J., and Zavala, A.: Neurochemistry and learning, Psychol. Bull. **61**:45-61, 1964.

Galambos, R., and Morgan, C. T.: The neural basis of learning. In Field, J., editor: Handbook of physiology, vol. 3, Baltimore, 1960, The William & Wilkins Co.

Glickman, S, E.: Perseverative neural processes and consolidation of the memory trace, Psychol. Bull. **58**:218-233, 1961.

Glickstein, M.: Neurophysiology of learning and memory. In Ruch, T. C., Patton, H. D., Woodbury, J. W., and Towe, A. L., editors: Neurophysiology, ed. 2, Philadelphia, 1965, W. B. Saunders Co.

Greenburn, R., and Pearlman, C.: Cutting the REM nerve: An approach to the adaptive role of REM sleep, Perspect. Biol. Med. **17**:513-521, 1974.

Hebb, D. O.: The organization of behavior, New York, 1961, Science Editions, Inc.

Hostetter, G.: Hippocampal lesions in rats weaken the retrograde amnesic effect of ECS, J. Comp. Physiol. Psychol. **66**:349-353, 1968.

Hudspeth, W. J., and Gerbrandt, L. K.: Electroconvulsive shock: Conflict, consolidation, and neuroanatomical functions, Psychol. Bull. **63**:377-383, 1965.

Hudspeth, W. J., McGaugh, J. L., and Thompson, C. W.: Aversive and amnesic effects of electroconvulsive shock, J. Comp. Physiol. Psychol. **57**:61-64, 1964.

Hudspeth, W. J., and Wilsoncroft, W. E.: Retrograde amnesia: Time dependent effect of rhinencephalic lesions, J. Neurobiol. **2**:221-232, 1969.

Hutt, L. D., and Elliot, L.: Chemical transfer of learned fear: Failure to replicate Ungar, Psychosom. Sci. **18**:57-59, 1970.

Jacobson, A., Babich, F., Bubash, S., and Jacobson, A.: Differential approach tendencies produced by injection of ribonucleic acid from trained rats, Science **150**:636-637, 1965.

John, E. R.: Mechanisms of memory, New York, 1967, Academic Press Inc.

John, E.: Switchboard vs. statistical theories of learning and memory, Science **177**:850-864, 1972.

Kennedy, D.: Nerve cells and behavior, Am. Sci. **59**:36-42, 1971.

Kimble, D. P.: The anatomy of memory, Palo Alto, Calif., 1965, Science & Behavior Books, Inc.

Landauer, T. K.: Two hypotheses concerning the biochemical basis of memory, Psychol. Rev. **71**:167-179, 1964.

Lashley, K.: In search of the engram, Symp. Soc. Exp. Biol., vol. 4, New York, 1950, Cambridge University Press.

Lewis, D. J., and Maher, B. A.: Neurol consolidation and electroconvulsive shock, Psychol. Rev. **72**:225-239, 1965.

Luttges, M., Johnson, T., Buck, C., Holland, J., and McGaugh, J.: An examination of "transfer of learning" by nucleic acid, Science **151**:834-837, 1966.

McGaugh, J. L.: Time-dependent processes in memory storage, Science **153**:1351-1358, 1966.

McGaugh, J. L.: Analysis of memory transfer and enhancement, Proc. Amer. Philosoph. Soc. **111**:347-351, 1967.

McGaugh, J. L.: Drug facilitation of learning and memory. In Effron, D. H., editor: Proceedings of the Sixth Annual Meeting of the American College of Neuropsychopharmacology, Dec. 12-15, 1967.

McGaugh, J. L.: A multi-trace view of memory storage processes, Atti Accad. Naz. Lincei Rend. **109**:13-24, 1968.

McGaugh, J. L., and Dawson, R. G.: Modification of memory storage processes, Behav. Sci. **16**:45-63, 1971.

Miller, G. A., Galanter, E., and Pribram, K. H.: Plans and the structure of behavior, New York, 1960, Henry Holt & Co.

Miller, N. E.: Learning of visceral and glandular responses, Science **163**:434-445, 1969.

Milner, B.: Visual recognition and recall after right temporal-lobe excision in man, Neuropsychologia **6**:191-209, 1968.

Milner, B. V., Branch, C., and Rasmussen, T.: Evidence for bilateral speech representation in some non-right-handers, Trans. Am. Neurol. Assoc. **91**:306-308, 1966.

Pearlman, C., and Becker, M.: Brief posttrial REM sleep deprivation impairs discrimination learning in rats, Physiol. Psychol. **1**:373-376, 1973.

Potts, A., and Bitterman, M. E.: Puromycin and retention in goldfish, Science **158**:1594-1596, 1967.

Rimland, B.: Infantile autism, New York, 1964, Appleton-Century-Crofts.

Robbins, K., and McAdam, D.: Interhemispheric alpha symmetry and imagery mode, Brain and Language **1**:189-193, 1974.

Rosensweig, M. R.: Environmental complexity, cerebral change and behavior, Am. Psychol. **21**:321-332, 1966.

Rosensweig, M. R., Krech, D., and Bennett, E. L.: A search for relations between brain chemistry and behavior, Psychol. Bull. **57**:476-492, 1960.

Rosensweig, M. R., Love, W., and Bennett, E. L.: Effects of a few hours a day of enriched experience on brain chemistry and brain weights, Physiol. Behav. **3**:819-825, 1968.

Russell, W. R.: Brain, memory, Learning, Oxford, England, 1959, The Clarendon Press.

Schiffrin, R. M., and Atkinson, R. C.: Storage and retrieval processes in long-term memory, Psychol. Rev. **76**:179-193, 1969.

Schmitt, F. O.: Macromolecular specificity and biological memory, Cambridge, Mass., 1962, The Technology Press of the Massachusetts Institute of Technology.

Schmitt, F. O.: Molecules and memory, New Scientist **23**:643-645, 1965.

Selnes, O.: The corpus callosum: Some anatomical and functional considerations with special reference to language, Brain and Language **1**:111-139, 1974.

Smith, D. D.: Mammalian Learning and behavior, Philadelphia, 1965, W. B. Saunders Co.

Sperry, R. W.: Cerebral organization and behavior, Science **133**:1749-1757, 1961.

Ungar, G.: Chemical transfer of learned behavior, Agent Action **1**:155-163, 1970.

Ungar, G., Gelson, L., and Clark, R. H.: Chemical transfer of learned fear, Nature **217**:1259-1261, 1968.

Walker, E. L.: Action decrement and its relation to learning, Psychol. Rev. **65**:129-142, 1958.

Chapter 18

Ax, A. F., Bamford, J. L., Beckett, P. G. S., Domino, E. F., and Gottlieb, J. S.: Autonomic response patterning of chronic schizophrenics, Psychosom. Med. **31**:353-364, 1969.

Benešová, O.: Neurophysiological and biochemical

aspects in the action of antidepressant drugs, Active. Nerv. Sup. **12**:226-234, 1970.

Berger, F. M.: Mental disease and the drugs affecting it, Prospect. Biol. Med. **13**:31-44, 1969.

Berry, H. K.: Hereditary disorders of amino acid metabolism associated with mental deficiency, Ann. N. Y. Acad. Sci. **166**:66-73, 1969.

Bliss, E. L., and Ailion, J.: The effect of lithium on brain monoamines, Brain Res. **24**:305-310, 1970.

Boakes, R. J., Bradley, P. B., Briggs, I., and Dray, A.: Antagonism of 5-hydroxytryptamine by LSD 25 in the central nervous system: A possible neuronal basis for the actions of LSD 25, Br. Med. J. Pharmacol. 40:202-218, 1970.

Boullin, D. J., Coleman, M., O'Brien, R. A., and Rimland, B.: Laboratory predictions of infantile autism based on 5-hydroxytryptamine efflux from blood platelets and their correlation with the Rimland E-2 score, J. Autism Childh. Schizophrenia 1:63-71, 1971.

Calloway, N. O.: The concept of biological half-life in relation to senescence, J. Am. Geriat. Soc. **17**:974-978, 1969.

Clancy, H., and McBride, G.: The autistic process and its treatment, J. Child Psychol. Psychiat. **10**:233-244, 1970.

Cochin, J.: Possible mechanisms in the development of tolerance, Fed. Proc. **29**:19-27, 1970.

Cohen, G., and Collins, M.: Alkaloids from catecholamines in adrenal tissue: Possible role in alcoholism, Science **167**:1749-1751, 1970.

Comfort, A.: Biological theories of aging, Hum. Dev. **13**:127-139, 1970.

Coons, E., and Miller, N. E.: Conflict vs. consolidation of memory traces to explain "retrograde amnesia" produced by ECS, J. Comp. Physiol. Psychol. **53**:524-531, 1960.

Davis, B. D.: Prospects for genetic intervention in man, Science **170**:1279-1283, 1970.

Dole, V. P.: Biochemistry of addiction, Annu. Rev. Biochem. **39**:821-840, 1970.

Eiduson, S., Geller, E., Yuwiler, A., and Eiduson, B. T.: Biochemistry and behavior, Princeton, N. J., 1964, D. Van Nostrand Co., Inc.

Farnsworth, N. R.: Hallucinogenic plants, Science **162**:1086-1092, 1968.

Frenkl, R., Csalay, L., Makara, G., and Harmos, G.: Antiulcerogenic effect of exercise in rats, Acta Physiol. Acad. Sci. Hung. **25**:97-100, 1964.

Fuller, J. L.: Experimental deprivation and later behavior, Science **158**:1645-1652, 1967.

Gershon, S.: Lithium in mania, Clin. Pharmacol. Ther. **11**:168-187, 1970.

Grossberg, J.: Behavior therapy: A review, Psychol. Bull. **62**:73-88, 1964.

Hartman, E.: Pharmacological studies of sleep and dreaming: Chemical and clinical relationships, Biol. Psychiat. **1**:243-258, 1969.

Heath, R. G.: Personal communication, 1970.

Heston, L. L.: The genetics of schizophrenic and schizoid disease, Science **167**:249-256, 1970.

Himwich, H. E., and Alpers, H. S.: Psychopharmacology, Annu. Rev. Pharmacol. **10**:313-334, 1970.

Hollister, L. E.: Marijuana in man: Three years later, Science **172**:21-29, 1971.

Humphrey, G., and Coxon, R. V.: The chemistry of thinking, Springfield, Ill., 1963, Charles C Thomas, Publisher.

Johnson, F. G.: LSD in the treatment of alcoholism, Am. J. Psychiat. **126**:481-487, 1969.

Johnson, L. C., Burdick, J. A., and Smith, J.: Sleep during alcohol intake and withdrawal in the chronic alcoholic, Arch. Gen. Psychiat. **22**:406-418, 1970.

Judd, L. J., Brandkamp, W. W., and McGlothin, W. H.: Comparison of the chromosomal patterns obtained from groups of continued users, former users, and nonusers of LSD 25, Am. J. Psychiat. **126**:626-635, 1969.

Lewis, D., and Adams, H.: Retrograde amnesia from conditioning competing responses, Science **141**:516-517, 1963.

Loew, D. M., and Taeschler, M.: Profiles of activity of psychotropic drugs: A way to predict therapeutic effects, Int. Pharmacopsychiat. **1**:1-20, 1968.

Lovaas, J.: Personal communication, 1970.

Mechoulam, R.: Marijuana chemistry, Science **168**:1159-1166, 1970.

Mirsky, A. F.: Neurophysiological bases of schizophrenia, Annu. Rev. Psychol. **20**:321-348, 1969.

Pauling, L.: Orthomolecular psychiatry, Science **160**:265-271, 1968.

Pollin, W., Martin, G. A., Hoffer, A., Stabenau, J. E., and Hrubec, Z.: Psychopathology in 15,909 pairs of veteran twins: evidence for a genetic factor in the pathogenesis of schizophrenia and its relative absence in psychoneurosis, Am. J. Psychiat. **126**:43-56, 1969.

Praag, H. M.: Monoamines and depression, pharmakopsychiat. Neuro-Pharm. **2**:151-160, 1969.

Ritvo, E. R., Yuwiler, A., Geller, E., Ornitz, E. M., Saeger, K., and Plotkin, S.: Increased blood serotonin and platelets in early infantile autism, Arch. Gen. Psychiat. **23**:566-572, 1970.

Rosenthal, S. H., and Wulfson, N. L.: Electrosleep: A preliminary communication, J. Nerv. Ment. Dis. **151**:146-151, 1970.

Schwartz, A. S., and Eidelberg, E.: Role of biogenic amines in morphine dependence, Life Sci. **9**:613-624, 1970.

Selye, H.: The physiology and pathology of exposure to stress, Montreal, 1960, Acta, Inc.

Selye, H.: Adaptive steroids: Retrospect and prospect, Prospect. Biol. Med. **13:**343-363, 1970.

Selye, H.: Stress and aging, J. Am. Geriatr. Soc. **18:**669-680, 1970.

Skalickova, O., Dejmal, V., and Pavlovski, P.: A study of the families of schizophrenics from the genetic aspect, Acta Univ. Carol. (Med.) **15:**343-363, 1969.

Snyder, S., Banerjeer, S., Yamamura, H., and Greenberg, D.: Drugs,, neurotransmitters, and schizophrenia, Science **184:**1243-1253, 1974.

Stein, L., and Wise, C. D.: Possible etiology of schizophrenia: Progressive damage to the noradrenergic reward system by 6-hydroxydopamine, Science **171:**1032-1036, 1971.

Towbin, A.: Mental retardation due to germinal matrix infarction, Science **164:**156-162, 1969.

Tsuboi, T.: Crimino-biologic study of patients with the XYY syndrome and Klinefelter's syndrome, Humangenetik **10:**68-84, Aug., 1970.

Ulrich, R.: Behavior modification: Research and practice, Mich. Ment. Health. Res. Bull. **2:**5-13, 1968.

Weil, A. T., Zinberg, N. E., and Nelsen, J. M.: Clinical and psychological effects of marijuana in man, Science **162:**1234-1242, 1968.

Winokur, G.: Genetic findings and methodological considerations in manic-depressive disease, Br. J. Psychiatry **117:**267-274, 1970.

Wynder, E. L., and Hoffman, D.: Experimental tobacco carcinogenesis, Science **162:**862-871, 1968.

Zigler, E.: Familial mental retardation: A continuing dilemma, Science **155:**292-298, 1967.

Zubek, J. P.: Sensory deprivation: Fifteen years of research, New York, 1969, Appleton-Century-Crofts.

Index